The DevelopMentor Series

Don Box, Editor

Addison-Wesley has joined forces with DevelopMentor, a premiere developer resources company, to produce a series of technical books written by developers for developers. DevelopMentor boasts a prestigious technical staff that includes some of the world's best-known computer science professionals.

*"Works in **The DevelopMentor Series** are practical and informative sources on the tools and techniques for applying component-based technologies to real-world, large-scale distributed systems."*
—Don Box

Titles in the Series:

Don Box, *Essential COM*, 0-201-63446-5

Don Box, Aaron Skonnard, and John Lam, *Essential XML: Beyond Markup*, 0-201-70914-7

Keith Brown, *Programming Windows Security*, 0-201-60442-6

Matthew Curland, *Advanced Visual Basic 6: Power Techniques for Everyday Programs*, 0-201-70712-8

Doug Dunn, *Java™ Rules*, 0-201-70916-3

Tim Ewald, *Transactional COM+L: Building Scalable Applications*, 0-201-61594-0

Jon Flanders, *ASP Internals*, 0-201-61618-1

Martin Gudgin, *Essential IDL: Interface Design for COM*, 0-201-61595-9

Stuart Halloway, *Component Development for the Java™ Platform*, 0-201-75306-5

Joe Hummel, Ted Pattison, Justin Gehtland, Doug Turnure, and Brian A. Randell, *Effective Visual Basic: How to Improve Your VB/COM+ Applications*, 0-201-70476-5

Stanley B. Lippman, *C# Primer: A Practical Approach*, 0-201-72955-5

Everett N. McKay and Mike Woodring, *Debugging Windows Programs: Strategies, Tools, and Techniques for Visual C++ Programmers*, 0-201-70238-X

Aaron Skonnard and Martin Gudgin, *Essential XML Quick Reference: A Programmer's Reference to XML, XPath, XSLT, XML Schema, SOAP, and More*, 0-201-74095-8

Watch for future titles in The DevelopMentor Series.

Java™ Rules

Douglas Dunn

Addison-Wesley

Boston • San Francisco • New York • Toronto • Montreal
London • Munich • Paris • Madrid
Capetown • Sydney • Tokyo • Singapore • Mexico City

The publisher offers discounts on this book when ordered in quantity for special sales. For more information, please contact:

Pearson Education Corporate Sales Division
201 W. 103rd Street
Indianapolis, IN 46290
(800) 428-5331
corpsales@pearsoned.com

Visit AW on the Web: *www.awl.com/cseng/*

Library of Congress Cataloging-in-Publication Data
Dunn, Douglas, 1958-
     Java rules / Douglas Dunn.
          p. cm.
     Includes bibliographical references and index.
     ISBN 0-201-70916-3 (pbk. : alk. paper)
     1. Java (Computer program language) I. Title.

   QA76.73.J38 D84 2001
   005.13'3—dc21

                                                              2001034111

0-201-70916-3

Text printed on recycled paper
1 2 3 4 5 6 7 8 9 10—DOC—0504030201
First printing, October 2001

There are only two people to thank for making the writing of this book possible:

Thank you, Gini. I finished.

And Mike, my undying gratitude.

— Doug

Table of Contents

Preface

This book has been under continuous development for over five years, since shortly after the JDK 1.0 release in 1995.

Married to the Java Specifications

This book is based on the *Java Language Specification* (*JLS*). In fact, I started out to write what I regarded as *The Java Language Specification for Application Programmers*. Shortly thereafter, however, I realized that material from *The Java Virtual Machine Specification* (*JVMS*) would have to be included as well. This work has grown to include everything of interest to mainstream business application programmers in a host of Java specifications, including the second editions of both the *JLS* and the *JVMS*.

The Target Audience

The main difference between the specifications and this book is the target audience. The *JVMS* is, of course, written for someone who wants to implement a JVM. What is not as generally understood is that the *JLS* is a grammar primarily intended for someone who wants to write a Java compiler, such as the `jikes` compiler team at IBM. Thus, it includes a lot of material that is of interest only to programmers who make a living in the arcane world of compilers. That is truly unfortunate because the *JLS* contains a wealth of information of interest to application programmers that rarely makes it into mainstream Java books. The same can be said of the *JVMS*. This book extracts all of that information, elaborates upon it where necessary, and presents it in a technical writing style appropriate for *mainstream business application programmers*.

Mainstream business application programmers are the target audience. By that I mean working programmers, most of whom will be found in corporations outside of Silicon Valley. They are experienced professionals who need to learn the language at a professional level in the first pass. This requires a serious and dedicated focus on the part of the reader.

Mainstream business application programmers have that focus. They bring to the subject years of experience and a strong motivation to learn.

More generally, this book is for any programmer who wants to truly master the basics of the Java programming language. While formalism and stylistic norms forbid me from including students in the target audience, I firmly believe that these books can be profitably used to teach the Java programming language (if not as the primary text, then as an auxiliary reference work).

Acknowledgements

I would like to take this opportunity to thank the people who have participated in this book project. One thing I can tell you is that the book I had 18 months ago, at the start of the Addison-Wesley (AW) technical review process, is nothing like the one I have now. First and foremost, I wish to thank the technical reviewers, especially Stuart Halloway. The following is an alphabetical listing of the technical reviewers who worked on this project:

> Orson Alvarez
> Simon Belanger
> Robert Brunner
> Carl Burnham
> John R. Collins
> Lisa Friendly
> Stuart Halloway
> Howard Lee Harkness
> Christian Paquin
> Gary Pavek
> Moshe Sambol
> Guy L. Steele, Jr.
> Anton Stiglic

Some technical reviewers have chosen to remain anonymous. My thanks are extended to them as well.

Then there is the editorial staff at AW. Mike Hendrickson, Editor-in-Chief at AW, saved me and this book from the garbage collector. Julie DiNicola and Heather Olszyk coordinated the 18-month-long technical review process with the greatest of care. Elizabeth Ryan was the Production Coordinator. It has been a joy working with all of you.

Finally, there is Sue Stark. Sue is a professional book editor in Boston. She was the first person with credentials to voice the opinion that I should continue the work. Sue copy edited the book through the first three drafts long before it was even sold in an electronic format on the Internet. Thank you, Sue. I owe you big.

A few last minute thanks: Don Box for approving Java Rules as the first Java book in the DevelopMentor series; Kenneth A. Dickey for commenting on a few of the math-oriented sections; Mike Hedrick for a really great copy edit; Darrell and Frank for easing the pain in the last few months prior to the publication of this first volume; and Jeffrey Kesselman and Steve Wilson for pointing out some problems with multi-threading in response to a posting on the Advanced-Java discussion group that Stuart Halloway manages for DevelopMentor.

About This Book

No Chapter on Inner Classes

As my understanding of how best to present the material on inner classes progressed, I determined that the subject of inner classes is so interwoven with the fabric of the language that it was a mistake to try to discuss inner classes as if they were a separate subject. Figuring out how to decompose the old chapter on inner classes and spread the material throughout the book was one of the tougher challenges I faced. As with the organization of the rest of the book, there was an untold number of permutations before arriving at the current organization. I believe that, as a result of having pursued the ideal of not treating inner classes as a special subject, the material on inner classes is actually much easier to understand.

Correct Terminology is Strongly Emphasized

Correct terminology is strongly emphasized throughout *Java Rules*. Whenever a term is used for the first time it appears in a **bold font** and is carefully and thoroughly defined. Entire sections of this book are sometimes dedicated to terminological discussions. *Standardization is essential to this effort, and* the Java Language Specification, the Java Virtual Machine Specification, *and a host of other officially released JavaSoft specifications are that standard.*

In matters of terminology, the author always defers to the software engineers and technical writers at JavaSoft.

Nonstandard Java terminology collected from dozens of Java books in and out of print is also considered when appropriate. Occasionally I introduce a new term of my own making or take exception with the usage in official JavaSoft specifications. This is never done without first alerting the reader.

Compiler Error Messages

This book makes extensive use of compiler error messages from the `javac` compiler. Compiler error messages are always improving at Sun, which is why I have recompiled most, if not all, of the examples using a 1.3 compiler prior to the publication of this book. If you use a different compiler or a different version of the same compiler, the compiler error messages may be different from those printed in the book. The *JLS* does not specify compiler error messages, only compiler errors.

API Tables

When there are a group of related methods to be discussed, I use a table similar to Table 0-1.

Table 0-1: Sample API Table

Method	Description

`return type`
`methodName`
`parameter list`
`throws clause`
	The method name is always in large print. Parameters are listed on separate lines in the same left-to-right order as they appear in the parameter list. The parameter type is followed by the same parameter name used in the API docs. The `throws` clause, if any, is always separated from the rest of the method header by a blank line.
	
	The following row is an example from the `java.io` package.

`boolean` **`isDirectory`**	Returns `true` if the abstract pathname exists and is a directory.

I refer to these as **API tables**. They are designed to minimize the page width required to display the full method header, while at the same time making it easy to find the discussion of a particular method.

Method Names

I use full method signatures throughout the book, even to the extent of using empty parentheses after the name of a no-argument method. This policy leaves no room for ambiguity. The exception is overloaded methods, which are referred to solely by their names, such as the fully overloaded `print` and `println` methods. Occasionally I make other exceptions. For example, I always use `main` instead of `main(String[] args)`. Furthermore, parameters names are always *exactly* the same as they appear in the API docs. This makes it easy to switch back and forth between my work and the API docs.

Qualifying the Names of Class Members

Many books on computer programming languages routinely qualify the names of instance methods with the name of the class in which the method is declared. The problem with doing so is that instance methods are never qualified with the name of the class in which they are declared. For example,

```
class Test {
    int i = Test.init();
    private int init() { return 0; }
}
```

Attempting to compile this program generates the following errors:

```
Test.java:2: non-static method init() cannot be referenced from a static context

    int i = Test.init();
                ^
1 error
```

For an instance method to be qualified by the name of the class in which it is declared is something you will never see in code. Instance variables and instance methods must be qualified with a reference to what this book refers to as the *target object*. Only class variables (which are often constants such an `Integer.MAX_VALUE`) and class methods declared `static` are qualified with the name of the class in which they are declared. For example, `trim()` is the name of an instance method in the `String` class. In my opinion, for a Java book to use `String.trim()` is misleading and awkward. I never qualifiy the name of instance methods with the name of the class in which they are declared. I use either the "trim() method in the String class" or "the trim() method declared in the String class," but never String.trim(). Only static members are qualified with type names, as they are in code. There is no exception to this rule.

Undocumented Examples

The overwhelming majority of the examples in this book are undocumented. By this I mean I do not include a blow-by-blow description of what the code is doing. This is deliberate. I personally do not like the long examples found in other books. Code is hard to read. You have to acquaint yourself with variable names and other intricacies of the code that have no long-term benefit to the reader. In this book I use numerous small examples. I keep them small because I *do* expect the reader to both read and understand the code. If I can demonstrate some point in a maximum of 10 to 15 lines of code, I don't think that asks too much of the reader.

Another thing that annoys me in other books is the lack of output. Not only are you expected to read and understand lengthy examples, there is an assumption that you know what the code outputs. I always include the output of code examples, which partially makes up for not documenting them.

Examples of Source Code from the Core API

These are always very short, usually no more than a few lines of code. Nevertheless, one must respect the copyright notices at the top of each of the compilation units in the core API. Therefore, the examples of source code from the core API are never the actual source code. They are simplified versions of the same code that are good only for instructional purposes. That is why I always qualify the introduction of these examples by saying that the source code "looks like this." That is, it is not the actual source code, but is close enough to make the salient point without bringing any disrepute to the software engineers at Sun. If I feel that a particular example is overly simplified, I will usually include a note explicitly reminding the reader that the actual source code is different.

The Inclusion of Bug Ids

I include many **Bug Ids** from the Bug Parade on the Java Developer Connection (JDC) Web site. The URL for looking up those bugs is

developer.java.sun.com/developer/bugParade/index.jshtml

You need to be a JDC member to access this Web address. Membership is free and highly recommended. Bug Ids are usually found solely in footnotes, but some bugs have aged so that they become de facto, undocumented features of the Java programming language. None comes more readily to mind in this context than Bug ID 4057172, dated June 6, 1997. This bug explains why `javac` and some other Java compilers tolerate extraneous semicolons. Such bugs are discussed in the main body of the text rather than in footnotes.

Miscellaneous Stuff

My general policy towards deprecated members and constructors is to pretend they do not exist. A deprecated member is something that should ideally be removed from the language. Why waste time explaining the way things used to be? The only exception is when explaining why something was deprecated helps to better understand the current language design or API.

A Java Tradition

There is a tradition in Java technical writing of quoting great thinkers that started with the first edition of *The Java Language Specification*. While there are many great thinkers I would like to quote, the following passage from *Walden* most often comes to mind when I think about some of the programmers I have met through the years.

> The laboring man has not leisure for a true integrity day by day. He cannot afford to sustain the manliest relations to men. His labor would be depreciated in the market. He has no time to be anything but a machine. How can he remember well his ignorance which his growth requires who has so often to use his knowledge. ... The finest qualities of our natures, like the bloom on fruits, can be preserved only by the most delicate handling. Yet we do not treat ourselves nor one another thus tenderly. The mass of men lead lives of quiet desperation.
>
> – Henry David Thoreau
> *Walden* or, *Life in the Woods*

My motivation in writing this book was to be of service to others. It was a labor of love, my effort to do some good in society by benefiting *the mass of programmers*. We are all in this together. The body of knowledge we strive to master is so vast that I have found it to be a verity that truly great programmers are humble people. Dr. James Gosling, the inventor of Java technology, is a perfect role model in this regard.

Chapter 1

Lexical Structure

Chapter Contents

1.1 Introduction

Before a Java compiler parses a compilation unit looking for what programmers refer to as *compiler errors*, the compilation unit must be tokenized. For example, consider the traditional Hello World! program as written in Java:

```
public class HelloWorld {
    public static void main (String[] args) {
        System.out.println("Hello World!");
    }
}
```

After tokenization the compilation unit would look something like this:

```
public
class
HelloWorld
{
public
static
void
main
(
String
[
]
args
)
{
System.out.println
(
"Hello World!"
)
;
}
}
```

This output was generated using an example of the `StreamTokenizer` class found in 5.8.3 The `StreamTokenizer` Class. If this source code was actually being compiled, each token would be stored in an array or other container in preparation for the next compilation step, parsing. Parsing is what generates the compiler errors.

Tokens are the basic unit of input to a parser. There are five different kinds of tokens:

- Identifiers
- Keywords
- Literals
- Separators
- Operators

Lexical structure is the study of these tokens and a number of other closely related subjects such as escape sequences and positional notation systems. If you look at the table of contents for this chapter you will see that all five tokens have their own sections. The other two main sections discuss white space and comments, which are discarded in the last step of the tokenization process.

Tokenizing in the Java programming language consists of the following three steps.

1. Unicode escape sequences are translated into their corresponding Unicode characters. That is, six locally encoded ASCII input characters are translated into a single 16-bit Unicode character. Source code does not necessarily have any Unicode escapes. It depends on the application.

2. The compilation unit is separated into lines. Separating the compilation unit into lines determines the end of what are called *traditional comments* in the Java programming language (comments that begin with the `//` characters).

3. White space and comments are discarded.

After white space and comments are discarded, only the tokens are left. This chapter discusses white space, comments, and tokens in that order.

The title of this chapter is the same as Chapter 3, "Lexical Structure," of the *Java Language Specification* (hereafter all references to the *JLS*, except where noted, will be to the second edition). The first two chapters of the *JLS* are an introduction and a very short chapter on grammars, which is of little or no interest to mainstream business application programmers. For that target audience *Java Rules* and the *JLS* begin with a discussion of the same subject. The two books diverge after that, but *Java Rules* is nonetheless more heavily indebted than most Java books to the authors of the *JLS*: James Gosling, Bill Joy, Guy Steele, and Gilad Bracha. (Gilad Bracha is responsible for changes in the second edition of the *JLS*.) In fact, Guy Steele provided some early feedback on the organization of this chapter as well as technically editing a limited number of other sections in the book.

1.2 White Space

The term **white space**[1] refers not only to spaces, but to other characters that appear as blanks or *white* on a computer screen or printed page. The classical definition of white space is represented by the characters in Table 1-1.

---

1. Opinion is evenly divided on this term being one or two words. I use two words in this book, as do the API docs.

Table 1-1: The Classical Definition of White Space

Character	Name
'\t'	Horizontal tab
'\n'	Line feed[a]
'\f'	Form feed
'\r'	Carriage return
' '	Space

a. This is the Unicode name for what is more commonly referred to as the *new line* character.

This definition of white space is now referred to as *ISO-Latin-1 white space* in the API docs and is represented by the now-deprecated `is-Space(char ch)` method.

There are two methods in the `Character` class that can be used to determine if a character is a space or white space. Their declarations are as follows:

```
public static boolean isWhitespace(char ch)
public static boolean isSpaceChar(char ch)
```

The `isWhitespace(char ch)` method is used in parsing source code. The `isSpaceChar(char ch)` method must be understood in the context of Java having an obligation to implement a full set of utility methods for working with the Unicode character set. Those methods are listed in 4.9.5 Unicode Utility Methods. You may never use some of those methods, but Java is nonetheless obligated to implement them for those few who will. The following program shows the difference in how these methods are implemented:

```
import java.util.*;
class Test {
    static Character.UnicodeBlock block, last = null;
    public static void main(String[] args) {
        ArrayList space = new ArrayList(),
            whitespace = new ArrayList(),
                both = new ArrayList(20);
        for (int i=0; i <= Character.MAX_VALUE; i++) {
            char ch = (char) i;
            Character wrapper = new Character(ch);
            if (Character.isSpaceChar(ch)) {
                if (Character.isWhitespace(ch))
                    both.add(wrapper);
                else
                    space.add(wrapper);
```

```
                } else {
                    if (Character.isWhitespace(ch))
                        whitespace.add(wrapper);
                }
            }
            System.out.println();
            System.out.println();
            System.out.println("isSpaceChar() ONLY...");
            for (Iterator i = space.iterator(); i.hasNext();) {
                print(((Character) i.next()).charValue());
            }
            last = null;
            System.out.println();
            System.out.println();
            System.out.println("isWhitespace() ONLY...");
            for (Iterator i = whitespace.iterator(); i.hasNext();) {
                print(((Character) i.next()).charValue());
            }
            last = null;
            System.out.println();
            System.out.println();
            System.out.println("BOTH...");
            for (Iterator i = both.iterator(); i.hasNext();) {
                print(((Character) i.next()).charValue());
            }
        }

        static void print(char ch) {
            block = Character.UnicodeBlock.of(ch);
            if (!block.equals(last)) {
                if (last == null) {
                    System.out.println(block.toString());
                } else {
                    System.out.println();
                    System.out.println(block.toString());
                }
                last = block;
            }
            System.out.print(toUnicodeEscape(ch) + "  ");
        }

        static String toUnicodeEscape(char ch) {
            String s = "" + Character.forDigit(((ch >>> 12) & 0xF), 16) +
                            Character.forDigit(((ch >>> 8) & 0xF), 16) +
                            Character.forDigit(((ch >>> 4) & 0xF), 16) +
                            Character.forDigit(((ch) & 0xF), 16);
            return "\\u" + s.toUpperCase();
        }
    }
```

Executing this program prints

```
isSpaceChar() ONLY...
LATIN_1_SUPPLEMENT
\u00A0

isWhitespace() ONLY...
BASIC_LATIN
```

```
\u\u0009  \u000A  \u000B  \u000C  \u000D  \u001C  \u001D  \u001E  \u001F

BOTH...
BASIC_LATIN
\u0020
GENERAL_PUNCTUATION
\u2000  \u2001  \u2002  \u2003  \u2004  \u2005  \u2006  \u2007  \u2008  \u2009
\u200A  \u200B  \u2028  \u2029
CJK_SYMBOLS_AND_PUNCTUATION
\u3000
```

The most commonly used space character is the ASCII space character
\u0020. Other space characters have different widths. The widest of
them is \u3000, which is an ideographic space for Asian languages.

The isWhitespace(char ch) method uses an internationalized
definition of white space that includes all but one of the space characters
in the *Unicode Standard*, as well as more of the C0 control charcters. That
one space character is the nonbreaking space in Latin-1, which can be
written using the Unicode escape \u00A0. For example,

```java
class Test {
    public static void main(String[] args) {
        System.out.println("Hello\u00A0World!");
    }
}
```

Executing this program prints

```
HelloáWorld!
```

As you can see, the space between Hello and World is not white.

Table 1-2: C0 **Control Characters that Are White Space**

Unicode Escape	Character Name
\u0009	Horizontal tab
\u000A	Line feed
\u000B	Vertical tab
\u000C	Form feed
\u000D	Carriage return
\u001C	File separator
\u001D	Group separator
\u001E	Record separator
\u001F	Unit separator

A complete list of the C0 control characters for which the isWhiteSpace(char ch) method returns true is shown in Table 1-2. The isSpaceChar(char ch) and isWhitespace(char ch) methods also return true for \u2028 and \u2029, which are the *Unicode Standard* line and paragraph separators discussed in 1.6.2.2.1 Line, Paragraph, and Page Separator Characters. Please note that this definition of white space is not based on the *Unicode Standard* because the *Unicode Standard* does not define white space. The internationalized definition of white space is uniquely Java but will likely be copied by the next programming language to implement the *Unicode Standard*.

1.2.1 Indenting

The single most important use of white space is indenting. Java is a **free format language.** Clear and regular indenting does more than anything else to make a program readable. The following is an example of poor indentation because the else appears to be bound to the wrong if:

```
if (expression)
    if (expression)
        statement;
else                    // dangling else
    statement;
```

Examples of code like this are sometimes referred to as the **dangling else** problem. The danger of a dangling else is that the implied control flow can lead to programming mistakes.

As an example of what is meant by a *free format language*, the following statements are exactly the same after tokenization:

```
System.out.println("Goodbye Cruel C++ World!");

System.out.println
(
"Goodbye Cruel C++ World!"
)
;
```

The second println method invocation helps to illustrate the relative terms *left* and *right* as used in expressing syntax rules. Although all of the tokens are written on separate lines, it is still proper to speak of one token as being "to the left of" or "to the right of" another. For example, when evaluating operator expressions, a binary operator is said to have a left- and a right-hand operand. That applies even to the following assignment operation:

```
x
=
2
+
4
```

The left-hand operand of the + operator is 2 and the right-hand operand is 4.

1.3 Comments

The C programming language uses what Java now calls a **traditional comment**. A traditional comment looks like this:

```
/* text of comment */
```

A traditional comment can span any number of lines. C++ added the **end-of-line comment**. An end-of-line comment looks like this:

```
int x;  // text of comment
```

The end-of-line and traditional comments are sometimes called *single-* and *multi-line comments*, respectively.

Java introduced another type of comment called the **documentation comment**, or **doc comment** for short, that begins with /**. To a Java compiler, a documentation comment looks the same as a traditional comment that begins with /*, but javadoc and other automatic documentation generation tools use the /** to parse for doc comments and generate sophisticated HTML documentation.

1.3.1 Commenting Out Large Blocks of Code

Using a traditional comment to comment out large blocks of code is problematic because of the likelihood that a large block of code will include other traditional or documentation comments. The first */ read by the compiler terminates a traditional or documentation comment, which is to say that traditional comments do not nest. For example,

```
class Test {
    public static void main(String[] args) {
/* trying to comment out a large block of code
    System.out.println("Hello World!") //end-of-line comment not a problem
    /*
     * But other traditional comments will genrate compiler errors
     * if you attempt to comment them out.
     */
    /**
     * The same is true for doc comments.
```

```
        */
  */        // THIS IS LINE 12
     }
  }
```

Attempting to compile this program generates the following compiler errors:

```
Test.java:12: illegal start of expression
*/
 ^
Test.java:12: ';' expected
*/
  ^
2 errors
```

The problem is that the first `*/` terminates any and all preceding `/*`, which strands the `*/` on line 12. Here are some possible solutions.

- Comment out each line of code using the end-of-line comment. However, doing so is tedious. The end-of-line comment is rarely used to comment out more than a few lines of code.
- Find each `*/` in the block of code to be commented out and change it to `//`. The compiler will not generate an error because of the `/*` and `/**` that remain. This, however, is also tedious and hard to undo.

A better way to comment out large blocks is to enclose them in an `if` statement that never executes. For example,

```
if (false) {
    /* SPECIAL NOTE:  (Document why code is commented out:
        why it is being preserved rather than simply deleted;
        who commented it out; when it was commented out;
        by what authority it was commented out;
        list any associated work orders, etc.) */

                            COMMENTED OUT CODE...
}
```

The `if (false)` statement does not generate an unreachable statement compiler error because of the special rules for conditional compilation.

1.4 Identifiers

A name is said to refer to an entity declared in a Java program. Within the actual declaration of an entity, however, the proper term is **identifier**. For example,

```
int x = 10;                      // x is an identifier
System.out.println(x);           // x is a name
```

An **entity** in the Java programming language is any of the following:

- Package
- Class
- Interface
- Method
- Constructor
- Field
- Local variable
- Parameter

There are a number of different declarations in the Java programming language, all of which correspond to one of the entities in this list. Those relationships are summarized in Table 1-3. Syntactically these declarations

Table 1-3: Entities and Declarations

Entity	Declaration(s)
Package	Package declarations
Class[a]	Single-type-import declarations Type-import-on-demand declarations Class declarations Local class declaration statements
Interface	Interface declarations
Field	Field declarations
Constructor	Constructor declarations
Method	Method declarations
Local variable	Local variable declaration statements
Parameter	Parameter declarations (a.k.a. parameter specifiers)

a. Anonymous classes are not included in the right-hand column because the declaration of an anonymous class is considered part of a class instance creation expression.

have little or nothing in common except that they all include an identifier that specifies the name of the entity declared. The only unnamed entities are the components of an array and anonymous classes.

Identifiers in Java can be any length. There are only three rules for identifiers. Unlike programmer conventions, failure to comply with these rules will generate a compiler error.

1. Identifiers cannot have the same spelling as a keyword, either of the Boolean literals `true` and `false` or the `null` literal.

2. The first character of an identifier must be a letter, dollar sign ($), or underscore (_) character. Only numeric literals can begin with the digits `0` to `9`. The `Character.isJavaIdentifier-Start(char ch)` method returns `true` "if the specified character is permissible as the first character in a Java identifier."[2]

3. All characters in an identifier other than the first must be a letter, digit, dollar sign ($), underscore (_) character, or one of the following unusual characters for identifiers:

   - A numeric letter (such as a Roman numeral character)
   - A combining mark
   - A nonspacing mark
   - An ignorable control character

   The `Character.isJavaIdentifierPart(char ch)` method returns `true` "if the specified character may be part of a Java identifier as other than the first character."[3]

In addition, there are some programmer conventions that apply to all names. Failure to comply with programmer conventions does not generate a compiler error.

- Programmers should not use a dollar sign as a character in identifiers primarily because $ is used in *mechanically generated* names or what the *JLS* calls *binary names*. (I am not fond of either of those terms and use *compiler-generated* class and interface names instead.) If Java is an internationalized programming language, why is the dollar sign a valid character for identifiers? It is used as a currency symbol in a limited number of countries. The following explanation is from the *JLS*.

---

2. API docs for the `isJavaIdentifierPart(char ch)` method in the `java.lang.Character` class.
3. Ibid.

... for historical reasons, the ASCII underscore (_, or \u005f) and dollar sign ($, or \u0024) [are allowed in Java identifiers]. The $ character should be used only in mechanically generated Java code or, rarely, to access preexisting names on legacy systems.[4]

- Except for constants, identifiers are mixed case. The first letter of each new word is capitalized. Constants such as MIN_VALUE and MAX_VALUE are all uppercase, requiring the use of the underscore character to separate words. This is the only use of the underscore character in Java naming conventions.
- Programmers should exercise restraint in the use of characters from other languages or scripts. English speaking programmers, for example, should only use the letters and digits that correspond to the ASCII character set. There are notably exceptions, however, especially in the use of mathematical symbols. Unicode makes it possible, for example, to use π as a variable name.

Limited keyboard interfaces have been sufficient up until now to discourage the use of foreign languages in computer programs. That will change, however, as operating systems become more sophisticated in terms of how the *Unicode Standard* is implemented. Something comparable to the input methods used in Asia will become common in the West. Until then, the only way to type characters not found on the keyboard is to use Unicode escape sequences. See also 4.9.5.5 Java Versus Unicode Identifiers.

1.4.1 Java Naming Conventions

In the Java programming language different kinds of entities can have the same name because the compiler can differentiate entities from the context in which they are used. There is nothing complicated about the use of context to *syntactically classify* a name, which means to determine what kind of entity (a field, method, type, etc.) that name refers to. Programmers do it all the time. For example, a method name is clear from the context in which it is used because method names are always followed by either an empty pair of parentheses or a parameter list enclosed in parentheses. So are constructors, but constructors are not confused with meth-

---

4. James Gosling, Bill Joy, Guy Steele, and Gilad Bracha, *The Java Language Specification, Second Edition* (Boston: Addison-Wesley, 2000), §3.8, "Identifiers."

ods because they have the same name as the class in which they are declared. These are two examples of what the *JLS* calls the *syntactic classification of names according to context*.

On a much larger scale a Java compiler does the same thing with all of the names in a compilation unit. The fact that entities can have the same name is usually discussed in terms of fields, methods, and types. With the exception of local variables and parameters not having the same name, however, there are no rules whatsoever in the *JLS* that say an entity cannot have the same name as a different kind of entity (both entities being in scope). Those entities are repeated here for your convenience:

- Package
- Class
- Interface
- Method
- Constructor
- Field
- Local variable
- Parameter

To this list of entities must be added *labels*, which can have the same name as any entity in scope. The Java programming language maximizes the use of context to classify names.

It is exactly because of the syntactic classification of names according to context that Java naming conventions are so important. What would happen if there were no naming conventions? Consider the following "pathological case" from *The Java Programming Language*:[5]

```
class Reuse {
    Reuse Reuse(Reuse Reuse) {
        Reuse:
        for (;;) {
            if (Reuse.Reuse(Reuse) == Reuse)
                break Reuse;
        }
        return Reuse;
    }
}
```

The importance of Java naming conventions should be clear from this example. Java naming conventions are specifically designed to counterbal-

---

5. Ken Arnold and James Gosling, *The Java Programming Language, Second Edition* (Reading: Addison-Wesley, 1998), p.113.

ance the syntactic classification of names according to context. They make it possible to readily distinguish one kind of entity from another. For example, field and method names always begin with a small letter (except constants). Class and interface names always begin with a capital letter. Without naming conventions the syntactic classification of names according to context could make Java programs difficult to read. That is why the naming conventions are part of the *JLS*. It is notable that the software engineers at Sun practice what they preach. There are very few exceptions to Java naming conventions in the core API.

On the other hand, some IT managers have been known to institute standards with such virility as to stifle creativity. In those cases the *JLS* says,

> These conventions should not be followed slavishly if long-held conventional usage dictates otherwise. So, for example, the `sin` and `cos` methods of the class `java.lang.Math` have mathematically conventional names, even though these method names flout Java convention because they are short and are not verbs.[6]

No standard should be followed slavishly. For example, compare the following two method names:

```
setXAndY()
setXandY()
```

The first method name slavishly follows the Java naming convention for capitalizing the first letter of each word in a method name, but the second method name is clearly more readable. Another example is the `IEEEremainder()` method in the `Math` class. If the naming standards were followed, that method name would be `IEEERemainder()`, which is less readable. To formalize these exceptions we might say that if the last letter of the previous word is capitalized, the rule that the first letter of a new word begins with a capital letter is not binding. That can happen when the previous word is either a single letter or an acronym.

---

6. Gosling et al., §6.8, "Naming Conventions." Please note that the *JLS* uses *flout* instead of *flaunt*. That is the correct verb. As noted in Webster's online edition, "flaunt undoubtedly arose from confusion with flout" (*www.m-w.com/cgi-bin/dictionary*). Nevertheless, I use *flaunt* in this book.

1.5 Keywords

Identifiers cannot have the same name as any of the logically grouped **keywords** in Table 1-4. The Boolean literals `true` and `false` and the `null` literal are omitted from this list for the following reason.

Table 1-4: Keywords

Group	Keyword	Group	Keyword
Primitive types + void	byte short int long char float double boolean void	Exception handling	throws try throw catch finally
		Class or interface declarations	class interface extends implements
Control flow statements	if else do while for break continue return case switch default	this and super	this super
		Package and import declarations	package import
		Object creation	new
		Type testing	instanceof
Modifiers	public protected private abstract static final synchronized native transient volatile		

While `true` and `false` might appear to be keywords, they are technically Boolean literals. Similarly, while `null` might appear to be a keyword, it is technically the null literal.[7]

They are considered to be literals and not keywords because they represent values.

There are also two **reserved words** in Java. As explained in the *JLS*,

The keywords `const` and `goto` are reserved, even though they are not currently used. This may allow a Java compiler to produce better error messages if these C++ keywords incorrectly appear in programs.[8]

Note that `const` and `goto` are the only reserved words in Java. Some outdated Java books list other reserved words:

- `var`
- `byvalue`
- `cast`
- `future`
- `generic`
- `inner`
- `operator`
- `outer`
- `rest`

None of these are reserved words, although some may have been in very early alpha and beta releases of Java.

1.6 Literals

The term **literal** as used in programming languages is short for *literal value*. Literal values are constants. To differentiate them from **named constants** declared using the `final` keyword, literals are sometimes referred to as **unnamed constants**.

There are six kinds of literals in the Java programming language. Table

---

7. Gosling et al., §3.9, "Keywords."
8. Ibid.

1-5 includes examples of each. Notice that character literals are enclosed with single quotation marks, whereas string literals are enclosed with double quotation marks.

Literal names are largely derived from their data type. For example, a Boolean literal has a `boolean` data type, a character literal has a `char` data type, and the default data type for integer literals is `int`. The exception to this naming convention for literals is *floating-point literals* that have a default data type of `double`. Floating-point literals have the `float` data type only if they use the `f` or `F` suffix (discussed below). The `null` literal is said to have the special `null` type, although the keyword `null` is not a type name.

1.6.1 Character Literals

The following character literals from Table 1-5 do not appear to be single characters, yet they must be because the literal value is enclosed by single quotes:

```
'\t'
'\\'
'\u03a9'
'\uFFFF'
'\177'
```

Any character literal that has more than one character between the single quotes is an escape sequence. Escape sequences are used in both character and string literals. They are discussed in the next section.

The `char` data type is unusual in that it can be initialized using a character literal, a number, or an escape sequence. For example, all of the following declarations are equivalent:

```
char copyright = '©';
char copyright = 169;
char copyright = '\u00A9';
```

The decimal number `169` is the Unicode character code for the copyright symbol, which is equal to the hexidecimal `A9` used in the Unicode escape sequence.

1.6.2 Escape Sequences

All **escape sequences** have the following two things in common.

Table 1-5: Examples of Literal Values

Kind of Literal	Data Type	Examples

Character	char	`'a'`
		`'%'`
		`'\t'`
		`'\\'`
		`'\''`
		`'\u03a9'`
		`'\uFFFF'`
		`'\177'`
		`'Ω'`

String	String	`""`
		`"\""`
		`"This is a string"`
		`"This is a " +`
		`"concatenated string"`

Integer	int	`0`
		`2`
		`0372`
		`0xCAFEBABE`

	long	`0l`
		`0777L`
		`0x100000000L`
		`2147483648L`
		`0xC0B0L`

Floating-point	float	`1e1f`
		`2.f`
		`.3f`
		`0f`
		`3.14f`
		`6.022137e+23f`

	double	`1e1`
		`2.`
		`.3`
		`0.0`
		`3.14`
		`1e-9d`
		`1e137`

Table 1-5: Examples of Literal Values (Continued)

Kind of Literal	Data Type	Examples
Boolean	`boolean`	`true` `false`
Null	Special `null` type	`null`

1. An escape sequence always begins with a backslash, which is known as an **escape character**.
2. An escape sequence is an alternative representation of a *single character*, which may be a nongraphic character. (Line separators are examples of nongraphic characters.)

The escape character signals the beginning of an escape sequence to the compiler. The end of an escape sequence depends on the second character in the escape sequence.

*   If the second character is a digit, then the escape sequence is an octal escape. The length of an octal escape sequence varies. There may be from one to three octal digits used in an octal escape. Valid octal digits are 0, 1, 2, 3, 4, 5, and 7

*   If the second character is a **Unicode marker** (a small letter u), then the escape sequence is a Unicode escape and the length of the escape sequence is six: the escape character, the Unicode marker, and four hexadecimal digits (0 to 9, a to f, or A to F)

*   If the second character is neither a digit nor the small letter u, the length of the escape sequence is two—the escape character plus one of the following:

    b, t, n, f, r, ", ', or \

If the second character is none of the above, the escape character always generates a compiler error. For example,

```
import java.io.File;

class Test {
    public static void main(String[] args) {
        File pathname = new File("C:\Windows");
    }
}
```

Attempting to compile this program generates the following compiler error:

```
Test.java:5: illegal escape character
        File pathname = new File("C:\Windows");
                                    ^

1 error
```

Programmers must be careful not to inadvertently use the escape character in a character or string literal. Here is another example:

```
static final char BACKSLASH = '\';        //COMPILER ERROR
```

The correct declaration follows:

```
static final char BACKSLASH = '\\';
```

There are four categories of escape sequences:

1. Octal escape sequences.
2. Escape sequences for C0 control characters.
3. Escape sequences for special characters.
4. Unicode escape sequences.

The first three categories of escape sequences were inherited from the C and C++ programming languages. They can only be used in character and string literals, whereas Unicode escape sequences can be used anywhere in a Java program, even as operators. This subject is discussed further in the section on Unicode escapes below.

1.6.2.1 Octal Escape Sequences

Octal escapes were the Unicode escapes of their day in that they were used as a means of expressing character codes. Their range of '\000' to '\377' corresponds to the character codes 0 to 255 in the ISO Latin-1 character set. It can be said that octal escapes were included in the Java programming language soley for the sake of backwards compatibility. They were obsolete even before the 1.0 release. As explained in the *JLS*,

> Octal escapes are provided for compatibility with C, but can express only Unicode values \u0000 through \u00FF, so Unicode escapes are usually preferred.[9]

The '\000' through '\377' limitation is only for octal escapes. The octal literals discussed in 1.6.4.1 Positional Notation Systems, Digits, and Radices have no such limitation.

---

9. Gosling et al., §3.10.6, "Escape Sequences for Character and String Literals."

1.6.2.1.1 *The NULL Character* The octal escape \0 is still used to express the NULL character in string literals.[10] The proper way to express the NULL character in the Java programming would be to use a Unicode escape. However, typing \0 is easier than the Unicode equivalent of \u0000. For that reason the NULL character is an exception to the rule that Unicode escapes should be used to express character codes in the Java programming language. Note that using the digit 0 in a character or string literal is not the same thing. The character code for the digit 0 is 48, not zero. Note also that '' (two single quotes with nothing between them) is not a valid char value and generates a compiler error.

> The only way to express the NULL character (which has a character code of zero) in a character or string literal is to use an escape sequence.

In other words, the NULL character must be typed as \0, \u0000, or 0x0 in a character or string literal. It is only in an assignment statement involving the char data type such as c = 0 that the NULL character can be expressed as zero.

As an example of using the NULL character in a string literal, consider the following methods declared in the SortedMap and SortedSet interfaces, respectively:

```
public SortedSet subSet(Object fromElement, Object toElement)
public SortedMap subMap(Object fromKey, Object toKey)
```

These methods use right-open intervals, meaning that the fromElement and fromKey are inclusive and the toElement and toKey are exclusive. Suppose you want a submap of all strings from Alpha to Omega. What should be the toKey string? Lexicographic ordering is such that if you want to stop at a precise point, such as Omega, you must take into consideration the length of the string. For example, what about Omegaa? That is between Omega and Omegb, but it is not the next string after Omega. For example,

```
SortedMap submap = map.subMap("Alpha", "Omega\0");
```

---

10. To help differentiate the NULL character from a null reference, the former is always capitalized. Doing so is consistent with the Unicode practice of always capitalizing character names.

> When expressing a range of `String` values in a right-open interval, you should always append the `NULL` character to the last string to be included (which is typically the second parameter).

That is `Omega` followed by an octal escape for zero. The answer then is `Omega\0`. You can think of this use of an octal escape as a kind of short-hand for the `NULL` character. In that sense the use of `\0` is comparable to using any of the other escape sequences inherited from C and C++. For example, when hard coding a line separator for an Internet protocol, you can type `\r\n` or `\u000D\u000A`. The older escape sequences are easier to type.

The following program illustrates some properties of the `NULL` character:

```
class Test {
    public static void main(String[] args) {
        char a = '\u0000', b = 0, c = ' ';
        String s = "" + 'X' + a + 'X';
        System.out.println("a = " + a);
        System.out.println("b = " + b);
        System.out.println("c = " + c);
        System.out.println("s = " + s);
         if (a == b)
                System.out.println("The NULL character is the same as zero");
    }
}
```

Executing this program prints

```
a =
b =
c =
s = X X
The NULL character is the same as zero
```

The `NULL` character does not print and is equal to zero. When displayed in a string the `NULL` character appears as a space.

1.6.2.2 Escape Sequences for C0 Control Characters

The **C0 control characters** have a long history in computer programming. They were originally used to control teletype machines. The ASCII character set, more formally known as ISO/IEC 646, has two subsets of characters. One is referred to as the *control character set* and the other is the *graphic character set*. C0 is the name of the control character set. The C in C0 stands for *control*. The 0 is a sequencing number (that is, C0 was the first control character set). These are simply naming conventions used for characters subsets in ISO/IEC. C0 is also used in Latin-1 and any other character set that builds on top of ISO/IEC 646, including the *Unicode Standard*. Latin-1 also includes the **C1** control character set. Though seldom used outside of ISO/IEC protocols, the name of the graphic character set used in ISO/IEC 646 is **G0**.

Because control characters are nongraphic, they have identifying acronyms such as FF for *form feed*. Those acronyms are used in code tables in place of the glyph used for graphic characters.

The category of control characters for which there are escape sequences in the Java programming language is referred to as **format effectors**, which "describe how the originator of the data stream wishes the information to be formatted or presented."[11] They are used when sending text to a display device such as the console or a printer. Table 1-6 includes the definitions of the control characters used in the Java programming language as found in ISO/IEC 6429.

The semantics of these escape sequences and their corresponding control characters are not part of the *Unicode Standard*. The *Unicode Standard* includes something of a disclaimer about these control characters.

> Programs that conform to the *Unicode Standard* may treat these 16-bit control codes in exactly the same way as they treat their 7- and 8-bit equivalents in other protocols, such as ISO/IEC 2022 and ISO/IEC 6429. Such usage constitutes a higher-level protocol and is beyond the scope of the *Unicode Standard*.[12]

Most of the time you use them when writing to standard output, as discussed in 5.10 Displaying Diagnostic Messages on the Console.

1.6.2.2.1 Line, Paragraph, and Page Separator Characters The
information and terminology used in this section is based in part on *Unicode Technical Report #13*, "Unicode Newline Guidelines." Note that the *JLS* uses the term *line terminator* instead of *line separator*. This usage is at odds with both the *Unicode Standard* and the name of the line.sepa-

---

11. ISO/IEC 6429, "Information Technology — Control functions for coded character sets," Third Edition (Genève: ISO/IEC, 1991), §4.2.41, "Formatter function."

12. Ken Whistler et al., *The Unicode Standard, Version 3.0* (Reading: Addison-Wesley, 2000), §2.8, "Controls and Control Sequences." Note that the *Unicode Standard* refers to control characters as control *codes*. I do not acknowledge this usage because it is contrary to ISO/IEC usage, and the ISO/ IEC defines the control characters, not the *Unicode Standard*.

Table 1-6: Escape Sequences for C0 Control Characters

Escape Sequence	Identifying Acronym	Character Name	ISO/IEC 6429 Definition[a]
\b	BS	Backspace	BS causes the active data position to be moved one character position in the data component in the direction opposite to that of the implicit movement.
\t	HT	Horizontal tab	HT causes the active data position to be moved to the following character tabulation stop in the presentation component.
\n	LF	Line feed[b]	LF causes the active presentation position to be moved to the corresponding character position of the following line in the presentation component.
\f	FF	Form feed	FF causes the active presentation position to be moved to the corresponding character position of the line at the page home position of the next form or page in the presentation component.
\r	CR	Carriage return	CR cause the active presentation position to be moved to the line home position of the same line in the presentation component.

a. These are not the complete definitions. They just give the flavor of the definitions as found in ISO/IEC 6429.
b. This is the Unicode name for what is more commonly referred to as the *new line* character.

rator system property. While both terms are acceptable, this book consistently uses *line separator*.

Programmers are mostly interested in the line separator characters. The most commonly used **line separators** are ASCII control characters, which explains why this is a subsection of "Escape Sequences for C0 Control Characters." That also explains why those line separator characters are almost universally recognized as commands by display devices; they have been around for a very long time. The line separator for Windows and Internet protocols requires the use of two C0 control characters. Table 1-7

Table 1-7: Line, Paragraph, and Page Separator Characters[a]

Type	Name	Acronym, Escape Sequence, and Character Code[b]			Platform(s)
Line	Carriage return	CR	\r	0D	MacIntosh
	Line feed	LF	\n	0A	Unix and some non-standard data transfer protocols based on Unix assumptions
	CRLF	CRLF	\r\n	0D0A	Windows and most Internet protocols such as HTTP
	Line separator	LS	\u2028	2028	*Unicode Standard*
Paragraph	Paragraph separator	PS	\u2029	2029	*Unicode Standard*
Page	Form feed	FF	\f	0C	Universally used as a page break character

a. There are other, less well-known line separators such as the vertical tab (VT) used by Word and a new line (NEL) character defined in ISO 6429 as a C1 control code.
b. The LF character maps to a different character code in EBCDIC systems.

summarizes the line, paragraph, and page separator characters that are important to Java programmers.

For the sake of HTML programmers, line separators correspond to the <BR> tag in HTML. Paragraph separators correspond to <P> and </P> tags.

The *Unicode Standard* has this say about the LS and PS characters.

> The *Unicode Standard* defines two unambiguous separator characters, Paragraph Separator (PS = 2029_{16}) and Line Separator (LS = 2028_{16}). In Unicode text, the PS and LS characters should be used wherever the desired function is unambiguous.[13]

Java will help usher in a day when these unambiguous line and paragraph separators characters are widely used, but until then a Java programmer needs to know how to generate a platform-neutral line separator using the older ASCII control characters. There are basically two options for generating platform-neutral line separators.

1. Invoke the `System.getProperty("line.separator")` method. The value returned can be stored in a `String` type variable and subsequently used in string concatenation operations.

2. Invoke the `newLine()` method in `BufferedWriter` or one of the overloaded `println` methods in `PrintWriter`, both of which use the `line.separator` system property. The no-argument `println()` is not always used to print a blank line. When used after a series of `print` method invocations, invoking the no-argument `println()` is a way of adding a platform-neutral line separator to the end of an existing line.

Neither of these options work if you are implementing a server or otherwise writing *network code*. Network protocols such as HTTP always use the same `\r\n` line separator as Windows regardless of the host system. In that case you should always hard code line separators.

Paragraph separators are typically only implemented in text editors, word processors, and the like. In practice, most text editors and word processors (including NotePad and Word) interpret line separators as paragraph separators because of automatic line wrapping. In other words, the ¶ symbol used by many word processors is actually a line separator interpreted as a paragraph separator. The difference is that paragraph separation includes formatting information such as indentation, line spacing, and alignment. A **page separator** is simply another name for the form feed character.

1.6.2.3 Escape Sequences for Special Characters

These escape sequences are required because the corresponding characters are used in Java to delimit character and string literals or to begin escape sequences. Table 1-8 shows the escape sequences.

---

13. Mark Davis, *Unicode Technical Report #13*, "Unicode Newline Guidelines" (*www.unicode.org/unicode/reports/tr13/tr13-5*, Unicode Inc., 1998–1999), §4, "Recommendations."

Table 1-8: Escape Sequences for Special Characters

Escape Sequence	Character Name
\\"	Quotation mark
\\'	Apostrophe
\\\\	Backslash

The quotation mark escape sequence must be used to include a quotation mark in a string; otherwise, the quotation mark by itself would terminate the string. For the same reason the apostrophe escape sequence is used to initialize a `char` field with an apostrophe. For example,

```
static final char APOSTROPHE = '\''
```

The backslash escape sequence must be used wherever the backslash character is not used in an escape sequence. The following is an example of using a Unicode escape to print the trademark sign in a string:

```
System.out.println("Java\u2122 is a trademark of Sun Microsystems, Inc.");
```

This prints

```
Java™ is a trademark of Sun MicroSystems, Inc.
```

If, on the other hand, a programmer wanted to display the Unicode escape sequence, an extra backslash must be used. For example,

```
System.out.println ("\\u2122 = \u2122")
```

This prints

```
\u2122 = ™
```

The first Unicode escape is not translated because there are an odd number of \ characters at the start of the escape sequence. This is discussed further in the next section.

1.6.2.4 Unicode Escape Sequences

The fourth and final category of escape sequences is **Unicode escapes**. Unicode escapes are not so much used by application programmers as they are by tools such as the `native2ascii` tool used to create resource bundles and the input methods used in Asia to type ideographs using a standard keyboard. There is usually going to be something between you, the application programmer, and the Unicode escape sequences written to source code or a resource file.

Unicode escape sequences always begin with the Unicode escape \u followed by four hexadecimal digits (0 to 9, a to f, or A to F). A compiler error is generated if there are fewer than four hexadecimal digits following a Unicode escape. This means leading zeros are required for Unicode escape sequences less than \u1000. Hexadecimal values have always been used to express character codes in the code tables of formal specifications such as those for the ASCII and Latin-1 character sets. Programmers, on the other hand, are just as likely, if not more, to use decimal values for characters in the ASCII or Latin-1 character sets because the range of values is from 0 to 255. With Unicode, however, the range of values is from 0 to 65,535. Programmers are a lot more likely to use hexadecimal values to express Unicode character codes because there are so many more of them. It is much easier, for example, to remember FFFD as the replacement character in the *Unicode Standard* than it is to remember the decimal equivalent of 65533. (The replacement character prints as a question mark. It is used when there is no glyph available in a particular font to represent a character.)

Unicode escape sequences are significantly different from other escape sequences because they can be used anywhere in a compilation unit, not just in character and string literals. You can even use them for operators. For example,

```
\u0063\u006c\u0061\u0073\u0073 Test {
    public static void main(String[] args) {
        int \u0069 = 2 \u002B 2;
        System.out.print("2 + 2 = " + i);
    }
}
```

Executing this program prints

```
2 + 2 = 4
```

The keyword class is typed as \u0063\u006c\u0061\u0073 \u0073. The identifier i is typed as \u0069, and subsequently referred to as i. Even the + operator is written as \u002B. It is actually possible to write an entire program using only Unicode escapes. In practice, however, hard coded Unicode escapes (versus the use of a tool that writes Unicode escapes) are usually limited to symbols and other unusual characters not found on a standard keyboard.

The following are some obscure points about using Unicode escape sequences.

- The first two characters of a Unicode escape must be \u. The \ cannot be written to a source code file as \u005C, which is the Unicode escape sequence for the backslash character. Likewise, the small letter u cannot be written as \u0075. For example, consider the following string:

  `"\u005cu005a"`

  You might think this is translated as \u005a, which is the character Z. If printed, however, what you would see is \u005a, not Z.

- There must always be an odd number of backslashes at the beginning of a Unicode escape sequence in order for it to be translated. For example, the Unicode escape sequence for the copyright symbol is \u00A9. However, \\u00A9 is read by the compiler as \u00A9 instead of ©. On the other hand, \\\u00A9 is translated as "\©".

- The Unicode escape sequences \u000d and \u000a cannot be used in character or string literals. Those are line separator characters, and after translation (which is the first step in the tokenization process) are indistinguishable from other line separator characters embedded into the text of a compilation unit. Lines separation, therefore, splits the character or string literal into multiple tokens. The effect is that the character or string literal appears to begin and end on different lines, which generates a compiler error in the parser. Note that this is true even though the equivalent \r and \n escape sequences can be used in character and string literals. Those line separators pass through the entire compilation process and are used to control display devices.

None of these are scenarios an application programmer is likely to encounter, but they are included here for the sake of completeness.

1.6.3 String Literals

The most important thing to remember about string literals is that they must begin and end on the same line. Java has no line continuation character as do some programming languages. Therefore, you cannot split a string literal across several lines. For example, the following code does not compile:

```
class Test {
    static String s = "Four score and seven years ago our fathers brought forth
                       on this continent, a new nation, conceived in Liberty,
                       and dedicated to the proposition that all men are created
                       equal." ;
    public static void main (String[] args) {
      System.out.println(s);
    }
}
```

Instead, you must break the string literal into parts so that each part fits on one line. For example,

```
class Test {
  static String s = "Fourscore and seven years ago our fathers brought forth" +
                    " on this continent, a new nation, conceived in Liberty," +
              "and dedicated to the proposition that all men are created equal." ;
    public static void main (String[] args) {
        System.out.println(s);
    }
}
```

The + symbol in this context is referred to as a *string concatenation operator*. The string concatenation operation can be optionally enclosed in parentheses for the sake of clarity.

Precisely because strings must begin and end on the same line, there are a lot of string concatenation operations in the Java programming language. This is not, however, a performance problem. A string concatenation operation that involves only string literals is computed at compile time and then stored as one string in the class file generated by the compiler. See 5.9 String Concatenation Operations for a discussion.

1.6.3.1 *The Empty String*

An **empty string** is represented as " ". There are two common uses of an empty string.

- Some programmers initialize fields (that is, class or instance variables) that are String objects and do not otherwise have an initial value with the empty string. Their rationale for doing so is that String objects such as addressLine2 are not always assigned a value and the standard default initialization of null for reference types may result in abrupt completion at run time should the field inadvertently be used. It is arguable whether or not that is a good coding practice. Nevertheless, it is one use for empty strings.

- String concatenation operations frequently begin with an empty string. In that context an empty string is referred to as a **primer string** in this book. Primer strings can be used as a quick method of converting primitive types to strings. For example,

```
System.setProperty("screen.width",  "" + getWidth());
System.setProperty("screen.height", "" + getHeight());
System.setProperty("screen.x",      "" + getX());
System.setProperty("screen.y",      "" + getY());
```

The use of a primer string in string concatenation operations is discussed further in 5.10 Displaying Diagnostic Messages on the Console. The empty string is sometimes called a *null string*. Because strings are objects in the Java programming language, however, that term can be misleading. The proper term in Java is *empty string*.

1.6.4 Numeric Literals

All numeric literals have one of four primitive numeric types: int, long, float, or double. There are a number of considerations when determining the data type of a numeric literal. The first thing to do is to determine if the numeric literal is an integral or floating-point type. Any of the following makes a numeric literal a floating-point type:

- A floating-point suffix (f, F, d, or D)
- A decimal point
- An exponent

Otherwise, a numeric literal is an integer. Note that any use of a decimal point makes the numeric literal a floating-point type. It does not matter if there are any digits to the right of the decimal point. For example:

```
class Test {
  public static void main(String args[]) {
    int i = 1.;
  }
}
```

Attempting to compile this program generates the following compiler error:

```
Test.java:3: possible loss of precision
found   : double
required: int
    int i = 1.;
            ^
```

The default data type of the 1. numeric literal is double, which cannot be assigned to an int without the use of an (int) cast operator.

In the absence of a numeric suffix the default data type of a numeric literal is used. The default type for integer literals is int. Floating-point literals default to the double data type. The **numeric suffixes** in Table 1-9 can be used to specify a type other than the default. They are required when the value of an integer literal exceeds the range of the int data type or when a floating-point literal is assigned to either an integral type or float. Use of the capital letter L is strongly preferred to the small letter l, which looks like the number 1. For example, what is the value of 1l1? Notice that there is no numeric suffix for int because that is the default data type for integer literals. There is a numeric suffix for double, however, which is the default data type for floating-point literals. That is an odd inconsistency that makes no sense unless you know that the d or D suffix was inherited from the C/C++ programming languages. In the Java programming language use of the d or D suffix is always redundant.

Table 1-10 shows the minimum and maximum values of numeric literals as given in the *JLS*. With one exception, these are the same numeric literals used to initialize the MIN_VALUE and MAX_VALUE fields in the respective primitive type wrapper class. The exception is float type literals. For comparison's sake, the values used to initialize Float.MAX_VALUE and Float.MIN_VALUE are included in the table. They are the longer, bracketed literals. Given the precision of the float data type, the different float type literals are mathematically the same. For example,

```
class Test {
   public static void main(String args[]) {
      float f1 = 3.40282347e+38f;           // largest float literal in JLS
      float f2 = 3.40282346638528860e+38f;  // Float.MAX_VALUE
      System.out.println(f1 == f2);
   }
}
```

Table 1-9: Numeric Suffixes

Suffix	Type
l or L	long
f or F	float
d or D	double

Table 1-10: Numeric Literal Ranges

Type	Negative Integer Range or Smallest Floating-Point Literal	Positive Integer Range or Largest Floating-Point Literal
int	-2147483648	2147483647
hexadecimal	0x80000000	0x7fffffff
octal	020000000000	017777777777
long	-9223372036854775808L	9223372036854775807L
hexadecimal	0x8000000000000000L	0x7fffffffffffffffL
octal	01000000000000000000000L	0777777777777777777777L
float	1.40239846e-45f	3.40282347e+38f
	[1.40129846432481707e-45f]	[3.40282346638528860e+38f]
double	4.94065645841246544e-324	1.79769313486231570e+308

Executing this program prints `true`.

Integer literals throw an exception if the literal value exceeds the range of the data type in which it is stored by a Java compiler. For example,

```
class Test {
  public static void main(String args[]) {
    long l = 2147483648; // Integer.MAX_VALUE + 1
  }
}
```

There are two assignment operations here. The one involving the l variable is explicit, but the integer literal is also implicitly assigned to an `int` type variable after being read by a Java compiler. That implicit assignment generates the following compiler error:

```
Test.java:3: integer number too large: 2147483648
    long l = 2147483648; // Integer.MAX_VALUE + 1
             ^

1 error
```

If, however, the L suffix is added to the end of the integer literal, the program compiles successfully.

There are three different positional notation systems used for writing integer literals. Floating-point literals can only be written using standard or scientific notation. The term **standard notation** refers to the decimal system. The following is an example of expressing the same value using all four of the notation systems available in the Java programming language:

```
int x = 29;           // standard notation
int x = 0x1d;         // hexadecimal notation
int x = 035;          // octal notation
double x = .29e2;     // scientific notation
```

All four of these notation systems are discussed in the following subsection.

1.6.4.1 Positional Notation Systems, Digits, and Radices

The **decimal system** of numbers used throughout the world is a **positional notation system** that uses the digits 0, 1, 2, 3, 4, 5, 6, 7, 8, and 9. The value of each digit in a positional notation system depends on where the digit appears in relation to what is commonly called the *decimal point*. However, that term is specific to the decimal system. For example, the binary system has a *binary point*. The generic term for the point used in positional notation systems is the **radix point** (or base point). I will come back to the term *radix* momentarily. The value of a digit in positional notation systems is referred to as the **place value**. In the decimal system, for example, digits in the number 1,024 have the following place values:

$$1,024 = (1 \times 10^3) + (0 \times 10^2) + (2 \times 10^1) + (4 \times 10^0)$$
$$1,024 = 1000 + 0 + 20 + 4$$

Notice that the place value to the immediate left of the radix point is one. That is true for all positional notation systems.

The decimal system is just one of many possible positional notation systems. Others include the **binary system**, the **octal system**, and the **hexidecimal system**, all of which are used in computer programming. In fact, the binary system can be described as *the language of digital computers*. In the binary, octal, and hexidecimal systems, 1,024 is represented as follows:

binary	$10000000000 = 1 \times 2^{10}$
octal	$2000 = 2 \times 8^3$
hexidecimal	$400 = 4 \times 16^2$

Each positional notation system is named after the base used to calculate the value of a digit. The binary system is base 2, the octal system is base 8, and the hexidecimal system is base 16. There are others though. For example, the *duodecimal system* is base 12. In fact, any whole number greater than one can be used as the base. All of which are derived from the Arabic system of numbers.

The base of a positional notation system is more formally known as the radix. For example, *radix 10* means the decimal system and *radix 16* means the hexidecimal system. In the core API of the Java programming language, the base of a positional notation system is always referred to as the radix. For example, there are the following **radix-conversion methods**, all of which return the numerical value of a string:

```
public static byte parseByte(String s, int radix)
public static short parseShort(String s, int radix)
public static int parseInt(String s, int radix)
public static long parseLong(String s, int radix)

public static Byte valueOf(String s, int radix)
public static Short valueOf(String s, int radix)
public static Integer valueOf(String s, int radix)
public static Long valueOf(String s, int radix)
```

These methods are discussed in 4.9.1 Parsing Strings for Primitive Type Values.

As noted above, any whole number greater than one can be used as the base in a positional notation system. However, there is a practical limitation in that you must have a symbol for each of the digits. The numbers 0 to 9 are used as digits in the decimal system. Beyond that, however, letters are used. The letter a or A equals 10, b or B equals 11, and so on up to z or Z, which equals 35. For example,

```
class Test {
    public static void main (String[] args) {
        System.out.println("a = " + Integer.valueOf("a", 16));
        System.out.println("b = " + Integer.valueOf("b", 16));
        System.out.println("c = " + Integer.valueOf("c", 16));
        System.out.println("d = " + Integer.valueOf("d", 16));
        System.out.println("e = " + Integer.valueOf("e", 16));
        System.out.println("f = " + Integer.valueOf("f", 16));
        System.out.println("A = " + Integer.valueOf("A", 12));
        System.out.println("B = " + Integer.valueOf("B", 12));
        System.out.println("Z = " + Integer.valueOf("Z", 36));
    }
}
```

Executing this program prints

```
a = 10
b = 11
c = 12
d = 13
e = 14
f = 15
A = 10
B = 11
Z = 35
```

Notice that the radix is 36, but the value of Z is 35. The radix is the number of digits used in a given notation system. For example, the binary system use 2 digits (0 and 1) whereas the hexidecimal system uses 16 digits (0 to 9, a to f, or A to F).

Because you must have a symbol for each of the digits in a positional notation system, the practical limits of the radix are 10 numbers (0 to 9) plus 26 letters in the English alphabet (a to z or A to Z), which is a total of 36 digits. This limitation is in place throughout the Java programming language and is represented by the following declarations in the Character class:

```
public static final int MIN_RADIX = 2;
public static final int MAX_RADIX = 36;
```

Positional notation systems are to numeric literals what escape sequences are to character literals. They are just different ways of representing the same character or number. For example,

```
class Test {
    public static void main (String[] args) {
        char c = 65;              // character code (decimal)
        System.out.print(c);
        c = '\101';               // octal escape
        System.out.print(c);
        c = '\u0041';             // Unicode escape
        System.out.print(c);
    }
}
```

Executing this program prints AAA. Now compare that program to the following:

```
class Test {
    public static void main (String[] args) {
        int i = 65;               // decimal system
        System.out.print(i);
        i = 0101;                 // octal system
        System.out.print(i);
        i = 0x41;                 // hexidecimal system
        System.out.print(i);
    }
}
```

Executing this program prints 656565.

The Java programming language directly supports three positional notation systems. Those are the decimal, octal, and hexidecimal systems. In the case of the octal and hexadecimal systems, that *direct support* takes the form of **radix specifiers** that can be used in numeric literals.

The radix specifier for the octal system is the digit 0. This means octal literals always have at least two digits. There is a need to point this out because, unlike hexidecimal literals, the radix specifier in an octal literal is easily overlooked. For example, what is the value of x after x = 097 is executed? This is a trick question. The assignment statement x = 097 will not compile because 9 is not a valid octal digit. However, x = 077 will compile and the value of x is 63, not 77. The lesson here is to beware of leading zeros in numeric literals. The radix specifier for the hexidecimal system is 0x or 0X. Leading zeros after the 0x or 0X are ignored. Thus, the literal value 0x1d is the same as 0x01d. Here is an example of expressing zero using all three of these positional notation systems:

```
decimal . . . . . . .  0
octal . . . . . . . . .  00
hexidecimal . . . .  0x0  or  0X0
```

All other numeric literals that begin with the digits 1 to 9 are decimal numbers.

The octal system is obsolete, but until direct support for the octal system is removed from the Java programming language, you must always remember that the radix specifier for octal literals is zero. This means integer literals with leading zeros are interpreted as octal numbers. The hexadecimal system, on the other hand, is used all of the time in computer programming.

Hexidecimal literals can be used in place of decimal literals anywhere numeric literals are used.

For example,

```
class Test {
   public static void main (String[] args) {
      for (int i=0x2000; i <= 0x2FFF; i++) {
         char ch = (char) i;
                if (Character.isJavaIdentifierPart(ch))
            System.out.print(toUnicodeEscape(ch) + "  ");
      }
   }
   static String toUnicodeEscape(char ch) {
      String s = "" + Character.forDigit(((ch >>> 12) & 0xF), 16) +
                 Character.forDigit(((ch >>> 8) & 0xF), 16) +
                 Character.forDigit(((ch >>> 4) & 0xF), 16) +
                 Character.forDigit(((ch) & 0xF), 16);
      return "\\u" + s.toUpperCase();
   }
}
```

This program asks the question *are there any characters in the Symbols Area (\u2000 through \u2FFF) of the Unicode code space that can be used in identifiers*. When I got the idea to use this as an example I thought the answer would be *No*. There are actually quite a few, including all of the Roman numerals.

The hexidecimal system is also used all the time as mask values when bit shifting. For example,

```
static String toUnicodeEscape(char ch) {
    String s = "" + Character.forDigit((((ch >>> 12) & 0xF), 16) +
                    Character.forDigit((((ch >>> 8) & 0xF), 16) +
                    Character.forDigit((((ch >>> 4) & 0xF), 16) +
                    Character.forDigit((((ch) & 0xF), 16);
    return "\\u" + s.toUpperCase();
}
```

I use this method to convert primitive `char` values to Unicode escape sequences. The `0xF` mask says *only consider the numeric value of the last four bits* (which is equal to one hexidecimal digit). Notice also the radix argument of `16` being passed to the `Character.forDigit(int digit, int radix)` method. There are many other uses of the hexidecimal notation system in computer programming. These are just a few examples.

1.6.4.2 Scientific Notation

Scientific notation is typically used by mathematicians, engineers, and the like to express very large or very small numbers. Any use of scientific notation is by definition a floating-point literal.

The exponent is written using the letter `e` or `E` followed by an integer representing the exponent value. The exponent value may be optionally signed. An unsigned exponent is positive. Everything to the left of the exponent is the **mantissa**. In this book I use mantissa exclusively in reference to scientific notation. (When discussing the floating-point formats I prefer to use the IEEE term *significand*.) Figure 1-1 displays the two main parts of a number written in scientific notation. This expression is read

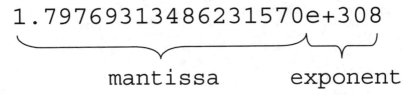

Figure 1-1: Scientific Notation

$1.79769313486231570 \times 10^{308}$, which is `Double.MAX_VALUE`. To convert a numeric literal written using computerized scientific notation to a decimal equivalent could not be easier. For example,

```
class Test {
    public static void main(String[] args) {
        System.out.println("1e3 = " + 1e3);
        System.out.println("1e-3 = " + 1e-3);
    }
}
```

Executing this program prints

```
1e3 = 1000.0
1e-3 = 0.0010
```

A positive exponent indicates the number of places to move the decimal point to the right and a negative exponent indicates the number of places to move the decimal point to the left. The conversion from scientific to standard notation is easy because both the mantissa and exponent are base 10. The fact that both the mantissa and exponent are always base 10 is why the scientific notation used in computer programming languages is sometimes referred to as **computerized scientific notation**.

1.6.5 Class Literals

Class literals were introduced in the Java 1.1 release along with inner classes. The rationale for class literals is given in the *Inner Classes Specification* as follows.

> Java APIs which require class objects as method arguments are much easier to use when the class literal syntax is available. Note that the compiler is responsible for taking into account the ambient package and import statements when processing the `TypeName` of a class literal.
>
> The older usage of `Class.forName` requires the programmer to figure out the desired package prefix and write it in a class name string. The difficulty of getting the string spelled right becomes greater in the presence of inner classes, since their names (as processed by `Class.forName`) are encoded with '$' characters instead of dots.[14]

---

14. John Rose, *Inner Classes Specification* (Mountain View: Sun Microsystems, 1997), "Other changes in the Java 1.1 language."

If a class has already be instantiated, you can always invoke the `get-Class()` method declared in the `Object` class. The question is how to get a reference to a class that has not yet been loaded. Before the 1.1 release the `Class.forName(String className)` utility method used by browsers to load applets was the only means of accomplishing this. However, that method requires a fully qualified class name, something not available for inner classes because the fully qualified name of an inner class is compiler-generated. Class literals are a much more natural way of accomplishing the same thing.

The general form of a **class literal** is *TypeName*.`class` where *TypeName* is the name of a class, interface, array, or primitive type. The class literal `void.class` is also valid. Class literals are better than the `Class.forName(String className)` method for the following reasons.

- The `className` argument in a `Class.forName(String className)` method invocation must be a fully qualified type name. Class literals, on the other hand, can be constructed using simple or partially qualified type names. Fully qualified type names can be used, but they are not necessary. The compiler disambiguates the type name used in class literals the same as it does any other simple or partially qualified type names using a procedure discussed in 2.5.4.1 Disambiguating Type Names.
- Misspelling when using `Class.forName(String className)` results in a `ClassNotFoundException` at run time, whereas misspelling the type name in a class literal is a compiler error.
- Both a class literal and the `Class.forName(String className)` method will dynamically load the named class or interface if it is not already loaded. That means the possibility exists that the named class or interface may not be found at run time. The `Class.forName(String className)` method throws a `ClassNotFoundException`, which is a checked exception. A class literal throws a `NoClassDefFoundError`. The difference in throwing a checked exception versus an error means that `Class.forName(String className)` must be coded in a `try` block.
- `Class.forName(String className)` does not work with primitive types or `void`.

For the primitive data types and `void` there, the special `TYPE` constant declared in each of the primitive type wrapper classes is an alternative to class literals. Table 1-11 lists all of the `TYPE` constants.

For any given primitive data type or `void` the class literal and `TYPE` constant reference the same `Class` object. Both are used in the core API. I believe the raison d'être for the `TYPE` fields is access time. In some way or another, class literals are implemented on top of `Class` objects. The problem is that `Class` objects are implementation defined. That at least suggests the possibility that access time could vary from one JVM implementation to the next. By storing a reference to the `Class` object for a primitive data type in the `TYPE` constant of the corresponding primitive type wrapper classes, access times are comparable to what they would be for any field access expression. Moreover, in most JVM implementations the primitive type wrapper classes are preloaded along with most of the `java.lang` package. In short, you should use the `TYPE` fields for primitive data types rather than the corresponding class literal.

The `Class.forName(String className)` method is referred to as "older usage" in the *Inner Classes Specification*. For all its shortcomings, however, there are times when only the `Class.for-Name(String className)` method will work, which is why it was not deprecated. When is that? When the class name is not known at compile

Table 1-11: The `TYPE` Field in Primitive Type Wrapper Classes

Primitive Types and `void`	Class Literal	Alternative `TYPE` Field
boolean	boolean.class	Boolean.TYPE
char	char.class	Character.TYPE
byte	byte.class	Byte.TYPE
short	short.class	Short.TYPE
int	int.class	Integer.TYPE
long	long.class	Long.TYPE
float	float.class	Float.TYPE
double	double.class	Double.TYPE
void	void.class	Void.TYPE

time. For example, the `Class.forName(String className)` method was originally used by browsers to load applets. The name of the applet class is not known until the HTTP page that includes the `<applet>` tag is loaded.

1.7 Separators

The **separator** tokens are shown in Table 1-12.

Table 1-12: Separators

Separator	Name	Uses
( )	LEFT and RIGHT PARENTHESIS	Formal parameter lists Argument lists Cast operators Operator precedence Control flow expressions
{ }	LEFT and RIGHT CURLY BRACKET[a] (BRACES)	Class body Interface body Method body Constructor body `static` initialization blocks Instance initialization blocks Array initializers Arbitrary blocks
[ ]	LEFT and RIGHT SQUARE BRACKET	Dimension expressions Index expressions
;	SEMICOLON	End of statements `for` loop header
,	COMMA	Formal parameter lists Argument lists `for` loop header `extends` clause (interfaces only) `implements` clause
.	FULL STOP (PERIOD)	Qualified names Method invocation expressions Field access expressions

a. I believe that *BRACES* is actually more common among programmers, at least in the United States.

1.8 Operators

There are a total of 40 operators in the Java programming language.

> 1 cast operator
> 1 `instanceof` operator
> <u>38</u> unary, binary, and ternary operators
>
> 40 total

In addition, the + operator is overloaded for string concatenation.

Java books sometimes refer to the following as operators.

- The so-called "membership operators" `[]`, ".", and `(params)` are separators, not operators. Hence, they should never be included in operator order of precedence tables. When they are shown they have the highest precedence of all operators. However, that is because they are only used in primary expressions, not because of operator order of precedence. Brackets are used in array access and array creation expressions. The "." operator is used in qualified names, field access expressions, and method invocation expressions. The parentheses at this level of precedence are those used to enclose an argument list in method invocation expressions and class instance creation expressions. All of these are primary expressions.

- The `new` keyword is not an operator for the same reason. It is only used in primary expressions.

There is no such thing as an operator in primary expressions; all expressions are either primary expressions or operator expressions.

Chapter 2

Compilation Units

Chapter Contents

2.1 Introduction

The more informal name for a **compilation unit** is a **source code file**. They are plain text files used for writing Java source code. At a different level compilation units are comparable to the blank sheet of paper on which an author or composer begins a creative work. Instead of writing a great novel or a symphony, computer programmers write applications, which usually consist of a number of compilation units. Like creative writing or composing, there is a basic structure that must be followed. This chapter serves to introduce the reader to the structure of compilation units without getting involved in the more complex subjects of defining what the `static` keyword actually means or explaining how the `this` and `super` keywords are used. Those are important subjects in understanding compilation units, but are not discussed until Chapter 3.

This chapter focuses on the organization of a compilation unit, most of which is within the opening and closing brace of a class or interface body. Class body declarations can appear haphazard at first until you learn about the compiler-generated **special initialization methods** used to initialize classes and objects.

A knowledge of the special initialization methods is essential to understanding the anatomy of a compilation unit.

I cannot exaggerate the importance of this subject. A knowledge of the special initialization methods will help you to understand much about how the Java programming language works.

One of the more important sections in this chapter discusses the five kinds of classes and interfaces:

- Package members
- Nested top-level classes and interfaces
- Inner member classes
- Local classes
- Anonymous classes

Only package members are declared directly in a compilation unit. All five kinds of classes and interfaces, however, should be discussed at the same time. This is by no means a complete discussion. The focus is on understanding the differences in the declaration syntax, but includes a limited discussion of how the five kinds of classes and interfaces are used. In the About This Book section, I mentioned that there is no chapter on inner classes. Three of the five kinds of classes are inner classes, and in Chapter 3 you also get a big dose of inner classes. This is unusual in that inner classes are generally considered an advanced subject. Then again, this is a reference work and not a book designed to teach Java programming from scratch. Type declarations are a major part of compilation units. I feel confident that including a discussion of all five kinds of classes and interfaces in this chapter is appropriate.

There are several references to the *Inner Classes Specification* in this chapter. That document was superseded by the second edition of the *JLS*. While I truly admire John Rose for taking on the job of introducing inner classes to Java programmers, I do not recommend reading the *Inner Classes Specification* unless you already have some experience using inner classes. There are significant differences between the *Inner Classes Specification* and the *JLS*, the most important of which I discuss at length in 2.7 The Definition of Top-Level Classes. Besides that, I quote John Rose extensively in this book.

The concept of *containment* and *inner class hierarchies* as distinct from *inheritance hierarchies* is also introduced in this chapter. Both describe the relationship of nested types to the top-level class or interface in which they are declared. The terms *containment hierarchy* and *inner class hierarchy* are not used in the *JLS*, the original *Inner Classes Specification*, or any other Java book that I have read. I developed the idea of containment and inner class hierarchies in an effort to simplify scope and access control rules involving nested types. As presented in the original *Inner Classes Specification*, those rules were very difficult to understand. As presented in the second edition of the *JLS*, I think those rules are oversimplified. The importance of containment and inner class hierarchies to my presentation of the Java programming language is such that there is an entire section in this chapter dedicated to explaining the rationale for them.

2.2 The Terminology of Class Body Declarations

As stated above, most of a compilation unit is within the opening and closing brace of a class or interface body. Before discussing the anatomy of a compilation unit you must be familiar with the basic terminology of class body declarations. That terminology is largely based on the use of the `static` keyword, which is a valid modifier in all class body declarations except the following.

- Constructors are inherently non-`static`
- Nested interfaces are implicitly `static`. The `static` keyword can be used in the declaration of a nested interface but is not required

The terms used to refer to an entity declared in a class body change (sometimes drastically) depending on whether or not the `static` modifier is used in their declaration. The `static` and non-`static` terms for each entity are shown in Table 2-1.

Table 2-1: Terms for Class Body Declarations

Entity	`static`	**Non-`static`**
Field	Class variable	Instance variable
Initialization block	`static` initialization block	Instance initialization block
Constructor		Constructor
Method	Class method	Instance method
Interface	Nested interface	
Class	Nested top-level class	Inner member class

Any class or interface declared in the body of another type (except for local and anonymous classes) is a member of that type, just like fields and methods are members. Another term used to describe such a nested class or interface is a **member type**. Member types may be more specifically referred to as either **member classes** or **member interfaces**. Member interfaces are implicitly `static`, which is why they are usually just referred to as **nested interfaces**. Member classes, however, as with the other members of a type, are either `static` or non-`static`. Instead of calling them *class classes* and *instance classes* like *class variables* and *instance variables*, or *class methods* and *instance methods*, however, they are called **nested top-level classes** and **inner member classes**.

The point here is simply that the `static` keyword makes a big difference in the declaration of an entity. The definition of most of the entities in Table 2-1 is based on the `static` modifier. Inner classes are a perfect example. The *JLS* defines an inner class as "a nested class that is not explicitly or implicitly declared `static`."[1] For the purpose of discussing the organization of compilation units, you only need to know the `static` and non-`static` names of the entities as shown in Table 2-1. The exact meaning of the `static` modifier is the subject of the next chapter, and the entities themselves are discussed throughout this book.

2.2.1 The Definition of Fields in Java

In the Java programming language the term **field** has a very specific meaning. It is used to differentiate the members of a class or interface type from local variables and parameters. Fields are variables that are not declared in a block (which includes initialization blocks, constructors, and methods). A variable declared in a block is said to be local to that block, or a **local variable**.

Fields are either class variables or instance variables, depending on whether or not the `static` keyword is used in their declaration. A **class variable** is declared using the `static` keyword. Another name for a class variable is a **`static` field**. An **instance variable** is any field that is not declared `static`. Another name for an instance variable is a **non-`static` field**. All fields declared in an interface are implicitly `static`. However, they are usually referred to as **interface constants** rather than

---

1. James Gosling, Bill Joy, Guy Steele, and Gilad Bracha, *The Java Language Specification, Second Edition* (Boston: Addison-Wesley, 2000), §8.1.2, "Inner Classes and Enclosing Instances."

class variables. The more substantial differences between class variables and instance variables are discussed in 3.2.1 `static` Fields.

2.2.2 Recognizing Constructors in Source Code

Constructors look like methods in that both can have parameter lists and a `throws` clause, but they are easy to recognize for several reasons, which are presented here in the order of their importance.

- The name of a constructor is the same as the name of the class in which it is declared. This is the easiest way to spot a constructor declaration in a compilation unit

- Access modifiers are the only modifiers used in the declaration of a constructor

- Constructor declarations do not have a result type because constructors always return a reference to the object created

After you get used to reading source code, constructors are easy to spot. They are also usually at the top of a compilation unit.

2.3 Anatomy of a Compilation Unit

The only compiler-enforced order to the declarations in a compilation unit is that a package declaration must be at the top of a compilation unit and any import declarations must immediately follow the package declaration. After the package and import declarations are one or more type declarations. In other words, compilation units have three parts:

1. Package declaration
2. Import declaration(s)
3. Type declaration(s)

Each of these is considered optional, which could be useful in compiling a template for reusable objects, application programs, utility classes, or any of the many other uses of reference types. You can even compile an empty file (at least using the latest version of the `javac` compiler) without generating a single compiler error or warning.

There can be only one package declaration and production code usually has one. There can be any number of import declarations, and anything other than the simplest of programs requires at least one or two import declarations. It is not uncommon to see full pages of import declarations in the source code of programmers who prefer to use single-type-import declarations (discussed below). Theoretically, there can be any number of type declarations in a compilation unit, but in practice there is usually only one. If more than one type is declared in a compilation unit only one of those types can be `public`.

Type declarations consist of a header and a body. The remainder of this section discusses the declarations in a class body. The declarations in an interface body are considerably simpler than class bodies and are discussed in 2.6.2.3 Interface Member Declarations.

Class bodies are a series of declarations inside of curly braces. Those declarations are one of the following:

1. Class variable (which is often a constant)
2. `static` initialization block
3. Class method
4. Instance variable
5. Instance initialization block
6. Constructor
7. Instance method
8. Inner member class
9. Nested top-level class
10. Nested interface

For the sake of simplicity, member types (8 to 10) are excluded from this discussion. Numbers 1 to 7 correspond to the circled numbers in Figure 2-1.

One of the main uses of this figure is to show how all executable code is part of some method. The dashed lines in Figure 2-1 represent the special initialization methods `<clinit>` and `<init>`, which are discussed below. Notice that there are two field declarations, two initialization blocks, and two method declarations (one `static` and the other non-`static`). Constructors are inherently non-`static`, which means that there are a total of seven different declarations in a class body (excluding member types). The `static` declarations are labeled using the circled digits ① ② ③, and the non-`static` declarations are labeled using the negative circled digits ❹ ❺ ❻ ❼. The character names *circled digit* and *negative cir-*

```
package declaration
import declaration(s)
class modifiers_opt class identifier extends_opt implements_opt
{
    <clinit>
    ┌──────────────────────────────────────────────────┐
    │ class variable declarations (including constants) │
    │  ┌─────────────────────────────────────────────┐  │
    │  │                 class variable initializers ① │  │
    │  │ static            = ┌─────────────────────┐ │  │
    │  │                     └─────────────────────┘ │  │
    │  └─────────────────────────────────────────────┘  │
    │ static initialization blocks ②                    │
    │  ┌─────────────────────────────────────────────┐  │
    │  │ static {                                     │  │
    │  └─────────────────────────────────────────────┘  │
    └──────────────────────────────────────────────────┘

    <init>
    ┌──────────────────────────────────────────────────┐
    │ instance variable declarations                    │
    │  ┌─────────────────────────────────────────────┐  │
    │  │            instance variable initializers ❹  │  │
    │  │      =  ┌─────────────────────────────────┐  │  │
    │  │         └─────────────────────────────────┘  │  │
    │  └─────────────────────────────────────────────┘  │
    │ instance initialization blocks ❺                  │
    │  ┌─────────────────────────────────────────────┐  │
    │  │      {                                    }  │  │
    │  └─────────────────────────────────────────────┘  │
    │ constructor declarations ❻                        │
    │  ┌─────────────────────────────────────────────┐  │
    │  └─────────────────────────────────────────────┘  │
    └──────────────────────────────────────────────────┘

    class method declarations ③
    ┌──────────────────────────────────────────────────┐
    │ static                                            │
    └──────────────────────────────────────────────────┘

    instance method declarations ❼
    ┌──────────────────────────────────────────────────┐
    │                                                   │
    └──────────────────────────────────────────────────┘
}
```

Figure 2-1: Anatomy of a compilation unit.

cled digit are from the *Unicode Standard*. Several discussions in this chapter and the next use the circled digits when referencing Figure 2-1.

2.3.1 Special Initialization Methods

The principle reason for discussing these methods is that they appear in stack traces. For example,

```
class Test {
    static {int i = 0/0;}
    public static void main(String args) { }
}
```

Attempting to execute this program throws the following exception:

```
Exception in thread "main" java.lang.ExceptionInInitializerError: java.lang.ArithmeticException: / by zero
        at Test.<clinit>(Test.java:2)
```

The code in `static` initialization blocks is added to the `<clinit>` method. It was the `<clinit>` method that abruptly completed, a fact that would be difficult to understand if you did not know something about the special initialization methods.

The same thing happens whenever an instance initialization block or constructor throws an uncaught exception. For example,

```
class Test {
    Test() {int i = 0/0;}
    public static void main(String[] args) {
        new Test();
    }
}
```

Attempting to execute this program throws the following exception:

```
Exception in thread "main" java.lang.ArithmeticException: / by zero
        at Test.<init>(Test.java:2)
        at Test.main(Test.java:4)
```

The larger lesson here is that all code is executed in some method, including variable initializers and the code in initialization blocks. Also, at run time the name of a constructor is always `<init>`.

The special initialization methods are like any other method in a class except that they are only executed by a Java Virtual Machine (JVM). They cannot be explicitly invoked by a programmer because `<` and `>` are not legal characters in identifiers. For example,

```
class Test {
    public static void main(String[] args) {
        <clinit>;
    }
}
```

Attempting to compile this program generates the following compiler error:

```
Test.java:3: illegal start of expression
        <clinit>;
        ^
1 error
```

The problem is not that the `<clinit>` method does not exist. It does. The problem is that the compiler does not recognize `<clinit>` as a method name (when used by a programmer).

Note that only the variable initializer of a field is properly part of the special initialization methods. (In Figure 2-1 the entire declaration for class and instance variables is shown inside the dashed boxes.) The actual declaration of a field is not included in the special initialization methods. For example,

```
class Test {
    int x = 10;
}
```

The `int  x` part of the variable declaration is properly part of the class body. Only the variable initializer is added to the `<init>` method. Inside of the `<init>` method for the `Test` class the variable initializer for `x` is just the assignment statement `x = 10`.

If you use `javap -c` to disassemble code, the `<init>` or `<clinit>` method names are not included in the output from the class file disassembler. The `<init>` methods still have what appears to be constructor names and `<clinit>` has no name. For example,

```
class Test {
    Test() { }
    static final long TIME_LOADED = System.currentTimeMillis();
    { if (true)
        throw new RuntimeException(); }
    public static void main(String[] args) {
      new Test();
    }
}
```

Using `javap -c` to disassemble the `Test.class` file prints

```
Compiled from Test.java
class Test extends java.lang.Object {
    static final long TIME_LOADED;
    Test();
    public static void main(java.lang.String[]);
    static {};
}

Method Test()
   0 aload_0
   1 invokespecial #1 <Method java.lang.Object()>
   4 new #2 <Class java.lang.RuntimeException>
   7 dup
   8 invokespecial #3 <Method java.lang.RuntimeException()>
  11 athrow
```

```
Method void main(java.lang.String[])
   0 new #4 <Class Test>
   3 dup
   4 invokespecial #5 <Method Test()>
   7 pop
   8 return

Method static {}
   0 invokestatic #6 <Method long currentTimeMillis()>
   3 putstatic #7 <Field long TIME_LOADED>
   6 return
```

The `RuntimeException` is being thrown in what appears to be a constructor:

```
Method Test()
   0 aload_0
   1 invokespecial #1 <Method java.lang.Object()>
   4 new #2 <Class java.lang.RuntimeException>
   7 dup
   8 invokespecial #3 <Method java.lang.RuntimeException()>
  11 athrow
```

However, executing this program throws the following exception:

```
Exception in thread "main" java.lang.RuntimeException
        at Test.<init>(Test.java:5)
        at Test.main(Test.java:7)
```

The method executing at the time the exception is thrown is `Test.<init>`, not the `Test()` constructor. This is further confirmed by the source code line number that is clearly pointing to the instance initialization block and not the `Test()` constructor.

The `<clinit>` method shows as follows:

```
Method static {}
   0 invokestatic #6 <Method long currentTimeMillis()>
   3 putstatic #7 <Field long TIME_LOADED>
   6 return
```

Not only is the method name not named `<clinit>`, there is no method name at all. These apparent discrepancies in the class file disassembler could be regarded as a bug. It is probably more accurate to say that the special initialization methods involve transformations that take place only after the class file is loaded. The fact is, if an uncaught exception is thrown in an instance variable initializer, instance initialization block, or constructor, the stack trace will always show `<init>` at the top of the stack. The method at the top of the stack is the one that threw the exception. The term used to refer to the method at the top of an execution stack is the **current method**. Likewise, if an uncaught exception is thrown in a class variable initializer or `static` initialization block, the stack trace will always show `<clinit>` at the top of the stack.

2.3.1.1 Class or Interface Initialization Methods `<clinit>`

Class initialization methods are used to initialize classes and interfaces when they are first loaded into a JVM. The code in a `<clinit>` method includes numbers ① and ② in Figure 2-1, which is all of the code from class variable initializers and `static` initialization blocks. That code is executed in the same textual order in which it appears in the compilation unit. There is at most one `<clinit>` method for every class or interface. The `<` and `>` characters are actually part of the method name. Class initialization methods have no parameters. The result type is always `void`.

To simplify the terminology I refer to all `<clinit>` methods as **class initialization methods**. The same method, however, is used to initialize interface constants when such initialization is required. There is a common misconception that all interface constants are inlined. This simply is not true. Some must be loaded into per-interface data structures and initialized just like class variables. For example, the `Test` class disassembled in the last section includes the following constant:

```
static final long TIME_LOADED = System.currentTimeMillis();
```

While this declaration meets the definition of a constant, it is not an inlined constant because of the method invocation expression in the variable initializer. Therefore, a `<clinit>` method is required, if that declaration were included in an interface, in order to invoke the `System.current-TimeMillis()` method. Such a `<clinit>` method would actually be an **interface initialization method**. If the variable initializer were changed to a compile-time constant expresssion, the `<clinit>` method would go away. In other words, if all of the interface constants are inlined, then there is no interface initialization method.

2.3.1.2 Instance Initialization Methods `<init>`

Instance initialization methods are used to initialize objects after they are created on the heap. They are the first method invoked after memory is allocated for an object and instance variables are initialized with standard default values. The code in an `<init>` method may include numbers ❹, ❺ and ❻ in Figure 2-1, which is all of the code from instance variable initializers, instance initialization blocks and one of the constructors. The compiler generates one **instance initialization method** for every constructor. The name of all instance initialization methods is `<init>`. That means `<init>` methods, like their corresponding constructors, are inherently overloaded. The `<init>` method has the same level of access as the corresponding constructor.

Instance initialization methods include at a minimum all of the code from the corresponding constructor. If the corresponding constructor begins with an explicit or implicit invocation of a superclass constructor, the `<init>` method also includes all of the instance variable initializers (transformed into assignment statements) and instance initialization blocks. Instance variable initializers and instance initialization blocks are executed in textual order followed by the code from the corresponding constructor. The other possibility is that one `<init>` method invokes another. That happens whenever the first line of a constructor explicitly invokes another constructor in the same class. If the corresponding constructor begins with an explicit invocation of another constructor in the same class, then the code from instance variable initializers and instance initialization blocks is omitted. Otherwise, that code could be executed twice when an object of that class is created.

If there are no constructors in the class, there is only one `<init>` method, which corresponds to the default constructor. Such an `<init>` method begins with an invocation of the superclass default constructor and has only the code from instance variable initializers and instance initialization blocks. A default constructor and, hence, the corresponding `<init>` method have the same level of access as the class in which the constructor is declared.

2.3.2 The Significance of Textual Order

The order in which the variable initializers and initialization blocks are added to the beginning of the special initialization methods is the same order in which they appear in source code. This is referred to as the **textual order**. For example,

```
public class Test {
    Test() {
        System.out.println("constructor");
    }
    int i = variableInitializer("instance variable initializer #1");
    { System.out.println("instance initialization block"); }
```

```
        double d = variableInitializer("instance variable initializer #2");
        public static void main(String[] args)  {
            new Test();
        }
        static int variableInitializer(String s) {
            System.out.println(s);
            return 0;
        }
    }
```

Executing this program prints

```
instance variable initializer #1
instance initialization block
instance variable initializer #2
constructor
```

All of these `println(String s)` method invocations are moved to an `<init>` method by the constructor. Only the textual order of variable initializers and initialization blocks is preserved. The code from a constructor is always executed last.

There is one notable exception to the use of textual order by the compiler. The variable initializers for inlined constants must be executed before all other variable initializers and initialization blocks. Therefore, the compiler moves them to the beginning of the special initialization methods in which they appear.

2.3.3 Limit of One `public` Package Member

There is a limit of one `public` package member per compilation unit when Java packages are stored in a filesystem. The specification for this is quoted and discussed at length in 2.8 Helper Classes are Not Fundamentally Different.

As used in that specification, *type* does not include member types. This is an important distinction because there is no limit to the number of nested top-level classes, nested interfaces, and inner member classes that can be declared `public`. That also explains why the name of this section had to be changed from *Limit of One public Type* to *Limit of One `public` Package Member* after the 1.1 release that introduced nested types.

2.4 Package Declarations

A package declaration consists of the `package` keyword followed by a fully qualified package name. Most declarations are thought of as creating

```
```

something. For example, a variable declaration allocates memory. This is not necessarily true of package declarations. The primary purpose of the package declaration at the top of a compilation unit is not to create a package but to declare the name of the package to which the compilation unit belongs. Just compiling the source code does not create the corresponding directories in the local file system unless the `-d <directory>` option is used.

The default behavior of a Java compiler, however, is to write class files to the same directory as the source code, even if it is not the directory where the same compiler would expect to find the class file based on the package statement. In other words, the default behavior of a Java compiler is to completely ignore the package declaration at the top of a compilation unit (at least in terms of where the generated class files are stored). Therefore, it is ultimately the responsibility of a Java programmer to make sure that class files find their way to the appropriate directory or Java Archive (JAR) file. If for any reason you compile something into the wrong directory, there is no reason to recompile. All you have to do is move the class file to where it belongs, or JAR it, as the case may be.

2.4.1 Package Names

Package naming conventions for widely distributed packages are designed to assure that package names are unique. The importance of unique package names increases proportionately with how widely a package is distributed. The ultimate challenge for creating unique package names is publishing on the Internet. Some kind of registry is needed. The JLS suggests piggybacking the Internet domain name registry. Reversed domain names are used as **package prefixes** for widely distributed Java packages. The `org.omg` packages in the core API are an example of using a package prefix. The `org.omg` package prefix is the reverse of the *www.omg.org* domain name.

If large corporations follow this naming convention, they will have *corporate namespace* on the Java platform. Furthermore, all of their Java packages will be organized into a single hierarchical directory structure. If Sun can write the entire core API using only the `java`, `javax`, and `org.omg` namespaces, then other large corporations should be able to follow its lead.

This does not mean you must have a Web site. It just means that if you want to distribute Java packages globally (perhaps as shrink-wrapped products in stores) you should start by applying for a domain name. If you do not intend to use it as a Web site, you are registering a Java package prefix. The reason for doing so is to make sure that your software can run anywhere in the world without the possibility of naming conflicts.

When applying for a domain name that is to be used as a package prefix, use legal Java identifiers as described in 1.4 Identifiers. If you already have a domain name and it has hyphens, subdomain names that begin with a number or are Java keywords, or for any other reason is an illegal identifier in Java, the *JLS* suggests using an underscore to solve the problem. For example, you could replace any hyphens with underscores. This solution does not appeal to me. I would spend the extra money to get a separate Java package prefix, one that uses only legal Java identifiers.

The use of package prefixes (that is, reversed Internet domain names) is all that distinguishes package naming conventions for widely distributed packages from those for packages intended for local use. The only Java naming convention for a package intended for local use is that the package name begin with a lowercase letter. The specification for package used locally actually says "a **first identifier** that begins with a lowercase letter" [emphasis added].[2] That brings up an interesting point about package naming standards. The first identifier in a package name is the top-level package such as `java`, `javax`, and `org`. The specification does not say anything whatsoever about the other identifiers in a package name (that is, the subpackage names). It does not say if they should begin with small or capital letters. Nor does the specifiction for package names say if the other identifies should be mixed case. In short, other than the *special* restriction on subpackage names discussed in the following subsection, there are no naming conventions for subpackage names, and for good reason. Reversed Internet domain names could be anything. Here are the examples from the *JLS*:

```
com.JavaSoft.jag.Oak
org.npr.pledge.driver
uk.ac.city.rugby.game
```

That is why naming conventions for subpackage names are wide open.

---

2. Gosling et al., *The Java Language Specification*, Second Edition, §6.8.1, "Package Names."

2.4.1.1 Special Restriction on Subpackage Names

No two members of a package can have the same name. Because both types and subpackages are members of a package, the name of this section is somewhat arbitrary. The special restriction on subpackage names applies to all package members, not just subpackages. It is strictly a Java platform restriction, unrelated to the filesystem of the underlying operating system. Filesystems generally allow subdirectories and files to have the same name.

It is obvious that no two types in the same package can have the same name. The significance of this rule is that subpackages (read subdirectories) and class files that are members of the same package and therefore stored in the same directory cannot have the same name. For example,

```
package com.javarules;
class examples { }
```

I use a package named `com.javarules.examples`, which is why attempting to compile this program generates the following compiler error:

```
examples.java:2: com.javarules.examples clashes with package of same name
class examples { }
      ^
1 error
```

If naming conventions are followed, this should never happen because package names begin with a lowercase letter and type names begin with an uppercase letter.

This restriction has been part of the *JLS* since the 1.0 release but was not implemented until the 1.2 release. There were problems with the Windows filesystem being case insensitive. While it is more generally true that no two members (of a package, class, interface, etc.) can have the same name, the primary reason for this restriction is to prevent ambiguity in the use of fully qualified class and package names.

2.4.1.2 Capitalization of Top-Level Domain Names

The original *JLS* said that top-level domain names should be capitalized (for example, COM, EDU, GOV, MIL, NET, and ORG). The following explanation for this specification is from the first edition of *The Java Programming Language*.

> The capital letters are used to prevent conflicts with package
> names chosen by those not following the convention, who are
> unlikely to use all uppercase, but might name a package the
> same as one of the many high-level domain names.[3]

The requirement that top-level domain names be capitalized was officially removed in the 1.2 release. The *JLS* now says,

> The first component of a unique package name is always written
> in all-lowercase ASCII letters and should be one of the top-level
> domain names, currently com, edu, gov, mil, net, org,
> or one of the English two-letter codes identifying countries as
> specified in ISO Standard 3166, 1981.[4]

This section is something of a historical note. I do not want to remove it, however, because there may be a number of package prefixes that follow the old naming convention.

2.4.2 The Members of a Package

Classes, interfaces, and subpackages are *members* of a package, whereas a compilation unit is said to be *part of* or *belong to* a package. If there is no package declaration, then the compilation unit is said to belong to the unnamed package.

2.4.3 Using the SDK to Develop Packages

This section is here to help programmers learn how to use the Software Development Kit (SDK) distributed by Sun, formerly known as the Java Development Kit (JDK). In regards to packages, there are three basic approaches to development work using the SDK. The simplest approach is to do all of your work in a single directory (the unnamed package). This approach is best suited for casual development, such as for someone learning the Java programming language. The advantages are that you do not have to bother with package declarations and, because the class files are in the same directory as the source code, typing DOS commands is easier. However, there are a number of disadvantages.

---

3. Ken Arnold and James Gosling, *The Java Programming Language* (Reading: Addison-Wesley, 1996), §10.1, "Package Naming."
4. Gosling et al., §7.7, "Unique Package Names." Note that these are the same country codes used by the Locale class, a complete list of which can be found on various Web sites by searching for "ISO 3166."

- The development directory quickly becomes cluttered with class files. This is especially true if you are using many inner classes

- There is always the risk that you will inadvertently use a locally developed class instead of one in the core API (precisely because there are class files in your development directory). This is a particularly nasty problem to debug the first time it happens. See 2.5.4.1 Disambiguating Type Names for a discussion

If you are going to use the unnamed package for casual development, the traditional directory name used for such purposes is `C:\Java\classes` for reasons dating back to the early releases when there was only one classpath.

The other approach is to use package declarations and the `-d` `<directory>` option to store class files in a directory structure that corresponds to the package name. When using this approach I strongly recommend making your top-level packages subdirectories of a single development directory such as `C:\Java\classes`. Doing so makes it possible to use "`.`" as a directory name in DOS commands, which is a special path notation used by the Java platform to mean the current working directory. Otherwise, you will be typing absolute or relative pathnames all the time. For example,

```
package com.javarules.examples;
class Test {}
```

The following DOS command compiles the `Test` class and puts `Test.class` in a subdirectory that corresponds to the package name:

```
c:\Java\classes>javac -d . Test.java
```

If any of the directories in the `C:\Java\classes\com\javarules\examples` pathname do not exist, they will be created by the compiler. Thus, and only thus, does a package statement result in the actual *creation* of a package, by which I mean creating directories in the local filesystem. The source code files remain in `C:\Java\classes` while the generated class files are written to subdirectories that correspond to the package name. The advantage to this approach is that it allows you to keep all your source code in one development directory while either reducing or eliminating the clutter of class files. There is a major disadvantage, however, in that you lose the automatic compilation (or recompilation) of dependencies. That means instead of compiling a single program, all of the classes and interfaces used in that program will have to be individually compiled. Of course, a Java Integrated Development Environment (IDE) would solve this problem, but that is a separate learning curve. If you go that route, I strongly recommend Forte, a version of which is available for free on the Java Web site.

The third approach to creating packages using the SDK is to use the `-d` `<directory>` compiler option as described in the last paragraph and also to store source code files in the same directory as the corresponding class file. That assures the automatic compilation of dependencies even when using the `-d` compiler option, but there is a cost. You have to type more at the DOS prompt either to change directories or enter relative pathnames. For example, the first and last DOS commands in the following sequence are equivalent:

```
C:\Java\classes>javac com\javarules\examples\Test.java

C:\Java\classes>cd com\javarules\examples

C:\Java\classes\com\javarules\examples>javac Test.java
```

I do not like to change directories all the time when working in DOS, so this approach does not work for me.

2.5 Import Declarations

Import declarations must immediately follow the package declaration at the top of a compilation unit. If there is no package declaration, then the import declarations come first. A programmer can import a single `public` class or interface using a **single-type-import** declaration or any of the `public` classes and interfaces in a package "on demand" using the **type-import-on-demand** declaration. Note that *on-demand* means those classes and interfaces actually referenced in a compilation unit. It does not mean all of the `public` classes and interfaces in the package. Otherwise, the declaration would be named something like *type-import-everything*. The hyphens in the terms *single-type-import* and *type-import-on-demand* are not mine. They are from the *JLS*. This book always defers to the *JLS* on matters of terminology. I do not mind them, but they bother some readers.

The first rule of importing is that only `public` classes and interfaces can be imported. For example, naming a non-`public` class or interface in a single-type-import declaration generates a compiler error. Syntactically, both import declarations look about the same. The keyword `import` is followed by a fully qualified package name. The difference is that, in a single-type-import declaration, the last identifier is the name of a `public` class or interface, whereas a type-import-on-demand uses an asterisk (sometimes called a *wild card*). Here are a few frequently used import declarations:

```
import java.util.ArrayList;   //single-type-import
import java.util.*;           //type-import-on-demand
```

Normally you would use one or the other because the type-import-on-demand declaration imports all of the `public` classes and interfaces in the `java.util` package, including `java.util.ArrayList`.

Import declarations import types, not subpackages. That is why they are called single-*type*-import and *type*-import-on-demand declarations (emphasis on *type*). For example, the following type-import-on-demand declaration does not generate any compiler errors or warnings:

```
import java.*;
```

It accomplishes nothing, however, because there are no types in the top-level `java` package, only the subpackages `java.lang`, `java.util`, `java.io`, etc.

Nor can you import types from a subpackage because package names must always be fully qualified. In fact, attempting to import from a subpackage generates the same compiler error as would a nonexistent package. For example,

```
import abracadabra.*;   //does not exist
import io.*;            //subpackage of java
```

These import declarations generate the following compiler errors:

```
Test.java:1: Package abracadabra not found in import.
import abracadabra.*;
               ^

Test.java:2: Package io not found in import.
import io.*;
       ^
```

Notice that these are essentially the same error messages.

The simple name of an imported class or interface has what this book calls *compilation unit scope*. This means the simple name of that type can be used anywhere in the same compilation unit as the `import` statement. It does not mean that you can use the simple name of any of the members of that type, only the simple name of the type itself. For example, all of the `public` classes in `java.lang` are automatically imported. This includes the `Math` and `System` classes. However, you cannot use the simple names `PI` or `gc()`. They must be qualified as `Math.PI` and `System.gc()`. What you do not have to type is `java.lang.Math.PI` and `java.lang.System.gc()`.

Importing types is a convenience, not a necessity. Every class or interface on your bootstrap, extension, or user classpath can be referenced in a compilation unit by using nothing more than fully qualified names. Use of import declarations is explained as follows in the *JLS*.

> An import declaration allows a named type to be referred to by a simple name that consists of a single identifier. Without the use of an appropriate `import` declaration, the only way to refer to a type declared in another package is to use its fully qualified name.[5]

Repeatedly typing fully qualified names is time-consuming. On the other hand, using a fully qualified name is sometimes self-documenting. In effect, using a fully qualified name says, "Look, I am typing a fully qualified name, so it is a good bet that this is the only use of this type in the entire compilation unit." For example, some Java programmers always use the fully qualified name of a tagging interface, such as `java.io.Serializable`, which is used only once in the `implements` clause of a class declaration. Doing so requires less coding than an import declaration.

2.5.1 Automatic Imports

In addition to being able to use the simple names of classes and interfaces in the current package, every compilation unit **automatically imports** the `public` classes and interfaces declared in the `java.lang` package. These classes and interfaces enjoy a special status in the Java programming language because they never need to be qualified. Moreover, most of the `java.lang` package is preloaded during system initialization. For example,

```
class Test {
   public static void main(String[] args) { }
}
```

---

5. Gosling et al., §7.5, "Import Declarations."

Execute this program using the -verbose option and count the number of java.lang classes loaded. You will find that almost the entire package, including the java.lang.ref and java.lang.reflect subpackages, are loaded. Of course, that is implementation specific. I always use the JVM distributed with the Windows version of the SDK. Note that java.io and java.util are not automatically imported.

The public classes and interfaces automatically imported from the java.lang package are listed in Table 2-2.

That all of the classes and interfaces in the current package are in scope is sometimes inaccurately described as an automatic import, as in "A package imports itself implicitly."[6] Such an explanation leaves a novice programmer wondering if he can use the members of the current package because they are in scope or because they are automatically imported. The answer is that the members of the current package are in scope. The concept of automatic imports really only applies to the java.lang package.[7]

2.5.2 Redundant Imports

Programmers sometimes import the current package or the java.lang package. This is not necessary because members of the current package are in scope, and java.lang is automatically imported. The Java compiler ignores such **redundant import declarations**. Even using a single-type-import declaration to import a member of a package named in a type-import-on-demand declaration or importing the same class or interface twice using a single-type-import declaration is ignored. For example,

```
import java.lang.*;
import java.lang.Object;
import java.lang.Object;
```

This compiles even though it is quadruply redundant.

There are, however, two restrictions on import declarations that are closely related to the discussion in 2.5.4.1 Disambiguating Type Names. Both involve the use of single-type-declarations, which rank high in terms of how the compiler disambiguates type names. The first is that single-type-import declarations cannot be used to import a class or interface with the

---

6. Arnold and Gosling, *The Java Programming Language*, p.186. *The Java Tutorial* makes the same mistake.
7. Gosling et al., §7.5.3, "Automatic Imports." In fairness to Arnold and Gosling (who, for all I know, wrote the specification), package scope and automatic imports are implemented using the same mechanism discussed in 2.5.4 How Import Declarations Are Used by a Compiler.

same simple name as a top-level class or interface declared in the compilation unit. Attempting to do so results in a compiler error. Nor can two dif-

Table 2-2: Automatically Imported Types[a]

Description		Standard Classes and Interfaces
Primordial class		`Object`

Primitive type wrappers		`Boolean`
		`Character`
		`Number`
		  `Byte`
		  `Short`
		  `Integer`
		  `Long`
		  `Float`
		  `Double`
		`Void`

Strings		`String` `StringBuffer`
Math		`Math` `StrictMath`

JVM	Run-time system	`Runtime`
		`RuntimePermission`
		`System`

	Security manager	`SecurityManager`

	Threads	`Thread`
		`ThreadLocal`
		`InheritableThreadLocal`
		`ThreadGroup`

	Class loader subsystem	`ClassLoader`
		`Package`
		`Class`

	External processes	`Process`

Standard interfaces		`Cloneable`
		`Comparable`
		`Runnable`

Exception processing		`Throwable`

Table 2-2: Automatically Imported Types[a] (Continued)

Description	Standard Classes and Interfaces
| Checked exceptions | ```
Exception
   ClassNotFoundException
   CloneNotSupportedException
   IllegalAccessException
   InstantiationException
   InterruptedException
   NegativeArraySizeException
   NoSuchFieldException
   NoSuchMethodException
   NullPointerException
``` |
| Run-time exceptions | ```
RuntimeException
   ArithmeticException
   ArrayStoreException
   ClassCastException
   IllegalArgumentException
   IllegalThreadStateException
      NumberFormatException
   IllegalMonitorStateException
   IllegalStateException
   IndexOutOfBoundsException
ArrayIndexOutOfBoundsException
StringIndexOutOfBoundsException
   SecurityException
   UnsupportedOperationException
``` |
| Errors | ```
Error
   LinkageError
      ClassCircularityError
      ClassFormatError
UnsupportedClassVersionError
      ExceptionInInitializerError
      IncompatibleClassChangeError
         AbstractMethodError
         IllegalAccessError
         InstantiationError
         NoSuchFieldError
         NoSuchMethodError
      NoClassDefFoundError
      UnsatisfiedLinkError
      VerifyError
   ThreadDeath
   VirtualMachineError
      InternalError
      OutOfMemoryError
      StackOverflowError
      UnknownError
``` |

a. Indentations indicate subclasses
```

ferent classes with the same simple name be imported using single-type-import declarations.

2.5.3 Importing Nested Classes of All Sorts (Top-Level or Inner)

The name of this section is taken directly from the following quotation in *Inner Classes Specification* because it took me so long to realize what the author, John Rose, means by "resolvable without reference to inheritance relations."

> Nested classes of all sorts (top-level or inner) can be imported by either kind of import statement. Class names in import statements must be fully package qualified, and be *resolvable without reference to inheritance relations* [emphasis added].[8]

Note that, in this discussion, nested types do not include local and anonymous classes. Local and anonymous classes cannot be imported because local classes scope to a method and anonymous classes do not have a name to use in an import declaration.

There are a number of subtleties involved in importing nested types (hereafter referred to more specifically as nested top-level classes, nested interfaces, and inner member classes).

1. Import statements require the use of fully qualified type names, which is usually thought of as being in the general form `packageName.TypeName`. The fully qualified name of a member type, however, includes not only a package name but also the names of one or more enclosing types.

2. Nested top-level classes, nested interfaces, and inner member classes are member types that are inherited by subclasses (assuming they are accessible and not hidden). Member types must be imported, however, using the fully qualified name of the class or interface *in which they are declared*. The *JLS* refers to this as the **canonical name** of a type.

3. Enclosing and deeply nested members types must be explicitly imported.

---

8. John Rose, *Inner Classes Specification* (Mountain View: Sun Microsystems, 1997), "How does the Java Language Specification change for inner classes?"

There are examples of each of these three points in the following subsections. Those examples are based on the following top-level class:

```
package com.javarules.examples;
public class TopLevelClass {
    public static String s = "TopLevelClass";
    public interface NestedInterface {
        public static String s = "NestedInterface";
    }
    public static class NestedTopLevelClass {
        public static String s = "NestedTopLevelClass";
        public static class DeeplyNestedTopLevelClass {
            public static String s = "DeeplyNestedTopLevelClass";
        }
    }
    class InnerMemberClass {
        public String s = "InnerMemberClass";
    }
}
```

As you read the subsections, please keep in mind that importing nested top-level classes and nested interfaces is unusual. Normally, qualified names are used instead. Importing an inner member class would be even more unusual because `private` inner member classes are the norm.

2.5.3.1 Importing Requires the Fully Qualified Name of a Type

The qualified names of nested top-level classes, nested interfaces, and inner member classes are different from classes and interfaces that are package members because the fully qualified name of such a type includes other type names. Those other type names cannot be left out when importing nested types using a single-type-import declaration because they are part of the fully qualified name. For example, the fully qualified name of `NestedTopLevelClass` is `com.javarules.examples.TopLevel-Class.NestedTopLevelClass`.

The single-type-import declaration required to import `Nested-TopLevelClass` is

```
import com.javarules.examples.TopLevelClass.NestedTopLevelClass;
```

This import declaration makes it possible to use the simple name of the `NestedTopLevelClass`. If using either of the following import declarations, `NestedTopLevelClass` would have to be qualified:

```
import com.javarules.examples.*;
import com.javarules.examples.TopLevelClass;
```

The second import declaration imports `TopLevelClass` and nothing else.

> Single-type-import declarations are just that. They
> import one type at most.

Likewise, type-import-on-demand declarations import only the `public` classes and interfaces that are *members of the named package*. In the above type-import-on-demand declaration, that would be members of the `examples` package, which does not include `NestedTopLevelClass`. `NestedTopLevelClass` is a member of `TopLevelClass`. It is not a member of the `examples` package. For example,

```
import com.javarules.examples.*;
class Test {
    public static void main(String[] args) {
        System.out.println(NestedTopLevelClass.s);
    }
}
```

Attempting to compile this program generates the following compiler error:

```
Test.java:4: cannot resolve symbol
symbol  : variable NestedTopLevelClass
location: class Test
        System.out.println(NestedTopLevelClass.s);
                           ^
1 error
```

You may wonder why this error message refers to `NestedTopLevelClass` as a variable. The answer is found in the following passage of the *JLS*.

> A simple name may occur in contexts where it may potentially be interpreted as the name of a variable, a type or a package. In these situations, the rules ... specify that a variable will be chosen in preference to a type, and that a type will be chosen in preference to a package.[9]

The compiler is required by the *JLS* to regard `NestedTopLevelClass` as a variable name in the context of qualified access.

2.5.3.2 Inherited Member Types Cannot Be Imported

Inherited member types cannot be imported. For example,

```
package com.javarules.examples;
class Superclass {
    class NestedTopLevelClass { }
```

---

9. Gosling et al., §6.3.2, "Obscured Declarations."

```
    }
class Subclass extends Superclass { }
```

The `NestedTopLevelClass` is inherited by `Subclass` and can be accessed using the fully qualified type name `Subclass.Nested-TopLevelClass`. However, only the canonical name `com.java-rules.examples.Superclass.NestedTopLevelClass` can be used to import that class. This is a simple matter of being able to find the class file. The compiler-generated name of that class is `Super-class$InnerMemberClass.class`, which could not be found given an import declaration such as the following:

```
import com.javarules.example.Subclass.NestedTopLevelClass;
```

Here is a more complete example involving classes `A` and `B` in the `com.javarules.examples` package:

```
public class A {
  public static class NestedTopLevelClass {}
  public class InnerMemberClass {}
}
public class B extends A { }
```

The following program is in a different package:

```
import com.javarules.examples.B.*;
class Test {
    public static void main(String[] args) {
        System.out.println(NestedTopLevelClass.class);
        System.out.println(InnerMemberClass.class);
    }
}
```

Attempting to compile this program generates the following compiler errors:

```
Test.java:4: cannot resolve symbol
symbol  : class NestedTopLevelClass
location: class Test
        System.out.println(NestedTopLevelClass.class);
                           ^

Test.java:5: cannot resolve symbol
symbol  : class InnerMemberClass
location: class Test
        System.out.println(InnerMemberClass.class);
                           ^

2 errors
```

All that has to be done to solve this problem is to change `B` to `A` in the import declaration and the program compiles. For example,

```
import com.javarules.examples.A.*;
class Test {
    public static void main(String[] args) {
        System.out.println(NestedTopLevelClass.class);
```

```
          System.out.println(InnerMemberClass.class);
      }
  }
```

Executing this program prints

```
class com.javarules.examples.A$NestedTopLevelClass
class com.javarules.examples.A$InnerMemberClass
```

The *JLS* addresses this issue by saying that the canonical name of a member type must be used in import declarations. The canonical name always includes the name of the class or interface in which the imported member type is actually declared.

2.5.3.3 *Importing Enclosing or Deeply Nested Member Types*

When importing nested top-level classes, nested interfaces, and inner member classes, the enclosing class is not imported as a result. For example, consider the following import declaration:

```
import com.javarules.examples.TopLevelClass.*
```

Using this import declaration, all of the following simple or partially qualified type names can be used:

```
          NestedInterface
          NestedTopLevelClass
          NestedTopLevelClass.DeeplyNestedTopLevelClass
          InnerMemberClass
```

However, the following program does not compile:

```
import com.javarules.examples.TopLevelClass.*;
class Test {
    public static void main(String[] args) {
        System.out.println(TopLevelClass.s);
    }
}
```

Attempting to compile this program generates the following compiler error:

```
Test.java:4: cannot resolve symbol
symbol  : variable s
location: class TopLevelClass
        System.out.println(TopLevelClass.s);
                          ^
1 error
```

The same is true if any of the other nested types contained in `TopLevelClass` were imported instead of actually importing `TopLevel-`

Class. `TopLevelClass` must be either fully qualified or imported using one of the following import declarations:

```
import com.javarules.examples.*;
import com.javarules.examples.TopLevelClass;
```

The same applies to inner classes. Should you ever import an inner member class, that does not mean the simple name of the enclosing class is in scope.

To use simple names for `TopLevelClass` and all of the nested types, both of the following import declarations are required:

```
import com.javarules.examples.TopLevelClass;
import com.javarules.examples.TopLevelClass.*;
```

The first import declaration gets you `TopLevelClass`. The second one gets you all of the following:

```
NestedInterface
NestedTopLevelClass
NestedTopLevelClass.DeeplyNestedTopLevelClass
InnerMemberClass
```

To use the simple name `DeeplyNestedTopLevelClass` would require a third import declaration.

2.5.4 How Import Declarations are Used by a Compiler

Import statements exist only in source code. They are used exclusively by the compiler to disambiguate type names and search for class files. The following subsections discus each of those uses.

2.5.4.1 Disambiguating Type Names

Simple and partially qualified type names are not considered ambiguous until the compiler has exhausted efforts to disambiguate them. In the language of the *JLS*, disambiguating a name is the same as determining the *meaning of a name*. The meaning of a type name is the fully qualified name of that type. *Import statements are of critical importance in determining the meaning of type names.*

There is a specific sequence used by the compiler to disambiguate type names. As soon as any one of the following is found, the process stops:

1. A local class in scope.
2. A member type in scope.

3. One of two inherited member types that have the same name (AMBIGUOUS TYPE NAME).

4. A type declared in the same compilation unit or imported using a single-type-import declaration.

5. A type declared in another compilation unit of the same package.

6. An imported type found using a type-import-on-demand declaration.

7. An imported type found using two or more type-import-on-demand declarations (AMBIGUOUS TYPE NAME).

8. Cannot find class or interface declaration.

If the type name is ambiguous or there is no such type, a compiler error is generated.

The first two rules for disambiguating type names are illustrated by the following program:

```
class Test {

    class Widget { }            // inner member class

    public static void main(String[] args) {
        class Widget { }        // local class
        System.out.println(Widget.class);
    }
}
class Widget { }                // helper class
```

Executing this program prints the following:

```
class Test$1$Widget
```

`Test$1$Widget` is the compiler-generated name of the local class. Now reverse the order of the two statements in the `main` method:

```
public static void main(String[] args) {
    System.out.println(Widget.class);
    class Widget { }
    }
```

The program now prints

```
class Test$Widget
```

This is the compiler-generated name of the inner member class. In neither case does the name mean `Widget`, which is the helper class.

The third rule concerning inherited types is illustrated by the following program:

```
class Superclass {
    class Widget { }
}
interface Superinterface {
    class Widget { }
}

class Test extends Superclass implements Superinterface {
    public static void main(String[] args) {
        System.out.println(Widget.class);
    }
}
class Widget { }
```

Attempting to compile this program generates the following compiler error:

```
Test.java:10: reference to Widget is ambiguous, both class Superclass.Widget in
Superclass and class Superinterface.Widget in Superinterface match
        System.out.println(Widget.class);
                           ^
```

```
1 error
```

Once again, the Widget helper class is completely ignored. Notice that it does not matter that one of the inherited member types is a nested top-level class and the other is an inner member class. (Superinterface.Widget is a nested top-level class because all member types declared in an interface are implicitly static.)

The next three rules (numbers 4 to 6 in the list) for disambiguating type names are the most interesting. The following quotation is found in 6.5.5, "Meaning of Types Names," of the *JLS*.

> This order of considering type declarations is designed to choose the most explicit of two or more applicable type declarations.[10]

Type names scope to a package, compilation unit, or other type. The first three rules for disambiguating type names were added to the second edition of the *JLS* to deal with type names that scope to other types (that is, nested types). The next three rules deal with the fact that package scope and compilation unit scope overlap. Consequently, the simple name of two different types can be in scope at the same time.

To solve this problem the language designers ordered the four declarations that have package or compilation unit scope according to their explicitness. That order is as follows:

---

10. Gosling et al., §6.5.5.1, "Simple Types Names."

1. Package members declared in the same compilation unit (PACK-AGE SCOPE).
2. Types imported using a single-type-import declaration (COMPILA-TION UNIT SCOPE).
3. Package members declared in another compilation unit of the same package (PACKAGE SCOPE).
4. Types found using a type-import-on-demand declaration (COMPI-LATION UNIT SCOPE).

Types imported using a single-type-import declaration are more explicit than package members declared in other compilation units for the simple reason that the single-type-import declaration has to be deliberately typed in the source code being compiled. If a type is neither declared in the current compilation unit nor imported using a single-type-import declaration, the compiler assumes that the programmer is referencing a type declared in a different compilation unit of the same package. That is, a type that has package scope is considered more explicit than one imported using a type-import-on-demand declaration.

Single-type-import declarations are on par with package members declared in the compilation unit in the above list of eight rules for disambiguating type names because of a special compiler rule that eliminates any possibility of ambiguity between the two. A single-type-import declaration cannot be used to import a type with the same simple name as a package member declared in the same compilation unit, nor can two different types with the same simple name be imported using single-type-import declarations. (In both cases you would be declaring two different types to have the same simple name.)

Single-type-import declarations are said to **shadow** other types that are in scope. This is new terminology introduced in the second edition of the JLS.[11] As an example of the order of declarations according to their explicitness, consider the following program.

```
package com.javarules.io;
import java.io.File;
class Test {
    public static void main(String[] args) {
        System.out.println(File.class);
    }
}
```

11. Gosling, et al., §7.5.1, "Single-Type-Import Declaration."

This program prints `java.io.File` because of the single-type-import declaration. The following program is exactly the same except that it uses a type-import-on-demand declaration:

```
package com.javarules.io;
import java.io.*;
class Test {
    public static void main(String[] args) {
        System.out.println(File.class);
    }
}
```

This program prints `com.javarules.io.File` because of a different implementation of the `File` class in the current package. Now suppose the programs were not part of the `com.javarules.io` package. For example,

```
import java.io.*;
class Test {
    public static void main(String[] args) {
        System.out.println(File.class);
    }
}
```

The program prints `java.io.File` again.

Whenever these rules for disambiguating type names do not work the way you want, you can always use a fully qualified type name instead. Alternatively, you can use a single-type-import declaration to make the use of one type name more explicit. When a single-type-import declaration is used to import a type that has the same simple name as a member of the current package, the programmer is making a choice as to which of these two types can be referenced using a simple name. That choice depends on which one is used more often. If the member of the current package is used more often, do nothing. If the other class or interface is used more often, use a single-type-import declaration to import that type.

After package scope and single-type-import declarations, the only thing left to use in disambiguating type names is type-import-on-demand declarations. A Java compiler searches all of the packages imported using type-import-on-demand declarations. It does not stop after finding a matching type name because the possibility exists that another package imported using a type-import-on-demand declaration will have a type with the same name. The compiler cannot arbitrarily decide which type-import-on-demand declaration you intended to use, which is exactly what it would be doing if the search stopped as soon as a matching type name was found. If more than one matching type name is found, the compiler generates an ambiguous type error. For example,

```
import java.awt.*;
import java.util.*;
class Test {
    List l;
}
```

Attempting to compile this program generates the following compiler error:

```
Test.java:4: reference to List is ambiguous, both class java.util.List in java.util and class
java.awt.List in java.awt match
    List l;
    ^
1 error
```

Both of these packages include a type named List. Any attempt to reference the List interface in the java.util package or the List class in the java.awt package using a simple name will be ambiguous. As noted above, you need only add a single-type-import declaration for one or the other List types to solve this problem. The other alternative is to use fully qualified names for both types.

On the other hand, simple type names are not ambiguous unless you try to use them. If no reference is made to such types, or if all of the references are fully qualified, then identically named types imported using type-import-on-demand declarations are no more ambiguous than if they were not imported at all.

2.5.4.1.1 Type Names in the Unnamed Package

If the current package is the unnamed package, the compiler will search for a type in the unnamed package before using a type from a type-import-on-demand declaration. This is a language feature that sooner or later comes to the attention of most Java programmers when they inadvertently declare a class that has the same simple name as a class in the core API. If that class is stored in the unnamed package, it is only a matter of time before you try to compile a program that attempts to import the like-named core API class using a type-import-on-demand declaration. The problem is that the compiler will find the class in the unnamed package because the unnamed package is more explicit than a type-import-on-demand declaration. In my case I thoughtlessly created a Properties class that sat in the unnamed package for months (like a time bomb waiting to explode) until one day when I tried importing `java.util.Properties` using import `java.util.*`. All sorts of compiler errors were generated because I was trying to use my `Proper-ties` class as if it were `java.util.Properties`. That is a very hard problem to diagnose the first time you encounter it.

2.5.4.2 Searching for Class Files

Import declarations are also used by a Java compiler to search for class files and their corresponding source code files on the bootstrap, extension, or user classpath. If both a class file and source code file are found, the compiler checks to see if the source code file has been updated since the last time it was compiled. This is accomplished by comparing the timestamp on the two files. Java compilers will replace an out-of-date class file by recompiling the source code. Although used by Java compilers to search for both class files and their corresponding source code files, the remainder of this section discusses only class files.

There is a tendency to think that the bootstrap, extension, and user classpaths provide all the information needed by a Java compiler or JVM to find class files. However, the classpath mechanism provides only the location where top-level packages are stored. I usually refer to that as a **development directory**. For example, if you do all your development work in a single development directory and use the `-d <directory>` option to store class files in subdirectories that correspond to package names, then all the classpath provides is the name of the development directory, which in my case is always `C:\Java\classes`. However, this is only the first part of the absolute pathname required in order to find a class file in the local filesystem. The rest of the absolute pathname is the fully qualified package name, the name of the class or interface (as found in the source code), and the `.class` file extension. The missing piece of the puzzle is the package name, which comes from one of three places:

1. The package statement for types declared in a compilation unit.
2. A fully qualified type name used in source code.
3. Import declarations.

Most of the time the package name is derived from import declarations. The fully qualified package name corresponds either to directories in the local file system or to the directory structure in a JAR file. In either case it effectively extends the pathname from the classpath mechanism. The extended pathnames are used in a string concatenation operation along with the simple or partially qualified type name and the `.class` file extension to provide the absolute path for a class file, which can then be read from the local file system. I refer to this string concatenation operation as the **classpath formula**. This is one of a handful of terms I have coined while writing this book.

Classpath formulas are either *simple* or *complex*. The defining difference between simple and complex classpath formulas is the availability of a fully qualified type name. A simple classpath formula does not involve type-import-on-demand declarations. It is used only when a programmer types a fully qualified type name or uses a single-type-import declaration (which in this context is roughly the equivalent of using fully qualified type names).

The complex classpath formula is imperfect. Instead of computing the absolute path for a class file (as does the simple classpath formula), the complex classpath formula computes every *mathematically possible combination* of pathnames from a user classpath and fully qualified type names. There is usually more than one pathname on a user classpath, and because of package scope, automatic imports, and type-import-on-demand declarations, there is always more than one fully qualified package name. That is, a simple or partially qualified type name may be a member of any number of packages (all of which must be searched). All of the mathematically possible combinations of pathnames and fully qualified package names are strung together with the simple or partially qualified type name and the `.class` file extension to create absolute paths. Then each of the absolute pathnames must be tried using something like the `exists()` method in the `File` class to determine if such a file actually exists. The pathnames on a user classpath are searched in the same left-to-right order in which they are written. Any uncompressed `.zip` files or JAR files on the user classpath are also searched using just the fully qualified type name plus the `.class` file extension.

One of the most significant differences between the simple and complex classpath formulas is the possibility of ambiguous type names. When using the simple classpath formula there is no possibility of an ambiguous type name. Therefore, the local filesystem is accessed once. When a Java compiler uses the complex classpath formula, the local filesystem must be accessed for each and every mathmatically possible combination because of the possibility of ambiguous type names. That the complex classpath formula must try every mathematically possible combination is primarily what makes the use of type-import-on-demand declarations slower than single-type-import declarations.

2.5.4.2.1 The Simple Classpath Formula Finding a class file is relatively simple given a fully qualified type name, hence the term **simple classpath formula**. The simple classpath formula is shown in Figure 2-2.

Java virtual machines always use the simple classpath formula because type names in a JVM are always fully qualified. For a compiler the availability of a fully qualified type name determines when the simple classpath formula can be used. There are two cases.

1. Programmers sometimes type fully qualified names. (This specifically does not include members of the unnamed package.)

2. When discussing classpath formulas the use of a single-type-import declaration is the equivalent of having typed the fully qualified type name.

The simple classpath formula is not used to locate the members of an unnamed package unless that member is imported using a single-type-import declaration (which is not something a programmer normally does).

path name \ fully qualified type name \ .class = absolute path

Figure 2-2: Simple classpath formula.

pathname \ package name or fully qualified type name \ simple or partially qualified type name \ .class = absolute path

Figure 2-3: Complex classpath formula.

Otherwise, members of the unnamed package are imported by means of a type-import-on-demand declaration that is implicitly added to all compilation units. That is how package scope is implemented in the Java programming language. There is an example of this in the next section.

2.5.4.2.2 The Complex Classpath Formula   The **complex classpath formula** involves type-import-on-demand declarations and is therefore only used by Java compilers. The complex classpath formula is shown in Figure 2-3. The package name or fully qualified type name in the second slot is from a type-import-on-demand declaration. The simple or partially qualified type name in the third slot is from the source code. The essential difference in the two formulas is that the fully qualified type name is now in two parts.

The compiler has no way of knowing which type-import-on-demand declaration goes with which class or interface name. It must append a simple or partially qualified type name from the source code to the end of the package name or fully qualified type name of each of the type-import-on-demand declarations used in the compilation unit in an attempt to find the class file. This increases the number of mathematically possible combinations exponentially. For example,

```
package com.javarules.examples;
import java.io.*;
import java.util.*;
```

Given this declaration, we must first include a type-import-on-demand declaration for the current package and `java.lang`. (That is how package scope and automatic imports are implemented in the Java programming language.)

```
package com.javarules.examples;
import java.com.javarules.examples.*;
import java.lang.*;
import java.io.*;
import java.util.*;
```

Now suppose you use the simple name of a class named `Widget`. There are five possibilities:

```
Widget
com.javarules.examples.Widget
java.lang.Widget
java.io.Widget
java.util.Widget
```

The first possibility in this list is that `Widget` is a member of an unnamed package, in which case `Widget` *is* the fully qualified type name. Now suppose there are five pathnames on the user classpath. After searching the bootstrap and extension classpath, the compiler must search 25 different mathematically possible combinations on the user classpath versus just one if a single-type-import declaration is used instead.

There are 25 different mathematically possible combinations on the user classpath in the previous example because a Java compiler does not assume that package names such as `java.lang`, `java.io` or `java.util` exists only on the bootstrap classpath. For example,

```
package java.lang;
public class Widget {
    public static void doSomething() {}
}
```

The following test program is declared in a different package.

```
import java.lang.*;
class Test {
    public static void main(String[] args) {
        Widget.doSomething();
    }
}
```

The `Test` program does compile, finding `java.lang.Widget` using the pathname `C:\Java\classes` from the user classpath. Of course, executing the `Test` program throws a `SecurityException` (because the `java.lang` package is sealed), but that is a different matter.

As explained in 2.5.4.1 Disambiguating Type Names, Java compilers cannot stop as soon as a class file is found. They must search all of the mathematically possible combinations to determine if there are ambiguous type names. That is one of the main reasons why the complex classpath formula is so inefficient. All of the mathematically possible combinations must be searched, even if the class file is found on the first try. In this case, that means accessing the local filesystem (that is, invoking the `exists()` method in the `java.io.File` class) 25 times. Only after the `exists()` method is invoked for all 25 mathematically possible combinations and only if exactly one of those method invocations is returned `true` is the class file actually read. Single-type-import declarations do not have this problem because they import at most one type.

Much has been done to make this process as efficient as possible—namely separating the bootstrap and extension classpaths so that only

JAR files have to be searched for the core API or installed extensions and the introduction of the `Index.list` file in the `Meta-inf` directory of a JAR file (which makes searching a JAR file lightning fast). There is nothing, however, that can be done to eliminate the 25 `exists()` method invocations because of the possibility of ambiguous types. The 25-to-1 ratio of this simple example explains why some programmers not only use single-type-import declarations all the time, but in extreme cases (that is, in large builds such as the core API) use them to import members of the current package.

2.5.5 The Efficiency of Type-Import-on-Demand Declarations

The term *import declaration* is something of a misnomer. The source code file(s) of the type or package named in an import declaration is(are) not actually imported into the body of the compilation unit at compile time (like goods are imported into the United States from other countries). This is a common misconception. Many Java books further this misconception by making authoritative statements to the effect that type-import-on-demand declarations are somehow inefficient without explaining what they mean or offering any detailed analysis of the problem. Import declarations define compilation unit scope. Without the use of import statements, only the members of the current package and `java.lang` are in scope.

The answer to the question *does using type-import-on-demand declarations somehow make my Java code less efficient* is an unqualified *No*. The class files generated by a Java compiler include symbolic references to only those classes and interfaces actually used in the compilation unit. In that sense *on-demand* means only those `public` classes and interfaces referenced in the body of a class or interface.

Does that mean that you should use type-import-on-demand declarations all the time? Yes and no. I find them useful while doing casual development work such as the examples in this book. However, there are four reasons not to use type-import-on-demand statements.

1. *Compilation Speed:* Arguably the most important reason for not using type-import-on-demand declarations is that, in a very large build (such as the core API), they noticeably slow the compilation process because the compiler must use the complex classpath formula discussed in the previous section. In smaller applica-

tions, however, the price paid at compile-time for using type-import-on-demand declarations is negligible.

2. *Naming Conflicts:* The use of type-import-on-demand declarations can be problematic if they introduce naming conflicts into a compilation unit. How are naming conflicts solved? The answer, in part, is by using fully qualified names, which is exactly the opposite of what you set out to accomplish by using import declarations in the first place.

3. *Documentation Issues:* As noted above, the use a fully qualified name is self-documenting. You are saying, "Look, I am typing a fully qualified name. So it is a good bet that this is the only use of this type in the entire compilation unit." In that sense, importing a package and then only using it once or twice is misleading. By contrast, using single-type-import declarations makes it clear the moment a compilation unit is opened exactly which classes and interfaces are used.

4. *The Unnamed Package Problem:* If there is no package declaration at the top of a compilation unit, Java compilers search for a type in the unnamed package before using type-import-on-demand declarations. As explained above, that can be problematic if the unnamed package includes a type with the same simple name as a type in the core API. This is only a problem during the early stages of development, but it can be systematically avoided by always using single-type-import declarations.

The best reason for not using type-import-on-demand declarations in production code is possibly that the software engineers at Sun generally do not use them. Look at the source code that comes with the SDK and see if you can find any type-import-on-demand declarations. They are hard to find. What you will find are lists of single-type-import declarations, some of which are very long—for example, the following import declarations in the `java.util.Properties` class:

```
import java.io.IOException;
import java.io.PrintStream;
import java.io.PrintWriter;
import java.io.InputStream;
import java.io.InputStreamReader;
import java.io.BufferedReader;
import java.io.OutputStream;
import java.io.OutputStreamWriter;
```

```
import java.io.BufferedWriter;
import java.util.Hashtable;
```

There are nine different classes imported from the `java.io` package, all using single-type-import declarations.

Even more interesting is the fact that `java.util.Hashtable` is imported from the current package. There are examples of classes in the core API with much longer lists of single-type-import declarations. I chose this one because it imports a class from the same package. Why? Classes and interfaces in the current package are in scope and do not need to be imported. The answer is that the package scope is implemented as if the compilation unit included a type-import-on-demand declaration for that package. This is also how automatic imports are implemented. For example, the following three lines of code are for the `java.util.Proper-ties` class:

```
package java.util;
import java.util.*;
import java.lang.*;
```

Normally you only see the first line of code, but all three are there as far as the compiler is concerned. So the question *why does `java.util.Proper-ties` import `java.util.HashTable`* is the same as asking why this programmer always uses single-type-import declarations. The answer may be any one of the four reasons listed above but is probably some combination of the four. Without asking, I cannot say for sure. What I do know is that many of the software engineers at Sun use single-type-import declarations for classes and interfaces in the current package.

You may wonder why the efficiency-minded software engineers at Sun do not extend the logic of using single-type-import declarations to members of the `java.lang` package. As described in this chapter, both package scope and automatic imports are implemented by adding type-import-on-demand declarations to a compilation unit. In the case of automatic imports, `import java.lang.*` is added to the top of every compilation unit. This is more didacticism than fact. I suspect that the algorithm that implements what I call the *complex classpath formula* always searches the `java.lang` package first. This makes sense because every class file includes symbolic references to members of the `java.lang` package.

My rule of thumb is to always use single-type-import declarations to import only what is necessary. Doing so is self-documenting and makes for faster builds on large projects. Based on what I have seen of the source code for the core API, that is what most of the software engineers at Sun also do. I use type-import-on-demand declarations like the unnamed package primarily as a convenience during development work. On the other hand, a more relaxed approach is to use type-import-on-demand declarations when many classes and interfaces from a particular package are used in a compilation unit. That often means using type-import-on-demand declarations for `java.io` and `java.util`. Type-import-on-demand declarations are much easier to type.

2.6 Type Declarations

Type declarations are either class types or interface types, depending on the keyword used. All type declarations share a common syntax except for anonymous classes.

2.6.1 Class Type Declarations

Classes provide the implementation for one or more types. A class declaration consists of a **class header** and **class body**. The class header has five parts, which are summarized in Table 2-3.

Table 2-3: The Five Parts of a Class Header

	Part	Notes
①	Class modifiers	**Class modifiers** are the access modifiers (`public`, `protected`, and `private`), `abstract`, `static`, `final`, and as of the 1.3 release, `strictfp`
②	`class` keyword	
③	Identifier	The name of the class
④	`extends` clause	Optional if the direct superclass is `Object`; otherwise required
⑤	`implements` clause	Optional list of comma-separated direct superinterfaces

Here are some examples from the core API:

```
public final class String implements java.io.Serializable, Comparable
public final class Integer extends Number implements Comparable
public abstract class FilterReader extends Reader
public class IOException extends Exception
public class ArrayList extends AbstractList implements List, Cloneable, java.io.Serializable
```

Anonymous classes are excluded from this discussion. There is no class header in the declaration of an anonymous class, only a class body. Nothing in the remainder of this section applies to anonymous classes.

There is a particular order in which class modifiers are usually listed. As always, the access modifiers are first.

```
[access modifier] abstract static final strictfp
```

This is a programmer convention. As stated in the *JLS*,

> If two or more class modifiers appear in a class declaration, then it is customary, though not required, that they appear in the [above] order ....[12]

That the `implements` clause follows the `extends` clause in the declaration of a class is also a programmer convention.

The class and interface types named in an `extends` or `implements` clause must be accessible, which implies that such types are one of the following:

- A member of the current package

- An imported class or interface type, which is necessarily `public`

- The fully qualified name of an accessible class or interface type

The class extended is said to be the **direct superclass** of the class being declared. Single inheritance in the Java programming language means that a class has only one direct superclass. The class being declared is said to be the **direct subclass** of the class named in the `extends` clause. A class declaration that does not use the `extends` clause implicitly extends the `Object` class as if the compiler added `extends Object` to the declaration of such a class.

The `implements` clause of a class declaration is a comma-separated list of the direct superinterfaces of a class. A direct superinterface is analogous to a direct superclass except that a class can implement any

---

12. Goslinget al., §8.1.1, "Class Modifiers."

number of direct superinterfaces. Unless a class is declared `abstract`, it must provide implementations for all of the `abstract` methods in the direct superinterface(s) that it implements as well as for any `abstract` methods inherited from what would necessarily be an `abstract` direct superclass.

2.6.1.1 Class Names

Class and interface names are mixed case. The first letter in each word is usually capitalized. With the notable exception of `Exception` and `Error` subclasses (which are usually long names), class names should not be overly long. According to the *JLS*, class names should be descriptive nouns or noun phrases. Some examples of class names in the core API are

```
Object
Class
String
Compiler
Dictionary
Process
Thread
```

Examples of noun phrases in the core API are

```
StringBuffer
ClassLoader
SecurityManager
ThreadGroup
```

It is sometimes said that a class name may be a *gerund* (a verbal noun ending in *-ing*). However, examples of this in the core API are rare.

2.6.1.2 The Members of a Class Type

The members of any reference type are fields, methods, and member types. Those members are either declared or inherited. The members of a class type are specifically

- Members declared in the body of the class
- Members inherited from the direct superclass either explicitly named in the `extends` clause or implicitly from the `Object` class
- Members inherited from any direct superinterfaces named in the `implements` clause

Constructors and initialization blocks are not members of a class type, which means they are not inherited by subclasses.

2.6.1.3 The Order of Class Body Declarations

There is no compiler-enforced order for the declarations in a class or interface body. That lack of order, particularly in class body declarations, is what makes compilation units appear so haphazard when learning the language. Programmers must impose an order of their own choosing on class body declarations. There should be some method to your madness. That is, the layout of your compilation units should be consistent and defensible.

One of the most important things to understand about the ordering of class body declarations is that no order, however well conceived, is appropriate for all reference types. For example, I use a different ordering for reusable objects and application programs. There is a compelling reason to keep instance variables together when they represent the state of an object. Likewise, all of the constants in a utility class should probably be kept together. There is an equally compelling reason, however, to declare the `static` variables in an application program immediately before their first use. Doing so makes it easier to find their declaration in order to determine if the variable is being correctly initialized. Declaring variables immediately before their first use is a structured programming practice that has been around for many years. There is no reason to stop doing it in application programs written in Java. Moreover, the top-down design of structured programming should not be abandoned for application programs written in an object-oriented programming language such as Java.

One popular ordering of class body declarations is to code all of the `public` methods at the top of the class body, presumably to make it easier for other programmers to find them. These are usually the same programmers that code all the fields at the bottom of a compilation unit, in part because they are usually declared `private` and also to keep them together. In between the `public` methods at the top of the compilation unit and the `private` fields at the bottom is the bulk of the source code. I do not use this ordering because I think coding `public` methods first is an invitation to read source code (instead of API docs). Nevertheless, this is one example of an ordering of class body declarations that, if used consistently, is easy to understand.

The ordering of class body declarations used in this book is explained in the following subsections. I have limited myself to the three most common uses of a reference type. Those are reusable objects, application programs, and utility classes. These brief sections not only help to explain to the reader the order of class body declarations used in this book but also help to show how each use of a reference type potentially justifies a different ordering of class body declarations.

2.6.1.3.1 *Class Body Declarations in Reusable Objects* For classes that are truly reusable objects, I use the order of class body declarations in Table 2-4. Fields and initialization blocks are placed at the top of a compilation unit for the following reasons.

Table 2-4: Order of Class Body Declaration for Reusable Objects

High-Level View		Declaration
Initialization Code	①	Constants
		Class variables
		`static` initialization blocks
	②	Instance variables
		Instance initialization blocks
	③	Constructors
Methods	④	Class methods
		Instance methods
Types	⑤	Member types
	⑥	Helper classes

- It is somewhat more natural to code fields before the methods that use them (although scoping rules allow for coding fields after the methods that use them)
- Field declarations and initialization blocks require far less space and tend to become "buried" under methods if coded at the bot-

tom of a compilation unit. Nevertheless, it should be noted that some programmers prefer to code all of the fields at the bottom of a compilation unit

The `static` declarations should come before the more numerous non-`static` declarations for essentially the same reason that fields come before methods. There are fewer of them.

2.6.1.3.2 Class Body Declarations in Application Programs

An application program written in Java should be structured the same as an application program written in a procedure-oriented programming language. That is, you should use a top-down design in which the `main` method is coded first.[13] In general, the `main` method should provide an overview of the execution path. In procedure-oriented programming, this is referred to as **structured programming**. A discussion of structured programming is beyond the scope of this book. Suffice it to say that if method A invokes method B, then method A should be declared above method B. That is why `main` is always at the top.

I also think that the variables in an application program should be declared immediately above the method in which they are used. This is a well-established practice in structured programming and one that some programmers have naturally carried over into object-oriented programming. Why code an instance variable miles above (or below) where it is actually used? If it made sense in procedure-oriented programming, why shouldn't it make sense in object-oriented programming? These are style issues, nothing more. They are subordinate to good interface design and to bug-free and efficient implementations.

2.6.1.3.3 Class Body Declarations in Utility Classes

I include this section to make two simple points. The first is the `private` constructor in a utility class such as the following one from the `System` class should be the very first thing coded:

```
/**
 * Do not instantiate this class.
 */
private System() {}
```

---

13. GUI applications are an exception because they are a hybrid (a cross between reusable objects and applications programs).

Doing so serves to notify the reader that this is a utility class. The second point is that the constants in a utility class should be coded before the utility methods. Placing the instance variables of a reusable object at the bottom of a class body is a generally accepted option, but not one that should be used for the constants in a utility class.

2.6.2 Interface Type Declarations

Interfaces are used to specify the behavior for a type that is expected to be implemented by a number of disparate classes. An interface declaration consists of an **interface header** and an **interface body**. The four parts to a interface header are summarized in Table 2-5.

Here are some examples from the core API:

```
public interface Cloneable
public interface Comparable
public interface Runnable
public interface Serializable
public interface ObjectInput extends DataInput
public interface ObjectOutput extends DataOutput
public interface SortedMap extends Map
public interface SortedSet extends Set
```

As you can see, most interfaces are declared `public`. In fact, that is the only access modifier that can be used for interfaces that are package members. If such an interface is not declared `public`, it is said to be non-`public` (which is synonymous with *default access* or *package-private*). Any access modifier can be used in the declaration of a nested interface. Nested interfaces can be declared `static`. However, the `static` modifier is optional because all interfaces, including nested interfaces, are implicitly `static`. Use of the `abstract` modifier in the declaration of an interface type is considered obsolete, though it does not generate a compiler warning using the latest version of the `javac` compiler. You may wonder why the `static` modifier is not also considered obsolete in the declaration of an interface type if they are implicitly both `abstract` and `static`. Used in the declaration of interfaces types, the `abstract` and `static` modifiers have completely different histories.

The use of the `abstract` modifier in interface declarations goes back to very early versions of Java, to a time when the Java programming language proper (as opposed to the API) was still very much under development. The use of the `static` modifier in the declaration of nested interfaces actually dates to the 1.1 release, when nested types were first introduced. No package member, whether a class or interface, can be

Table 2-5: The Four Parts of an Interface Header

Part		Notes
①	Interface modifiers[a]	**Interface modifiers** are the access modifiers (`public`, `protected`, and `private`), `static`, and as of the 1.3 release, `strictfp`
②	`interface` keyword	
③	Identifier	The name of the interface
④	`extends` clause	Optional list of comma-separated direct superinterfaces

a. The `abstract` interface modifier (used before the 1.0 release) is obsolete because interfaces are implicitly `abstract`. The *JLS* specifically says that this modifier should not be used.

declared `static`. That was true before and after nested types were introduced to the language. Nested top-level classes require the `static` modifier to differentiate them from inner member classes. As stated in the *JLS*, "Its effect is to declare that [the nested class] is not an inner class."[14] By making the `static` modifier optional for nested interfaces, the 1.1 release made the use of the `static` modifier consistent for all nested types, whether they be class or interface types.

Interfaces extend superinterfaces using the same `extends` clause that classes use, and they inherit from those superinterfaces in much the same manner as classes do. The `extends` clause in an interface type declaration is a comma-separated list of direct superinterfaces. Much like a class can implement any number of direct superinterfaces, an interface can extend any number of direct superinterfaces. The terms **direct superinterface**, **superinterface**, **direct subinterface**, and **subinterface** are used to describe the resultant interface hierarchies much like direct superclass, superclass, direct subclass, and subclass describe class hierarchies.

If there is no `extends` clause the interface implicitly extends the following imaginary `Object` interface:

```
public interface Object {
```

---

14. Gosling et al., §8.5.2, "`static` Member Type Declarations."

```
    Class getClass();
    int hashCode();
    boolean equals(Object obj);
    String toString();
    void notify();
    void notifyAll();
    void wait(long timeout) throws InterruptedException;
    void wait(long timeout, int nanos) throws InterruptedException;
    void wait() throws InterruptedException;
}
```

At least, that is my view of things. As stated in the *JLS*,

> If an interface has no direct superinterfaces, then the interface implicitly declares a `public abstract` member method *m* with signature *s*, return type *r*, and `throws` clause *t* corresponding to each `public` instance method *m* with signature *s*, return type *r* and `throws` clause *t* declared in `Object`, unless a method with the same signature, same return type, and a compatible `throws` clause is explicitly declared by the interface.[15]

It goes without saying that interfaces cannot inherit method implementations as do classes. The *JLS* is simply defining a concrete example of the concept of interface inheritance. I think the above quotation should be interpreted to mean that interface types do indeed extend the `Object` class, but only in terms of interface inheritance.

2.6.2.1 Interface Names

Like class naming conventions, interface names usually begin with a capital letter, are mixed case, and should be "short and descriptive, not overly long."[16]

The *JLS* has a separate naming convention for "interfaces used as if they were abstract superclasses."[17] That naming convention is the same naming convention used for class names. The two examples provided in the *JLS* are `java.io.DataInput` and `java.io.DataOutput`.

How do you know when an interface is being "used as if it were an `abstract` superclass"? The answer is simple. If the would-be subclasses in question exist primarily to implement the interface, then the interface is being "used as if it were an `abstract` superclass." Other examples of this are the core collection interfaces `Collection`, `Set`, `List`, `Map`, `SortedSet`, and `SortedMap`. The *general-purpose implementations*,

---

15. Gosling et al., §9.2, "Interface Members."
16. Gosling et al., §6.8.2, "Class and Interface Type Names."
17. Ibid.

as they are called, exist primarily to implement one of the core collection interfaces (for example, `ArrayList` and `HashMap`). The rule is that if the classes exists primarily to implement the interface, then the interface abides by class naming conventions.

Adjectives typically ending in *-able* are used for other interface names. Some important examples from the core API are the following standard interfaces:

```
java.lang.Cloneable
java.lang.Comparable
java.lang.Runnable
java.io.Serializable
```

As another example of this naming convention, this book uses a `Computer` class hierarchy in which `Networkable` is an interface.

2.6.2.2 The Members of an Interface

The members of any reference type are fields, methods, and member types. Those members are either declared or inherited. The members of an *interface type* are specifically

- Members declared in the body of an interface
- Members inherited from any direct superinterfaces named in the `extends` clause

If there is no `extends` clause, the interface implicitly declares all of the methods in the *imaginary* `Object` interface discussed at the bottom of 2.6.2 Interface Type Declarations.

2.6.2.3 Interface Member Declarations

The constants declared in the body of an interface are implicitly `public static final`. These are called **constant modifiers**, and they are the only modifiers that can be used when declaring what are generally referred to as **interface constants**. The use of constant modifiers is actively discouraged "as a matter of style" in the original *JLS*.

> Every field declaration in the body of an interface is implicitly `public`, `static`, and `final`. It is permitted, *but strongly discouraged as a matter of style*, to redundantly specify any or all of these modifiers for such fields [emphasis added].[18]

The emphasized text, however, is absent in the second edition of the *JLS*. One assumes that the use of constant modifiers in interface types is now considered an acceptable style of coding. I would add that, if you are going to use them, you should probably use all three.

The methods declared in an interface are implicitly `public abstract`. These are called **abstract method modifiers**, and they are the only modifiers that can be used when declaring methods in an interface. The use of `abstract` method modifiers in an interface is actively discouraged "as a matter of style" in the *JLS*.

> For compatibility with older versions of the Java platform, it is permitted *but discouraged, as a matter of style*, to redundantly specify the `abstract` modifier for methods declared in interfaces.
>
> It is permitted, *but strongly discouraged as a matter of style*, to redundantly specify the `public` modifier for interface methods. [emphasis added].[19]

Unlike interface constants, no one thinks modifiers should be used when declaring `abstract` methods in an interface. Note that a semicolon is used as a place holder for the method body in the declaration of an `abstract` method, much like it is in the declaration of a `native` method.

Nested top-level classes and interfaces can also be declared in interfaces. For example,

```
interface Interface {
    class NestedTopLevelClass {}
    interface NestedInterface {}
}
```

Notice that the declaration of `NestedTopLevelClass` does not require the `static` keyword. Much like interface constants, all nested classes declared in the body of an interface are implicitly `static`.

This chapter does not have much to say about nested top-level classes declared in the body of an interface, but I think that interfaces that come with their own objects are going to be more fully exploited as object-oriented programming in the Java programming language matures.

---

18. James Gosling, Bill Joy, and Guy Steele, *The Java Language Specification* (Reading: Addison-Wesley, 1996), §9.3, "Field (Constant) Declarations."
19. Gosling et al., §9.4, "Abstract Method Declarations."

2.7 The Definition of Top-Level Classes

This is one of the sharpest departures in my work concerning the terminology in official Sun specifications, in this case the *JLS*. I therefore dedicate an entire section to an explanation for that departure. Understanding exactly what is meant by the term *top-level class* is a prerequisite for the next section.

The second edition of the *JLS* introduced some new terms to the Java programming language, clarified others, and in a few cases redefined important terms such as *hiding* and *top-level class*. The need for a comprehensive review of the terminology of inner classes was indisputable. For example, one of the new terms introduced in the second edition of the *JLS* is *inner member class*, which is a badly needed replacement of the *non-static member class* used in the *Inner Classes Specification*. Before the introduction of this term I had to use long, awkward expressions such as *top-level classes, nested interfaces, and inner classes (non-static member classes to be exact)*. The problem was that I wanted to say *inner classes*, but then needed to immediately qualify which kind of inner class. The new term *inner member class* solves that problem.

On the other hand, I ardently disagree with the new definition of top-level class as given in the *JLS*.

> A *nested class* is any class whose declaration occurs within the body of another class or interface. A *top-level class* is a class that is not a nested class.[20]

Using this definition the term top-level class becomes little more than a synonym for package members. It is a lexical definition that is not very useful. Furthermore, it could not be more contrary to what John Rose says in the original *Inner Classes Specification* in which a top-level class is defined as one that has no enclosing instance. Here are some relevant quotations:

> A static class is a top-level class, not an inner class.[21]
>
> The static keyword may also modify the declaration of a class *C* within the body of a top-level class *T*. Its effect is to declare that *C* is also a top-level class.[22]

---

20. Gosling et al., Introduction to Chapter 8, "Classes."
21. Rose, "How do inner classes affect the idea of this in Java code?"
22. Rose, "Can a nested class be declared final, private, protected, or static?"

> Classes which are `static` class members and classes which are package members are both called top-level classes.[23]
>
> Top-level classes do not have multiple current instances. Within the non-`static` code of a top-level class *T*, there is one current instance of type *T*. Within the `static` code of a top-level class *T*, there are no current instances. This has always been true of top-level classes which are package members, and is also true of top-level classes which are `static` members of other top-level classes.[24]

The last quotation is a much more intellectually rigorous definition of **top-level class**, one that I fully support. Furthermore, I implore the authors of the *JLS* to reconsider the definition of this term in future editions of the *JLS*, of which there are certain to be many.

The difference is that in the *JLS*, *all classes are either top-level or nested*. That is their high-level view of things. In this book, as well as in the original *Inner Classes Specification*, *all classes are either top-level or inner*. This is no small difference. It is based on different definitions of the term top-level class. The definition of top-level class in the *JLS* says,

> A *top-level* class is a class that is not a nested class.[25]

The opposing view is

> All top-level classes have one thing in common. They are either implicitly or explicitly `static`. The `static` keyword is what makes them *top-level*.

Oddly, the two views do agree on the definition of inner class. As stated in the *JLS*,

> An *inner class* is a nested class that is not explicitly or implicitly declared `static`.[26]

This is precisely where I think the *JLS* approach falls apart. Allow me to explain.

---

23. Rose, "What are top-level classes and inner classes?"
24. Rose, "How do inner classes affect the idea of this in Java code?"
25. Gosling et al., Introduction to Chapter 8, "Classes."
26. Gosling et al., §8.1.2, "Inner Classes and Enclosing Instances."

Using the definitions from the *JLS*, the implication is that there are nested classes that are neither top-level nor inner classes. That makes for three fundamentally different categories of classes: top-level, nested (and `static`), and inner classes. The difference between top-level classes and inner classes is confused using this approach, whereas the difference between top-level classes and inner classes is a fundamental one using the definition of top-level class from the original *Inner Classes Specification*.

The distinction that the *JLS* is seeking is not lost using the older definition of top-level class. The more general term that applies to all nested top-level classes, nested interfaces, and inner classes is still **nested types** (not inner classes). All types are indeed either package members or nested.

The lord giveth and the lord taketh away. If you adopt the definition of top-level class in the *JLS*, you lose the term *nested top-level class*. A nested top-level class is so called because it is declared in the body of another type using the `static` keyword. The *JLS* would refer to such a class as just a *nested class*. Therefore, on the one hand the *JLS* gives us *inner member class*, but then it takes away *nested top-level class*. You are back where you started terminologically, and there are examples of this in the *JLS*.

> Nested classes that are not inner classes may declare `static` members freely ....[27]

"Nested classes that are not inner classes" are nested top-level classes. You can see how the term *nested top-level class* is useful.

There are more important issues at stake here than a term. I would say what is at stake here is the whole concept of *top-level*. The top-level is procedure-oriented. There is no current object. John Rose may have opened a door through which we all must pass because as object-oriented theory advances the role of the top-level will certainly diminish. Before that happens, however, it will be the subject of intense study and debate. The starting point for that research may be the precise definition of *top-level* given in the original *Inner Classes Specification*. Adding a lexical definition of the term *top-level class* to the *JLS* only muddies the water.

---

27. Gosling et al., §8.1.2, "Inner Classes and Enclosing Instances."

2.8 Helper Classes are Not Fundamentally Different

A **helper class** is a non-`public` package member that does not have a separate compilation unit. The source code for a helper class is found in a `.java` file that bears the name of some other class. They are typically declared at the bottom of the compilation unit in which they are found. For example,

```
public class PackageMember {
   ...
}
class HelperClass {
   ...
}
```

I have seen core API programmers use "helper class" (in quotation marks), as if sceptical of the whole concept, and with good reason. The problem with the term *helper class* is it suggests there is something fundamentally different about classes that do not have their own compilation unit. That is self-evidently absurd because compilation units have no bearing whatsoever on the run-time system.

A helper class is a package-private class like any other. The only thing special about the so-called helper classes is that they are not declared in their own compilation unit, but that does not make them helper classes. Any package-private class is a helper class in the sense the it is part of the implementation (that is, it "helps" to implement a `public` class or interface type). Such classes are sometimes called *support classes*.

Why all the confusion? I think this is largely a terminological problem, but the specification is partly to blame. I will quote that specification momentarily, but before I do I want to mention one of the most widely held misconceptions about helper classes. Many Java programmers labor under the misconception that helper classes are inaccessible outside of the compilation unit in which they are declared. That simply is not true. These are package-private classes just like any other. The basis for that misconception is probably the following passage from the *JLS*, which indirectly defines what most people think of as helper classes.

> When packages are stored in a file system, the host system may choose to enforce the restriction that it is a compile-time error if a type is not found in a file under a name composed of the type name plus an extension (such as `.java` or `.jav`) if either of the following is true:

- The type is referred to by code in other compilation units of the package in which the type is declared.
- The type is declared `public` (and therefore is potentially accessible from code in other packages).

This restriction implies that there must be at most one such type per compilation unit. This restriction makes it easy for a compiler for the Java programming language or an implementation of the Java Virtual Machine to find a named class within a package ....[28]

These restrictions leave only top-level classes and interfaces that meet all of the following criteria:

- Non-`public`
- Package member
- Not referenced outside of the compilation unit in which it is declared

A non-`public` class that is a package member and not referenced outside of the compilation unit in which it is declared is the very definition of what most people think of as a helper class. Can you see the relationship between this specification and the common definition of helper class? The problem is that this is a fiction. Helper classes can be referenced by other classes in the same package because they have default access. There is nothing about their being a helper class that changes how the access control mechanism works in a Java compiler or a JVM at run time. This is where there is a major disconnect for many Java programmers.

The problems with the wording in this passage are numerous. I am going to document them in this section on helper classes not as a criticism of the *JLS*, but to help clear the air of any notion that helper classes are a fundamentally different kind of class. They are not. That becomes important in the next section because if there is something fundamentally different about the so-called helper classes, there would be *six kinds of classes and interfaces* instead of five. Before I can even discuss the problem with the wording of this specification, however, I must explain this use of the term *host system*.

---

28. Gosling et al., §7.6, "Top-Level Type Declarations."

For most mainstream business application programmers *host system* means *host operating system* or the operating system of the host platform, but this use of the term is defined in the *JLS*, which is quoted here in its entirety.

> Each host determines how packages, compilation units, and subpackages are created and stored, and which compilation units are observable in a particular compilation; and which packages are accessible.

> The packages may be stored in a local file system in simple implementations of Java. Other implementations may use a distributed file system or some form of database to store Java source and/or binary code.[29]

As you can see from this quotation, the *host* is an implementation of the Java platform, which notably includes the compile-time environment as well as the run-time system. In the context of a discussion of helper classes the *host system* is just a Java compiler.

One of the subtleties of this specification is the wording of the first sentence, which reads in part "the host system may choose to enforce [this file naming] restriction ... if either of the following is true" (emphasis on *either*).[30] Now look again at what I am calling the *common definition* of helper classes (because there is no formal definition for this term):

- Non-`public`
- Package member
- Not referenced outside of the compilation unit in which it is declared

The inclusion of both the first and third item has no correspondence to the *either-or* language used in the specification. In short, what I am saying is that I think the common definition of the term *helper class* is based on a misunderstanding of a short passage in the *JLS* that was intended primarily to support the automatic compilation of dependencies (as discussed in the following subsection).

The Java implementations used by mainstream business application programmers will never implement this file naming restriction based on the

---

29. Gosling et al., §7.2, "Host Support for Packages."
30. Ibid.

first condition. I have a hard time understanding how any host system or Java implementation could enforce this. Once a so-called helper class is compiled, there is nothing whatsoever to keep another class that has access from doing so. How could a compiler know that? It would have to be a closed system in which the compiler can determine exactly which compilation units do or do not access a particular helper class. That would likely be a very small system in which the definition of helper classes would probably be meaningless.

That leaves only the second condition, which is not an option in the file-system of Java implementations such as J2EE used by mainstream business application programmers. For example,

```
package com.javarules;
public class Test {
    public static void main(String[] args) {
        System.out.println(HelperClass.x);
    }
}
public class HelperClass {
    public static int x = 0;
}
```

Attempting to compile this program generates the following compiler errors:

```
Test.java:7: class HelperClass is public, should be declared in a file named HelperClass.java
public class HelperClass {
       ^
1 error
```

Were that restriction not enforced the simple and complex classpath formulas discussed in this chapter would be meaningless. The main point of this section, however, is that none of this fundamentally differentiates helper classes from package-private classes that are declared in their own compilation unit. In that sense, there is no such thing as a helper class unless by that you mean all package-private classes. As stated above, package-private classes are also sometimes referred to as *support classes*.

The term *helper class* should signify nothing more or less than a package member that does not have its own compilation unit. That is not the case, however. I suspect that many Java programmers think there is something fundamentally different about helper classes, which may be a testament to the power of terminology. In that sense, it is important to note the following.

Where the term helper class came from I do not know. It is not properly part of the Java lexicon.

Normally, helper classes are used only in the compilation unit in which they are declared, but that is nothing more than a programmer convention. There is nothing to keep you from declaring any number of non-public classes in the same compilation unit and using them anywhere in the package. In fact, I am sure somewhere in the universe of Java programming there is an application for which doing so makes a lot of sense.

The introduction of inner classes in the Java 1.1 release seriously eroded the raison d'être for helper classes. Why? Because most helper classes were small. A small class that is only used by one other class should be nested. This is one point on which there appears to be universal agreement. For example, one of the primary uses of helper classes before the Java 1.1 release was as adapter classes. Almost all adapter classes are now inner classes. Large helper classes are another matter altogether. They continue to be used in the core API (including even the newer packages such as `javax.swing`). A `private` member class is the equivalent of a helper class in that it cannot be used outside of the class in which it is declared and is not inherited. In purely syntactic terms the only difference between a `private` member class and a helper class is the closing brace of the package member. For example,

```
public class PackageMember {
    class InnerMemberClass {
    }
}
```

Move the closing brace of `PackageMember` and `InnerMember-Class` becomes a `HelperClass`. For example,

```
public class PackageMember {
}
class HelperClass {
}
```

Many helper classes of yore are now `private` member classes. Why not all of them? Why do some programmers continue to use helper classes? My guess is that they do not want to indent an entire class (which is often done when using nested types). Consequently, they tend to use helper classes, especially when the class in question is a very large one.

Or it may be something as simple as wanting to see the closing brace of one class before starting another.

Based on my analysis of the `java` and `javax` namespaces in the 1.3 release, 1 in every 8.5 source code files (or approximately 12 percent of them) have member classes compared to 1 in every 50 (or 2 percent) that have helper classes. Helper classes are here to stay, but they will never be used as much as they were before the introduction of nested types in the 1.1 release.

2.8.1 Technical Arguments Against the Use of Helper Classes

I think that anything that is not interface related, a bug fix, or a performance optimization ultimately should be regarded as programmer preference so as not to stifle creativity with a bunch of arbitrary rules. That is the art of computer programming, and includes the choice of using a so-called "helper class" (that is, a package-private class not declared in its own compilation unit).

Having said that, this section discusses three technical reasons why not to use helper classes, preferring instead `private` member classes (that really do not have to be indented if they are declared at the bottom of a compilation unit). The three technical reasons for not using helper classes are listed here in the order of their importance:

1. One-to-one correspondence of source code and class file names
2. No automatic compilation of dependencies
3. Unintended overwriting of class files

The first reason for not using helper classes is as old as the language itself. Even before the introduction of inner classes, many programmers chose not to use helper classes because it makes it difficult to find the source code for a helper class if all you know is the class name. Even the *JLS* points this out.

> In practice, many Java programmers choose to put each class or interface type in its own compilation unit, whether or not it is public or is referred to by code in other compilation units.[31]

This is a simple maintenance issue. If all package members are declared in their own compilation unit, then for every `.class` file there is a corre-

---

31. Ibid.

sponding `.java` file. There is much to be said for the simplicity of this design.

Helper classes are never automatically compiled when referenced outside of the compilation unit unless both of the following are true.

- The `public` class declared in the same compilation unit is also referenced
- The class file is out of date

I believe this to be the entire intent of the specification in question. For example, suppose the following compilation unit was saved to the unnamed package but not compiled:

```
public class Dummy { }
class HelperClass {
    static String s = "The so-called helper classes are " +
                      "just package-private package members";
}
```

Then in a different compilation unit you declare the following `Test` program:

```
class Test {
    public static void main(String[] args) {
        System.out.println(HelperClass.x);
    }
}
```

Normally you would expect this to compile because of the automatic compilation of dependencies. Instead, attempting to compile this program generates the following compiler error:

```
Test.java:3: cannot resolve symbol
symbol  : variable HelperClass
location: class Test
        System.out.println(HelperClass.x);
                           ^
```

```
1 error
```

The problem is that there is no `HelperClass.java` file to compile. Now if you go back and reread the *JLS* specification, you will see why I think it is directed at the automatic compilation of dependencies.

The third technical argument against the use of helper classes is the possibility of two helper classes having the same name. If they are members of the same package, compiling one of the helper classes overwrites the class file of the other. The compiler has no way of knowing that the class file being overwritten is actually from a different compilation unit and does not issue a warning. You could even do this to yourself while copying code that includes a helper class. For example,

```
class HelloWorld {
    public static void main(String[] args) {
        Message message = new Message();
        message.print();
    }
}
class Message {
    String message = "Hello World!";
    void print() {
        System.out.println(message);
    }
}
```

This program uses a helper class to print the `Hello World!` message. Now suppose you add the following program to the same package:

```
class GoodbyeCruelWorld {
    public static void main(String[] args) {
        Message message = new Message();
        message.print();
    }
}
class Message {
    String message = "Goodbye Cruel C++ World!";
    void print() {
        System.out.println(message);
    }
}
```

The problem is that now the `HelloWorld` program prints `Goodbye Cruel C++ World` and there is no warning of the change. Even worse is the following implementation of `GoodbyeCruelWorld`, which includes what the programmer probably thinks is a minor change in one of the method names from `print()` to `printMessage()`:

```
class GoodbyeCruelWorld {
    public static void main(String[] args) {
        Message message = new Message();
        message.printMessage();
    }
}
class Message {
    String message = "Goodbye Cruel C++ World!";
    void printMessage() {
        System.out.println(message);
    }
}
```

After compiling this class, attempting to execute the `HelloWorld` program generates the following error:

```
Exception in thread "main" java.lang.NoSuchMethodError at HelloWorld.main(HelloWorld.java:4)
```

Nested classes never have such problems because they exist within a type namespace that is under the complete control of a single programmer rather than in a shared package namespace.

2.9 The Five Kinds of Classes and Interfaces

There of five kinds of classes and interfaces, which are summarized in Table 2-6. The following `PackageMember` class includes examples of each kind of reference type except for an anonymous class:

```
public class PackageMember {

    public interface NestedInterface {…}

    public static class NestedTopLevelClass {
            public static class DeeplyNestedTopLevelClass {…}
    }

    /* THE FOLLOWING ARE INNER CLASS DECLARATIONS */

    private class InnerMemberClass {…}

    public void instanceMethod() {
        …
        class LocalClass {…}
        …
    }
}
```

Notice that the only difference between the declaration of a nested top-level class and an inner member class is the `static` keyword. Remove the `static` keyword from the declaration of a nested top-level class and it becomes an inner member class.

Nested types have compiler-generated names when viewed as class files in the local filesystem. The complete list of class file names generated by this compilation unit is as follows:

```
PackageMember.class
PackageMember$NestedInterface.class
PackageMember$NestedTopLevelClass.class
PackageMember$NestedTopLevelClass$DeeplyNestedTopLevelClass.class
PackageMember$InnerMemberClass.class
PackageMember$1$LocalClass.class
```

One of the important differences in the five kinds of classes and interfaces is the choice of an access modifier. There is only one access modifier for package members. That is the `public` modifier. If a package member is not declared `public`, it is said to be non-`public` (which is synonymous

Table 2-6: The Five Kinds of Classes and Interfaces

Kind	`static` Keyword	Description
❶ Package Members	The `static` keyword is implicit. Use of the `static` keyword in the declaration of a package member will generate a compiler error.	A class or interface declared directly in a compilation unit. This includes the so-called "helper classes."
❷ Nested top-level classes and interfaces	The `static` keyword must be explicit for nested top-level classes declared in the body of another class. It can be omitted in the body of an interface because all types declared in the body of an interface are implicitly `static`. Nested interfaces are implicitly `static` in either a class or interface body. Their declaration never requires use of the `static` keyword.[a]	Top-level classes and interfaces declared in the body of another type. The type in which a nested top-level class or interface is declared is always another top-level class or interface because `static` members cannot be declared in inner classes. It may be either a package member or another nested top-level class or interface.
❸ Inner member classes	Inner member classes are extremely versatile. Any class declared in the body of another class (versus a class declared in a block) that is not also declared `static` is an inner member class. Such declarations can occur anywhere, even in the body of a local or anonymous class.	
❹ Local classes	Named classes declared in a block. The term *local class* is analogous to *local variable*. The difference between a local class and a member type is that the enclosing block is not a class or interface body.	
❺ Anonymous classes	Unnamed classes declared using a special form of the class instance creation expression. An anonymous class can be declared anywhere in the body of another class, even as a variable initializer for fields (that is, not in a block of code).	

a. Hence, the term *inner classes* applies only to classes. There are no "inner interfaces."

with default access or package-private). Any access modifier can be used in the declaration of a member type (nested top-level classes, nested interfaces, and inner member classes). Helper classes as well as local and anonymous classes do not have access modifiers.

A purely academic approach towards the subject of inner classes always suggests an *Alice in Wonderland* world of infinite possibilities. This is one subject that must be taught on a more practical basis. For example, while qualifying the `super` keyword (discussed in the next chapter) has been called the *pathological case*, the truth is that the `new` keyword is not being explicitly qualified either. And not only are examples of bizarre nesting such as a local or inner member class declared in an anonymous class virtually nonexistent, but examples of deeply-nested member types are extremely rare.

Each of the five kinds of classes and interfaces is discussed in the following subsections. They largely correspond to Table 2-6, with one important exception. Nested top-level classes declared `public` and package members are discussed together. The only other discussion of member types is of non-`public` member classes.

2.9.1 `public` Top-Level Classes

Package members are either `public` or non-`public`. Non-`public` package members are not seen by the users of a package, but they are an important part of the implementation of the package. This section only discusses `public` top-level classes, which includes some nested top-level classes while excluding non-`public` package members such as helper classes. A nested top-level class declared `public` has more in common with a `public` package member than do helper classes.

A nested top-level class declared `public` is an important part of the package member interface. For example, `java.lang.Character.UnicodeBlock` is described as follows in the API docs.

> A family of character subsets representing the character blocks defined by the Unicode 2.0 specification.[32]

Yet the `Character` class does not instantiate `UnicodeBlock`. The definition of `Character.UnicodeBlock` is purely a service to users of the `Character` class. (There is an example of using this class in 1.2 White Space.) The only real difference between this use of nested top-level classes and package members is that the fully qualified name of a nested top-level class includes the name of the enclosing class as well as the package name. For example, the fully qualified name of `UnicodeBlock` is `java.lang.Character.UnicodeBlock`. John Rose refers to this use of nested top-level classes as a *class-based API*.

---

32. API docs for the `java.lang.Character.UnicodeBlock` class.

2.9.1.1 A Note About *public* Inner Member Classes

Java compilers went to school after inner classes were introduced to the language. There was a "parade" of bugs reported against both the compiler and inner classes, many of which concerned `protected` inner classes. The primary Bug Ids are still available in the Bug Parade. They are listed here in their order of importance:

> 4158650
>
> 4109894
>
> 4087314

They have all been fixed, but they leave behind a legacy of inner member classes declared `public`. That was a common workaround for many of these problems.

Here is a sampling of the documentation comments you will find for such classes in the core API.

> This inner class is marked "public" due to a compiler bug. This class should be treated as a "protected" inner class. Instantiate it only within subclasses of `<Foo>`.[33]

> This is here because of a bug in the compiler. When a protected-inner-class-savvy compiler comes out we should move this into `MetalComboBoxLayoutManager`.[34]

> This class is not meant to be used directly by application developers, but is instead meant only to be subclassed by component developers. Due to a restriction that `protected` inner classes cannot be subclassed outside of a package, this inner class has been made `public`. When this restriction is lifted for JDK 1.1.7, this class will be made `protected`.[35]

Were it not for those compiler errors in the 1.1 release, examples of `public` inner member classes would be much harder to find.

---

33. This documentation comment is included in many `public` member classes in the core API, particularly those in the `javax.swing` package. Here `<Foo>` replaces the actual class name.
34. API docs for the `layoutComboBox(Container parent, MetalComboBoxLayoutManager manager)` method in the `javax.swing.plaf.metal.MetalComboBoxUI` class.
35. API docs for `javax.swing.JComponent` class.

2.9.2 Non-`public` Member Classes

Here is where the term *member classes* is useful. The choice between a nested top-level class and an inner member class is better thought of as a choice between a `static` or non-`static` member class. Then you do not have to wrestle with the idea of nested top-level classes versus inner member classes. In this context I believe those terms do more harm than good.

The choice between a `static` and non-`static` member class is straightforward. There are three considerations, which are listed here in their order of importance:

1. Full access to the `private` members of the enclosing class.
2. Access to `static` members.
3. Instantiation in a `static` context.

Each of these is discussed in the following subsections.

2.9.2.1 Full Access to the `private` Members of an Enclosing Class

Non-`static` member classes have what is best described as *full access to the private members of the enclosing class.* You have to be careful with the language used here. What we are most interested in is access to the `private` instance variables required for the implemetation of the member class. Inner member class do indeed have full access to the `private` instance variables of the enclosing class, but it is not true that inner member classes have full access to all of the instance variables in the enclosing class. Inner member classes do not have access to `protected` members that the enclosing class inherited from one or more superclasses. That is a detail about access control that escapes some programmers. Here is an example of accessing the `private` instance varaible of an enclosing class:

```
class Test {

    private String s = "this is a private instance variable";

    public static void main(String[] args) {
        new Test().new InnerMemberClass().print();
        new NestedTopLevelClass().print();
    }
    class InnerMemberClass {
        void print() {System.out.println(s);}
    }
```

```
        static class NestedTopLevelClass {
            void print() {System.out.println(s);}
        }
    }
}
```

Attempting to compile this program generates the following compiler error:

```
Test.java:13: non-static variable s cannot be referenced from a static context
        void print() {System.out.println(s);}
                                         ^
1 error
```

This is not an access control issue. If `s` were declared `static`, the program would compile and execute without a problem. For example,

```
class Test {

    private static String s = "this is a private class variable";

    public static void main(String[] args) {
        new Test().new InnerMemberClass().print();
        new NestedTopLevelClass().print();
    }
    class InnerMemberClass {
        void print() {System.out.println(s);}
    }
    static class NestedTopLevelClass {
        void print() {System.out.println(s);}
    }
}
```

Executing this program prints

```
this is a private class variable
this is a private class variable
```

The problem is that in the body of `NestedTopLevelClass` there is only one current instance. There is no instance of the enclosing `Test` class. Therefore, you cannot access an instance variable of that class. Instance variables, like instance methods and inner member classes, cannot exist apart from an instance of the class of which they are a member. As the last program shows, access to the `static` members of the enclosing class is a given. Any nested type has access to the `static` members of an enclosing type.

It is precisely because inner member classes have full access to the `private` members of the enclosing class that inner member classes are the first choice when declaring a member class. This is true even if the inner member class does not actually access the instance variables of the enclosing class. An evolving implementation of the class may want to access those members at a later date. The alternative would be to declare a member class `static` (that is, use a nested top-level class) and then later remove the `static` keyword from the declaration if access to the `private` instance variables of the enclosing class is required. Declaring a member class `static` and later removing the `static` modifier is probably not compatible with existing binaries. Unfortunately, Chapter 13, "Binary Compatibility," of the *JLS* does not address this question. In the absence of any statement in the *JLS*, I do not want to commit to saying that such a change is or is not compatible with existing binaries. The fact is, however, that most member classes are declared non-`static`.

2.9.2.2 The `static` Keyword and Inner Classes

Generally speaking, inner classes cannot use the `static` keyword. More precisely, inner classes cannot include any of the following declarations:

- `static` initialization blocks
- Class variables (except inlined constants)
- Class methods
- Nested top-level classes
- Interfaces

For example,

```
class Test {
    class InnerMemberClass {
        static void staticMethod() {}
    }
}
```

Attempting to compile this program generates the following compiler error:

```
Test.java:3: inner classes cannot have static declarations
        static void staticMethod() {}
                    ^
1 error
```

John Rose addresses this in the *Inner Classes Specification* when he writes,

> As opposed to top-level classes (whether nested or not), inner classes cannot declare any `static` members at all. To create a class variable for an inner class, the programmer must place the desired variable in an enclosing class.[36]

For example,

```
class Test {
    static void print() {
        System.out.println("this is a class method");
    }
    public static void main(String[] args) {
        new Test().new InnerMemberClass().print();
    }
    class InnerMemberClass {
        void print() {
            Test.print();
        }
    }
}
```

This program does compile and prints the message *this is a class method.*

If an inner class requires a top-level entity, that entity must be declared in the top-level class at the top of the inner class hierarchy. The top-level class at the top of an inner class hierarchy is the only class in an inner class hierarchy that can declare `static` members. Those `static` members are in scope throughout the inner class hierarchy. The term *inner class hierarchy* is discussed in 2.12 Containment and Inner Class Hierarchies.

Member classes are sometimes extended by the subclasses that inherit them. The reason for doing so is the same as overriding a method. You make the implementation specific to the subclass. Examples of extending member classes in the same class in which they are declared can also be found. For example, `java.util.Character.UnicodeBlock` extends the following simplified implementation of the `java.util.Character.Subset` class:

```
public static class Subset {
    private String name;
    protected Subset(String name) {
        this.name = name;
    }
    public final boolean equals(Object obj) {
        return (this == obj);
    }
    public final int hashCode() {
        return super.hashCode();
    }
    public final String toString() {
        return name;
    }
}
```

---

36. Rose, "How do inner classes affect the idea of this in Java code?"

As you can see, the rationale behind this superclass is like that of any superclass. In this case, `Character.Subset` provides default implementations for three of the housekeeping methods inherited from the `Object` class. Note that all three of the housekeeping methods in this class are declared `final`. All Unicode character subsets have the same `toString()` policy, and the fact that `hashCode()` is consistent with `equals()` is guaranteed for all subclasses. That is part of the reason for declaring the `SubSet` superclass in the first place. Housekeeping methods are discussed at the end of Chapter 4.

The reason for discussing the extension of inner classes in this section is that I have seen examples of non-`static` member classes extending `static` member classes (that is, an inner member classes extending a nested top-level class). One reason you might extend a nested top-level class with an inner member class is that inner member classes can inherit `static` members. They just cannot declare them.

2.9.2.2.1 Declaring Inlined Constants in Inner Classes

The JLS does allow for the declaration of inlined constants in inner classes. The exception was made because, in compiled code, an inlined constant is indistinguishable from numeric or string literals. That is, however, the only exception to the rule that inner classes cannot use the `static` keyword. Inlined constants are `String` or primitive type class variables that are declared `final` and initialized with a compile-time constant expression. For example,

```
class Test {

    public static void main(String[] args) {
        new Test().new InnerMemberClass().print();
    }
    class InnerMemberClass {
        static final int ZERO = 0;
        void print() {System.out.println(ZERO);}
    }
}
```

This code does compile and, when executed, prints 0.

2.9.2.3 Instantiating Member Classes in a static Context

Inner member classes cannot be instantiated in a `static` context such as a `static` method. For example,

```
class Test {
    public static void main(String[] args) {
        InnerMemberClass inner = new InnerMemberClass();
    }
    class InnerMemberClass {}
}
```

Attempting to compile this program generates the following compiler error:

```
Test.java:3: non-static variable this cannot be referenced from a static context
        InnerMemberClass inner = new InnerMemberClass();
                                 ^
```

```
1 error
```

The term *static context* is defined in 3.3 The Definition of `static` Context.

An inner member class cannot exist apart from an instance of the enclosing class. What the compiler sees in this example is a class instance creation expression that defaults to the current instance of the enclosing class. The following code is exactly the same to a Java compiler:

```
class Test {

    public static void main(String[] args) {
        InnerMemberClass inner = this.new InnerMemberClass();
    }
    class InnerMemberClass {}
}
```

Implicitly or explicitly, the `new` keyword in a class instance creation expression for an inner member class is always qualified. This makes inner member classes different from every other kind of class in the Java programming language. The program does not compile because the `this` keyword cannot be used in a `static` method. These subjects are discussed at length in the next chapter.

This problem is easily corrected by declaring the member class `static`. For example,

```
class Test {

    public static void main(String[] args) {
        NestedTopLevelClass topLevel = new NestedTopLevelClass();
    }
    static class NestedTopLevelClass {}
}
```

This is essentially the same code using a nested top-level class instead of an inner member class. The good news is that a nested top-level class can be instantiated anywhere. The bad news is that you must choose between full access to the `private` members of the enclosing class and instantiation in a `static` context.

2.9.3 Local and Anonymous Classes

I avoid discussing anonymous classes as much as possible in this chapter. While they are most definitely a kind of inner class, anonymous classes are better thought of as an alternative form of the class instance creation expression. The transition from thinking of anonymous classes as a *kind of inner class* to *an alternative form of the class instance creation expression* was something of an epiphany for me. That may be hard to understand unless have you read the original *Inner Classes Specification*, in which the emphasis was on anonymous classes as being a *kind of inner class* with a *special syntax*. The "syntactic sugar" expression from the following line of the *Inner Classes Specification* always comes to mind in this context.

> As noted previously, not every inner class should be anonymous,
> but very simple "one-shot" local objects are such a common
> case that they merit some syntactic sugar.[37]

This approach makes anonymous classes harder to understand than thinking of them as another way of writing a class instance creation expression. Therefore, I was glad to see the *JLS* treat anonymous classes as an *optional class body* at the end of a class instance creation expression.

> ... class instance creation expressions may optionally end with a
> class body. Such a class instance creation expression declares
> an anonymous class and creates an instance of it.[38]

An anonymous class is a class body tacked on to the end of a class instance creation expression. The type name in such a class instance creation expression can be either a class or an interface. If a class, then the class is implicitly subclassed. If it is an interface, then it is implicitly implemented. In either case the class body implements a class that has no name and the object created must be referenced as an instance of the type name used in the class instance creation expression. The use of interface types in *class* instance creation expressions is unique to anonymous classes.

---

37. Rose, "Why does Java need inner classes?"
38. Gosling, et al., §15.9, "Class Instance Creation Expressions."

A local class is any class declared in a block of code that is not an anonymous class. Here are examples of a local class, an anonymous subclass, and an anonymous class that implements an interface:

```
class Test {

    public static void main(String[] args) {

        class LocalClass {
            void printMessage() {
                System.out.println("this is a local class");
            }
        }
        LocalClass local = new LocalClass();
        A a = new A() {
                void printMessage() {
                    System.out.println("this is an anonymous subclass of A");
                }
            };
        B b = new B() {
                public void printMessage() {
                    System.out.println("this anonymous class implements " +
                                            "interface B");
                }
            };

        local.printMessage();
        a.printMessage();
        b.printMessage();
    }
}
class A {
    void printMessage() {
        System.out.println("this message will be overridden in " +
                                "the anonymous subclass");
    }
}
interface B {
    void printMessage();
}
```

Executing this program prints

```
this is a local class
this is an anonymous subclass of A
this anonymous class implements interface B
```

The difference between a local and anonymous class is slight. Anonymous classes are used only once. The next step up from a class that is used only once is a local class that is used only in a block of code. What is the difference? Anonymous classes can be used to initialize fields (in which case there is no block of code involved), but most of the time an anonymous class is declared in some block of code. So we have two different kinds of classes that can be declared in a block of code. Both have access to local variables and parameters.

The main difference between a local and an anonymous class is that local classes can be instantiated more than once in the same block of code, but this is rarely a requirement. Unless instantiating a local class more than once, an anonymous class is always an alternative. An anonymous class can be created and assigned to a local variable as easily as a local class. In the above example the local variables `local`, a, and b can be used again. It does not matter how they were created. The only thing left to differentiate local and anonymous classes is the size of the class.

Anonymous classes tend to be small, especially when they are used as argument expressions. For example,

```
someGuiComponent.addEventListener(
    new Eventadapter() {
        public void eventMethod(EventObject e) {
            actionMethod();
        }
    });
```

This anonymous class has only four lines of code. You can always assign an anonymous class to a local variable if it becomes too large to use as an argument expression. The following example is equivalent to the one above:

```
EventAdapter listener = new Eventadapter() {
    public void eventMethod(EventObject e) {
    actionMethod();
        }
    };
someGuiComponent.addEventListener(listener);
```

The name of the local variable will help the reader understand how the anonymous class is being used. There is, however, an extreme indentation in such an anonymous class, which makes it difficult to code larger classes. The next step up in terms of the size of the class is to use a local class. Local classes require less indentation than anonymous classses. The choice between a local or an anonymous class can be that simple.

2.9.4 Nested Interfaces

Nested interfaces are less common than interfaces that are package members. One of the most widely known nested interfaces is `Map.Entry` in the `java.util` package. Note that `java.util.Map` is also an interface. Something I have never seen is deeply nested interfaces (three or more levels deep) or classes declared in nested interfaces. In other words, the nesting of types involving interfaces usually stops at the second level. This, however, is more generally true of all nested types.

2.10 Choosing Which Kind of Class to Use

Why are there five kinds of classes? There are at least three questions that need to be answered here.

- What are the fundamental differences between package members and nested types?

- What is the difference between `static` and non-`static` member classes?

- When using an inner class, how do I decide which kind to use?

This section provides answers to these questions. You should remember, however, that most of this chapter is only an introduction to the terminology of compilation units. A full answer to these questions requires delving into the details of access control, inheritance, and other subjects.

There are two general characteristics of nested types that make them useful. John Rose refers to them in the *Inner Classes Specification* when he says,

> Here are some of the properties that make [nested types] useful:
>
> - The [nested types]'s name is not usable outside its scope, except perhaps in a qualified name. This helps in structuring the classes within a package.
> - The code of a [nested type] can use simple names from enclosing scopes, including both class and instance members of enclosing classes, and local variables of enclosing blocks.[39]

For example,

```
public class PackageMember {

    private static String privateField = "private field";
    private String privateMethod() {
        return "private method.";
    }

    public static class NestedTopLevelClass {
        public static String s = privateField;
```

---

39. Rose, "What are top-level class and inner classes?"

```
        }
    private class InnerMemberClass {
        String s = privateMethod();
    }
}
```

The limited scope of a nested type and full access to the `private` members of an enclosing class (or to the local variables and parameters of an enclosing block) are what make nested types special. I refer to this as *full access to the `private` members of an enclosing class*, with the emphasis on *private*. In this context `private` means class `private`, `containment-hierarchy-private`, `inner-class-hierarchy-private`, or even `package-private`—anything but `protected`.

The answer to questions like *when should I use a top-level class versus an inner class* depends on where the class is used. For example, a top-level class declared `public` can be used by anyone who has access to the package, whereas a local class can only be used in a block of code.

> The general rule is to declare a class as close as possible to where it is used.

You will find that if you follow this simple rule then you will naturally take full advantage of nested types without having to master all of their intricacies. Exceptions to this rule are made when the class is too large to be declared close to where it is used. Maybe a class is used in only one method, but if the implementation of that class is unwieldy and requires many hundreds of lines of code, declaring it as a local class is impractical. In that case you will probably want to use a `private` inner member class.

In deciding what kind of class to use I consider the different kinds of classes in the following order:

1. Package members.
2. Anonymous classes.
3. Member classes.

Local classes are absent from this list because they are seldom used.

Deciding on a package member is relatively easy. Is the class used in other packages or by other classes in the same package? If so, then you probably want to declare a package member. Nested top-level classes are an alternative to package members when the class is clearly subordinate to an existing package member. `Character.UnicodeBlock` is a perfect example.

If the class is only used in the compilation unit in which you are working, you have to choose what kind of nested class to use. Most of the time this is an easy decision. First ask yourself if the class is instantiated more than once. Many, if not most, nested classes are only instantiated once. Any class that is only instantiated once is a logical candidate to be declared as an anonymous class. Anonymous classes use a special syntax designed specifically for classes that are used only once. That is precisely why they are *anonymous*. A class that is only used once does not require a name. The declaration and use of such a class are one and the same.

Anonymous classes are an extreme case of declaring a class close to where it is used. That is why they are second on the list after package members. I think they should be used as much as possible, although some programmers prefer not to use them because the use of `private` inner member classes allows for a greater separation of code.

This leaves only member classes. Most nested classes that are not anonymous are non-`public` member classes. The difference between `static` and non-`static` member classes is discussed at length in 2.9.2 Non-`public` Member Classes.

There are two special considerations when deciding which kind of nested class to use. The first is that only local and anonymous classes have access to local variables and parameters. If this is a requirement, then member types are out of the question. The second is that anonymous classes do not have constructors. If an instance initialization block does not work as a replacement for a constructor, then an anonymous class is not an option.

I want finish this section by reiterating that I regard the choice as to which kind of class to use to be purely a matter of style (unless you are doing something like implementing a design pattern based on using certain kinds of classes). The choice of what kind of class to use in Java is analogous to making decisions about how to organize code in structured programming. Having plied my trade for years as a structured programmer, I know all too well the feeling of someone else trying to impose their ideas on my designs. No matter what I say about the use of one kind of class over another, if you have other ideas on the subject, do what looks or feels right to you. None of the issues at stake here are important enough to override the responsible programmer's sense of proper design. The important things are that a class has a good interface design, is bug free, and runs efficiently. Beyond that there has to be a healthy respect that software engineering is creative (but hopefully not *too* creative).

The reality is that, no matter how the subject of inner classes is presented, some programmers (including some of those working on the core API) are going to use non-`public` inner member classes to implement `Listener` interfaces, which is precisely why anonymous classes were added to the language in the 1.1 release. Is that wrong? Yes and no. There is a basis from which to argue that `Listener` interfaces should be implemented as anonymous classes except in the rare case when the implementation requires more than a dozen or so lines of code. John Rose did as much when he wrote the original *Inner Classes Specification*. Another programmer with the same amount of experience may see an opportunity to replace a dozen or so lines of code with a single class instance creation expression by moving those lines to a non-`public` inner member class.

Imagine the following `createChangeListener` method in a large and complex class implementation:

```
protected ChangeListener createChangeListener() {
    return new ChangeListener() {
        public void stateChanged(ChangeEvent e) {
            fireStateChanged();
            };
    }
}
```

Now see how much simpler the `createChangeListener` method looks if `ChangeListener` is implemented as an inner member class:

```
private class ModelListener implements ChangeListener, Serializable {
    public void stateChanged(ChangeEvent e) {
        fireStateChanged();
    }
}

protected ChangeListener createChangeListener() {
    return new ModelListener();
}
```

I am playing the devil's advocate here because my preference would be to use the anonymous class in the first example. As I see them, the first is actually the simpler implementation. The second, however, is actual code from the `javax.swing.JSlider` class in the core API. To my way of thinking anonymous classes are not used as often as they should be. There are plenty of examples of using inner member classes to implement `Lis-`

`tener` interfaces in the core API that I think should be anonymous classes. Nevertheless, I understand and respect that choice of a member type instead of an anonymous class is a matter of programmer preference.

2.10.1 From `VectorEnumerator` to an Anonymous Class

This section is a case study of how one class in the core API went from being a helper class in the 1.0 release to an anonymous class in the current release. Before the Java 1.1 release introduced inner classes to the Java programming language, there was a helper class declared at the bottom of the `java.util.Vector` compilation unit. The name of that helper class was `VectorEnumerator` because it implemented the `Enumeration` interface. Classes that implement the `Enumeration` interface are called *enumerators*. The gradual transformation of this class from a helper class to a `private` inner member class to a local class and finally to an anonymous class will help you to understand some of the practical differences in these four kinds of classes.[40] Many, but not all, *top-level adapter classes* (as John Rose calls them) have gone the same route. An example of a helper class that has not been so transformed is `java.security.PermissionsEnumerator`, which in the 1.3 release is nearly identical to the original `java.util.VectorEnumerator` helper class discussed in this section.

From beginning to end the only use of that class is in the `elements()` method of the `Vector` class, which returns an instance of the `Enumeration` interface. That enumerator is used to enumerate the elements of a `Vector`. Hence, the method name `elements()`. The original `VectorEnumerator` helper class looked like this:

```
final class VectorEnumerator implements Enumeration {
    Vector vector;
    int loopCount;
    VectorEnumerator(Vector v) {
        vector = v;
    }
    public boolean hasMoreElements() {
        return loopCount < vector.elementCount;
    }
    public Object nextElement() {
        synchronized (vector) {
            if (loopCount < vector.elementCount)
```

---

40. This section has been part of the book for so long that I am no longer sure if I embellished along the way. In particular, the core API may have bypassed the use of a local class and gone straight to an anonymous class.

```
                        return vector.elementData[loopCount++];
                }
                throw new NoSuchElementException("VectorEnumerator");
        }
}
```

When that same class was declared a `private` inner member class in a subsequent release, the class name was changed from `VectorEnu-`merator to just `Enumerator` because the *Vector* part of the name became redundant once the class was nested. Here is `VectorEnumer-`ator implemented as a `private` inner member class:

```
public class Vector {
    ...
    private class Enumerator implements Enumeration {
        int loopCount;
        public boolean hasMoreElements() {
            return loopCount < elementCount;
        }
        public Object nextElement() {
            synchronized (Vector.this) {
                if (loopCount < elementCount) {
                    return elementData[loopCount++];
                }
            }
            throw new NoSuchElementException("Enumerator");
        }
    }
}
```

Other than moving the declaration inside of the `Vector` class, there is not much difference. The only difference between the declaration of the original helper class and the `private` inner member class is that the `vector` field and the constructor that initializes it are no longer required. They are replaced by a compiler-generated link variable.

Next, the same `Enumerator` class is declared as a local class in the `elements` method of the `Vector` class:

```
public synchronized Enumeration elements() {
    class Enumerator implements Enumeration {
        int loopCount;
        public boolean hasMoreElements() {
            return loopCount < elementCount;
        }
        public Object nextElement() {
            synchronized (Vector.this) {
                if (loopCount < elementCount) {
                    return elementData[loopCount++];
                }
            }
            throw new NoSuchElementException("Enumerator");
        }
    }
```

```
        return new Enumerator();
    }
```

The problem with this local class is that it is only used once and so does not require a name. Furthermore, that this is an enumerator is obvious from the fact that the class implements the `Enumeration` interface. In short, the class name is useless. Therefore, a better implementation is as an anonymous class:

```
public synchronized Enumeration elements() {
return new Enumeration() {
    int loopCount = 0;
    public boolean hasMoreElements() {
        return loopCount < elementCount;
    }
    public Object nextElement() {
        synchronized (Vector.this) {
            if (loopCount < elementCount) {
                return elementData[loopCount++];
            }
        }
        throw new NoSuchElementException("Vector Enumeration");
    }
};
}
```

You can compare this to the actual implementation in the current release of the core API. The two implementations are close.

Now you can begin to see some of the advantages of inner classes. The number of lines of code has dropped substantially. More importantly, the `elements()` method, which is the only method that used the original `Vec-torEnumerator` helper class, now contains the declaration of the same.

2.11 The Rationale for Containment and Inner Class Hierarchies

The idea of containment and inner class hierarchies developed as a result of a prolonged effort to simplify scope and access control rules involving nested types. I must have approached this subject a hundred different ways before arriving at the idea of containment and inner class hierarchies, which is why the first thing I did when opening the long-awaited second edition of the *JLS* was to flip to the pages on scope and access control to see how the authors had incorporated the *Inner Classes Specification* relative to those subjects. In particular, I was eager to see if the *JLS* had hit upon the idea of containment or inner class hierarchies.

Imagine my surprise when I discovered that the extent of the coverage was a few short sentences. It was like digging all day in the hot sun of a tropical island for a buried treasure chest, only to find a few gold coins. My initial reaction was that the authors deliberately skirted some of the more complex issues. After a thorough review of my work, I am still of that opinion. For example, I do not think the following statement goes far enough to explain access control in a containment or inner class hierarchy.

> ... if the member or constructor is declared private, then access is permitted if and only if it occurs within the body of the top level class that encloses the declaration of the member.[41]

The equivalent statement from the *Inner Classes Specification* reads:

> Access protection never prevents a class from using any member of another class, as long as one encloses the other, or they are enclosed by a third class.[42]

Neither of these statements is entirely true. For example,

```
class PackageMember {
    private String s = "PackageMember is the top-level class that " +
                       "encloses the private variable s";
    class MemberClass {
        void print() {
            System.out.println(s);
        }
    }
}
```

Access to the s variable occurs in `MemberClass`, which is clearly within the body of the top level class that encloses the declaration of s. As would be expected, this compiles. If, however, the `static` keyword is added to the declaration of `MemberClass` the same code generates the following compiler error:

```
PackageMember.java:6: non-static variable s cannot be referenced from a static context
            System.out.println(s);
                               ^
1 error
```

See 3.3.1 The `static` Context in an Inner Class Hierarchy for a discussion. I just think there is too much left unsaid using the *JLS* approach to access control involving nested types, at least for mainstream business application programmers.

---

41. Gosling et al., §6.6.1, "Determining Accessibility."
42. Rose, "Can a nested class be declared final, private, protected, or static?"

Although the *JLS* approach requires fewer words, this does not necessarily mean the use of containment and inner class hierarchies is more complicated. Take, for example, access control rules for nested types. Instead of nested types complicating access control rules, access control is greatly simplified by the use of containment and inner class hierarchies. As seen in Figure 2-4, there are four levels of access control. Everything is either `public` or `private` to some lesser scope. The `private` keyword by itself always means "class `private`". That this approach blends well with the *package-private* terminology used at Sun is an added bonus.

Containment hierarchies are lexical units similar to packages. Both packages and containment hierarchies are lexical units comprised of multiple classes and interfaces. The main difference is that the uses of a containment hierarchy are mostly at the language level. For example, all of the

Figure 2-4: Four levels of access control.

anonymous classes in a containment hierarchy are named after the package member at the top of the containment hierarchy. And, as can be seen in the last quotation from the *JLS*, there are access control rules that regard containment hierarchies as lexical units.

The *JLS* masks this reality by defining *top-level class* to mean only package members and then uses the term top-level class to refer to containment hierarchies. I think this is an oversimplification. Lexical units require a name, much like package, compilation unit, type, etc. That name is naturally a *containment hierarchy*. *Top-level class* is a poor substitute.

Furthermore, individual containment hierarcies require a name, much like packages and other entities have names. The difference is that containment and inner class hierarchies are not explicitly declared. Therefore, there must be a programmer convention for naming them. The anonymous class naming convention suggests that containment hierarchies should be named after the package member at the top of the containment hierarchy. I agree.

If I go overboard in my approach to the subject, it is in the definition of inner class hierarchies as distinct from containment hierarchies. I cannot say how many times I have questioned the validity of separating containment and inner class hierarchies. So far I have found two reasons for doing so. The first is the simplification of access control. Types are either `public` or `private` to some lesser scope. The other technical justification is in 3.3.1 The `static` Context in an Inner Class Hierarchy. The truth of the matter is—at least until I fully flesh out the idea of how to present this subject—I maintain the distinction as much on instinct as anything else. The concept of containment and inner class hierarchies is introduced in the following sections and used throughout this book.

2.12 Containment and Inner Class Hierarchies

The terms *containment hierarchy* and *inner class hierarchy* are defined in this chapter because they must be understood in terms of the five kinds of classes and interfaces. In both containment and inner class hierarchies there is only one class or interface at the top of the hierarchy. In a containment hierarchy that class or interface is always a package member. In an inner class hierarchy that class may be either a package member or a nested top-level class. In either case the class at the top of an inner class hierarchy is always a top-level class.

Both of the following subsections refer to the same example. The source code for that example follows:

```
public class PackageMember {

    public void instanceMethod() {
        class LocalClass { }
    }
    public static class NestedTopLevelClass { }

    private class InnerMemberClass {
        HelperClass helper = new HelperClass() { };
```

```
        public void instanceMethod() {
            HelperClass.doSomething(new HelperClass() {
                        });  /* these three characters together (usually on
                            * a separate line) indicates the use of an anony-
                            * mous class as an argument in a method invocation
                            * expression or class instance creation expression
                            */
        }
    }
    public interface NestedInterface {
        class DeeplyNestedInnerMemberClass { }
        interface DeeplyNestedInterface { }
    }
}
class HelperClass {
    static void doSomething(HelperClass dummy) {}
}
```

Note that `NestedInterface.DeeplyNestedTopLevelClass` is implicitly `static` because it is declared in an interface.

2.12.1 Containment Hierarchies

A **containment hierarchy** describes the relationship between nested top-level classes and interfaces and the package member in which they are declared. For every package member in which one or more nested top-level class or interface is declared, there is exactly one containment hierarchy. *All of the types in a containment hierarchy are either top-level classes or interfaces.*

One of the rules of the Java programming language that greatly simplifies containment hierarchies is stated as follows in the *JLS*.

> The `static` keyword may modify the declaration of a member type *C* within the body of a non-inner class *T*.[43]

The important point here is that `static` member classes (that is, nested top-level classes) cannot be declared in inner classes. That rule is the same as saying that `static` fields and methods cannot be declared in inner classes. Nested top-level classes and interfaces can only be declared in the body of another top-level class or interface. That gives top-level classes and interfaces a definite hierarchical relationship in which the package member is completely analogous to a root directory in a hierarchical filesystem or the `Object` class in an inheritance hierarchy.

The containment hierarchy for the `PackageMember` class is depicted in Figure 2-5. The important thing to notice about this example of

---

43. Gosling et al, §8.5.2, "Static Member Type Declarations."

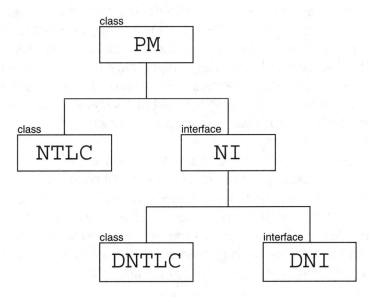

Figure 2-5: Example of a containment hierarchy.

a containment hierarchy is that inner classes are completely ignored. They have nothing to do with the concept of containment hierarchies. Containment hierarchies are straightforward. They only show the relationship of nested top-level classes and interfaces to the package member in which they are declared.

2.12.2 Inner Class Hierarchies

This section is an introduction to inner class hierarchies. You should also read 3.6 Multiple Current Instances (a.k.a. Levels). That section completes this introduction to inner class hierarchies by discussing the concept of different levels within an inner class hierarchy.

An **inner class hierarchy** describes the relationship between inner classes and the top-level class in which they are declared. The type at the top of an inner class hierarchy is always a top-level *class* because classes declared in the body of an interface are implicitly `static`. In other words, it is impossible to declare an inner class in an interface. For every top-level class in which one or more inner classes is declared, there is exactly one inner class hierarchy. All of the classes in an inner class hierarchy are inner classes except for the top-level class at the top of the hierarchy. In other words, the only top-level class in an inner class hierarchy is literally at the top.

Nested top-level classes and interfaces may also be contained in the body of a class at the top of an inner class hierarchy. For example, `Pack-age-Member` is at the top of both a containment and inner class hierarchy. In the last section I said inner classes "have nothing to do with the concept of containment hierarchies." The reverse, however, is not true. Inner class hierarchies are sometimes part of a larger containment hierarchy. That is why inner classes can access the `static` members of any enclosing class or interface.

The `PackageMember` inner class hierarchy is shown in Figure 2-6. Notice that the boxes in an inner class hierarchy do not need to be labeled *class* or *interface* because they are always classes. The abbreviated names `PM$1` and `PM$2` are anonymous classes. The actual class names are `PackageMember$1` and `PackageMember$2`. Anonymous classes are always named after the package member in which they are declared, followed by a $ sign and a sequencing number that starts at one.

2.12.2.1 Orphaned Local and Anonymous Classes

The intervening `static` context in which some local and anonymous classes are declared effectively isolates those classes from participating in an inner class hierarchy. For example,

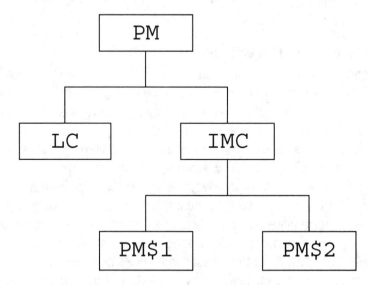

Figure 2-6: Example of an inner class hierarchy.

```
class PackageMember {
    public static void staticMethod() {
        class LocalClass { }
    }
}
```

LocalClass is not part of the PackageMember inner class hierarchy. The technical difference, which will be explained in detail in Chapter 3, is that LocalClass (or more generally any local or anonymous class declared in a static context) has no enclosing instance. An inner class with no enclosing instance only has access to local variables and parameters in an enclosing block (assuming they are declared final) and the static members of any enclosing type(s). One of the static contexts discussed in 3.3 The Definition of static Context has no enclosing block. Anonymous classes declared in the variable initializer of a field have no enclosing block. Such an anonymous class can only access the static members of enclosing types.

Local and anonymous classes declared in a static context should have a name. Therefore, I am introducing a new term not found in the *JLS*: **orphaned local and anonymous classes**. Such classes are orphaned by the static context in which they are declared. They are like top-level classes in that there is no enclosing instance.

Chapter 3

The `static` Modifier, `this`, and `super`

Chapter Contents

3.1 Introduction

The `static` keyword is the opposite of `this` and `super`. Where one exists the others do not. Consequently, this chapter has two major divisions. The first is an elaborate definition of the `static` keyword. The second is about the `this` and `super` keywords. To my knowledge this is the first Java book to present these subjects together and in their own chapter.

The realization that these subjects are so closely related and of sufficient weight to justify their inclusion in a separate chapter came about as a result of my efforts to define the `static` keyword. A defining moment in that effort was when I realized the utter futility of trying to find a single definition. Just as there is no one definition for expressions, there is no one definition for the `static` keyword. The meaning of `static` depends upon the entity, which is a field, method, or class. This chapter includes sections on `static` fields, `static` methods, and `static` classes in which the `static` keyword is defined for that particular kind of entity.

3.2 The `static` Modifier

In early releases of the JVM (now called the classic JVM), one could point to the Method Area as a definition of `static`. In a classic JVM main memory is divided into the Method Area and the heap. Anything defined in the Method Area of a classic JVM is by definition `static`. This includes, notably, the internal table of loaded classes and interfaces (which are basically class files after they are loaded into a JVM), method dispatch tables (from which the Method Area derives its name), and class variables. The Method Area of a classic JVM is literally more "static" than the heap. Early implementations of the JVM did not even unload classes. Once a class was loaded it remained in memory until the JVM was exited.

I retain this discussion of the Method Area for historical reasons. A familiarity with the Method Area helps to understand the use of `static` as a keyword. The newer HotSpot JVM is completely object-oriented. Run-time data structures used exclusively by the JVM are now allocated as objects on the heap. What makes these objects unique is that they are neither created by a programmer nor directly referenced in application programs. They are part of the JVM implementation. The point is that there is no Method Area in the latest implementations of the JVM. This requires a new definition of `static`. It can no longer be defined in terms of memory usage.

In a section entitled "Members that can be marked `static`" in the original *Inner Classes Specification*, John Rose begins by explaining how the `static` modifier was used before inner classes were introduced to the language.

The static declaration modifier was designed to give programmers a way to define *class methods* and *class variables*
which pertain to a class as a whole, rather than any particular
instance. They are "top-level" entities.[1]

The static keyword is used in the declaration of *top-level entities*. Table
3-1 includes a complete list of top-level entities in the column marked
static. Initialization blocks are executed in special initialization methods. Therefore, we can eliminate them from this discussion. That leaves
the following **top-level entities**:

- Class variables (including interface constants)
- Class methods
- All interfaces
- Classes that are either implicitly or explicitly declared static

Interfaces are excluded from this discussion because they are always
either implicitly or explicitly static. That leaves only the following three
kinds of top-level entities that can be either static or non-static:

- Fields
- Methods
- Classes

Table 3-1: Terms for Class Body Declarations

Entity	static	non-static
Field	Class variable	Instance variable
Initialization block	static initialization block	Instance initialization block
Constructor		Constructor
Method	Class methods	Instance method
Interface	Nested interface	
Class	Nested top-level class	Inner member class

---

1. John Rose, *Inner Classes Specification* (Mountain View: Sun Microsystems, 1997), "Can a nested class be declared final, private, protected, or static?"

The meaning of the `static` keyword in relation to each of these three kinds of top-level entities is the subject of the following three subsections.

The remainder of this section discusses the one thing that all top-level entities have in common.

The value of a `static` field can be accessed, a utility method can be invoked, and a nested top-level class can be instantiated without having to instantiate the class in which they are declared.

The `Character` class has all three kinds of top-level entities. For example,

```
class Test {
    public static void main(String[] args) {
        int i = Character.MAX_VALUE;
        System.out.println(i);
        System.out.println(Character.toLowerCase('A'));
    }
}
```

Executing this program prints

```
65535
a
```

Nowhere in this program is the `Character` class instantiated. Nor is the `Character` class instantiated anywhere in the example of the `Character.Unicode` nested top-level class in 1.2 White Space. All you have to do to access the value of a `static` field, to invoke a utility method, or to instantiate a nested top-level class is to qualify the name of the `static` member with the name of the class or interface in which it is declared.

The following entities do not exist unless you first instantiate the class in which they are declared:

- Instance variables
- Instance methods
- Inner classes

For example,

```
class Test {
    public static void main(String[] args) {
        Character c = new Character('a');
        System.out.println(c.hashCode());
    }
}
```

Executing this program prints the character code for the letter a, which is 97. The `hashCode()` method is an instance method. It cannot be invoked until the `Character` class has been instantiated. The `c` variable is the "particular instance" referred to in the above quotation from the *Inner Classes Specification*. This is the fundamental difference between `static` and non-`static` entities.

3.2.1 `static` Fields

An object in memory is little more than a list of instance variables, the values of which collectively represent the state of the object at any given point in time. The value of an instance variable can be different for every instance of the class because instance variables are used as a template when creating objects. Every time the template is used to stamp out a new object, a copy is made of each of the instance variables. You cannot reference an instance variable without first implicitly or explicitly naming an object. Class variables are entirely different. The value of a class variable is the same for all instances of the class.

Class variables have only one value for the entire class.

That is the essential meaning of the `static` keyword in relation to fields. Here is a playful example:

```
class Human {
    public static final String GOD = "good";
    private char sex;
    private int age;
    private float height;
    private float weight;
    private Fingerprint[] fingerprints;
    private DNA dna;
}
```

No matter how many `Human` objects are created, there is only one GOD. The value of GOD is always `good`, unless hidden in subclasses by the declaration of a different `static` field with the same name.

That "class variables have only one value" is only part of the story. The real question is how `static` fields are used. Answering this question is more difficult than one may think. My analysis is as follows:

- Convenience constants and enumerated types

- True mathematical constants
- Program variables (that is, non-`public` variables declared `static` so they can be used in more than one method)
- One-of-a-kind, system-wide values
- Take-a-number variables (rare)

I believe this analysis is complete but welcome any comments from readers. The list is partly based on the idea of *inconstant constants*. Constants should be either true mathematical constants such as `Math.PI` or what are referred to as *convenience constants* in API docs. Convenience constants take the place of enumerated types, which Java does not support (at least not at the language level).

Non-`public` variables used in more than one method are just a programmer using the `static` keyword to scope a variable to the type in which it is declared. This is a scope issue in application programs, utility classes, and other nonobject-oriented uses of reference data types. That use of `static` fields is entirely different from analyzing the uses of class variables declared `public`. Class variables declared `public` are very special.

In a `public` type, `static` variables declared `public` have a de facto system-wide scope.

Combined with the fact that class variables only have one value, you have one value with a system-wide scope, or a system-wide value. The defining characteristic of a system-wide value is that there is only one such value for the entire system. True mathematical constants, convenience constants, enumerated types, and take-a-number variables are different kinds of system-wide values. The following subsection discusses some one-of-a-kind system-wide values.

3.2.1.1 One-of-a-Kind System-Wide Values

One-of-a-kind **system-wide values** may be either references to objects or primitive data types. Here are some examples from the `java.lang.System`, `java.io.File`, and `java.util.Locale` classes of one-of-a-kind system-wide values that reference objects:

```
private static Properties props;
private static SecurityManager security = null;
private static String tmpdir;
private static Locale defaultLocale;
```

There is only one system `Properties` object, just as there is only one `SecurityManager`, one temporary directory, and one default `Locale`. Here are some more examples from the `File` class of one-of-a-kind system-wide values that are primitive data types:

```
public static final char separatorChar;
public static final char pathSeparatorChar;
```

There is only one file and path separator for any given system.

3.2.1.2 Take-a-Number Variables

I named these variables after the take-a-number dispensers at the deli counter of your local grocery store. They are usually `int` type `static` fields. For example, threads have either names or numbers. Threads that do not have names are referred to as anonymous threads. They are assigned a number in `Thread` class constructors by invoking the `next-ThreadNum` method. Here are the relevant declarations:

```
private static int threadInitNumber;
private static synchronized int nextThreadNum() {
   return threadInitNumber++;
}
```

The `static` field `threadInitNumber` is an example of a take-a-number variable.

3.2.2 `static` Methods

The meaning of `static` in the declaration of a class method is that there is no current object. That is why using the `this` keyword in class methods generates a compiler error. I defer that discussion, however, until 3.4.1 The Current Object (`this`). There is only one point I would like to make in this section.

Any `public static` method is a **utility method** regardless of the class in which it is declared.

A utility method is comparable to a function in procedure-oriented programming languages. By this I mean a named sequence of statements that, when executed, may also return a value. There is nothing object-oriented about `static` methods because there is no current object. They do not need to be declared in a utility class in order to be utility methods. Some utility methods such as `Math.pow(double a, double b)` are declared in utility classes, but most are not.

Why declare utility methods in the body of a reusable object or other non-utility class? In a word, encapsulation. They require access to the non-`public` members of the class in which they are declared. For example, the `ClassLoader.getSystemResource(String name)` utility method in the `java.util` package does not load anything; it only returns an instance of the `URL` class. Why not declare `ClassLoader.getSystemResource(String name)` in a utility class (or even the `URL` class)? Doing so would have created encapsulation problems for the `ClassLoader` class. The utility method in question invokes a `private` method in the `ClassLoader` class.

Sometimes utility methods are at best only logically related to objects of the class in which they are declared. Consider, for example, the `Integer.parseInt(String s)` method. The implementation of this method does not reference any of the fields or methods declared in the `Integer` class. Why not declare `parseInt(String s)` in the `String` class? The `String` class is a reasonable choice because `Integer.parseInt(String s)` parses a `String` object and also invokes the `length()` and `charAt(int index)` methods declared in the `String` class. In this sense it has a stronger affinity to the `String` class than it does to the `Integer` class. The `length()` and `charAt(int index)` methods, however, are `public`. There are, therefore, no encapsulation issues. Because the string argument is supposed to be an integer (in the range of an `int`), the `Integer` class was deemed a logical place to declare this utility method.

3.2.3 `static` Classes

This section is a summary of 2.7 The Definition of Top-Level Classes and is included here for the sake of completeness. The meaning of the `static` keyword in the declaration of a class is the difference between a top-level class and an inner class. As stated in the *JLS*, the effect of the `static` keyword in the declaration of a nested class "is to declare that [the nested class] is not an inner class."[2] Package members are implicitly `static` and therefore top-level. Nested classes are top-level only if they are implicitly or explicitly declared `static`; otherwise they are inner classes.

To say that a class is top-level or inner is only part of the story. You have to understand the difference between a top-level class and an inner class. That difference is summarized in the following sentence.

> There is only one current instance in the non-`static` code of a top-level class, whereas inner classes always have at least two current instances depending on how deeply nested the inner class is (except for orphaned local and anonymous classes declared in a `static` context).

Notice how this parallels the "class variables have only one value" definition of a `static` field. Multiple current instances are discussed in 3.6 Multiple Current Instances (a.k.a. Levels). The definition of top-level class in that section is much more meaningful than simply saying that the class is implicitly or explicitly `static`.

3.3 The Definition of `static` Context

Many a compiler error message includes the term **static context**. For example,

```
class Test {
  int instanceVariable;
  public static void main(String[] args) {
      System.out.println(instanceVariable);
  }
}
```

Attempting to compile this program generates the following compiler error:

```
Test.java:4: non-static variable instanceVariable cannot be referenced from a static context
      System.out.println(instanceVariable);
                         ^
1 error
```

---

2. James Gosling, Bill Joy, Guy Steele, and Gilad Bracha, *The Java Language Specification, Second Edition* (Boston: Addison-Wesley, 2000), §8.5.2, "Static Member Type Declarations."

The term static *context* has a very precise definition in the *JLS*. There are four static contexts in the *JLS*:

- static method
- static initialization block
- Class variable initializer
- Argument expressions in explicit constructor invocation expressions

The only surprise here is argument expressions in explicit constructor invocation expressions. The constructor body that begins with the explicit constructor invocation expression is not a static context, just the argument expressions in the first line of code. For example,

```
class Superclass {
    Superclass(int i) {}
    Superclass(int i) {}
}

class Test extends Superclass {
  int instanceVariable;
  Test() {
      this(instanceVariable);
  }
  Test(int i) { }
}
```

Attempting to compile this program generates the following compiler error:

```
Test.java:9: cannot reference instanceVariable before supertype constructor has
been called
        this(instanceVariable);
            ^
 1 error
```

If this is changed to super, almost the exact same error message is generated.

There are at least two other static contexts besides those included in the *JLS*. Qualified access involving type names is a static context. That is just another way of saying that only class variables and interface constants can be accessed using the TypeName.fieldName general form of field access expressions, and only class methods can be invoked using the TypeName.methodName general form method invocation expressions. The other static context not mentioned in the *JLS* is static context in an inner class hierarchy, which is critically important in terms of the default qualifying instance. The following section explains in part why I separate containment and inner class hierarchies.

3.3.1 The `static` Context in an Inner Class Hierarchy

An inner member class can be instantiated anywhere in an inner class hierarchy using the default qualifying instance. It is important to remember, however, that the definition of an inner class hierarchy as given in 2.12.2 Inner Class Hierarchies does not include any nested top-level classes or interfaces declared in the body of the top-level class at the top of the inner class hierarchy.

See what happens when I try to instantiate `InnerMemberClass` in a nested top-level class:

```
public class Top {
    public static class NestedTopLevelClass {
        InnerMemberClass inner = new InnerMemberClass();
    }
    class InnerMemberClass {}
}
```

Attempting to compile this class generates the following compiler error:

```
Top.java:3: non-static variable this cannot be referenced from a static context
        InnerMemberClass inner = new InnerMemberClass();
                                 ^
1 error
```

Insofar as the inner class hierarchy is concerned, anywhere in the body of a nested top-level class or interface is a `static` *context*.

3.4 The `this` and `super` Keywords

The and `super` keywords cannot be used in a `static` context. That includes the `static` code numbered ①, ②, and ③ in Figure 2-1. Everywhere else in a compilation unit (numbers ❹, ❺, ❻, and ❼ in the same figure, as well as inner classes) the `this` keyword represents a complex mechanism that allows a Java programmer to reference the current object. I refer to that mechanism as the **`this` mechanism**. What follows is a brief overview of how the `this` mechanism works.

Instance methods cannot be invoked without first implicitly or explicitly naming an object. That object is known as the **target object**. The target object (as with all objects) has what is called an *object header*, which includes a reference to the `Class` object. The first thing that happens when an instance method is invoked is that the JVM uses the `Class` object referenced in the header of the target object to locate the method dispatch table.[3] After searching the method dispatch table to find the matching method, the bytecodes for that method are executed. Figure 3-1 is a diagram of the `this` mechanism.

The JVM passes a reference to the target object to instance methods much like it passes a reference to the array in which command-line arguments are stored to the `main(String[] args)` method in an application program. Instead of storing that reference in the `args` parameter, however, the reference to the target is always stored in the first component of the local variable array. The local variable array is an array in which the JVM allocates local variables and parameters during the execution of a method. Supposing that array were called `locals`, the `this` keyword is always a reference to `locals[0]`, which is more commonly referred to as *local variable zero*.

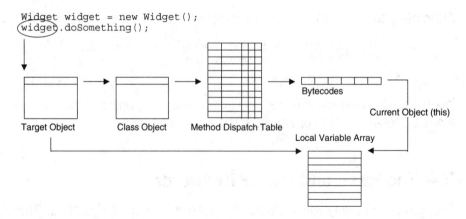

```
Widget widget = new Widget();
widget.doSomething();
```

Figure 3-1: The `this` mechanism.

---

3. While most, if not all, JVM use object headers, they are nevertheless implementation defined. As always, I base my description of the JVM on what I understand to be the latest Sun implementations. I think it is more important to describe one JVM in detail rather than just saying something is implementation defined and leaving it at that. In this case, however, it is reasonable to assume that some JVM implementations do not use the `Class` object to find the method dispatch table. An obvious alternative would be to store a reference to the method dispatch table directly in the object header, thus eliminating a layer of indirection. That, however, increases the size of every object in the system. In general, JVM implementations strive for the smallest memory footprint possible.

Class methods are entirely different. Class methods are almost always invoked using the `TypeName.methodName` general form of a method invocation expression, where `TypeName` is the name of the class in which the method is declared. The JVM uses that type name to go directly to the `Class` object. There is no object involved in locating the method dispatch table for a class method. Moreover, there is no target object to pass to the method invoked.

In the body of the instance method invoked the target object is known as the current object. There are two names for the object involved in invoking an instance method or constructor because that object is seen from two different perspectives. On one hand a client programmer is invoking an instance method. On the other hand is the programmer responsible for implementing that method. Figure 3-2 shows the object from both perspectives. Although the `this` mechanism is completely hidden from both programmers, you know it is there because you are able to reference the current object using the `this` keyword. Think about that for a moment. Unlike every other entity in a compilation unit, there is no declaration for `this`.

Figure 3-2: Target object and current object are the same.

The `this` keyword is one of the most important mechanisms in the whole of the JVM. Understanding how this mechanism works is something like pulling the curtain back on the Wizard of Oz. I strongly encourage all readers to pursue an uncompromising understanding of the `this` keyword.

3.4.1 The Current Object (`this`)

The current object is always an instance of the class in which the `this` keyword appears. A programmer must think abstractly about an entire class of objects when writing instance methods. However, instance methods are always invoked with respect to a particular instance of that class. From the perspective of the programmer defining the state and behavior of an object, that instance is referred to as either the **current object** or **current instance** (both terms are acceptable). The current object is an abstraction of every object for which the instance method will ever be executed. Because those objects do not exist when the instance method is written, they obviously cannot be referred to by name. Thus, the generic `this` keyword is used in source code to refer to the current object.

3.4.1.1 *this* is Polymorphic, *super* is Not

The compile-time type of the `this` keyword is always the class type in which the keyword appears. At run time, however, `this` is polymorphic. If the member in which the `this` keyword appears is inherited by a subclass, the class of the object referenced by the `this` keyword is the subclass. For example,

```
class Test {
  public static void main(String[] args) {
    Subclass sub = new Subclass();
    sub.print();
  }
  void print() {
    System.out.println(this.getClass().getName());
  }
}
class Subclass extends Test { }
```

Executing this program prints `"Subclass"`. This much you would expect because the `print()` method is inherited.

The strange thing about the fact that `this` is polymorphic is overridden instance methods and constructors. Constructors are not members of a class and are not, therefore, inherited by subclasses. Nor are overridden instance methods. Nevertheless, the `this` keyword is polymorphic in both. For example,

```
class Superclass {
  void print() {
      System.out.println(this.getClass().getName());
  }
}
class Test extends Superclass {
  public static void main(String[] args) {
      new Test().print();
  }
  void print() {
    super.print();
  }
}
```

Executing this program prints `"Test"`. The reason for this is explained in detail in the next section. It is not hard to understand what is happening if you know how `super` is implemented in a Java compiler.

The method invoked using the `super` keyword is always found in the method dispatch table of the direct superclass because a special machine instruction is used. The only question is *what reference to pass the instance method invoked*. The answer is to pass a reference to the current object using the `this` keyword, which is polymorphically also an instance of the superclass. Think of `super` as one part of the complex `this` mechanism, all of which is hidden from view.

When using the `super` keyword to invoke an overridden instance method, `this` is implicitly used as the target object.

In simpler terms, using `super` is the same as using `this`. That is why the `super` keyword cannot be used in class variable initializers, `static` initialization blocks, or class methods.

Here is an example of a polymorphic `this` keyword in a constructor:

```
class Test  {
  Test() {
      System.out.println(this.getClass().getName());
  }
  public static void main(String[] args) {
     Subclass sub = new Subclass();
  }
}
class Subclass extends Test { }
```

Executing this program prints "Subclass". The name of the class printed in the Test() constructor is Subclass because a Subclass object is being created, not a Test object.

The class of the object referenced by the this keyword in constructors is always the class of the object under construction.

The explanation for this is exactly the same as when using the super keyword to invoke an overridden superclass method. There is no such thing as a constructor in the JVM. Constructors are incorporated into the instance initialization methods named <init>. When subclasses are instantiated, the design of the JVM is such that one of the instance initialization methods (which may correspond to the default constructor) of the direct superclass is always invoked. Again, the only question is *what reference to pass the instance method invoked*. This time the answer is to pass a reference to the object under construction, which, again, is an instance of the super-class.

3.4.2 The Direct Superclass (super)

As explained in the *JLS*, the super keyword is implemented in Java compilers "as if" it were replaced with a cast of the this keyword. The type name in the cast operator is always the direct superclass of the class in which the super keyword appears. As much as I would like to include an example of how the compiler implements the super keyword using this explanation, doing so within the body of an overriding instance method (which is the primary use of the super keyword) is impossible. For example,

```
class Superclass {
  void print() {
      System.out.println(Superclass.class.getName());
  }
}
class Test extends Superclass {
  public static void main(String[] args) {
      new Test().print();
  }
  void print() {
      ((Superclass)this).print();
  }
}
```

Executing this program results in infinite recursion. The `print` method in the `Test` class is no different than if it were written

```
void print() {
    print();
}
```

The infinite recursion is much more obvious when written like this. That is why the *JLS* must say the `super` keyword is implemented *as if* it were a cast of the `this` keyword. The point of such an example would be to show that the following two lines of code are identical:

```
super.print();
((Superclass)this).print();
```

They are identical for field access expressions or method invocation expressions that invoke anything other than an overridden instance method. For example,

```
class Superclass {
  void print() {
      System.out.println(Superclass.class.getName());
  }
}
class Test extends Superclass {
  public static void main(String[] args) {
      new Test().whatever();
  }
  void whatever() {
      ((Superclass)this).print();
      super.print();
  }
}
```

This program completes normally and prints

```
Superclass
Superclass
```

The difference between a programmer typing `((Superclass)this).print()` in the body of the overriding print method and what the compiler does is the invocation mode. The invocation mode for `((Superclass)this).print()` is virtual, which corresponds to the `invokevirtual` machine instruction. The `virtual` invocation mode uses the run-time class of the object referenced to determine which method dispatch table to search, not the compile-time type of the variable or other expression used as the target object in the method invocation expression. Therefore, the `virtual` invocation mode always invokes an overriding method in the class of the object referenced, which explains the infinite recursion in the example at the top of this section.

Casting the variable or other expression used as the target object in such a method invocation expression has no effect.

You'd think that things like invocation modes would be discussed in the *JVMS*, but they are not. There is not a single reference to *invocation mode* anywhere in either edition of the *JVMS*. Invocation modes are *JLS* bytecode mnemonics mentioned only once in the entire *JLS*, in 15.12.3 Compile-Time Step 3: Is the Chosen Method Appropriate?

> Invocation modes are implicit in the machine instruction used to invoke a method.

The *JVMS* uses different bytecode mnemonics. For example, the `super` invocation mode in the *JLS* corresponds to the `invokespecial` machine instruction, which is the *JVMS* mnemonic for bytecode 183.[4] It is a special machine instruction that always uses the method dispatch table of the direct superclass. It is used to implement the `super` keyword, invoke `private` instance methods (that cannot be overridden), and to invoke `<init>` methods when compiling class instance creation expressions.

3.5 Practical Uses of the `this` and `super` Keywords

This section *introduces* the reader to the practical uses of the `this` and `super` keywords. I stress the word *introduce* because fully understanding the practical uses of the `this` and `super` keywords is a sign that you have "arrived" in terms of your understanding of the Java programming language. It is not a subject that can be completely addressed in one chapter. The main goal of Table 3-2 is to show the reader that there are a finite number of practical uses for the `this` and `super` keywords. As presented in that table, there are exactly four uses of both and they closely parallel one another, making them even easier to learn. If you become acquainted with these uses and are able to recall some or all of them, then I have achieved the goal of this chapter. It is my belief that defining the boundaries of something that must be eventually learned in much greater detail is useful.

---

4. I use a fixed font for both *JLS* invocation modes and the corresponding *JVMS* machine instructions. That is just my preference. The `invokespecial` instruction was named `invokenonvirtual` prior to the JDK 1.0.2 release. I do not know the story behind the name change.

Doing so provides a kind of mental picture frame that serves to make the learning process more manageable. In this case the open question of how the `this` and `super` keywords are used is reduced from an infinite unknown to four possibilities. The remainder of this section includes simple examples of each of the uses in Table 3-2.

Table 3-2: Uses of the `this` and `super` Keywords

Description of Use	this	super
Primary use	A reference to the current object.	Invoking overridden superclass methods from within the body of the overriding subclass.
Accessing shadowed or hidden fields and hidden class methods	When a local variable or parameter is shadowing the name of a field in non-`static` code, the general form `this.fieldName` is used to refer to the hidden field. This is normally done only in constructors. If a class variable is shadowed in a `static` context, it must be referenced using the `TypeName.fieldName` general form.	When a field or class method declared in the current class is hiding a superclass member, the `super.fieldName` and `super.methodName` general forms are used in non-`static` code to refer to the hidden members. If class variables or class methods are hidden in a `static` context, the `TypeName.fieldName` and `TypeName.methodName` general forms must be used.
Explicit constructor invocations	The `this` keyword is used as the first statement in a constructor body to explicitly invoke another constructor in the same class.	The `super` keyword is used as the first statement in a constructor body to explicitly invoke a constructor in the direct superclass.
Miscellaneous uses	Fields are sometimes qualified with the `this` keyword in non-`static` code as a matter of style to differentiate them from local variables and parameters. To achieve the same effect in a `static` context, class variables and interface constants must be qualified with their type name.	The `super.fieldName` general form of the field access expression can be used to access a superclass field when the simple name of the field would be ambiguous because an interface constant with the same name was inherited.

The Java programming language is designed so that the `this` keyword is implicit in most of the contexts in which it is needed. However, `this` must be explicitly coded when referencing the current object in the following three contexts:

- As an argument expression in a method invocation expression or class instance creation expression

- As a return value in a `return` statement

- As the expression in a `synchronized` statement

This is what I characterize as the primary use of the `this` keyword. Examples of this use of the `this` keyword are as simple as `return this`. Used in these contexts the `this` keyword is sometimes referred to as the **`this` reference**.

The primary use of the `super` keyword is to invoke overridden superclass instance methods from within the body of the overriding subclass. Were it not for the `super` keyword, doing so would be impossible. Except for the `super.methodName` general form invoked from within the body of the overriding subclass, access to the overridden instance method in the superclass is impossible given a reference to an instance of the overriding subclass. Were that not so it would be possible to defeat the design of the subclass in which the overriding method is declared. For example, the following program does everything it can to invoke the overridden `print()` method in T2 given only a reference to a T3 class object:

```
class T1 {
    String print() { return "NEVER HAPPEN"; }
}

class T2 extends T1 {
    String print() { return "YES"; }
}

class T3 extends T2 {
    String print() { return "NO"; }
    void test() {
        System.out.println("print() = " + print());
        System.out.println("super.print() = " + super.print());
        System.out.println("((T2)this).print() = " + ((T2)this).print());
        System.out.println("((T1)this).print() = " + ((T1)this).print());
        System.out.println();
    }
}

public class Test {
    public static void main(String[] args) {
```

```
        T3 t3 = new T3();
        t3.test();
    /* Try casting the t3 variable */
        System.out.println("t3.print() = " + t3.print());
        System.out.println("((T2)t3).print() = " + ((T2)t3).print());
        System.out.println("((T1)t3).print() = " + ((T1)t3).print());
    /* Try converting t3 to a superclass type and then invoking
        the print() method */
        T2 t2 = t3;
        System.out.println("t2.print() = " + t2.print());
        T1 t1 = t3;
        System.out.println("t1.print() = " + t1.print());
    }
}
```

Executing this program prints

```
print() = NO
super.print() = YES
((T2)this).print() = NO
((T1)this).print() = NO

t3.print() = NO
((T2)t3).print() = NO
((T1)t3).print() = NO
t2.print() = NO
t1.print() = NO
```

The best way to remember this is that when a subclass overrides a super-class instance method, the `super.methodName` general form is "the only way back."

Note that, although the method invoked by the `super.methodName` general form is a member of the direct superclass, it may be declared in any of the superclasses in the class hierarchy. For example, if the `print()` method were removed from the T2 class in the example above, a `super.print()` method invocation in the T3 class would invoke the `print()` method declared in the T1 class, and NEVER HAPPEN would be printed.

The `this` and `super` keywords are also used to access hidden or shadowed fields and hidden class methods. The following program is an example of accessing hidden fields:

```
class Superclass {
  static String msg = "hidden field";
}
public class Test extends Superclass {
  String msg = "shadowed field";
  public static void main(String[] args) {
      /* instantiate Test in order to invoke an instance method */
      new Test().print();
  }
  void print() {
```

```
            String msg = "local variable";
            System.out.println(msg);
            System.out.println(this.msg);
            System.out.println(super.msg);
        }
    }
```

Executing this program prints

```
local variable
shadowed field
hidden field
```

Hiding is generally discouraged in the Java programming language. The same could be said of local variables or parameters shadowing fields except for one important exception. Constructor parameters usually shadow the name of the instance variable to which they are assigned. This programmer convention makes coding constructors much easier because you do not have to think of names for all of the constructor parameters. For example,

```
class Widget {
    int x;
    Widget(int x) {
        this.x = x;
    }
}
```

Note that if `this` were not used to qualify the instance variable x, $x = x$ would assign the value of the constructor parameter to itself.

One special use of the `this` and `super` keywords is in explicit constructor invocations. Explicit constructor invocations invoke either another constructor in the same class (the `this` keyword) or a superclass constructor (the `super` keyword). They are always the first statements in a constructor. For example,

```
class Superclass {
    Superclass(String s) {
        System.out.println(s);
    }
}
public class Test extends Superclass {
    Test() {
        this("Test(String s)");
        System.out.println("Test()");
    }
    Test(String s) {
        super("Superclass(String s)");
        System.out.println(s);
    }
    public static void main(String[] args) {
```

```
        new Test();
    }
}
```

Executing this program prints

```
Superclass(String s)
Test(String s)
Test()
```

The other uses of the `this` and `super` keywords are described as *miscellaneous* in Table 3-2. They include qualifying members of the current class when doing so is unnecessary. For example,

```
public class Test {
    static int x;
    public static void main(String[] args) {
        /* instantiate Test in order to invoke an instance method */
        new Test().print();
    }
    void print() {
        System.out.println(this.x);
    }
}
```

The `x` field does not need to be qualified. The simple name of a field or method is implicitly qualified with the `this` keyword. For whatever reason, programmers sometimes choose to make that qualification explicit. To achieve the same effect in a `static` context a type name is used to qualify the simple name of a class variable or class method. For example,

```
public class Test {
    static int x;
    public static void main(String[] args) {
        System.out.println(Test.x);
    }
}
```

Again, the `x` field does not have to be qualified like this.

Finally, there is one very obscure use of the `super` keyword. The simple name of a field is ambiguous if inherited from both a superclass and superinterface. For example,

```
interface Superinterface { double x = 3.3; }
class Superclass { int x = 3; }
class Test extends Superclass implements Superinterface {
    public static void main(String[] args) {
        /* instantiate Test in order to invoke an instance method */
        new Test().print();
    }
    void print() {
        {System.out.println(x);}      //COMPILER ERROR
    }
}
```

Attempting to compile this program generates the following compiler error:

```
Test.java:9: reference to x is ambiguous, both variable x in Superclass and variable x in
Superinterface match
        {System.out.println(x);}      //COMPILER ERROR
                          ^
1 error
```

If the reference to x in Subclass is changed to super.x, the same code compiles and prints 3.

3.5.1 Using super to Reference Members in Different Packages

A member must be accessible for the general form super.fieldName or super.methodName to compile. A superclass member declared private or that has default access is not accessible from subclasses declared in different packages. Therefore, such a member cannot be accessed using the general form super.fieldName or super.methodName. For example,

```
package com.javarules.examples;
public class Superclass {
    int x;
    int getX() {return x;}
}
```

```
import com.javarules.examples.Superclass;
class Test extends Superclass {
    public static void main(String[] args) {
      /* instantiate Test in order to invoke an instance method */
      new Test().print();
    }
    void print() {
      System.out.println(super.x);          //COMPILER ERROR
      System.out.println(super.getX());      //COMPILER ERROR
    }
}
```

Superclass and Test are members of different packages. (Test is a member of the unnamed package.) Attempting to compile this program generates the following compiler errors:

```
Test.java:8: x is not public in com.javarules.examples.Superclass; cannot be accessed from
outside package
        System.out.println(super.x);              //COMPILER ERROR
                                ^
Test.java:9: getX() is not public in com.javarules.examples.Superclass; cannot be accessed
        from outside package
        System.out.println(super.getX());      //COMPILER ERROR
                                ^
```

In other words, there is nothing special about the `super` keyword that would allow access to an otherwise inaccessible superclass member.

3.6 Multiple Current Instances (a.k.a. Levels)

The term *current instance* is synonymous with *current object*, which is another name for the `this` keyword. I prefer *current instance* in this context. As with the discussion of the five kinds of classes and interfaces in the last chapter, the discussion of multiple current instances in this chapter is a result of my decision not to have a separate chapter on inner classes.

This section is more or less a continuation of 2.12.2 Inner Class Hierarchies in that the idea of *levels* (as in *top-level*) in an inner class hierarchy is defined.

The members of an inner class cannot be accessed unless two or more objects are first created. For example,

```
public class Dog {
    public class Tail {
        public void wag () {…}
    }
}
```

To create a dog and then wag its tail requires three lines of code:

```
Dog dog = new Dog();
Dog.Tail tail = dog.new Tail();
tail.wag();
```

From an interface design perspective, the problem here is that most dogs come with their tails already attached. Notice that the `Tail` class must be instantiated using a reference to a *particular instance* of the `Dog` class. This is referred to as a *qualified* class instance creation expression, which is discussed in the following subsection. There are two levels of code involved here. One corresponds to the `Dog` class and the other to the `Tail` class. Both of these classes must be instantiated before you can wag the tail of a dog. The inner class hierarchy for this example is shown in Figure 3-3. The lines in an inheritance hierarchy connect subclasses to their direct superclass. In an inner class hierarchy lines are used to connect inner classes to their innermost enclosing class. In other words, the innermost enclosing class in an inner class hierarchy is just like a direct superclass in an inheritance hierarchy. There is only one innermost enclos-

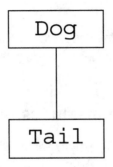

Figure 3-3: The Dog inner class hierarchy.

ing class, and there is a line connecting the inner class to the innermost enclosing class.

Dog is the top-level class. The second level is the Tail class, which has two current instances. A third level would have three current instances and so on. Therefore, level numbers correspond to the number of objects that must be created before a member at that level can be accessed. The following example is used throughout this section as well as in some of the subsections that follow:

```
public class Test {

    interface Printable {
        void print();
    }

    class M1 {}

    class M2 {
        class M1 {
            Printable getPrint() {
                return new Printable() {
                    public void print() {
                        System.out.println(this.getClass().getName());
                        System.out.println(Test.this.getClass().getName());
                        System.out.println(Test.M2.this.getClass().getName());
                        System.out.println(Test.M2.M1.this.getClass().getName());
                    }
                };
            }
        }
        M1 m1 = new M1();
    }
    static M2.M1 m1 = new Test().new M2().new M1(); /* TOTALLY WEIRD CODE */

    public static void main(String[] args) {
        /* instantiate Test so that an instance method can be invoked */
        new Test().print();
```

```
    }
    void print() {
        M2 m2 = new M2();
        Printable p = m2.m1.getPrint();
        p.print();
    }
}
```

The M in the type names stands for *member type*. Executing this program prints

```
Test$1
Test
Test$M2
Test$M2$M1
```

The inner class hierarchy for this example is shown in Figure 3-4.
Notice the following line of code:

```
static M2.M1 m1 = new Test().new M2().new M1();
```

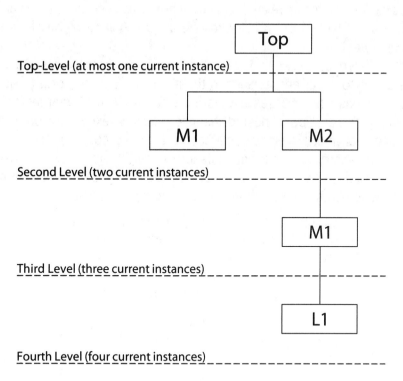

Figure 3-4: Multiple current instances (a.k.a. levels).

This is an example of using qualified class instance creation expressions to instantiate a deeply nested inner member class. It shows that three objects must be created before the anonymous class in the `print()` method of `Test.M2.M1` can be instantiated. Java programmers are normally shielded from the complexity of qualified class instance creation expressions for reasons that are explained in 3.6.3.1 Default Qualifying Instances.

Another indication of multiple current instances in this program are the following qualified and unqualified `this` keywords used in the body of the anonymous class:

```
this
Test.this
Test.M2.this
Test.M2.M1.this
```

They clearly show that there are four current instances in the body of the anonymous class. Qualified `this` keywords are discussed in 3.6.2 Qualifying the `this` Keyword.

The difference between top-level classes and inner classes is that there is only one current instance in the non-`static` code of a top-level class, whereas inner classes always have at least two current instances depending on how deeply nested the inner class is (except for orphaned local and anonymous classes declared in a `static` context). The reason that there is only one current instance is that there is no enclosing instance. That is what defines a top-level class. John Rose says as much in the following quotation from the *Inner Classes Specification*.

> It is helpful at this point to abuse the terminology somewhat, and say, loosely, that the `static` keyword always marks a "top-level" construct (variable, method, or class), which is never subject to an enclosing instance.[5]

Elsewhere in the *Inner Classes Specification* he says,

> Top-level classes do not have multiple current instances. Within the non-`static` code of a top-level class *T*, there is one current instance of type *T*. Within the `static` code of a top-level class *T*, there are no current instances. This has always been true of

---

5. Rose, *Inner Classes Specification* (Mountain View: Sun Microsystems, 1997), "Can a nested class be declared `final`, `private`, `protected`, or `static`?"

top-level classes which are package members, and is also true of top- level classes which are `static` members of other top-level classes.[6]

This observation is fully supported by the concept of inner class hierarchies as presented in this book because at the top level of an inner class hierarchy there is at most one current instance. The difference is that the current instance in a top-level class cannot be referenced in `static` contexts. In other words, there are current instances everywhere except in `static` contexts, which can only be found in top-level classes. Current instances are what make a programming language such as Java object-oriented.

3.6.1 A Note About Deeply Nested Types

The definition of **deeply nested** is anything at level three or below. Deeply nested local and anonymous classes are common. Deeply nested member types, however, are unusual. Nevertheless, there are no restrictions whatsoever on the placement of inner classes. For example,

- An inner member class can enclose a local or anonymous class (normal inner class usage)

- A local class can enclose an inner member class or an anonymous class (unusual coding)

- An anonymous class can enclose an inner member class or a local class (highly questionable coding)

Nor is there a limit on the depth to which inner classes can be nested. For example, an anonymous class can enclose an inner member class, which in turn can enclose a local class that encloses yet another anonymous class, and so on.

Programmers should guard against this *Alice in Wonderland* world of unlimited possibilities. Local and anonymous classes especially should be kept simple. By that I mean nested types generally should not be declared in local and anonymous classes. John Rose specifically warns against this in the *Inner Classes Specification* when he warns:

...avoid deeply nested code.

---

6. Rose, "How do inner classes affect the idea of this in Java code?"

Nested types are typically no more complex than the relationships suggested in Figure 3-5. Half of the local and anonymous classes in this figure are deeply nested (level three and below). Typically only local and anonymous classes are deeply nested, but because they always use the default qualifying instance, you are not usually aware of the fact that they are deeply nested. Figure 3-5 is intended primarily to show that the other

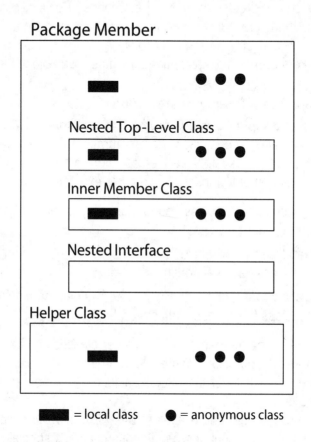

Figure 3-5: Typical uses of nested types.

nested types (nested top-level classes and interfaces and inner member classes) are generally not nested more than one level deep. In other words, most uses of nested types are conservative. This is not my opinion but based upon a very time-consuming and thorough study of nested types in the core API.

3.6.2 Qualifying the `this` Keyword

An unqualified `this` keyword always refers to the current instance of the class in which the `this` keyword appears. In an inner class hierarchy current instances are referred to as either the **innermost current instance** or an **enclosing instance**. To refer to enclosing instances the `this` keyword must be qualified by the name of the corresponding enclosing class. The following `nextElement()` method from an implementation of the `Enumerator` interface includes an example of a qualified `this` keyword:

```
public Object nextElement() {
    synchronized (Vector.this) {
        if (count < elementCount) {
            return elementData[count++];
        }
    }
    throw new java.util.NoSuchElementException("Enumerator");
}
```

An unqualified `this` keyword in the `nextElement()` method would be a reference to the `Enumerator` object. The `nextElement()` method uses `Vector.this` to lock the enclosing `Vector` object while an element is being accessed.

As can be seen in this example, the uses of qualified `this` keywords are the same as those of an unqualified `this` keyword. Another one of those uses is to reference a field shadowed by a local variable or parameter. Likewise, a qualified `this` can be used to reference a field shadowed by an unqualified `this`. For example,

```
class Test {
    class Superclass {
        String s = "inheritance takes precedence over scope";
    }
    public static void main (String[] args) {
        EnclosingClass enclose = new EnclosingClass();
        EnclosingClass.Subclass inner = enclose.new Subclass();
        inner.print();
    }
}

class EnclosingClass extends Test {
    String s = "this is the enclosing class";
    class Subclass extends Superclass {
        void print() {
            System.out.println(this.s);
            System.out.println(EnclosingClass.this.s);
        }
    }
}
```

Executing this program prints

```
inheritance takes precedence over scope
this is the enclosing class
```

If the simple name s is used in the `Subclass`, the following compiler error is generated:

```
Test.java:18: s is inherited from Test.Superclass and hides variable in outer class Enclosing-
Class. An explicit 'this' qualifier must be used to select the desired instance.
            System.out.println(s);
                               ^
1 error
```

In other words, the simple name s is ambiguous in the `InnerClass`.

3.6.2.1 Special Restriction on Nested Type Names

Nested types cannot have the same name as an enclosing type. For example,

```
class Top {
    class Inner {
        class Inner { }
    }
}
```

Attempting to compile this class generates the following compiler error:

```
Top.java:3: Top.Inner is already defined in Top
        class Inner { }
              ^
1 error
```

The same error message would be generated if nested top-level classes were used instead of inner member classes. This restriction applies to all nested types. Using class names to qualify the `this` keyword works precisely because of this restriction on nested type names.

NOTE

3.1

The remainder of this chapter discusses qualifying the `new` and `super` keywords. As mentioned in the last chapter, while qualifying the `super` keyword has been called "the pathological case," the truth is that the `new` keyword is not being explicitly qualified either. I will go out on a limb and say that 99.9 percent of the time you do not need to know this stuff. For that reason, I earnestly recommend that inexperienced programmers bypass these sections. They have been deliberately placed at the bottom of the chapter for this very reason. You can always come back and read these sections after having coded your first inner member class.

3.6.3 Qualifying the `new` Keyword

Class instance creation expressions are either qualified or unqualified. Usually they are unqualified. Unqualified class instance creation expressions begin with the `new` keyword. For example,

```
new Object()
```

The general form of a qualified class instance creation expression is as follows:

```
primaryExpression.new Identifier ( ArgumentList_opt ) ClassBody_opt
```

The primary expression must evaluate to an instance of the innermost enclosing class. In the context of a qualified class instance creation expression, an instance of the innermost enclosing class is referred to as the **qualifying instance** in this book. There is also a default qualifying instance, which is the subject of the next section.

Only inner member classes can be instantiated using a qualified class instance creation expression, which explains why they are so unusual. Top-level classes are only used in unqualified class instance creation expressions because they have no enclosing instance. Local and anonymous classes always use the default qualifying instance. An unqualified class instance creation expression for an inner member class also defaults to the current instance of the innermost enclosing class. As John Rose states,

> By default, a current instance of the caller becomes the enclosing instance of a new inner object. In an earlier example, the expression `new Enumerator()` is equivalent to the explicitly qualified `this.new Enumerator()`. *This default is almost always correct*, but some applications (such as source code generators) may need to override it from time to time [emphasis added].[7]

I do not want to make too much of this quotation, but "source code generators" is a long way from mainstream business applications. If you consider that quotation and the general tenor of the following one, also from the original *Inner Classes Specification*, it appears obvious to me that John Rose did not envision inner member classes being instantiated outside of the class in which they are declared.

> The inner class's name is not usable outside its scope, except perhaps in a qualified name.[8]

---

7. Rose, "How do inner classes affect the idea of this in Java code?"
8. Rose, "What are top-level classes and inner classes?"

Inner classes are declared close to where they are used. Qualified class instance creation expressions imply that an inner member class is being used far from where it is declared. This is an inherent contradiction. That is why qualified class instance creation expressions are so unusual.

The following example is repeated from 3.6 Multiple Current Instances (a.k.a. Levels):

```
public class Dog {
    public class Tail {
        public void wag () {…}
    }
}
```

The innermost enclosing class of `Tail` is `Dog`. Therefore, in a qualified class instance creation expression for the `Tail` class, the primary expression must evaluate to an instance of the `Dog` class. Here is the rest of the code from that example:

```
Dog dog = new Dog();
Dog.Tail tail = dog.new Tail();
tail.wag();
```

The variable `dog` is the primary expression. As can be seen, the variable `dog` evaluates to an instance of the `Dog` class.

Java programmers are usually shielded from the complexity of qualified class instance creation expressions for reasons that are explained in the following subsection.

3.6.3.1 Default Qualifying Instances

Unqualified class instance creation expressions for inner classes always default to the current instance of the innermost enclosing class. This is called the **default qualifying instance**. It is precisely this language feature that shields Java programmers from the inherent complexity of inner classes. For example,

```
class Top {
    public Top() {
        InnerMemberClass inner = new InnerMemberClass(); //implicit
        System.out.println(inner.getClass().getName());
    }
    class InnerMemberClass {}
}
```

Now consider the following program:

```
class Test {
    public static void main(String[] args) {
        new Top();
    }
}
```

Executing this program prints

```
Top$InnerMemberClass
```

The `Top` class could have just as easily been written using the `this` keyword to qualify the class instance create expression. For example,

```java
class Top {
    public Top() {
        InnerMemberClass inner = this.new InnerMemberClass(); //explicit
        System.out.println(inner.getClass().getName());
    }
    class InnerMemberClass {}
}
```

The only difference in this implementation is that the default qualifying instance is made explicit by use of the `this` keyword.

The default qualifying instance of an inner member class is not always the unqualified `this`. For example,

```java
public class Test {
    class M1 { }
    class M2 {
        M1 m1 = new M1(); //implicit
    }
    public static void main(String[] args) {
        /* instantiate Test so that an instance method can be invoked */
        new Test().print();
    }
    void print() {
        M2 m2 = new M2();
        System.out.println(m2.m1.getClass().getName());
    }
}
```

Executing this program prints `"Test$M1"`. The compiler first determined that `Test` was the innermost enclosing class of `M1` and then used `Test.this` as the default qualifying instance. The following program produces exactly the same results:

```java
public class Test {
    class M1 { }
    class M2 {
        M1 m1 = Test.this.new M1(); //explicit
    }
    public static void main(String[] args) {
        /* instantiate Test so that an instance method can be invoked */
        new Test().print();
    }
    void print() {
        M2 m2 = new M2();
        System.out.println(m2.m1.getClass().getName());
    }
}
```

The ability of Java compilers to determine the innermost enclosing class and then use the appropriate current instance is what makes it possible to instantiate an inner member class anywhere in the inner class hierarchy in which it is declared without having to use a qualified class instance creation expression.

3.6.4 Qualifying the `super` Keyword

Qualifying the `super` keyword in an explicit constructor invocation is analogous to qualifying the `new` keyword in a class instance creation expression for an inner member class. The general form of a qualified superclass explicit constructor invocation is

```
primaryExpression.super (ArgumentListopt);
```

A compiler error is generated if the `primaryExpression` does not evaluate to an instance of the innermost enclosing class of the direct superclass.

Inner member classes are sometimes extended by the subclasses that inherit them. Doing so is well within the limits of normal inner class usage. For example,

```
class Top {
    class Inner {
        String s;
        Inner(String s) {
            this.s = s;
        }
    }
}
```

```
class Test extends Top {
    class InnerSubclass extends Inner {
        InnerSubclass(String s) {
            super(s);
        }
        void print() {
            System.out.println(s);
        }
    }
    public static void main (String[] args) {
        /* instantiate Test so that an instance method can be invoked */
        new Test().print();
    }
    void print() {
        InnerSubclass innersub = new InnerSubclass("Hello World!");
        innersub.print();
    }
}
```

Executing this program prints "Hello World!". These are inner classes at their best. A Java programmer who extends an inner member class in this fashion is shielded from a ton of complexity.

So why would you want to qualify the super keyword? That is a good question. Although doing so is technically possible, a qualified super keyword is a rare bird indeed. Suppose Test did not extend Top. For example,

```java
class Top {
    class Inner {
        String s;
        Inner(String s) {
            this.s = s;
        }
    }
}

class Test {
    class InnerSubclass extends Top.Inner {
        InnerSubclass(String s) {
            super(s);
        }
        void print() {
            System.out.println(s);
        }
    }
    public static void main (String[] args) {
        /* instantiate Test so that an instance method can be invoked */
        new Test().print();
    }
    void print() {
        InnerSubclass topinnersub = new InnerSubclass("Hello World!");
        topinnersub.print();
    }
}
```

Other than putting the classes in the same compilation unit and dropping the extends clause in the declaration of Test, nothing has changed. Attempting to compile this example, however, generates the following compiler error:

```
Test.java:13: no enclosing instance of type Top is in scope
                super(s);
                   ^
1 error
```

The problem here is that there is no instance of Top being created that can be used in creating the Inner class. In the previous example there was. Test extended Top and was therefore an instance of the Top class.

If for some reason you ever find a need to code like this, what you need to do is pass the Test constructor an instance of the Top class that can be used to qualify the super keyword. For example,

```
class Top {
    class Inner {
        String s;
        Inner(String s) {
            this.s = s;
        }
    }
}

class Test {
    class InnerSubclass extends Top.Inner {
        InnerSubclass(Top top, String s) {
            top.super(s);
        }
        void print() {
            System.out.println(s);
        }
    }
    public static void main (String[] args) {
        /* instantiate Test so that an instance method can be invoked */
        new Test().print();
    }
    void print() {
        Top top = new Top();
        InnerSubclass topinnersub = new InnerSubclass(top, "Hello World!");
        topinnersub.print();
    }
}
```

The program now compiles and prints "Hello World!" as before.

Chapter 4

Primitive Data Types
and `Object`

Chapter Contents

4.1 Introduction

All data types are either **primitive data types** or **reference types**. Primitive data types are so called because they are built into the language. (The term **built-in data type** is an acceptable alternative to *primitive data type*.) There are eight primitive data types in the Java programming language. Reference types are either **class types** or **interface types**. Within class types, arrays are special. The dynamically created array classes are orthogonal to the type system, which means that for every type there is a corresponding array type. Figure 4-1 summarizes all of the data types in the Java programming language.

This chapter discusses all of the primitive data types, the reference data type (singular), the special `null` type, and `Object`. If you look at Figure 4-1 again, you will see that this chapter discusses all of the data types except for those in Figure 4-2 .

This represents the vast majority of classes and interfaces, but the focus is narrowed considerably. The last three chapters of this book discuss the most common data types in the Java programming language. Understanding how to use the most common data types is the fastest way to gain a familiarity with the language. Table 4-1 provides an overview of the three chapters on common data types.

All Data Types			
Primitive Data Types		**Reference Types**	

Primitive Data Types		Reference Types		
char 16-bit Unicode characters	boolean type	**The Object Class**		
		Class Types		Interface Types
Primitive Numeric Types		*nonarray classes* includes the all-important String class	*arrays*	*interfaces*
two's compliment integers 8-bit byte 16-bit short 32-bit int 64-bit long				
IEEE 754 floating-point single precision float double precision double		the null reference (a.k.a. the special null type)		

Figure 4-1: All data types.

Class Types		Interface Types
nonarray classes includes the all-important String class	*arrays*	*interfaces*

Figure 4-2: The remaining data types.

Table 4-1: Common Data Types

Chapter	Data Types
4	Primitive data types (integers, decimal numbers, characters, and Boolean values), primitive type wrapper classes, BigInteger, BigDecimal, and Object
5	String, StringBuffer, other string related classes, dates, times, and currency.
6	Arrays and other containers

The idea is that after these three chapters you should have a mastery of the most common data types and be ready to begin the process of acquiring knowledge of other classes and interfaces in the core API.

As represented in the *JLS*, the primitive data types are divided into integral types, floating-point types, and `boolean`. One of the integral types is `char`. While this is technically correct in that the format of `char` is an unsigned 16-bit integer, I do not agree with representing `char` as an integral type. Doing so blurs the distinction between the kinds of data that can be stored in primitive data types, which are integers, decimal numbers, characters, and Boolean values. I point this out because the first sentence in 4.3.1 Integral Types begins: "There are four integral types in Java ...." Technically speaking, there are five, the fifth being `char`. This also explains why I consistently describe the format of the `char` data type as two-byte Unicode character codes instead of unsigned 16-bit integers.

4.2 The Definition of Data Types

Though not often discussed, the term **data type** has two fundamentally different meanings in an object-oriented programming language such as Java that supports primitive (or built-in) data types. The older meaning of data type is used when we speak of the primitive data types or of the reference data type (singular), both of which are the focus of this chapter. The older *data types* and the newer class and interface *types* are used interchangeably, but they have fundamentally different meanings. You will notice that I prefer using *data type* when referring to primitive data types and *type* by itself when referring to class and interface types. I am not suggesting that such a distinction should be adopted by everyone; it just helps me to remember the difference between the older definition of data types and the newer meaning of type as used in object-oriented programing.

4.2.1 Data Type as a Set of Values

The primitive data types are a *set of values*, meaning that the data type determines the set of values that can be stored in a variable. Using the term *set of values* to describe data types is well-established usage. Those sets of values are described as follows:

- Only integers in the range of 0 to 255 can be stored in a `byte` type variable

- Only Unicode character codes in the range of 0 to 65535 can be assigned to a `char`

- Section 3.1 Sets of Values, in *IEEE Standard for Binary Floating-Point Arithmetic (ANSI-IEEE Std 754–1985)* describes the sets of values for `float` and `double`

- Only `true` or `false` can be stored in a `boolean` type variable

This definition of data type is based on two things: the data format and length. The data format determines what kind of values can be stored (integers, decimal numbers, characters, or Boolean values). The length determines the range of the values that can be stored. The formula is

---

data type = data format + length

Different data types may have the same format but different lengths, or the same length but different formats. Table 4-2 shows the format and length of the primitive data types in the Java programming language. Two's complement is used for integers, *IEEE 754* for floating-point types, and two-byte Unicode character codes for the `char` data type. A knowledge of data formats is not a prerequisite for programming. All you really need to understand is the difference between integers, decimal numbers, characters, and Boolean values.

What then are class and interface types such as `Object`? In one sense (the older definition of data type), they are reference data types. The reference data type is only defined as a reference to an object in the *JVMS*, but in practice the format of a reference data type is usually a pointer (that is, a memory address) in newer JVM. The length of a reference data type depends on the system architecture. In the current state-of-the-art, a **reference** is usually a 32-bit pointer. However, on 64-bit systems, a reference would be a 64-bit pointer. What is the set of values that can be stored in a reference type variable? They are the memory addresses of the host operating system. This is the older definition of data type as applied to class and interface types. The class and interface types used in object-oriented programming have an entirely different meaning.

Table 4-2: Format of the Primitive Data Types[a]

Format	Primitive Data Type	Length in bytes
Two's complement	`byte`	1
	`short`	2
	`int`	4
	`long`	8
IEEE 754	`float`	4
	`double`	8
Sixteen-bit Unicode character codes	`char`	2

a. The `boolean` data type is omitted from this table to simplify the discussion.

4.2.2 The Object-Oriented Definition of Type

The newer definition has nothing to do with the format and length of a data type. A class or interface type is defined by an identifier (the class or interface name), the method signatures of `public` methods, and the interface specification (more commonly referred to as **API docs** in Java) that describes the behavior of those methods. The formula is

type = identifier + the method signatures of `public`
methods + API docs

A method signature is the method name and the number and type of each parameter. They serve to identify a particular behavior (the name alone being insufficient to identify a behavior because overloaded methods by definition have the same name). The reason this definition stresses *method signatures* instead of just *methods* is that although the definition of type varies slightly from one book to the next there is universal agreement that the definition of a type does not include method implementations. Types are defined by their external behavior (that is, `public` methods), which is described in their API docs.

Some programmers will argue that `protected` methods also define a class type. I agree with this perspective. I just think they muddy the water in this context. For example, a method can be declared pro-

`tected` in a class that is not extended. Do we then define the type by a `protected` method that is not inherited?

Where the older definition of *data type* and the newer class and interface *type* meet is that class and interface types further restrict the set of values that can be stored in a reference type variable to memory addresses of assignment compatible types. Java uses a system of compile-time and run-time type checking to "guarantee" that only references to objects of a compatible class will be stored in a reference type variable. For example,

```
Locale defaultLocale;
```

`Locale` is a `final` class (in the `java.util` package), which means there are no subclasses. A `Locale` "represents a specific geographical, political, or cultural region" of the world.[1] They are discussed in Chapter 5. Given this declaration, only references to a `Locale` object could ever be assigned to the `defaultLocale` variable. Therefore, `default-Locale` is both a reference data type and a `Locale` class type variable, depending on how you want to think about it at any given moment. Most of the time, however, you just say that it is a `Locale` type variable. The same is true of all class and interface types.

4.3 Numeric Data Types

The numeric data types are divided into **integers** and **real numbers**. These are mathematical terms with very precise meanings. Integers are sometimes described as **counting numbers**. Subsets of integers include *whole numbers* {0,1,2,3,4 ...} and *natural numbers* {1,2,3,4 ...}. There are four **integral types** in Java: `byte`, `short`, `int`, and `long`.

The mathematical definition of *real numbers* is much more complex (no pun intended). In strictly mathematical terms, real numbers are complex numbers with no *imaginary* part. That explains the adjective *real*, but such a definition is useless unless you understand complex numbers. A more common term for real numbers is **decimal numbers**. Decimal numbers have a **decimal point**. Any digits to the right of the decimal point are the fractional part of the number. The fractional part differentiates real numbers from integers. In the Java programming language real numbers are

---

1. API docs from the `java.util.Locale` class.

implemented in the **floating-point types** `float` (single precision), `double` (double precision), or `BigDecimal` (arbitrary precision). I like to think of these data types as small, medium, and large precision sizes. Learning which to use is one of the basic goals of this chapter. The term *floating point* is also explained in detail.

4.3.1 Integral Types

There are four integral types in Java. They differ, of course, in the range of values that can be stored. The range of each of the primitive types is defined by the constants `MIN_VALUE` and `MAX_VALUE` declared in their respective wrapper classes. Those values are given in Table 4-3. The `byte` and `short` data types do not have many uses in mainstream business applications. The `byte` data type is used a lot in the `java.io` package, but even there it is mostly used as if it were unsigned (by means of bit shifting into and out of a modulo 256 `int`). The `short` data type in particular is a relic of the 1980s when the 8086 processor and 16-bit architectures were state of the art. This data type exists largely for compatibility with C and C++ programming languages.

The range of an `int` is best remembered as ±2 billion, which is not a very large number even in mainstream business applications. That is why the primary use of the `int` data type is characterized as small counting numbers. The range of a `long` is discussed in the following subsection.

4.3.1.1 How Long is `long`?

The range of a `long` is approximately ±9 quintillion, which for those readers unfamiliar with the American system of numeration is shown in relation to the more common million, billion, and trillion in Figure 4-3.

Table 4-3: Fixed-Precision Integer Ranges[a]

Type	MIN_VALUE	MAX_VALUE
byte	-128	127
short	-32768	32767
int	-2147483648	2147483647
long	-9223372036854775808L	9223372036854775807L

a. Ranges are inclusive.

sextillion

quintillion

quadrillion

trillion

billion

million

thousand

hundred

ten

Figure 4-3: Quintillion is the fifth "illion," or 10^{18}.

Is ±9 quintillion a bigger number than will ever be used in mainstream business applications? Some caution is required here. A number of Java books make comparisons that suggest the range of a `long` is absurdly large for nonscientific applications. For example,

> The maximum number for a long is enough to provide a unique ID for one transaction per second for every person on the planet for the next 50 years. It is also the number of grains in about a cubic mile of sand.[2]

> Consider if you were counting seconds in time. A `byte` can hold a few minutes, a `short` could count a whole day at the office. An `int` can count up your entire lifetime, and a `long` can count from the big bang till the end of time, over 300 billion years.[3]

---

2. Joe Webber et al., "Limits on Integer Values," *Special Edition Using Java, Second Edition* (Indianapolis: Que Corporation, 1996), p. 118.
3. Patrick Naughton, *The Java Handbook* (Berkeley: McGraw-Hill, 1996), Ch. 4, "Types."

These are great descriptions of ±9 quintillion. Range is everything, however, when deciding on which integral type to use. A mainstream business application that exceeds the range of the `long` data type is not out of the question, in which case the `BigInteger` class can be used. Using one of the floating-point types is not an option because the whole number precision of a `long` exceeds that of a `double`.

4.3.2 Floating-Point Types

One of the most remarkable things about floating-point types is how you visualize the number line. Unlike the more familiar integral types, zero is not a dividing point between negative and positive numbers. Figure 4-4 displays a number line for integral types.

-3 -2 -1 0 +1 +2 +3 +4 +5 +6 +7 +8 +9 +10

Figure 4-4: Number line for integral types.

In a floating-point type any value can be either positive or negative, including zero and `Infinity`. The number line for floating-point types is shown in Figure 4-5. Unlike the more familiar integers, zero is not the dividing point between negative and positive numbers in a floating-point type. The set of real numbers is instead divided by one, which in this context is expressed as 2^0.

Everything to the left of 2^0 is a fraction and has a negative exponent such as $1.0E-3$, which is 0.001. Everything to the right of 2^0 has a pos-

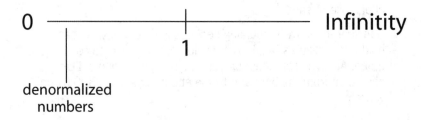

0 ————————————————————— Infinitity

1

denormalized
numbers

Figure 4-5: Number line for floating-point types (real numbers).

itive exponent such as `1.0E3`, which is `1000`. Table 4-4 shows some of those powers of two and their decimal place values. Positive and negative exponents are very different from positive and negative numbers. For example, both negative and positive 4 have the same exponent, which is 2^{+2}. Likewise, both negative and positive `0.25` have the same exponent, which is 2^{-2}.

Table 4-4: Powers of Two

2^e	Decimal Value
2^{+10}	1024
2^{+9}	512
2^{+8}	256
2^{+7}	128
2^{+6}	64
2^{+5}	32
2^{+4}	16
2^{+3}	8
2^{+2}	4
2^{+1}	2
2^0	1
2^{-1}	.5
2^{-2}	.25
2^{-3}	.125
2^{-4}	.0625
2^{-5}	.03125
2^{-6}	.015625
2^{-7}	.0078125
2^{-8}	.00390625
2^{-9}	.001953125

Table 4-5: Floating-Point Ranges[a] as Shown in the JLS

Type Name	MIN_VALUE	MAX_VALUE
float	1.40129846432481707e-45f	3.40282346638528860e+38f
double	4.94065645841246544e-324	1.79769313486231570e+308

a. Remember, on the floating-point number line any number can be either positive or negative. MIN_VALUE and MAX_VALUE for floating-point types is always expressed as positive numbers. Consequently, the range is neither inclusive nor exclusive.

The range of each of the floating-point types is defined by the constants MIN_VALUE and MAX_VALUE declared in their respective wrapper classes. Those values are shown in Table 4-5. MIN_VALUE for a floating-point type is the smallest denormalized number that can be expressed before zero is reached. Likewise, MAX_VALUE is the largest number that can be expressed before Infinity is reached.

That is how the range of the floating-point types is normally expressed. Using floating-point literals to express the range of the floating-point types does not, however, effectively communicate anything to the average programmer. I prefer to express those ranges as powers of two, as seen in Table 4-6.

Zero is sometimes referred to as the **floor**, and infinity is referred to as the **ceiling**. For example, two of the rounding modes discussed below are ROUND_CEILING and ROUND_FLOOR. This does not change the fact that these ranges involve incomprehensibly small or large numbers. A float reaches infinity at about one duodecillion. A double reaches infinity at 2^{1024}. There is no name for that number. The largest number for

Table 4-6: Floating-Point Ranges as Powers of Two[a]

Type	0	MIN_VALUE	Zero Exponent		MAX_VALUE	Infinity
		Denormalized numbers		1		
float	2^{-150}	2^{-149}	2^{-127}	2^0	2^{127}	2^{128}
double	2^{-1075}	2^{-1074}	2^{-1023}	2^0	2^{1023}	2^{1024}

a. All columns are exact except MAX_VALUE. MAX_VALUE is reached somewhere between 2^{127} and 2^{128} for a float. Likewise, MAX_VALUE for a double is actually reached somewhere between 2^{1023} and 2^{1024}.

which there is a name in the American system of numeration is a centillion, which is *only* 10^{303}. The point is that the range of a floating-point type involves numbers so small and so large that the average person cannot comprehend them.

When deciding on which floating-point type to use, there are three things to take into consideration.

1. *Are exact results required?* For example, financial applications require exact results. If the result of an arithmetic operation must be exact, you should always use `BigDecimal`. Some programmers would argue that speed is a factor in this decision, but I am not one of them. Here *exact* results means that a programmer expects results consistent with the arithmetic taught in grade school.

2. *Are exponential expressions involved?* Scientific notation is used by scientists, astronomers, structural engineers, and the like, not by mainstream business application programmers. Most of the time the answer to this question will be *No*.

3. *What is the require precision?* Precision comes in three sizes: single precision (`float`), double precision (`double`), and arbitrary precision (`BigDecimal`). Think of them as small, medium, and large. You must know the required precision. How can you tell? The answer is to use the significant digits measurement of precision. From 1 to 7 significant digits is small. Eight to 15 is medium, and 16 or greater is large. In other words, a `float` is precise up to 8 significant digits. A `double` is precise up to 16 significant digits. Beyond that you have to use a `BigDecimal`.

Figure 4-6 is a decision tree for deciding on which floating-point types to use. Precision is to the floating-point types what range is to the integral types. Range is the deciding factor when deciding on which integral data type to use. When deciding on a floating-point type, precision (the *significant digits* measurement of precision to be exact) is the deciding factor. This is why *IEEE 754* calls them the single and double *precision* formats (emphasis on *precision*). The following subsection discusses the precision of a floating-point type.

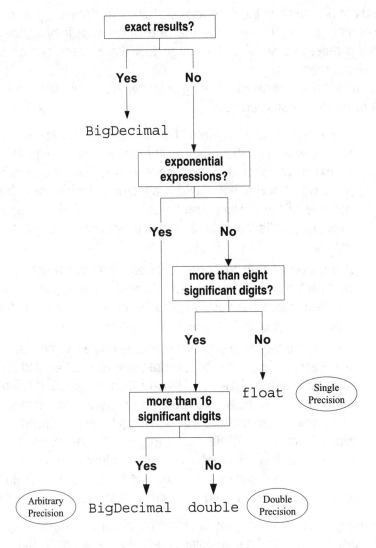

Figure 4-6: A decision tree for floating-point types.

4.3.2.1 The Precision of a Floating-Point Type

All numeric data types have either a *fixed-length* precision or an *arbitrary* precision. These are opposites. The primitive numeric data types have a **fixed-length precision**. This means that an `int` or `float` has only four bytes of storage to work with and a `long` or `double` has only eight. There is a limit to how large or small a number you can store using a fixed amount of storage. If you exceed that limit in an integral type the value is said to *overflow* or *underflow*. If you exceed that limit in a floating-point type you reach infinity or zero. `BigInteger` and `BigDecimal` are objects that have an **arbitrary precision**, which means that the amount of storage used is automatically increased to accommodate larger or smaller numbers, just as the size of a `StringBuffer` is automatically increased when necessary. In this context *arbitrary* basically means unlimited.

The **precision** of a floating-point type is simply a factor of how many bits are used to store the significand. The format of the `float` data type is shown in Figure 4-7.

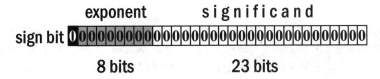

exponent   **s i g n i f i c a n d**

sign bit

8 bits   **23 bits**

Figure 4-7: The format of the `float` data type.

The sizes of both the exponent and the significand are increased for the `double` data type, as shown in Figure 4-8.

11 bits   **52 bits**

Figure 4-8: The format of the `double` data type.

Neither the exponent nor the significand actually doubles in size, but as a result of the increased size of both, the significant digits measurement of precision is doubled. Hence, the name of the `double` data type.

In terms of whole number precision, an `int` has a greater range than a `float` because an `int` uses 31 bits versus the 23 bits of a `float` significand. The same can be said for the `long` and `double` types. Table 4-7 lists the four larger primitive numeric data types in the order of their whole number precision. The least precise type is listed first. The precision is shown in bits, powers of two, and the ranges in which the type can store a whole number without any loss of precision. One normally uses the significant digits measurement of precision when discussing floating-point types. Whole number precision is not useful in deciding on which floating-point type to use, but it does emphasize the loss of precision in floating-

Table 4-7: Whole Number Precision

Type	bits[a]	2^e	whole number precision
float	23	2^{24}	±16777216
int	31	2^{31}	–2147483648 +2147483647
double	52	2^{53}	±9007199254740992
long	63	2^{63}	–9223372036854775808 +9223372036854775807

a. For the floating-point types this is the number of bits in the significand only.

point types in terms that the average programmer can readily understand. For example, a `float` begins to lose whole number precision at 16,777,217. Compare that to `Float.MAX_VALUE`:

16,777,217	Loss of whole number precision
3,402,823,46,638,528,860,000,000,000,000,000,000,000	`Float.MAX_VALUE`

Where whole number precision can be misleading is that for many numbers between 16,777,217 and `Float.MAX_VALUE` there is no loss of precision. There is never a loss of precision in an exact power of two. Many whole numbers greater than 16,777,217 that end in zeros also do not lose precision if all the bits that do not fit in the significand are zeros.

There is a more fundamental reason for including whole number precision in a discussion of the floating-point types. I believe it helps to understand how the exponent and significand in the floating-point types relate to the real number line. Most programmers know that place values in the binary system are double that of the place value to the immediate right. For example, the place values for a `byte` are `128`, `64`, `32`, `16`, `8`, `4`, `2`, and `1`. If you think of those powers of two as the values stored in the exponent of a floating-point type, each new power of two is not only a step in the direction away from zero, but each time the distance between those steps is double that of the last step. The steps are the magnitude of a number. The significand represents the distance between each step. This is what makes the whole number measurement of precision so intriguing to me: at some point along the real number line, a floating-point type is no longer able to accurately measure the distance between those steps because the significand is too small. That point is whole number precision.

4.3.2.1.1 *The Meaning of* Significant Digits The term **significant digits** just means the number of digits in a numeric literal. Whether they're before or after the decimal point does not matter. Trailing zeroes do not count. (Leading zeros imply an octal literal, in which case this discussion does not apply.) The number 123.50, for example, has four significant digits. The number of significant digits is used as a measurement of precision in floating-point types. Table 4-8 includes some examples.

Table 4-8: The Measurement of Precision in Floating-Point Types

Data Type	Precision	Examples[a]
float	Eight significant digits	12345678
		12345.678
		.12345678
double	Sixteen significant digits	1234567890123456
		1234567890.123456
		.1234567890123456

a. These are examples of numbers that could be represented precisely in the given floating-point type. The purpose of these examples is to show that the placement of the decimal point does not matter when counting significant digits.

So what happens if you use a number that has a greater precision than the floating-point type in which it is stored? The answer is that the least significant digits are rounded. The following examples use the `double` data type:

```
import java.math.BigDecimal;
class Test {
    public static void main (String[] args) {
        System.out.println();
        System.out.println("Maximum Whole Number Precision");
        double d = 9007199254740992L;
        BigDecimal exact = new BigDecimal(d);
        System.out.println("The literal value is 9007199254740992L");
        System.out.println("The value stored is  " + exact);

        System.out.println();
        System.out.println("Significant Digits ALL FRACTION");
        d = 0.123456789012345678;    //18 SIGNIFICANT DIGITS
        exact = new BigDecimal(d);
        System.out.println("The literal value is 0.123456789012345678");
        System.out.println("The value stored is  " + exact);

        System.out.println();
```

```
System.out.println("Significant Digits HALF WHOLE NUMBER/HALF FRACTION");
d = 9876543210.12345678;
exact = new BigDecimal(d);
System.out.println("The literal value is 9876543210.12345678");
System.out.println("The value stored is  " + exact);

System.out.println();
System.out.println("Significant Digits MOSTLY WHOLE NUMBER");
d = 43210987654321.12345;
exact = new BigDecimal(d);
System.out.println("The literal value is 43210987654321.12345");
System.out.println("The value stored is  " + exact);
    }
}
```

Executing this program prints

```
Maximum Whole Number Precision
The literal value is 9007199254740992L
The value stored is  9007199254740992

Significant Digits ALL FRACTION
The literal value is 0.123456789012345678
The value stored is  0.12345678901234567736988623209981597028672695159912109375

Significant Digits HALF WHOLE NUMBER/HALF FRACTION
The literal value is 9876543210.12345678
The value stored is  9876543210.1234569549560546875

Significant Digits MOSTLY WHOLE NUMBER
The literal value is 43210987654321.12345
The value stored is  43210987654321.125
```

Count the number of significant digits in each of the floating-point literals and then observe where rounding begins. As you can see, the placement of the decimal point does not matter.

That the significant digits measurement of precision works regardless of the decimal point is what makes it so valuable to computer programmers. For example, if you are storing body temperature, the precision of a float is more than adequate. Using a double would only waste storage. Body temperature is normally 37.0°C (or 98.6°F), which have two and three significant digits, respectively.

A note of caution if you are going to store 8 significant digits in a float or 16 significant digits in a double: whole numbers from 16,777,217 to 99,999,999 may be imprecise in a float even though this range of values has 8 significant digits. For example,

```
class Test {
  public static void main (String[] args) {
    System.out.println();
    System.out.println("Take significant digits with a grain of salt...");
    float f = 99999999f; //eight significant digits
```

```
        System.out.println("99999999f == " + f);
    }
}
```

Executing this program prints

```
Take significant digits with a grain of salt...
99999999f == 1.0E8
```

The `double` data type suffers from the same problem in that not all numbers with 16 significant digits can be precisely represented. That is why some books list the precision of the `float` and `double` data types at 7 and 15 significant digits, respectively, to be on the safe side.

4.3.2.2 Floating-Point Modes

The term **floating-point mode** is used in both the *JLS* and *JVMS*. All methods have a floating-point mode, which defaults if not specified. At present, there is only one non-default floating-point mode. It is **FP-strict**, which corresponds to the use of the `strictfp` modifier. The FP-strict floating-point mode is not new. That is the way the language worked prior to the 1.2 release. The default floating-point mode is what's new.

Java Specification Request 84 (JSR-000084), "Floating Point Extensions," may add an FP-fast floating-point mode that uses the `fastfp` modifier, but that is still in the works. If the `fastfp` modifier is introduced to the Java programming language, there will be three speeds of floating-point operations: slow (`strictfp`), medium (`default`), and fast (`fastfp`).

4.3.2.2.1 The Default Floating-Point Mode   The **default floating-point mode** was introduced to the Java programming language in the 1.2 release by the following sentence in the "Summary of New Features" document.

Floating Point Changes

The Java programming language and virtual machine specifications have been modified slightly to permit implementations to perform floating point calculations more efficiently on popular microprocessors.[4]

---

4. Java™ Development Kit, Version 1.2, "Summary of New Features."

Some JVM implementations now use a larger exponent for intermediate results. Those formats are referred to as **float-extended-exponent** and

Table 4-9: Comparison of Floating-Point Formats[a]

Field	float	float-extended-exponent	double	double-extended-exponent
Exponent	8	≥ 11	11	≥ 15
Significand	24	24	53	53

a. These numbers are the size of the field in bits.

double-extended-exponent. They are not the same as the extended formats in *IEEE 754* because they only have a larger exponent (hence, the names). Table 4-9 compares the floating-point formats.

The size of the significand is the same, which means that `float` has the same precision as float-extended-exponent and `double` has the same precision as double-extended-exponent.

What does all this mean for Java programmers? As stated in the *JLS*,

> … the net effect, roughly speaking, is that a calculation might produce "the correct answer" in situations where exclusive use of the float value set or double value set might result in overflow or underflow.[5]

Overflow or underflow in the floating-point types implies the use of very large or very small numbers. Mainstream business application programmers do not work with values in those ranges. Hence, the difference between the default floating-point mode and the use of the `strictfp` modifier is negligible. Most mainstream business applications should use the default floating-point mode.

4.3.2.2.2 The FP-Strict Floating-Point Mode (`strictfp`)

All declarations in a `strictfp` class or interface type are `strictfp`, including methods (declared or inherited), constructors, initialization blocks, the variable initializers for fields, and all of the declarations in nested types. In addi-

---

5. James Gosling, Bill Joy, Guy Steele, and Gilad Bracha, *The Java Language Specification, Second Edition* (Boston: Addison-Wesley, 2000), §15.4, "FP-strict Expressions."

tion, the `strictfp` modifier can be used in the declaration of individual methods.

The "strict" in `strictfp` stands for *strict reproducibility*. The results of floating-point operations are strictly reproducible if they are the same across all platforms. Strict reproducibility is achieved by specifying the behavior of floating-point types to such a degree that performance suffers. The Java platform uses *IEEE 754* as a standard to enforce strict reproducibility in the floating-point types. As stated in the original *JVMS*: "Operators on floating-point numbers behave exactly as specified by *IEEE 754*."[6] There was initially much enthusiam for strict reproducability. Here are some relevant quotations from white papers dated May 1996.

> For numeric programming, the Java Language has platform-independent data types, array bounds-checking, and well-defined IEEE arithmetic. These capabilities provide good grounding for writing stable numerical algorithms that give repeatable results.[7]

> Real numeric types and their arithmetic operations are as defined by the *IEEE 754* specification ....

> C and C++ both suffer from the defect of designating many fundamental data types as "implementation dependent". Programmers labor to ensure that programs are portable across architectures by programming to a lowest common denominator.

> Java eliminates this issue by defining standard behavior that will apply to the data types across all platforms. Java specifies the sizes of all its primitive data types and the behavior of arithmetic on them.[8]

That initial enthusiasm is now tempered by the realization that speed is more important than strict reproducibility when the only numbers that are not strictly reproducible involve intermediate results that would overflow or underflow a `float` or a `double` without an extended exponent. In other words, there was an intelligent compromise to be made.

---

6. Tim Lindholm and Frank Yellin, *The Java Virtual Machine Specification* (Reading: Addison-Wesley, 1997–1999), Section 2.4.3, "Operators on Floating-Point Values." Note that *IEEE 754* is an abbreviated reference to *IEEE Standard for Binary Floating-Point Arithmetic, ANSI/IEEE Standard 754-1985.*
7. Douglas Kramer , *The Java Platform: A White Paper* (Mountain View: Sun Microsystems, 1996), "What is the Java Platform?"
8. James Gosling and Henry McGilton, *The Java Language Environment: A White Paper* (Mountain View: Sun Microsystems, 1996), §4.2, "Portable."

JSR-000084 is an interesting read in this context. The following is an excerpt from the description.

> Version 1.1 of the Java platform specification gave strict rules for floating point semantics, using the *IEEE 754 Standard for Binary Floating-Point Arithmetic*. These rules enforced bit-by-bit reproducibility of floating point results across implementations. As a result, in some cases, the rules also significantly impaired floating point performance by effectively prohibiting certain code generation optimizations and the use of certain native operations on some processors. Version 1.2 of the Java platform specification permitted a relaxation of the rules for floating point semantics. These new rules allow a larger exponent (larger than that specified by earlier versions of Java) to be used in certain situations. This improved the achievable performance of Java platform implementations for certain popular microprocessors at the cost of bit-by-bit reproducibility of floating point calculations on those processors. However, the relaxed rules still impair performance in many important cases ....

> While it is sometimes desirable to maintain bit-by-bit reproducibility of floating-point operations, such strictness is not always required. Floating-point arithmetic is an approximation to real arithmetic, and rounding errors are unavoidable. From a numeric viewpoint, in order to improve performance and/or accuracy, it is often acceptable to replace a computation with another. This relaxation of floating-point rules can be adopted as an option by the Java platform, provided that strict reproducibility can be enforced when needed and that suitable restrictions are set on implementations exploiting the relaxed rules.[9]

It is unclear to me under what circumstances a mainstream business application programmer would be concerned about strict reproducibility. Otherwise, I would suggest you ignore the `strictfp` modifier.

4.3.2.3 *Printing the Value of Floating-Point Types*

One of the truly remarkable things about computer programming languages is that more often than not the value of a floating-point literal is not the same as the value stored by the computer. For the uninitiated, the

---

9. Mark Snir et al., JSR-000084, "Floating Point Extensions" (*java.sun.com/ aboutJava/communityprocess/jsr/jsr_084_fpe.html*, Sun Microsystems, 2000), §2.1, "Please describe the proposed Specification."

inability to reconcile what is seen in source code with what the computer actually does can seem like a grand deception perpetrated against computer programmers. The `print` and `println` methods are co-conspirators in that deception. They are never to be trusted to print the actual value stored in a floating-point type. For example,

```
class Test {
    public static void main (String[] args) {
        double d = 1.1;
        System.out.println(d);
    }
}
```

Executing this program prints `1.1`. This is unfortunate because it reinforces the mistaken notion that the value stored is the same as the floating-point literal. This is true only when the floating-point literal does not exceed the precision of the floating-point type and there either is no fraction or the fraction is one of the few that has an exact binary equivalent (for example, `0.125`, `0.25`, `0.375`, `0.5`, `0.625`, `0.75`, `0.875`, etc.). Most, but not all, programmers know that the value stored is not actually `1.1`, and some of those who do know are not exactly sure why.

What is the value stored in the variable `d`? To determine this you must use the `BigDecimal` class in the `java.math` package. For example,

```
import java.math.BigDecimal;
class Test {
    public static void main (String[] args) {
        double d = 1.1;
        BigDecimal exact = new BigDecimal(d);
        System.out.println(exact);
    }
}
```

Executing this program prints

1.100000000000000088817841970012523233890533447265625

The infinitesimally small differences between the value of floating-point literals and the value actually stored is explained in 4.3.3 Understanding the Floating-Point Types. The `BigDecimal` class never lies about the contents of a `float` or `double` when the `BigDecimal(double value)` constructor is used in string concatenation operations. The API docs for the `BigDecimal` class recommend not using this constructor because the value stored has the same precision problems as the `double` data type. If the new `BigDecimal("1.1")` is used instead, the value stored is precisely `1.1`.

Now that you know how to determine the actual values of a `float` or `double` using the `BigDecimal` class, the rest of this section discusses the behavior of the `toString()` methods for floating-point types without differentiating between the `float` and `double` types. The implicit string conversions in string concatenation invoke the `toString()` methods in the `Float` and `Double` classes to print the value of a floating-point type. Unlike other `toString()` methods, the `toString()` methods in the `Float` and `Double` classes are anything but easy to understand. They are implemented as follows:

```java
public static String toString(float f){
    return new FloatingDecimal(f).toJavaFormatString();
}

public static String toString(double d){
    return new FloatingDecimal(d).toJavaFormatString();
}
```

The `FloatingDecimal` class is a package-private class in the `java.lang` package. Notice that the same `toJavaFormat-String()` method is used to print both `float` and `double` values. That is why the specification for the `toString()` methods in both the `Float` and `Double` classes is the same.

Values in the range of `.001` to `9999999` (inclusive) are printed using standard notation. This range includes many, if not most, of the numbers in mainstream business applications. Smaller or larger numbers are printed using scientific notation. For example,

```java
class Test {
    public static void main (String[] args) {
        System.out.println(.000999);
        System.out.println(Math.pow(10, -3));
        System.out.println(Math.pow(10, 7) - 1);
        System.out.println(Math.pow(10, 7));
    }
}
```

Executing this program prints

```
9.99E-4
0.0010
9999999.0
1.0E7
```

Negative numbers are printed with a - prefix.

The main question when printing the value of floating-point types is *how many digits will print to the right of the decimal point*. The answer is the same for both standard and nonstandard scientific notation. For example,

```
class Test {
    public static void main (String[] args) {
        double d1 = 123456789012345678901234567890123456789.0;
        double d2 = 1.2345678901234567890123456789;
        double d3 = 0.00012345678901234567890123456789;
        System.out.println(d1);
        System.out.println(d2);
        System.out.println(d3);
    }
}
```

This is a very large number followed by a number within the `0.001` to `9999999` range (and therefore printed in standard format) and then a very small number. Executing this program prints

```
1.2345678901234568E28
1.2345678901234567
1.2345678901234567E-4
```

In this case, 16 digits were printed to the right of the decimal point. That is the most that will ever be printed given the precision of the `double` data type, which is 15 or 16 digits depending on the book you are reading. The remainder of this section explains the new *no loss of information* policy behind the number of digits that now print to the right of the decimal point when the `toString()` method for a `float` or `double` is invoked.

Before the 1.1 release the answer to the question *how many digits will print to the right of the decimal point* was simple. The `toString()` methods for the floating-point types were originally based on the `%g` format of the `printf` function in C and would print at most six digits after the decimal point. For example, `Integer.MAX_VALUE`, which is `+2147483647`, would print as `2.14748e+009` in both a `float` and `double`. That same value now prints differently depending on which data type is used. Why? Because a `double` is more precise than a `float` and the new rule of thumb is that there should be no loss of information when a `float` or `double` is printed. For example,

```
class Test {
    public static void main (String[] args) {
        System.out.println((float) Integer.MAX_VALUE);
        System.out.println((double) Integer.MAX_VALUE);
    }
}
```

Executing this program prints

```
2.14748365E9
2.147483647E9
```

In the case of a `double`, which can precisely represent the value of `Integer.MAX_VALUE`, the exact number is now printed.

Some programmers miss the simplicity of the `toString()` methods in the 1.0 release and are sometimes baffled by the ever-changing number of digits that prints to the right of the decimal point since the 1.1 release. The truth is that the `toString()` methods are not much more difficult to understand than they were in the early releases. The specification reads in part,

> There must be at least one digit to represent the fractional part, and beyond that as many, but only as many, more digits as are needed to uniquely distinguish the argument value from adjacent values of [that type].[10]

The new implementation of the `toString()` methods is designed not to lose information if the printed value were parsed and the resultant number stored in the same data type (a full cycle numeric-string-numeric conversion). In short, the fraction is printed to the greatest precision possible for the given floating-point type. For example,

```java
import java.math.BigDecimal;

class Test {
    public static void main (String[] args) {
        double d1 = 1.1;
        double d2 = 1.2;
        double d3 = 1.3;
        double d4 = 1.2 - .1;
        System.out.println(new BigDecimal(d1));
        System.out.println(d1);
        System.out.println(new BigDecimal(d2));
        System.out.println(d2);
        System.out.println(new BigDecimal(d3));
        System.out.println(d3);
        System.out.println(new BigDecimal(d4));
        System.out.println(d4);
        System.out.println(new BigDecimal(Math.PI));
        System.out.println(Math.PI);
    }
}
```

---

10. API docs for the `toString(double d)` method in the `java.lang.Double` class.

In the following output from this program I have inserted pipe symbols after the 16th "significant" digit of the `BigDecimal` value:

```
1.100000000000000|0888178419700125232338905334472656 25
1.1
1.199999999999999|9555591079014993738383054733276367 1875
1.2
1.300000000000000|0444089209850062616169452667236328 125
1.3
1.099999999999999|8667732370449812151491641998291015 625
1.0999999999999999
3.141592653589793|1159979634685441851615905761718 75
3.141592653589793
```

The `toString()` method is rounding after about 16 significant digits. It does the same thing for the `float` data type after about eight significant digits. In effect, the `toString()` methods now print what might be described as *the most meaningful string* for a given `float` or `double` value.

There is still a difference, however, between *the most meaningful string* representation of a value and the actual value stored in a `float` or `double`. The rule is

---

Never assume the printed value is exactly the same as
the value stored in a floating-point type.

If you ever want to know the actual value of a `float` or `double`, use it as an argument in a `BigDecimal (double value)` constructor and then print the value of the `BigDecimal`. This is the only way to know the exact value of a `float` or `double` for sure.

4.3.2.3.1 *Printing Overly Precise Floating-Point Literals* Some of the floating-point literals used to initialize constants in the core API, such as `Math.PI`, have a precision greater than the precision of the data type to which they are assigned. For example,

```
public static final double PI = 3.14159265358979323846;
```

Does the printed value of `Math.PI` lose information because it is not as long as the original? No, given the precision of the `double` data type. For example,

```
class Test {
    public static void main (String[] args) {
```

Table 4-10: Printing ±0, ±∞, **and** NaN

Special Floating-Point Values	Prints as...
Negative zero	-0.0
Positive zero	0.0
Negative infinity	-Infinity
Positive infinity	Infinity
Not-a-Number (NaN)	NaN

```
        String pi = Double.toString(Math.PI);
        double d = new Double(pi).doubleValue();
        if (d == Math.PI)
            System.out.println("the toString methods do not lose information");
    }
}
```

Executing this program prints

```
the toString methods do not lose information
```

4.3.2.3.2 Printing ±0, ±∞, and NaN Special floating-point values are printed as shown in Table 4-10.

Before the 1.1 release Infinity would print as Inf.

4.3.3 Understanding the Floating-Point Types

What follows is an introduction to the *IEEE 754* format for the float and double types. Normally, mainstream business application programmers do not require a knowledge of data formats. I make an exception for the floating-point types. The average programmer would like to understand the loss of precision in floating-point types, what a *floating point* is, etc. The discussion of *IEEE 754* formats in the following subsections, however, is minimal. All of the examples use the float data type for aesthetic reasons. Examples involving the float data type fit better on the page (double is too wide). This should not matter because the functions of the sign bit, exponent, and significand are the same for both floating-point types.

Floating-point types are imprecise for two reasons. The most obvious is that they are designed that way. Specifically, the significand is designed to be imprecise. That is what makes it possible for floating-point types to store very small and very large numbers as powers of two in the exponent. More on this in the following subsection. There is another, completely unrelated reason why floating-point types are imprecise. Most decimal fractions cannot be precisely represented in a floating-point type because the binary and decimal number systems have what are described as *incommensurable bases*. Both the fact that floating-point types are designed to be imprecise and the problem of incommensurable bases are discussed in detail in the following subsections.

4.3.3.1 The Significand is Designed to be Imprecise

When storing a number that is not an exact power of two in a floating-point type, the value is stored in two fields, the exponent and the significand. The highest power of two is stored in the exponent. You can think of the exponent field of a floating-point type as a compression algorithm for very small or very large numbers. The problem is that it only works for powers of two. The remainder is stored in the significand as a normal binary number. For example,

```
float f = 100;
```

The highest power of two in 100 is 2^6, or 64. The remainder of $100-64$ is 36. Therefore, 36 is stored in the significand.

If the remainder is too large for the significand, only the most significant digits are stored. The least significant digits are rounded using the *IEEE 754* default rounding mode of *round to the nearest*, which is the equivalent of `BigDecimal.ROUND_HALF_EVEN` in the core API. That results is a loss of precision.

A loss of precision always occurs when the remainder must be rounded in order to fit in the significand.

As with all rounding, the resulting number is reasonably close to the original. It is just not precise.

Before explaining the mechanics of a loss of precision in detail, I want to make a quick comparison to gasoline prices. In the United States the signs that advertise the price of a gallon of gasoline usually include a small nine or nine-tenths following the cents. For example, the sign at my local gas station currently reads as follows in Table 4-11. The small 9 means the price of a gallon of gas is actually nine-tenths of a cent more than what the larger numbers say. Americans have gotten so used to gasoline prices

Table 4-11: Typical Gasoline Prices in the US

Regular	1.51^9
Plus	1.59^9
Supreme	1.67^9

such as these that most of the time they completely ignore the extra nine-tenths of a cent in the price of a gallon of gasoline.

Now, what does this have to do with floating-point numbers? The answer is that it illustrates on a scale that most people can readily under-stand how part of a number can be ignored because it is not that signifi-cant. The same thing happens when the remainder is too large to store in the significand, only sometimes on a much larger scale. For example, if you are computing a number close to a nonillion, a trillion or so is no more significant than that nine-tenths of a cent at the local gas station. It is hard to imagine rounding off a trillion or more, but this is not unusual when work-ing with very large numbers. For the average programmer, however, round-ing on that scale makes *imprecise* or a *loss of precision* sound like a euphemism.

Next, I want to use examples to show how the significand works. In the process you will learn what a floating-point is. Doing so requires a method for printing the bit pattern of a `float`. The core API offers the following solution:

```
class Test {
    public static void main (String[] args) {
        System.out.println(Integer.toBinaryString(Float.floatToIntBits(100.5f)));
    }
}
```

Executing this program prints the bit pattern of a `float` for the number `100.5`. Unfortunately, the `toBinaryString(int i)` method in the `Integer` class does not print leading zeros (which might be inadvertently mistaken for an octal radix specifier). That marginalizes the usefulness of the `toBinaryString(int i)` method when used to print the bit pat-

tern of a binary number. For example, the actual bit pattern for `100.5` is
as follows:

```
0 10000101 1001001000000000000000000
```

However, the `toBinaryString(int i)` method in the `Integer`
class prints only

```
10000101100100100000000000000000
```

It is very confusing and requires that you count the number of bits printed,
subtract that from 32, and then add the remainder as leading zeroes.
Something better is needed.

I use the following `BitPattern` utility class, which has overloaded
print methods to print the bit pattern of an `int`, `long`, `float` or `double`:

```java
package com.javarules.utilities;
public class BitPattern {

    /**
     * Do not instantiate this class.
     */
    private BitPattern() {}

    static final long[] BIT_MASK = new long[64];
    static {
        BIT_MASK[0] = 1;
        for (int i = 1; i < BIT_MASK.length; i++)
            BIT_MASK[i] = BIT_MASK[i-1] << 1;
    }

    public static void print(int n)    { System.out.print(getBitPattern(n)); }
    public static void print(long n)   { System.out.print(getBitPattern(n)); }
    public static void print(float n)  { System.out.print(getBitPattern(n)); }
    public static void print(double n) { System.out.print(getBitPattern(n)); }

    public static String getBitPattern(int n) {
        StringBuffer bitPattern = new StringBuffer(35);
        for (int i = 31; i >= 0; i--) {
            bitPattern.append((n & BIT_MASK[i]) == 0 ? '0' : '1');
            if (i % 8 == 0) bitPattern.append(" ");
        }
        return bitPattern.toString();
    }
    public static String getBitPattern(long n) {
        StringBuffer bitPattern = new StringBuffer(67);
        for (int i = 63; i >= 0; i--) {
            bitPattern.append((n & BIT_MASK[i]) == 0 ? '0' : '1');
            if (i % 8 == 0) bitPattern.append(" ");
        }
        return bitPattern.toString();
    }
    public static String getBitPattern(float n) {
        StringBuffer bitPattern = new StringBuffer(34);
        int bits = Float.floatToIntBits(n);
```

```
            for (int i = 31; i >= 0; i--) {
                bitPattern.append((bits & BIT_MASK[i]) == 0 ? '0' : '1');
                if (i == 23 || i == 31) bitPattern.append(" ");
            }
            return bitPattern.toString();
        }
        public static String getBitPattern(double n) {
            StringBuffer bitPattern = new StringBuffer(66);
            long bits = Double.doubleToLongBits(n);
            for (int i = 63; i >= 0; i--) {
                bitPattern.append((bits & BIT_MASK[i]) == 0 ? '0' : '1');
                if (i == 52 || i == 63) bitPattern.append(" ");
            }
            return bitPattern.toString();
        }
    }
```

A sample program follows:

```
import com.javarules.utilities.BitPattern;
class Test {
    public static void main(String args[]) {
        System.out.println("100.5 = " + BitPattern.print(100.5f));
    }
}
```

Executing this program prints

```
100.5f = 0 10000101 10010010000000000000000
```

Now that we have the desired bit pattern, the first thing I want to consider is the exponent.

In this chapter I ignore the bit pattern of the exponent. We already know that the highest power of two in the number 100.5 is 2^6 or 64, so the exponent is 6, even though it does not appear so given the above bit pattern of 10000101. That bit pattern has a value of 133, not the 6 expected. To understand the bit pattern of an exponent you need to know about the exponent *bias*, which is 127 for the float data type. To get the actual (or unbiased) exponent, the exponent bias must be subtracted from 133. In this example, $133-127$ is 6, which is what we expected. Instead of using this computation in the remainder of this section, I will avoid the complexity of biased and unbiased exponents by just stating what the highest power of two is for a given number.

Now we are ready to take a closer look at the significand. For the number 100.5 the remainder is $100.5-64$ or 36.5. The bit pattern of the significand is as follows:

```
10010010000000000000000
```

The first thing you need to know is where to place the floating point, which is the binary equivalent of a decimal point. That depends on the exponent. In this case the exponent is 6, so the floating point is placed after the sixth digit in the significand. For example,

```
100100.10000000000000000
```

Now you can see the remainder. The bit pattern `100100` is equal to `36`, and `0.1` is the binary equivalent of decimal `0.5`.

Here is another example using `1100.25`:

```
0 10001001 00010011000100000000000
```

The highest power of two is 2^{10}, which is `1024`. That makes the remainder that must be stored in the significand `76.25`. To verify this we must first determine how far to *float* the binary point. The exponent is `10`, so the floating point should be placed after the 10th digit in the significand as follows:

```
0001001100.0100000000000
```

Does this check out? Yes. The binary value of `1001100` is `76`, and `0.01` is the binary equivalent of decimal `0.25`.

Here is one more example involving a much larger number, `2100000.75`. The bit pattern is

```
0 10010100 00000000010110010000011
```

The highest power of two is 2^{21}, which is `2097152`. The remainder is `2848.75`. The significand with a binary point would look like this:

```
000000000101100100000.11
```

The bit pattern `101100100000` is equal to `2848`, and `0.11` is the binary equivalent of decimal `0.75`. The reason for including this final example is to introduce the technical explanation for a loss of precision.

If the binary point floats far enough, there is no more room in the significand. What happens in the last example if more room is needed for a larger number or the same number with a larger fraction? *The answer is a loss of precision.* The first thing to go is the fraction. At 2^{23} (8,388,608), the binary point floats all the way to the right edge of a 23-bit `float` significand, as shown in Figure 4-9.

Consequently, there is no room left for the binary equivalent of a decimal fraction. At 2^{24} (16,777,216), the `float` data type begins to lose whole

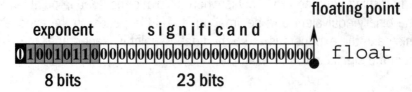

Figure 4-9: 2^{23} uses all of a `float` significand.

number precision. The binary point has floated so far to the right that the low-order bit is effectively truncated, as shown in Figure 4-10.

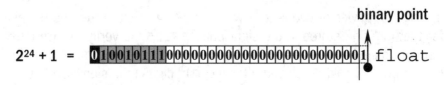

Figure 4-10: A loss of ±1 precision in the `float` data type.

The result is that numbers greater than 2^{24} are *potentially* ±1 imprecise. I stress *potentially* because not all numbers greater than 2^{24} actually lose precision. Sometimes all of the least significant bits that do not fit in the significand are zeros. For example,

```
import java.math.BigDecimal;
class Test {
    public static void main (String[] args) {
        System.out.println("BigDecimal = " +
                new BigDecimal("2e24").add(new BigDecimal("2e25")));
        double d = 2e24 + 2e25;
        System.out.println("double = " + d);
    }
}
```

Executing this program prints

```
BigDecimal = 22000000000000000000000000
double = 2.2E25
```

Many numbers greater than 2^{24}, however, must be rounded, the effect of which is a loss of precision.

The next highest power of two causes another low-order bit to be truncated, as shown in Figure 4-11.

With each new power of two the imprecision more than doubles. Table 4-12 illustrates how imprecise conversions from `int` or `long` to `float` can be. Notice that the loss of precision is equal to two raised to the

binary point

$$2^{25} + 3 = \texttt{01001011100000000000000000000000011} \quad \texttt{float}$$

Figure 4-11: A loss of ±3 precision in the `float` data type.

Table 4-12: Potential Loss of Whole Number Precision in a `float`

Powers of Two		Integer Range		Bits Truncated	Potential Loss of Precision
From	To	From	To		
0	2^{24}	0	16,777,216	0	0
$2^{24} + 1$	2^{25}	16,777,217	33,554,432	1	1
$2^{25} + 1$	2^{26}	33,554,433	67,108,864	2	3
$2^{26} + 1$	2^{27}	67,108,865	134,217,729	3	7
$2^{27} + 1$	2^{28}	134,217,729	268,435,456	4	15
$2^{28} + 1$	2^{29}	268,435,457	536,870,912	5	31
$2^{29} + 1$	2^{30}	536,870,913	1,073,741,824	6	63
$2^{30} + 1$	2^{31}	1,073,741,825	2,147,483,648	7	127
$2^{62} + 1$	2^{63}	4,611,686,018, 427,387,905	9,223,372,036, 854,776,000	39	549,755,813, 887

power of the number of bits truncated minus one. Therefore, in the range of $2^{28}+1$ to 2^{29}, the loss of precision is $2^5 - 1 = 31$. The `float` data type reaches infinity at 2^{128}, which has a potential loss of precision of means the maximum imprecision of the `float` data type at $2^{104} - 1$, which is 20,282,409,603,651,670,000,000,000,000,000. Again, I have to say that calling ±20 nonillions *imprecise* or a *loss of precision* must sound like a euphemism to the average programmer. This is pocket change, however, when computing numbers in the range of 2^{128}.

4.3.3.1.1 Integer to Floating-Point Type Conversions There are three type conversions that are relevant to any discussion of a loss of precision in the floating-point types. They are the only three primitive type conversions in which there is the potential for a loss of precision. The focus in this section is on explaining the counterintuitive classification of the following type conversions as safe:

```
int to float
long to float
long to double
```

Discussing them necessarily involves introducing the reader to the terminology of type conversions such as *widening conversions*. I make every effort to minimize the distraction of this new terminology. On the other hand, there is no way I can fully explain all the terms used.

A *widening* primitive conversion generally refers to the length of the primitive data types involved. For example,

```
int i = Integer.MAX_VALUE;
long l = i;
```

A `long` is literally wider than an `int` because there are eight bytes in a `long` and only four in an `int`. That makes `l = i` a widening primitive conversion. In these three widening primitive conversions, however, the length of the *to* format is equal to or smaller than the length of the *from* format. A `long` to `float` type conversion is superficially a narrowing type conversion, so why are these type conversions described as *widening* in the terminology of type conversions?

The technical classification of these conversions as *widening* is based on the fact that they are considered safe. All widening conversions are supposed to be safe, the technical definition of which is that there is *no loss of data* (sometimes expressed as a *loss of information*) and *no possibility of an exception being thrown* at run time. Hence, no cast operator is required. Cast operators are the compiler's way of making a programmer acknowledge that a requested conversion is classified as unsafe. The technical definition of a *loss of data*, however, specifically does not include a *loss of precision*, and for good reason. The significand of a floating-point type is designed to be imprecise.

In the context of the type conversions under consideration, however, to classify such type conversions as safe is counterintuitive. An `int` has a greater whole number precision than a `float`, and a `long` has a greater whole number precision than a `double`. Thus, a *loss of precision* in this context means a *different number*. Programmers do not expect whole numbers to change as the result of storing them in a different data type. Nevertheless, this can happen.

An important distinction is made between a loss of magnitude and a loss of precision in the floating-point types. Primitive type conversions from integral to floating-point types are categorized as widening primitive conversions (that is, safe) because there is no loss of magnitude. A **loss of magnitude** is defined as a change in the exponent as a result of the type conversion. When discussing floating-point types, always remember,

---

Magnitude is to the exponent what precision is to the significand.

There is no potential for a loss of magnitude in the three type conversions under consideration, only a loss of precision. When converting from `int` to `float` or from `long` to `float` or `double`, the highest power of two is always stored in the exponent. Specifically, the highest power of two in `Integer.MAX_VALUE` can be stored in the exponent of a `float`. Likewise, the highest power of two in `Long.MAX_VALUE` can be stored in the exponent of a `float` or `double`. In fact, the exponents of the floating-point types can store powers of two that are much greater than `Integer.MAX_VALUE` and `Long.MAX_VALUE`. A loss of precision always refers to the significand.

The following example of a loss of precision in an `int` to `float` type conversion is from the *JLS*:

```
class Test {
    public static void main(String[] args) {
        int big = 1234567890;
        float approx = big;
        System.out.println(big - (int)approx);
    }
}
```

which prints

```
-46
```

thus indicating that information was lost during the conversion from `int` to type `float` because values of type `float` are not precise to nine significant digits.[11]

---

11. Gosling et al., §5.1.2, "Widening Primitive Conversion."

How can two numbers that are the same have a difference of 46? This is the intuitive reaction to this code from readers who do not know about the loss of precision in floating-point types. In this case that loss of precision occurred in the following line of code:

```
float approx = big;
```

That is an `int` to `float` type conversion, which is classified as safe because, technically speaking, there is no loss of data. The highest power of two in the number 1234567890 is 2^{30}, or 1073741824. There is a loss of precision when storing this integer literal in a floating-point type because the remainder of 160,826,066 cannot be precisely stored in the significand of a `float`. There is no loss of magnitude because the number stored is still at least 2^{30}, which we already know because the difference was only 46. This is an example of counterintuitive loss of precision in what is supposed to be a safe type conversion.

Note the use of the `(int)` cast operator in this example. Before subtracting two numbers of different types, one type must be "promoted" to the other type. If that were allowed to happen, `big` would be converted to a `float` and therefore would be as imprecise as `approx`. The difference would be zero. By using the `(int)` cast operator the value stored in `approx` is shown to be less than expected.

There is a natural inclination to think that a loss of magnitude is much more serious than a loss of precision. Indeed, a loss of magnitude implies something went wrong, whereas a loss of precision is considered normal. A loss of magnitude does not always mean a big change in the number, though. For example,

```java
class Test {
    public static void main(String[] args) {
        double d = Math.pow(2,31);
        int i = (int) d;    //loss of magnitude
        System.out.println("d - i = " + (d - i));
        System.out.println(i == Integer.MAX_VALUE);
        System.out.println(i > Math.pow(2,30));
        System.out.println(i < Math.pow(2,31));
    }
}
```

Executing this program prints

```
d - i = 1.0
true
true
true
```

There is a loss of magnitude because 2^{31} is one greater than `Integer.MAX_VALUE`. The example of a loss of precision from the *JLS* involved a difference of 46. Here we have a loss of magnitude that involves a difference of only 1. Nevertheless, a loss of precision is considered safe and a loss of magnitude is considered unsafe.

4.3.3.2 The Problem of Incommensurable Bases

The problem of **incommensurable bases** begins at the compiler. Floating-point literals are decimal numbers, not binary. The compiler, however, parses those string literals, using something like the methods discussed in 4.10.1 Parsing Strings for Primitive Type Values, and saves the result in a binary format (UTF-8). Floating-point literals are base 10. Binary data formats are base two. These are incommensurable bases, which means they are like the metric system and the U.S. system of measurement in which the fundamental unit of measurement is different. More precisely, most decimal fractions have no binary equivalent.

The problem is always fractions, never whole numbers. For example, the following program appears to store the value 0.1 in a `double`, when in fact the value stored is slightly more than that because the decimal fraction 0.1 has no binary equivalent:

```
import java.math.BigDecimal;

class Test {

    public static void main (String[] args) {

        System.out.println();
        System.out.println("Things are not as they appear to be...");
        double d = .1;
        BigDecimal exact = new BigDecimal(d);
        System.out.println("The literal value is 0.1");
        System.out.println("The value stored is " + exact);

    }
}
```

Executing this program prints

```
Things are not as they appear to be...
The literal value is 0.1
The value stored is 0.1000000000000000055511151231257827021181583404541015625
```

The difference between

```
0.1
```

and

```
0.1000000000000000055511151231257827021181583404541015625
```

is infinitesimally small. Depending on how the value is used, it may never be noticed. When used in even the simplest of arithmetic operations, however, these differences are pronounced. For example,

```
class Test {
    public static void main (String[] args) {
        double d = 1.2 - .1;
        System.out.println(d == .1);
        System.out.println("1.2 - .1 = " + d);
    }
}
```

Executing this program prints

```
false
1.2 - .1 = 1.0999999999999999
```

Notice that this example uses the `double` data type, whereas the last example used a `float`. The problem of incommensurable bases is the same for both the `float` and `double` data types.

It is important to understand that this happens with almost every floating-point literal that has a fraction. For example,

```
import java.math.BigDecimal;
class Test {
    public static void main (String[] args) {
        System.out.println();
        System.out.println("Only the following cents are stored exactly...");
        for (int i = 1; i < cents.length; i++) {
            BigDecimal exact = new BigDecimal(cents[i]);
            if (exact.scale() <= 2)
                System.out.println(exact);
        }
    }

    static double[] cents = {.00, .01, .02, .03, .04, .05, .06, .07, .08, .09,
                             .10, .11, .12, .13, .14, .15, .16, .17, .18, .19,
                             .20, .21, .22, .23, .24, .25, .26, .27, .28, .29,
                             .30, .31, .32, .33, .34, .35, .36, .27, .38, .39,
                             .40, .41, .42, .43, .44, .45, .46, .37, .48, .49,
                             .50, .51, .52, .53, .54, .55, .56, .47, .58, .59,
                             .60, .61, .62, .63, .64, .65, .66, .57, .68, .69,
                             .70, .71, .72, .73, .74, .75, .76, .67, .78, .79,
                             .80, .81, .82, .83, .84, .85, .86, .77, .88, .89,
                             .90, .91, .92, .93, .94, .95, .96, .87, .98, .99};
}
```

Executing this program prints

```
Only the following cents are stored exactly...
```

```
0.25
0.5
0.75
```

Those are the only decimal fractions from 0.00 to 0.99 (when incrementing by 0.01) that have equivalent binary fractions and therefore do not introduce a loss of precision.

The following program does the same thing but can be scaled:

```
import java.math.BigDecimal;
import java.util.*;
class Test {
    public static void main (String[] args) {
        System.out.println();
        SortedSet set = new TreeSet();
        System.out.println("Only the following fractions are stored exactly...");
        for (int i = 1; i <= 99999; i++) {  //SET SCALE HERE
            String s = "0." + Integer.toString(i);
            BigDecimal exact = new BigDecimal(Double.parseDouble(s));
            if (exact.scale() <= 10)  //MUST BE GREATER THAN SCALE
                set.add(exact);
        }
        Iterator iterator = set.iterator();
        while(iterator.hasNext()) {
            System.out.println((BigDecimal)iterator.next());
        }
    }
}
```

Executing this program prints

```
0.125
0.15625
0.1875
0.21875
0.25
0.28125
0.3125
0.34375
0.375
0.40625
0.4375
0.46875
0.5
0.53125
0.5625
0.59375
0.625
0.65625
0.6875
0.71875
0.75
0.78125
0.8125
0.84375
0.875
0.90625
```

```
0.9375
0.96875
```

As you can see, very few decimal fractions have an exact binary equivalent. The rule is as follows.

Floating-point literals are decimal numbers. Floating-point types approximate the value of floating-point literals. They are not exact because decimal numbers and the floating-point types have incommensurable bases.

That is why `BigDecimal` is discussed in this chapter. If you want exact results, use `BigDecimal`.

I am reluctant to end this section with an example that could make the floating-point types even more difficult to understand, but this code serves a useful purpose in showing that the value stored in a floating-point type is also dependant on the size of the significand:

```java
import java.math.BigDecimal;

class Test {
    public static void main (String[] args) {

        float[] floats = {.1f, .2f, .3f};
        double[] doubles = {.1, .2, .3};
        for(int i=0; i < 3; i++) {
            System.out.println();
            System.out.println(new BigDecimal(floats[i]));
            System.out.println(new BigDecimal(doubles[i]));
        }
    }
}
```

Executing this program prints

```
0.100000001490116119384765625
0.1000000000000000055511151231257827021181583404541015625

0.20000000298023223876953125
0.200000000000000011102230246251565404236316680908203125

0.300000011920928955078125
0.299999999999999988897769753748434595763683319091796875
```

This example is enough to make one characterize the actual value stored in a floating-point type as *wildly unpredictable* (which, of course, is not true). You just have to accept that the values stored in floating-point types are usually approximations of the floating-point literals seen in source code. They are not always exact.

4.4 The `char` Data Type

The `char` data type holds two-byte Unicode character codes in the range of `'\u0000'` (the NULL character) to `'\uFFFF'` (decimal 65535). Normally a `char` is initialized with a character literal such as `'a'`. However, an integer literal can also be used to initialize a `char` if the value is that of a Unicode character code between 0 and 65535. For example,

```
class Test {
    public static void main(String[] args) {
        char abc[] = {97,98,99};
        for (int i=0; i < abc.length; i++)
            System.out.print(abc[i]);
    }
}
```

Executing this program prints `abc`. But if the integer literal is not a Unicode character code, a compiler error is generated. For example,

```
class Test {
    public static void main(String[] args) {
        char c1 = -1;
        char c2 = 65536;
    }
}
```

Attempting to compile this program generates the following compiler errors:

```
Test.java:3: possible loss of precision
found   : int
required: char
        char c1 = -1;
                  ^
Test.java:4: possible loss of precision
found   : int
required: char
        char c2 = 65536;
                  ^
2 errors
```

The value of a `byte`, `short`, or `int` type variable (versus an integer literal) can never be assigned to a `char` without the use of a cast operator.

4.5 The `boolean` Data Type

The `boolean` data type is said to represent a *logic quantity*, and to have one of two possible **truth values**. Those values are the Boolean literals `true` and `false`. The standard default value for a `boolean` type field is `false`.

Wherever Java syntax requires a Boolean expression, a `boolean` type variable can be used. For example,

```
class Test {
    public static void main (String[] args) {
        boolean b = true;
        if (b)
            System.out.println("a variable is an expression");
    }
}
```

Executing this program prints

```
a variable is an expression
```

Bit flags are an alternative to using the `boolean` data type.

4.6 The `null` Type

Because expressions can evaluate to `null`, `null` is sometimes referred to as the **null type**. As stated in the *JLS*:

> There is also a special *null type*, the type of the expression `null`, which has no name. Because the null type has no name, it is impossible to declare a variable of the null type or to cast to the null type. The null reference is the only possible value of an expression of the null type. The null reference can always be cast to any reference type. In practice, the programmer can ignore the null type and just pretend that `null` is merely a special literal that can be of any reference type.[12]

One usually speaks of a *null reference* more so than a *null type*. Any reference type variable can be assigned a `null` reference, resulting in a `null` reference of that type.

---

12. Gosling, et al., §4.1, "The Kinds of Types and Values."

A **null reference** means the variable or other reference type expression currently does not reference an object on the heap. Null references appear in code as one of the following.

1. The `null` literal.
2. An uninitialized field that has a reference type. (The standard default value for all reference types is `null`.)
3. A reference type variable that has been assigned a `null` reference.

The important thing to remember is that the `null` literal is not a type name. Specifically, the `null` literal cannot be used as a type name in variable declarations, in a cast operator, or as the right-hand operand of the `instanceof` operator.

4.7 The `Number` Class

The `Number` class is important because it is the superclass of all the primitive type wrapper classes, `BigInteger`, and `BigDecimal`. All `Number` subclasses are immutable objects.

The idea behind this class is to allow users to convert a `Number` to any of the primitive data types without having to use a cast operator. There are six accessor methods that return the values stored in a `Number` subclass, one for each of the integral and floating-point types. It is important to remember that all `Number` subclasses inherit all six of the methods in Table 4-13. Note that the names of these methods are consistent with the `booleanValue()` and `charValue()` methods in the `Boolean` and `Character` primitive type wrapper classes, respectively.

The documentation comments for these methods include the warning that *this may involve rounding*. That is an understatement if you are going to do something like invoke `byteValue()` on a `long`, `double`, or `BigDecimal` in which a large number is stored. You are expected to know that the method you are invoking is appropriate for the value stored in an instance of one of the `Number` subclasses.

4.8 The `java.math` Package

There are only two `public` classes in the `java.math` package. They are both arbitrary precision numeric data types: one for integers, which is called `BigInteger`, and one for decimal numbers, which is called `Big-`

Table 4-13: `Number` **Class Accessor Methods**

Result Type	Method
byte	byteValue()
short	shortValue()
int	intValue()
long	longValue()
float	floatValue()
double	doubleValue()

`Decimal`. As explained in 4.3.2.1 The Precision of a Floating-Point Type, *arbitrary* in this context basically means unlimited, or *big*. Mainstream business applications do not use `BigInteger` as much as they do `BigDecimal`. The primary use of `BigInteger` is to store the unscaled value of a `BigDecimal`.

4.8.1 The `BigInteger` Class

With few exceptions, instance methods in the `BigInteger` class such as `negate()`, `remainder(BigInteger val)`, `shiftLeft(int n)`, `shiftRight(int n)`, `add(BigInteger val)`, `subtract(BigInteger val)`, `multiply(BigInteger val)`, and `divide(BigInteger val)` behave exactly as do the corresponding primitive type operators. All six of the comparison operators (<, >, <=, >=, ==, and !=) are implemented by means of the `compareTo(BigDecimal val)` method, which is discussed in 4.8.2.3 Comparison Operators for the `BigDecimal` Class. Relevant methods in the `java.lang.Math` class such as `pow(int exponent)` have also been declared in the `BigInteger` class. This covers all of the basic arithmetic operations. Beyond that, there are methods for "modular arithmetic, GCD calculation, primality testing, prime generation, bit manipulation, and a few other miscellaneous operations."[13]

4.8.2 The `BigDecimal` Class

The value of a `BigDecimal` is stored in two fields. One is the **unscaled value**, which is stored in a `BigInteger`. The other is the scale, which is stored in an `int`. The **scale** is the number of digits to the right of the decimal point. For example,

```
import java.math.*;
class Test {
    public static void main (String[] args) {
        BigDecimal value = new BigDecimal("12345.6789");
        int scale = value.scale();
        BigInteger unscaledValue = value.unscaledValue();
        System.out.println("value: " + value);
        System.out.println("scale: " + scale);
        System.out.println("unscaled value: " + unscaledValue);
    }
}
```

Executing this program prints

```
value: 12345.6789
scale: 4
unscaled value: 123456789
```

If you do something like multiply or divide a `BigDecimal` that results in a larger unscaled value, the `BigDecimal` class allocates a larger `BigInteger`. That is how arbitrary precision is implemented in the `BigDecimal` class.

There are four constructors in the `BigDecimal` class. You must be careful about the arguments passed to these constructors:

```
public BigDecimal(String val)
public BigDecimal(double val)
public BigDecimal(BigInteger val)
public BigDecimal(BigInteger unscaledVal, int scale)
```

The `BigDecimal(String val)` constructor is used most of the time. The number is passed as a string. For example,

```
new BigDecimal("100.5")
```

Enhancements to the 1.3 release included the following.

---

13. API docs from the `java.math.BigInteger` class.

The `BigDecimal(String)` constructor has been enhanced to allow signed strings (for example, `"+2.71828"`) and exponential notation (for example, `"1.23E-23"`) as input.[14]

Now any numeric literal written using either standard or scientific notation can be enclosed in parentheses and passed as an argument to a `BigDecimal` constructor.

The `BigDecimal(double val)` constructor is characterized as *unpredictable* in the API docs because of the problem of incommensurable bases.

> The results of this constructor can be somewhat unpredictable. One might assume that new `BigDecimal(.1)` is exactly equal to `.1`, but it is actually equal to `.1000000000000000055511 15123125782702118158340454101562`5. This is so because `.1` cannot be represented exactly as a `double` (or, for that matter, as a binary fraction of any finite length). Thus, the `long` value that is being passed in to the constructor is not exactly equal to `.1`, appearances nonwithstanding [sic].

> The `(String)` constructor, on the other hand, is perfectly predictable: new `BigDecimal(".1")` is *exactly* equal to `.1`, as one would expect. Therefore, it is generally recommended that the `(String)` constructor be used in preference to this one.[15]

I use the `BigDecimal(double val)` constructor in this chapter for that very reason (to show the actual value of a `float` or `double`).

The last two constructors in the above list are unusual. `BigDecimal(BigInteger val)` "translates a `BigInteger` into a `BigDecimal`," and therefore has a scale of zero.[16]

4.8.2.1 The Scale of a `BigDecimal`

There are two important details to understand about the scale of a `BigDecimal`. The first is that any zeroes at the end of the fractional part of a decimal number passed as an argument to a `BigDecimal` constructor are counted in determining the scale. They are not discarded. The second

---

14. Java™ 2 SDK, Standard Edition, Version 1.3, "Summary of New Features and Enhancements."
15. API docs for the `BigDecimal(double val)` constructor in the `java.math.BigDecimal` class.
16. API docs for the `BigDecimal(String val)` constructor in the `java.math.BigDecimal` class.

is that because `BigDecimal` is immutable, invoking one of the instance methods in the `BigDecimal` class usually results in a new `BigDecimal` being created, the scale of which depends on the operation. Table 4-14 is for basic arithmetic operations.

Table 4-14: Scaling the Result of a `BigDecimal` Operation

Method	Scale of the Result
`add(BigDecimal val)`	`max(this.scale(), val.scale())`
`subtract(BigDecimal val)`	`max(this.scale(), val.scale())`
`multiply(BigDecimal val)`	`this.scale() + val.scale()`

`divide(BigDecimal val,`
`        int scale,`
`        int roundingMode)`
	As specified by the `scale` parameter

`divide(BigDecimal val,` `        int roundingMode)`	`this.scale()`

The `multiply(BigDecimal val)` method is the one to notice in this context. Every time you multiply two `BigDecimal` numbers, the scale of the result grows. For example,

```java
import java.math.*;
class Test {
   public static void main (String[] args) {
      BigDecimal amount = new BigDecimal("1.50");      // $1.50
      BigDecimal value;
      value = amount.multiply(new BigDecimal("10"));   //no scale
      print(value);
      value = amount.multiply(new BigDecimal("10.0")); //scale of one
      print(value);
      value = amount.multiply(new BigDecimal(10.0));   //different constructor
      print(value);
   }
   static void print(BigDecimal value) {
       int scale = value.scale();
       System.out.println(value + " has a scale of " + scale);
    }
}
```

Executing this program prints

```
15.00 has a scale of 2
15.000 has a scale of 3
15.00 has a scale of 2
```

You should know the scale of the result before invoking a `BigDecimal` instance method that returns a new `BigDecimal`. Failing that, there is a `FormatUtilities` utility class in 5.16 The Localization of Common Data Types that will allow you to ignore the scale while working with monetary values. (The scale is automatically set to two when the format methods in the utility class are invoked.)

The scale of a `BigDecimal` can be deliberately changed in one of two ways. The first is to invoke one of the following `setScale` methods:

```
public BigDecimal setScale(int scale)
public BigDecimal setScale(int scale, int roundingMode)
```

The first `setScale` method invokes the second one using the `ROUND_UNNECESSARY` rounding mode. An `ArithmeticExeception` is thrown if rounding is necessary. Because these methods round their result when necessary, they are described as *scaling/rounding operations*.

The other way to change the scale of a `BigDecimal` is to invoke the `movePointLeft(int n)` or `movePointRight(int n)` methods. Assuming that the `int` argument is nonnegative, the `movePointLeft(int n)` method adds the `int` argument to the `scale` field without changing the unscaled value. Assuming that the `int` argument is greater than the `scale`, the `movePointRight(int n)` method subtracts the `int` argument from `scale` without changing the unscaled value. These methods are described as *decimal point motion operations*.

4.8.2.2 `BigDecimal` Rounding Modes

`BigDecimal` includes a comprehensive set of eight rounding modes, which are described in Table 4-15.

BigDecimal.ROUND_HALF_EVEN is the same as *IEEE 754 "round to nearest"* (the default rounding mode for the `float` and `double` data types).

ROUND_HALF_UP is the more familiar rounding mode, but ROUND_HALF_EVEN may be a better choice of rounding modes, depending on the application. The difference is whether people are involved or not. For example, in 5.16.1.2 Formatting Currency I strongly recommend using ROUND_HALF_UP because that is what most people expect. When there is no one standing across from the cash register, `ROUND_HALF_EVEN` is the best general-purpose rounding mode and what you should regard as the general-purpose rounding mode, especially because *round to nearest* (the other name for the same rounding mode) is specified as the default rounding mode in *IEEE 754*.

Table 4-16 was populated using variations of the following program:

```
import java.math.BigDecimal;
class Test {
    public static void main(String[] args) {
        BigDecimal d1 = new BigDecimal("1.1");
        BigDecimal d2 = new BigDecimal("1.5");
        BigDecimal d3 = new BigDecimal("1.6");
        BigDecimal d4 = new BigDecimal("1.9");
        BigDecimal d5 = new BigDecimal("-1.1");
        BigDecimal d6 = new BigDecimal("-1.5");
        BigDecimal d7 = new BigDecimal("-1.6");
        BigDecimal d8 = new BigDecimal("-1.9");
        System.out.print(d1.setScale(0, BigDecimal.ROUND_HALF_UP) + "  " +
                         d2.setScale(0, BigDecimal.ROUND_HALF_UP) + "  " +
                         d3.setScale(0, BigDecimal.ROUND_HALF_UP) + "  " +
                         d4.setScale(0, BigDecimal.ROUND_HALF_UP) + "  " +
                         d5.setScale(0, BigDecimal.ROUND_HALF_UP) + "  " +
                         d6.setScale(0, BigDecimal.ROUND_HALF_UP) + "  " +
```

Table 4-15: Rounding Modes in the `BigDecimal` Class

Mode	Description
ROUND_UP	Rounds *away from zero*.
ROUND_DOWN	Rounds *towards zero*, which is what most programmers refer to as *truncation* (that is, not rounding).
ROUND_CEILING	Rounds *towards positive infinity*.
ROUND_FLOOR	Rounds *towards zero*.
ROUND_HALF_UP	This is the rounding mode that most of us were taught in grade school.
ROUND_HALF_DOWN	Same as ROUND_HALF_UP except for five, which rounds down.

Table 4-15: Rounding Modes in the `BigDecimal` Class (Continued)

Mode	Description
ROUND_HALF_EVEN	Same as ROUND_HALF_UP and ROUND_HALF_DOWN except for five. Five is rounded up if the digit to the left of the five is odd. If that digit is even, five is rounded down. The API docs say "this is the rounding mode that minimizes cumulative error when applied repeatedly over a sequence of calculations."[a] This is a different name for the same rounding mode used in the `float` and `double` primitive data types and described in *IEEE 754* as well as the *JLS* as *round to nearest*.
ROUND_UNNECESSARY	Do not round.

a. API docs for the ROUND_HALF_EVEN field in `java.math.BigDecimal`.

Table 4-16: Rounding Mode Examples

Mode	1.1	1.5	1.6	1.9	-1.1	-1.5	-1.6	-1.9
ROUND_UP	2	2	2	2	-2	-2	-2	-2
ROUND_DOWN	1	1	1	1	-1	-1	-1	-1
ROUND_CEILING	2	2	2	2	-1	-1	-1	-1
ROUND_FLOOR	1	1	1	1	-2	-2	-2	-2
ROUND_HALF_UP	1	2	2	2	-1	-2	-2	-2
ROUND_HALF_DOWN	1	1	2	2	-1	-1	-2	-2

```
            d7.setScale(0, BigDecimal.ROUND_HALF_UP) + "  " +
            d8.setScale(0, BigDecimal.ROUND_HALF_UP));
    }
}
```

The `setScale()` method used in this example is one of three methods that can lose precision and therefore requires a rounding mode to be specified.

The ROUND_HALF_EVEN mode is not included in this table because the results would have been the same as ROUND_HALF_UP. The ROUND_HALF_EVEN mode rounds five up "if the digit to the left of the discarded fraction is odd."[17] The digit to the left in all of the examples is one, which is odd. Had `2.5` been used instead, the result of

---

17. API docs for the ROUND_HALF_EVEN field in `java.math.BigDecimal` class.

ROUND_HALF_EVEN would have been the same as ROUND_HALF_DOWN (2 or -2). Notice also that ROUND_UNNECESSARY is not included in the table. If that rounding mode is specified in an operation that actually requires rounding, an ArithmeticException is thrown at run time.

4.8.2.3 Comparison Operators for the *BigDecimal* Class

There are two groups of primitive type operators that comprise the comparison operators. The first is the relational operators `<`, `>`, `<=`, and `>=`. The second group is the equality operators `==` and `!=`. The compareTo(BigDecimal val) method in the BigDecimal class replaces all of them. As explained in the API docs for that method,

> Compares this BigDecimal with the specified BigDecimal. Two BigDecimals that are equal in value but have a different scale (like 2.0 and 2.00) are considered equal by this method. This method is provided in preference to individual methods for each of the six boolean comparison operators (`<`, `==`, `>`, `>=`, `!=`, `<=`). The suggested idiom for performing these comparisons is: (x.compareTo(y) *<op>* 0), where *<op>* is one of the six comparison operators.[18]

This method does not implement the Comparable interface because the parameter type is BigDecimal, not Object. (Using a different parameter type changes the method signature.) It is invoked by the compareTo(Object o) method in the BigDecimal class, but the fact that a second method was declared with a more specific parameter type shows that this method is intended primarily as a replacement for the comparison operators.

The main point of the (x.compareTo(y) *<op>* 0) idiom referred to in the above quotation is that zero should always be used as the right-hand expression. It is important that you understand why. For example,

```
import java.math.BigDecimal;
class Test {
    public static void main (String[] args) {
        print(new BigDecimal("1"), new BigDecimal("99"));
        print(new BigDecimal("99"), new BigDecimal("1"));
        print(new BigDecimal("99"), new BigDecimal("99"));
    }
    static void print(BigDecimal x, BigDecimal y) {
```

---

18. API docs for the compareTo(BigDecimal val) method in the java.math.BigDecimal class.

```
     if (x.compareTo(y) < 0)
        System.out.println(x + " < " + y);
     else if (x.compareTo(y) > 0)
        System.out.println(x + " > " + y);
     else if (x.compareTo(y) == 0)
        System.out.println(x + " == " + y);
     else
        throw new RuntimeException("should never happen");
  }
}
```

Executing this program prints

```
1 < 99
99 > 1
99 == 99
```

The comparison operator used to test the return value always reads as if it were placed between the target object and the argument. In this example the method invocation (x.compareTo(y) < 0) is the same as (x < y) would be when comparing primitive values, (x.compareTo(y) > 0) is the same as (x > y), and (x.compareTo(y) == 0) is the same as (x == y). All of the other comparison operators work the same way when the right-hand operand is zero.

Another good thing about this programmer convention is that you do not have to think about the return value, which is -1, 0, or 1, depending on whether the target object is less than, equal to, or greater than the argument. Note that these are not exactly the same return values as the compareTo(Object o) method in the Comparable interface. That method only specifies returning "a negative integer, zero, or a positive integer as this object is less than, equal to, or greater than the specified object,"[19] whereas the more specific BigDecimal comparison method returns "-1, 0 or 1 as this BigDecimal is numerically less than, equal to, or greater than val."[20]

4.9 Currency Calculations

Historically, programmers have compensated for a loss of precision in the floating-point types in one of three ways:

1. Not using floating-point values in equality expressions.

---

19. API docs for the compareTo(Object o) method in the java.jang.Comparable interface.
20. API docs for the compareTo(BigDecimal val) method in the java.math.BigDecimal class.

2. Rounding the result of floating-point operations.

3. Using integral types to store and process monetary values (for example, $1.50 would be 150 in an `int` or `long`) and then multiplying by 0.01 (or dividing by 100) on output for dollars and cents or the equivalent in other currencies.

Each of these approaches is discussed in order in the following subsections.

4.9.1 Inexact Results and Comparison Operators

As noted in the previous section, there are six comparison operators. Four are the relational operators `<`, `>`, `<=`, and `>=`. The other two are the equality operators `==` and `!=`. That floating-point values should not be used in equality tests can be seen in the following simple program:

```
class Test {
    public static void main (String[] args) {
        float f = 1.2f;
        double d = 1.2;
        if (f == d)
            System.out.println("equal");
        else
            System.out.println("not equal");
    }
}
```

Unless the decimal fraction is one of the relatively few that has an exact binary equivalent (for example, `0.125`, `0.25`, `0.375`, `0.5`, `0.625`, `0.75`, `0.875`, etc.), `"not equal"` always prints. The same thing happens if `float` values are compared to floating-point literals because the latter have a default literal type of `double`. For example,

```
class Test {
    public static void main (String[] args) {
        float f = 1.2f;
        if (f == 1.2)
            System.out.println("equal");
        else
            System.out.println("not equal");
    }
}
```

This program also prints `"not equal"`.

The equality operators are just the most obvious cases, however, because the relational operators suffer from the same problem. For example,

```
import java.math.*;
class Test {
    public static void main (String[] args) {
```

```
double d = 1.2 - .1;
if (d > 1.1)
    System.out.println("greater than");
if (d < 1.1)
    System.out.println("less than");
if (d >= 1.1)
    System.out.println("greater than or equal to");
if (d <= 1.1)
    System.out.println("less than or equal to");
if (d == 1.1)
    System.out.println("equal");
if (d != 1.1)
    System.out.println("not equal");
double a = d;
double b = 1.1;
System.out.println("a = " + new BigDecimal(1.2 - .1));
System.out.println("b = " + new BigDecimal(1.1));
System.out.println(a < b);
    }
}
```

Executing this program prints

```
less than
less than or equal to
not equal
a = 1.0999999999999998667732370449812151491641998291015625
b = 1.100000000000000088817841970012523233890533447265625
true
```

The problem is not the equality tests. The problem is that floating-point types can only approximate the value of floating-point literals that have a decimal fraction other than 0.125, 0.25, 0.375, 0.5, 0.625, 0.75, 0.875, etc. This is the problem of incommensurable bases.

4.9.2 Rounding the Result of a Floating-Point Operation

Another way of dealing with the problem of floating-point types is to round results. For example,

```
class Test {
    public static void main(String[] args) {
        double d = 1.2 - .1;
        double r = ((int)(100*d+0.05))/100.0;
        System.out.println("1.1 = " + r);
        }
}
```

Executing this program prints

```
1.1 = 1.1
```

Less mathematically inclined programmers use the NumberFormat class to round the value of a floating-point type. For example,

```
import java.text.NumberFormat;
class Test {
    public static void main(String[] args) {
        double d = 1.2 - .1;
        NumberFormat format = NumberFormat.getInstance();
        format.setMaximumFractionDigits(2);
        String s = format.format(d);
        d = Double.parseDouble(s);
        System.out.println("1.1 = " + d);
    }
}
```

Using `NumberFormat` to round is an efficiency nightmare. However, both approaches leave much to be desired because you have to continually round the results of floating-point operations.

4.9.3 Using Integral Types to Store Monetary Values

The third and final way of dealing with the problem of floating-point types is to store monetary values in integral types as *the number of pennies* (or the equivalent for other currencies). Hence, `590` in an `int` or `long` would represent $5.90. The following examples use U.S. dollars but are equally applicable to other currencies:

```
class Test {
    public static void main (String[] args) {
        int amount = 150;              //$1.50
        int quantity = 4;
        int tax = 20;                  //5% sales tax
        int coupon = 40;               //.40¢ off
        amount *= quantity;            //four items @ $1.50 each = $6.00
        amount += amount/tax;          //plus tax = $6.30
        amount -= coupon;              //less coupon = $5.90
        double total = amount * 0.01;  //change to dollars and cents
        System.out.println("total = $" + total);
    }
}
```

Executing this program prints

```
total = $5.9
```

The `BigDecimal` class does substantially the same thing in that a `Big-Integer` is used to store the unscaled value. Here is the same program written using `BigDecimal` instead of `int`:

```
import java.math.BigDecimal;
import java.text.NumberFormat;

class Test {
    public static void main (String[] args) {
        BigDecimal amount = new BigDecimal("1.50");
```

```
BigDecimal quantity = new BigDecimal("4");
BigDecimal tax = new BigDecimal(".05");
BigDecimal coupon = new BigDecimal(".40");
amount = amount.multiply(quantity);
amount = amount.add(amount.multiply(tax));
amount = amount.subtract(coupon);
NumberFormat currencyFormatter = NumberFormat.getCurrencyInstance();
String s = currencyFormatter.format(amount);
System.out.println(s);
    }
}
```

Executing this program prints $5.90. Leaving aside the more formal formatting of the output in the second example, the same number of lines of code is used. The two implementations are very similar.

In the 1.3 release the `BigInteger` class was implemented in pure Java. An "Enhancements to `java.math`" document in that release noted the following.

> Class `java.math.BigInteger` has been reimplemented in pure Java programming-language code. Previously, `BigInteger`'s implementation was based on an underlying C library. On a high-quality VM [read *HotSpot*], the new implementation performs all operations faster than the old implementation. The speed-up can be as much as 5x or more, depending on the operation being performed and the length of the operands.[21]

That also affects the speed and efficiency of the `BigDecimal` class because `BigDecimal` is implemented on top of `BigInteger`.

Still, arithmetic operators will always be faster than their corresponding method invocations in the `BigDecimal` class. Hence, it is to be expected that some programmers will continue storing and processing monetary values in an `int` or `long`. This reminds me of one of the truly great articles that occasionally surface in the Java periodicals. "Getting the Numbers Right" was written by Kenneth A. Dickey for the February 1998 issue of *Java Report*. He points out that "Many people consider IEEE floats as 'the wrong answer fast,'" and goes on to say:[22]

I favor using `BigDecimal` for all currency calculations except in the most extreme of circumstances, where everything must be sacrificed at the altar of performance. Java may be the first programming language in

---

21. Java™ 2 SDK, Standard Edition, Version 1.3, "Enhancements to `java.math`."
22. Kenneth A. Dickey, "Getting the Numbers Right, A Cautionary Tale," *Java Report 3*, no. 2 (Feb 1998): 48.

> "As computing power doubles every 18 months, isn't
> it time to take some of this power and make sure we
> get the answers right?"

which using a class such as `BigDecimal` instead of primitive data types becomes the norm for mainstream business application programmers.

That a reference type is used for currency calculations may surprise some programmers. Nevertheless, that is the case. Instead of normal arithmetic operations, a programmer must invoke methods declared in the `BigDecimal` class such as `add(BigDecimal val)`, `subtract(BigDecimal val)`, `multiply(BigDecimal val)`, and `divide(BigDecimal val, int roundingMode)`. If it helps, just think of `BigDecimal` objects as bills and coins.

4.10 Primitive Type Wrapper Classes

Each of the primitive data types has a corresponding **primitive type wrapper class**. A primitive type wrapper class literally *wraps* a primitive type value so that it can be used as an object. For example, the letter `'a'` can be assigned to a primitive `char` data type or it can be wrapped in the `Character` type and used as an object. The primitive type wrapper classes, all of which are discussed in the following subsections, are also storehouses of utility methods (that is, `public static` methods) used when working with primitive values. The names of the primitive type wrapper classes are

```
Byte
Short
Integer
Long
Float
Double
Character
Boolean
```

Notice that, with the exception of the `Integer` and `Character` classes, the name of the primitive type wrapper class is the same as the corresponding primitive data type, only capitalized.

In understanding the term *wrapper class*, taking a look at the source code for one of these classes in the core API is immensely helpful. The following declaration uses a simplified version of the `Character` class to show the basic structure of all primitive type wrapper classes:

```
public final class Character extends Object
    implements java.io.Serializable, Comparable {

    public Character(char value) {
        this.value = value;
    }

    public static final char   MIN_VALUE = '\u0000';
    public static final char   MAX_VALUE = '\uFFFF';
    public static final Class TYPE = Class.getPrimitiveClass("char");

    private char value;

    public char charValue() {
        return value;
    }

    public int compareTo(Character anotherCharacter) {
        return this.value - anotherCharacter.value;
    }

    public int compareTo(Object o) {
        return compareTo((Character)o);
    }

    public int hashCode() {
        return (int)value;
    }

    public boolean equals(Object obj) {
        if ((obj != null) && (obj instanceof Character)) {
            return value == ((Character)obj).charValue();
        }
        return false;
    }

    public String toString() {
        char buf[] = {value};
        return String.valueOf(buf);
    }
}
```

The primitive type `value` field is literally *wrapped* in the `Character` class declaration. All of the primitive type wrapper classes are designed more or less exactly like this.

The numeric type object wrappers include a second constructor for passing numbers as strings. Here is an example of one of those constructors from the `Integer` class:

```
public Integer(String s) throws NumberFormatException {
    this.value = parseInt(s, 10);
}
```

All of these constructors throw `NumberFormatException` and therefore are usually coded in `try` blocks (which makes them harder to use). The `Float` class has a third constructor that allows a `double` argument to be passed without having to use a cast operator.

Notice that the `char` value is stored in a `private` instance variable named `value`. All of the primitive type wrapper classes have a `value` field in which the primitive type value is stored. The `Character(char value)` constructor assigns the `value` parameter to the `value` field. The primitive type wrapper classes are immutable objects, which means the primitive type value cannot be changed once the object is created. There are no mutator methods (that is, no `set` methods) declared in these classes.

All of the primitive type wrapper classes also have a `public` accessor method such as `charValue()` that returns the primitive value. The names of those accessor methods in the other primitive type wrapper classes are

> `byteValue()`
> `shortValue()`
> `intValue()`
> `longValue()`
> `floatValue()`
> `doubleValue()`
> `booleanValue()`

The result types of these methods correspond to the primitive type in their name. For the numeric types, these accessor methods are inherited from the `Number` superclass discussed in 4.7 The `Number` Class.

With the exception of the `Boolean` class, all of the primitive type wrapper classes declare MIN_VALUE and MAX_VALUE constants, which define the range of values that can be assigned not only to that particular primitive type wrapper class but also to the corresponding primitive data type. Instead of MIN_VALUE and MAX_VALUE, the Boolean class includes the following declarations:

```
public static final Boolean TRUE = new Boolean(true);
public static final Boolean FALSE = new Boolean(false);
```

These allow you to test a Boolean object using the equals (object o) method much as you would a boolean type variable. For example,

```
class Test {
   public static void main (String[] args) {
      Boolean wrapper = new Boolean(true);
      if (wrapper.equals(Boolean.TRUE))
         System.out.println("Boolean.FALSE and Boolean.TRUE are like" +
                            "Boolean literals for object wrappers");
   }
}
```

Executing this program prints

```
Boolean.FALSE and Boolean.TRUE are like Boolean literals for object wrappers
```

Remember to use the equals(Object o) method and not reference equality.

In addition to being object wrappers for the primitive data types, these classes are also storehouses of utility methods that programmers can use when working with primitive values. The following subsections discuss all of those utility methods in detail.

4.10.1 Parsing Strings for Primitive Type Values

All of the methods discussed in this section do the same thing, namely, parse strings for numeric values. They differ only in the result type and whether or not a radix specifier can be used in the argument string. One example of parsing a primitive type value passed as a String is the args parameter of the main method, which is an array of strings that corresponds to command-line arguments. Sometimes those command-line arguments are numbers and have to be parsed before they can be stored in a numeric data type.

All of the methods discussed in this section are declared in the primitive type wrapper class that corresponds to the result type. They all throw a NumberFormatException if the String argument passed is not a number. There are five sets of methods to consider:

```
public static byte parseByte(String s)
public static short parseShort(String s)
public static int parseInt(String s)
```

```
public static long parseLong(String s)
public static float parseFloat(String s)
public static double parseDouble(String s)

public static byte parseByte(String s, int radix)
public static short parseShort(String s, int radix)
public static int parseInt(String s, int radix)
public static long parseLong(String s, int radix)

public static Byte valueOf(String s)
public static Short valueOf(String s)
public static Integer valueOf(String s)
public static Long valueOf(String s)
public static Float valueOf(String s)
public static Double valueOf(String s)

public static Byte valueOf(String s, int radix)
public static Short valueOf(String s, int radix)
public static Integer valueOf(String s, int radix)
public static Long valueOf(String s, int radix)

public static Byte decode(String nm)
public static Short decode(String nm)
public static Integer decode(String nm)
public static Long decode(String nm)
```

The second group of methods in bold are the workhorses. Without exception, all of the other methods call these to do the bulk of the actual parsing. I refer to these as the `parse`, `valueOf`, and `decode` methods for now, ignoring the optional `radix` argument for integers. Note that there is also a `valueOf` method in the `Boolean` class. Obviously, this method does not throw a `NumberFormatException`. Invoking the `valueOf` method in the `Boolean` class is exactly the same as using the `Boolean(String s)` constructor. Both are implemented as follows:

```
return ((name != null) && name.toLowerCase().equals("true"))
```

They return `false` for any string other than a case-insensitive `"true"`.

The `parse` and `valueOf` methods differ only in that the former returns a primitive data type and the latter returns an instance of the corresponding primitive type wrapper class. The source code for parsing integers is always found in the two-argument `parse` method. The other method implementations are based on that method, as can be seen in the following examples from the `Integer` class:

```
public static int parseInt(String s) throws NumberFormatException {
    return parseInt(s,10);
}
public static Integer valueOf(String s, int radix) throws NumberFormatException {
    return new Integer(parseInt(s,radix));
}
public static Integer valueOf(String s) throws NumberFormatException {
```

```
        return new Integer(parseInt(s, 10));
    }
```

In the case of the `Float` and `Double` classes, all four methods are based on the `FloatingDecimal.readJavaFormatString(s)` method. (`FloatingDecimal` is a package-private class in the `java.lang` package.) Discussing the method implementations helps to show that the only real difference between the `parse` and `valueOf` methods is the result type.

The string passed to one of the `decode` methods is different from the `parse` and `valueOf` methods in that it can include a radix specifier, as discussed in 1.5.3.2 Positional Notation Systems, Digits, and Radices. The radix specifier, if any, must be `0x`, `0X`, `#`, or `0`. The following code is used to *decode* the radix:

```
int radix = 10;
if (string.startsWith("0x") || string.startsWith("0X")) {
    radix = 16;
} else if (string.startsWith("#", index)) {
    radix = 16;
} else if (string.startsWith("0") && string.length() > 1) {
    radix = 8;
}
```

This code is an oversimplification because it ignores the possibility that the string may begin with a negative sign. Nevertheless, it is instructive. As can be seen, the default radix is `10` if no radix specifier is used. The first argument is the remainder of the string (after the optional negative sign and radix specifier). The second argument is the decoded radix. My reason for explaining this again is to emphasize that the source code for parsing integers is always found in the two-argument `parse` method.

4.10.2 Converting Primitive Numeric Types to Strings

You should not have to instantiate one of the primitive type wrapper classes just to convert a number to a string. Therefore, the primitive type wrapper classes include `toString()` class methods that accept a corresponding primitive type argument. Those methods are

```
public static String toString(byte b)
public static String toString(short s)
public static String toString(int i)
public static String toString(int i, int radix)
public static String toString(long l)
public static String toString(long l, int radix)
public static String toString(float f)
public static String toString(double d)
```

The range of radices that can be passed to one of the two-argument methods is from `Character.MIN_RADIX` to `Character.MAX_RADIX` (which is from 2 to 36). Radices are discussed in 1.5.2.3 Positional Notation Systems, Digits, and Radices. As would be expected, the one-argument `toString(int i)` and `toString(long l)` methods assume that the primitive value is a decimal number.

4.10.2.1 *Converting Integral Types to Hex, Octal, and Binary Strings*

All of the methods discussed in this section are declared in the `Integer` and `Long` classes. There are two sets of methods to consider, one of which accepts `int` type arguments. The three methods with `int` type parameters also work for `byte` and `short` values because of the method invocation conversion context. The other three methods have `long` type parameters:

```
public static String toHexString(int i)
public static String toOctalString(int i)
public static String toBinaryString(int i)

public static String toHexString(long i)
public static String toOctalString(long i)
public static String toBinaryString(long i)
```

There is no real explaination as to why there are two groups of methods, except perhaps as a memory optimization. I checked the implementations in the 1.3 release and there is no performance gain for using `int` type parameters. I think this is a case where built-in method overloading would have made for a better, simpler interface. This is not the natural interface because it forces the client programmer to think about which set of methods to use. As an example of using one of these methods, the `toHexString(int i)` method is invoked as follows in the default implementation of the `toString()` method in the `Object` class:

```
getClass().getName() + '@' + Integer.toHexString(hashCode())
```

The output from one execution of this line of code is

```
java.lang.Object@73d6a5.
```

I have often wished that the `toBinaryString` methods would print the entire bit pattern, including leading zeros. That would make it useful in a classroom setting. The `toHexString` methods have a similar shortcoming if you are using them to print Unicode escape sequences. Neither of those methods include leading zeros in the result because to do so would be to produce a string that could inadvertently be interpreted as an octal literal.

The `toHexString` or `toOctalString` methods do not include a radix specifier (`0x`, `0X`, or `0`) in the result. For example,

```
class Test {
    public static void main (String[] args) {
        int i = (int) (Math.pow(2, 0) +
                       Math.pow(2, 1) +
                       Math.pow(2, 2) +
                       Math.pow(2, 3) +
                       Math.pow(2, 4) +
                       Math.pow(2, 5) +
                       Math.pow(2, 6) +
                       Math.pow(2, 7));
        System.out.println(Integer.toHexString(i).toUpperCase());
        System.out.println(Integer.toOctalString(i));
        System.out.println(Integer.toBinaryString(i));
    }
}
```

Executing this program prints

```
FF
377
11111111
```

Notice that the `toUpperCase()` method is invoked on the return value of `toHexString(int i)`. Lowercase digits are normally returned by the `toHexString` methods.

In all cases either 2^{32} or 2^{64} is added to the result if the argument is negative. Those powers of two represent the sign bit in a four-byte `int` and an eight-byte `long`, respectively. The value 1 in a sign bit means negative. For example,

```
class Test {
    public static void main (String[] args) {

        int i = -1;
        System.out.println(Integer.toHexString(i).toUpperCase());
        System.out.println(Integer.toOctalString(i));
        System.out.println(Integer.toBinaryString(i));
    }
}
```

Executing this program prints

```
FFFFFFFF
37777777777
11111111111111111111111111111111
```

Notice that because the sign bit is set to 1 the entire bit pattern now prints. These are two's complement bit patterns for negative integers, which are not easily understood.

4.10.3 Bit Pattern Manipulation

These methods in the Float and Double classes are also not easily understood unless you already know something about the format of floating-point types. They do not pass numeric values (at least not the numeric values that you might expect). They pass bit patterns from integral types to floating-point types and vice versa. There are two sets of methods to consider:

```
public static native float intBitsToFloat(int bits);
public static native int floatToIntBits(float value);
public static native int floatToRawIntBits(float value);

public static native double longBitsToDouble(long bits);
public static native long doubleToLongBits(double value);
public static native long doubleToRawLongBits(double value);
```

The first set of methods is used to manipulate the four-byte bit patterns of an int or float. The second set of methods is used to manipulate the eight-byte bit patterns of a long or double. The *raw* methods return the actual bit pattern of a NaN instead of either Float.NaN or Double.NaN.

NaN is a constant defined in both the Float and Double classes and is used to represent a range of values, all of which are defined as *Not-a-Number* in *IEEE 754*. That range of values is "collapsed" into Float.NaN or Double.NaN when the floatToIntBits(float value) or doubleToLongBits(double value) methods are invoked. This is not an issue that concerns mainstream business application programmers. It is therefore doubtful that you will ever use the raw methods.

When invoking these methods you must remember that what you are passing is a bit pattern, not a number. A two's complement bit pattern will be interpreted very differently in a floating-point type. For example,

```
class Test {
  public static void main (String[] args) {
    float f1 = Float.intBitsToFloat(256);
    System.out.println(f1);
  }
}
```

Executing this program prints $3.59E-43$, which is a very different number from the two's complement 256 passed.

4.10.4 Accessing Primitive Type System Properties

All of the following methods are declared in the `Integer`, `Long`, and `Boolean` classes. There are three sets of methods to consider:

```
public static Integer getInteger(String nm)
public static Integer getInteger(String nm, int val)
public static Integer getInteger(String nm, Integer val)

public static Long getLong(String nm)
public static Long getLong(String nm, long val)
public static Long getLong(String nm, Long val)

public static boolean getBoolean(String name)
```

System properties are stored as strings. These methods are used to access system properties whose strings represent integers or `Boolean` values.

4.10.5 Unicode Utility Methods

In the current release there are 22 utility methods in the `Character` class (excluding deprecated methods). Table 4-17 is a concise listing of all 22 utility methods in the current version of the `Character` class. Many of these methods are defined in terms of the **Unicode character database**. For example, the case mappings used to implement the `toUpperCase(char ch)` and `toLowerCase(char ch)` methods are part of the Unicode character database, the latest version of which can be found at

www.unicode.org/Public/UNIDATA/UnicodeCharacterDatabase.html

All of these methods are discussed in the following subsections.

4.10.5.1 Case

The utility methods discussed in this section are declared in the `Character` class. They are for working with individual characters and should not be confused with the `toLowerCase()` and `toUpperCase()` methods declared in the `String` class. There are three sets of methods to consider: the first is for lowercase, the second is for uppercase, and the third is for titlecase.

Table 4-17: Unicode Utility Methods in the `Character` Class

Subject	Methods
Case	`public static char toLowerCase(char ch)`
	`public static char toUpperCase(char ch)`
	`public static char toTitleCase(char ch)`
	`public static boolean isLowerCase(char ch)`
	`public static boolean isUpperCase(char ch)`
	`public static boolean isTitleCase(char ch)`
Character types	`public static int getType(char ch)`
	`public static boolean isISOControl(char ch)`
	`public static boolean isLetter(char ch)`
	`public static boolean isDigit(char ch)`
	`public static boolean isLetterOrDigit(char ch)`
	`public static boolean isDefined(char ch)`
	`public static boolean isSpaceChar(char ch)`
	`public static boolean isWhitespace(char ch)`
`char` to digit conversions and vice versa	`public static int digit(char ch, int radix)`
	`public static char forDigit(int digit, int radix)`
Decimal equivalents	`public static int getNumericValue(char ch)`
Identifiers	`public static boolean isUnicodeIdentifierStart(char ch)`
	`public static boolean isUnicodeIdentifierPart(char ch)`
	`public static boolean isJavaIdentifierStart(char ch)`
	`public static boolean isJavaIdentifierPart(char ch)`
	`public static boolean isIdentifierIgnorable(char ch)`

```
public static boolean isLowerCase(char ch)
public static char toLowerCase(char ch)

public static boolean isUpperCase(char ch)
public static char toUpperCase(char ch)

public static boolean isTitleCase(char ch)
public static char toTitleCase(char ch)
```

In all likelihood, a mainstream business application programmer will never use the titlecase methods. The other four methods are based directly on case mappings in the Unicode character database.

In the *Unicode Standard* there are three case forms:

UPPERCASE (a.k.a. *capital letter* or *majuscule*)

Titlecase

lowercase (a.k.a. *small letter* or *minuscule*)

The **titlecase** (spelled as one word, like *lowercase* and *uppercase*) is used when the first character of a word is capitalized, as in the title of a book. This case form is rare. There are only four characters in the whole of the *Unicode Standard* that have the titlecase form. For example,

```
class Test {
    public static void main (String[] args) {
        for (int i=0; i <= Character.MAX_VALUE; i++) {
            char c = (char) i;
            if (Character.isTitleCase(c))
                System.out.println(Integer.toHexString(i).toUpperCase());
        }
    }
}
```

Executing this program prints

```
1C5
1C8
1CB
1F2
```

The first three are Croatian digraphs matching Serbian Cyrillic letters. The last one is Dz, which is the titlecase for the small letter dz or capital DZ in the Latin Extended-B block.

There are only four modern scripts that have case. Those scripts are

- Latin

- Greek

- Cyrillic

- Armenian

The Latin script includes much of the world's population. But for all other languages that are not derived from those scripts, the concept of upper- and lowercase is foreign. Consequently, most letters in the Unicode Standard do not have case. For example,

```
import java.text.NumberFormat;
import java.util.*;
class Test {
    public static void main (String[] args) {
        int letters = 0;
        int noCase = 0;
        float hasCase = 0;  //to facilitate percentage calculations
        int latin = 0;
        Map map = new TreeMap();   // frequency table
        final Integer ONE = new Integer(1);
```

```
/* This must be local class because of the constructor */
class LatinScript extends Character.Subset {
    LatinScript(String name) {
        super(name);
    }
}
/* The Character class is exceptionally well designed. See
   how naturally the interface is used to group a bunch of
   existing Unicode blocks */
final Character.Subset LATIN_SCRIPT = new LatinScript("LATIN_SCRIPT");
for (int i=0; i <= Character.MAX_VALUE; i++) {
    char c = (char) i;
    if (Character.isLetter(c)) {
        letters++;
        if (Character.isUpperCase(c) == false &&
            Character.isTitleCase(c) == false &&
            Character.isLowerCase(c) == false)
            noCase++;
        else {
            hasCase++;
            Character.Subset block = Character.UnicodeBlock.of(c);
            if (block == Character.UnicodeBlock.BASIC_LATIN ||
                block == Character.UnicodeBlock.LATIN_1_SUPPLEMENT ||
                block == Character.UnicodeBlock.LATIN_EXTENDED_A ||
                block == Character.UnicodeBlock.LATIN_EXTENDED_B ||
                block == Character.UnicodeBlock.LATIN_EXTENDED_ADDITIONAL) {
                    latin++;
                    block = LATIN_SCRIPT;
            }
            /* convert to string for lexicographical sort */
            String key = block.toString();
            Integer count = (Integer)map.get(key);
            if (count == null)
                count = ONE;
            else
                count = new Integer(count.intValue() + 1);
            map.put(key, count);
        }
    }
}
NumberFormat percentage = NumberFormat.getPercentInstance();
System.out.println("Only " + (int)hasCase + " or " +
                percentage.format(hasCase/letters) +
               " of the " + letters + " letters in Unicode have case, ");
System.out.println("and of those " + latin + " or " +
                percentage.format(latin/hasCase) +
               " are letters in the Latin script.");
System.out.println();
System.out.println("The breakdown is as follows...");
Iterator iterator = map.entrySet().iterator();
Map.Entry entry = (Map.Entry)iterator.next();
while(iterator.hasNext()) {
    System.out.println(entry.getKey() + "=" + (Integer)entry.getValue());
    entry = (Map.Entry)iterator.next();
}
```

Executing this program prints

```
Only 1506 or 4% of the 36121 letters in Unicode have case,
and of those 631 or 42% are letters in the Latin script.

The breakdown is as follows...
ALPHABETIC_PRESENTATION_FORMS=12
ARMENIAN=77
CYRILLIC=220
GEORGIAN=77
GREEK=97
GREEK_EXTENDED=218
HALFWIDTH_AND_FULLWIDTH_FORMS=52
IPA_EXTENSIONS=89
LATIN_SCRIPT=631
LETTERLIKE_SYMBOLS=32
```

If characters that do not have case are passed to `toLowerCase(char ch)`, `toUpperCase(char ch)`, or `toTitleCase(char ch)` methods, the same character is returned.

4.10.5.2 Character Types

Every `char` value maps to exactly one **character type** (or what the API docs refers to as an *enumerated Unicode general category type*). There are exactly 28 character types in Java. They are type `int` convenience constants, the value of which is returned by the `Character.getType(char ch)` method. For example,

```java
class Test {
    public static void main (String[] args) {
        int count = 0;
        for (int i=0; i < Character.MAX_VALUE; i++) {
            char c = (char) i;
            int charType = Character.getType(c);
            if (charType == Character.LINE_SEPARATOR)
                System.out.println(Integer.toHexString(i).toUpperCase());
        }
    }
}
```

Executing this program prints `2028`, which is the hexadecimal character code for the Unicode line separator character.

The 28 character types in Java are listed in the Table 4-18. As you can see, some character types have related class methods that make it easier to determine if a character is or is not that type. These methods are sometimes used to group character types, as is the case with the `isLetter(char ch)` method. In addition, the `isLetterOrDigit(char ch)` method returns `true` if either the `isLetter(char ch)` or `isDigit(char ch)` methods would return `true` when passed the same character. The `isWhiteSpace(char ch)` method does not directly correspond to character types. That method is discussed in 1.2 White Space.

Character types in Java are largely based on the Unicode character database, which explains character types as follows.

> General Category. This is a useful breakdown into various 'character types' which can be used as a *default categorization* in implementations [emphasis added].[23]

There are minor differences, however, between the general categories in Unicode and character types as used in Java. For example, one of the Unicode character types is `Cc`, which is defined as follows:

```
Cc = Other, Control or Format
```

General categories in Unicode are two-letter codes with the first letter capitalized. The corresponding character types in Java are CONTROL and FORMAT. This deviation from the default categorization in the Unicode Standard makes it easy for Java to implement the `isISOControl(char ch)` method. The important thing to remember about the methods based on character types is that they work the same for all languages. For example, the `isLetter(char ch)` method works the same for European, African, and Asian programmers, as well as for programmers in America.

Table 4-18: Character Types in Java

Convenience Method	==	Character Type
`public static boolean isDefined(char ch)`	`!=`	UNASSIGNED
		UPPERCASE_LETTER
		LOWERCASE_LETTER
`public static boolean isLetter(char ch)`	`==`	TITLECASE_LETTER
		MODIFIER_LETTER
		OTHER_LETTER
		NON_SPACING_MARK

---

23. Ken Whistler et al., *The Unicode Standard, Version 3.0* (Boston: Addison-Wesley, 2000), "Unicode Character Database" on the CD-ROM.

Table 4-18: Character Types in Java (Continued)

Convenience Method	==	Character Type
		ENCLOSING_MARK
		COMBINING_SPACING_MARK
public static boolean isDigit(char ch)	==	DECIMAL_DIGIT_NUMBER
		LETTER_NUMBER
		OTHER_NUMBER
public static boolean isSpaceChar(char ch)	==	SPACE_SEPARATOR
		LINE_SEPARATOR
		PARAGRAPH_SEPARATOR
public static boolean isISOControl(char ch)	==	CONTROL
		FORMAT
		PRIVATE_USE
		SURROGATE
		DASH_PUNCTUATION
		START_PUNCTUATION
		END_PUNCTUATION
		CONNECTOR_PUNCTUATION
		OTHER_PUNCTUATION
		MATH_SYMBOL
		CURRENCY_SYMBOL
		MODIFIER_SYMBOL
		OTHER_SYMBOL

4.10.5.3 *char to Digit Conversions and Vice Versa*

Letters in the English alphabet correspond to digits when used to represent numbers. There are two methods discussed in this section:

```
public static int digit(char ch, int radix)
public static char forDigit(int digit, int radix)
```

They convert `char` values to digits and vice versa. For example,

```
class Test {
    public static void main (String[] args) {
        char character = 'f';
        int digit = 15;
        int radix = 16;
        if (character == Character.forDigit(digit, radix) &&
            digit == Character.digit(character, radix))
            System.out.println("the character " + character +
                                    " is equal to " + digit);
    }
}
```

Executing this program prints

```
the character f is equal to 15
```

Most programmers think only of the letters a to f in this context because of hexadecimal numbers, but the range of valid radices in Java is 2 to 36, which correspond to 0 to 9 plus a to z. For example, the following program prints the English alphabet:

```
class Test {
    public static void main (String[] args) {
        for (int digit = 10; digit < Character.MAX_RADIX; digit++)
            System.out.print(Character.forDigit(digit, Character.MAX_RADIX));
    }
}
```

This is a simple matter of a table lookup. It is just as easy and in some cases more efficient to convert the values yourself.

If a programmer wants to use capital A to Z instead of the lowercase a to z, the `toUpperCase()` method can be invoked on the `forDigit (int digit, int radix)` return value. For example,

```
static String toUnicodeEscape(char ch) {
    String s = "" + Character.forDigit(((ch >>> 12) & 0xF), 16) +
                    Character.forDigit(((ch >>> 8) & 0xF), 16) +
                    Character.forDigit(((ch >>> 4) & 0xF), 16) +
                    Character.forDigit(((ch) & 0xF), 16);
    return "\\u" + s.toUpperCase();
```

This method prints the Unicode escape for a given character.

The `digit(char ch, int radix)` method returns -1 and the `forDigit(int digit, int radix)` method returns the NULL character if either of the arguments are invalid. The numeric value of the character or digit must be greater than or equal to zero and less than the radix, and the radix must be in the range of `Character.MIN_RADIX` and `Character.MAX_RADIX`.

4.10.5.4 *The* `getNumericValue()` *Method*

This method does not return a character code from 0 to 65535.[24] The behavior of this method is described in the API docs as follows.

> Returns the Unicode numeric value of the character as a non-negative integer. If the character does not have a numeric value, then -1 is returned. If the character has a numeric value that cannot be represented as a *nonnegative integer* (for example, a fractional value), then -2 is returned [emphasis added].[25]

The salient point is that the character must have a *numeric value* that can be represented as a nonnegative integer, which excludes fractions and some other Unicode characters that would otherwise be thought of as numeric values.

The phrase *numeric value* is a reference to the actual value of the character, not to the character code. If you want the character code, just assign the `char` value to an `int`. For example,

```
class Test {

    public static void main(String[] args) {

        char ch = 'a';
        int code = (int) ch;
        String escape = toUnicodeEscape(ch);
        int numericValue = Character.getNumericValue(ch);
        System.out.println("The character code for the small letter '" +
                        ch + "' is " +  code + " (or " + escape +
                        "), but the numeric value of '" + ch +
                        "' is " + numericValue + ".");

    }

    static String toUnicodeEscape(char ch) {
        String s = "" + Character.forDigit(((ch >>> 12) & 0xF), 16) +
                        Character.forDigit(((ch >>> 8) & 0xF), 16) +
                        Character.forDigit(((ch >>> 4) & 0xF), 16) +
                        Character.forDigit(((ch) & 0xF), 16);
        return "\\u" + s.toUpperCase();
    }
}
```

Executing this program prints

```
The character code for the small letter 'a' is 97 (or \u0061), but the numeric
value of 'a' is 10.
```

---

24. Hence, Bug ID 4233482, which is *not* a bug.
25. API docs for the `getNumericValue(char ch)` method in the `java.lang.Character` class.

Alternatively, you can invoke the `hashCode()` method in the `Character` class, which also returns the character code as an `int` (at least in Sun implementations).

The numeric value of `'a'` is 10 because `Character.getNumericValue(char ch)` returns the same integer values as `Character.digit(char ch, int radix)` for the letters a to z or A to Z. There are many Unicode characters other than the Arabic numerals and letters in the English alphabet, however, that have numeric values that can be expressed as nonnegative integers. These include digits found in scripts other than Latin as well as many Unicode characters that return `false` when the `isDigit()` method is invoked. Examples of the latter include Roman numerals and circled numbers. For example,

```
class Test {
public static void main(String[] args) {

// Tibetan Digit 7
System.out.println(Character.isDigit('\u0F27'));
System.out.println(Character.getNumericValue('\u0F27'));

    // Roman Numeral XII
    System.out.println(Character.isDigit('\u216B'));
    System.out.println(Character.getNumericValue('\u216B'));

    // Circled 1
    System.out.println(Character.isDigit('\u2460'));
    System.out.println(Character.getNumericValue('\u2460'));
  }
}
```

Executing this program prints

```
true
7
false
12
false
1
```

The `getNumericValue()` method returns `-1` if the `char` does not have a numeric value. If the `char` does have a numeric value but cannot be expressed as a nonnegative integer, `-2` is returned. It is difficult to imagine when you would need this method, but if you did there would be no substitute for it because it requires such a broad knowledge of Unicode characters to implement.

4.10.5.5 *Java Versus Unicode Identifiers*

I deliberately did not discuss these methods in 1.4 Identifiers because I think they are obscure and would only confuse that straightforward discussion of identifiers. Part of the problem is that these methods differentiate between Java and Unicode identifiers. The Java programming language only uses **Java identifiers**. That is why they are called Java identifiers in the first place. The *Unicode Standard* includes a specification for identifiers that is slightly different from Java identifiers. Those are called **Unicode identifiers**. There are three sets of methods to consider. The first is used to determine if a `char` can be used as the first character in an identifier. The second is used to determine if a `char` can be used anywhere else in an identifier other than as the first character. The third "determines if the specified character should be regarded as an ignorable character in a Java or Unicode identifier."[26]

```
public static boolean isJavaIdentifierStart(char ch)
public static boolean isUnicodeIdentifierStart(char ch)

public static boolean isJavaIdentifierPart(char ch)
public static boolean isUnicodeIdentifierPart(char ch)

public static boolean isIdentifierIgnorable(char ch)
```

The only difference between `isJavaIdentifierStart(char ch)` and `isUnicodeIdentifierStart(char ch)` is that only Java identifiers can start with a dollar sign or underscore. The only difference between

Table 4-19: Identifier Ignorable Characters

Ignorable Characters	Description
0x0000 through 0x0008 0x000E through 0x001B 0x007F through 0x009F	ISO control characters that are not white space
0x200C through 0x200F	Join controls
0x200A through 0x200E	Bidirectional controls
0x206A through 0x206F	Format controls
0xFEFF	Zero-width no-break space

---

26. API docs for the `isIdentifierIgnorable(char ch)` method in the `java.jang.Character` class.

`isJavaIdentifierPart(char ch)` and `isUnicodeIdentifi-erPart(char ch)` is that only Java identifiers can include a dollar sign. The `isIdentifierIgnorable(char ch)` is the same for both Java and Unicode identifiers. The **identifier ignorable characters** are listed in Table 4-19. While the `isJavaIdentifierStart(char ch)` and `isJavaIdentifierPart (char ch)` methods are used in a few obscure `com.sun.tools` and `sun.misc` classes, the other three methods are not used at all in either the core API or any of the other packages that ship with the SDK. I believe they are included in the core API as a matter of compliance with the *Unicode Standard*.

4.11 The `Object` Class

The focus in this section is on the five housekeeping methods routinely implemented when declaring a new class of objects. Four of the five housekeeping methods are declared in the `Object` class. A knowledge of how these methods are implemented is the first step towards declaring your own classes.

Before discussing the housekeeping methods, though, it is helpful to have an understanding of the `Object` class. I get a kick out of the following list of names for the `Object` class, particularly the "cosmic" ones:

Base class
Base-of-all-classes
Class from which all other classes are built
Common ancestor class
Cosmic baseclass
Cosmic superclass
Cosmic root class
Generic class
Grand-daddy of all classes
Most general class in the hierarchy
One universal type
Primordial class
Root class
Root class of all classes
Root of the class hierarchy
Root of the total class hierarchy

Standard root class
Supertype of all class and interface types
Top-most class
Ultimate parent
Ultimate ancestor
Ultimate baseclass
Ultimate superclass

If these names were made up it would not be so funny. This list was faithfully compiled over many years from Java books in print. At first the list began as a standard exercise of including alternative terminology from other Java books, but soon I realized that something special was going on here. This particular list just kept growing, far beyond any of the others. Then I realized that, for whatever reason, software engineers and technical writers are given to a kind of hyperbole when trying to come up with a name that reflects the importance of the `Object` class in a single-inheritance, object-oriented programming language such as Java. Ever since then this list has become a hobby. If nothing else, it is an exercise in the need for a standard vocabulary. The *JLS* uses the **primordial class**, though seldom. I prefer to use the `Object` class.

One of the most important concepts for a student of the Java programming language to grasp is that an object in memory is little more than a list of instance variables in which the state of the object is stored. The comparison to records in a legacy system is hard to ignore. The object is the record and the class is the file, if you will, only records all of a sudden can go off and do things on their own. (There was indeed a paradigm shift.)

Conceptually, you begin by listing all of the instance variables in the base class. (As used in this book, *base class* always means a direct subclass of `Object`.) You begin at the base class because `Object` declares no instance variables, and I think it is safe to say that will never change. The `extends` clause used to create a new subclass literally extends the list of instance variables in which the state of an object is stored by adding new ones to the bottom of it. Conceptually, the memory is allocated in contiguous layers, where each layer represents all the instance variables from one of the classes in the hierarchy. As is the case with inheritance hierarchies, superclasses are at top and subclasses at the bottom.

One of the reason for thinking about an object like this is to emphasize that each layer includes *all* of the instance variables declared in that particular class (emphasis on *all*), including `private` or hidden instance variables that are technically not inherited by subclasses. *They are nonetheless still part of the object.* For example,

```
class Test {
    public static void main(String[] args) {
        Subclass subclass = new Subclass();
        subclass.print();
        System.out.println(subclass.s);
        System.out.println(((Superclass)subclass).s);
        subclass.print();
    }
}

class Superclass {
    String s = "superclass";
    private int x = 0;
    void print() {
        System.out.println(x);
    }
}

class Subclass extends Superclass {
    String s = "subclass";
    private double x = Math.PI;
    void print() {
        super.print();
        System.out.println(x);
    }
}
```

Executing this program prints

```
subclass
superclass
0
3.141592653589793
```

Four values are printed using the same `subclass` object. This proves that there are two `String` type instance variables named `s` and two instance variables named `x`. One is type `int` and the other is type `double`.

Figure 4-12 illustrates what a `PC` object might look like in memory. An *object header* is a few bytes of data at the start of each object. Object headers are used by the run-time system for garbage collection, method dispatch, and the like.

The **heap**, also known as the **memory allocation pool**, is a name given to the memory a JVM uses to create objects. The heap is actually managed by the garbage collector, which is another way of saying that memory allocation is an important part of any garbage collection algorithm. All objects are allocated on the heap. The `<init>` instance initial-

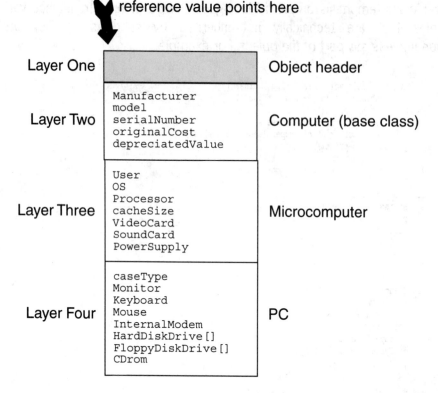

reference value points here

Layer One		Object header
Layer Two	Manufacturer model serialNumber originalCost depreciatedValue	Computer (base class)
Layer Three	User OS Processor cacheSize VideoCard SoundCard PowerSupply	Microcomputer
Layer Four	caseType Monitor Keyboard Mouse InternalModem HardDiskDrive[] FloppyDiskDrive[] CDrom	PC

Figure 4-12: Memory allocation for a PC object.

ization methods are used to initialize objects. They are the first methods invoked after memory is allocated for an object and instance variables are initialized with standard default values. In the body of an `<init>` method, instance variable initializers and instance initialization blocks are executed in textual order followed by code from the corresponding constructor.

If an object is little more than a list of instance variables in memory, and the `Object` class has no instance variables, how is the `Object` class used? The two uses of the `Object` class are

- Untyped references
- Inheritance

The first use of the `Object` class is discussed in 6.4 Untyped References Versus Parameterized Types. The second use of the `Object` class is inheritance.

By *behavior* I mean instance methods. There are 11 instance methods declared in the `Object` class. Nine of them are `public`. The other two are protected.

The nine `public` methods are

```
public int hashCode()
public boolean equals(Object obj)²⁷
public String toString()

public final Class getClass()
public final void notify()
public final void notifyAll()
public final void wait(long timeout) throws InterruptedException
public final void wait(long timeout, int nanos) throws InterruptedException
public final void wait() throws InterruptedException
```

The first three methods in this list are three of the five housekeeping methods mentioned above. The last six are `final` methods that you only need to learn how to use. The two `protected` methods are

```
protected Object clone() throws CloneNotSupportedException
protected void finalize() throws Throwable
```

The `clone()` method is another one of the housekeeping methods. I am undecided as to whether or not `finalize()` is used often enough to make it a housekeeping method. It is tempting to want to cover all of the non-`final` methods declared in the `Object` class, but there is a significant learning curve that comes with a discussion of finalizers, and they are not used as much as they were when the language was new. For now the `finalize()` method is not discussed in this chapter. The fifth housekeeping method is `compareTo()` in the `java.lang.Comparable` interface.

Before discussing the housekeeping methods further in 4.11.3 The Five Housekeeping Methods, it is important to understand the difference between reference equality and an equivalence relationship and how hash tables work. You need to understand how hash tables work in order to know how to implement the `hashCode()` method, which is one of the five housekeeping methods.

---

27. Although `Object` declares `equals(Object obj)`, I always use `equals(Object o)` because that is how the method is declared in the `Comparable` interface. Details!

4.11.1 Reference Equality Versus the Equivalence Relationship

The == operator is referred to as the *reference equality operator* if the operands are reference types (or possibly the null literal). Any use of a reference equality operator is **reference equality**. This is an important term in object-oriented programming. Reference equality means that the references are the same. References are usually pointers (that is, memory addresses). If two references are equal, they both point to the same object on the heap. On the other hand, if the references are not equal they either point to different objects or one of the two reference values is null. For example,

```java
class Test {
    public static void main(String[] args) {
        Car carNo1 = new Car("Cadilac", "Coupe DeVille", 2001, "black");
        Car carNo2 = new Car("Cadilac", "Coupe DeVille", 2001, "black");
        if (carNo1 != carNo2)
            System.out.println("carNo1 != carNo2");
        if (carNo1.equals(carNo2))
            System.out.println("carNo1.equals(carNo2)");
    }
}
class Car {
    String make;
    String model;
    int year;
    String color;
    Car(String make, String model, int year, String color) {
        this.make = make;
        this.model = model;
        this.year = year;
        this.color = color;
    }
    public boolean equals(Object o) {
        if (o == this) return true;
        if (o == null) return false;
        if (o.getClass() != this.getClass())
            return false;
        Car argument = (Car) o;
        if (make.equals(argument.make)    &&
            model.equals(argument.model)  &&
            year == argument.year         &&
            color.equals(argument.color))
                return true;
        return false;
    }
}
```

Executing this program prints

```
carNo1 != carNo2
carNo1.equals(carNo2)
```

It is clear that these two cars are different objects. However, they have the same `make`, `model`, `year`, and `color`. *Most people would say they are the same car,* which is why this implementation of the `equals(Object o)` method returns `true`. It is, simply put, a more common-sense definition of equals. That is the problem with reference equality. It is too narrowly defined. Two objects are equal using reference equality only if they are the same object *in memory.* This is often referred to as testing for *object identity* versus using the `equals(Object o)` method to test for *object equality.*

The `equals(Object o)` method is declared in the `Object` class and therefore is inherited by all other classes. The following is the default implementation of the `equals(Object o)` method in the `Object` class:

```
public boolean equals(Object obj) {
    return (this == obj);
}
```

The default implementation is based on reference equality. A number of classes inherit this default implementation, in effect saying that two objects of that class are not equal unless they are the same object in memory.

Much like compiling the `instanceof` type comparison operator, the compiler checks to make sure that it is at least possible for reference type operands in an equality expression to be equal. If it is not possible, the equality expression will not compile. For example,

```
class Test {
    public static void main(String[] args) {
        String s = null;
        StringBuffer sb = null;
        if (s == sb) //compiler error
            System.out.println("never happen");
    }
}
```

Attempting to compile this program generates the following compiler error:

```
Test.java:5: incomparable types: java.lang.String and java.lang.StringBuffer
        if (s == sb) //compiler error
              ^
    1 error
```

Variables of type `String` and `StringBuffer` could never be equal because those classes are not even related to each other.

As stated in the API docs, the `equals(Object o)` implements an **equivalence relationship** in the Java programming language. For example, if `equals(Object o)` returns `true`, the two objects are regarded as the same element in a collection. The importance of equivalence relationships to collections is discussed in 6.6 The Equivalence Relationship and Elements.

4.11.2 Understanding Hash Tables

In the Java programming language every object has a hash code because of the default implementation of the `hashCode()` method in the `Object` class. This section discusses the importance of hash codes and how they are used. Examples include the use of `java.util.HashMap`, which is somewhat in advance of Chapter 6, which covers the Collections Framework. This is unavoidable if 4.11.3.3 The `hashCode()` Method is to be fully understood.

The importance of hash codes is simple. The only collection faster than a hash table is an array. Arrays are of limited use because they are fixed length. If you want to find something fast in a variable-length (or resizable) collection of objects, there is nothing faster than a hash table. Because of their speed, hash tables are used all of the time. They are used so much that the `hashCode()` method is declared in the `Object` class.

Hash codes are required in order to store and retrieve values from a hash table. Each entry in a hash table has a key and a value. The purpose of the key is to find the value. It is not like the primary keys in a relational database, which are retrieved along with the other columns in a table. In a hash table such as `HashMap` you invoke the `get(Object key)` method, which returns the value. That is, you pass the key and get back the value. Unlike SQL, there is no way to ask for all of the entries that have keys meeting certain criteria and then return the key and value (unless you want to consider submaps as something like an SQL query). In a hash table you always look up a specific key. Because you must know the key in advance, there is no reason to return the key. There is, in fact, no method that returns the key, only the `get(Object key)` method, which returns the value. In short, in order to find something in a hash table, you must either know the key in advance or iterate over all the entries in the table (sort of like a SQL engine would).

A good example of keys and their values is system properties. The keys in the system properties table are strings such as `user.language`. Strings are frequently used as keys in hash tables. They are immutable, which is important when a class of objects is used either as elements in a set or as keys in a map. Table 4-20 shows some examples of system properties. The idea is that, while the value may change, the key remains the same. In a sense, the key is used much like an index value is used in an array. If you know the key, you can go more or less straight to the value.

In the Java programming language the key is always an object. That every object has a hash code means any class of objects can be used as keys in a hash table. What is the relation of the hash code to the key? As discussed in 4.11.3.3 The `hashCode()` Method, the hash algorithms typically written by Java programmers use the numeric value of the same instance variables used in the `equals(Object o)` method to generate a hash code. For example, in the case of `boolean` data types, zero or one is used, a `char` uses the character code, etc. However, hash codes are not the numerical equivalent of their key. This is a common misconception made when first learning how hash tables work. Keys must be unique, whereas the design of hash tables is such that two or more keys can have the same hash code. This is perhaps the most difficult thing to understand about hash tables.

The remainder of this section discusses how hash codes are used, and then a subsection on hash collisions explains in detail what happens when two keys have the same hash code.

Table 4-20: Keys and Values

Key	Value
user.language	en
user.name	Billy Bob Thornton
user.dir	C:\Java\classes
user.region	US
user.timezone	null
user.home	C:\WINDOWS

The result type of the hashCode() method is int, which may be either positive or negative. The int is the **hash code**, which is to say that in the Java programming language hash codes range in value from -2147483648 to 2147483647, some 4,294,967,296 potential hash codes. Both the put(Object key, Object value) and get(Object key) methods in HashMap (as well as the older Hashtable) invoke key.hash-Code() and then use the int value returned to generate an index. Here is the code used to generate the index:

```
hashCode = key.hashCode();
index = (hashCode & 0x7FFFFFFF) % hashTable.length;
```

All hashCode & 0x7FFFFFFF does is to change a negative sign bit to positive, which is why it is okay for hashCode() to return a negative number. In a remainder operation the left-hand operand is the dividend and the right-hand operand is the divisor. It is a mathematical certainty that the remainder is always less than the divisor (in this case, the length of the hash table) and has the same sign as the dividend (which is positive because of hashCode & 0x7FFFFFFF). That is how a hash code is converted into an index in the core API.

4.11.2.1 Hash Collisions

A **hash collision** is when two different objects (as defined by the equivalence relationship) generate the same index. Hash collisions are at the very heart of understanding how hash tables work. There are actually two kinds of collisions and they are entirely unrelated. One is rare. The other is common.

The rare kind of hash collision happens in the hashCode() method. As stated above, there are only 4,294,967,296 potential hash codes in the Java programming language because of the int result type. This is not enough for some sets of keys, such as strings. There are infinitely more strings than there are int values. A well-designed hash algorithm will *evenly distribute* hash codes. Sooner or later, however, any hash algorithm is going to return the same hash code for two different strings. Obviously, different objects with the same hash code are going to generate the same index value. This is rare (unless the hash algorithm is poorly written) but expected in the overall design of hash tables.

The more common hash collision is a result of two different hash codes generating the same index value. If there are fewer int values than there are keys, there are even fewer index values in an average-sized hash table than there are `int` values. For example, the length of the hash table created by the no-argument `HashMap()` or `HashSet()` constructors is 11. Given a ratio of 4,294,967,296 to 11 in converting from possible hash codes to actual indices, there are going to be some hash collisions. That is, the following line of code is going to result in the same index value for different hash codes because of the remainder operator:

```
index = (hashCode & 0x7FFFFFFF) % hashTable.length;
```

Regardless of the kind of hash collision, they always mean the same thing: different keys have the same index value.

You cannot tell just by looking at two hash codes whether they will collide. It does not matter if the difference between two hash codes is one or a million; they can still collide. Nor are hash collisions the result of an *overcrowded* map (though frequent collisions imply an overcrowded map). This kind of hash collision happens because of the size of the hash table. The smaller the table, the fewer the index values, the more likely a hash collision. For example,

```java
import java.util.*;
import java.math.BigInteger;
class HashCollision {

    public static void main(String[] args) {

        //use PRIME NUMBERS to level the playing field
        hashCollisions(11);    //default size of "empty" map
        hashCollisions(prime(100));
        hashCollisions(prime(1000));
        hashCollisions(prime(10000));
        hashCollisions(prime(Character.MAX_VALUE/2));
        hashCollisions(prime(Character.MAX_VALUE));
    }
    static void hashCollisions(int size) {

        Character ch = new Character('A');
        int index = (ch.hashCode() & 0x7FFFFFFF) % size;
        int hashCode = 0;

        int hashCollisions = 0;
        for(int i=0; i<=Character.MAX_VALUE; i++) {
            hashCode = (new Character((char)i)).hashCode();
            if ((hashCode & 0x7FFFFFFF) % size == index)
                hashCollisions++;
        }
        System.out.println("With " + size + " buckets, there are " +
                        hashCollisions + " hash collisions");
    }
    static int prime(int n) {
        BigInteger bigInt;
        int certainty = 50;
```

```
                int i=0;
            while(true) {
                bigInt = new BigInteger(Integer.toString(n+i++));
                if (bigInt.isProbablePrime(certainty)) {
                    return bigInt.intValue();
                }
            }
        }
    }
}
```

Executing this program prints

```
With 11 buckets, there are 5957 hash collisions
With 101 buckets, there are 649 hash collisions
With 1009 buckets, there are 65 hash collisions
With 10007 buckets, there are 7 hash collisions
With 32771 buckets, there are 2 hash collisions
With 65537 buckets, there are 1 hash collisions
```

Each time the `hashCollisions()` method is invoked the number of collisions with an arbitrary hash code (the letter A) is counted. The hash function used is identical to that used in the collections framework. Note that these collisions would occur regardless of the number of entries in the map. In fact, there is no map.

This program uses the hash codes for Unicode characters, which is the same as their character code. So long as the hash table is at least as large as the number of entries, the keys are evenly distributed. *Do not take this to mean that larger is better.* This example forced hash collisions by using table sizes that were deliberately made too small. The core API uses an initial capacity that is approximately twice the number of keys. Beyond that, however, the larger a map is, the more memory is wasted and, more importantly, *the longer it takes to iterate over a collection view of the map.* The initial capacity of a hash table is discussed in 6.9.2 Performance Tuning a General-Purpose Implementation. The consequences of using larger maps in terms of iterator performance is discussed at length in 6.12.2 Using Collection Views to Iterate Over a Map.

Here is an example of hash collisions using a `HashMap` with an initial capacity that is approximately twice the number of keys:

```
import java.util.*;
import java.text.*;
class Test {
    public static void main(String[] args) {
        DecimalFormat indexFormatter = new DecimalFormat("00");

        /*
         * As the output shows, there are 45 system properties.
         * (That number varies from JVM to JVM.) The initial
```

```
 * capacity is set to 97 because that is the first
 * prime number after 90.
 */
 int length = 97;
 HashMap map = new HashMap(length);
 ArrayList list = new ArrayList(length);
 map.putAll((Map) System.getProperties());
 Iterator iterator = map.keySet().iterator();
 int lastIndex = 0;
 while (iterator.hasNext()) {
     String key = (String) iterator.next();
     int index = (key.hashCode() & 0x7FFFFFFF) % length;
     String s = "[" + indexFormatter.format(index) + "] ";
     if (index == lastIndex)
         list.add(s + key + " COLLISION");
     else
         list.add(s + key);
     lastIndex = index;
 }
 iterator = list.iterator();
 while (iterator.hasNext())
     System.out.println(iterator.next());
 }
}
```

Executing this program prints

```
[96] java.awt.graphicsenv
[94] user.timezone
[91] file.encoding
[85] sun.cpu.endian
[85] path.separator COLLISION
[84] line.separator
[83] user.region
[81] java.vm.specification.version
[79] sun.io.unicode.encoding
[77] java.vm.info
[77] java.class.version COLLISION
[74] java.vendor
[74] java.vendor.url COLLISION
[73] java.vm.name
[71] sun.cpu.isalist
[65] file.separator
[65] java.specification.vendor COLLISION
[64] os.name
[61] java.vm.version
[58] java.vendor.url.bug
[58] file.encoding.pkg COLLISION
[49] awt.toolkit
[45] java.runtime.name
[44] java.ext.dirs
[41] user.dir
[39] sun.boot.class.path
[38] java.awt.fonts
[38] java.vm.vendor COLLISION
[35] java.vm.specification.name
[32] java.specification.version
[31] java.io.tmpdir
[30] os.arch
```

```
[29]  java.awt.printerjob
[28]  java.class.path
[20]  java.vm.specification.vendor
[19]  java.runtime.version
[15]  user.name
[12]  java.specification.name
[11]  user.home
[09]  os.version
[07]  java.library.path
[05]  java.version
[05]  user.language COLLISION
[04]  sun.boot.library.path
[01]  java.home
```

The hash collisions in this output are any two or more lines with the same index value in brackets.

How does a hash table solve the problem of hash collisions? That is, how is it possible for different keys to have the same index value? As implemented in the collections framework, a hash table is an array of singly linked lists in which two or more entries with the same index value are linked together. The declaration of a hash table looks like this:

```
private Entry[] table;
```

Entry is an instance of the Map.Entry class, which is not discussed in detail until 6.10.1.3 HashMap and Map.Entry. There are four fields in each Entry:

```
int hashCode;
Object key;
Object value;
Entry next;
```

The next field is used to link entries that have the same index value. This design allows for there to be any number of entries for a given index value. Because there is only a next field (and not a previous field, as in the Node class of a LinkedList), these are singly linked lists. A hash table is an array of singly linked lists. In the terminology of hash tables they are referred to as **buckets**.

The index value is used only to get to the right bucket.
After that, object equality is used to find the right key.

If you look back at the output from the last example you will see that not all the buckets are used, some have only one entry, and others have more than one entry. If there is more than one entry in a bucket the singly linked list used to connect them is sometimes referred to as a **collision list**. There are two collision lists in Figure 4-13.

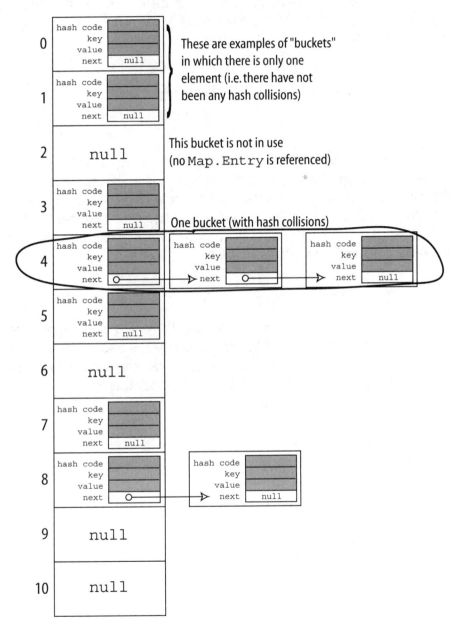

Figure 4-13: Hash tables.

Now that you can see how collision lists are used when more than one key has the same index value, the last piece of the puzzle is understanding how the `get(Object key)` method is implemented. Assuming that the key passed is not `null`, the implementation of the `get(Object key)` method looks like this:

```
int hashCode = key.hashCode();
int index = (hashCode & 0x7FFFFFFF) % hashTable.length;
for (Entry e = hashTable[index]; e != null; e = e.next) {
   if ((e.hashCode == hashCode) && key.equals(e.key))
      return e.value;
}
return null;
```

Notice how the index is used in the *ForInit* part of the `for` loop header, not actually in the loop. The loop control mechanism is assigning the next element in a collision list to `e` until there are no more elements in the collision list. Most of the time, however, the index is all you need because there is no collision list. In other words, there is usually only one element in a bucket and the code executes as follows:

```
Entry e = hashTable[index];
if ((e.hashCode == hashCode) && key.equals(e.key))
   return e.value;
```

Note that most of the time there is only one element in a bucket and the `for` loop exits in the middle of the first iteration. The Boolean expression (`e.hashCode == hashCode`) in the `if` statement is a performance optimization explained in 4.11.3.2.1 Performance Optimizations for the `equals(Object o)` Method.

4.11.3 The Five Housekeeping Methods

The following subsections discuss four methods declared in the `Object` class and one in a standard interface in the `java.lang` package. I refer to these methods as **housekeeping methods** because they are routinely implemented *when creating a new class of objects*. You will want to become expert at implementing the housekeeping methods because these are the methods that everybody must write. Generic implementations of the housekeeping methods should be included in any sort of template you use when coding a reusable object from scratch. The following subsections include examples of generic implementations that can be used for this purpose. You may want to copy these implementations to a template as you read each of the sections on housekeeping methods. When doing so, make sure you understand how to modify the implementation to make it work for a particular class of objects.

Several of the subsections are very heavily indebted to *Java Report* articles written by Dr. Mark Davis, in particular the entire section on the `equals(Object o)` method and the `HashCode` utility class in the section on the `hashCode()` method. These articles are in a class of their own. The following subsections are also heavily indebted to the API docs in that the method contracts for all five housekeeping methods is quoted in full. 4.12.5 The `Comparable` Interface includes an example of all five housekeeping methods in one class.

4.11.3.1 The `toString()` Method

The implicit string conversions in string concatenation operations automatically invoke the `toString()` method that is a member of every class of objects. The general contract for the `toString()` method is

> Returns a string representation of the object. In general, the `toString` method returns a string that "textually represents" this object. The result should be a concise but informative representation that is easy for a person to read. It is recommended that all subclasses override this method.

> The `toString` method for class `Object` returns a string consisting of the name of the class of which the object is an instance, the at-sign character `'@'`, and the unsigned hexadecimal representation of the hash code of the object. In other words, this method returns a string equal to the value of:

```
getClass().getName() + '@' + Integer.toHexString(hashCode())
```

For example,

```
class Test {
    public static void main(String[] args) {
        Object o = new Object();
        System.out.println(o);
    }
}
```

Executing this program prints something like `java.lang.Object@73d6a5`. Of course, the hash code will be different every time the program is executed. This is not very meaningful, which is why the default implementation of the `toString()` method in the `Object` class is usually overridden. Here is an example from the `Thread` class:

```
Thread[main,5,main]
```

This is a string representation of the main thread in an application program. The first `main` in the brackets is the name of the thread, which is followed by the thread priority. The second `main` is the name of the thread group to which the `main` thread belongs. The programmer is showing the state of the thread by printing the value of some of the instance variables. This is what all `toString()` methods do: print the value of some or all of the instance variables in which the state of an object is stored. This information is primarily used by client programmers for debugging purposes. It's just a question of how creative you want to be in printing the state of an object.

Either a string concatenation operation or a `StringBuffer` can be used to implement the `toString()` method. Here is an example using a string concatenation operation:

```java
if (getThreadGroup() != null) {
    return "Thread[" + getName() + "," + getPriority() + "," +
            getThreadGroup().getName() + "]";
} else {
    return "Thread[" + getName() + "," + getPriority() + "," +
            "" + "]";
}
```

This is the `toString()` method in the `Thread` class. Here is an example using a `StringBuffer`:

```java
public String toString() {
    int max = size() - 1;
    StringBuffer buffer = new StringBuffer();
    Iterator iterator = entrySet().iterator();
    buffer.append("{");
    for (int i = 0; i <= max; i++) {
        Entry e = (Entry)(iterator.next());
        buffer.append(e.getKey() + "=" + e.getValue());
        if (i < max)
            buffer.append(", ");
    }
    buffer.append("}");
    return buffer.toString();
}
```

This example is from the Collections Framework. It really does not matter how you implement this method because `toString()` methods are primarily used for debugging.

Should line separators be used to format the output of a `toString()` method? There is nothing in the method contract that precludes the use of line separators in a `toString()` method implementation. For example,

```
public String toString() {
    String newLine = System.getProperty("line.separator");
    return "State of SomeClass Object" + newLine +
        "-------------------------" + newLine +
            "instanceVariable1 = " + instanceVariable1 + newLine +
            "instanceVariable2 = " + instanceVariable2 + newLine +
            "instanceVariable3 = " + instanceVariable3 + newLine;
        ...
}
```

I have never seen this done in the core API. Is there a de facto standard that the string returned by the `toString()` method should not include embedded line separators? I think the answer is *Yes*. There is a reasonable expectation that the string returned by the `toString()` method does not include any embedded line separators. You should use commas or any of the other separator characters listed in Table 1-12 to separate the output values (as does the `Thread` class), but not line separators.

When implementing `toString()` be careful not to use the `this` keyword by itself as an argument in a string concatenation operation or an `append` method invocation. Doing so causes `this.toString()` to be invoked, which results in infinite recursion. For example,

```
class Test {
    public static void main(String[] args) {
        Widget widget = new Widget();
        System.out.println(widget);
    }
}
class Widget {
    String s = "Widget";
    private int x = 0;
    public String toString() {
        return s + ": " + this + x;
    }
}
```

This program compiles but when executed throws a `StackOverflow-Error`.

4.11.3.2 The `equals(Object o)` Method

The implementation of the `equals(Object o)` method is critical for a number of reasons, the most important of which is collections. Dr. Davis says: "In general, if a class does not override equals, its implementation is just plain wrong."[28] I think that is an overstatement, but you might what to check to make sure a class is overriding the `equals(Object o)` method. If not, ask yourself if reference equality is what you expect.

What follows is the entire contract for `equals(Object o)` from the API docs for the `Object` class.

> It indicates whether some other object is *equal to* this one.
>
> It implements an equivalence relation.
>
> - It is *reflexive*: for any reference value x, `x.equals(x)` should return `true`
> - It is *symmetric*: for any reference values x and y, `x.equals(y)` should return `true` if and only if `y.equals(x)` returns `true`
> - It is *transitive*: for any reference values x, y, and z, if `x.equals(y)` returns `true` and `y.equals(z)` returns `true`, then `x.equals(z)` should return `true`
> - It is *consistent*: for any reference values x and y, multiple invocations of `x.equals(y)` consistently return `true` or consistently return `false`, provided no information used in equals comparisons on the object is modified
> - For any non-null reference value x, `x.equals(null)` should return `false`
>
> The `equals` method for class `Object` implements the most discriminating possible equivalence relation on objects; that is, for any reference values x and y, this method returns `true` if and only if x and y refer to the same object ($x==y$ has the value `true`)[29]

Equivalence relationship is a purely mathematical term. A carefully thought-out, systematic approach to the implementation of this method is required.

In order to simplify this discussion I have created the following four subsections:

4.11.3.2.1   Performance Optimizations for the `equals (Object o)` Method

4.11.3.2.2   Comparing Classes in an `equals(Object o)` Method

4.11.3.2.3   Chaining `equals(Object o)` Method Invocations

4.11.3.2.4   Comparing Instance Variables for Equality

---

28. Mark Davis, "Liberté, equalité, fraternité," *Java Report* 5, no. 1 (Jan. 2000): 47.
29. API docs for the `equals(Object o)` method in the `java.lang.Object` class.

The order of these subsections is like four steps in coding an equals(Object o) method. The purpose of the performance optimizations is to obviate the need for the other three steps.

4.11.3.2.1 Performance Optimizations for the `equals(Object o)` Method

There are two standard performance optimizations when implementing the equals(Object o) method. The first is a **reference equality optimization**. The two objects are compared using the following line of code:

```
if (o == this) return true;
```

This is usually the first line of code in an equals(Object o) method implementation.

The second performance optimization is called the **cached hash code optimization**. The cached hash code optimization is used in the following line of code from the get(Object key) method in the Hash-Map class:

```
if ((e.hashCode == hashCode) && key.equals(e.key))
```

When the get(Object key) method is invoked, this line of code is executed for every entry in a map until the key is found (or there are no more entries). Invoking the equals(Object o) method is relatively slow compared to using the == operator. A conditional-and operator is used because

---

If the hashCode() and equals(Object o)
methods are properly implemented, two objects cannot be equal if they have different hash codes.

How is that a performance optimization? Other than when the key you are searching for is found, the only other time the right-hand operand in the above line of code is evaluated is in the case of hash collisions.

The same optimization can be used in the equals(Object o) method in classes that cache their hash code:

```
if (!hashCodeCached) {
    hashCode = hashCode();
    hashCodeCached = true;
}
if (hashCode != argument.hashCode)
    return false;
```

The explanation is the same: if the `hashCode()` and `equals(Object o)` methods are properly implemented, two objects cannot be equal if they have different hash codes. Thus, you can return `false` without having to compare instance variables for equality. The problem with this performance optimization is that the hash code for immutable objects must be recomputed if the value of any of the instance variables used in the `equals(Object o)` method changes. Immutable objects do not have that problem.

4.11.3.2.2 Comparing Classes in an `equals(Object o)` Method

This is one subject about which there is appreciable subtlety. I think Dr. Davis deserves a lot of credit for pointing out the problem with using the `instanceof` operator in the `equals(Object o)` method for extensible classes. It is a serious problem, and one that I believe many Java programmers are completely unaware of. The `instanceof` operator is used all the time in `equals(Object o)` method implementations. That is not a problem in `final` classes. In an extensible classes, however, use of the `instanceof` operator in your `equals(Object o)` method could lead to program failures elsewhere in the system. While I have heard no reports of this happening, the problem is real enough that there needs to be a new programmer convention for implementing the `equals(Object o)` method, one based on the suggestions made by Dr. Davis in an article entitled "Liberté, equalité, fraternité" in the January 2000 issue of *Java Report*.[30] Here is how the `instanceof` operator is typically used in an `equals(Object o)` method implementation:

```
if (!(o instanceof Widget))
    return false;
Widget argument = (Widget)o;
```

The remainder of this section discusses how these three lines of code can lead to program failures in extensible classes.

There is no requirement in the `equals(Object o)` method contract for two objects to be the same class. On the contrary, the API docs strongly recommends that natural ordering be consistent with equals and then goes on to say "all elements in [a] list must be *mutually comparable*," implying that those elements may in fact have different class types.[31] For

---

30. Mark Davis, "Liberté, equalité, fraternité," *Java Report*, Vol. 5, No. 1 (Jan. 2000): 47.
31. API docs for the `sort(List list)` method in the `java.util.Collections` class.

example, the Number class could have implemented an equals(Object o) method that made it possible for a Byte and BigDecimal to be equal. Such *mutually comparable* classes, however, are rare.

It is important to point out that there is no such requirement in the API docs for the equals(Object o) method. Nevertheless, most classes of objects can only be equal to other instances of the same class, which means that the following two lines of code are what they appear to be, namely, a performance optimization:

```
if (!(o instanceof Widget))
    return false;
```

The intent of the programmer 99.9% of the time is to say that the class of the object being compared must be the same as this class. That is not, however, what this code says. It says the object being compared must be *an instance of* this class, which includes subclasses.

The problem is that subclasses do not return false. That is a direct violation of the equals(Object o) method contract from above, specifically the requirement for symmetry, which states that "for any reference values x and y, x.equals(y) should return true if and only if y.equals(x) returns true."[32] For example,

```
import java.util.*;
class Test {
    public static void main(String[] args) {
        X x = new X(0);
        Y y = new Y(0,0);
        System.out.println(x.equals(y));
        System.out.println(y.equals(x));
    }
}
class X {
    int a;
    X(int a) {
        this.a = a;
    }
    public boolean equals(Object o) {
        if (o == this) return true;
        if (!(o instanceof X))
            return false;
        X argument = (X)o;
        if (this.a == argument.a)
            return true;
        return false;
    }
}
```

---

32. API docs for the equals(Object o) method in the java.lang.Object class.

```
final class Y extends X {
    int a;
    int b;
    Y(int a, int b) {
        super(a);
        this.b = b;
    }
    public boolean equals(Object o) {
        if (o == this) return true;
        if (!(o instanceof Y))
            return false; //test fails here
        Y argument = (Y)o;
        if ((this.a == argument.a) &&
            (this.b == argument.b))
            return true;
        return false;
    }
}
```

Executing this program prints

```
true
false
```

This is clearly a violation of the method contract. Depending on how a client programmer invokes the `equals(Object o)` method, x may or may not equal y. And that can lead to program failures elsewhere in the system.

What is the solution? A class literal could be used to test for a specific class. For example,

```
if (o.getClass() != Widget.class)
    return false;
```

The problem with this solution is that it does not work if the `equals(Object o)` method is inherited by subclasses. A better solution is the one recommended by Dr. Davis:

```
if (o == null) return false;
if (o.getClass() != this.getClass())
    return false;
```

The test for `null` is not necessary when using the `instanceof` operator, but it is when coding like this to avoid a `NullPointerException`. This solution to the problem of the `instanceof` operator becomes a minor performance optimization when `equals(Object o)` method invocations are chained together, requiring only a single type check where poorly implemented class hierarchies might repeatedly type check the same object using the `instanceof` operator. More on this in the following subsection.

4.11.3.2.3 Chaining `equals(Object o)` *Method Invocations*

Implementations of the `equals(Object o)` method should be chained together, much like constructors or `finalize()` methods. Doing so requires the following line of code:

```
if (!super.equals(o)) return false;
```

The following is a modification of the `equals(Object o)` method in the `Y` class from the example in the previous section:

```
public boolean equals(Object o) {
    if (o == this) return true;
    if (!super.equals(o))
        return false;
    Y argument = (Y)o;
    if (this.b != argument.b) return false;
    return true;
}
```

This may look trivial in such a small example, but in more sophisticated classes attempting to compare instance variables declared in a superclass is problematic. First there is the problem of read access. The `private` instance variables declared in superclasses cannot be directly compared. Access methods must be used instead. The trouble starts when there is no access method for `private` superclass instance variables. Even if you do have access to all of the superclass instance variables, a change such as adding a new instance variable to one of the superclasses would require a corresponding change in the `equals(Object o)` method of every subclass. These kinds of manual update dependencies are never good in software design.

Each class should be responsible for comparing only those instance variables declared in that class.

It is important to realize that `o.getClass() != this.getClass()` is comparing the class of the argument against the class of the current object. That same line of code placed in the `equals(Object o)` method of a base class (that is, a direct subclass of `Object`) will work for all subclasses. Hence, there are two fundamentally different implementations of the `equals(Object o)` method. One is for base classes, which includes the following preliminary equality checks:

```
if (o == this) return true;
if (o == null) return false;
if (o.getClass() != this.getClass())
    return false;
```

The other is for subclasses, which includes the following preliminary equality checks:

```
if (o == this) return true;
if (!super.equals(o))
    return false;
```

Only after invoking the superclass `equals(Object o)` method should the argument be cast to the type of the current object. You can remember that if you regard the type conversion as the first step in comparing instance variables.

4.11.3.2.4 Comparing Instance Variables for Equality If you want to compare all of the instance variables in a class for equality, a *Java Report* article written by Scott Oaks includes the following use of reflection to avoid always having to update the `equals(Object o)` method when an instance variable is added to or removed from a class:[33]

```
Class c = getClass();
try {
    Field[] fields = c.getDeclaredFields();
    for(int i=0; i < fields.length; i++) {
        Field f = fields[i];
        Object o1 = f.get(this);    //automatically wraps primitive values
        Object o2 = f.get(o);       //automatically wraps primitive values
        if (!o1.equals(o2))
            return false;
    }
} catch(Exception e) { return false; }
return true;
```

This example is not the same as the one in the article. It has been modified to work with the `equals(Object o)` method implementation discussed in the previous example where subclasses invoke their superclass `equals(Object o)` method using the following two lines of code:

```
if (!super.equals(o))
    return false;
```

---

33. Scott Oaks, "Using the REfletion API", Java Report, Vol. 4, No. 10, Oct. 1999, p. 80.

In other words, this modified example only compares the instance variables declared in the current class, not instance variables that are inherited from superclasses. This is why the `getDeclaredFields()` method is invoked instead of the `getFields()` method, which returns superclass fields as well. Again, each class should be responsible for comparing their own instance variables.

This code works for both primitive and reference type instance variables because the `get(Object obj)` method in the `java.lang.reflect.Field` class automatically wraps primitive type fields. The only checked exception thrown by this code is `Illegal-AccessException`, which is thrown by the `get(Object obj)` method if `obj` is not an instance of the same class as the reflected field. That should never happen if the `equals(Object o)` method is implemented as suggested in the previous section. If it does happen, however, the correct thing to do is return `false`.

The problem with the use of reflection is that deciding which instance variables to compare for equality is at the heart of an `equals(Object o)` method implementation. No one can tell you how to do this. You must think about the class of objects and what it means for two such objects to be the same. For example, suppose the `Car` class in 4.11.1 Reference Equality Versus the Equivalence Relationship had a `price` field. Should that be compared? No! Two cars are the same regardless of the price paid. There are no shortcuts here. Only the responsible programmer can decide which instance variables to compare.

To some extent these decisions are a matter of common sense. Just ask yourself: What are people thinking of when they say two of these objects are the same? What makes two toasters the same? Two horses? Two invoices? As in the example of a car, the answer has more to do with the perception of the average person than it does computer programming. Two cars are the same if they are the same `make`, `model`, `year`, and `color`. Another `Car` class may ignore all of those fields and use only the serial number. It depends on how the class is being used. About the only rule that is available when deciding which fields to use in the `equals(Object o)` method is that cached information such as `transient` fields should not be compared.

There are several rules to observe when comparing instance variables.

- Use == with primitive type fields and `equals(Object o)` with reference types
- Fields that can be `null` require special code. You want to make sure the instance variable is not `null` before invoking the `equals(Object o)` method. If it is `null`, then you want to compare for `null` in the other field. For example,

```
if (instanceVariable == null {
    if (o.instanceVariable != null)
        return false;
} else {
    if (!instanceVariable.equals(o.instanceVariable))
        return false;
}
```

- When comparing arrays, always use the fully overloaded `equals` methods in the `Arrays` utility class. Otherwise, what you get is reference equality. Likewise, always be aware that some classes may not implement `equals(Object o)` correctly. You have to work around this on a case by case basis

Here is an example of the last point:

```
import java.util.Arrays;
class Test {
    public static void main(String[] args) {
        char[] a1 = {'a', 'b', 'c'};
        char[] a2 = {'a', 'b', 'c'};
        System.out.println(a1.equals(a2));
        System.out.println(Arrays.equals(a1, a2));
    }
}
```

Executing this program prints

```
false
true
```

4.11.3.3 The `hashCode()` Method

When you implement the `hashCode()` method you are actually implementing a simple hash algorithm. It is nothing like the complex hash algorithms you read about in research papers, but it is nonetheless a hash algorithm. Hashing takes an object and uses it to generate a hash code, which in the Java programming language is an `int`.

Here is the complete interface contract for the `hashCode()` method from the API docs for the `Object` class.

Returns a hash code value for the object. This method is supported for the benefit of hashtables such as those provided by `java.util.Hashtable`.

The general contract of `hashCode` is:

- Whenever it is invoked on the same object more than once during an execution of a Java application, the `hashCode` method must consistently return the same integer, provided no information used in `equals` comparisons on the object is modified. This integer need not remain consistent from one execution of an application to another execution of the same application.
- If two objects are equal according to the `equals(Object)` method, then calling the `hashCode` method on each of the two objects must produce the same integer result.
- It is *not* required that if two objects are unequal according to the `equals(java.lang.Object)` method, then calling the `hashCode` method on each of the two objects must produce distinct integer results. However, the programmer should be aware that producing distinct integer results for unequal objects may improve the performance of hashtables.

As much as is reasonably practical, the `hashCode` method defined by class `Object` does return distinct integers for distinct objects. (This is typically implemented by converting the internal address of the object into an integer, but this implementation technique is not required by the Java™ programming language.)[34]

The main question when implementing the `hashCode()` method is which instance variables to use in computing the hash code. That depends on the `equals(Object o)` method.

> The set of instance variables used to generate a hash code must be the same set of instance variables used in the `equals(Object o)` method when comparing two objects for equality, or a subset thereof.

This is what is meant by "equal objects must have equal hash codes," which is usually expressed as follows.

---

34. API docs for the `hashCode(Object o)` method in the `java.lang.Object` class.

If `x.equals(y)`, then `x.hashCode() == y.hashCode()` must be true.

This will always be true if the set of instance variables used in the `hashCode()` method is the same set used in the `equals(Object o)` method, or a subset thereof. As discussed in 4.11.3.3.1 Performance Optimizations for The `hashCode()` Method, there is no requirement to use all of those instance variables when generating a hash code. The `hashCode()` method may only *sample* a small percentage of the instance variables used in the `equals(Object o)` method. More on that subject momentarily.

Is "equal objects must have equal hash codes" true for the default implementations of the `equals(Object o)` and `hashCode()` methods in the `Object` class? Here is the source code:

```
public boolean equals(Object obj) {
    return (this == obj);
}
public native int hashCode();
```

Although it is not so obvious, the answer is *Yes* because, as stated in the API docs for the `hashCode()` method,

> As much as is reasonably practical, the `hashCode` method defined by class `Object` does return distinct integers for distinct objects. (This is typically implemented by converting the internal address of the object into an integer, but this implementation technique is not required by the Java™ programming language.

That the same set of instance variables compared in the `equals(Object o)` method must be used to generate the hash code is fundamental to the design of the language and explains why classes that override the `equals(Object o)` methods should override the `hashCode()` method too.

If you do not override these methods, but want to make sure that subclasses do not violate "equal objects must have equal hash codes," you can provide overriding implementations that do little more than add the `final` keyword to the housekeeping method declarations. Here is an example from the `Character.Subset` class:

```
/**
 * Compares two Subset objects for equality.  This method returns
 * true if and only if x and y refer to the same object, and because
 * it is final it guarantees this for all subclasses.
```

```
 */
public final boolean equals(Object obj) {
    return (this == obj);
}

/**
 * Returns the standard hash code as defined by the hashCode method.
 * This method is final in order to ensure that the equals and hashCode
 * methods will be consistent in all subclasses.
 */
public final int hashCode() {
    return super.hashCode();
}
```

Note that these are essentially the same as the default implementations they override. The only real difference is that they are now `final` methods.

4.11.3.3.1 Performance Optimizations for The `hashCode()` Method

There is a premium placed on the performance of the `hashCode()` method because it is automatically invoked all the time when accessing hash-based containers. The precise reason for maximizing the performance of the `hashCode()` method is that it directly contributes to the constant time of every container operation that accesses a hash-based container. In simple English, mess this up and your mistake will be magnified many thousands of times over, perhaps millions, billions, or even trillions of times over for well used classes that have a long shelf life. For example, `HashMap` and `HashSet` invoke the `hashCode()` method every time an element is added, removed, or just accessed. The importance of an efficient `hashCode()` implementation cannot be overstated.

There are two performance optimizations for the `hashCode()` method:

- Caching the hash code
- Sampling optimization

Caching the hash code is not the same as the cached hash code optimization discussed in 4.11.3.2.1 Performance Optimizations for the `equals(Object o)` Method. They are, however, closely related. Any class that does one is likely to do the other, in which case the same cached hash code would be used.

Here is an example of caching the hash code:

```
if (!hashCodeCached) {

    ... generate hash code here ...
```

```
    hashCodeCached = true;
}
    return hashCode;
```

In an immutable class the hash code only needs to be computed once. In an immutable class that may have to recompute the hash code from time to time, hashCodeCached would have to be set to false immediately before changing the value of one of the instance variables used in the implementation of the equals(Object o) method.

Sampling is the single most important performance optimization for the hashCode() method, one that is infinitely more important than tweaking the simple hash algorithms Java programmers write when implementing the hashCode() method. I do not think it is possible to overemphasize the relative importance of thoughtfully selecting which of the instance variables in the equals(Object o) method you will use when hashing the same objects. Never assume you should use all of them.

> There is no rule in writing a hash algorithm that says
> you must hash all of the instance variables used in the
> corresponding equals(Object o) method. A sub-
> set will do just fine.

Let us call this the **sampling optimization**. Sampling large containers (which include arrays as well as the container classes in the java.util package) is not really an option. Otherwise you are penny wise and pound foolish (minimizing hash collisions at the cost of an increased constant time for all operations that access hash-based containers).

Notice this says *large* containers. Sampling small containers can be problematic, especially if the container is the only thing being hashed. There was an example of this in the early implementations of the equals(Object o) method. The String class used to sample the array in which the Unicode characters are stored (that is, the character buffer) for strings longer than 15 characters. The programmer obviously was allowing for the possibility that some strings may be very large. However, the decision to sample unexpectedly backfired. A number of bug reports were filed, stating that the incidence of hash collisions in the String class was too high. I recall one bug report in which the only difference in a bunch of absolute URL was the rightmost directory or file name. The `String` class was returning the same hash code for practically all of them, resulting in unacceptable performance when accessing those elements in hash-based containers. The `String` class no longer samples. That is a lesson we can all learn from.

The `HashCode` class includes the following methods for sampling arrays:

```
public void add(byte[] a, int samplingRate)
public void add(short[] a, int samplingRate)
public void add(char[] a, int samplingRate)
public void add(int[] a, int samplingRate)
public void add(long[] a, int samplingRate)
public void add(float[] a, int samplingRate)
public void add(double[] a, int samplingRate)
public void add(Object[] a, int samplingRate)
```

You can specify any sampling rate from one to `Integer.MAX_VALUE`. To sample one out of every three elements in an array, invoke the following:

```
HashCode hashCode = new HashCode();
hashCode.add(array, 3)
```

Sampling large arrays and other containers is a *quantitative* sampling. Equally important is a *qualitative* sampling in which you intelligently choose which subset of instance variables to sample.

Some instance variables make for better hash codes. For example, think about generating a hash code for a person. Two of the instance variables used in the `equals(Object o)` method are `sex` and `birthDate`. If you had to chose only one of those two instance variables to generate a hash code, which do you think is better? The answer is `birthDate`. An instance variable such as `sex` is close to useless in generating hash codes that are evenly distributed. Why? Because `sex` only has two values, male and female. Two in, Two out. The most hash codes you could ever generate using the `sex` field is two. The goal of sampling is to use the smallest selection of fields that have the greatest diversity of values. The ideal is something like `serialNumber`, which distinquishes one object from all of the other objects in the same class and therefore can be returned as the hash code. In that case, there really is no hash algorithm. The unique (or almost unique) value returned is best thought of as an *arbitrary index value for that element* that the Collections Framework knows how to convert to an actual index value once the size of the hash-based container is known.

It is important to realize that the sampling optimization includes the decision to invoke `super.hashCode()` in a class hierarchy.

Knowing how to sample, more so than tweaking hash algorithms, is where application programmers should focus their attention. You can do more towards generating evenly distributed hash codes by intelligently selecting which fields to hash in the first place than you can by a hundred tweakings of the actual hash algorithm. Seriously! Be careful selecting which fields to use. Some instance variables may have the potential for a great diversity of values when in fact the actual values are bunched together.

> Always remember, hash codes do not have to be perfect. Equal hash codes mean the two objects are very likely the same, but only the `equals(Object o)` method can say that for sure.

Your goal is to intelligently select which instance variables to hash without a noticeable increase in hash collisions. Hash too many instance variables and not only is your `hashCode()` method is slow but so are all container operations that access hash-based containers; too few and there are hash collisions, which means more traversing of collision lists. Either way the performance of the container classes in the `java.util` package suffers. Modifications of the second program in 4.11.2.1 Hash Collisions can be used to test your assumptions about hash tables. In particular it can be used to see if any adjustments you make to the implementation of the `hashCode()` method results in more or fewer hash collisions. This information is needed to balance any attempt to minimize the number of instance variables hashed. You have to carefully balance the two requirements in situations in which performance is at a premium, or as I like to say, *when everything is being sacrificed at the altar of performance.*

For mainstream business application programmers, however, maintenance costs make writing simple code sometimes just as important as writing code that runs as fast as possible. I would strongly emphasize, therefore, that something like testing for hash collisions because you are not sure if you went too far sampling in the `hashCode()` method is a bit in the extreme. Most mainstream business applications will not require anymore thought to performance tuning of hash-based containers than to writing a reasonably good `hashCode()` implementation (one that does not go so far as to require testing for hash collisions) and then using an optimum hash table size, which is some prime number over twice the required size. See 6.9.2 Performance Tuning the General-Purpose Implementations for a discussion of selecting the optimum container size. Certainly if you are new to hash tables you should keep it that simple until there is a compelling reason to performance tune the `hashCode()` method.

4.11.3.3.2 The Simplicity of a *HashCode* Class This section discusses a HashCode class that is not part of the core API but perhaps should be. It can be used by all Java programmers to simplify the implementation of the `hashCode()` method. After all, the design of hashing is to routinely overflow or underflow the `int` in which the hash code is stored. I usually shy away from oversimplified analogies, but you understand hashing when you realize that this is like spinning a roulette wheel. All you want is some number that can be used as an alias in a container (an arbitrary index, if you will). It should not be so complicated. For example, here is the hashCode() method in the `Locale` class:

```
/**
 * Placeholder for the object's hash code.  Always -1.
 */
private int hashcode = -1;        // lazy evaluated

/**
 * Override hashCode.
 * Since Locales are often used in hashtables, caches the value
 * for speed.
 */
public synchronized int hashCode() {
    if (hashcode == -1) {
        hashcode =
    language.hashCode() ^
    country.hashCode() ^
    variant.hashCode();
    }
    return hashcode;
}
```

Notice that this implementation caches the hash code as discussed in the last section on performance optimizations. The `hashCode()` method must be synchronized because `Locale` objects are mutable. This is a good approach to combining the hash codes of other objects and as such represents one of a practically unlimited number of hash algorithms that can be used to implement the `hashCode()` method. Some may work better than others, but there is a growing consensus that something like the `HashCode` class would make life easier for Java programmers. Though an admittedly imperfect general-purpose hash algorithm for the Java language, it is one that I am certain builds on a concensus of opinion of what such a hash algorithm should look like. At any rate, it gets the job done. It spins the roulette wheel.

Using the `HashCode` class, the implementation of the `hashCode()` method in the `Locale` class would be replaced by the following:

```java
public synchronized int hashCode() {
    if (hashcode == -1) {
        HashCode x = new Hashcode();
        x.add(language);
        x.add(country);
        x.add(variant);
        hashcode = x.get();
    }
    return hashcode;
}
```

If you're not sampling, all you need to do is look at your `equals(Object o)` method, list all of the instance variables used, and then add them together using the fully overloaded `add` method in the `HashCode` class.

I want to strongly emphasize that the following `HashCode` class is an outgrowth of one written by Dr. Davis in an article on hashing in the April 2000 issue of *Java Report*. Other influences on the design of this class are numerous `hashCode()` implementations in the core API. Here is the `HashCode` class:

```java
public final class HashCode {

    /*
     * Use whatever prime number you want, but
     * 31 has become the prime number of choice
     * in the core API.
     */
    private int PRIME = 31;
    private int hashCode = 0;

    public int get() { return hashCode; }

    public void add(boolean x) {
        hashCode += PRIME*hashCode + (x ? 1:0);
    }

    public void add(int x) {
        hashCode += PRIME*hashCode + x;
    }

    public void add(long x) {
```

```
            hashCode += PRIME*hashCode + (int)((x >>> 32) +
                                        (x & 0xFFFFFFFF));
    }


    /*
     * The following two methods can handle signed
     * zero and NaN
     */
    public void add(float x) {
        add(x == 0.0f ? 0 : Float.floatToIntBits(x));
    }

    public void add(double x) {
        add(x == 0.0 ? 0L : Double.doubleToLongBits(x));
    }

    public void add(Object x) {
        hashCode += (x == null) ? 0 : PRIME*hashCode + x.hashCode();
    }

    /*
     *  User responsible for the processing
     *  of multidimensional arrays.
     *
     */
    public void add(byte[] a) { add(a, 1); }
    public void add(byte[] a, int samplingRate)     {
        if (samplingRate <= 0) throw new IllegalArgumentException
            ("Illegal sampling rate: " + samplingRate);
        for(int i = 0  ; i < a.length; i += samplingRate) {add(a[i]);}
    }

    public void add(short[] a) { add(a, 1); }
    public void add(short[] a, int samplingRate)     {
        if (samplingRate <= 0) throw new IllegalArgumentException
            ("Illegal sampling rate: " + samplingRate);
        for(int i = 0  ; i < a.length; i += samplingRate) {add(a[i]);}
    }

    public void add(char[] a) { add(a, 1); }
    public void add(char[] a, int samplingRate)     {
        if (samplingRate <= 0) throw new IllegalArgumentException
            ("Illegal sampling rate: " + samplingRate);
        for(int i = 0  ; i < a.length; i += samplingRate) {add(a[i]);}
    }

    public void add(int[] a) { add(a, 1); }
    public void add(int[] a, int samplingRate)     {
        if (samplingRate <= 0) throw new IllegalArgumentException
            ("Illegal sampling rate: " + samplingRate);
        for(int i = 0  ; i < a.length; i += samplingRate) {add(a[i]);}
    }

    public void add(long[] a) { add(a, 1); }
    public void add(long[] a, int samplingRate)     {
        if (samplingRate <= 0) throw new IllegalArgumentException
```

```
                    ("Illegal sampling rate: " + samplingRate);
            for(int i = 0  ; i < a.length; i += samplingRate) {add(a[i]);}
    }

    public void add(float[] a) { add(a, 1); }
    public void add(float[] a, int samplingRate)    {
        if (samplingRate <= 0) throw new IllegalArgumentException
            ("Illegal sampling rate: " + samplingRate);
        for(int i = 0  ; i < a.length; i += samplingRate) {add(a[i]);}
    }

    public void add(double[] a) { add(a, 1); }
    public void add(double[] a, int samplingRate)    {
        if (samplingRate <= 0) throw new IllegalArgumentException
            ("Illegal sampling rate: " + samplingRate);
        for(int i = 0  ; i < a.length; i += samplingRate) {add(a[i]);}
    }

    public void add(boolean[] a) { add(a, 1); }
    public void add(boolean[] a, int samplingRate)    {
        if (samplingRate <= 0) throw new IllegalArgumentException
            ("Illegal sampling rate: " + samplingRate);
        for(int i = 0  ; i < a.length; i += samplingRate) {add(a[i]);}
    }

    public void add(Object[] a) { add(a, 1); }
    public void add(Object[] a, int samplingRate)    {
        if (samplingRate <= 0) throw new IllegalArgumentException
            ("Illegal sampling rate: " + samplingRate);
        for(int i = 0  ; i < a.length; i += samplingRate) {add(a[i]);}
    }

    public String toString() {
        return Integer.toString(get());
    }
}
```

Note the absence of synchronization. This is a performance optimization
that requires references to HashCode objects never be passed out of the
hashCode() method except by invoking the get() method in the
return statement. The add methods for arrays are necessary because
the dynamically created array classes do not override the hashCode()
method. For example,

```
class Test {
    public static void main(String[] args) {
        char[] cb1 = {'a', 'b', 'c'};
        char[] cb2 = {'a', 'b', 'c'};
        System.out.println(cb1.hashCode());
        System.out.println(cb2.hashCode());
    }
}
```

Executing this program prints

This output will vary from one JVM to the next as well as from one execution to the next, but serves to show that two arrays with the same component types and the exact same elements return different hash codes. This is an example of a class that should override the `hashCode()` method but does not. There are others. What you need to do is write your own hash algorithm for such a class and use it instead of invoking the `hash-Code()` method for that object. In the case of an array that means coding a `for` loop to add all of the elements to the value of the hash code. Workarounds for other classes that should, but do not, override the `hashCode()` method may not be as simple.

The container classes in the `java.util` package do not have this problem. They correctly implement the `hashCode()` method but have no methods for sampling large collections or maps. I do not offer such methods in the `HashCode` class. They could, however, be added easily.

In order to make sure the `add` method in the `HashCode` class was fully overloaded, I used the following `Test` program:

```java
import java.math.BigDecimal;
class Test {
    public static void main(String[] args) {

        byte b = 5;
        short s = 5;
        char c = 5;
        int i = 5;
        long l = 5L;
        float f = 5.0f;
        double d = 5.0;
        boolean one = true;
        Integer hundred = new Integer(100);
        BigDecimal bd = new BigDecimal("5000.0005");
        String str = "abc";

        HashCode hashCode = new HashCode();
        hashCode.add(b);
        System.out.println("byte b = 5 " + hashCode);
        hashCode.add(s);
        System.out.println("short s = 5 " + hashCode);
        hashCode.add(c);
        System.out.println("char c = 5 " + hashCode);
        hashCode.add(i);
        System.out.println("int i = 5 " + hashCode);
        hashCode.add(l);
        System.out.println("long l = 5L " + hashCode);
        hashCode.add(f);
        System.out.println("float f = 5.0f " + hashCode);
        hashCode.add(d);
```

```
System.out.println("double d = 5.0 " + hashCode);
hashCode.add(one);
System.out.println("boolean one = true " + hashCode);
hashCode.add(hundred);
System.out.println("Integer hundred = new Integer(100) "
                    + hashCode);
hashCode.add(bd);
System.out.println("BigDecimal bd = new BigDecimal(\"5000.0005\") "
                    + hashCode);
hashCode.add(str);
System.out.println("String str = \"abc\" " + hashCode);
    }
}
```

Executing this program prints

```
byte b = 25 5
short s = 25 165
char c = 25 5285
int i = 25 169125
long l = 25L 5412005
float f = 25.0f 1257411744
double d = 25.0 -1637444608
boolean one = true -858619903
Integer hundred = new Integer(Integer.MAX_VALUE) 441450527
BigDecimal bd = new BigDecimal("5000.0005") -1503452161
String str = "abc" -865732542
```

This example brings up an interesting point about hash codes that is rarely
discussed. The `int` in which a hash code is stored is designed to underflow or overflow ad infinitum. Every time a new instance value is added to
the hash code, the previous value of the hash code is multiplied by 31. It is
easy to see how fast that will overflow an `int`. This aspect of hashing is,
again, like spinning a roulette wheel. Do you see the roulette wheel spinning in this example? The hash code starts at zero and overflows the `int`
data type twice, going from positive to negative, back to positive, and
finally stopping at `-865732542` (*and where she stops nobody knows*).

4.11.3.4 The `clone()` Method

This section is about copying objects. The `clone()` method in the
`Object` class is a `native` method. Therefore, you have to rely solely on
the API docs to tell you what the method does. Here is the entire method
contract for the `clone()` method in the `Object` class.

Creates and returns a copy of this object. The precise meaning
of "copy" may depend on the class of the object. The general
intent is that, for any object x, the expression:

```
x.clone() != x
```

will be `true`, and that the expression:

```
x.clone().getClass() == x.getClass()
```

will be `true`, but these are not absolute requirements. While it is typically the case that:

```
x.clone().equals(x)
```

will be `true`, this is not an absolute requirement. Copying an object will typically entail creating a new instance of its class, but it also may require copying of internal data structures as well. No constructors are called.

The method `clone` for class `Object` performs a specific cloning operation. First, if the class of this object does not implement the interface `Cloneable`, then a `CloneNotSupportedException` is thrown. Note that all arrays are considered to implement the interface `Cloneable`. Otherwise, this method creates a new instance of the class of this object and initializes all its fields with exactly the contents of the corresponding fields of this object, as if by assignment; the contents of the fields are not themselves cloned. Thus, this method performs a "shallow copy" of this object, not a "deep copy" operation.

The class `Object` does not itself implement the interface `Cloneable`, so calling the `clone` method on an object whose class is `Object` will result in throwing an exception at runtime. The `clone` method is implemented by the class `Object` as a convenient, general utility for subclasses that implement the interface `Cloneable`, possibly also overriding the `clone` method, in which case the overriding definition can refer to this utility definition by the call:

```
super.clone()
```

[end of quotation][35]

Understanding the default implementation of the `clone()` method in the `Object` class (referred to as the *utility definition* in the above quotation) is very important. This `native` method can create a **bitwise copy** of any object on the heap. Every bit in the clone is the same as the original. It is a powerful method, which explains the security precautions and why overriding implementations always begin with `super.clone()`.

---

35. API docs for the `clone()` method in the `java.lang.Object` class.

Does cloning an object mean the same thing as copying? *Yes* and *No*. Cloning is the first step in copying an object. It may or may not be the only step, depending on the object being cloned. The bitwise copy of an object is more commonly known as a **shallow copy**. Why shallow? The bitwise copy of a primitive type is indeed a copy of the original value (two numbers with the same primitive data type and bit pattern). If the copy is changed the original remains the same. The bitwise copy of a reference type, however, is simply another reference to the same object. Here is an example of a shallow copy of a container:

```
import java.util.*;
class Test {
    public static void main(String[] args) {
        List list = new ArrayList();
        list.add(new StringBuffer("Josh says: \"All things being equal, "));
        List clone = (List) ((ArrayList)list).clone();
        StringBuffer sb = (StringBuffer) clone.get(0);
        sb.append("immutable types are the way to go.\"");
        System.out.println(list.get(0));
    }
}
```

Executing this program prints

```
Josh says: "All things being equal, immutable types are the way to go."
```

In this example an `ArrayList` is cloned. The `ArrayList` has one element, a `StringBuffer`. After cloning the `ArrayList`, the `String-Buffer` in the clone is appended. Finally, the `StringBuffer` in the original is converted to a string, showing that both the original and the clone reference are the same `StringBuffer`. The essential definition of a shallow copy is that objects are not copied. The definition of *shallow copy* is particularly important when discussing containers. See 6.14.3 Cloning Versus Copying a Container for a discussion.

In the context of a discussion of cloning an object, instance variables fall into one of three categories. They are primitive data types, immutable objects, or mutable objects. For primitive data types and immutable objects there is no difference between cloning and copying. Everything is a copy. In other words, a shallow copy and a deep copy are the same if all of the instance variables are either primitive data types or immutable objects. There is only a difference between cloning and copying in mutable objects. When mutable objects are involved, all clones start life as a shallow copy, whereas there is a general expectation that a **copy** does not share any implementation with the original.

It is the definition of *copy* (or *deep copy*) that makes cloning such an ugly business. On the one hand, the API docs for the `clone()` method are completely open-ended. The `clone()` method can return a shallow or a deep copy. The choice is yours. Or is it?

> Although the `clone()` method contract is very open-ended in the definition of a copy, other programmers are not. For mutable objects, other programmers expect a clone that is a deep copy.

If the clone is in any way a shallow copy it is regarded as a failure. As a general rule, the `clone()` method should return a regular copy, a.k.a. a **deep copy**, in which all references to mutable objects have been cloned. This is not a requirement, but it is what other programmers expect.

As a performance optimization, immutable objects can use the following implementation of the `clone()` method:

```
public Object clone() {
    return this;
}
```

Otherwise, the minimum declaration for a class that supports cloning looks something like this:

```
public Object clone() {
    try {
        Widget clone = (Widget)super.clone();
        return clone;
    } catch (CloneNotSupportedException e) {
        throw new InternalError();
    }
}
```

This is all that is required to implement the `clone()` method if none of the instance variables references mutable objects.

If there are mutable objects you must clone those in order to make your clone a deep copy. Here is an example from the core API:

```
public Object clone () {
    try {
        GridBagConstraints clone = (GridBagConstraints)super.clone();
        clone.insets = (Insets)insets.clone();
        return clone;
    } catch (CloneNotSupportedException e) {
        throw new InternalError();
    }
}
```

In this case, `Insets` is a mutable class of objects. Therefore, the object referenced by `insets` must be cloned before returning. The reference to the original is then replaced by the clone. If there were more references to mutable objects in the object being cloned, you would just add more assignments statements such as `clone.insets = (Insets)insets.clone()`. The cast operator is always necessary because the result type of `clone()` is `Object` (or what this book calls an *untyped reference*).

Some classes may not implement `clone()`, or the implementation may be a shallow copy that includes references to mutable objects. In this case you must try to clone the object yourself using the available access methods and constructors. This is not always possible.

4.11.3.4.1 *The* `Cloneable` *Interface* `Cloneable` is a tagging interface used to determine if a class of objects can be cloned. Unless the `Cloneable` interface is implemented, the powerful default implementation of the `clone()` method in the `Object` class cannot be executed. The JVM throws a `CloneNotSupportedException` instead. That is a fundamental security precaution in the overall design of the Java platform. The potential security threat of unwanted clones also explains why the default implementation in the `Object` class is a `protected` method. Why a tagging interface in addition to normal access control? Members declared `protected` can still be accessed from within the same package. That is not enough security for a method as powerful as the default implementation of the `clone()` method in the `Object` class. The `Cloneable` interface is the first line of defense against unwanted clones. Do not implement the `Cloneable` interface and a JVM will never clone your objects. That is important because in a sense cloning completely accesses control. A bitwise copy knows nothing of the `private`, `protected`, and `public` access modifiers used in the declaration of the fields it is copying.

`CloneNotSupportedException` is a checked exception that requires the use of a `try` statement. The `catch` clause in such a `try` statement usually throws an `InternalError` because the programmer invoking the `clone()` method already knows the class supports cloning. Thus, the `CloneNotSupportedException` should never be thrown. See the example in the last section.

Some classes that do not support cloning override the `clone()` method with a `final` implementation that unconditionally throws a `CloneNotSupportedException`. For example,

```
protected final Object clone() throws CloneNotSupportedException {
    throw new CloneNotSupportedException()
}
```

Doing so means that subclasses no longer have the option of implementing the `clone()` method and can be regarded as the final nail in the coffin in terms of shutting down the clone mechanism within a given class hierarchy.

4.11.3.4.2 Copy Constructors

When you think of *copying* an object, your first thought should be of the `clone()` method. Copy constructors are a nonstandard means of copying objects. A **copy constructor** creates a new instance of the class and then copies all of the fields. If a field in the original object references a mutable object, you are faced with the same decisions that must be made when implementing the `clone()` method. Should the mutable object be cloned? The answer is usually *Yes*.

The problem with copy constructors is a question of interface design. If the `clone()` method is used to copy objects, what is the difference between cloning an object and passing it to a copy constructor? For example, there is very little difference between the use of a copy constructor and cloning a container in the Collections Framework. This makes for a slightly confusing interface. When do I clone a container and when do I copy one? Does it make a difference? See 6.14.3 Cloning Versus Copying a Container for a discussion.

There is another, more serious problem with copy constructors. Copy constructors in non-`final` classes can be passed an instance of a subclass. In that case the class of the object created is not the same as the class of the object copied, which is a basic requirement of the `clone()` method contract. Otherwise, it is not really a copy because the original and clone are different classes of objects. Cloning does not suffer from this problem because the class of the object returned by the `clone()` method in the `Object` class is always the same class as the target object.

4.12 The Comparison Methods

It is important to remember the purpose of each of the five housekeeping methods. Otherwise, you may forget to implement them. The purpose of the compareTo(Object o) method in the Comparable interface is to specify the **default ordering** for a class of objects. The compareTo(Object o) method in the Comparable interface (natural ordering) and the compare(Object o1, Object o2) method in the Comparator interface are known as **comparison methods**.

The term *comparison methods* suffers from a small problem. The de facto standard for naming different kinds of methods (for example, *conversion methods* for methods such as toString() that start with to, or *accessor methods* that begin with get) are based on method names and are therefore very loosely defined. This is not the case with comparison methods. As discussed in Table 4-21, comparison methods all have the same semantics. The Comparable interface is the more general of the

Table 4-21: Comparison Methods

Interface	Method	Notes
Comparable	int **compareTo** Object o	The current object (this) in the Comparable interface loosely corresponds to the first parameter (o1) in the Comparator interface. The other object is the "object being compared" and is usually referred to as such in this book. If this or o1 is less than the other object, a negative integer is returned. If they are equal, zero is returned. If this or o1 is greater than the other object, a positive integer is returned.
Comparator	int **compare** Object o1 Object o2	

two and is a member of the java.lang package. The Comparator interface is a member of the java.util package.

There are other comparison methods in the core API. For example, in the String class there is

```
public int compareTo(String anotherString)
public int compareToIgnoreCase(String str)
```

Another example of a comparison method that has the same semantics is the compareTo(BigDecimal val) method, which is discussed in 4.8.2.3 Comparison Operators for the BigDecimal Class. Some of the comparison methods in the core API have the more specific return values of -1, 0, and 1. For example, the return value specification for the `compareTo(BigDecimal val)` method is as follows.

Returns:

-1, 0 or 1 as this `BigDecimal` is numerically less than, equal to, or greater than `val`.

The semantics is nevertheless the same.

Comparison methods are implemented by first casting the `Object` type parameter(s) to the class type used in the comparison. For example,

```
public int compareTo(Object o) {
    Widget argument = (Widget)o;
    ...
}

public int compare(Object o1, Object o2) {
    Widget target = (Widget)o1;
    Widget argument = (Widget)o2;
    ...
}
```

Next, the instance variable(s) must be compared. If you are only sorting by one field, return the value of that single comparison. It is that simple. Sorting by more than one field is discussed in 4.12.4 Sorting By More Than One Field.

Reference type instance variable are compared by invoking the `compareTo(Object o)` method. Primitive numeric type instance variables must be compared as follows:

```
this.x < argument.x ? -1 : (this.x == argument.x ? 0 : 1)
```

The alternative of `this.x - argument.x` can overflow if the primitive value in the object being compared is negative. This is a very serious problem in the implementation of comparison methods.

4.12.1 What is Default Ordering?

What makes the `compareTo(Object o)` method the default ordering for a class of objects that implements the `Comparable` interface? The `compareTo(Object o)` method is automatically invoked by the no-argument `sort` methods in the `Collections` and `Arrays` utility classes, as well as by methods in `TreeMap` and `TreeSet`, much like `toString()` is automatically invoked in a string concatenation operation.

If these methods are invoked for a class that does not implement the `Comparable` interface, a `ClassCastException` is thrown. In that case the user must pass a `Comparator` as an alternative means of specifying the sort order. The key to understanding this design is that users should not have to create a `Comparator` as a means of specifying the *natural ordering* for a class of objects. If there is a natural ordering for a given class of objects and that class does not implement the `Comparable` interface, then the interface for that class of objects is incomplete. Users will have to compensate by writing a `Comparator` for the natural ordering, which may not even be possible.

4.12.2 What is Natural Ordering?

The terms *default ordering* and *natural ordering* are used interchangeably, but they are not necessarily synonymous. As stated in the API docs for the `Comparable` interface,

> This interface imposes a total ordering on the objects of each class that implements it. This ordering is referred to as the class's *natural ordering*, and the class's `compareTo` method is referred to as its *natural comparison method*.[36]

The **default ordering** for a class of objects, however, is only *natural* if the programmer who implements the `compareTo(Object o)` method chooses a sort order that is what a user would expect. In other words, to call the default ordering *natural* is subjective. The default ordering is simply the `compareTo(Object o)` method in a class that implements the `Comparable` interface.

4.12.3 Reverse Order (or Descending) Sorts

The API docs refer to descending sorts are **reverse order sorts** instead of a descending sort, and for good reason. That natural ordering is ascending or that the reverse of any sort order is a descending sort is an assumption, but one that holds true a lot of the time. Therefore, I consistently make that assumption in this chapter for the sake of simplifying the terminology.

There are two objects involved in every comparison. You must know which to use as the target object and which to use as the argument when

---

36. API docs for the `java.lang.Comparable` interface.

invoking the `compareTo(Object o)` method. I refer to the argument as the **object being compared**. That one simple terminological device and the following rule are intended to help you tell the two objects apart when implementing either of the comparison methods:

The object being compared is always the last parameter
in the parameter list of a comparison method.

This is true of all comparison methods and can rightly be regarded as part of the semantics of those methods.

Why is this so important? The answer is **descending sorts**. If you switch the target object and argument, in effect you implement a descending sort. Some programmers make the switch deliberately as a means of implementing a descending sort. This should not be regarded as a matter of style because it is too easily overlooked by maintenance programmers. The correct way to implement a descending sort is to negate the return value. For example,

```
public int compareTo(Object o) {
    Name argument = (Name)o;
    return -(fileAs.compareTo(argument.fileAs));
}
```

This is the same implementation used in the `Name` class example in 4.12.5 The `Comparable` Interface except for negating the return value. This `compareTo(Object o)` method implementation is a descending sort. Of course, you would never do that because a descending sort is not the natural ordering for a list of names. If sorting by more than one field, which is the subject of the next section, be careful to negate the return value of all the `return` statements.

4.12.4 Sorting By More Than One Field

When sorting by more than one field, the order in which the fields are compared determines the sort order. For example,

```
public int compareTo(Object o) {
    Widget argument = (Widget)o;
    int result = x.compareTo(argument.x);
    if (result != 0)
        return result;
    result = (y < argument.y ? -1 :
             (y == argument.y ? 0 : 1));
    if (result != 0)
```

```
        return result;
    return = z().compareTo(argument.z());
}


public int compare(Object o1, Object o2) {
    Widget target = (Widget)o1;
    Widget argument = (Widget)o2;
    int result = (target.x.compareTo(argument.x);
    if (result != 0)
        return result;
    result = (target.y < argument.y ? -1 :
            (target.y == argument.y ? 0 : 1));
    if (result != 0)
        return result;
    return = target.z().compareTo(argument.z());
}
```

Check for a non-zero return value after each comparison. If the return value is non-zero, return that value. Otherwise, compare the next instance variable. In the end, if all of the instance variables compare equally, zero is returned. This either tells a stable partial sort not to reorder the objects or means that two objects in a total ordering are the same.

4.12.5 The `Comparable` Interface

Comparison methods are rarely implemented from scratch. Instead they build on top of the natural ordering for one of the classes in the core API. What this means is that, instead of having to decide what the return value is when implementing the `compareTo(Object o)` method, most of the time you invoke the `compareTo(Object o)` method of classes in the core API and return that value. For example,

```
public int compareTo(Object o) {
    Widget argument = (Widget)o;
    return (fileAs.compareTo(argument.fileAs));
}
```

This is an example of implementing a lexicographic sort that builds on top of the natural ordering of the `String` class. Likewise, chronological sorts use `Date` type objects to invoke the `compareTo(Object o)` method in the `Date` class. Numeric sorts invoke the `compareTo(Object o)` method in one of the primitive type wrapper classes, `BigDecimal`, or `BigInteger`. This is what is meant when I say that most sorts are *built on top* of the natural ordering of one of the classes in the core API. Those are the classes that have to make the more fundamental choice of which object comes first in a lexicographic, chronological, or numeric sort.

There are surprisingly few classes in the core API that implement the Comparable interface. Table 4-22 is a complete list except for java.io.ObjectStreamField. Note that all of these are reference types. Sorting an array of primitive types never requires the use of the Comparable or Comparator interface. See 6.14.1.1 Sorting an Array for a discussion. There is an example of a compareTo(Object o) from one of these classes (the String class, which is used for lexicographical sorts) in 4.12.6.4 Coding a Comparison Method From Scratch.

Table 4-22: Natural Ordering in the Core API

Natural Order	Core API Classes
Signed numerical	Byte Short Integer Long Float Double BigInteger BigDecimal
Unsigned numerical	Character
System-dependent lexicographic on pathname	File
Lexicographic	String
Chronological	Date
Locale-specific lexicographic	CollationKey

Here is an example of a Name class with a default lexicographic sort that builds on top of the natural ordering of the String class. Notice the shift in terminology in the last sentence. Whether you call the compareTo(Object o) method implementation a *default ordering*, *default sort*, *default sort order*, or *default order* does not matter. I use *default ordering* most of the time because it is consistent with *natural ordering*. The default ordering is lastName, firstName, middleName. I would say this is natural ordering of the Name class:

```
public class Name implements Comparable, java.io.Serializable {

    private String fileAs;
```

```java
    private String firstName;
    private String lastName;
    private String middleName;
    private String fullName;

    public Name(String lastName,
                String firstName) {
      if (firstName == null || lastName == null)
        throw new NullPointerException
        ("name arguments cannot be null");
      this.firstName = firstName.intern();
      this.lastName = lastName.intern();
      fullName = (firstName + " " + lastName).intern();
      fileAs = (lastName + ", " + firstName).intern();
    }

    public Name(String lastName,
                String firstName,
                String middleName) {
      if (firstName == null ||
          lastName == null ||
          middleName == null)
          throw new NullPointerException
          ("name arguments cannot be null");
      this.firstName = firstName.intern();
      this.lastName = lastName.intern();
      if (middleName.length() == 1)
          middleName += ".";
      this.middleName = middleName.intern();
      fullName = (firstName + " " +
                  middleName + " " +
                  lastName).intern();
      fileAs = (lastName + ", " +
                firstName + " " +
                middleName ).intern();
    }

    public String getFullName()   {return fullName;}
    public String getFirstName()  {return firstName;}
    public String getLastName()   {return lastName;}
    public String getMiddleName(){return middleName;}

// Housekeeping Methods

    public String toString() {
       return fullName;
    }
    public boolean equals(Object o) {
       if (o == this) return true;
       if (o == null) return false;
       if (o.getClass() != this.getClass())
           return false;
     //Compare Instance Variables for Equality
       Name argument = (Name)o;
       return this.fileAs.equals(argument.fileAs);
    }
    public int hashCode() {
       return 31*fileAs.hashCode();
```

```
      }
      public Object clone() {
         return this;
      }
      public int compareTo(Object o) {
         Name argument = (Name)o;
         return (fileAs.compareTo(argument.fileAs));
      }
   }
}
```

Now watch what happens when a list of names is "automatically" sorted:

```
import java.util.*;
class Test {
   public static void main(String[] args) {
      List list = new ArrayList();
      list.add(new Name("McNealy", "Scott"));
      list.add(new Name("Naughton", "Patrick"));
      list.add(new Name("Gosling", "James"));
      list.add(new Name("Bloch", "Joshua"));
      Collections.sort(list);
      Iterator iterator = list.iterator();
      while (iterator.hasNext())
         System.out.println(((Name)(iterator.next())).getFullName());
   }
}
```

Executing this program prints

```
Joshua Bloch
James Gosling
Scott McNealy
Patrick Naughton
```

That is the natural ordering for a list of names.

Learning how to implement this method is easy enough. The big question is which instance variable(s) to compare. This decision is governed by the rule that *natural ordering must be consistent with equals*. The API docs for the `Comparable` interface state

> Virtually all Java core classes that implement comparable have natural orderings that are consistent with equals.
>
> It is strongly recommended, but *not* strictly required that `(x.compareTo(y)==0) == (x.equals(y))`. Generally speaking, any class that implements the `Comparable` interface and violates this condition should clearly indicate this fact. The recommended language is "Note: this class has a natural ordering that is inconsistent with equals." [37]

---

37. API docs for the `java.lang.Comparable` interface.

What the last paragraph says is that the code equivalent of *natural ordering must be consistent with equals* as follows:

```
(x.compareTo(y)==0) == (x.equals(y))
```

This line of code, however, is not actually used in implementing the `compareTo(Object o)` method. You could add it to either the `compareTo(Object o)` or `equals(Object o)` methods, but if the class of objects being compared properly implemented the `compareTo(Object o)` method, the above line of code would always return `true`. The question is how to properly implement the `compareTo(Object o)` method so that `(x.compareTo(y)==0) == (x.equals(y))` is always true.

Once again, you must think in terms of the `equals(Object o)` method defining a set of instance variables. For the natural comparison method to be consistent with equals, *the exact same set of instance variables* must be compared in both the `compareTo(Object o)` method and the `equals(Object o)` method. Notice how this is comparable to the fact that the `hashCode()` method must use a subset of the instance variables compared in the `equals(Object o)` method.

Why the exact same set? The reason why the *natural ordering must be consistent with equals* rule exists is that the `equals(Object o)` method is not always used to implement the equivalence relationship in Java. Sometimes the comparison methods are used instead.

The definition of a duplicate element in a set or of a matching key in a map is defined in the API docs in terms of the `equals(Object o)` method but is sometimes implemented using one of the comparison methods.

When are the comparison methods used instead of the `equals(Object o)` method to determine if two objects are the same? The answer is when adding an element to a `TreeSet` or a key to a `TreeMap`. If either of the comparison methods returns zero, *the objects are assumed to be the same*. Thus, the exact same set of instance variables must be compared in the `compareTo(Object o)` methods as well as any `Comparator` passed when creating a `SortedSet` or `SortedMap`. Such a `Comparator` is referred to as a **total ordering**. The `compareTo(Object o)` method in the `Comparable` interface is a total ordering. Natural ordering is always a total ordering. A **partial ordering** is a `Comparator` that does not use all of the instance variables compared in the `equals(Object o)` method. Such a `Comparator` may compare any of the instance variables declared in the class that is being sorted.

Partial orderings are not consistent with equals. In a partial ordering zero means something entirely different than the zero returned by a total ordering. In a total ordering zero means the same thing as `true` when the `equals(Object o)` method is invoked. The objects being compared are the same. The zero returned by a partial ordering does not necessarily mean the objects being compared are the same. The zero returned by a partial ordering is essentially an instruction to stable sorts not to reorder the objects just compared.

As a final note about the `Comparable` interface, there is a very subtle confusion that stems from the fact that the two important rules to remember when implementing the housekeeping methods look and sound alike. First there is *equal objects must have equal hash codes*, which is usually expressed as follows:

If `x.equals(y)`, then `x.hashCode() == y.hashCode()` must be true.

Then there is *natural ordering must be consistent with equals*, which is usually expressed as follows.

`(x.compareTo(y)==0) == (x.equals(y))`

Furthermore, the requirement in both cases is to work with the same set of instance variables as the `equals(Object o)` method, or, in the case of the `hashCode()` method, a subset thereof. They are easily confused because they look and sound alike. What you do not want to confuse, however, is when to implement the housekeeping methods. Most classes that override `equals(Object o)` will also override `hashCode()`. The exception would be classes of objects that are never stored in a container, which may be an assumption that programmers should not make. The same is not true, however, of the `Comparator` interface. Only classes that have a natural or obvious default ordering are obligated to implement the `compareTo(Object o)` method.

4.12.6 The `Comparator` Interface

The `compare(Object o1, Object o2)` method in the `Comparator` class is a comparison method, but it is definitely not a housekeeping method. It is used primarily to override default ordering and therefore is not *a method routinely implemented when creating a new class of objects.* A discussion of the `Comparator` interface is necessary at this time because the `Comparator` and `Comparable` interfaces help to define each other. They are part of the same sort mechanism in the Collections Framework.

All implementations of the `Comparator` are either partial or total orderings. Ad hoc sorts are usually partial orderings. Partial orderings work well with the stable `sort` methods in the `Arrays` and `Collections` utility classes. The only time a `Comparator` must be a total ordering is when passed to a constructor in a class that implements the `SortedSet` or `SortedMap` interfaces, including the general-purpose `TreeSet` or `TreeMap` implementations in the `java.util` package. Such a `Comparator` is used to override the default ordering (one total ordering overriding another) or perhaps to compensate for a class that fails to implement the `compareTo(Object o)` method when there is clearly a natural order.

Comparators have four uses.

1. The primary use of a `Comparator` is to sort an `Object[]` or `List`. There are two reasons why a `Comparator` must be used in a sort. The first is for classes that do not implement the `Comparable` interface, either because there is no natural default ordering or the responsible programmer forgot to implement the `compareTo(Object o)` method. The second reason why a `Comparator` must be used in a sort is to override the default ordering of a class that implements the `Comparable` interface. The `Comparator` used in a sort is usually a partial ordering but could be a total ordering. They are most likely to be total orderings when a programmer has forgotten to implement the `compareTo(Object o)` method for a class that has a natural default ordering.

2. A use closely related to sorting is searching an `Object[]` or `List` using one of the overloaded `binarySearch` methods in the `Collections` utility class. The same comparator used to

sort an `Object[]` or `List` must be used when searching. Otherwise, the behavior of the binary search is undefined.

3.   `Comparators` are used when instantiating a `SortedSet` or `SortedMap`, including the general-purpose `TreeSet` and `TreeMap` implementations in the `java.util` package. These are the `Comparators` that must be a total ordering.

4.   A partial or total ordering `Comparator` can be passed to one of the following methods in the `Collections` utility class:

```
min(Collection coll, Comparator comp)
max(Collection coll, Comparator comp)
```

Unlike a binary search which requires a sorted list, the order of a `Collection` prior to invoking the `min` or `max` methods does not matter.

To understand the `min` and `max` methods you must think of the elements in a list or set as rows in a spreadsheet. The instance variables are the columns. Invoking the `min` or `max` method is like clicking on one of the columns to alternately sort the list in ascending or descending value. These methods return an `Object` that I like to refer to as an *untyped reference* to one of the elements in a set or list. In the spreadsheet analogy, the object returned corresponds to the first row in the table after clicking on a given column. The "click" is not actually accomplished by sorting the set or list. Rather an iterator is used to loop through all of the elements, comparing them one at a time and always saving a reference to whichever element comes first using the natural ordering or the `Comparator` passed. I usually shy away from analogies because they always fall apart. In this case the analogy works pretty good if the natural ordering or `Comparator` is sorting by a single instance variable. Otherwise, the analogy falls apart.

Unlike lists that can be completely reordered, the ordering of a `SortedMap` or `SortedSet` cannot be changed. If that `SortedMap` or `SortedSet` was created using a `Comparator` and you invoke the one-argument `min(Collection coll)` or `max(Collection coll)`, the natural comparison method will be used to find the minimum or maximum element instead of the `Comparator` that corresponds to the actual order of the `SortedMap` or `SortedSet`. There is therefore a `comparator()` method declared in both the `SortedMap` and `SortedSet` interfaces. The `comparator()` method either returns `null` if natural ordering is used or a reference to the `Comparator` used to automatically sort elements as they are added to the map or set. Here is an example of invoking the `min` or `max` methods for a `SortedMap` or `SortedSet` when you do not have a reference to the `Comparator` or are not sure if natural ordering or a `Comparator` is being used:

```
max(set, set.comparator())
```

It is not necessary to check if `comparator()` returns `null` because if the value of the `Comparator` passed to one of these methods is `null` the method defaults to using the natural ordering of the element type.

4.12.6.1 Partial Orderings (Ad Hoc Sorts)

The following is the generic code for a partial ordering `Comparator` such as those used in ad hoc sorts:

```
public int compare(Object o1, Object o2) {
    return ((Widget)o1).accessorMethod().compareTo
        (((Widget)o2).accessorMethod());
}
```

Change `Widget` to the appropriate type name and `accessorMethod()` to the name of some accessor method for the field you wish to sort by and you are done. The result type of the accessor method determines if the sort is lexicographic, chronological, or numeric, and is typically one of those listed in Table 4-22.

4.12.6.2 Total Orderings

A `Comparator` passed to a `TreeSet` or `TreeMap` constructor must be a total ordering of the elements. An easy way to make a partial ordering such as those used in ad hoc sorts a total ordering so that it can be passed to a `SortedMap` or `SortedSet` constructor is to return the value of a `compareTo(Object o)` method invocation if all of the instance variables compare equal. The following example is from 4.12.6.3 Important `Comparator` Implementations in the Core API at the bottom of this chapter:

```
public int compare(Object o1, Object o2) {
    int cmp =
    String.CASE_INSENSITIVE_ORDER.compare(o1, o2);
    return cmp==0 ?
      -((Comparable)o1).compareTo((Comparable)o2) : cmp;
}
```

This is an unusual implementation but follows the basic formula, which has three parts.

1. Implement the `Comparator` as you would for a sort (that is, a partial ordering).

2. Check the value returned by the `compare(Object o1, Object o2)` method. If it's non-zero, return that value. Otherwise, continue comparing instance variables.

3. Repeat the same code used to implement the natural ordering of the element type. It does not matter if you use a descending sort in this part of the `Comparator` (as in the above example), only that you repeat the same code used in the natural ordering. The easiest way to do this is to invoke the `compareTo(Object o)` method using `o1` as the target object and `o2` as the argument (exactly as is done in the example above).

Here is an example of a total ordering that extends the generic code from above:

```
public int compare(Object o1, Object o2) {
    int cmp = ((Widget)o1).accessorMethod().compareTo
            (((Widget)o2).accessorMethod());
    return cmp==0 ?
    ((Comparable)o1).compareTo((Comparable)o2) : cmp;
}
```

Assuming that both `o1` and `o2` have a natural ordering, the last line of code can be used as is to make any partial ordering a total ordering. Negate the return value of the `compareTo(Object o)` method invocation for a descending sort.

What happens if the element type has no natural ordering? The answer is that instead of invoking the `compareTo(Object o)` method in step three you have to provide a total ordering for that element type. In effect, you have to implement a `compareTo(Object o)` method at the bottom of the `compare(Object o1, Object o2)` method. When doing so be sure to follow the same guidelines for implementing the `equals(Object o)` method. That way you will be sure to have a total ordering.

4.12.6.3 *Important* `Comparator` *Implementations in the Core API*

The `Collections.reverseOrder()` utility method returns one of two important `Comparator` implementations available in the core API. The **reverse order comparator** is used to reverse the default order. This comparator is used when you want a descending sort based on the default ordering. It is used the same as any other `Comparator`, but the elements in the container must implement the `Comparable` interface. Otherwise, a `ClassCastException` is thrown at run time when the reverse comparator attempts to reverse the default ordering by invoking the `compareTo(Object o)` method and negating the results. See also 4.12.3 Reverse Order (or Descending) Sorts.

The other important `Comparator` in the core API is a constant in the `String` class named `String.CASE_INSENTIVE_ORDER`. Here is an example of using that `Comparator` to sort a list of strings:

```
import java.util.*;
class Test {
    public static void main(String[] args) {
        List list = new ArrayList();
        list.add("TOMMORROW");
        list.add("tommorrow");
        list.add("Tommorrow");
        list.add("hello");
        list.add("HELLO");
        list.add("Hello");
        Collections.sort(list, String.CASE_INSENSITIVE_ORDER);
        Iterator i = list.iterator();
        while (i.hasNext())
            System.out.println(i.next());
    }
}
```

Executing this program prints

```
hello
HELLO
Hello
TOMMORROW
tommorrow
Tommorrow
```

This program demonstrates an important point about the sort algorithms used in the `Arrays` and `Collections` utility classes: they are stable. A **stable sort** is one that does not reorder equal elements. The classic example is an e-mail inbox. A good e-mail program uses stable sorts. Suppose you sort your inbox by date so the most recent e-mails are at the top, but then need to find all the e-mails from a particular person. After the second sort (clicking on the *From* column header) you expect to find the most recent e-mails from that person at the top. For that to happen the e-mail package must use stable sorts.

For indices (such as the index for the API docs), glossaries, and some other such lists the desired output is

```
hello
Hello
HELLO
tommorrow
Tommorrow
TOMMORROW
```

This makes stable sorts a problem. As an exercise in making a partial ordering such as those used in ad hoc reports a total ordering so that it can be passed to a `SortedMap` or `SortedSet` constructor, let us solve the problem.

First you need to know that lexicographic sorts have two distinct properties.

- Shorter strings always come before longer strings. For example, "at" comes before "atom" or "atoll," and "age" comes before "agent" or "agency"

- In a case-sensitive lexicographical sort involving the English alphabet, capital letters come before small letters. That is because their character code is less. For example, the character code for 'A' is 41 and 'a' is 61

The sort putting shorter strings first is not the problem we are trying to solve. The problem is that a normal lexicographic sort will place capital letters before small letters. This works for a telephone book but is the opposite of what is wanted here. What we need is small letters before capital letters, but only when two words compare equal using a case-insensitive `Comparator`. Here is the solution:

```java
import java.util.*;
class Test {
    public static void main(String[] args) {
        List list = new ArrayList();
        list.add("TOMMORROW");
        list.add("tommorrow");
        list.add("Tommorrow");
        list.add("hello");
        list.add("HELLO");
        list.add("Hello");
        Collections.sort(list, new Comparator() {
                public int compare(Object o1, Object o2) {
```

```
                int cmp = String.CASE_INSENSITIVE_ORDER.compare(o1, o2);
                return cmp==0 ? -((Comparable)o1).compareTo((Comparable)o2) : cmp;
            }
        });
        Iterator i = list.iterator();
        while (i.hasNext())
            System.out.println(i.next());
    }
}
```

Executing this program prints the strings in the desired order.

4.12.6.4 *Coding a Comparison Method From Scratch*

When coding a comparison method from scratch, you think in terms of the return value. It is a completely different mindset than when building on top of the natural ordering of one of the classes in the core API, which is what mainstream business application programmers do most of the time when implementing a lexicographic, chronological, or numeric sort. This section takes a look at one of the compareTo(Object o) methods in the core API, namely, the String class, as a lesson in how to implement a comparison method from scratch. Notice that I did not say a natural comparison method. All comparison methods have the same semantics. Their implementation is virtually the same whether building on top of the natural ordering of one of the classes in the core API or implementing from scratch.

The implementation of a lexicographic comparison is of some interest. It requires a left-to-right comparison of individual characters in the two strings. There are three possibilities.

1. The strings are different.
2. The strings are the same.
3. The strings have different lengths but each character in the shorter string is the same as the corresponding character in the longer string.

As characters from both strings are compared from left to right, if any two characters are not the same, the difference between their Unicode character codes is returned using a subtraction expression such as the following:

```
return this.charAt(i) - argumentString.charAt(i);
```

If the two strings in Figure 4-14 were compared, the value returned would be 32 - 110 = -78.

J	a	v	a		R	u	l	e	s	!
74	97	118	97	32	82	117	108	101	115	33

J	a	v	a	n	e	s	e
74	97	118	97	110	101	115	101

Figure 4-14: Character values in a string comparison.

A negative return value means the target string lexicographically precedes the argument string. A positive return value means the target string lexicographically follows the argument string.

If the loop in which the left-to-right comparison of individual characters is made completes, this still does not mean that the strings are the same. If the length of the strings is different, the loop only executes until the end of the shorter string. Then the length of the strings must be compared using another subtraction expression.

```
return this.length() - anotherString.length();
```

The effect is the same as the previous subtraction of the character codes. For example, if *Java Rules!* is lexicographically compared to *Javanese*, the value returned is `11 - 4 = 7`, which means that *Java Rules!* follows *Javanese*, as would be expected in a lexicographic sort. If the lengths are the same, zero is returned, which means that the strings are equal.

Chapter 5

Strings and Other Common Data Types

Chapter Contents

5.1 Introduction

This chapter has two major divisions: "all things string" and "other data types." There are two string classes, both of which are members of the `java.lang` package. `String` is an immutable, fixed-length string. `StringBuffer` is a mutable, variable-length string. Strings are one of the most important data types in computer programming. My goal in the first half of this chapter is to discuss all of the class and interface types related to string processing, which is significantly more than just the `String` and `StringBuffer` classes. For example, there are the

`StringReader` and `StringWriter` classes in the `java.io` package. These classes are a `String` and `StringBuffer` that implement the `Reader` and `Writer` interfaces, respectively. After discussing all of the string-related classes and interfaces in the core API, the closely related subjects of text boundaries (or *breaks*), tokenization, and string concatenation operations are discussed.

Displaying diagnostic messages on the console (usually for debugging purposes) is discussed next. Diagnostic messages are formatted strings, but beyond that the relationship to the rest of this chapter is at best tentative. Displaying diagnostic messages on the console and related subjects such as standard I/O and abnormal program termination need to be discussed as early as possible in any book that covers the basics of the Java programming language. That is why I have placed the section on diagnostic messages between the sections on *all things string* and the rest of the chapter on *other common data types*. Frankly, I expect to move these sections to a planned third volume of *Java Rules* when and if it is published. They are being included in this chapter for the sake of novice programmers using this first volume as an introduction to the language.

The other common data types are primarily dates, times, and currency. None of these data types are built into the Java programming language. They are all reference types such as `Date` and `GregorianCalendar`. These reference types all have one thing in common: the numerical data are stored in a primitive data type and then formatted prior to output. This must be done because the format of these data types involves localization. In other words, dates, times, and currency print differently from one language or country to the next. Localization is part of internationalization. The difference between the two is thoroughly explained in this chapter. However, only localization is discussed in detail. The localization of common data types is something every Java programmer must understand. You may never write an internationalized application in your entire career, but that does not matter. You still need to understand the localization of common data types in order to format dates, times, and currencies using the default locale.

5.2 Would-Be Mutator Methods

One of the more interesting details about the `String` and `StringBuffer` classes is that many of the instance methods in the *immutable* `String` class appear to be mutator methods, particularly the following ones:

```
public String concat(String str)
public String replace(char oldChar, char newChar)
public String toLowerCase()
public String toLowerCase(Locale locale)
public String toUpperCase()
public String toUpperCase(Locale locale)
public String trim()
```

If these were mutator methods, they would probably be declared `void`, but as you can see they return a reference to a `String`. String data are usually passed as `String`, not `StringBuffer`. The reason for declaring these methods in the `String` class is simply a matter of convenience. All they do is return a new `String` rather than modifying the target string. The declaration of such methods in an immutable class such as `String` is a minor design pattern that I call **would-be mutator methods**. Would-be mutator methods do not actually modify the target object. They return a copy of what the target object would look like were it modified by an actual mutator method.

There is more to the would-be mutator method design pattern. If, for whatever reason, execution of one of these methods results in the same sequence of characters, *a reference to the same immutable object is returned as a performance optimization.* Therefore, if the intent is to modify the target object, would-be mutators methods are always invoked as follows:

```
s = s.toUpperCase();
```

This is how you implement a mutator method in an immutable class.

5.3 The Length of a `String` or `StringBuffer`

The length of a `String` or `StringBuffer` is returned by the `length()` method. Programmers are sometimes frustrated by the need to remember that `length` is a `final` field in the dynamically created array classes, but an accessor method in the string classes.

The length of a `StringBuffer` is implicitly changed by the overloaded `insert` and `append` methods and explicitly changed by the `set-Length(int newLength)` method, which throws a `StringIndex-OutOfBoundsException` if the `newLength` argument is negative. If the `newLength` argument is less than the current length of the string buffer, *the character sequence is truncated.* Setting the length of a `StringBuffer` to zero effectively clears out the `StringBuffer`. If the `newLength` argument is longer than the current length of the `String-Buffer`, the new characters are initialized to the `NULL` character.

5.4 The Capacity of a `StringBuffer`

The **growth policy** of a character-based container such as `String-Buffer` is the formula used to control the relationship between the length of the string and the capacity of the container. The length is the number of characters in the character string. The **capacity** is the size of the `char[]` in which those characters are stored. From time to time a larger character array must be allocated. The question of how much larger is answered by the growth policy of a particular character-based container. The length is returned by the `length()` method and the capacity is returned by the `capacity()` method.

There are three constructors in the `StringBuffer` class, and the **initial capacity** of a `StringBuffer` is determined by which of those constructors is invoked:

```
public StringBuffer()
public StringBuffer(String str)
public StringBuffer(int length)
```

The first constructor uses the **default initial capacity** of 16 characters. In other words, the `char[]` (or buffer) in which the string is stored is created as follows:

```
char[] buffer = new char[16];
```

The default initial capacity of 16 for `StringBuffer` is an industry standard. Years of experience have shown that to be a good initial capacity for general-purpose string buffers. The next constructor sets the initial capacity equal to the length of the `String` passed plus the default initial capacity. For example,

```
class Test {
    public static void main(String[] args) {
        StringBuffer buffer = new StringBuffer("Java");
        System.out.println(buffer.length());
        System.out.println(buffer.capacity());
    }
}
```

Executing this program prints

```
4
20
```

The third constructor allows a programmer to specify the initial capacity. If the capacity argument is negative, a `NegativeArraySizeException` is thrown.

5.4.1 Ensuring the Capacity of a `StringBuffer`

The growth policy of a `StringBuffer` is encapsulated in the `ensureCapacity(int minimumCapacity)` method. If the `minimumCapacity` argument is not greater than `capacity()`, the method returns without doing anything. Otherwise, executing the `ensureCapacity(int minimumCapacity)` method for a `StringBuffer` "ensures" that the length of the `char[]` (or character buffer) in which the string is stored is at least as much as the `minimumCapacity` argument. The new capacity is calculated as follows:

```
int newCapacity = (buffer.length + 1) * 2;
if (minimumCapacity > newCapacity)
   newCapacity = minimumCapacity;
```

The new capacity is the `minimumCapacity` or twice the old capacity, whichever is greater. That is the "growth policy" of a `StringBuffer`.

The default sizes of variable-length (or resizable) containers in the Java programming language are small. You should always pass an initial capacity argument when creating such a container. That is generally understood when it comes to regular containers such as `ArrayList`, but is not as well understood when it comes to character-based containers such as `StringBuffer`. The default capacity of any variable-length (or resizable) container can be very inefficient at times. Character-based containers such as `StringBuffer` are no exception.

5.5 `String` Indices

The term *string* is short for *character string*. Specifically, strings in the Java programming language are sequences of Unicode characters. Those characters are stored in a `private char[]`, which is accessed using indices that are completely analogous to the indices used to access any other array. For example,

```
class Test {
  public static void main(String[] args) {
    String string = "Hello World!";
```

```
char[] array = {'H','e','l','l','o',' ','W','o','r','l','d','!'};
System.out.println("the length of the string is " + string.length());
System.out.println("the length of the array is " + array.length);
System.out.println("string.charAt(0) = " + string.charAt(0));
System.out.println("array[0] = " + array[0]);
System.out.println("string.charAt(11) = " + string.charAt(11));
System.out.println("array[11] = " + array[11]);
    }
}
```

Executing this program prints

```
the length of the string is 12
the length of the array is 12
string.charAt(0) = H
array[0] = H
string.charAt(11) = !
array[11] = !
```

The index of the first character in a string is zero. The index of the last character is the length of the string minus one. The only difference between string and array indices is that if the index value is negative or greater than the length of the string minus one, methods in the `String` and `StringBuffer` classes throw `StringIndexOutOfBounds-Exception` instead of `ArrayIndexOutOfBoundsException`. (As of this writing and the 1.3 release, the API docs for the entire `String` class are wrong on this point. They consistently say `IndexOutOf-Bounds` is thrown. The code says otherwise. This is just an API docs maintenance issue.)

All indices and dimension expressions are type `int`, which implicitly limits the length of arrays and strings to `Integer.MAX_VALUE`. For example,

```
class Test {
    public static void main (String[] args) {
        long dim = 10;
        int[] array = new int[dim];
    }
}
```

Attempting to compile this program generates the following compiler error:

```
Test.java:5: possible loss of precision
found   : long
required: int
        int[] array = new int[dim];
                              ^
1 error
```

If the smaller integral types `byte` or `short` are used as index values, the value is promoted to `int`.

The index parameters in the `String` and `StringBuffer` classes have many different names:

```
index
fromIndex
beginIndex
endIndex
start
end
```

They are also referred to as offsets:

```
offset
toffset (this offset)
ooffset (other offset)
```

Whatever the parameter name, the value passed is simply an `int` type index value. Many of the methods in the `String` and `StringBuffer` classes return `int` values, which are also indices. The index value returned is typically passed as is to one of the other methods. By that I mean you typically do not need to add or subtract one from the value returned before using it somewhere else. For example,

```
class Test {
    public static void main(String[] args) {
        String s = "How much wood would a woodchuck chuck, " +
                   "if a woodchuck could chuck wood?";
        int w = s.indexOf('w');
        int wood = s.lastIndexOf("wood");
        System.out.println(s.charAt(w));
        System.out.println(s.substring(wood, wood+4));
    }
}
```

Executing this program prints

```
w
wood
```

Notice how the `endIndex` argument in the `substring(int beginIndex, int endIndex)` method is the value of the `beginIndex` plus the length of the substring.

5.5.1 Right-Open Intervals in `String` and `StringBuffer`

There are four methods in the `String` and `StringBuffer` classes that are passed a range of indices:

```
public String substring(int beginIndex, int endIndex)
public void getChars(int srcBegin, int srcEnd, char[] dst, int dstBegin)
public synchronized void delete(int start, int end)
public synchronized replace(int start, int end, String str)
```

The first two methods are declared in both the `String` and `String-Buffer` classes. The last two methods are declared only in `String-Buffer`. The behavior of all four methods is consistent with that of the canonical form of a `for` loop used to iterate over the elements of an array, or what is described in Chapter 6 as *right-open intervals*. In a right-open interval (that is, when expressing a range of indices), the first index is inclusive and the second is exclusive. In terms of these four methods, the significance of right-open intervals in the `String` and `StringBuffer` classes is as follows:

- The last character in a substring is `endIndex - 1`

- If you want a substring that reaches to the end of the string, pass it the length of the string

- The last character in a string copied using the `getChars` method is `srcEnd - 1`. If you want to copy the whole string, pass it the length of the string

- The last character deleted or replaced in a `StringBuffer` is `end-1`

You should not have any problem remembering that the "to" index in a range of indices is exclusive because right-open intervals are always used when passing a range of indices in the Java programming languages.

5.6 Checked Exceptions in `String` and `StringBuffer`

There is only one checked exception thrown by any of the constructors or methods in the `String` and `StringBuffer` classes. That is `java.io.UnsupportedEncodingException`, which is a subclass of `java.io.IOException`. This checked exception is thrown by the following constructors and method, none of which is used very often:

```
public String(byte bytes[], int offset, int length, String enc)
public String(byte bytes[], String enc)
public byte[] getBytes(String enc)
```

Consequently, the general rule is that methods and constructors in the `String` and `StringBuffer` classes never need to be coded in try blocks. The `UnsupportedEncodingException` is discussed in 5.7.5 Translating Locally Encoded Strings.

5.7 The `String` Class

There are no general-purpose constructors in the `String` class, which brings up an interesting point. How do you create a string? You do not have to use the `new` keyword to instantiate the `String` class. String literals implicitly create new `String` objects when the class file is loaded. For example,

```
String s = "Hello World!";
```

This code implicitly creates a `String` object with the value `"Hello World"`. Other than the use of array initializers, which implicitly create arrays, the `String` class is the only class that can be instantiated without using the `new` keyword.

All of the `public` fields, constructors, and methods declared in the `String` class are discussed in the following subsections.

5.7.1 Case Mappings

These methods convert all of the characters in a string to either lowercase or uppercase. There are two groups of methods to consider:

```
public String toLowerCase()
public String toLowerCase(Locale locale)

public String toUpperCase()
public String toUpperCase(Locale locale)
```

As you might expect, the first method in each group invokes the second method using the default locale.

If the first method is implemented as `return toLower-Case(Locale.getDefault())` or `return toUpper-Case(Locale.getDefault())`, there is a certainty that the behavior of these methods is the same. The API docs are misleading in this regard. They suggest that `toLowerCase(Locale locale)` and `toUpper-Case(Locale locale)` include special mappings for the Turkish language. This is not the case (no pun intended). That a few case mappings for the Turkish language require special handling is an implementation detail that should not be exposed in the API docs.

The case mappings are the same for all of these methods. This includes the unusual case mappings in Figure 5-1.

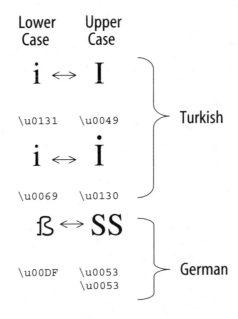

Figure 5-1: Unusual case mappings.

Case mappings are not always reversible. For example,

```
class Test {
    public static void main(String[] args) {
        String name = "John Brown";
        System.out.println("name = " + name);
        name = name.toUpperCase();
        System.out.println("name = " + name);
        name = name.toLowerCase();
        System.out.println("name = " + name);
    }
}
```

Executing this program prints

```
name = John Brown
name = JOHN BROWN
name = john brown
```

By reversible, I mean that some programmers expect the following output:

```
name = John Brown
```

```
name = JOHN BROWN
name = John Brown
```

The capitalization of the name is "reversed" (back to the original), but that is not how these methods work. As with all of the would-be mutator methods in the `String` class, sometimes a copy of the original string must be saved.

For Germans at least, there is the distinct possibility that the length of the string returned will be different from the original because the ß character in that language maps to "SS" in uppercase and vice versa.

5.7.2 Comparing Strings

These methods return `true` if two strings are the same or if different "regions" of the strings *match*. There are three groups of methods to consider as well as the only `public` field in the `String` class:

```
public boolean equals(Object anObject)
public boolean equalsIgnoreCase(String anotherString)

public int compareTo(String anotherString)
public int compareToIgnoreCase(String str)

public boolean regionMatches(int toffset,
                             String other,
                             int ooffset,
                             int len)
public boolean regionMatches(boolean ignoreCase,
                             int toffset,
                             String other,
                             int ooffset,
                             int len)

public static final Comparator CASE_INSENSITIVE_ORDER
```

The first group of methods includes the `equals(Object o)` method, only the parameter name has been changed from `o` to `anObject`. This is the same case-sensitive `equals(Object o)` method that all classes inherit from `Object`. The `equalsIgnoreCase(String anotherString)` method is case insensitive. Both methods return `false` if the strings are different lengths.[1]

The `compareTo(String anotherString)` method implements the `Comparator` interface in the `String` class. It is a lexicographic sort that is used all the time by application programmers. Lexicographic sorts

---

1. This would appear to be a bug considering the German case mapping of ß to "SS" discussed in the last section.

are discussed further in 4.12.5 The Comparable Interface. The second `compareToIgnoreCase(String str)` method allows for case-insensitive sorts. Alternatively, there is the `CASE_INSENSITIVE_ORDER` field, which is one of two very important `Comparator` objects in the core API. See 6.15.1 Sorting Containers for a discussion.

The funny thing about being case insensitive in the world of Unicode, in which lowercase may be unequal and uppercase equal or vice versa, is that you must decide which case to ignore, upper or lower. This leads to the following interface specification.

> Two characters, `c1` and `c2`, are considered the same, ignoring case if at least one of the following is true.
>
> - The two characters are the same (as compared by the `==` operator)
> - Applying the method `Character.toUpperCase(char)` to each character produces the same result
> - Applying the method `Character.toLowerCase(char)` to each character produces the same result[2]

Notice that this says "at least one" of these must be true, not all of them. In other words, *equals ignore case* means if there is any possibility of the strings being equal, not that the strings are equal when mapped to both upper- and lowercases.

The first `regionMatches` method invokes the second with `ignoreCase` set to `false`. Note that the regions are necessarily the same length (because different length strings are never equal), but they do not have to begin at the same position. The `toffset` and the `ooffset` are the index values for the first character in their respective regions. Often the `ooffset` is zero and the `length` argument is equal to the length of the other string. For example,

```
if (regionMatches(toffset, other, 0, other.length())
    ...
```

In this case the `other` string is sometimes called a **pattern string** because it is being used to search for a pattern of characters in the target string.

The overloaded `regionMatches` methods return `false` rather than throw a `StringIndexOutOfBoundsException`. This makes

---

2. API docs for the `equalsIgnoreCase()` method in the `java.lang.String` class.

them easier to use in certain loops such as those discussed at the bottom of the next section.

5.7.3 Accessing Individual Characters or Substrings

Individual characters or substrings are directly accessed using indices. There are two groups of methods to consider:

```
public char charAt(int index)

public String substring(int beginIndex)
public String substring(int beginIndex, int endIndex)
```

The `charAt(int index)` method returns an individual character at the specified position. The first `substring` method invokes the second using zero as the `beginIndex` and the length of the string as the `endIndex`. Note that `endIndex` is always `beginIndex` plus the length of the substring (that is, a right-open interval). The `charAt(int index)` method throws `StringIndexOutOfBoundsException`. The other two methods, however, return an empty string rather than throw an `StringIndexOutOfBoundsException`.

There are four groups of methods to consider when searching for an individual character or substring:

```
public int indexOf(int ch)
public int indexOf(int ch, int fromIndex)

public int lastIndexOf(int ch)
public int lastIndexOf(int ch, int fromIndex)

public int indexOf(String str)
public int indexOf(String str, int fromIndex)

public int lastIndexOf(String str)
public int lastIndexOf(String str, int fromIndex)
```

In all cases the first method invokes the second with `fromIndex` equal to zero. The first two groups of methods find the first or last occurrence of an individual character. The last two groups find the first or last occurrence of a substring. The return value is always the index of the individual character or substring. If the individual character or substring is not found, -1 is returned.

To find all occurrences of an individual character or substring, the search methods are invoked in a loop until the beginning or end of the string is reached. For example,

```
class Test {
    public static void main(String[] args) {
        String s = "How much wood would a woodchuck chuck, " +
```

```
                "if a woodchuck could chuck wood?";
        int index;

        //indexOf(int ch, int fromIndex)
        index = s.indexOf('w', 0);
        while(index != -1) {
            System.out.print(index + "  ");
            index = s.indexOf('w', ++index);
        }
        System.out.println();

        //lastIndexOf(int ch, int fromIndex)
        index = s.lastIndexOf('w', s.length());
        while(index != -1) {
            System.out.print(index + "  ");
            index = s.lastIndexOf('w', --index);
        }
        System.out.println();

        //indexOf(String str, int fromIndex)
        index = s.indexOf("wood", 0);
        while(index != -1) {
            System.out.print(index + "  ");
            index = s.indexOf("wood", index+4);
        }
        System.out.println();

        //lastIndexOf(String str, int fromIndex)
        index = s.lastIndexOf("wood", s.length());
        while(index != -1) {
            System.out.print(index + "  ");
            index = s.lastIndexOf("wood", index-4);
        }
    }
}
```

Executing this program prints

```
2 9 14 22 44 66
66 44 22 14 9 2
9 22 44 66
66 44 22 9
```

These methods are specifically designed to be executed in such loops (until -1 is returned and regardless of the fromIndex value passed). That is why they do not throw a StringIndexOutOfBoundsException.

The following three boolean methods test for substrings at the beginning or end of a string:

```
public boolean startsWith(String prefix)
public boolean startsWith(String prefix, int toffset)
public boolean endsWith(String suffix)
```

The `startsWith(String prefix, int toffset)` method is just an `indexOf(String str, int fromIndex)` with a boolean result type. The first `startsWith` method invokes the second with `toffset` equal to zero. The only exception these methods throw is a `NullPointerException` if the `prefix` or `suffix` is null. If the `prefix` or `suffix` are empty strings, `toffset` is negative, or if `toffset` is greater than or equal to the length of this string, `false` is returned.

One of the common uses of the `endswith(String suffix)` method is to test for a particular file extension. For example,

```java
import java.io.*;
import java.util.*;
class Test {
    public static void main(String[] args) {
        File directory = new File(System.getProperty("user.dir"));
        String[] list = directory.list(new FilenameFilter() {
                public boolean accept(File directory, String name) {
                    return name.endsWith(".java");
                }
            });
        Arrays.sort(list);
        for (int i=0; i < list.length; i++)
            System.out.println(list[i]);
    }
}
```

This program prints all of the `.java` source code files in the current working directory.

5.7.4 `char[]` to `String` Conversions and Vice Versa

Constructors are generally used for `char[]` to `String` conversions. However, the `valueOf` and `copyValueOf` utility methods discussed in this section can also be used. The following is a list of all of the constructors and utility methods that can be used for `char[]` to `String` conversions:

```java
public String(char[] value)
public String(char[] value,
              int offset,
              int count)

public static String valueOf(char[] data)
public static String valueOf(char[] data,
                             int offset,
                             int count)

public static String copyValueOf(char data[])
public static String copyValueOf(char data[],
                                 int offset,
                                 int count)
```

In all cases the first constructor or method invokes the second with an offset of zero and a count equal to the length of the character array. Only two of the fully overloaded valueOf methods are shown here. They are used for the implicit string conversions in a string concatenation operation. See 5.11.2 Implicit String Conversions for a complete discussion of the valueOf utility methods in the String class.

Except for the method names, the copyValueOf methods are the same as the valueOf methods. The copyValueOf methods should have been deprecated long ago because they are redundant and only serve to confuse the String class interface. They are holdovers from a time when constructors in the String class copied the reference to the char[] argument rather than copying the actual data (that is, creating a new character array). As explained by Patrick Naughton,

> The runtime didn't copy the char array in earlier pre-release versions of the system. In fact there was a second version called copyValueOf, which did do the copy. As of JDK 1.0, both valueOf and copyValueOf, and subsequently substring, all make copies of the array. This was introduced as a security measure ....[3]

That is the story of why there are two groups of related methods for copying the contents of a character array. This is ancient history, though. As already stated, you should use the constructors to copy the contents of a character array. The fully overloaded valueOf methods are used in implicit string conversions and the copyValueOf methods should be deprecated.

The rest of this section discusses String to char[] conversions in the opposite direction. There are two utility methods to consider:

```
public char[] toCharArray()
public void getChars(int srcBegin, int srcEnd, char dst[], int dstBegin)
```

Both of these methods are layered on top of the arraycopy(Object src, int src_position, Object dst, int dst_position, int length) method discussed in 6.15.3.1 System.arraycopy. Much like the method it is built directly on top of, the getChars(int srcBegin, int srcEnd, char dst[], int dstBegin) is a workhorse in the core API. It adds a bounds check before invoking Sys-

---

3. Patrick Naughton, *The Java Handbook* (Berkeley: McGraw-Hill, 1996), 161.

tem.arraycopy. The toCharArray() method in turn is built on top of the getChars method. It creates the character array for you and then invokes the getChars method to copy the elements.

5.7.5 Translating Locally Encoded Strings

These constructors and methods are used to translate locally encoded character strings. There are two groups of constructors and one group of methods to consider. String class constructors are always used to translate from local character encodings to Unicode. The overloaded getBytes methods are used to go the other direction:

```
public String(byte[] bytes)
public String(byte[] bytes, String enc)

public String(byte[] bytes, int offset, int length)
public String(byte[] bytes, int offset, int length, String enc)

public byte[] getBytes()
public byte[] getBytes(String enc)
```

In all three cases the first constructor or method is exactly the same as the second except for the addition of an enc parameter. The enc parameter is called a **character encoding string**. They are also known as *encoding identifiers*. The first constructor or method in each of these sets invokes the second passing a reference to the **default character encoding**. As stated in the API docs for the java.lang package,

> Various constructors and methods in the java.lang and java.io packages accept string arguments that specify the character encoding to be used when converting between raw eight-bit bytes and sixteen-bit Unicode characters ....
>
> Every instance of the Java virtual machine has a default character encoding. The default encoding is determined during virtual-machine startup and typically depends upon the locale and encoding being used by the underlying operating system [emphasis added].[4]

The default character encoding is stored in the file.encoding system property. For example,

```
class Test {
    public static void main(String[] args) {
        System.out.println(System.getProperty("file.encoding"));
```

---

4. API docs for the java.lang package.

```
        }
    }
```

Executing this program on a Windows machine prints `Cp1252`, which is the Latin-1 character encoding scheme used by the Windows operating system.[5] There are hundreds of character encoding schemes in use throughout the world. Hence, there are hundreds of character encoding strings in the Java programming language to identify them. If the character encoding string passed to one of these constructors or methods is not supported by a particular JVM, an `UnsupportedEncodingException` is thrown at run time.

Translating between the default character encoding (or any character encoding for that matter) and Unicode is normally the domain of the `InputStreamReader` and `OutputStreamReader` classes in the `java.io` package. Those classes translate entire files. However, `String` constructors can do the same thing and are much easier to use. For example,

```
FileInputStream fis = new FileInputStream("Whatever.txt");
byte[] data = new byte[fis.available()];
fis.read(data);
String text = new String(data);
```

These four lines of code read the contents of any text file into a string, converting from the default character encoding to Unicode along the way. Whether or not reading the entire contents of a file into memory in a single read statement is a good idea is a separate issue. It depends on the size of the file.

5.7.6 Miscellaneous Methods in the `String` Class

These are miscellaneous methods that do not fit in any of the other sub-sections:

```
public String trim()
public String replace(char oldChar, char newChar)
```

The API docs for the `trim()` method say that this method removes white space from the beginning and end of a string and cross references the deprecated `isSpace(char ch)` method in the `Character` class. The `isSpace(char ch)` method, as you may recall from Chapter 1, is

---

5. The full name is "Microsoft Windows Codepage: 1252 (Latin I)," which is documented at *www.microsoft.com/globaldev/reference/sbcs/1252.htm*. The "Cp" stands for *codepage*, which is the Microsoft term for what the *Unicode Standard* calls a code chart.

now described as *ISO Latin-1 white space*, which includes the ASCII space character as well as 4 of the 32 CO control characters. The isWhiteSpace(char ch) method is an internationalized definition of white space that includes all but 4 of the space characters in the *Unicode Standard* as well as 9 of the 32 CO control characters. The trim() method in the String class trims the ASCII space character and all 32 CO control characters. It is not a very significant point, but you should be aware that these are three different definitions of white space. See also 1.2 White Space.

The semantics of the replace(char oldChar, char newChar) is fairly obvious. Every occurrence of oldChar is replaced by newChar in the string returned. This method is case sensitive. For a more powerful replace method, use replace(int start, int end, String str) in StringBuffer.

5.7.7 Unusual Constructors in the String Class

The following String class instructors all have highly specialized uses:

```
public String()
public String(String value)
String(StringBuffer buffer)
```

The no-argument (or no-arg) constructor is rarely invoked by application programmers. It represents an empty string and is primarily used when loading class files that include the "" empty string literal. Remember, string literals are instances of the String class. Whenever a string literal with a length of zero is loaded from the constant pool of a class file, the String() constructor is invoked. There is only ever one such string added to the pool of unique strings privately maintained by the String class. Therefore, for any given execution of the JVM, this constructor would only be invoked once. Note that it could also be used in place of an empty string, if for some reason you do not want to use "" as a string literal.

The String(String value) constructor is a copy constructor. It copies the contents of the argument string. For example,

```
class Test {
    public static void main(String[] args) {
        String original = "whatever";
        String copy = new String(original);
        System.out.println(copy.equals(original));
        System.out.println(copy == original);
    }
}
```

Executing this program prints

```
true
false
```

`String` objects are immutable, so this constructor is seldom used. Note that the string returned by this constructor is by definition a computed string. For example,

```
class Test {
    public static void main(String[] args) {
        String copy = new String("whatever");
        System.out.println(copy == "whatever");
    }
}
```

Executing this program prints `false` because computed strings are not automatically interned as are string literals and compile-time constants of type `String`. That means the following two lines of code are not the same:

```
String s = "Hello World!";
String s = new String("Hello World!");
```

One creates a string that is equal to `"Hello World!"` using reference equality, and the other does not. Normally strings are copied by simply assigning the string to a different `String` type variable. In other words, the reference is copied, not the contents.

The last of the specialized constructors is discussed in 5.11.4 Shared Character Buffers. That constructor is used in the `toString()` method for the `StringBuffer` class, which is what an application programmer would invoke rather than directly using this constructor.

5.8 The `StringBuffer` Class

The most important methods in the `StringBuffer` class are the fully overloaded `append` and `insert` methods. Then there are what might be called the *infrastructure* methods: `length()`, `setLength()`, `capacity()`, and `ensureCapacity(int minimumCapacity)`. These methods are discussed in 5.3 The Length of a `String` or `StringBuffer` and 5.4 The Capacity of a `StringBuffer`. The 1.2 release more than doubled the number of other methods in the `StringBuffer` class. However, there is still only a handful of them. They are discussed in 5.8.2 Other Methods in the `StringBuffer` Class.

5.8.1 The Overloaded `insert` and `append` Methods

These methods are described as the *principle operations* of the `String-Buffer` class. They are **fully overloaded** in that any data type can be passed to them.[6] Here is a complete list of the methods:

```
public StringBuffer append(Object obj)
public StringBuffer append(String str)
public StringBuffer append(char[] str)
public StringBuffer append(boolean b)
public StringBuffer append(char c)
public StringBuffer append(int i)
public StringBuffer append(long l)
public StringBuffer append(float f)
public StringBuffer append(double d)

public StringBuffer append(char[] str,
                           int offset,
                           int len)

public StringBuffer insert(int offset, Object obj)
public StringBuffer insert(int offset, String str)
public StringBuffer insert(int offset, char[] str)
public StringBuffer insert(int offset, boolean b)
public StringBuffer insert(int offset, char c)
public StringBuffer insert(int offset, int i)
public StringBuffer insert(int offset, long l)
public StringBuffer insert(int offset, float f)
public StringBuffer insert(int offset, double d)
```

The `insert` and `append` methods can produce the same results when the offset argument passed to an `insert` method is equal to the length of the `StringBuffer`. To add something to the front of a `String-Buffer`, invoke one of the `insert` methods using a zero `offset` argument.

As discussed in 5.11.2 Implicit String Conversions, the `append` methods are responsible for the implicit string conversions in a string concatenation operation. The `insert` methods make the same string conversions. As in string concatenation operations, passing a `null` reference to one of these methods will result in `"null"` being appended or inserted.

---

6. As used in this book, *fully overloaded* always includes all of the primitive data types and `Object`, but is loosely defined in terms of which arrays can be passed. The term usually includes at least an `Object []` but not always (as is the case here). I would say that the `print` and `println` used when writing to standard output as well as the append and insert methods in the `StringBuffer` should be used to define the term *fully overloaded*. This term is of my own making.

5.8.2 Other Methods in the `StringBuffer` Class

Except for synchronization, the following four methods are the exact same in both the `String` and `StringBuffer` classes:

```
public char charAt(int index)
public void getChars(int srcBegin, int srcEnd, char[] dst, int dstBegin)
public String substring(int start)
public String substring(int start, int end)
```

You can read about these four methods in the sections on the `String` class. A few of the parameters names are different, but the method signatures and semantics are the same.

This leaves only the following four methods in the `StringBuffer` class, the semantics of which is fairly obvious:

```
public synchronized void setCharAt(int index, char ch)
public synchronized void deleteCharAt(int index)
public synchronized void delete(int start, int end)
public synchronized StringBuffer reverse()
public StringBuffer replace(int start,
                            int end,
                            String str)
```

The `deleteCharAt(int index)` and `delete(int start, int end)` methods are interesting in that they actually shorten the length of a `StringBuffer`. Although the result type of the `reverse()` method is `StringBuffer`, it does not create a new `StringBuffer`. A reference to the same `StringBuffer` is returned. This is consistent with the older `append` and `insert` methods. The newer methods added in the 1.2 release broke ranks and have a `void` result type. A `StringBuffer` result type makes sense for the `append` methods, invocations of which are chained together by the compiler, but not for methods such as `reverse()`. In that case returning a value that is probably never used is inefficient. Note that the parameters and semantics of the `replace(int start, int end, String str)` method in `String-Buffer` are different from the like named `replace(char oldChar, char newChar)` in the `String` class.

5.9 Other String-Related Classes

There are several other classes that can be used to read or write a string. Each offers something a little different. One is a container for passing text, especially to methods in the `java.text` package. Others wrap a `String` and `StringBuffer` in the `Reader` and `Writer` interfaces used in the `java.io` package. The intent in both cases is to pass strings around using standard interfaces (other than `String` and `StringBuffer`). Each offers something different. They are summarized in Table 5-1. Except for `String` and `StringBuffer`, which have already been discussed, each of these string-related classes is discussed in the following subsections.

5.9.1 The `StringCharacterIterator` Class

The `StringCharacterIterator` class implements the `CharacterIterator` interface, which allows for bidirectional iteration over text using the following methods:

```
current()
first()
last()
next()
previous()
```

Note that these have become standard method names for iterators in both the `java.util` and `java.text` packages.

This container offers a convenient alternative to the `for` loop for iterating over the characters in string. For example, the following loops are identical:

```
import java.text.*;
class Test {
    public static void main(String[] args) {
        String text = "testing, testing, testing";
        final int DONE = CharacterIterator.DONE;  //get rid of long name
        CharacterIterator iterator = new StringCharacterIterator(text);
        for (char ch=iterator.first(); ch != DONE; ch=iterator.next())
            System.out.print(ch);
        System.out.println();
        for (int i=0; i < text.length(); i++)
            System.out.print(text.charAt(i));
    }
}
```

Executing this program prints the `text` string twice.

`CharacterIterator` is different from `StringBuffer` in that the user has total control of the characters in the container. What this means is that there are no methods, such a `insert` and `delete`, in the `StringBuffer` class that do element shifting. (Element shifting is discussed in 6.10.1.1 `ArrayList` and `LinkedList` and is depicted in Figure 6-9.) Dr. Davis explains the necessity for the `CharacterIteator` interface in a February 1999 *Java Report* article as follows.

Table 5-1: String Classes

Class	Description
String	As already discussed, String is immutable. It is used to store string literals and has many useful methods for manipulating strings.
StringBuffer	StringBuffer is the general-purpose class for mutable strings. It includes a number of useful methods for manipulating strings.
StringCharacterIterator	A container for text primarily used in the java.text package for internationalization but also very handy for bidirectional iteration over the characters in a String.
StringReader	Unlike StringWriter, there has always been something like StringReader in the Java programming language. The method was originally called StringBufferInputStream. Before there was a StringCharacterIterator, these classes were particularly useful in reading a String one character at a time.
StringWriter	StringWriter is an *append only* alternative to StringBuffer in which the write primitives in the java.io package take the place of the append methods. It is only an alternative interface. The engine under the hood is still a StringBuffer.

Why Have CharacterIterator?

The CharacterIterator [interface] is used in BreakIterator and a few other places in the JDK and is used even more in Java 2. Sometimes we are asked why we didn't use String or StringBuffer instead.

String and StringBuffer are simple classes that store their characters contiguously. Insertion or deletion of characters in a StringBuffer end up shifting all the characters that follow, which works fine for reasonably small number of characters. However, this model doesn't scale well. Consider a word processor, for example, where shifting many kilobytes of characters just to insert or delete one character involves far too much extra work. For acceptable performance in these circumstances, text needs to be stored in data structures that use internally discontiguous chunks of storage.

We needed some way to have a more abstract representation of text that could be used both for `String` and for larger-scale text models. Unfortunately, we couldn't change `String` and `StringBuffer` to descend from an abstract class that would provide this sort of representation. To resolve this problem, we added a very minimal interface, `CharacterIterator`. This interface allows both sequential (forward and backward) and random access to characters from any source, not just from a `String` or `Stringbuffer`.[7]

The API docs describe this as a *protocol*.

The `for` loop in the previous example is the one suggested by the API docs. There are, however, alternatives. For example,

```
/*
 * Forward iteration
 */
final int DONE = CharacterIterator.DONE;
char c = iterator.first();
while (c != DONE) {
   System.out.print(c);
   c=iterator.next();

/*
 * Backward iteration
 */
char c = iterator.last();
while (c != DONE) {
   System.out.print(c);
   c=iterator.previous();
}
```

Other than the canonical form of the `for` loop used to loop through an array, I generally prefer this construct for iteration. It is a very clean read.

`CharacterIterator` has four methods for getting and setting the index:

```
public int getIndex()
public char setIndex(int p)
public int getBeginIndex()
public int getEndIndex()
```

---

7. Mark Davis, "The Java Internationalization API," *Java Report*, Vol. 4, No. 2 (Feb. 1999): 32.

The beginning and ending of the text is determined during object initialization and cannot be changed. There are three contructors to consider:

```
public StringCharacterIterator(String text)
public StringCharacterIterator(String text, int pos)
public StringCharacterIterator(String text, int begin, int end, int pos)
```

The first two constructors set the begin index to zero and the end index to the length of the string. For example,

```
import java.text.*;
class Test {
    public static void main(String[] args) {
        String text = "testing, testing, testing";
        CharacterIterator iterator = new StringCharacterIterator(text);
        System.out.print(iterator.getBeginIndex() == 0);
        System.out.print(iterator.getEndIndex() == text.length());
    }
}
```

Executing this program prints `true` twice. The last two constructors allow you to specify the *position*, or initial index value. If the argument passed is not a valid index for the `String`, an `IllegalArgumentException` is thrown with a detailed error message of "`Invalid position`". For the first two constructors the entire string is editable. The third constructor sets the begin and end index, which thereafter cannot be changed. This means a window on the text is opened when the `StringCharacter-Iterator` is created. Any text before or after that window is not editable because attempting to do so throws an exception. For example:

```
import java.text.*;
class Test {
    public static void main(String[] args) {
        String text = "testing, testing, testing";
        CharacterIterator iterator = new StringCharacterIterator(text, 9, 16, 9);
        iterator.setIndex(0);
    }
}
```

Attempting to execute this program throws the following exception:

```
Exception in thread "main" java.lang.IllegalArgumentException: Invalid index at
java.text.StringCharacterIterator.setIndex(Unknown Source) at Test.main(test.java:6)
```

Text outside of the window is not editable.

5.9.2 The `StringReader` and `StringWriter` Classes

`StringReader` and `StringWriter` are members of the `java.io` package. They implement the `Reader` and `Writer` interfaces in the same package. In this context those interfaces can be regarded as alternatives to the interface implicitly defined by the `String` and `StringBuffer` class types, respectively.

`StringReader(String s)` is the only constructor in the `StringReader` class. The following implementation of that constructor and related instance variables should help you more fully appreciate how `StringReader` is a thin wrapper for a `String`:

```
private String s;
private int length;

public StringReader(String s) {
    this.s = s;
    this.length = s.length();
}
```

Likewise, the `StringWriter` class has two constructors and these directly correspond to the `StringBuffer` constructors. Here are all four of the constructors:

```
public StringBuffer()
public StringBuffer(int length)

public StringWriter()
public StringWriter(int initialSize)
```

The second constructor from both classes allows you to specify the initial capacity of the `StringBuffer`.

The parameter names used in both the `StringBuffer(int length)` and `StringWriter(int initialSize)` constructors is unfortunate. It should be `initialCapacity` for both constructors. That would be consistent with the `ensureCapacity(int minimumCapacity)` method. Because of this parameter name I should point out that the length of a `StringBuffer` or `StringWriter` using either of these constructors is initially zero, no matter what argument is passed.

The implementation of the `StringWriter` constructors and related instance variables is also instructive in showing how the `StringReader` and `StringWriter` are thin wrappers for `String` and `StringBuffer`, respectively:

```
private StringBuffer buffer;
public StringWriter() {
    buffer = new StringBuffer();
}
public StringWriter(int initialSize) {
    if (initialSize < 0)
        throw new IllegalArgumentException("Negative buffer size");
    buffer = new StringBuffer(initialSize);
}
```

The question is *what do the* `StringReader` *and* `StringWriter` *interfaces offer that other string-related classes do not*. This is an interesting question because, if you look carefully at the `Reader` and `Writer` interfaces they implement, the answer is that they offer no functionality that cannot be easily replicated in string classes outside of the `java.io` package.

That explains why, as of this writing, `StringReader` is used only once in the core API and `StringWriter` is not used at all. More than anything else, this should serve to inform you of the usefulness of these classes. They are not so much used for their interfaces to read and write strings are they are to wrap a `String` in a `Reader` or `Writer` interface. There does not, however, appear to be a great need for that. This explains `StringReader` but does not do much in explaining `String-Writer` because a `CharacterArrayWriter` would do just as well in passing a character string as a `Writer` and is more flexible. I believe `StringWriter` was included in the 1.1 release largely for the sake of symmetry. It is notable that, even though there was a `StringBuffer-InputStream` in the original `java.io` package of the 1.0 release, there was nothing equivalent to the current `StringWriter` class.[8]

5.10 Lexical Analysis

There is always more than one way to solve a programming problem, and this is certainly the case when tokenizing a string or text file. The Java programming language has steadily grown from the simplicity of `String-Tokenizer` to the sophistication of `BreakIterator`. In a `StringTokenizer` the characters between tokens are referred to as delimeters. Tokens are usually returned. Delimeters are not, although delimeters can be optionally returned along with the tokens if the `String-Tokenizer` (`String str, String delim, boolean returnDelim`) constructor is invoked with `returnDelim` set to true. This is when `StreamTokinizer` behaves most like `BreakIterator` because you do not know for sure if the first `String` returned by `nextToken()` is a token or delimiter, and the only way to know for

---

8. The `StringBufferInputStream` had to be deprecated because the byte-to-char conversion requisite to read a Unicode string into a byte stream used only the second, low-order byte in each Unicode character. In other words, this class suffered from the same problem all byte streams had when trying to convert to and from Unicode characters. It worked, but only for one-byte character encodings.

sure is to test the first character of the `String` returned to see if it is one of the delimiter characters. The same is sometimes true when working with text boundaries. Word boundaries in particular behave like this, only instead of testing the first character of the `String` returned to see if it is a delimiter, the `Character.isLetter(char ch)` method is invoked for all the characters between two word boundaries. If any of them return `true`, the characters between those boundaries is a word. But I am getting ahead of myself.

The subject of text boundaries requires that an application programmer think globally or face the prospect of having to rewrite parts of a program should they ever be used in an internationalized program. For example, consider the following `WordCount` program that uses a `switch` statement to count the number of characters, words, and lines in a plain text file:

```java
import java.io.*;
class SimpleWordCount {
    public static void main(String[] args) {
        int characters= 0, words = 0, lines = 0;
        boolean word = false;
        File file = new File("Shakespeare.txt");
        /*
         *  process file one character at a time
         */
        try {
            BufferedReader inputFile = new BufferedReader(new FileReader(file));
            int ch = inputFile.read();
            while(ch != -1) {
                if (Character.isWhitespace((char)ch)) {
                    if (ch == '\n')
                        lines++;
                    if (word)
                        words++;
                    word = false;
                } else {
                    characters++;
                    word = true;
                }
                ch = inputFile.read();
            }
            inputFile.close();
        }
        catch (IOException e) {System.err.println(e);}

        System.out.println("The file " + file + " has " + characters +
            " characters, " + words + " words, and " + lines + " lines.");
    }
}
```

While this program works, it is hopelessly backward as far as international-ization is concerned because it only works with ASCII or Latin-1 files (and even then is somewhat simplistic in that it counts every single character in the input file instead of distinguishing between characters and spaces). In 5.10.1.2 Iterating Over Word Boundaries, this program is internationalized through the use of a `BreakIterator`.

An important distinction is made between natural languages and pro-gramming languages. The newer `BreakIterator` class is designed for use with natural languages such as English, French, or Spanish, not pro-gramming languages. There is no replacement for the `StreamToken-izer` class for tokenizing source code files. All of the available classes for lexical analysis are summarized in Table 5-2.

All of the classes mentioned in this table that are directly related to string processing are discussed in the following subsections.

5.10.1 The `BreakIterator` Class[9]

A **break** is another term for a text boundary. They are completely synony-mous, hence the class name `BreakIterator`, which is said to iterate over text boundaries. The behavior of a `BreakIterator` is similar to a `StringTokenizer`, but instead of returning a token, a `BreakItera-tor` returns the boundaries of a glyph, word, line, or sentence, which are collectively referred to as **text boundaries**. The boundaries are returned by the following methods:

```
public int first()
public int last();
public int next();
public int previous();
public int next(int n);
public int following(int offset);
public int preceding(int offset)
```

All of these methods return an `int` type value which can be used to access the `String` using some other class. That is an important point to

---

9. `BreakIterator` is an `abstract` class that is routinely instantiated by invoking a factory method. This is a favorite design of the software engineers at Taligent, Inc., who wrote most of the software used in the localization of common data types. Common functionality is captured in the `abstract` superclass (which is also used as an interface). One of their "Simple" subclasses, for example, the package-private `SimpleTextBoundary`, is the main implementation class. I do not like this design. One of the more serious problems with this approach is that adding `abstract` methods to a class breaks compatibilty with existing binaries. In order to add methods they need to use bogus implementations. See the source code for the `preceding(int offset)` method for an example.

Table 5-2: Lexical Analysis Classes

Use	Class
Finding text boundaries in a natural language	The `java.text.BreakIterator` class should always be used to make the program "amenable to internationalization and localization," to quote Dr. Gosling.
Tokenizing a source code file	While not so obvious in the class name the `java.io.StreamTokenizer` is designed specifically for this purpose.
Reading binary data or `.dat` files	Binary data include strings that are read and written using `DataInputStream` and `DataOutputStream` classes.
Tokenizing numbers in a plain text file	The `StreamTokenizer` class reads all numbers into the `nval` field, which is of type `double`. If you are reading mixed primitive numeric data types and need to preserve the type information, try using something like the code in the `PrintReader` and `KeyboardReader` classes. The exception is if you have a text file of numbers separated by white space or line separators and do not care if they are all read into the `double` type. In that case, the `StreamTokenizer` class would work well. There is an example of doing just this in the `StreamTokenizer` class subsection.
Tokenizing configuration files (or more generally, files in `name=value` format)	Configuration files written in Java should be referred to as *property lists*. The `Property` class is designed specifically for reading and writing such files. (See also 4.10.4 Accessing Primitive Type System Properties)
A general-purpose class for tokenizing strings	The `StringTokenizer` class remains useful because an application programmer can set the delimiters to anything. However, it is expected that any serious program that must iterate over text that includes punctuation would use a `BreakIterator`.

grasp. The `BreakIterator` class only tells you where the breaks are. To access the string using the index values returned by any of these methods you must use the `String` or `StringCharacterIterator` passed to the overloaded `setText` methods. At that point the so-called "breaks" are indistinguishable from other indices. For example,

```
import java.text.*;
class Test {
    public static void main(String[] args) {

        BreakIterator words = BreakIterator.getWordInstance();
        String text = "Testing, testing, testing";
        words.setText(text);

        System.out.println();
        System.out.println("012345678901234567890012345");
        System.out.println(text);
        System.out.println("first() ...... " + words.first());
        System.out.println("next() ....... " + words.next());
        System.out.println("next() ....... " + words.next());
        System.out.println("next() ....... " + words.next());
        System.out.println("next() ....... " + words.next());
        System.out.println("next() ....... " + words.next());
        System.out.println("previous() ... " + words.previous());
        System.out.println("last() ....... " + words.last());
    }
}
```

Executing this program prints

```
012345678901234567890012345
Testing, testing, testing
first() ...... 0
next() ....... 7
next() ....... 8
next() ....... 9
next() ....... 16
next() ....... 17
previous() ... 16
last() ....... 25
```

The first word in this text is "Testing," which begins at zero and ends at seven. The second word is "testing," which begins a 9 and ends at 16. The last break is at 25. All of these are index values that can be used *as is* in a right-open interval. Repeated invocations of the `next()` or `previous()` method continue until the end or beginning of the text is reached, as indicated by the `BreakIterator.DONE` return value. The word iterator requires a little explanation. See 5.10.1.2 Iterating Over Word Boundaries for a discussion.

Notice my use of *glyph* instead of character. Despite the name `getCharacterInstance()` factory method, only a `CharacterIter-`

ator iterates over characters. The `BreakIterator` returned by the `getCharacterInstance()` factory method iterates over glyphs, not characters. And, *Yes*, some glyphs comprise multiple characters. More on this in a moment.

Which text boundaries you iterate over depends on the factory method invoked. There are four groups of factory methods to consider:

```
public static BreakIterator getCharacterInstance()
public static BreakIterator getCharacterInstance(Locale where)

public static BreakIterator getWordInstance()
public static BreakIterator getWordInstance(Locale where)

public static BreakIterator getLineInstance()
public static BreakIterator getLineInstance(Locale where)

public static BreakIterator getSentenceInstance()
public static BreakIterator getSentenceInstance(Locale where)
```

These four possibilities are discussed in the following four subsections. The order in which they are discussed is glyph, word, line, and sentence.

After invoking one of the factory methods and before iterating over the text boundaries, however, one of the `setText` methods must be invoked. There are two groups of methods to consider:

```
public void setText(String newText)
public void setText(CharacterIterator newText)

public CharacterIterator getText()
```

The `setText` methods are used to pass the text to the `BreakIterator`. The first method invokes the second as follows:

```
setText(new StringCharacterIterator(newText));
```

You can see that a `BreakIterator` always uses an instance of the `CharacterIterator` interface, which is, notably, a bidirectional iterator. This also explains why `getText()` returns a `CharacterIterator`.

5.10.1.1 *Iterating Over Glyph Boundaries*

The `BreakIterator` returned by the `getCharacterInstance` factory methods in the `BreakIterator` class is fundamentally different from a `StringCharacterIterator`. A `StringCharacterIterator` iterates over the characters in a string. The `BreakIterator` returned by the `getCharacterInstance` factory methods in `Brea-`

`kIterator` iterates over the corresponding glyphs as they would appear on the console or a printed page.

The main differences are the **diacritical marks** used most frequently in European languages and which have both canonical mappings and Latin-1 characters, such as the following accented small letters a:

àáâãäå

The **Latin-1 diacritics** combine the base character and the combining diacritical mark of the canonical mappings into one glyph. These same glyphs can be represented by the same small letter a followed by a **combining diacritical mark**:

a`a´a^a~a¨a°

The Unicode names for the combining diacritical marks in this character string are (from left to right) *grave accent*, *acute accent*, *circumflex accent*, *tilde*, *diaeresis*, and *ring above*. I am using glyphs for characters which always adds some confusion to the discussion. The Unicode equivalent of àáâãäå is `"\u00E0\u00E1\u00E2\u00E3\u00E4\u00E5"`. The Unicode equivalent of a`a´a^a~a¨a° is `"\u0061\u0300\u0061\`
`u0301\u0061\u0302\u0061\u0303\u0061\u0308\u0061\`
`u030A"`. The difference is that one string has 6 characters and one has 12. When rendered on a display device, however, both strings should appear as àáâãäå. This is what is meant by a *combining* diacritical mark. The display device is responsible for rendering characters correctly.

Where you notice the difference in these two character strings is in the `BreakIterator` returned by the `getCharacterInstance` factory method. That `BreakIterator` understands what a combining diacritical mark is and will treat it and the base character as one. For example,

```
import java.text.*;
class Test {
    public static void main(String[] args) {
        int length=0;
        final int DONE = CharacterIterator.DONE;   //get rid of long name
        CharacterIterator iterator;
        iterator = new StringCharacterIterator
                ("\u00E0\u00E1\u00E2\u00E3\u00E4\u00E5");
        for (char ch = iterator.first(); ch != DONE; ch=iterator.next())
            length++;
        System.out.println("Latin-1 diacritics string length is " + length);
        length = 0;
        ((StringCharacterIterator)iterator).setText
                ("\u0061\u0300\u0061\u0301\u0061\u0302" +
```

```
                            "\u0061\u0303\u0061\u0308\u0061\u030A");
        for (char ch = iterator.first(); ch != DONE; ch=iterator.next())
            length++;
        System.out.println("Combining character diacritics string length is " +
                            length);
    }
}
```

Executing this program prints

```
Latin-1 diacritics string length is 6
Combining character diacritics string length is 12
```

This shows that the *canonical mappings* are not the same as Latin-1 diacritics until the glyphs are rendered on a display device, the difference being that there are twice as many characters using the canonical mappings.

The following `for` loop is suggested by the API docs when iterating over the glyphs in text:

```
BreakIterator boundary = BreakIterator.getCharacterInstance();
boundary.setText(text);
int start = boundary.first();
for (int end = boundary.next();
     end != BreakIterator.DONE;
     start = end, end = boundary.next()) {
    System.out.print(text.charAt(start));
}
```

However, this code seems unnecessarily complicated to me. The following example does exactly the same thing and is much easier to read:

```
BreakIterator cb = BreakIterator.getCharacterInstance();
cb.setText(text);
int boundary = cb.first();
while (boundary != BreakIterator.DONE) {
System.out.print(text.charAt(boundary));
    boundary = cb.next();

}
```

This code is from the internationalized `WordCount` program in the next section.

5.10.1.2 *Iterating Over Word Boundaries*

The API docs have this to say about the `BreakIterator` returned by the `getWordInstance()` factory method.

> Word boundary analysis is used by search and replace functions, as well as within text editing applications that allow the user to select words with a double click. Word selection provides correct interpretation of punctuation marks within and following words.

Characters that are not part of a word, such as symbols or punctuation marks, have word-breaks on both sides.[10]

With every other iteration using a word `BreakIterator` the boundaries are going to be the beginning and end of the space(s), punctuation and space(s), or some other combination of characters that separates the words. This requires reading the characters to see if one of them is a letter. *If at least one character is a letter, the boundaries are for a word.* Because the implementation of `Character.isLetter(char ch)` is based on the *Unicode Standard*, this works for any language.

There is an example of using the `BreakIterator` returned by a `getWordInstance()` method invocation in the following internationalized `WordCount` program:

```java
import java.io.*;
import java.text.*;
class WordCount {
    public static void main(String[] args) throws IOException {

        int charNoWS = 0, allChar = 0, words = 0, sentences = 0;

        /*
         * read text file into byte buffer and then use a
         * String constructor for conversion to Unicode
         */
        File file = new File("Shakespeare.txt");
        FileInputStream fis = new FileInputStream(file);
        byte[] data = new byte[fis.available()];
        fis.read(data);
        String text = new String(data);

        /* count the number of characters */
        BreakIterator cb = BreakIterator.getCharacterInstance();
        cb.setText(text);
        int boundary = cb.first();
        while (boundary != BreakIterator.DONE) {
            allChar++;
            if (!Character.isWhitespace(text.charAt(boundary)))
                charNoWS++;
            boundary = cb.next();                              }

        /* count the number of words */
        BreakIterator wb = BreakIterator.getWordInstance();
        wb.setText(text);
        int lastBoundary = wb.first();
        int nextBoundary = wb.next();
        while (nextBoundary != BreakIterator.DONE) {
            testForWord:
                for (int i = lastBoundary; i < nextBoundary; i++) {
                    if (Character.isLetter(text.charAt(i))) {
```

---

10. API docs for the `java.text.BreakIterator` class.

```
                    words++;
                    break testForWord;
                }
            }
        lastBoundary = nextBoundary;
        nextBoundary = wb.next();
    }

    /* count the number of sentences */
    BreakIterator sb = BreakIterator.getSentenceInstance();
    sb.setText(text);
    while (sb.next() != BreakIterator.DONE)
        sentences++;

    System.out.println("Statistics:");
    System.out.println();
    System.out.println("  words                    " + words);
    System.out.println("  characters (no spaces)   " + charNoWS);
    System.out.println("  characters (with spaces) " + allChar);
    System.out.println("  sentences                " + sentences);
    }
}
```

Executing this program prints

```
Statistics:

words                    183
characters (no spaces)   812
characters (with spaces) 994
sentences                10
```

The file is the Polonius speech from Act I, Scene iii of Shakespeare's *Hamlet*. This is a much cleaner program that offers more possibilities than just counting the number of words and is fully internationalized.

5.10.1.3 *Line Wrapping*

The `BreakIterator` returned by the `getLineInstance()` factory method is not used to find the start and end of a line. It is used to find where a line can be broken, as would be required in a text editor or word processor. This is usually referred to as **line wrapping**. For example, if such a `BreakIterator` were used in the `WordCount` program, the line break count would have been 184, one more than the word count.

5.10.1.4 *Iterating Over Sentence Boundaries*

This is perhaps the simplest `BreakIterator` of all. For example,

```
import java.io.*;
import java.text.*;
```

```
class Test {
    public static void main(String[] args) {
        String text = "I came. I saw. I conquered.";
        BreakIterator iterator = BreakIterator.getSentenceInstance();
        iterator.setText(text);
        int last = iterator.first();
        int next = iterator.next();
        while(next != BreakIterator.DONE) {

            /*
             *  Process sentence here. For example...
             */
            System.out.println(text.substring(last, next));

            last = next;
            next = iterator.next();
        }
    }
}
```

Executing this program prints

```
I came.
I saw.
I conquered.
```

There are three sentences in this text.

5.10.2 The `StringTokenizer` Class

There are three constructors in the `StringTokenizer` class:

```
public StringTokenizer (String str)

public StringTokenizer (String str,
                        String delim)

public StringTokenizer (String str,
                        String delim,
                        boolean returnDelim)
```

The first constructor uses the **default delimiter string** `"\t\n\r"`, which includes a space, tab, and the line separator control characters. A **delimiter** is a character that separates the tokens in a string. A token is any sequence of characters that does not include a delimiter. By passing a delimiter string to one of these constructors you implicitly define the tokens to be returned.

A string is used for the `delim` parameter to allow a programmer to specify more than one delimiter. Delimiters are normally skipped (that is, not returned). If the `returnDelim` parameter in the third constructor is true, however, delimiters are returned one at a time by the `next-Token()` method, which means that at least every other value returned will be a d+Oelimiter. If `returnDelim` is `true`, delimiters are also necessarily counted by the `countToken()` method. For example,

```
import java.util.StringTokenizer;
class Test {
    public static void main(String[] args) {
        String s = "$123.00#10.5#99%##";
        StringTokenizer tokenizer = new StringTokenizer(s, "#", true);
        System.out.println("count = " + tokenizer.countTokens());
        while (tokenizer.hasMoreTokens()) {
            System.out.println(tokenizer.nextToken());
        }
    }
}
```

Executing this program prints

```
count = 7
$123.00
#
10.5
#
99%
#
#
```

Change the `returnDelim` argument to `false` (or just use a different constructor), and the same program prints

```
count = 3
$123.00
10.5
99%
```

A `while` loop is typically used for string tokenization.

There are only six methods in the `StringTokenizer` class. Two of those are overriding implementations of `public` methods in the `Enumeration` interface, which the `StringTokenizer` class implements:

```
public boolean hasMoreElements()
public Object nextElement()
```

These are alternatives to the `hasMoreTokens()` and `nextToken()` methods. They are less convenient to use because `nextElement()` returns an `Object` that must be cast to a `String`, whereas `nextToken()` returns a `String`. Three of the other four methods are used in the example above. The last is the `nextToken(String delim)` method, which allows a programmer to specify a different delimiter or set of delimiters than was passed to the constructor. The no-argument `nextToken()` always uses the delimiter(s) passed to the constructor or the default delimiters if none were passed. Note that it is possible to alternate between the two `nextToken` methods.

5.10.3 The `StreamTokenizer` Class

This class is specifically designed for tokenizing programming languages and as such complements the `BreakIterator` class, which is used for natural languages. The following example uses the `StreamTokenizer` class to print a compilation unit much as it would be input to a parser, which is the next step in the compilation process after tokenizing:

```
package javarules;
import java.io.*;

class Tokenizer {

    public static void main(String[] args) throws IOException {

        File compilationUnit;

        if (args.length == 0)
            //default compilation unit for tokenizing
            compilationUnit = new File("javarules\\Tokenizer.java");
        else
            compilationUnit = new File(args[0]);

        if (!compilationUnit.exists() || !compilationUnit.isFile() ||
            !compilationUnit.getName().endsWith(".java"))
        {
            System.err.println(compilationUnit + " is not a compilation unit");
            System.exit(1);
        }

        Reader reader = new BufferedReader(new FileReader(compilationUnit));
        StreamTokenizer tokenizer = new StreamTokenizer(reader);

        /*
         * Traditional comments such as this one are not removed by default.
         * Invoking these methods causes them to be removed.
         */
        tokenizer.slashStarComments(true);
        tokenizer.slashSlashComments(true);

        while (tokenizer.nextToken() != StreamTokenizer.TT_EOF) {
            switch(tokenizer.ttype) {
                case StreamTokenizer.TT_NUMBER:
                    System.out.println(tokenizer.nval);
                    break;
                case StreamTokenizer.TT_WORD:
                    System.out.println(tokenizer.sval);
                    break;
                case 34:
                    /* This is a "quoted string" in StreamTokenizer terminology.
                     * The value 34 is a double quote, which is NOT output by the
```

```
                             * StringTokenizer class.
                             */
                            System.out.println("\"" + tokenizer.sval + "\"");
                            break;
                        default:
                            System.out.println((char)tokenizer.ttype);
                            break;
                    }
                }
            }
        }
    }
```

The `TT` and `tt` stand for *token type*. Token types are described in Table 5-3.

Table 5-3: Token Types

Token Type	Description
`StreamTokenizer.TT_WORD`	A word stored in the `sval` field
`StreamTokenizer.TT_NUMBER`	A number stored in the `nval` field
`StreamTokenizer.TT_EOL`	End-of-Line (EOL), which is treated as white space and therefore can be ignored unless `eolIsSignificant(true)` is invoked
`StreamTokenizer.TT_EOF`	End-of-File (EOF)
Value passed to the `quoteChar` method, which is typically a double quote (character code 34)	A *quoted string* that is stored in the `sval` field
None of the above	An *ordinary character*, the value of which is stored in `ttype`

Besides tokenizing source code, there is one other use I have found for the `StreamTokenizer` class. If you have a text file of decimal numbers separated by white space, the following program is probably the easiest way to read those values:

```
import java.io.*;
import java.util.*;
class ReadNumbers {
    public static void main(String[] args) throws IOException {

        File inputFile = new File("javarules\\random numbers.txt");
        Reader reader = new BufferedReader(new FileReader(inputFile));
        StreamTokenizer tokenizer = new StreamTokenizer(reader);

        ArrayList numbers = new ArrayList();
```

```
while (tokenizer.nextToken() != StreamTokenizer.TT_EOF) {
    if (tokenizer.ttype == StreamTokenizer.TT_NUMBER)
        numbers.add(new Double(tokenizer.nval));
    else {
        System.err.println("file is corrupted");
        System.exit(1);
    }
}

int count = 0;
Iterator iterator = numbers.iterator();
while(iterator.hasNext()) {
    count++;
    System.out.println(((Double) iterator.next()).doubleValue());
}
System.out.println(count + " numbers in file");
    }
}
```

This use of the `StreamTokenizer` class works well in this isolated case because it does not matter if the numbers are separated by spaces or on separate lines, either of which is a likely scenario.

5.11 String Concatenation Operations

The **string concatenation operator +** was introduced in 1.6.2 String Literals. In that section only string literals were concatenated. You may recall this example of a string concatenation operation:

```
static String s = "Fourscore and seven years ago our fathers brought forth" +
        " on this continent, a new nation, conceived in Liberty," +
        "and dedicated to the proposition that all men are created equal.";
```

This is an example of how the string concatenation operator should be used. When should the string concatenation operator not be used? The string concatenation operator generally should not be used to compute strings. What is a computed string? Good question. What you see above is not a computed string. It is a compile-time constant expression.

> All string concatenation operations either evaluate to a compile-time constant expression or are written to the class file and executed as a series of `append` method invocations. That latter are referred to as *computed strings*.

Understanding the difference between the two is very important in terms of knowing when to use the string concatenation operator. A compile-time constant expression of type `String` is strictly limited to the following:

- String literals
- The simple name or qualified name in the `TypeName.field-Name` general form of an inlined constant
- The string concatenation operator +
- A cast operator for any of the primitive data types or `String`

Note that any use of the += operator in a string concatenation operation is by definition a computed string. Here is a more elaborate example of a string concatenation operation that is a compile-time constant expression:

```
class Test {
    public static void main(String[] args) {
        final double NUM_CHAR = 49194;
        String s = "Not all of the " + (int)Character.MAX_VALUE +
                   " character codes in Unicode are, in fact, " +
                   "characters. Moreover, as of Version 3.0 " +
                   "of the Unicode Standard, there are only " +
                   (int) NUM_CHAR + " characters in use.";
        System.out.println(s);
    }
}
```

Executing this program prints

```
Not all of the 65535 character codes in Unicode are, in fact, characters. Moreover, as of Ver-
sion 3.0 of the Unicode Standard, there are only 49194 characters in use.
```

The compiler performed the entire string concatenation operation. If the code for the `main` method is disassembled using `javap -c`, the output is

```
Compiled from Test.java
class Test extends java.lang.Object {
    Test();
    public static void main(java.lang.String[]);
}

Method Test()
   0 aload_0
   1 invokespecial #1 <Method java.lang.Object()>
   4 return

Method void main(java.lang.String[])
   0 ldc #2 <String "Not all of the 65535 character codes in Unicode are, in fact, characters.
               Moreover, as of Version 3.0 of the Unicode Standard, there are only 49194
               characters in use.">
   2 astore_3
```

```
 3 getstatic #3 <Field java.io.PrintStream out>
 6 aload_3
 7 invokevirtual #4 <Method void println(java.lang.String)>
10 return
```

As you can see, there is only one string. There is no run-time performance penalty for this use of the string concatenation operator because the operation is performed by the compiler. Furthermore, all compile-time constant expressions of type `String` are interned when the class file is loaded along with the string literals. This is not so with computed strings. Computed strings are not automatically interned.

The API docs for the `StringBuffer` class are surprisingly misleading when it comes to differentiating between a compile-time constant expression and a computed string. They include the following example.

> String buffers are used by the compiler to implement the binary string concatenation operator +. For example, the code:
>
> ```
> x = "a" + 4 + "c"
> ```
>
> is compiled to the equivalent of:
>
> ```
> x = new StringBuffer().append("a").append(4).append("c").toString()
> ```
> [11]

That is not true. The compiler writes `"a" + 4 + "c"` to the class file as `"a4c"`. Write the code and disassemble it to see for yourself. If you have never done this before I encourage you to try now. Assuming a default DOS prompt of `C:\Java\classes>` on a Windows machine, the DOS command looks like this:

```
C:\Java\classes>javap -c Test
```

`Test` is the name of the class file you want to disassemble. Do not use the `.class` file extension.

Before discussing computed strings, there is a trick you can use if you're not sure if a string concatenation operation is a compile-time constant expression. Compare the value of the string concatenation operation to an equivalent string literal using reference equality. If they compare equal, the string concatenation operation is a compile-time constant expression. If they do not compare equal, the string concatenation operation is a computed string. For example,

```
class Test {
    public static void main(String[] args) {
```

---

11. API docs for the `java.lang.StringBuffer` class.

```
            String goodbye = "Good"+"bye";
            System.out.print(goodbye == "Goodbye");
        }
    }
```

Executing this program prints `true`, which means that `"Good"+"bye"` must be a compile-time constant expression.

The remainder of this section discusses computed strings which are implemented in the compiler using the `append` methods of a `StringBuffer` (as shown in the last example from the API docs). The moment you add a variable or invoke a method in the variable initializer for a `String` type variable, you have a **computed string**. These are sometimes referred to as *manufactured strings*. For example,

```
class Test {
    public static void main(String[] args) {
        int NUM_CHAR = 49194;
        String s = "There are " + NUM_CHAR + " characters in " +
                   "the latest version of the Unicode Standard.";
        System.out.println(s);
    }
}
```

This is an example of a computed string (because `NUM_CHAR` is no longer `final`). A computed string is the opposite of a compile-time constant expression in that the string concatenation operation must be executed at run time. The disassembled code is very different. For example,

```
Compiled from Test.java
class Test extends java.lang.Object {
    Test();
    public static void main(java.lang.String[]);
}

Method Test()
   0 aload_0
   1 invokespecial #1 <Method java.lang.Object()>
   4 return

Method void main(java.lang.String[])
   0 ldc #2 <Integer 49194>
   2 istore_1
   3 new #3 <Class java.lang.StringBuffer>
   6 dup
   7 invokespecial #4 <Method java.lang.StringBuffer()>
  10 ldc #5 <String "There are ">
  12 invokevirtual #6 <Method java.lang.StringBuffer append(java.lang.String)>
  15 iload_1
  16 invokevirtual #7 <Method java.lang.StringBuffer append(int)>
  19 ldc #8 <String " characters in ">
  21 invokevirtual #6 <Method java.lang.StringBuffer append(java.lang.String)>
  24 ldc #9 <String "the latest version of the Unicode Standard.">
```

```
26 invokevirtual #6 <Method java.lang.StringBuffer append(java.lang.String)>
29 invokevirtual #10 <Method java.lang.String toString()>
32 astore_2
33 getstatic #11 <Field java.io.PrintStream out>
36 aload_2
37 invokevirtual #12 <Method void println(java.lang.String)>
40 return
```

Even though this string is substantially shorter than the original, there is much more code. The string concatenation operation results in the following lines of code being written to the class file:

```
StringBuffer sb = new StringBuffer();
sb.append("There are ");
sb.append(NUM_CHAR);
sb.append(" characters in ");
sb.append("the latest version of the Unicode Standard.");
```

The problem with the compiler-generated code is that the String-Buffer allocated always uses the default initial capacity of 16, even if it is perfectly clear that the length of the String produced by the string concatenation operator is greater than that.

The default initial capacity is not an arbitrary number. As with all default initial capacities, it has been the subject of years of study. Another container that has a default initial capacity is ArrayList. The default initial capacity of an ArrayList is 11. Both the StringBuffer and ArrayList class have an ensureCapacity(int minimumCapacity) method that is invoked when the container is no longer large enough. This is where the inefficiency arises. A new array must be allocated. Then the contents of the old array must be copied to the new one. The code looks like this:

```
char newValue[] = new char[newCapacity];
System.arraycopy(value, 0, newValue, 0, count);
value = newValue;
```

Essentially the same thing happens in ArrayList. My reason for continually making this comparison to ArrayList is that it is generally understood that setting the initial capacity of an ArrayList is important to the performance of that container. However, the same is not true of StringBuffer (at least not the StringBuffer used in string concatenation operations). For example, in the last example of a string concatenation operation the ensureCapacity(int minimumCapacity) method has to be invoked twice. This is a high price to pay for something as simple as a computed string.

To understand how this works you must be familiar with the "growth policy" of a `StringBuffer`. If the length of the string to be appended would exceed the current capacity of the `StringBuffer`, the `ensureCapacity(int minimumCapacity)` method is invoked. The `minimumCapacity` argument is the number of characters already in the buffer plus the length of the string to be appended. The `ensure-Capacity(int minimumCapacity)` method uses either the `minimumCapacity` argument or twice the current capacity, whichever is greater. In the last example the initial capacity of the `StringBuffer` is 16, which is sufficient for `sb.append("There are ")` and `sb.append(NUM_CHAR)`. At that point `"There are 49194"` is in the buffer, which is a total of 15 characters. The `sb.append(" characters in ")` method invocation increases the size of the buffer to 16+1*2=33 characters, 27 of which are in use. However, `sb.append("the latest version of the Unicode Standard.")` is an additional 45 characters, requiring yet another array to be allocated. Allocating the new arrays and copying the contents of one array to another is costly and is to be avoided for something as simple as a computed string.

The question is *how do you wrest control of string concatenation operations away from the compiler so that you can specify the correct initial capacity for a `StringBuffer`*. The answer is simple. In performance-critical code you should not use the string concatenation operator for computed strings. This requires being able to differentiate a compile-time constant from a computed string in a glance and then knowing what to do if it is a computed string. What to do is the easy part. As already stated, the problem with computed strings is that the compiler always uses the default initial capacity of 16 when allocating a `StringBuffer`. You need only allocate the `StringBuffer` yourself, setting the initial capacity to an appropriate value. For example,

```
StringBuffer sb = new StringBuffer(75);
sb.append("There are ");
sb.append(NUM_CHAR);
sb.append(" characters in ");
sb.append("the latest version of the Unicode Standard.");
s = sb.toString();
```

There are a number of benchmark tests that show that specifying an adequate initial capacity and writing the string concatenation operation yourself is on average six times faster than letting the compiler do the job for you. There is much more work because you also have to code all the `append` method invocations. I call this coding the string concatenation operation *by hand*. The alternative string concatenation operation is always much easy to type. For example,

```
String s = "There are " + NUM_CHAR + " characters in " +
           "the latest version of the Unicode Standard.";
```

Getting used to the idea that you have to do the work yourself is the hard part, but it shows that you know how costly computed strings can be. What everyone needs is something like the following `concat(String[] strings)` utility method in the `String` class:

```
class Test {
    public static void main(String[] args) {
        int NUM_CHAR = 49194;
        String s = concat(new String[] {"There are ",
                                        String.valueOf(NUM_CHAR),
                                        " characters in the latest ",
                                        "version of the Unicode Standard."});
        System.out.println(s);

    }
    public static String concat(String[] strings) {
        int capacity = 0;
        for(int i=0; i<strings.length; i++)
            capacity += strings[i].length();
        StringBuffer sb = new StringBuffer(capacity);
        for(int i=0; i<strings.length; i++)
            sb.append(strings[i]);
        return sb.toString();
    }
}
```

Java compilers could also do a limited analysis of the length of the resultant string prior to generating the code that allocates a `StringBuffer`.

There is one more important lesson to take away from all this. *Do not use string concantenation operators in loops.* For example,

```
class Test {
    public static void main(String[] args) {
        String ascii = "";
        for(int i=0; i<256; i++)
            ascii += (char)i;
        System.out.println(ascii);
    }
}
```

Every time `ascii += (char)i` is evaluated a new `StringBuffer` is created. It is often said that a new `String` is also created, which is true, but the new `String` shares the same `char[]` (or character buffer) that the `StringBuffer` created. Buffer sharing in string concatenation operations is discussed in 5.11.4 Shared `StringBuffers`. The point is that it is mostly the `StringBuffer` that is wasted. The same is true whenever the + operator is used in a loop.

Every time an expression in which the + and += string concatenation operators is evaluated, a `StringBuffer` is created. Therefore, string concatenation operators should never be used in a loop. Doing so is highly inefficient.

You should always code string concatenation operations inside of loops by hand. For example,

```
class Test {
    public static void main(String[] args) {
        StringBuffer ascii = new StringBuffer(256);
        for(int i=0; i<256; i++)
            ascii.append((char)i);
        System.out.println(ascii);
    }
}
```

This is a much more efficient implementation.

There is one other alternative to the string concatenation operator and coding by hand. For any two strings (regardless of their length), the most efficient concatenation operation is the `concat(String str)` method declared in the `String` class:

```
public String concat (String str)
```

This method creates a new string that is a concatenation of the target string and the argument string. The *JLS* includes a clever example of how `concat()` method invocations can be chained *together*. The method invocation expression `"to".concat("get").concat("her")` returns a `String` object equal to *together*. However, the following string concatenation expression implicitly creates a `String` object with the same sequence of characters, is much easier to type, and is less costly:

```
"to" + "get" + "her"
```

Each `concat(String str)` method invocation creates a new array in which to store the result. The contents of both the target and argument strings are then copied to the array, which is used to create a `String`. For two strings that total more than 16 characters, the `concat(String` `str`) method is the most efficient way to go. For more than two strings (such as in the `"to".concat("get").concat("her")` example), however, you are back to coding by hand if efficiency is a priority.

To summarize, your options for string concatenation are as follows.

1. Use the string concatenation operator + or += for all compile-time constant expressions or computed strings of 16 characters or less.

2. Use the `concat(String str)` method in the `String` class to concatenate two strings of any length.

3. Code it by hand, being careful to specify an adequate initial capacity for the `StringBuffer` used, or use something like the `concat(String[] strings)` utility method above.

The options are listed here in the order in which they should be used. This reduces everything said in this section to three choices that you can easily remember.

5.11.1 A Note about the Overloaded Binary + Operator

Care must be taken when using the string concatenation operator to format diagnostic messages. The binary + operator may be either an addition operator or a string concatenation operator depending on the types of the operands. This is called **operator overloading**. It is sometimes said that the Java programming language has no operator overloading. This statement is correct to the extent that it is intended as a comparison to the C and C++ programming languages. The binary + operator is the only example of operator overloading in the Java programming language. A *binary* operator is one that has two operands. As with most of the binary operators, the + operator is left associative. Expressions that use the binary + operator are evaluated from left to right, performing one operation at a time. For example,

```
a + b + c
```

Because the + operator is left-associative, the expression is read as

```
(a + b) + c
```

Now it is clear that there are two operations involved.

Are these addition operations or string concatenation operations? Without knowing the types of variables a, b, and c, there is no way of answering that question. They could be addition operations, string concatenation operations, or an addition operation followed by a string concatenation operation. What it cannot be is a string concatenation operation followed by an addition operation, because if the first operation is a string concatenation then by definition the second is too. If either the left-hand or the right-hand operand is a string (that is, a string literal or a reference to a `String` type object), the operation is a string concatenation. If neither operand is a string, then the operation is addition. This last point is significant because both operands in an additive expression must be primitive numeric types. Otherwise, the compiler will generate an `incompatible type` error message. Figure 5-2 summarizes these rules.

"NOT a string or primitive numeric type" means either a Boolean value or any reference type other than `String`. For example,

```
class Test {
    public static void main(String[] args) {
        Integer two = new Integer(2);
        System.out.println(two + two);
    }
}
```

Attempting to compile this program generates the following compiler error:

```
Test.java:4: operator + cannot be applied to java.lang.Integer,java.lang.Integer
        System.out.println(two + two);
                               ^
1 error
```

You can do two things here. The first is to add a `toString()` method invocation to one of the objects:

```
System.out.println(two.toString() + two);
```

The second is to add what I call a **primer string**. A primer string is another name for the empty string "". For example,

```
System.out.println("" + two + two);
```

The first subexpression "" + `two` is carried out as a string concatenation operation because the left-hand operand is an empty string. The result is a string equal to "2". This then becomes the left-hand operand in the second subexpression and "22" is printed. This use of a primer string at the start of a string concatenation operation is very common.

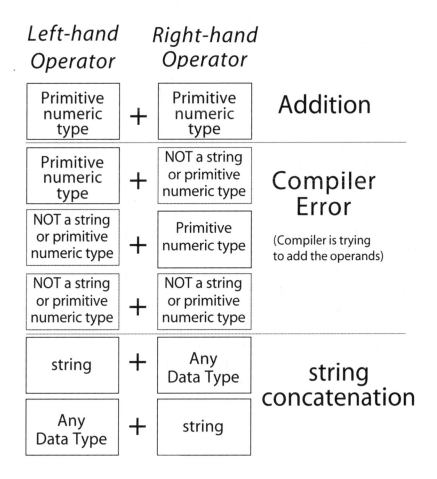

Figure 5-2: Operator Overloading and the Binary + Operator

5.11.2 Implicit String Conversions

The design of the Java programming language is such that any data type in a string concatenation operation is automatically converted to a string. These are known as **implicit string conversions**. There are three possibilities.

- For the primitive numeric data types the results are as would be expected. The numbers are printed as numeric literals

- A `boolean` value will print the Boolean literals `true` or `false`. This includes expressions that evaluate to the `boolean` type. For example, the following diagnostic message prints "`true`":

```
System.out.println(2 + 2 == 4);
```

  Printing the results of Boolean expressions like the above to prove that the expression is either `true` or `false` is a common use of implicit string conversions

- Reference types either print "`null`" or are converted to a string by invoking the `toString()` method

String conversion is primarily the responsibility of the overloaded `value-Of` methods in the `String` class. Those methods encapsulate the *string conversion policy* for the Java programming language. Hence, they are discussed primarily in this section.

As discussed in the last section, at least one of the operands in a string concatenation operation must be a string. That is what defines it as a string concatenation operation rather than an additive operation. The other operand of a string concatenation operation can be any data type. As noted above, the compiler implements string concatenation by replacing the + operator with an equivalent `append` method invocation in the `StringBuffer` class. For example,

```
int x = 10;
String s = "x = " + x;
```

The code output from a compiler is

```
int x = 10;
String s = new StringBuffer().append("x = ").append(x).toString();
```

Thus, the overloaded `append` methods in the `StringBuffer` class are responsible for converting the operands in a string concatenation operation. They do so by invoking one of the following `valueOf` methods in the `String` class:

```
public static String valueOf(Object obj) {
    return (obj == null) ? "null" : obj.toString();
}

public static String valueOf(char data[]) {
    return new String(data);
}

public static String valueOf(boolean b) {
    return b ? "true" : "false";
```

```
    }

    public static String valueOf(char c) {
        char data[] = {c};
        return new String(0, 1, data);
    }

    public static String valueOf(int i) {
        return Integer.toString(i, 10);
    }

    public static String valueOf(long l) {
        return Long.toString(l, 10);
    }

    public static String valueOf(float f) {
        return Float.toString(f);
    }

    public static String valueOf(double d) {
        return Double.toString(d);
    }
```

Studying the implementation of these overloaded `valueOf` methods in the `String` class, you can see how implicit string conversions are implemented. For example, the following line of code from the first `valueOf(Object obj)` method in this list shows why string conversion operations never throw a `NullPointerException`:

```
    return (obj == null) ? "null" : obj.toString();
```

Note that this is only a partial listing of the fully overloaded `valueOf` utility methods in the `String` class.

It took me a long time to appreciate this design, and I still have my reservations. You may wonder why the overloaded `append` methods do not copy these implementations instead of invoking another method. For example,

```
    public synchronized StringBuffer append(Object obj) {
        return append(String.valueOf(obj));
    }
```

Instead of this implementation, why not just

```
    public synchronized StringBuffer append(Object obj) {
        return append((obj == null) ? "null" : obj.toString());
    }
```

The same could be asked for all the other overloaded `append` methods in the `StringBuffer` class. The answer is that there must be one central place where string conversion policy is defined. The `String` class is the obvious place and the overloaded `valueOf` methods encapsulate that policy.

Is a centralized string conversion policy really necessary? The implicit string conversions in a string concatenation operation are the single most important application of that policy. There are others, however, the most important of which are the overloaded `print` and `println` methods in the `PrintStream` and `PrintWriter` classes. All of the primitive type wrapper classes also invoke the `valueOf` methods in their `toString()` methods. This is mind boggling because for numeric types the overloaded `valueOf` method in the `String` class turns around and invokes the `static toString()` methods in the primitive type wrapper classes (as can be seen above). It makes no sense unless understood from the point of view of encapsulating string conversion policy in the `String` class. Even then I would say that, in the case of the primitive type wrapper classes, this is unnecessary. The need for consistency, for example, between the `append(int i)` method in the `StringBuffer` class (used for implicit string conversions of `byte`, `short`, and `int` values) and the `toString()` utility methods in the `Byte`, `Short`, and `Integer` classes could have been handled through the API docs, saving two completely unnecessary method invocations (although such method invocations tend to be inlined by state-of-the-art JVM).

5.11.3 The Intern Mechanism

String literals are constants, not unlike `Math.PI` or other numerical constants. If I assign a constant to a variable, I expect that variable to compare equal when later compared to the same constant. This is not a problem with primitive constants such as `Math.PI`, but strings are objects. *Two objects are never equal using reference equality unless they are the same object.* Consider the following code:

```
String s = "Hello World!";
...
if (s == "Hello World!")
    ...
```

The design of the Java programming language is such that the variable `s` will always be equal to the string literal `"Hello World!"` using reference equality. Yet, as discussed in the introduction to this chapter, every string literal represents a `String` object in an executing Java program.

Based on that, one might think that the expression s == "Hello World!" in the if statement evaluates to false. Yes, the operands have the same value, but they reference two different objects. I have just said that two objects are never equal using reference equality unless they are the same object. The implication is that if the expression s == "Hello World!" evaluates to true, the variable s and the string literal "Hello World!" must reference the same object. They do. Inside of a JVM, the expression reads more like if (s == s).

To understand the intern mechanism you must first know about the **pool of strings** maintained by the String class. *Every string in the pool of strings is unique.* That is, no two String objects in the pool of strings have the same sequence of Unicode characters. Hence, the pool of strings is sometimes referred to as the *pool of unique strings*. The API docs have this to say about the pool of strings:

> A pool of strings, initially empty, is maintained privately by the class String.
>
> When the intern method is invoked, if the pool already contains a string equal to this String object as determined by the equals(Object) method, then the string from the pool is returned. Otherwise, this String object is added to the pool and a reference to this String object is returned.
>
> It follows that for any two strings s and t, s.intern() == t.intern() is true if and only if s.equals(t) is true.
>
> All literal strings and string-valued constant expressions are interned.[12]

Programmers can add strings to the pool of strings by invoking the intern() method, which is why I call this the **intern mechanism**. The intern() method is discussed in 5.11.3.1 Interning Computed Strings.

Interning is a two-stage process that begins at the compiler. For example,

```
class Test {
    public static void main(String[] args) {
        String goodbye = "Goodbye";
        System.out.print(goodbye == ("Good"+"bye"));
    }
}
```

---

12. API docs for the intern() method in the java.lang.String class.

Executing this program prints `true`, but not because of the pool of unique strings maintained by the `String` class. This stage of interning is about writing the most compact class file possible. The constant pool of a class file is always checked before adding a new value. If the value is already in the constant pool, the compiler refers to that value. It is, after all, a constant pool, which means that it is safe to use the same value in a different context. For example,

```
class Test {
    public static void main(String[] args) {
        String goodbye = "Goodbye";
        System.out.print(goodbye == ("Good"+"bye"));
    }
}
```

Using `javap` with the `-c` option to disassemble this code shows that there is only one `Goodbye` string in the class file:

```
Compiled from Test.java
class Test extends java.lang.Object {
    Test();
    public static void main(java.lang.String[]);
}

Method Test()
   0 aload_0
   1 invokespecial #1 <Method java.lang.Object()>
   4 return

Method void main(java.lang.String[])
   0 ldc #2 <String "Goodbye">
   2 astore_1
   3 getstatic #3 <Field java.io.PrintStream out>
   6 aload_1
   7 ldc #2 <String "Goodbye">
   9 if_acmpne 16
  12 iconst_1
  13 goto 17
  16 iconst_0
  17 invokevirtual #4 <Method void print(boolean)>
  20 return
```

This will always happen whenever two compile-time constant expressions of type `String` in the same class are equal. That these strings are also equal using reference equality (that is, they are the same object) is not because they were interned at run time but because the values in the constant pool of a class file are as unique as the strings in the pool of strings maintained by the `String` class. However, this only applies to two or more string literals or other compile-time constant expressions of type `String` *in the same class.*

The next stage of interning happens when class files are loaded. This is what most programmers think of as interning. Before loading a string from the constant pool of a class file, the pool of strings is searched for an existing string with the same sequence of characters, much like the compiler does when searching the constant pool of a class file. If no matching sequence of characters is found, a `String` object is created and added to the pool of strings.

Java compilers and JVM have two very different motivations for adding only unique strings to their respective pools. Duplicate strings (or any other duplicate constants) are not written to the constant pool of a class file as a means of compacting the file. The raison d'être for maintaining a pool of unique strings is that string literals from different classes must compare equal. That maintaining a pool of unique strings also reduces the memory footprint of a Java program is serendipitous. Nevertheless, the effect is the same: no two `String` objects in the constant pool of a class file or the pool of strings maintained by the `String` class represent the same sequence of Unicode characters. In a JVM that means different objects are necessarily different strings, making it possible to use reference equality to compare `String` objects.

Here is an example of why the part of the intern mechanism in a JVM is necessary:

```
class Test {
    public static void main(String[] args) {
        if (AnotherClass.s == "abc")
            System.out.println("This is the raison d'etre " +
                                "for the pool of strings");
    }
}
class AnotherClass {
    static String s = "abc";
}
```

These are two different classes. Executing the `Test` program prints

```
This is the raison d'etre for the pool of strings
```

Imagine how perplexing it would be if this diagnostic message did not print. A Java compiler can only guarantee that no two string constants are the same in a given class file. The JVM must do the same across all class files.

There is much misinformation about the intern mechanism in older Java books because of a bug in Java 1.0.2 and earlier releases. That bug is explained as follows in the *JVMS*.

> String literal resolution is not implemented correctly in Sun's JDK release 1.0.2. In that implementation of the Java Virtual Machine, resolving a `CONSTANT_String` in the constant pool always allocates a new string. Two string literals in two different classes, even if they contained the identical sequence of characters, would never be `==` to each other. A string literal could never be `==` to a result of the `intern` method.[13]

The 1.1 release was not in full compliance with the *JLS* either (in that the compiler was not executing string concatenation operations for compile-time constant expressions of type `String`). As of the 1.2 release (or *Java 2*), however, the SDK is in full compliance. I am not sure about other implementations.

5.11.3.1 Interning Computed Strings

String literals and other compile-time constant expressions of type `String` in the constant pool of a class file are automatically added to the pool of unique strings maintained by the `String` class whenever a class file is loaded. All strings are either compile-time constant expressions or computed at run time. The latter are referred to as *computed strings* in this book. There is no mechanism for automatically interning computed strings. *They are therefore never equal to other strings using reference equality.* For example,

```
class Test {
    public static void main(String[] args) {
        String good = "Good";
        String s1 = good + "bye";
        String s2 = good + "bye";
        System.out.println(s1.equals(s2));
        System.out.println(s1 == s2);
    }
}
```

Executing this program prints

```
true
false
```

---

13. Tim Lindholm and Frank Yellin, *The Java Virtual Machine Specification* (Reading: Addison-Wesley, 1997), §5.4, "String Resolution."

Now watch what happens if the computed strings are interned:

```
class Test {
    public static void main(String[] args) {
        String good = "Good";
        String s1 = (good + "bye").intern();
        String s2 = (good + "bye").intern();
        System.out.println(s1.equals(s2));
        System.out.println(s1 == s2);
    }
}
```

The same program now prints

```
true
```

The intern() method makes it possible for programmers to use reference equality when comparing computed strings, which is much more efficient than invoking the equals(Object o) method. Doing so is generally thought to be a performance optimization. Interning computed strings, however, is an expensive operation. There must be enough string comparisons to compensate for the additional overhead of invoking the native intern() method. This is one performance optimization about which I would not want to make any generalizations. I think benchmark tests are required on a per-application basis to make sure that it really is a performance optimization.

The danger is that you are piggybacking a JVM mechanism that in all probability dwarfs whatever programming problem you are trying to solve. The pool of strings includes every string literal from every class and interface loaded, and there are hundreds of them in even the smallest application. The pool of strings is doubtless a hash table that offers constant-time access, but just imagine what will happen if you cause that table to be rehashed! Most mainstream business applications do not require the interning of computed strings because there are not enough computed strings compared to compensate for the additional overhead of invoking the native intern() method.

When interning a computed string so that it can be compared to other strings using reference equality, the intern() method must always be coded as follows:

```
s = s.intern();
```

The original string is replaced by the intern() return value. Unless you save a reference to the original string, there is no way of knowing if the string was added to the pool or a reference to a different string was returned, but that does not matter. The important thing is that the string is now "guaranteed" to be in the pool.

The language designers had no choice but to make the `intern()` method part of the `public` interface of the `String` class, but that does not automatically make it the best solution even if there is no question about the importance of string comparisons in a given application. The functionality of interning is easily replicated. For example,

```java
import java.util.HashMap;
class Test {
    private static final HashMap poolOfStrings = new HashMap(101);
    public static void main(String[] args) {
     String computed = "computed";
     String s1 = computed + " string";
     String s2 = computed + " string";
     System.out.println(s1 == s2);
     s1 = intern(s1);
     s2 = intern(s1);
     System.out.println(s1 == s2);
    }
    private static String intern(String s) {
        if (s==null)
            throw new NullPointerException();
        String value = (String)poolOfStrings.get(s);
        if (value == null) {
            poolOfStrings.put(s, s);
            return s;
        }
        return value;
    }
}
```

Executing this program prints

```
false
true
```

Now you have an intern mechanism that can be custom tailored to meet your needs. It is doubtless faster than piggybacking the intern mechanism in the `String` class.

5.11.4 Shared Character Buffers

This is an obscure point about the `String` and `StringBuffer` classes but is of interest in fully understanding string concatenation operations and the `String(StringBuffer buffer)` constructor.

The `char[]` array in which the sequence of Unicode characters are stored for a `String` object is sometimes shared with a `StringBuffer` object. This happens because of the way string concatenation operations are implemented. A string concatenation operation for a computed string implicitly creates a `String` and `StringBuffer` object. The latter is a byproduct of the string concatenation operation and is immediately eligible for garbage collection. The `String` object is created by invoking the `toString()` method in the `StringBuffer` class. This method uses the following constructor in the `String` class.

```
public String (StringBuffer buffer)
```

Rather than allocating a new `char[]` in which to store the sequence of Unicode characters, the `String` class marks the `StringBuffer` as shared and copies a reference to the `char[]` in the `StringBuffer`. Creating a new `char[]` is out of the question because string concatenations are so common. Moreover, the `StringBuffer` is eligible for garbage collection as soon as the string concatenation operation is complete, so it makes sense to reuse the existing `char[]`.

If the `StringBuffer` object created as a byproduct of string concatenation operations is immediately eligible for garbage collection, why mark it as shared? The answer to this question is that a programmer may explicitly create a `StringBuffer` object and then either invoke the `toString()` method or use it in a string concatenation operation (in which case the `toString()` method is implicitly invoked). In either case an immutable `String` object is going to be created that references the same `char[]` array as a mutable `StringBuffer` object. The difference is that `StringBuffer` is no longer a byproduct of string concatenation, is not immediately available for garbage collection, and may be subsequently modified. If that should happen the `StringBuffer` class is designed to make a copy of the shared `char[]` array before any operations that would normally modify the sequence of characters, length, or capacity of the string buffer.

5.12 Displaying Diagnostic Messages on the Console

Programmers display messages on their console when debugging a program. The following subsections discuss diagnostic messages at length, including the closely related subjects of the fully overloaded `print` and `println` methods in the `PrintStream` and `PrintWriter` classes, standard I/O, and abnormal program termination. Diagnostic message and the related subjects of standard I/O and abnormal program termination are thoroughly discussed in the following subsections.

5.12.1 Standard I/O

The first program almost every student of the Java programming language writes is something like the one Dennis Ritchie wrote in 1972 that displays the message "Hello World!" In Java that message is displayed using the following `println` method invocation:

```
System.out.println("Hello World!");
```

The `System.out` part of this statement is commonly referred to as *standard output*.

`System.out` is one of three class variables declared in the `System` utility class that are collectively referred to as **standard I/O**. The names of those variables are `System.in`, `System.out`, and `System.err`. Table 5-4 includes a brief description of each.

While there are still plenty of command-line programs written, the primary use of standard I/O is to print diagnostic messages when debugging a program. There are three things that make Standard I/O so well suited for this purpose.

- The three standard I/O streams are automatically opened when the `System` class is loaded

- Both output streams are automatically flushed whenever one of the overloaded println methods is invoked. That means you do not have to worry about closing the streams. (The primary reason for closing an output stream is to flush buffers.)

- Both output streams are instances of the `PrintStream` class. None of the methods in the `PrintStream` class (notably the overloaded `print` and `println` methods) throw exceptions

Automatic flushing of the buffer means that as soon as you invoke one of the overloaded `println` methods the diagnostic message appears on the screen (unless `System.out` has been redirected).

Table 5-4: Standard I/O

Field Name	Common Name	Description
System.in	Standard input	Reads one line at a time from the keyboard.
System.out	Standard output	By default prints diagnostic messages to the console. If the application is run inside of a browser the Java console is used. Standard output can be redirected using the System.setOut() method discussed below. Typically, standard output is redirected to a file to save the output from a command-line program.
System.err	Standard error	By default, prints error messages to the console. The raison d'être for standard error is that if standard output has been redirected to a file the user still sees error messages on the console. For example, many programmers use standard error in exception handlers.

5.12.1.1 Redirecting Standard I/O

The following methods in the System class can be used to **redirect** System.in, System.out, and System.err:

```
public static void setIn(InputStream in)
public static void setOut(PrintStream out)
public static void setErr(PrintStream err)
```

Usually only standard output is redirected. The purpose of standard error is so that error messages continue to be displayed on the console if standard output is redirected. Therefore, it would be unusual to redirect standard error. Standard input is redirected to simulate keystrokes during a test.

As an example of using one of these methods to redirect standard I/O, the redirect(String fileName) method in the following program can be used as is in any Java program to redirect standard output to a file:

```
import java.io.*;
class Test {
    public static void main(String[] args) {
        redirect("debug.txt");
        System.out.println("This line should be written to the file.");
    }
    public static void redirect(String fileName) {
```

```
        File out = new File(fileName);
        PrintStream ps = null;
        try {
            ps = new PrintStream(new BufferedOutputStream
                            (new FileOutputStream(out),128), true);
        }
        catch (IOException e) {
            System.err.println(e);
            System.exit(1);
        }
        System.setOut(ps);
    }
}
```

It is important to use a buffer that is automatically flushed when redirecting standard output. Otherwise, you would have to remember to invoke `System.out.flush()` before exiting the program.

Standard output can be redirected to a dummy `OutputStream` as a means of disabling debugging code without having to change a single line of code. Doing so is as easy as invoking `setOut(new DummyOutputStream())` during program initialization. The `DummyOutputStream` is declared as follows:

```
import java.io.*;
public class DummyOutputStream extends OutputStream {
    public void write(int b) { }
    public void write(byte[] b) { }
    public void write(byte[] b, int off, int len) { }
}
```

There are also DOS alternatives for redirecting both standard input and standard output. For example, the following DOS command on a Windows machine saves the output from the `Test` program to a file named `output.txt` in the current working directory:

```
C:\Java\classes>java Test > output.txt
```

To append the output to the end of a file use the following command:

```
C:\Java\classes>java Test >> output.txt
```

To redirect to your default printer, use this command:

```
C:\Java\classes>java Test > prn
```

Standard input can be redirected to read from a file using the following command:

```
C:\Java\classes>java Test < input.txt
```

The DOS redirect commands can also be used in combination. For example,

```
C:\>java Test < input.txt >> output.txt
```

DOS redirect commands are easier to use than the `setIn`, `setOut`, and `setErr` methods, assuming you are only redirecting for a single run.

5.12.1.2 *The Standard Output Problem*

Standard output is seriously flawed. The `PrintStream` class was originally designed for writing text files. The problem is that the following methods in the `PrintStream` class do not output text:

```
public void write(int b)
public void write(byte buf[])
public void write(byte buf[], int off, int len)
```

For example,

```
import java.io.*;

class Test {
    public static void main(String[] args) throws IOException {
        byte[] buf = {1,2,3};
        System.out.write(buf);
        for(int i=0; i < buf.length; i++)
            System.out.write(buf[i]);
    }
}
```

The output from this program is not text. That is, it cannot be read by a human. This interface problem is quickly and easily eliminated by using `System.out` to create an instance of the `PrintWriter` class. For example, the following code does not compile:

```
import java.io.*;

class Test {
    public static void main(String[] args) throws IOException {
        byte[] buf = {1,2,3};
        PrintWriter debug = new PrintWriter(System.out);
        debug.write(buf);
        for(int i=0; i < buf.length; i++)
            System.out.write(buf[i]);
    }
}
```

The interface problem goes away because there are no `write(int b)`, `write(byte[] buf)`, or `write(byte[] buf, int off, int len)` methods in the `PrintWriter` class.

Another, albeit minor, problem with the `PrintStream` class is that it auto flushes too often. This is not something you are likely to notice, but the `PrintStream` class auto flushes "whenever a byte array is written, one of the `println` methods is invoked, or a newline character or byte (\n) is written."[14] This behavior was greatly simplified in `PrintWriter`, which only automatically flushes whenever one of the overloaded `println` methods is invoked. For example,

```
import java.io.*;
public class Test {
    public static void main(String[] args) throws Exception {
        PrintStream console = new PrintStream
                    (new FileOutputStream(FileDescriptor.out), true);
        console.print("PrintWriter would not\n" +
                    "print this line at all");
    }
}
```

Executing this program prints

```
PrintWriter would not
print this line at all
```

Note that the stream would have been flushed regardless of where the '\n' appears in the string. Auto flushing whenever '\n' is written is usually cited as a problem because this behavior is not platform neutral. The '\n' character is only a line separator on Unix platforms. The `PrintWriter` class, on the other hand, would not print this line even with auto flushing on. For example,

```
import java.io.*;

public class Test {
    public static void main(String[] args) throws Exception {
        PrintWriter console = new PrintWriter
                    (new FileOutputStream(FileDescriptor.out), true);
        console.print("PrintWriter would not\n" +
                    "print this line at all");
    }
}
```

Executing this program prints nothing because a `print` method was invoked instead of a `println` method.

5.12.1.2.1 Solving the Standard Output Problem Standard output is an instance of the `PrintStream` class. This section discusses the alter-

---

14. API docs for the constructor in the `PrintStream` class.

native of using a `PrintWriter` to display messages on the console. There are two ways to solve this problem. The first involves using one of the following `PrintWriter` constructors:

```
public PrintWriter(OutputStream out)
public PrintWriter(OutputStream out, boolean autoFlush)
```

These constructors are essentially the same. The first constructor simply invokes the second one with `autoFlush` set to `false`. The second constructor is implemented as follows:

```
public PrintWriter(OutputStream out, boolean autoFlush) {
    this(new BufferedWriter(
        new OutputStreamWriter(out)), autoFlush);
}
```

As you can see, these constructors wrap the `OutputStream` in a `BufferedWriter` that uses the default character encoding.

These constructors were included in the `PrintWriter` class to help ease the introduction of the `PrintWriter` class as a replacement for the `PrintStream` class. One possible use of these constructors is to wrap `System.out` in an instance of `PrintWriter`, which solves the problems discussed in the last section. For example,

```
import java.io.*;
class Test {
    public static void main(String[] args) throws IOException {
        PrintWriter console = new PrintWriter(System.out, true);
        console.println("Testing, testing, testing");
    }
}
```

A more efficient way to solve this problem is to use `FileDescriptor.out` to create an instance of `PrintWriter` that can be used to display messages on the console without using an instance of the `PrintStream` class. For example,

```
import java.io.*;
class Test {
    public static void main(String[] args) throws IOException {
        PrintWriter console = new PrintWriter
                        (new FileOutputStream(FileDescriptor.out), true);
        console.println("Testing, testing, testing");
    }
}
```

There is no need to buffer this stream because a `BufferedWriter` is attached to the output stream in the `PrintWriter(OutputStream` out, boolean `autoFlush`) constructor. This solution is more desirable because it eliminates the much-troubled `PrintStream` class.

5.12.1.3 Reading the Keyboard Using Standard Input

The keyboard can be read one character or one line at a time. The following example reads the keyboard one character at a time and displays the character code for that key:

```java
class Unicode {
    public static void main(String[] args) throws java.io.IOException {
        System.out.println();
        System.out.println("PROGRAM INSTRUCTIONS");
        System.out.println("--------------------");
        System.out.println("Type one or more characters, and then press enter.");
        System.out.println("The Unicode codepoint(s) are then displayed.");
        System.out.println();
        System.out.println("STOPPING THE PROGRAM");
        System.out.println("Press Ctrl-Z on Windows or Ctrl-D on Unix or Macs");
        System.out.println("to simulate an end-of-file or EOF marker. It may be");
        System.out.println("necessary to input the EOF marker on a separate line.");
        System.out.println();

        char c;
        int i = System.in.read(); /* INITIAL READ */
        while(i != -1) {          {
            c = (char) i;
            if (c != '\r' && c != '\n')
                System.out.println(c + " = " + i);
            i = System.in.read();  /* LOOPED READ */
        }
    }
}
```

Note that this program reads one character at a time from standard input, not from the keyboard. There is a difference. You cannot read every keystroke using standard input. Were it otherwise, the backspace key could not be used to correct mistakes. Keystrokes are not available to standard input until the enter key is pressed. In other words, data is sent from the keyboard to standard input one line at a time.

The one exception to the rule that standard input does not receive data from the keyboard until the enter key is pressed is the EOF marker. Pressing Z while holding down the control key (`Ctrl`), sometimes written as `Ctrl-Z` or `^Z`, is the standard input equivalent of an EOF marker in the Windows operating systems. `Ctrl-D` or `^D` does the same thing in other operating systems. The EOF marker is sent immediately to standard input. You may have to type the EOF marker on a separate line in some systems.

The following program is an example of reading standard input one line at a time:

```java
import java.io.*;
class Test {
    public static void main(String[] args)  {
        BufferedReader in  = new BufferedReader
                          (new InputStreamReader(System.in));
        System.out.println("PRESS ENTER ON AN EMPTY LINE TO END THE PROGRAM");
        try {
            String s = in.readLine();  /* INITIAL READ */
            while (!(s.equals("") || s == null)) {
                ...your code for processing one line at a time goes here...
                s = in.readLine();  /* LOOPED READ */
            }
        }
        catch (IOException e) { System.err.println(e); }
    }
}
```

The `s == null` is necessary in case standard input is redirected to a file. The `readline()` method returns `null` if the end-of-file is reached.

5.12.1.4 *Standard Error and Abnormal Program Termination*

Standard error is most often used in an exception handler to print error messages before exiting a program. For example,

```java
try {
    ...
}
catch (Exception e) {
    System.err.println(e);
    System.exit(1);
}
```

Alternatively, a stack trace can be printed to standard error as follows:

```java
try {
    ...
}
catch (Exception e) {
    e.printStackTrace();
    System.exit(1);
}
```

Printing both a string representation of the exception object and a stack trace is redundant because stack traces include a string representation of the exception object as the first line of code.

The argument passed to the `exit(int  status)` method is referred to as the **status code**. By convention, a non-zero status code indicates abnormal termination. The non-zero value is usually one. It is interesting to note that the only use of the status code is to determine if finalizers should be run on exit. If `runFinalizersOnExit(true)` is invoked before exiting, finalizers are run when the `exit(int status)` method is invoked, but only if the status code is zero. However, the `runFinal-izersOnExit(boolean value)` methods have been deprecated. Assuming that they are not invoked, the status code currently has no practical use. That could change in the future, though, and you should continue to use zero and one (or another non-zero value) to indicate normal and abnormal termination, respectively.

5.12.2 The `print` and `println` Methods

The `print` and `println` methods in the `PrintStream` and the `PrintWriter` classes are fully overloaded so that you can easily print anything. Here is a list of all of the `print` and `println` methods:

```
public void print(boolean b)
public void print(char c)
public void print(int i)
public void print(long l)
public void print(float f)
public void print(double d)
public void print(char[] c)
public void print(String s)
public void print(Object obj)

public void println()      //terminates an existing line or prints a blank line

public void println(boolean b)
public void println(char c)
public void println(int i)
public void println(long l)
public void println(float f)
public void println(double d)
public void println(char[] c)
public void println(String s)
public void println(Object obj)
```

The difference is that the `print` methods do not terminate the line whereas the `println` methods do. The no-argument `println()` method is invoked to print a blank line. If the argument passed to `print(String s)`, `println(String s)`, `print(Object obj)`, or `println(Object obj)` is a `null` reference, the word "null" is printed. Printing `null` instead of throwing a `NullPointerExcep-tion` is also what happens when a `null` reference is used in a string concatenation operation.

5.13 The `Locale` Class

A **locale-sensitive operation** is any operation that uses a `Locale`. The operation may use the default locale, or it may be passed a `Locale`. The following specification is from the `Locale` class.

> Each class that performs locale-sensitive operations allows you to get all the available objects of that type. You can sift through these objects by language, country, or variant, and use the display names to present a menu to the user. For example, you can create a menu of all the collation objects suitable for a given language. Such classes must implement these three class methods:
>
> ```
> public static Locale[] getAvailableLocales()
> public static String getDisplayName(Locale objectLocale,
>                                     Locale displayLocale)
> public static final String getDisplayName(Locale objectLocale)
>         // getDisplayName will throw MissingResourceException if the locale
>         // is not one of the available locales.15
> ```

The important point to grasp is that locales are supported at the class level, not the core API. The locales supported by any given class are returned by the `getAvailableLocales()` method in that class.

A `Locale` is an immutable string that encodes information used in localization. The general format is

```
ISOlanguageCode_ISOcountryCode_variant
```

Each of the components is separated by an underscore. The language and country codes must be in the order shown here. The **ISO language code** is one of the lowercase, two-letter codes defined by ISO-639, a complete list of which can be found on any number of Web sites by searching for *ISO 639*. All locales have a language code. The **ISO country code** is one of the uppercase, two-letter codes defined by ISO-3166. The country code is optional, allowing for differences in the same language from one country to the next. Perhaps you have heard the expression *the British and the Americans are two peoples divided by a common language*. (For example, what we call a *period* in the United States is a *full stop* in the U.K.)

Both the country code and variant are optional when creating a `Locale`, a fact that is not immediately obvious looking at the only two constructors in the `Locale` class:

---

15. API docs for the `java.util.Locale` class.

```
public Locale(String language, String country, String variant)
public Locale(String language, String country)
```

This is a painfully obvious interface problem. There really should be a third constructor that accepts only a language code. The only explanation for not having such a constructor would be that all of the language-only locales are already supported in the SDK, but such an explanation is dubious and would be contrary to *supported locales* design. (Just because the SDK supports all of them does not mean other implementations support them.) Instead, to create a `Locale` that has only a language code, an empty string must be passed as the second argument. For example,

```
Locale locale = new Locale("en", "");
```

This `Locale` is the same as the `Locale.English` convenience constant.

Variants have no standard, except perhaps the EURO discussed below. The variants WIN, MAC, and UNIX might be considered programmer conventions. Beyond that, variants can be anything. They are used to create "custom locales" if you will. Although both of the variants in the locales that the SDK supports (NY and EURO) are uppercase as well as the three variants mentioned in the API docs (WIN, MAC, and POSIX), variants are nevertheless mixed case. If there is more than one variant they are separated by an underscore. *List them from left to right in the order of their importance.*[16] Most locales, however, do not have a variant. I will return to the subject of variants shortly.

A `Locale` has been described as a **cultural nexus**. Most of them consist of a language and country code. Most countries have only one language, which means that the `Locale` is basically an identifier for that country. Here is a complete list of the English-language locales supported in the SDK:

```
en_AU  English (Australia)
en_CA  English (Canada)
en_GB  English (United Kingdom)
en_IE  English (Ireland)
en_NZ  English (New Zealand)
en_ZA  English (South Africa)
en_US  English (United States)
```

---

16. API docs for the `java.util.Locale` class.

The last one is the default locale in the United States, just as all the others are the default locales in their respective countries. The **default locale** is returned by the `Locale.getDefault()` method.

These are not dialects. Almost any dictionary definition of *dialect* will confirm that dialects are generally thought of as *regional dialects within the same country*. That is why I do not use the term *regional* to describe locales as implemented in the Java programming language.

Adding regional dialects would be tricky from a translation point of view. However, were it done, the dialect would be a variant. For example, the Norwegian language has two literary forms. One is Bokmål, which is based on the spoken dialects of Norway. The other is Nynorsk, which has developed through the gradual reform of written Danish. There are, therefore, two Norwegian locales:

```
no_NO Norwegian (Norway)
no_NO_NY Norwegian (Norway,Nynorsk)
```

The first local assumes Bokmål, which makes sense because that is the more natural of the two literary forms. The *NY* is the variant.

The Chinese locales are a good example of the idea of a cultural nexus. There are three Chinese locales:

```
zh_CN   Chinese (China)
zh_HK   Chinese (Hong Kong)
zh_TW   Chinese (Taiwan)
```

However, locales can also be multiple languages in the same country. For example,

```
en_CA English (Canada)
fr_CA French (Canada)
ca_ES Catalan (Spain)
es_ES Spanish (Spain)
fr_BE French (Belgium)
nl_BE Dutch (Belgium)
de_LU German (Luxembourg)
fr_LU French (Luxembourg)
```

The Yugoslavia question aside, these are the only two-language countries I could find using the `Locale.getAvailableLocales()` method and a frequency table. There is only one three-language country. That is Switzerland, which has the following locales:

```
de_CH German (Switzerland)
fr_CH French (Switzerland)
it_CH Italian (Switzerland)
```

Were we to stop here you could say that a `Locale` identifies either a language or a language within a country.

Variants are a third component of some locales. The API docs say this about the use of variants:

> The Variant codes are vendor and browser-specific. For example, use WIN for Windows, MAC for Macintosh, and POSIX for POSIX [or UNIX for UNIX].[17]

This is somewhat misleading, however, because the two variants used in the locales that the SDK supports (`NY` and `EURO`) have nothing to do with operating systems or browsers. One of the two is the Nynorsk literary form of the Norwegian language mentioned above. The other is the ECU (*European Currency Unit*), which is more commonly referred to as the *Euro*. For example,

```java
import java.util.*;
class Test {
  public static void main(String[] args) {
      Locale[] availableLocales = Locale.getAvailableLocales();
      String variant;
      for(int i=0; i<availableLocales.length; i++) {
        variant = availableLocales[i].getVariant();
        if(variant.equals("EURO"))
            System.out.println(availableLocales[i] + " " +
                               availableLocales[i].getDisplayCountry());
      }
   }
}
```

Executing this program prints

```
ca_ES_EURO  Spain
de_AT_EURO  Austria
de_DE_EURO  Germany
de_LU_EURO  Luxembourg
en_IE_EURO  Ireland
es_ES_EURO  Spain
fi_FI_EURO  Finland
fr_BE_EURO  Belgium
fr_FR_EURO  France
fr_LU_EURO  Luxembourg
it_IT_EURO  Italy
nl_BE_EURO  Belgium
nl_NL_EURO  Netherlands
pt_PT_EURO  Portugal
```

---

17. API docs for the `java.util.Locale` class.

These are all of the European countries that have adopted the new Euro currency. Each of these countries also has another `Locale` that does not include the `Euro` variant. For example,

```
it_IT
it_IT_EURO
```

These are two different locales for Italy. The first assumes the national currency, which is the lira. The second specifies the Euro. The difference is an important one if you are using the `Locale` to format currency.

The `locale` strings such as `"en_US"` used in the Java programming language are much simpler than the locales used by some operating systems because they encode much less information. For example, locales in Microsoft operating systems include the default codepage.[18]. As stated in the API docs,

> A `Locale` is the mechanism for identifying the kind of object (`NumberFormat`) that you would like to get. The locale is just a mechanism for identifying objects, not a container for the objects themselves.[19]

It is interesting to note that at the same time that locales were introduced into the language the `file.encoding` system property was changed from `ISO8859-1` to `Cp1252` (on Windows machines in the United States and Western Europe). It appears as if there was a recognition that the codepage had to be available somewhere.

5.13.1 The Default Locale

The question of how the default locale is set is a curiosity. The API docs for the `getDefault()` method have always included a sentence such as the following from the current release.

> The Java Virtual Machine sets the default locale during startup based on the host environment.[20]

Programmers have looked at the code for the `Locale` class to see how the default locale is set. A simplified version of that code is included here:

---

18. See *www.microsoft.com/globaldev/FAQs/Locales.asp*.
19. API docs for the `java.util.Locale` class.
20. API docs for the `getDefault()` method in the `java.utl.locale` class.

```
private static Locale defaultLocale;

static {
    String language = System.getProperty("user.language","EN");
    String country =  System.getProperty("user.region","");
    defaultLocale = new Locale(language, country);
}
```

The default locale is set in a `static` initialization block using system properties. This implies that the `System` class is loaded before the `Locale` class, which can be verified using the `-verbose` option of the `java` command. I recommend using an empty main method such as

```
class Test {
    public static void main(String[] args) { }
}
```

This way you see only the preloaded classes. Even if it were not loaded first, the `System` class would necessarily be loaded at the same time as the `Locale` class because there are symbolic references to the `System` class in the `Locale.class` file. It is the `System` class that creates the system properties object. A curious programmer would look in the `System` class to find out how the `user.language` and `user.region` properties were set. This, however, is accomplished by invoking a `native` method in a class variable initializer. Consequently there is nothing to be learned about the default locale in the `System` class because the source code for `native` methods is not made available to the general public.

The reason why programmers are interested in how the default locale is set is so that they can reset it during program initialization. This is usually atttempted using the `javac -Dproperty=value` option to set the `user.language` and `user.region` system properties. For example,

```
java -Duser.language=en -Duser.region=US Test
```

Japanese programmers in particular are trying to do this (for example, see Bug ID 4127375). Using command-line options to set the default locale does not work, at least not in all implementations. You can accomplish the same thing as follows:

```
import java.util.Locale;
class Test {
    public static void main(String[] args) {

        //set default locale
        switch (args.length) {
            case 1:
```

```
          System.setProperty("user.language", args[0]);
          System.setProperty("user.region", "");
          Locale.setDefault(new Locale(args[0], ""));
          break;
      case 2:
          System.setProperty("user.language", args[0]);
          System.setProperty("user.region", args[1]);
          Locale.setDefault(new Locale(args[0], args[1]));
          break;
      default:
          System.err.println("Usage: java Test user.language <user.region>");
          System.exit(0);
      }
      System.out.println(Locale.getDefault());
    }
}
```

Here are the DOS commands and output from a single execution:

```
C:\Java\classes>java Test ja JP
ja_JP
```

5.13.2 Supported Locales

The closest thing there is to a specification for supported locales is the following quotation from the *Internationalization* document in the 1.2 release.

> On the Java™ platform, there does not have to be a single set of supported locales, since each class maintains its own localizations. Nevertheless, there is a consistent set of localizations supported by the Java platform classes. Other implementations of the Java platform may support different locales .... Subsequent releases of the platform may include additional locales.[21]

These locales are listed in Tables 5-5 and 5-6, which include the corresponding convenience constants declared in the Locale class (if there is one). This table does not include the EURO variants listed above.

Note that supported locales in the SDK are still very volatile and changes are to be expected in at least the next few releases. You may want to write a program that invokes all of the getAvailable-Locales() methods in the core API and check to see that they are consistent. I use such a program to maintain the tables in this section.

The getAvailableLocales() method in the Locale class is not special in this regard. It returns an array of locales supported by the Locale class. It specifically does not return an array of all of the locales supported in the core API. There can be no such method because there is

---

21. API docs from the *Internationalization* document in the Java™ 2 SDK, Standard Edition.

Table 5-5: SDK-Supported Locales (Language Only)

Locale	Description[a]	Convenience Constant
ar	Arabic	
be	Byelorussian	
bg	Bulgarian	
ca	Catalan	
cs	Czech	
da	Danish	
de	German	Locale.German
el	Greek	
en	English	Locale.English
es	Spanish	
et	Estonian	
fi	Finnish	
fr	French	Locale.French
hr	Croatian	
hu	Hungarian	
is	Icelandic	
it	Italian	Locale.Italian
iw	Hebrew	
ja	Japanese	Locale.Japanese
ko	Korean	Locale.Korean
lt	Lithuanian	
lv	Latvian (Lettish)	
mk	Macedonian	
nl	Dutch	
no	Norwegian	
pl	Polish	

Table 5-5: SDK-Supported Locales (Language Only) (Continued)

Locale	Description[a]	Convenience Constant
pt	Portuguese	
ro	Romanian	
ru	Russian	
sh	Serbo-Croatian	
sk	Slovak	
sl	Slovenian	
sq	Albanian	
sr	Serbian	
sv	Swedish	
th	Thai	
tr	Turkish	
uk	Ukrainian	
zh	Chinese	`Locale.Chinese`

a. This is what the `getDisplayName()` method prints.

no specification that says all of the locale-sensitive operations in the core API have to support some minimum number of locales.

All of the following methods in the `Locale` class either use the default locale or are passed a `Locale`:

```
public String getISO3Language() throws MissingResourceException
public String getISO3Country() throws MissingResourceException

public final String getDisplayLanguage()
public final String getDisplayCountry()
public final String getDisplayVariant()
public final String getDisplayName()

public String getDisplayLanguage(Locale inLocale)
public String getDisplayCountry(Locale inLocale)
public String getDisplayVariant(Locale inLocale)
public String getDisplayName(Locale inLocale)
```

These are locale-sensitive operations in the `Locale` class. The strings returned by these methods must be translated into all of the languages

Table 5-6: SDK-Supported Locales (Less Euro Variants)

Language[a]	Locale	Country[b]	Convenience Constant
Arabic	ar_AE	United Arab Emirates	
	ar_BH	Bahrain	
	ar_DZ	Algeria	
	ar_EG	Egypt	
	ar_IQ	Iraq	
	ar_JO	Jordan	
	ar_KW	Kuwait	
	ar_LB	Lebanon	
	ar_LY	Libya	
	ar_MA	Morocco	
	ar_OM	Oman	
	ar_QA	Qatar	
	ar_SA	Saudi Arabia	
	ar_SD	Sudan	
	ar_SY	Syria	
	ar_TN	Tunisia	
	ar_YE	Yemen	
Byelorussian	be_BY	Belarus	
Bulgarian	bg_BG	Bulgaria	
Catalan	ca_ES	Spain	
Czech	cs_CZ	Czech Republic	
Danish	da_DK	Denmark	
German	de_AT	Austria	
	de_CH	Switzerland	
	de_DE	Germany	Locale.GERMANY
	de_LU	Luxembourg	
Greek	el_GR	Greece	

Table 5-6: SDK-Supported Locales (Less Euro Variants) (Continued)

Language[a]	Locale	Country[b]	Convenience Constant
English	en_AU	Australia	
	en_CA	Canada	Locale.CANADA
	en_GB	United Kingdom	Locale.UK
	en_IEE	Ireland	
	en_NZ	New Zealand	
	en_ZA	South Africa	
	en_US	United States	Locale.US
Spanish	es_AR	Argentina	
	es_BO	Bolivia	
	es_CL	Chile	
	es_CO	Colombia	
	es_CR	Costa Rica	
	es_DO	Dominican Republic	
	es_EC	Ecuador	
	es_ES	Spain	
	es_GT	Guatemala	
	es_HN	Honduras	
	es_MX	Mexico	
	es_NI	Nicaragua	
	es_PA	Panama	
	es_PE	Peru	
	es_PR	Puerto Rico	
	es_PY	Paraguay	
	es_SVr	El Salvador	
	es_UY	Uruguay	
	es_VE	Venezuela	
Estonian	et_EE	Estonia	
Finnish	fi_FI	Finland	

Table 5-6: SDK-Supported Locales (Less Euro Variants) (Continued)

Language[a]	Locale	Country[b]	Convenience Constant
French	fr_BE	Belgium	
	fr_CA	Canada	Locale.CANADA_FRENCH
	fr_CH	Switzerland	
	fr_FR	France	Locale.FRANCE
	fr_LU	Luxembourg	
Croatian	hr_HR	Croatia	
Hungarian	hu_HU	Hungary	
Icelandic	is_IS	Iceland	
Italian	it_CH	Switzerland	
	it_IT	Italy	Locale.ITALY
Hebrew	iw_IL	Israel	
Japanese	ja_JP	Japan	Locale.JAPAN
Korean	ko_KR	South Korea	Locale.KOREA
Lithuanian	lt_LT	Lithuania	
Latvian (Lettish)	lv_LV	Latvia	
Macedonian	mk_MK	Macedonia	
Dutch	nl_BE	Belgium	
	nl_NL	The Netherlands	
Norwegian	no_NO	Norway	
Norwegian	no_NO_NY	Norway (Nynorsk)	
Polish	pl_PL	Poland	
Portuguese	pt_BR	Brazil	
	pt_PT	Portugal	
Romanian	ro_RO	Romania	
Russian	ru_RU	Russia	
Serbo-Croatian	sh_YU	Yugoslavia	
Slovak	sk_SK	Slovakia	

Table 5-6: SDK-Supported Locales (Less Euro Variants) (Continued)

Language[a]	Locale	Country[b]	Convenience Constant
Slovenian	sl_SI	Slovenia	
Albanian	sq_AL	Albania	
Serbian	sr_YU	Yugoslavia	
Swedish	sv_SE	Sweden	
Thai	th_TH	Thailand	
Turkish	tr_TR	Turkey	
Ukrainian	uk_UA	Ukraine	
Chinese	zh_CN	China	Locale.CHINA Locale.PRC Locale.SIMPLIFIED_ CHINESE
	zh_HK	Hong Kong	
	zh_TW	Taiwan	Locale.TAIWAN Locale.TRADITIONAL _CHINESE

a. This is what the getDisplayLanguage() method prints.
b. This is what the getDisplayCountry() method prints, except for *Norway (Nynorsk)*.

listed in Table 5-5. The requisite translations are stored in resource bundles that ship with the SDK. In short, the Locale class in the core API has been internationalized. For example, the getDisplayLanguage() and getDisplayLanguage(Locale inLocale) methods in Sun implementation of the Locale class can translate the strings "United States" and "English" into about 40 languages. That is the meaning of the Locale.getAvailableLocales() method. Again, it specifically does not return a list of all the locales supported in the core API.

5.13.2.1 Supported Locales in *NumberFormat*

This section is a criticism of one small aspect of the overall internationalization design and not anything a mainstream business application programmer necessarily needs to know.

All implementations should be required to support the same locales in the NumberFormat class (at least in the Standard and Enterprise editions). There should be a `ResourceBundle` for every country included in ISO-3166. *What we are talking about here is a full complement of pattern strings*. This is not a difficult task. Application programmers need this as much as they do the *Unicode Standard*. Otherwise, the localization of common data types in an internationalized application is not robust. I am surprised that the internationalization team at IBM missed this opportunity to standardize the Java platform. Another way of looking at this is that the resource bundles used by `NumberFormat` should be as *universal* as Unicode or as global as the `TimeZone` class.

The problem with this design is the following line from the API docs for the `java.util.ResourceBundle` class.

> `ResourceBundles` are used internally in accessing `Number-Formats`, `Collations`, and so on. The lookup strategy is the same.[22]

The lookup strategies for a currency formatter should not be the same because *there is a substantial difference between text translations and currency pattern strings*.

The lookup strategy specified in the `ResourceBundle` class works fine for text translations because you can always fall back to an international language such as French, English, or Spanish. For example, a button may be labeled *Cancel* instead of *Abbrechen*. However, the entire interface will fall back to the same language. A German user will recognize at once that this in an English interface instead of the desired German one. The fallback, however, may include an unwanted currency conversion. For example, U.S. $10,259.89 instead of 10.259,89 DM. That is a big difference, and there is no warning that the price should be in Deutsche marks. Furthermore, if enough of the resource bundles that normally ship with the Java run times distributed by Sun are missing in a substandard implementation, an application that would normally run to completion will throw a `MissingResourceException`. This specification in inconsistent with the Java design goal of a robust programming language as well as to *write once, run anywhere*.

---

22. API docs for the `java.util.ResourceBundle` class.

5.14 The `Date` Class

The `Date` class underwent a radical change in the 1.1 release when most of the methods in the class were deprecated. If you ignore the deprecated methods and the usual housekeeping methods, a simplified implementation of the `Date` class looks like this:

```
public class Date implements java.io.Serializable {

    private long time;

    public Date() {
        this(System.currentTimeMillis());
    }

    public Date(long date) {
        time = date;
    }

    public long getTime() {
        return time;
    }

    public void setTime(long time) {
        this.time = time;
    }

    public boolean before(Date when) {
        return getTime() < when.getTime();
    }

    public boolean after(Date when) {
        return getTime() > when.getTime();
    }

}
```

This is the `Date` class as you should think of it except that I removed the `Clonable` and `Comparable` interfaces from the `implements` clause because I am not showing any of the housekeeping methods. If you look at the source code for the `Date` class, it is immensely more complicated than this, but that is only because a "phantom" `GregorianCalendar` must be used for the deprecated methods.

Computer systems use an arbitrary instant in time as zero when measuring time in milliseconds. This instant in time is called the **epoch**. The epoch differs from one operating system to the next. Java technology uses the UNIX epoch, which is January 1, 1970, 0:00:00 GMT. All dates and times are measured as offsets from January 1, 1970, 00:00:00 GMT in milliseconds. For example,

```
class Test {
    public static void main(String[] args) {
        System.out.println(System.currentTimeMillis());
    }
}
```

Executing this program prints `981593820020`, which is almost a trillion milliseconds, a billion seconds, 16,359,897 minutes, 272,665 hours, 11,361 days, or 31 years and 12 days ago as of this writing. This is what makes the `Date` class conceptually difficult.

> An instance of the `Date` class is actually a measure-
> ment in *time* (the number of milliseconds since Janu-
> ary 1, 1970 to be exact), not a date. It is essentially a
> timestamp.

This inherent contradiction can be seen in the names of the accessor and mutator methods in the `Date` class, which are `getTime()` and `set-Time(long time)`. Likewise, the `getTime()` method in the `Cal-endar` class returns an instance of the `Date` class. Moreover, the raw milliseconds have no meaning apart from a `GregorianCalendar` because only `Calendar` subclasses know how to interpret a `Date` using the epoch. In a sense, the `Date` class is inseparable from `Gregorian-Calendar`.

Dr. Davis referred to the `Date` class as "purely a storage class."[23] Classes in the `Calendar` hierarchy expect the raw milliseconds used to represent dates and times to be passed as instances of the `Date` class, not as a `long`. You should never pass raw milliseconds in a `long` if they represent a time. They should always be encapsulated in a `Date`. This is the only use of the `Date` class to pass the raw milliseconds used in date and time computations. The actual computations are based on a particular calendar system (that is, a `Calendar` subclass), of which there is at present only one in the core API. That is `GregorianCalendar`. If you want to know how to work with dates and times in the Java programming language, you must learn the `GregorianCalendar` class, not `Date`.

---

23. Mark Davis, "The Java Internationalization API," *Java Report*, Vol. 4, No. 2 (Feb. 1999): 28.

5.14.1 Date Comparisons

The one thing you can do well with raw millisecond time measurements based on the same epoch is compare them. The following methods are declared in the `Date` class:

```
public boolean before(Date when)
public boolean after(Date when)
```

These methods are also declared in the `Calendar` class so as to obviate the necessity of invoking `getTime()` just to make date comparisons. The only difference is that the parameter type is `Object` instead of `Date`:

```
public boolean before(Object when)
public boolean after(Object when)
```

There is no explanation in the API docs as to why the `when` parameter type is `Object`. On the contrary, the API docs describe the `when` parameter as "the `Calendar` to be compared with this `Calendar`."

5.15 The `GregorianCalendar` Class

I think of `GregorianCalendar` class as a monstrous adding machine with levers, buttons, spinning dials, and smoke coming out of the top, and in the end you invoke the `getTime()` method and out pops a `Date` that you can pocket and use elsewhere. If you want to know how to work with dates and times in the Java programming language, you must learn the `GregorianCalendar` class, not `Date`. The API docs have much to say about the **Gregorian calendar**, the most important of which is that it is "the standard calendar used by most of the world."[24] For most readers it is just a technical name for the calendar hanging on your wall at work or home.

Note that the `GregorianCalendar` class does not use the `Date` class except to wrap the milliseconds in the `return` statement in the `getTime()` method. For example,

```
public final Date getTime() {
    return new Date( time );
}
```

---

24. API docs for the `java.util.GregorianCalendar` class.

The milliseconds are stored in a highly unusual *write only* field named `time`. As would be expected, you cannot directly read the `time` field. There is a `getTime()` method, but that returns a `Date`. Client programmers can set the `time` field, however, either directly using the `setTime(Date date)` method or indirectly by setting the value of a date or time field using one of the field manipulation methods. There is also a `protected setTimeInMillis(long millis)` method available in subclasses.

The explanation for this particular write only field is twofold. First, `System.currentTimeInMillis()` is used to set the current date and time. This explains why client programmers must be able to assign a millisecond value to the `time` field. The reason why they cannot read the same field is that the software engineers at Sun do not want you passing around millisecond measurements that should be encapsulated in the `Date` class.

While it is normally my practice to shun oversimplified analogies, in the case of the `Calendar` class I make an exception. Understanding this class is greatly facilitated if you approach the subject as follows.

Think of the `long` in which the millisecond measurement of time is stored as the odometer in your car.

Using the odometer analogy, there are three mental models. The first mental model, in Figure 5-3, is comparable to a regular calendar.

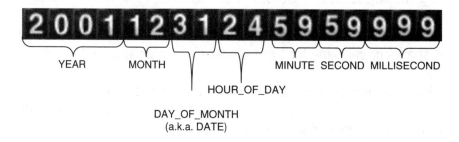

Figure 5-3: The standard calendar mental model.

The field names shown in these figures are the field names in the `Calendar` class. When explaining rules for changing the value of a `Calendar`, they are referred to as **units of time**. The units of time to the left are "larger" than the units of time to the right. Each field can be set independently.

The second mental model, in Figure 5-4, is 365 days in a year.

Figure 5-4: 365 days in a year mental model.

Note that all three of these mental models use the HOUR_OF_DAY field, which is comparable to military time. You can easily substitute the use of HOUR and AM_PM. HOUR has a range of 0 to 11, which is like the hours on a normal clock. Merely by setting the HOUR and AM_PM fields, the Calendar class knows your preference. You can, however, clear the HOUR_OF_DAY if it makes you feel more comfortable. The clear methods are discussed below.

The third and final mental model in Figure 5-5 is 52 weeks in a year.

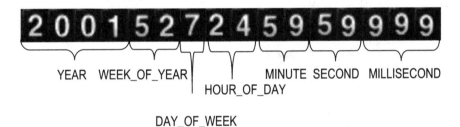

Figure 5-5: 52 weeks in a year mental model.

This mental model is used by businesses in Europe. Allowing for the substitution of HOUR and AM_PM (normal clock time) for HOUR_OF_DAY (military time) and the ERA field (which is seldom explicitly set), there are only 2 of the 15 date and time fields that do not fit into one of these three mental models based on the odometer analogy. Those two fields are WEEK_OF_THE_MONTH and DAY_OF_WEEK_IN_MONTH. They are not discussed in this chapter. You can read about them in the API docs. Otherwise, these three mental models cover all of the date and time fields in the `Calendar` class.

5.15.1 Instantiating the `GregorianCalendar` Class

Some of the constructors and `set` methods in this section include a possible implementation so that you can seen how things are connected together. I ignore those constructors and methods that have `TimeZone` and `Locale` parameters. Doing so greatly simplifies the presentation. Most of the time the default `TimeZone` and `Locale` are used.

For the sake of brevity, the examples in this section invoke a `print-Fields()` utility method that I have removed from the examples. The implementation of that method is as follows:

```
static void printFields(Calendar calendar, boolean printTime, String title) {

    System.out.println();
    System.out.println();
    System.out.println();
    System.out.println(title);
    System.out.println();

    int loopControl;
    if (printTime)
        loopControl = 15;
    else
        loopControl = 9;

    for (int i=0; i<loopControl; i++) {
        switch(i) {
            case  0: System.out.print("ERA ....................");
                     break;
            case  1: System.out.print("YEAR ...................");
                     break;
            case  2: System.out.print("MONTH ..................");
                     break;
            case  3: System.out.print("WEEK_OF_YEAR ...........");
                     break;
            case  4: System.out.print("WEEK_OF_MONTH ..........");
                     break;
            case  5: System.out.print("DAY_OF_MONTH (or DATE)...");
                     break;
            case  6: System.out.print("DAY_OF_YEAR ............");
                     break;
            case  7: System.out.print("DAY_OF_WEEK ............");
                     break;
            case  8: System.out.print("DAY_OF_WEEK_IN_MONTH ....");
                     break;
            case  9: System.out.print("AM_PM ..................");
                     break;
            case 10: System.out.print("HOUR ...................");
                     break;
            case 11: System.out.print("HOUR_OF_DAY ............");
```

```
                break;
      case 12: System.out.print("MINUTE ...............");
                break;
      case 13: System.out.print("SECOND ...............");
                break;
      case 14: System.out.print("MILLISECOND ..........");
                break;
    }
    System.out.print(calendar.get(i));
    if (i==Calendar.MONTH)
      System.out.print("    (remember MONTH is zero-origin)");
    System.out.println();
  }
}
```

Consequently, some of the examples in this section and the sections to follow will not actually compile.

When instantiating the `GregorianCalendar` class for the current date and time, there is a choice of using a `getInstance()` factory method inherited from the `Calendar` class or a `GregorianCalendar` constructor. There is no substantial difference between the two:

```
public static synchronized Calendar getInstance() {
    return new GregorianCalendar();
}

public GregorianCalendar() {
    this(TimeZone.getDefault(), Locale.getDefault());
}
```

It is natural for the default implementation of the `getInstance()` factory method in the `Calendar` class to return an instance of the `GregorianCalendar` subclass because that is the calendar used in most of the world. Both of these invoke the following constructor using the default `TimeZone` and `Locale`:

```
public GregorianCalendar(TimeZone zone, Locale aLocale) {
    super(zone, aLocale);
    setTimeInMillis(System.currentTimeMillis());
}
```

As you can see, this constructor initializes the `long` field (our odometer) by invoking the `System.currentTimeMillis()` method.

For a `GregorianCalendar` that is set to something other than the current date and time when instantiated, you always have a choice between using one of the other `GregorianCalendar` constructors or the corresponding `set` method. For every constructor there is a corresponding `set` method. For example,

```
public GregorianCalendar(int year, int month, int date) {
      super(TimeZone.getDefault(), Locale.getDefault());
```

```
        this.set(ERA, AD);
        this.set(YEAR, year);
        this.set(MONTH, month);
        this.set(DATE, date);
    }
```

Invoking this constructor is equivalent to the following:

```
Calendar calendar = Calendar.getInstance();
calendar.set(year, month, date);
```

If you prefer to use the set methods, invoke the no-arg Gregorian-Calendar() constructor. Then overwrite the current date and time by invoking the appropriate set method.

There are two other such sets of matching constructors and set methods.

```
public GregorianCalendar(int year, int month, int date,
                         int hour, int minute) {
    super(TimeZone.getDefault(), Locale.getDefault());
    this.set(ERA, AD);
    this.set(YEAR, year);
    this.set(MONTH, month);
    this.set(DATE, date);
    this.set(HOUR_OF_DAY, hour);
    this.set(MINUTE, minute);
}

public final void set(int year, int month, int date,
                      int hour, int minute) {
    set(YEAR, year);
    set(MONTH, month);
    set(DATE, date);
    set(HOUR_OF_DAY, hour);
    set(MINUTE, minute);
}

public GregorianCalendar(int year, int month, int date,
                         int hour, int minute, int second) {
    super(TimeZone.getDefault(), Locale.getDefault());
    this.set(ERA, AD);
    this.set(YEAR, year);
    this.set(MONTH, month);
    this.set(DATE, date);
    this.set(HOUR_OF_DAY, hour);
    this.set(MINUTE, minute);
    this.set(SECOND, second);
}

public final void set(int year, int month, int date,
                      int hour, int minute, int second) {
    set(YEAR, year);
    set(MONTH, month);
    set(DATE, date);
    set(HOUR_OF_DAY, hour);
    set(MINUTE, minute);
    set(SECOND, second);
}
```

It is important to note that these constructors are setting the HOUR_OF_DAY fields and not HOUR and AM_PM. The HOUR_OF_DAY field (military time) is the norm. One detail to note is that all three sets of these constructors and set methods are using the standard calendar mental model. If you want to use the 365 days in a year or 52 weeks in a year mental model, you have to use the overloaded set method.

5.15.2 The Inconsistent Field Rule

While I am to blame for the odometer analogy in this chapter, the three mental models have a strong foundation in the *inconsistent information* policy expressed in the API docs for the Calendar class.

> **Inconsistent information.** If fields conflict, the calendar will give preference to fields set more recently. For example, when determining the day, the calendar will look for one of the following combinations of fields. The most recent combination, as determined by the most recently set single field, will be used.
>
> ```
> MONTH + DAY_OF_MONTH
> MONTH + WEEK_OF_MONTH + DAY_OF_WEEK
> DAY_OF_YEAR[25]
> ```

You can interpret this as the core API giving preference to the standard calendar, the 52 weeks in a year (European business) and the 365 days in a year mental models, in that order. All of these are different ways of expressing a date. The **inconsistent field rule** says that when there is more than one field in which essentially the same datum can be expressed, the most recently set field is used. For example,

```
import java.text.*;
import java.util.*;
class Test {
    static Calendar calendar = new GregorianCalendar();
    public static void main(String[] args) {
        DateFormat df = DateFormat.getDateInstance(DateFormat.LONG);
        calendar.set(Calendar.DAY_OF_YEAR, 365);
        calendar.set(Calendar.YEAR, 1945);
        calendar.set(Calendar.MONTH, Calendar.MAY);
        calendar.set(Calendar.DATE, 8);
        System.out.println(df.format(calendar.getTime()));
    }
}
```

---

25. API docs for the java.util.Calendar class.

Executing this program prints May 8, 1945. DAY_OF_YEAR is ignored because it was set first.

Preference is given to HOUR and AM_PM using the same inconsistent fields rule. Merely by setting those fields, the HOUR_OF_DAY field is ignored in the same way DAY_OF_YEAR is ignored in the example above.

5.15.3 The Maximum DAY_OF_MONTH Rule

When setting, adding, or rolling MONTH, DAY_OF_MONTH, or DATE, there is one rule that always applies. The API docs refer to this as *ADD rule 1*, yet the same rule applies to both adding and rolling. I call it the **maximum DAY_OF_MONTH rule**, with the understanding that it applies equally to the DATE field.

This rule explains the setting, adding, and rolling behavior of a Calendar when the DAY_OF_MONTH or DATE field has a value higher than what the getActualMaximum(Calendar.MONTH) method would return. There are two behaviors, one for setting MONTH, DAY_OF_MONTH, DATE or some combination thereof, and one for either adding or rolling those same fields. In this example I will use February and 31 as the values, simply because everyone knows that February does not have 31 days. The following program shows what happens when setting the fields:

```
import java.text.*;
import java.util.*;
class Test {

    static Calendar calendar = new GregorianCalendar();

    public static void main(String[] args) {
        DateFormat df = DateFormat.getDateInstance(DateFormat.LONG);
        calendar.clear();                    //CLEAR FOR READABILITY
        calendar.set(Calendar.YEAR, 2001);
        calendar.set(Calendar.MONTH, Calendar.FEBRUARY);
        calendar.set(Calendar.DAY_OF_MONTH, 31);
        System.out.println("DAY_OF_MONTH set last: " +
                            df.format(calendar.getTime()));
        calendar.set(Calendar.DAY_OF_MONTH, 31);
        calendar.set(Calendar.MONTH, Calendar.FEBRUARY);
        System.out.println("MONTH set last: " +
                            df.format(calendar.getTime()));
    }
}
```

Executing this program prints

```
DAY_OF_MONTH set last: March 3, 2001
MONTH set last: March 3, 2001
```

My reason for trying this both ways is that there is an interesting relationship between the inconsistent fields and maximum DAY_OF_MONTH rules. In a sense the MONTH (February) and DAY_OF_MONTH (31) are inconsistent, but if you reread the discussion of the inconsistent fields rule you will see that it applies to fields that have essentially the same datum. For example, HOUR_OF_DAY versus HOUR and AM_PM. In that case the inconsistent fields rule says to use the field(s) most recently set. However, MONTH and DAY_OF_MONTH, while closely related, are not the same datum. Therefore, a different rule is needed.

The maximum DAY_OF_MONTH rule used in the add(int field, int value), roll(int field, int value), and roll(int field, boolean up) methods is different from the inconsistent fields rule. In the following example a month is added to January 31, 2001. Then the same date is rolled one month using both of the overloaded roll methods. The result in all three cases is different from the March 3, 2001 result you would expect using the inconsistent fields rule:

```
import java.text.*;
import java.util.*;
class Test {

    static Calendar calendar = new GregorianCalendar();

    public static void main(String[] args) {
        DateFormat df = DateFormat.getDateInstance(DateFormat.LONG);
        calendar.clear();                    //CLEAR FOR READABILITY
        calendar.set(Calendar.YEAR, 2001);
        calendar.set(Calendar.MONTH, Calendar.JANUARY);
        calendar.set(Calendar.DAY_OF_MONTH, 31);
        Date date = calendar.getTime();      //SAVE DATE
        calendar.add(Calendar.MONTH, 1);
        System.out.println(df.format(calendar.getTime()));
        calendar.setTime(date);
        calendar.roll(Calendar.MONTH, true);
        System.out.println(df.format(calendar.getTime()));
        calendar.setTime(date);
        calendar.roll(Calendar.MONTH, 1);
        System.out.println(df.format(calendar.getTime()));
    }
}
```

Executing this program prints February 28, 2001 three times.

There is an interesting comment about this rule in the API docs.

> **Usage model.** To motivate the behavior of add() and roll(), consider a user interface component with increment and decrement buttons for the month, day, and year, and an underlying GregorianCalendar. If the interface reads

January 31, 1999 and the user presses the month increment button, what should it read? If the underlying implementation uses `set()`, it might read March 3, 1999. A better result would be February 28, 1999. Furthermore, if the user presses the month increment button again, it should read March 31, 1999, not March 28, 1999. By saving the original date and using either `add()` or `roll()`, depending on whether larger fields should be affected, the user interface can behave as most users will intuitively expect.[26]

The trick is that you need to save the original date (as in the example above). Otherwise, after rolling from `January 31` to `February 28`, `February 28` rolls to `March 28`. The same holds true for repeated invocations of the `add(int field, int value)` method.

5.16 Date and Time Fields in the `Calendar` Class

Most of the date and time fields are declared in the `Calendar` base class. Only the `ERA` field is unique to the `GregorianCalendar` subclass. The date and time fields in a calendar are summarized in Table 5-7. Besides the fact that there is a *least maximum* column, there are several interesting details to notice in this table:

- The change from `Calender` to `GregorianCalendar` for the `BC` and `AD` constants. The notion of *BC* and *AD* is strictly Gregorian calendar and you must use the longer type name qualifier. All of the other convenience constants are declared in the `Calendar` class. Of course, they are inherited by `Gregorian-Calendar`, but you will probably want to use the shorter of the two type names to qualify them.

- `MONTH` is zero-based. Valid ranges are 0 to 11. (See Dr. Davis' quotation below.)

- `DAY_OF_MONTH` and `DATE` are *two names for the same constant*. They will therefore always be equal. The valid range of values for both is from 1 to 31.

---

26. API docs for the `java.util.Calendar` class.

- The `DST_OFFSET` and `ZONE_OFFSET` fields are omitted because I generally ignore time zones in this chapter. The default time zone is used most of the time, which makes these two fields very different from the rest. Time zones are discussed in 5.17 The `TimeZone` Class.

Table 5-7: Date and Time Fields in the `Calendar` Class

Field	Minimum[a]	Least Maximum	Maximum	Convenience Constants
ERA	0		1	`GregorianCalendar.BC` `GregorianCalendar.AD`
YEAR	1	292269054	292278994	

MONTH
(zero-origin)
	0		11	`Calendar.JANUARY`
				`Calendar.FEBRUARY`
				`Calendar.MARCH`
				`Calendar.APRIL`
				`Calendar.MAY`
				`Calendar.JUNE`
				`Calendar.JULY`
				`Calendar.AUGUST`
				`Calendar.SEPTEMBER`
				`Calendar.OCTOBER`
				`Calendar.NOVEMBER`
				`Calendar.DECEMBER`

WEEK_OF_YEAR	1	52	53	
WEEK_OF_MONTH	0	4	6	
DATE DAY_OF_MONTH	1	28	31	
DAY_OF_YEAR	1		366	

DAY_OF_WEEK	1		7	`Calendar.SUNDAY`
				`Calendar.MONDAY`
				`Calendar.TUESDAY`
				`Calendar.WEDNESDAY`
				`Calendar.THURSDAY`
				`Calendar.FRIDAY`
				`Calendar.SATURDAY`

DAY_OF_WEEK_ IN_MONTH	-1	4	6	
AM_PM	0		1	`Calendar.AM` `Calendar.PM`

a. In a `GregorianCalendar`, the `getMinimum(int field)` and `getGreatestMinimum(int field)` methods always return the same value.

The fact that months are zero-origin irks a lot of people. Dr. Mark Davis had this to say in a February, 1999 article in *Java Report*:

Why is January Zero?

We probably get more complaints about this than any other issue. Here's what happened. The JDK 1.0 `Date` API and implementation were very specific to the Gregorian calendar, and were not terribly Y2K friendly. Although the Gregorian calendar is used in most of the world, many countries use other calendar systems. For instance, businesses in Europe often use a calendar that measures by day, week, and year, rather than day, month, year. There are also a large number of traditional calendars in widespread use in the Middle East and Asia. To deal with these problems, we split out the date computations into another class, `Calendar`, and retained `Date` purely as a storage class.

The zero-based month numbers in `Date` were a vestige of old C-style programming—originally month names were stored in a zero-based array and the months were numbered accordingly for convenience. JavaSoft felt that consistency with the old `Date` APIs was important, so we needed to keep this convention in `Calendar`. So calling `calendar.set(1998, 3, 15)` gives April 15th, not March 15th.[27]

There you have it. Straight from the horse's mouth, as they say. As I read it, Dr. Davis is placing the blame squarely on the conservative compatibility policy at Sun, and maybe he is right. Maybe they could have bent just this once. Then again, I have seen a lot of misplaced blame in my own career when even minor interface changes were made *in code that had not even reached production.* I believe that Sun's very conservative policy in matters of backwards compatibility has served them (or rather all of us) well.

The remainder of this section is a discussion of the valid range of values that can be stored in the date or time fields and will explain the least maximum column along the way.

The valid range of values that can be stored in one of the date and time fields of a `Calendar` is complicated by answers to questions such as *how many days are there in a month.* Instead of the usual MIN_VALUE and MAX_VALUE fields used to express a range of values, a total of six

---

27. Mark Davis, "The Java Internationalization API," *Java Report,* Vol. 4, No. 2 (Feb. 1999): 28. Please note that I corrected a minor mistake in the "`calendar.set(1998, 3, 5)`" method invocation in the original, and also changed "were" to was" in the previous sentence for readability.

instance methods in the `Calendar` class are required to return the valid range of values that can be stored in one of these fields. The first four methods are

```
public int getMinimum(int field)
public int getGreatestMinimum(int field)
public int getLeastMaximum(int field)
public int getMaximum(int field)
```

For example, 28 is the least maximum DAY_OF_MONTH or DATE for the month of February. Using a GregorianCalendar, getMinimum(int field) and getGreatestMinimum(int field) always return the same values. Hence, there are only three columns in Table 5-7. The other two methods are

```
public int getActualMinimum(int field)
public int getActualMaximum(int field)
```

These methods return values based on the current date. As with get-GreatestMinimum(int field), the getActualMinimum(int field) method for a GregorianCalendar always returns the same values as the getMinimum(int field) method. In other words, the two minimum values for the date and time fields in a GregorianCalendar are always the same. The getActualMaximum(int field) method is particularly useful for determining the number of days in February. For example,

```
import java.util.*;
class Test {
    public static void main(String[] args) {
        Calendar notLeapYear = new GregorianCalendar(1997, Calendar.FEBRUARY, 1);
        Calendar leapYear = new GregorianCalendar(1996, Calendar.FEBRUARY, 1);
        System.out.println(notLeapYear.getActualMaximum(Calendar.DAY_OF_MONTH));
        System.out.println(leapYear.getActualMaximum(Calendar.DAY_OF_MONTH));
    }
}
```

Executing this program prints

```
28
29
```

The following subsections discuss default values for date and time fields, normalizing date and time fields, and what the API docs call the *field manipulation methods*.

5.16.1 Standard Default Values for Date and Time Fields

This is actually a curious subject because *standard default values* are usually thought of as the value of a primitive data type after memory allocation and before being assigned a value. Furthermore, the standard default values for numeric fields such as dates and times is usually zero. In a `Date` or `Calendar`, however, zero is the epoch. For example,

```java
import java.text.*;
import java.util.*;
class Test {
    public static void main(String[] args) {
        Date epoch = new Date();
        epoch.setTime(0);
        Calendar calendar = new GregorianCalendar();
        calendar.setTime(epoch);
        DateFormat df = DateFormat.getDateTimeInstance();
        df.setTimeZone(TimeZone.getTimeZone("GMT"));
        ((SimpleDateFormat)df).applyPattern("yyyyMMddHHmmssSSS zzz");
        System.out.println(df.format(calendar.getTime()));
    }
}
```

Executing this program prints

```
19700101000000000 GMT
```

These are reasonable defaults for the time fields, but January 1, 1970 is not a very good standard default value for dates. Therefore, the standard default values for date and time fields is the current date and time when the `Date` or `Calendar` is created. For example,

```java
import java.text.*;
import java.util.*;
class Test {
    public static void main(String[] args) {
        DateFormat df = DateFormat.getDateTimeInstance();
        Date now = new Date();
        Calendar calendar = new GregorianCalendar();
        System.out.println(df.format(calendar.getTime()));
        calendar.setTime(now);
        System.out.println(df.format(calendar.getTime()));
    }
}
```

The first time this program was executed it printed

```
Aug 1, 2001 10:39:30 PM
Aug 1, 2001 10:39:30 PM
```

The problem with this is what to do when one of the following clear methods is invoked.

```
public final void clear()
public final void clear(int field)
```

You cannot "reset" a `Calendar` back to the date and time it was created. Therefore a calendar is set to zero when the `clear()` method is invoked. Zero, however, as was shown in a previous example, is the epoch. If printed, the value of a cleared `Calendar` is as shown in Figure 5-6.

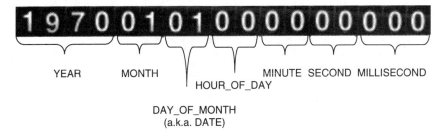

Figure 5-6: A cleared `Calendar` is equal to the epoch.

In short, invoking the `clear()` method sets a `Calendar` to January 1, 1970. Clearing the individual date fields yields the same results. For example,

```
import java.text.*;
import java.util.*;
class Test {
    public static void main(String[] args) {
        DateFormat df = DateFormat.getDateTimeInstance();
        Calendar calendar = new GregorianCalendar();
        System.out.println(df.format(calendar.getTime()));
        calendar.clear();
        System.out.println(df.format(calendar.getTime()));
        calendar.clear(Calendar.YEAR);
        calendar.clear(Calendar.MONTH);
        calendar.clear(Calendar.DATE);
        System.out.println(df.format(calendar.getTime()));
    }
}
```

The first execution of this program prints

```
Aug 1, 2001 11:22:29 PM
Jan 1, 1970 12:00:00 AM
Jan 1, 1970 12:00:00 AM
```

Notice that the `HOUR` field is 12, not 0. That is just because `AM_PM` is being used instead of military time.

5.16.2 Normalizing Date and Time Fields

Calendars are **lenient** by default. If a calendar is not lenient, and one of the values passed to the `set(int field, int value)` method is not in the `getActualMinimum()` to `getActualMaximum()` range, an `IllegalArgumentException` is thrown. For example,

```
import java.text.*;
import java.util.*;
class Test {
    public static void main(String[] args) {
        DateFormat df = DateFormat.getDateInstance(DateFormat.LONG);
        Calendar calendar = new GregorianCalendar();
        calendar.setLenient(false);
        System.out.println(df.format(calendar.getTime()));
        System.out.println(calendar.getActualMaximum(Calendar.DATE));
        calendar.set(Calendar.DATE, 29);
        System.out.println(df.format(calendar.getTime()));
    }
}
```

Attempting to executing this program prints

```
February 9, 2001
28
Exception in thread "main" java.lang.IllegalArgumentException
        at java.util.GregorianCalendar.computeTime(Unknown Source)
        at java.util.Calendar.updateTime(Unknown Source)
        at java.util.Calendar.getTimeInMillis(Unknown Source)
        at java.util.Calendar.getTime(Unknown Source)
        at Test.main(Test.java:11)
```

The `set` method threw an `IllegalArgumentException` because `29` is not in the `getActualMinimum()` to `getActualMaximum()` range. A lenient calendar would have been set to `March 1, 2001`.

The change from `February 29, 2001` to `March 1, 2001` in a lenient calendar is called **normalizing** the date and time fields. Normalizing allows you to compute dates using any unit of time. For example,

```
import java.text.*;
import java.util.*;
class Test {
    public static void main(String[] args) {
        DateFormat df = DateFormat.getDateInstance(DateFormat.LONG);
        Calendar calendar = new GregorianCalendar();
        System.out.println(df.format(calendar.getTime()));
        final int FIVE_YEARS_IN_MINUTES = 5*365*24*60;
        calendar.add(Calendar.MINUTE, FIVE_YEARS_IN_MINUTES);
        System.out.println(df.format(calendar.getTime()));
    }
}
```

Executing this program prints

```
February 9, 2001
February 8, 2006
```

The same can be done with either the set(int field, int value) or roll(int field, int value) methods.

5.16.3 Date and Time Field Manipulation Methods

The set, add, and roll methods in the Calendar class are referred to as **field manipulation methods**. They are one of two fundamentally different ways of changing the value of the write only time field in which the milliseconds are stored in a Calendar. The other is to invoke the setTime(Date date) method. It is important to grasp that when invoking the setTime(Date date) method you are directly setting the milliseconds in the time field. This measurement of time is fundamentally different from the date and time fields. The date and time fields can be thought of as dates the way they appear in print. At any given time only one of these two sets of instance variables can be in use. Setting any of the date and time fields invalidates the milliseconds and vice versa. Both the application programmer and the Calendar class must keep track of which is in use.

The GregorianCalendar class has a method to compute the milliseconds based on the settings of the date and time fields and vice versa, but these methods are expensive and never invoked unless absolutely necessary. For example, if the date and time fields are in use, multiple set method invocations will not cause the milliseconds to be recomputed. An invocation of getTime(), however, would.

The set, add, and roll field manipulation methods are discussed in that order in the following subsections.

5.16.3.1 Setting Date and Time Fields

One method is used to set all of the date and time fields:

```
public final void set(int field, int value)
```

Convenience constants such as Calendar.YEAR, Calendar.MONTH, and Calendar.DATE are always used as the first argument when invoking this method. Note that while it is possible to set all the fields, setting the WEEK_OF_THE_MONTH and DAY_OF_WEEK_IN_MONTH fields is not easy. You should study the API docs before attempting to do so. These fields are mostly useful on output.

5.16.3.2 *Adding Date and Time Fields*

The odometer analogy works best when adding to a field. For example, if you add one month to December 1, 2000, the new date is January 1, 2001. The larger unit of time is incremented or decremented as necessary. There is one add method for all of the date and time fields:

```
public void add(int field, int amount)
```

Here is a real odometer at work

```java
import java.text.*;
import java.util.*;
class Test {

    static Calendar calendar = new GregorianCalendar();

    public static void main(String[] args) {
        DateFormat df = DateFormat.getDateInstance(DateFormat.LONG);
        System.out.println(df.format(calendar.getTime())); //CURRENT DATE AND TIME
        final long ONE_YEAR  = 365*24*60*60; //ONE YEAR IN SECONDS
        for (int i=0; i<=ONE_YEAR; i++)
            calendar.add(Calendar.SECOND, 1);
        System.out.println(df.format(calendar.getTime()));
    }
}
```

Executing this program prints

```
February 5, 2001
February 5, 2002
```

That adding to a smaller unit of time increments larger units of time is referred to as *Add rule 1* in the API docs, but because I have changed *Add rule 2* to the *maximum DAY_OF_MONTH rule*, we will just call it the **add rule**. As you will see in the next section, the add rule is what makes adding different from rolling.

There is no subtract method, but you can pass a negative value to the add(int field, int value) method to achieve the same result. For example,

```java
import java.text.*;
import java.util.*;
class Test {
    static Calendar calendar = new GregorianCalendar();
    public static void main(String[] args) {
        DateFormat df = DateFormat.getDateInstance(DateFormat.LONG);
```

```
        System.out.println(df.format(calendar.getTime()));
        calendar.add(Calendar.MONTH, -12);
        System.out.println(df.format(calendar.getTime()));
    }
}
```

Executing this program prints

```
February 9, 2001
February 9, 2000
```

Notice the add rule at work in that the larger unit of time (in this case a YEAR) changed as a result of the add(int field, int value) method invocation.

5.16.3.3 Rolling Date and Time Fields

Oversimplified analogies always break down at some point. We are at that point for the odometer analogy, which is ironic because of all the places you would want the analogy to work, *rolling* the odometer would be one of them. There are two roll methods:

```
public void roll(int field, boolean up)
public void roll(int field, int amount)
```

The first method can be used to increment or decrement the value of a field and is comparable to the -- and ++ operators. The second method is different from add(int field, int value) only in that the roll methods use the roll rule instead of the add rule.

The **roll rule** states that larger units of time are unchanged as a result of rolling a field. It is the opposite of the add rule. The following example rolls the DATE past the end of the month, but the month field is left unchanged. Instead of constants such as MIN_VALUE and MAX_VALUE, the range of values for a given field is returned by the getActualMinimum(field) and getActualMaximum(field) methods. For example,

```
import java.text.*;
import java.util.*;
class Test {
    static Calendar calendar = new GregorianCalendar();
    public static void main(String[] args) {
        DateFormat df = DateFormat.getDateInstance(DateFormat.LONG);
        calendar.set(Calendar.DATE, 3);    //February 3, 2001
        System.out.println("getActualMinimum() = " +
                        calendar.getActualMinimum(Calendar.DATE));
        System.out.println(df.format(calendar.getTime()));
        for (int i=0; i<5; i++) {
```

```
            calendar.roll(Calendar.DATE, false);
            System.out.println(df.format(calendar.getTime()));
        }
        System.out.println();
        System.out.println();
        calendar.set(Calendar.DATE, 26);     //February 26, 2001
        Date date = calendar.getTime();
        System.out.println("getActualMaximum() = " +
                        calendar.getActualMaximum(Calendar.DATE));
        System.out.println(df.format(calendar.getTime()));
        for (int i=0; i<5; i++) {
            calendar.roll(Calendar.DATE, true);
            System.out.println(df.format(calendar.getTime()));
        }
        calendar.setTime(date);
        System.out.println();
        System.out.println();
        calendar.roll(Calendar.DATE, 5);
        System.out.println(df.format(calendar.getTime()));
    }
}
```

Executing this program prints

```
getActualMinimum() = 1
February 3, 2001
February 2, 2001
February 1, 2001
February 28, 2001
February 27, 2001
February 26, 2001

getActualMaximum() = 28
February 26, 2001
February 27, 2001
February 28, 2001
February 1, 2001
February 2, 2001
February 3, 2001

February 3, 2001
```

Notice that the result of invoking `roll(Calendar.DATE, true)` five times is the same as `roll(Calendar.DATE, 5)`. As with the `add(int field, int value)` method, the `roll(int field, int value)` method can be passed a negative number to move "the instant in time"[28] in a counter clockwise direction. Here is the same code used in the example of passing a negative value to the `add(int field, int value)` method, only the method name has been changed from `add` to `roll`:

---

28. API docs for the `java.io.Date` class.

```
import java.text.*;
import java.util.*;
class Test {
    static Calendar calendar = new GregorianCalendar();
    public static void main(String[] args) {
        DateFormat df = DateFormat.getDateInstance(DateFormat.LONG);
        System.out.println(df.format(calendar.getTime()));
        calendar.roll(Calendar.MONTH, -12);
        System.out.println(df.format(calendar.getTime()));
    }
}
```

Executing this program prints

```
February 9, 2001
February 9, 2001
```

As you can see, the YEAR is unchanged.

5.17 The `TimeZone` Class

Mainstream business application programmers do not usually use the Time-Zone class. It is, however, very important to the time computations in GregorianCalendar, and therefore is mentioned briefly in this chapter.

Most of the time the default time zone is used. That time zone is returned by the `TimeZone.getDefault()` utility method. For example,

```
import java.util.*;
class Test {
    public static void main(String[] args) {
        TimeZone timeZone = TimeZone.getDefault();
        System.out.println("getID() = " + timeZone.getID());
        System.out.println("getDisplayName(false, TimeZone.SHORT) = " +
                timeZone.getDisplayName(false, TimeZone.SHORT));
        System.out.println("getDisplayName(false, TimeZone.LONG) = " +
                timeZone.getDisplayName(false, TimeZone.LONG));
        System.out.println("getDisplayName(true, TimeZone.SHORT) = " +
                timeZone.getDisplayName(true, TimeZone.SHORT));
        System.out.println("getDisplayName(true, TimeZone.LONG) = " +
                timeZone.getDisplayName(true, TimeZone.LONG));
        System.out.println("useDayLightTime() = " +
                timeZone.useDaylightTime());
        System.out.println("inDayLightTime(new Date()) = " +
                timeZone.inDaylightTime(new Date()));
    }
}
```

Executing this program prints

```
getID() = America/New_York
getDisplayName(false, TimeZone.SHORT) = EST
getDisplayName(false, TimeZone.LONG) = Eastern Standard Time
getDisplayName(true, TimeZone.SHORT) = EDT
```

```
getDisplayName(true, TimeZone.LONG) = Eastern Daylight Time
useDayLightTime() = true
inDayLightTime(new Date()) = false
```

The `inDayLightTime(Date date)` method should have been declared in the `GregorianCalendar` class and is scheduled to be "moved" to that class in a future release, at which time this declaration will be deprecated.

As with the default locale, the default time zone can be set by invoking the `setDefault(TimeZone zone)` method. In addition, there are two time fields (the two time fields that were not discussed in the sections on the `GregorianCalendar`) in the `Calendar` class that can be used to set the time zone using a millisecond measurement:

```
ZONE_OFFSET
DST_OFFSET          // DST = Daylight Savings Time
```

The `ZONE_OFFSET` is used in `get(int field)` and `set(int field int value)` for the "raw offset from GMT in milliseconds."[29] `DST_OFFSET` is used in the same methods for "the daylight savings offset in milliseconds."[30] These fields are not likely to be used by mainstream business application programmers. There are more user-friendly accessor and mutator methods declared in the `Calendar` class:

```
public TimeZone getTimeZone()
public void setTimeZone(TimeZone value)
```

These can be used to access or change the time zone used by a particular instance of the `Calendar` class. If for some reason you needed to maintain calendars in several time zones, these are the methods you would most likely use.

5.18 Understanding the Difference between i18n and l10n

Understanding the relationship between internationalization and localization is the first step in becoming an internationally aware programmer. These are two very different yet closely related subjects:

- Internationalization (**i18n**)
- Localization (**l10n**)

---

29. API docs for ZONE_OFFSET field in the `java.util.Calendar` class.
30. API docs for DST_OFFSET field in the `java.util.Calendar` class.

The abbreviation *i18n* means there are 18 letters between the *i* and *n*. Likewise, the *10* in l10n means there are 10 letters between the *l* and *n*.

Internationalization defines localization. It is therefore necessary to define internationalization before discussing localization. Internationalization has two distinct levels. One level is the computer programming language itself. The other level is when an application programmer makes a conscious decision to write an internationalized application. This involves, among other things, translating text into different languages and storing the translations in "resource bundles." The first level of internationalization is the responsibility of software engineers such as Dr. Gosling and Dr. Davis, who designed the Java programming language and the `java.text` package, respectively. The other level of internationalization is the responsibility of application programmers. It is the internationalization of a computer programming language the defines localization, not the internationalization done by application programmers. That level of internationalization is the process of systematically identifying and removing all of the cultural biases from a computer programming language. The Java platform (with the help of IBM's Center for Java Technology in Silicon Valley) has taken internationalization further than any computer programming language in history. It has been nothing less than ground breaking in that regard.

As a very small example of cultural bias in a computer programming language, the original definition of *white space* was encapsulated in the `isSpace()` method of the `Character` class. That definition of white space is now recognized as *ISO-Latin-1 white space*. The `isSpace()` method was deprecated in the 1.1 release in favor of `isWhitespace()`, which includes all of the space characters in the Unicode standard.

The most critical decision regarding the internationalization of the Java platform was made by Dr. Gosling. That was the use of the 16-bit Unicode character set. Java is the first and only widely used computer programming language to adopt the *Unicode Standard*. In *The Java Language Environment: A White Paper*, Dr. Gosling states

> By adopting the Unicode character set standard for its character data type, Java language applications are amenable to internationalization and localization, greatly expanding the market for world-wide applications.[31]

This internationalization began in earnest on August 20, 1996 when IBM and Sun announced an agreement to integrate internationalization technology developed by Taligent, Inc. (a wholly-owned subsidiary of IBM) into what would become the Java 1.1 release. The internationalization of the Java platform continues to this day with the development of Hebrew, Islamic, Buddhist, and Japanese calendars, text-rendering support for Thai and Hindi scripts, and on many other fronts. This work will continue for many years, and Java technology will be the proving ground for that work.

If internationalization at the language level is the process of systematically identifying and removing all of the cultural biases from a computer programming language, what is **localization**? It is the opposite of internationalization. Localization makes a culturally neutral computer program look as if it were written in a particular language. The means by which this is accomplished is a simple **fill-in-the-blank mechanism** left in place by the software engineers who internationalized the programming language. The relationship can be summarized as follows.

Localization is the residual product of internationalization at the language level.

In the Java programming language the fill-in-the-blank mechanism is a `ResourceBundle`, which is a collection of plain text files or class files in which **locale-specific data** is stored. Non-ASCII translations can be stored as Unicode escape sequences in plain text files using the `native2ascii` tool. This tool actually writes a Latin-1 encoded file in which all of the characters are ASCII. That is how text is stored for use by the fill-in-the-blank mechanism. Text is not the only information used to *fill in the blank*. Other resources such as culturally sensitive audio clips and images can also be used to *fill in the blank*. If the resource is anything other than text, it must be stored in a class file. Only text can be optionally stored in a plain text file. `Accessor` methods in the `ResourceBundle` class access the appropriate file and return the translation or other locale-specific data used to fill in the blank. If the default `Locale` is France, for example, the file containing the French translation is accessed. (There may be a different file with translations for French-speaking Canadians.)

---

31. James Gosling and Henry McGilton, *The Java Language Environment: A White Paper* (Mountain View: Sun Microsystems, 1996), §2.1.1, "Primitive Data Types."

Some resource bundles are included in the core API. These bundles contain pattern strings (discussed below) for formatting the following numeric data types:

- Numbers
- Date and times
- Currency

The following sections discuss how to format these data types using the default locale. This level of localization is inescapable for any application programmer. It is the localization of common data types so that numeric data can be read by users who live in the same country and speak the same language as the application programmer.

5.19 The Localization of Common Data Types

Many classes are involved in the localization of common data types. It is helpful to start by looking at the relationship between these classes. The package in which they are declared is `java.text`. I refer to them as *the formatting classes*, although not all of them are in the `Format` class hierarchy, which is shown in Figure 5-8. In the sections on the localization of common data types, the focus is on the six classes in the bold boxes. The formatting classes are unusual in that you typically invoke utility methods in the `abstract NumberFormat` and `DateFormat` base classes, which return instances of the `DecimalFormat` and `SimpleDateFormat` subclasses. The `DecimalFormat` class is used to format "integers (123), decimal numbers (123.4), scientific notation (1.23E4), percentages (12%), and currency amounts ($123)," not just decimal numbers as the name would suggest.[32]

The following subsections use a `FormatUtilities` class, the source code for which follows:

```
import java.text.*;
import java.util.Locale;
import java.math.BigDecimal;

public final class FormatUtilities {

    /* Utility Class */
    private FormatUtilities() { }
```

---

32. API docs for the `java.text.DecimalFormat` class.

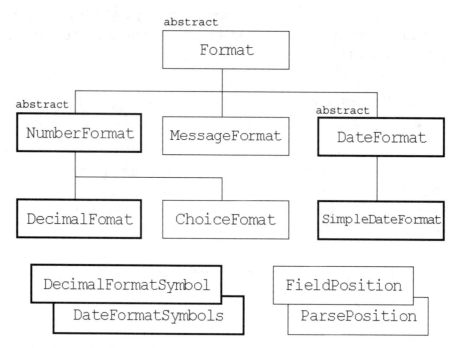

Figure 5-7: The formatting classes.

```
/*
 * REPLACES SOME DEFAULT SYMBOLS USED WHEN FORMATING DATES AND TIMES
 * Change Jan to JAN for all twelve months, and xDT to xST for
 * all daylight savings time zones.
 */
private static DateFormatSymbols symbols = new DateFormatSymbols();
static {
    symbols.setShortMonths(new String[]
            {"JAN", "FEB", "MAR", "APR", "MAY", "JUN",
             "JUL", "AUG", "SEP", "OCT", "NOV", "DEC"});
    String[][] zones = symbols.getZoneStrings();
    for (int i=0; i < zones.length; i++) {
        zones[i][3] = zones[i][1];
        zones[i][4] = zones[i][2];
    }
    symbols.setZoneStrings(zones);
}


/*
 * Return the same set of formatters as DateFormat (except for
 * DateFormat.getInstance()), but with customized date symbols
 */

public static DateFormat getTimeInstance() {
  DateFormat formatter = DateFormat.getTimeInstance();
  ((SimpleDateFormat)formatter).setDateFormatSymbols(symbols);
```

```
    return formatter;
  }

  public static DateFormat getTimeInstance(int style) {
    DateFormat formatter = DateFormat.getTimeInstance(style);
    ((SimpleDateFormat)formatter).setDateFormatSymbols(symbols);
    return formatter;
  }

  public static DateFormat getTimeInstance(int style, Locale aLocale) {
    DateFormat formatter = DateFormat.getTimeInstance(style, aLocale);
    ((SimpleDateFormat)formatter).setDateFormatSymbols(symbols);
    return formatter;
  }

  public static DateFormat getDateInstance() {
    DateFormat formatter = DateFormat.getDateInstance();
    ((SimpleDateFormat)formatter).setDateFormatSymbols(symbols);
    return formatter;
  }

  public static DateFormat getDateInstance(int style) {
    DateFormat formatter = DateFormat.getDateInstance(style);
    ((SimpleDateFormat)formatter).setDateFormatSymbols(symbols);
    return formatter;
  }

  public static DateFormat getDateInstance(int style, Locale aLocale) {
    DateFormat formatter = DateFormat.getDateInstance(style, aLocale);
    ((SimpleDateFormat)formatter).setDateFormatSymbols(symbols);
    return formatter;
  }

  public static DateFormat getDateTimeInstance() {
    DateFormat formatter = DateFormat.getDateTimeInstance();
    ((SimpleDateFormat)formatter).setDateFormatSymbols(symbols);
    return formatter;
  }

  public static DateFormat getDateTimeInstance(int dateStyle,
                                               int timeStyle) {
    DateFormat formatter = DateFormat.getDateTimeInstance(dateStyle,
                                                          timeStyle);
    ((SimpleDateFormat)formatter).setDateFormatSymbols(symbols);
    return formatter;
  }

  public static DateFormat getDateTimeInstance(int dateStyle,
                                               int timeStyle,
                                               Locale aLocale) {
    DateFormat formatter = DateFormat.getDateTimeInstance(dateStyle,
                                                          timeStyle,
                                                          aLocale);
    ((SimpleDateFormat)formatter).setDateFormatSymbols(symbols);
    return formatter;
  }

/*
 * These utility methods either uses what most people think of as
```

```
 * rounding, or else they truncate.
 */

public static String formatCurrency(BigDecimal amount) {
   return formatCurrency(amount, true);
}
public static String formatCurrency(BigDecimal amount, boolean round) {
   NumberFormat formatter = NumberFormat.getCurrencyInstance();
   BigDecimal rounded;
   if (round)
      rounded = amount.setScale(2, BigDecimal.ROUND_HALF_UP);
   else
      rounded = amount.setScale(2, BigDecimal.ROUND_DOWN);

   return formatter.format(rounded.doubleValue());
}
public static String formatPercentage(double value) {
   NumberFormat formatter = NumberFormat.getPercentInstance();
   String s = Double.toString(value);
   BigDecimal rounded = new BigDecimal(s).setScale
                     (2, BigDecimal.ROUND_HALF_UP);
   return formatter.format(rounded.doubleValue());
}
}
```

This utility class includes functionality that I use on a routine basis when formatting numbers, currency, dates, times, and percentages.

Before delving into the details of formatting numbers, dates, times, and currency, there is the interesting problem of where and when to format numbers that must be effectively translated (much like text). The most obvious example is currency. Currency conversion is little different from text translation. It necessitates storing the converted amount along with other locale-specific data in a resource bundle. The question is *should you go ahead and format converted currency that is already being stored in the ResourceBundle for a particular country anyway.* Or should all formatting be done on the client as a matter of policy?

Conceptually at least, all formatting should be done on the client using the default locale, but in this case I think that may be a purist argument. If I have converted a dollar amount into a dozen or so national currencies, what harm can come of formatting those amounts and then just accessing them as strings? Is that not in fact a minor performance optimization? The same would hold true for other numeric values such as GNP, literacy rate, population, and other numbers that are effectively translated in that there is a different number for each country. I believe you should go ahead and format such values. Doing so does not detract from the default locale mechanism.

5.19.1 Formatting Numbers

The formatting of numbers includes currency and percentages. It may come as a surprise to a few readers that percentages are formatted differently in other languages. There are three subsections, one for formatting numbers (both integers and decimal numbers), one for formatting currencies, and one for percentages. Using the factory methods in the `NumberFormat` class makes formatting numbers, currency, and percentages easy. These factory methods use default pattern strings stored in special resource bundles that ship with the core API. Most of the complexity in formatting numbers is in creating your own pattern strings.

5.19.1.1 *Formatting Integers and Decimal Numbers*

When formatting integers and decimal numbers using the default locale, the following factory methods in the `NumberFormat` class are equivalent:

```
public static final NumberFormat getInstance()
public static final NumberFormat getNumberInstance()
```

The API docs for the first methods say

> Returns the default number format for the current default locale. The default format is one of the styles provided by the other factory methods: `getNumberInstance`, `getCurrencyInstance` or `getPercentInstance`. Exactly which one is locale dependant.

But that makes no sense if you look at the source code. Both methods are implemented the same. Any change in the default locale would affect both in the same manner.

In the case of formatting an integer or decimal number, it helps to know something about the defaults used. The following program uses accessor methods in the `DecimalFormat` class to peer into the resource bundle for the default locale:

```
import java.text.*;
class Test {
   public static void main (String[] args) {

      /*
       * Yes, I realize that I could have used a Decimalformat
       * constructor. This is being done for instructional
       * purposes.
       */
```

```
DecimalFormat numberFormatter =
(DecimalFormat)NumberFormat.getNumberInstance();

/* Print info about the default formatter */
System.out.println("toPattern()......................" +
    numberFormatter.toPattern());
System.out.println("getNegativePrefix() ............" +
    numberFormatter.getNegativePrefix());
System.out.println("getMaximumIntegerDigits() ......" +
    numberFormatter.getMaximumIntegerDigits());
System.out.println("getMaximumFractionDigits() ....." +
    numberFormatter.getMaximumFractionDigits());
System.out.println("getMinimumIntegerDigits() ......" +
    numberFormatter.getMinimumIntegerDigits());
System.out.println("getMinimumFractionDigits() ....." +
    numberFormatter.getMinimumFractionDigits());
    }
}
```

Executing this program prints

```
toPattern()....................#,##0.###
getNegativePrefix() ............-
getMaximumIntegerDigits() ......309
getMaximumFractionDigits() .....3
getMinimumIntegerDigits() ......1
getMinimumFractionDigits() .....0
```

Compare the return value of `getMaximumIntegerDigits()` to `Double.MAX_VALUE`, which is `1.79769313486231570e+308`. The implication is that you can format any double, though the length of the string returned may be extraordinary. At higher values you may want to consider using scientific notation, in which case `Float.toString(float f)` or `Double.toString(double d)` should be used instead. The implementation of those methods involves some highly sophisticated code that is not easily replicated.

Our primary focus is on the default pattern string for formatting numbers, which is `#,##0.###`. The `toPattern()` method returns only the numeric part of the positive subpattern. The whole pattern string used by the `getNumericInstance()` factory method with a default locale of `Locale.US` is `"#,##0.###;-#,##0.###"`. Compared to the pattern strings used by the other factory methods, this one is more likely to be replaced by mainstream business application programmers. To do that you need to invoke the `applyPattern(String pattern)` method as discussed in 5.19.2.1 The `applyPattern(String pattern)` Methods.

Otherwise, formatting a number is as simple as invoking the `format()` method. For example,

```
import java.text.*;
class Test {
    public static void main (String[] args) {
        NumberFormat numberFormatter = NumberFormat.getNumberInstance();
        System.out.println(numberFormatter.format(Double.MAX_VALUE));
    }
}
```

Executing this program prints

```
179,769,313,486,231,570,000,000,000,000,000,000,000,000,000,000,000,000,000,000,000,000,0
00,000,000,000,000,000,000,000,000,000,000,000,000,000,000,000,000,000,000,000,000,000,00
0,000,000,000,000,000,000,000,000,000,000,000,000,000,000,000,000,000,000,000,000,000,000
,000,000,000,000,000,000,000,000,000,000,000,000,000,000,000,000,000,000,000,000,000,000,
000,000,000,000,000,000,000,000,000,000
```

Using `Double.toString(double d)` the same number prints as
`1.7976931348623157E308`. See also 4.3.2.3 Printing the Value of
Floating-Point Types.

Note that a decimal point was not printed in the last example. There
are two methods in the `DecimalFormat` class that control the printing
of decimal points:

```
public boolean isDecimalSeparatorAlwaysShown()
public void setDecimalSeparatorAlwaysShown(boolean newValue)
```

By default they do not print unless there is a fraction, which means they
would never print for an integer such as `Double.MAX_VALUE` in the last
example. Invoking `setDecimalSeparatorAlwaysShown(true)`
and setting the minimum number of *fraction digits* to print using the `set-
MinimumFractionDigits(int newValue)` method discussed in
the next paragraph is useful in solving column-alignment problems when
working with both integers and decimal numbers.

You can change the minimum and maximum number of digits to the left
or right of the decimal point using one of the following methods:

```
public void setMaximumIntegerDigits(int newValue)
public void setMinimumIntegerDigits(int newValue)
public void setMaximumFractionDigits(int newValue)
public void setMinimumFractionDigits(int newValue)
```

Be very careful in the use of these methods, particularly `setMaximu-
mIntegerDigits(int newValue)`. If I were to add a `number-
Formatter.setMaximumIntegerDigits(5)` method invocation
to the last example, `Double.MAX_VALUE` would print as `00,000` without throwing an exception. The `setMinimumFractionDigits(int
newValue)` method uses a rounding mode that makes it inappropriate for

formatting currency and percentages, a fact that is discussed at length in the following subsections.

The rounding mode used is comparable to that used by the primitive floating-point types. It is referred to as *round to nearest* in the *IEEE 754* standard but is best referred to as *IEEE 754 default rounding* by Java programmers. If you want to use a different rounding mode than that which the `NumberFormat` class uses, you can add a utility method to the `FormatUtilities`. The pattern for doing so can be seen in the implementation of the `formatCurrency` and `formatPercentage` methods in the `FormatUtilities` class. I have deliberately omitted comparable `formatNumber` methods so that the reader could add them as an exercise. You should finish reading the following subsections, however, before attempting to do so because I discuss rounding at length there.

5.19.1.2 Formatting Currency

The formatting in this section assumes that `BigDecimal` is being used for currency calculations. In solving the problem of formatting currency, I think it is important that the solution leaves the application programmer free from having to think about the scale of `BigDecimal` objects while doing the actual currency calculations. Setting the scale (and the consequent rounding) should be part of the formatting. This makes currency calculations using `BigDecimal` much more fluid. For example,

```
import java.math.BigDecimal;
class Test {
    public static void main (String[] args) {
        BigDecimal price = new BigDecimal("6.78");
        BigDecimal quantity = new BigDecimal("2.5");
        BigDecimal subtotal = price.multiply(quantity);
        BigDecimal tax = subtotal.multiply(new BigDecimal(".05"));
        BigDecimal total = subtotal.add(tax);
        System.out.println(FormatUtilities.formatCurrency(total));
    }
}
```

The total is 17.7975, which is rounded and prints as $17.80.

There is a difference between localizing currency and currency conversions. Do not forget to do currency conversions and store the results in your resource bundles along with the translations of text. This is only an issue in internationalized applications. It is usually mentioned by way of pointing out that the `NumberFormat` class does not do currency conversions. That is the responsibility of whoever creates the resource bundles used in an internationalized program.

5.19.1.3 Formatting Percentages

Based on the sheer number of Bug IDs, the rounding of percentages in the `NumberFormat` class is even more of a problem than with currency. Programmers do not expect *IEEE 754* default rounding when formatting a number. There is a difference, however, between this problem and the same problem when formatting currency. When formatting currency some programmers do not expect any rounding. Others expect what most of us think of as rounding, which is the equivalent of `BigDecimal.ROUND_HALF_UP`. When it comes to formatting percentages, almost all programmers expect rounding equivalent to `BigDecimal.ROUND_HALF_UP`. In other words, all `NumberFormat` instances suffer from the same problem, which is a poor choice of default rounding mode.

My solution, again, is a utility method, but this time there is no rounding option. Instead, the number is automatically rounded using a combination of the `Double.toString(double d)` method and `BigDecimal`. The `Double.toString (double d)` method is necessary to compensate for the tiny imprecisions in the floating-point types. The utility method is repeated here for your convenience:

```
public static String formatPercentage(double value) {
    String s = Double.toString(value);
    BigDecimal rounded = new BigDecimal(s).setScale(2, BigDecimal.ROUND_HALF_UP);
    return percentageFormatter.format(rounded.doubleValue());
}
```

For example,

```
import java.text.NumberFormat;
class Test {
    public static void main (String[] args) {
        NumberFormat percentageFormatter = NumberFormat.getPercentInstance();
        System.out.println(".005 ......" + percentageFormatter.format(.005) +
                        "    " + FormatUtilities.formatPercentage(.005));
        System.out.println(".015 ......" + percentageFormatter.format(.015) +
                        "    " + FormatUtilities.formatPercentage(.015));
        System.out.println(".025 ......" + percentageFormatter.format(.025) +
                        "    " + FormatUtilities.formatPercentage(.025));
        System.out.println(".035 ......" + percentageFormatter.format(.035) +
                        "    " + FormatUtilities.formatPercentage(.035));
        System.out.println(".045 ......" + percentageFormatter.format(.045) +
                        "    " + FormatUtilities.formatPercentage(.045));
        System.out.println(".055 ......" + percentageFormatter.format(.055) +
                        "    " + FormatUtilities.formatPercentage(.055));
```

```
System.out.println(".065 ......" + percentageFormatter.format(.06) +
              "    " + FormatUtilities.formatPercentage(.065));
System.out.println(".075 ......" + percentageFormatter.format(.075) +
              "    " + FormatUtilities.formatPercentage(.075));
System.out.println(".085 ......" + percentageFormatter.format(.085) +
              "    " + FormatUtilities.formatPercentage(.085));
System.out.println(".095 ......" + percentageFormatter.format(.095) +
              "    " + FormatUtilities.formatPercentage(.095));
    }
}
```

Executing this program prints

```
.005 ......0%    1%
.015 ......2%    2%
.025 ......2%    3%
.035 ......4%    4%
.045 ......4%    5%
.055 ......6%    6%
.065 ......6%    7%
.075 ......8%    8%
.085 ......8%    9%
.095 ......10%  10%
```

The first column of percentages was returned by the NumberFormat class. The second column of percentages based on the same set of numbers was returned by the utility method in FormatUtilities. As you can see, there is a big difference.

As a point of interest, the pattern string used by the getPercentInstance() factory method for Locale.US is "#,##0%". Knowing this might save you the trouble of creating such a pattern string.

5.19.2 Formatting Dates and Times

When formatting dates and times there are a number of different **predefined formats** that can be used by specifying one of the following constants when a formatter is created (see tables 5-8 and 5-9). Note that all of

Table 5-8: Predefined Date Formats

Style	General Description	Example for United States
DEFAULT	The default format is one of the other four predefined formats. Which one depends on the Locale. Usually it is MEDIUM.	Apr 24, 2001
SHORT	Completely numeric	4/24/01

Table 5-8: Predefined Date Formats (Continued)

Style	General Description	Example for United States
MEDIUM	Abbreviated month	Apr 24, 2001
LONG	Full month name	April 24, 2001
FULL	Includes day-of-week	Tuesday, April 24, 2001

Table 5-9: Predefined Time Formats

Style	General Description	Example for United States
DEFAULT	The default format is one of the other four predefined formats. Which one depends on the Locale. Usually it is MEDIUM.	6:53:23 AM
SHORT	Hours and minutes only	6:53 AM
MEDIUM	Hours, minutes, and seconds	6:53:23 AM
LONG	Hours, minutes, seconds, and time zone	6:53:23 AM EDT
FULL	Same as LONG	6:53:23 AM EDT

the predefined formats include AM or PM instead of using military time. The *general descriptions* in these tables are applicable to most predefined formats. They may not, however, be accurate descriptions of the predefined formats in all locales.

The following program was used to populate these tables:

```
import java.text.DateFormat;
import java.util.Date;
class Test {
    public static void main(String[] args) {
        Date today = new Date();
        System.out.println();
        System.out.println("predefined date formats...");
        System.out.println("DEFAULT = " +
        DateFormat.getDateInstance(DateFormat.DEFAULT).format(today));
        System.out.println("SHORT = " +
        DateFormat.getDateInstance(DateFormat.SHORT).format(today));
        System.out.println("MEDIUM = " +
        DateFormat.getDateInstance(DateFormat.MEDIUM).format(today));
        System.out.println("LONG = " +
```

```
           DateFormat.getDateInstance(DateFormat.LONG).format(today));
           System.out.println("FULL = " +
           DateFormat.getDateInstance(DateFormat.FULL).format(today));
           System.out.println();
           System.out.println("predefined time formats...");
           System.out.println("DEFAULT = " +
           DateFormat.getTimeInstance(DateFormat.DEFAULT).format(today));
           System.out.println("SHORT = " +
           DateFormat.getTimeInstance(DateFormat.SHORT).format(today));
           System.out.println("MEDIUM = " +
           DateFormat.getTimeInstance(DateFormat.MEDIUM).format(today));
           System.out.println("LONG = " +
           DateFormat.getTimeInstance(DateFormat.LONG).format(today));
           System.out.println("FULL = " +
           DateFormat.getTimeInstance(DateFormat.FULL).format(today));
       }
   }
```

You can change the name of the `DateFormat` class in the method invocation expressions to `FormatUtilities` to see the different symbols used by the utility class. The default predefined format for a *date and time* formatter returned by one of the overloaded `DateFormat.getDateTimeInstance` methods is simply a combination of the default date format followed by the default time format. For example,

```
import java.text.DateFormat;
import java.util.Date;
class Test {
    public static void main(String[] args) {
        Date today = new Date();
        System.out.println(DateFormat.getDateTimeInstance().format(today));
    }
}
```

Executing this program prints dates and times such as `Jul 4, 2001 7:25:40 PM`.

The alternative to using the predefined formats for a given `Locale` is to build your own pattern strings and invoke the `applyPatterns(String pattern)` method discussed in the next section.

5.19.2.1 The `applyPattern(String pattern)` *Methods*

Both the `DecimalFormat` and `SimpleDateFormat` subclasses declare an `applyPattern(String pattern)` method for creating a custom format. Because formatters are typically stored in `NumberFormat` and `DateFormat` type variables, a cast is required to invoke these methods. For example,

```
DateFormat df = DateFormat.getInstance();
```

```
((SimpleDateFormat)df).applyPattern("h 'o''clock' a, z");
```

The API docs encourage this style of programming (instead of instantiating the subclasses `DecimalFormat` and `SimpleDateFormat`) in the following quotation.

> `SimpleDateFormat` allows you to start by choosing any user-defined patterns for date-time formatting. However, you are encouraged to create a date-time formatter with either `get-TimeInstance`, `getDateInstance`, or `getDateTimeInstance` in `DateFormat`. Each of these class methods can return a date/time formatter initialized with a default format pattern. You may modify the format pattern using the `applyPattern` methods as desired.[33]

The API docs for the `DecimalFormat` class includes a similar note in regard to invoking the factory methods in the `NumberFormat` superclass. Essentially they want you to regard the subclasses as what I call *implementation only classes*. I think that I am about to say the king has no clothes, but this is a flawed design. Furthermore, the flaw is not difficult to understand. Implementation only classes are never referenced outside of their own compilation unit. This is what makes them *implementation only*. They are usually referenced by interface types. When an implementation only class is referenced by a superclass type, as is the case here, there must be pure inheritance. That is, the subclass cannot declare any new methods (or define any new behaviors in OO speak). This is not true of the formatting classes, and the `applyPattern(String pattern)` method is such an example. There is no such method in the `DateFormat` and `NumberFormat` superclasses.

Thus, the `SimpleDateFormat` and `DecimalFormat` subclasses are not implementation only. For example, the API docs for `Decimal-Format` says that "if you need to customize the format object, do something like this":

```
NumberFormat f = NumberFormat.getInstance(loc);
if (f instanceof DecimalFormat) {
    ((DecimalFormat) f).setDecimalSeparatorAlwaysShown(true);
}[34]
```

`NumberFormat` and `DateFormat` say something similar.

---

33. API docs for the `java.text.SimpleDateFormat` class.
34. API docs for the `java.text.DecimalFormat` class.

> If you want even more control over the format or parsing, or want to give your users more control, you can try casting the NumberFormat you get from the factory methods to a DecimalNumberFormat. This will work for the vast majority of locales; just remember to put it in a try block in case you encounter an unusual one.[35]
>
> If you want even more control over the format or parsing, or want to give your users more control, you can try casting the DateFormat you get from the factory methods to a SimpleDateFormat. This will work for the majority of countries; just remember to put it in a try block in case you encounter an unusual one.[36]

What does "in case you encounter an unusual one" mean? As of this writing, there is nothing—I repeat, *nothing*—about the locale that is going to cause the factory methods in the NumberFormat class to return anything other than an instance of the DecimalFormat class. Nor is there anything that is going to cause the factory methods in the DateFormat class to return anything other than an instance of SimpleDateFormat. So what does it mean?

The only thing it can mean is that the java.text programmers are reserving the right to change the implementation of those methods. Consequently, the factory methods guarantee you only what their result type says, a NumberFormat or a DateFormat. My guess is that the designers were hedging against the possibility that, as Java grows into a full-blown international programming language, there may be some obscure locale that requires a separate subclass to implement the NumberFormat and DateFormat interfaces.

This is not in and of itself a problem. The problem is the type check required before casting to the would-be implementation only subclasses. The example from the API docs is repeated here for your convenience:

```
NumberFormat f = NumberFormat.getInstance(loc);
if (f instanceof DecimalFormat) {
    ((DecimalFormat) f).setDecimalSeparatorAlwaysShown(true);
}
```

The setDecimalSeparatorAlwaysShown(boolean newValue) method allows you to include a decimal point when formatting integers. If a

---

35. API docs for the java.text.NumberFormat class.
36. API docs for the java.text.DateFormat class.

new `NumberFormat` subclass were added to the core API, does that mean this behavior goes away? That is the flaw in this design. And what about something more critical such as the `applyPattern(String pattern)` methods? Might they not be supported in the new subclass? Even if these behaviors are supported in the new subclass, what good will it do me if I have used something like `if (f instanceof DecimalFormat)`? This is not proper object-oriented design.

The following subsections discuss how to build **pattern strings** using the available symbols. Pattern strings are also known as **custom formats**. There are two classes that encapsulate the symbols used in pattern strings. One is the `DateFormatSymbols` class, which is used to build date and time pattern strings. The other is `DecimalFormatSymbols`, which is a comparatively simple class.

5.19.2.2 The `DecimalFormatSymbols` Class

A pattern string for formatting numbers always includes a positive subpattern and may include an optional negative subpattern. If present, the negative subpattern follows the positive subpattern. They are separated by a semicolon. The semicolon is not required if the negative subpattern is omitted. Here is a typical pattern string that has both a positive and negative subpattern:

```
"##,###,##0.00;(##,###,##0.00)"
```

The meaning of the negative subpattern `"(#,##0.00)"` is that negative numbers should be enclosed in parentheses, as is often done in accounting.

The **decimal format symbols** are summarized in Table 5-10. The so-called "nonlocalized" decimal format symbols used in tables such as this one are actually for the default U.S. locale. The decimal format symbols the Java programmers use in pattern strings vary from one language or country to the next. They are localized. Only the ¤ and ¤¤ **currency symbols** are used by all Java programmers. That is why there are accessor and mutator methods.

The currency symbol ¤ is actually part of the Latin-1 character set. It is not something you can type using a standard keyboard and therefore must be represented using a Unicode escape sequence of `\u00A4`. For example, here is the pattern string used by `getCurrencyInstance()` factory method with a default locale of `Locale.US`:

```
"\u00a4#,##0.00;(\u00a4#,##0.00)"
```

Table 5-10: Decimal Format Symbols[a]

Symbol	Behavior	Accessor and Mutator Methods
0	Always print digit.	`getZeroDigit()` `setZeroDigit()`
#	Do not print leading zeros.	`getDigit()` `setDigit(char digit)`
.	Decimal point for numbers.	`getDecimalSeparator()` `setDecimalSeparator(char decimalSeparator)`
.	Decimal point for monetary value (e.g., between dollars and cents) is not the same as decimal point for numbers in some languages.	`getMonetaryDecimalSeparator()` `setMonetaryDecimalSeparator()`
–	Minus sign	`getMinusSign()` `setMinusSign()`
,	Grouping separator used between hundreds, thousands, millions, etc.	`getGroupingSeparator()` `setGroupingSeparator(char groupingSeparator)`
%	Using the percent sign in a pattern string actually causes the number to be multiplied by 100.	`getPercent()` `setPercent()`
∞	Infinity sign (localized but "almost always left unchanged" according to API docs).	`getInfinity()` `setInfinity()`
?	This is the Unicode replacement character `u\FFFD`, which prints as a question mark (localized but "almost always left unchanged" according to API docs).	`getNaN()` `setNaN()`

Table 5-10: Decimal Format Symbols[a] (Continued)

Symbol	Behavior	Accessor and Mutator Methods
;	**Pattern separator** character used to separate the positive and negative patterns (not required if negative pattern is omitted).	`getPatternSeparator()` `setPatternSeparator()`
¤	Prints the normal currency symbol, such as $ for the U.S.	`getCurrencySymbol()` `setCurrencySymbol(String currency)`
¤¤	Prints the three-letter ISO 4217, "Codes for the representation of currencies and funds" (such as USD for United States Dollars). See Dr. Mark Davis quotation below.	`getInternationalCurrencySymbol()` `setInternationalCurrencySymbol()`

a. The *per mille* symbol is considered obscure and is therefore omitted from the table.

If there is a sequence of two international currency symbols (¤¤ which is typed as `"\u00A4\u00A4"`) in a pattern string, the three-letter international currency code is used instead. Dr. Davis explains why.

> These are necessary in an application that deals with many different currencies because the regular, one-character currency symbols are often shared by many different currencies. For example, both the US and Canada use "$" in their default currency format. An application dealing with both currencies will probably want to use "USD" and "CAD" instead. In Java 2, this is now possible, using a sequence of two international currency symbols ("¤¤" = "\u00A4\u00A4") in the pattern.[37]

Another event that occurs if the `\u00a4` escape sequence appears in a pattern string is that the monetary decimal separator is used instead of the decimal separator. In effect, the presence of this character in a pattern string makes it a **currency pattern string**.

---

37. Mark Davis, "The Java Internationalization API," *Java Report* 4, no. 2 (Feb. 1999): 34.

As with the date and time format symbols, if you want any of the decimal format symbols in Table 5-10 to appear in the formatted output, they must be enclosed in single quotes. The example used in the API docs is "'#'#", which formats 123 as #123.

Every pattern string for numbers has a prefix, a numeric part, and a suffix. The numeric part is any of the decimal formatting symbols in Table 5-10 except the minus sign. Anything that comes before those symbols is the prefix. Anything that comes after them is the suffix. This is important because only the prefix and suffix of the negative subpattern is used. The rest is ignored. Consequently, the following patterns strings are the same:

```
"##,###,##0.00;(##,###,##0.00)"
"##,###,##0.00;(#)"
```

Both of these pattern strings enclose negative numbers in parentheses. The prefix is an open parenthesis, and the suffix is a close parenthesis. All the character in between are decimal formatting symbols found in Table 5-10. Hence, they are ignored in a negative subpattern. If the negative subpattern is omitted, a localized minus sign is used to prefix negative numbers. Given that a localized minus sign is used as the default prefix for negative numbers and that the negative subpattern is used only for the prefix and suffix, all of the following pattern strings are equivalent:

```
"##,##0.00"
"##,##0.00;-#"
"##,##0.00;-##,##0.00"
```

I would use the third one just to be explicit.

Pattern strings for numbers have what is called a **grouping size**. This is the number of digits between the **grouping separator**. For example,

```
import java.text.*;
import java.util.Locale;
class Test {
    public static void main(String[] args) {
        Locale[] locales = {Locale.US, Locale.GERMANY};
        for (int i=0; i<locales.length; i++) {
            NumberFormat nf = NumberFormat.getCurrencyInstance(locales[i]);
            switch(i) {
                case 0: System.out.print("USA ........... ");
                        break;
                case 1: System.out.print("Germany ....... ");
                        break;
            }
            System.out.println(nf.format(1000000000.00));
        }
    }
}
```

Executing this program prints

```
USA .......... $1,000,000,000.00
Germany ....... 1.000.000.000,00 DM
```

As suggested by this output, a grouping size of three is very common. The grouping separator (as well as the monetary decimal separator), however, varies from country to country. If you specify a pattern string in which the grouping size is inconsistent, the last group in the string determines the grouping size. For example,

```
"##,###,###0.00" //LIKELY ERROR
```

The grouping size for this format is four. Were it used to format 1000000000, the result would be 10,0000,0000.00, using a comma as the group separator. The grouping size is returned by the `getGroupingSize()` method in the `DecimalFormat` class. The following methods in the `NumberFormat` class can be used to turn groupings off:

```
public boolean isGroupingUsed()
public void setGroupingUsed(boolean newValue)
```

Groupings are used in all of the locales supported in the core API.

Some pattern strings are illegal, such as `"#.#.#"` and `"#.####,###"`, and throw an `IllegalArgumentException`.

5.19.2.3 The `DateFormatSymbols` Class

The symbols in this class are used in either date or time pattern strings. The date symbols are summarized in Table 5-11.

Table 5-11: Date Format Symbols[a]

Default Symbol	Corresponding Date Field	Default English Values	Explanation of Numeric Symbols or Accessor and Mutator Methods
G	ERA	BC AD	`getEras()` `setEras(String[] newEras)`
y yy yyy	YEAR		Two-digit year with a range of 1 to well past the usefulness of the Java platform. ALWAYS USES LEADING ZERO
yyyy	YEAR		Four-digit year (for example, 2001).

Table 5-11: Date Format Symbols[a] (Continued)

Default Symbol	Corresponding Date Field	Default English Values	Explanation of Numeric Symbols or Accessor and Mutator Methods
M	MONTH		One- or two-digit month (that is, no leading zeroes) with a range of 1 through 12. USE MM FOR LEADING ZERO
MMM	MONTH	Jan Feb Mar Apr May Jun Jul Aug Sep Oct Nov Dec	`getShortMonths()` `setShortMonths(String[] newShortMonths)`
MMMM	MONTH	January February March April May June July August September October November December	`getMonths()` `setMonths(String[] newMonths)`

Table 5-11: Date Format Symbols[a] (Continued)

Default Symbol	Corresponding Date Field	Default English Values	Explanation of Numeric Symbols or Accessor and Mutator Methods
d	DATE DAY_OF_MONTH		One- or two-digit date or day of month (whichever you prefer, but in either case no leading zeroes) with a range of 1 through 31. USE dd FOR LEADING ZERO
D	DAY_OF_YEAR		One-, two-, or three-digit day of year (that is, no leading zeroes) with a range of 1 through 366. USE DD FOR ONE LEADING ZERO USE DDD FOR TWO LEADING ZEROES
E EE EEE	DAY_OF_WEEK	Sun Mon Tue Wed Thur Fri Sat	getShortWeekdays() setShortWeekdays(String[], newShortWeekDays)
EEEE	DAY_OF_WEEK	Sunday Monday Tuesday Wednesday Thursday Friday Saturday	getWeekdays() setWeekdays(String[], newWeekDays)
F	DAY_OF_WEEK_IN_MONTH		One-digit day or week in month with a range of 1 through 5 (note that this range is substantially different than the minimum and maximum value of the corresponding date field) Used in strings such as "2nd Wed in July" that require substantial coding (for 1st, 2nd, 3rd, 4th, 5th).

Table 5-11: Date Format Symbols[a] (Continued)

Default Symbol	Corresponding Date Field	Default English Values	Explanation of Numeric Symbols or Accessor and Mutator Methods
w	WEEK_OF_YEAR		One- or two-digit week of year (i.e., no leading zeroes) with a range of 1 through 53. USE ww FOR LEADING ZERO
W	WEEK_OF_MONTH		One-digit day or week in month with a range of 1 through 5 (note that this range is substantially different than the minimum and maximum value of the corresponding date field).

a. This table extrapolates on the single character symbols to capture what should be the most common uses.

Note that month-based tables are zero-based, whereas day of the week tables include an empty string in the first element so that a more natural indexing of Sunday=1, Monday=2, Tuesday=3, etc. can be used. The historical basis for this difference is explained by Dr. Davis in a quotation in 5.16 Date and Time Fields in the `Calendar` Class.

The numeric date and time fields can have any number of leading zeroes simply by repeating the symbol. For example,

```
import java.text.*;
import java.util.*;
class Test {
    public static void main(String[] args) {
        DateFormat df = DateFormat.getInstance();
        Calendar calendar = Calendar.getInstance();

        // GyMdkHmsSEDFwWahKz
        ((SimpleDateFormat)df).applyPattern("GGGGGGGGGGGGGGGGGGGGGGGG");
        System.out.println(df.format(calendar.getTime()));
        ((SimpleDateFormat)df).applyPattern("yyyyyyyyyyyyyyyyyyyyyyyy");
        System.out.println(df.format(calendar.getTime()));
        ((SimpleDateFormat)df).applyPattern("MMMMMMMMMMMMMMMMMMMMMMMM");
        System.out.println(df.format(calendar.getTime()));
        ((SimpleDateFormat)df).applyPattern("dddddddddddddddddddddddd");
        System.out.println(df.format(calendar.getTime()));
        ((SimpleDateFormat)df).applyPattern("kkkkkkkkkkkkkkkkkkkkkkkk");
        System.out.println(df.format(calendar.getTime()));
        ((SimpleDateFormat)df).applyPattern("HHHHHHHHHHHHHHHHHHHHHHHH");
        System.out.println(df.format(calendar.getTime()));
        ((SimpleDateFormat)df).applyPattern("mmmmmmmmmmmmmmmmmmmmmmmm");
```

```
System.out.println(df.format(calendar.getTime()));
((SimpleDateFormat)df).applyPattern("sssssssssssssssssssssssss");
System.out.println(df.format(calendar.getTime()));
((SimpleDateFormat)df).applyPattern("SSSSSSSSSSSSSSSSSSSSSSSSS");
System.out.println(df.format(calendar.getTime()));
((SimpleDateFormat)df).applyPattern("EEEEEEEEEEEEEEEEEEEEEEEEE");
System.out.println(df.format(calendar.getTime()));
((SimpleDateFormat)df).applyPattern("DDDDDDDDDDDDDDDDDDDDDDDDD");
System.out.println(df.format(calendar.getTime()));
((SimpleDateFormat)df).applyPattern("FFFFFFFFFFFFFFFFFFFFFFFFF");
System.out.println(df.format(calendar.getTime()));
((SimpleDateFormat)df).applyPattern("wwwwwwwwwwwwwwwwwwwwwwwww");
System.out.println(df.format(calendar.getTime()));
((SimpleDateFormat)df).applyPattern("WWWWWWWWWWWWWWWWWWWWWWWWW");
System.out.println(df.format(calendar.getTime()));
((SimpleDateFormat)df).applyPattern("aaaaaaaaaaaaaaaaaaaaaaaaa");
System.out.println(df.format(calendar.getTime()));
((SimpleDateFormat)df).applyPattern("hhhhhhhhhhhhhhhhhhhhhhhhh");
System.out.println(df.format(calendar.getTime()));
((SimpleDateFormat)df).applyPattern("KKKKKKKKKKKKKKKKKKKKKKKKK");
System.out.println(df.format(calendar.getTime()));
((SimpleDateFormat)df).applyPattern("zzzzzzzzzzzzzzzzzzzzzzzzz");
System.out.println(df.format(calendar.getTime()));
    }
}
```

Executing this program prints

```
AD
2001
February
0000000000000000000000010
0000000000000000000000013
0000000000000000000000013
0000000000000000000000015
0000000000000000000000047
0000000000000000000000110
Saturday
0000000000000000000000041
0000000000000000000000002
0000000000000000000000006
0000000000000000000000002
PM
0000000000000000000000001
0000000000000000000000001
Eastern Standard Time
```

As this output suggests, the additional leading zeroes can be used for column alignment.

The symbols used in time pattern strings are summarized in Table 5-12. When using **date and time pattern strings**, all of the English letters ('a' through 'z' and 'A' through 'Z' in the ASCII range) are reserved for use as symbols. If you use any of those characters as text, they must be enclosed in a single quotation. Therefore, to use a single quotation mark

Table 5-12: Time Format Symbols[a]

Default Symbol	Corresponding Time Field	Explanation of Numeric Symbols or Accessor and Mutator Methods
h	HOUR	One- or two-digit hour (that is, no leading zeroes) with a range of 1 through 12, used with a (AM/PM). USE hh FOR LEADING ZERO
H	HOUR_IN_DAY (military time)	One- or two-digit hour (that is, no leading zeroes) with a range of 0 through 23 (military time). USE HH FOR LEADING ZERO
k	HOUR_IN_DAY (military time)	One- or two-digit hour (that is, no leading zeroes) with a range of 1 through 24 (military time). USE kk FOR LEADING ZERO
K	HOUR	One- or two-digit hour (that is, no leading zeroes) with a range of 0 through 11, used with a (AM/PM). USE KK FOR LEADING ZERO
m	MINUTE	One- or two-digit minute (that is, no leading zeroes) with a range of 0 through 59. USE mm FOR LEADING ZERO
s	SECOND	One- or two-digit second (that is, no leading zeroes) with a range of 0 through 59. USE ss FOR LEADING ZERO
S	MILLISECOND	One-, two-, or three-digit millisecond (i.e., no leading zeroes) with a range of 0 through 999. USE SS FOR ONE LEADING ZERO USE SSS FOR TWO LEADING ZEROES
a	AM_PM	The is the only time formatting symbol that results in the printing of text instead of numbers. It is therefore localized. The default English values are AM and PM. The accessor and mutator methods are: getAmPmStrings() setAmPmStrings(String[] newAmpms)

Table 5-12: Time Format Symbols[a] (Continued)

Default Symbol	Corresponding Time Field	Explanation of Numeric Symbols or Accessor and Mutator Methods
z		Uses the short time zone display name such as "EST."
zz		
zzz		
zzzz		Uses the long time zone display name such as "Eastern Standard Time."

a. This table extrapolates on the single character symbols to capture what should be the most common uses.

you must use two of them in a row. The classic example for both of the rules is adding *o'clock* (*of the clock*) to a time. For example,

```
import java.text.*;
import java.util.*;
class Test {
    public static void main(String[] args) {
        DateFormat df = DateFormat.getInstance();
        Calendar calendar = Calendar.getInstance();
        ((SimpleDateFormat)df).applyPattern("h 'o''clock' a, z");
        System.out.println(df.format(calendar.getTime()));
    }
}
```

Executing this program prints times in a format such as 3 o'clock PM, EST. Notice how the comma printed. As with all patterns strings, characters that are not formatting symbols print as and where they appear in the pattern string. They specifically do not need to be enclosed in single or double quotation marks.

You can experiment with these symbols using the following program until you get the date or time exactly the way you want it.

```
import java.text.*;
import java.util.Date;
class Test {
    public static void main(String[] args) {
        DateFormat df = DateFormat.getInstance();
        ((SimpleDateFormat)df).applyPattern("EEE, MMM d, ''yy");
        System.out.println(df.format(new Date()));   //try on current date and time
    }
}
```

This particular pattern prints a date such as Sat, Feb 10, '01.

If, however, your experimentation requires the setting of date and time fields in order to test very specific formats, you can use something like this:

```
import java.text.*;
import java.util.Date;
class Test {
    public static void main(String[] args) {
        DateFormat df = DateFormat.getInstance();
        Calendar calendar = Calendar.getInstance();
        calendar.set(Calendar.HOUR, 24);
        ((SimpleDateFormat)df).applyPattern("H HH");
        System.out.println(df.format(calendar.getTime()));
    }
}
```

Executing this program prints 0 00.

The time zones strings returned by getZoneStrings() are stored in a table of type String[][].There are two rows for every time zone, one for the short, three-letter zone ID, which has been deprecated, and one for the long zone ID that replaced them. The zone ID is in the first column, which is referred to as the key. The second column is an array of five strings. The first string is the key followed by two sets of strings. The first set is regular time. The second set is daylight savings time. Within each set the first string is a long name such as Eastern Standard Time. The second string is a short name such as EST. Note that while strings such as EST have been deprecated as zone IDs, they are still valid as display names. Here is an example of four rows from the table:

```
{"EST", new String[] {"EST",
                      "Eastern Standard Time", "EST",
                      "Eastern Daylight Time", "EDT"}},

{"America/New_York", new String[] {"America/New_York",
                      "Eastern Standard Time", "EST",
                      "Eastern Daylight Time", "EDT"}},

{"JST", new String[] {"JST",
                      "Japan Standard Time", "JST",
                      "Japan Standard Time", "JST"}},

{"Asia/Tokyo", new String[] {"Asia/Tokyo",
                      "Japan Standard Time", "JST",
                      "Japan Standard Time", "JST"}},
```

Notice that Japan does not use daylight savings time, which is why I included that country in this example.

The reason for showing you how this table is built in detail is that, while technically correct, display names such as Eastern Daylight Time or EDT are not always desirable. For example, can you recall hearing a voice on a TV say that a show started at *Eastern Daylight Time, Central Daylight Time,* or *Pacific Daylight Time?* No. They always say *Eastern Stan-*

dard Time, Central Standard Time, or Pacific Standard Time, regardless of what time of the year it is. The following code solves that problem by replacing all of the daylight savings display names with the standard time display names:

```
/*
 * REPLACES SOME DEFAULT SYMBOLS USED WHEN FORMATING DATES AND TIMES
 * Change Jan to JAN for all twelve months, and xDT to xST for
 * all daylight savings time zones.
 */
DateFormatSymbols symbols = new DateFormatSymbols();
symbols.setShortMonths(new String[] {"JAN", "FEB", "MAR", "APR", "MAY", "JUN",
                          "JUL", "AUG", "SEP", "OCT", "NOV", "DEC"});
String[][] zones = symbols.getZoneStrings();
for (int i=0; i < zones.length; i++) {
    zones[i][3] = zones[i][1];
    zones[i][4] = zones[i][2];
}
symbols.setZoneStrings(zones);
```

This code also replaces the short month names with all caps. I routinely include this code when updating date format symbols because I prefer to format dates as 10 FEB 01. Of course, you must remember to invoke the `setDateFormatSymbols(DateFormatSymbols newFor-matSymbols)` method for the new symbols to take effect. This method is declared in the `SimpleDateFormat` class and requires a cast in order to invoke. For example,

```
DateFormat df = DateFormat.getInstance();
((SimpleDateFormat)df).setDateFormatSymbols(symbols);
```

This is the same cast required as when invoking the `applyPat-tern(String pattern)` method. See the `FormatUtilities` class in 5.19 The Localization of Common Data Types for an example replacing default symbols.

5.20.2.3.1 Formatting for Different Time Zones The API docs for the `DateFormat` class include the following sentence.

You can also set the time zone on the format if you wish.[38]

As of this writing, that is the extent to which the API docs for `DateFor-mat` and `SimpleDateFormat` say anything about formatting for different time zones. I searched through the Bug Parade before figuring out why

---

38. API docs for the `java.text.DateFormat` class.

invoking the setTimeZone(TimeZone zone) method in the Calendar class was having no effect on the output from the z or zzzz time symbol. There is a lot going on here, but the API docs say nothing on this subject.

In retrospect, maybe it was not so smart to assume that you have to invoke the setTimeZone(TimeZone zone) method in the Calendar class in order to format a time in a different time zone. Doing so would effectively change the time, requiring that you set it back to the original time zone. You might think of that as "destructive formatting." DateFormat has the same setTimeZone(TimeZone zone) method as Calendar, which allows the application programmer to format for a different time zone without changing the time stored in the Calendar. This is an interesting method because it adjusts the time stored in the Calendar for the time zone used in formatting. For example,

```java
import java.text.*;
import java.util.*;
class Test {
    public static void main(String[] args) {
        DateFormat df = DateFormat.getInstance();
        Calendar calendar = Calendar.getInstance();

        System.out.println();
        ((SimpleDateFormat)df).applyPattern("h:m:s a");
        System.out.println(df.format(calendar.getTime()));
        ((SimpleDateFormat)df).applyPattern("z");
        System.out.println(df.format(calendar.getTime()));
        ((SimpleDateFormat)df).applyPattern("zzzz");
        System.out.println(df.format(calendar.getTime()));

        //HAS NO EFFECT WHATSOEVER ON FORMATTED DATE!!!
        calendar.setTimeZone(TimeZone.getTimeZone("America/Los_Angeles"));

        System.out.println();
        ((SimpleDateFormat)df).applyPattern("h:m:s a");
        System.out.println(df.format(calendar.getTime()));
        ((SimpleDateFormat)df).applyPattern("z");
        System.out.println(df.format(calendar.getTime()));
        ((SimpleDateFormat)df).applyPattern("zzzz");
        System.out.println(df.format(calendar.getTime()));

        //THIS IS WHAT DOES THE JOB
        df.setTimeZone(TimeZone.getTimeZone("America/Los_Angeles"));

        System.out.println();
        ((SimpleDateFormat)df).applyPattern("h:m:s a");
        System.out.println(df.format(calendar.getTime()));
        ((SimpleDateFormat)df).applyPattern("z");
        System.out.println(df.format(calendar.getTime()));
        ((SimpleDateFormat)df).applyPattern("zzzz");
        System.out.println(df.format(calendar.getTime()));
```

```
      }
    }
```

Executing this program prints

```
2:54:31 PM
EST
Eastern Standard Time

2:54:31 PM
EST
Eastern Standard Time

11:54:31 AM
PST
Pacific Standard Time
```

Notice how the time was adjusted three hours for the difference between EST and PST.

Chapter 6

Arrays and The Collections Framework

Chapter Contents

6.1 Introduction

This chapter primarily discusses arrays and the Collections Framework (hereafter not capitalized) added to the `java.util` package in the 1.2 release. The terminological standard used for sections on the collections framework is the "Collections Framework" document that introduced collections in the 1.2 release and the "Collections" chapter of *The Java Tutorial*, which was written by Joshua Bloch. They are equally important because Bloch both designed and implemented the collections framework. No study of the collections framework is complete without reading what he says in *The Java Tutorial*. I quote him extensively in this chapter. His chapter on the collections framework is available online at

> *java.sun.com/docs/books/tutorial/collections*

The footnotes for quotations from *The Java Tutorial* use relative URLs that begin after the `collections` subdirectory. This is done to save space. For example, the first quotation is from *intro/index.html*. The complete Web address for that page of *The Java Tutorial* is *java.sun.com/docs/books/tutorial/collections/intro/index.html*.

There is a minor terminological problem in the collections framework. Because of the name *collections* framework, there is a presumption that all of the data structures in the framework are collections. They are and they are not. They are in the sense that **collections** is a generic term for all data structures that represent groups of objects. As Bloch states in *The Java Tutorial*,

> Collection implementations in earlier versions of Java included `Vector`, `Hashtable`, and array.[1]

Here Bloch uses the term *collection* to refer to arrays and legacy containers. All of the containers in the collections framework are not collections in the

---

1. Joshua Bloch, *The Java Tutorial: A Short Course on the Basics*, Third Edition (Reading: Addision-Wesley, 2000), "What Is a Collection?", *intro/index.html*.

sense that all of the general-purpose containers in the `java.util` package implement either the `Collection` or `Map` interface. The `Map` interface is not an extension of the `Collection` interface. This is a problem because it brings into question what exactly is meant by the term *collection*. If used in reference to the `Collection` interface, a collection is either a set or a list. If used generically it includes maps.

The terms *collection* and *container* as used in computer programming are historically synonymous. The only way to solve this problem is to use **container** as the generic reference to all collections, including arrays, the collections framework, and the legacy containers `Vector` and `Hashtable`. Containers have three general uses, each of which is as important as the next:

- To store and retrieve data
- To facilitate manipulating data
- To pass data to other methods or constructors

Generally I try to restrict my use of the term *collection* to mean instances of the `Collection` interface, but this does not help much. Any use of the term *collection* is potentially ambiguous. Therefore, I usually say *set* or *list* or use the `Set` and `List` interface names when referring to a `Collection`. One notable exception is the term **collection variable**. A collection variable is any variable that has one of the six core collection interface types. An **array variable** is any variable that has an array type. Both terms are short for *core collection interface type variable* and *array type variable*, respectively.

While on the subject of terminology, the plural of *index* is *indices*, but this is one of the words that common usage is in the process of changing. I use both *indexes* and *indices* in this book, whichever sounds more natural in a given context.

Arrays, `Vector`, and `Hashtable` are now referred to as **legacy collections**. Inasmuch as *legacy* carries the meaning of *old technology*, however, I do not include arrays in my definition of legacy collections. Arrays are here to stay because of speed, compile-time type checking, and primitive component types. Having explained this, the general organization of this chapter is as follows:

1. Arrays
2. The collections framework

3. Legacy containers

I deliberately say as little as possible about the legacy containers. Some readers will object on the basis that legacy containers such as `Vector` and `Hashtable` are here to stay. That is true to the extent that most of the core API, including the `javax.swing` packages, were largely completed before the collections framework. Nevertheless, for the sake of those readers who are new to the language, I try not to inadvertently give the impression that legacy containers should continue to be used. They should not.

The collections framework is the first major API covered in this book. That means you will see many of the API tables for the first time. In this case they are carefully designed so that you will not see the same method twice in any of the API tables. This is important in the collections framework because there are subinterfaces and multiple implementations of the same interface, etc. If a technical writer is not mindful of the design of the collection framework in this regard, the same method may be discussed over and over again in the context of different types. I studiously avoid this possibility even to the point that Table 6-4 is composed of the three methods that are common to both the `Collection` and `Map` interfaces (which do not have a common superinterface), namely, `size()`, `isEmpty()`, and `clear()`. This approach allows the reader to focus on what makes a particular core collection interface or general-purpose implementation unique. Because most of the behavior in the collections framework is defined in the core collection interfaces, there are only two very small API tables for the general-purpose implementations.

I want to add a personal note here. The notion that the entire universe of computer programming can be reduced to *data structures and algorithms* is bonkers.

Programming, at its best, approaches art—the art of simplicity expressed in logical constructs.

James Gosling is a great computer programmer, not only because of his vast technical knowledge, but also because of his flawless design instincts. There is also a certain beauty in the design of the collections framework. Given the current state of the art, I seriously doubt that more than a handful of programmers could have done as superb a job. If it were a building, Joshua Bloch would be celebrated in the press for his work, but the beauty of logical constructs can be appreciated only by other computer programmers.

6.2 Array, Component, and Element Types

Before discussing arrays I want to tackle a somewhat difficult terminological problem when working with arrays. There are three types for every array: the *array type*, the *component type*, and the *element type(s)*. Having a firm understanding of the difference between these three types is essential to understanding why an `ArrayStoreException` is thrown.

The **unnamed variables** in an array are referred to as the **components** of the array. The lifetime of an array component is comparable to instance variables in other classes. They are created when an array initializer or array creation expression is evaluated (that is, when an array is created) and destroyed when the array is garbage collected. The **component type** is the type name used in the declaration of an array variable. *All of the components in a given array have the same component type.* The **array type** is the component type followed by one or more pairs of empty brackets indicating the number of dimensions. Two array types are the same if they have the same component type and the same number of dimensions. For example,

```
class Test {
    public static void main(String[] args) {
        String[] array = {""};
        if (array.getClass() == args.getClass())
            System.out.println("these arrays are instances " +
                               "of the same class");
    }
}
```

The component type in this example is `String`. The array type is `String[]` (a one-dimensional array of `String`). The diagnostic message `"these arrays are instances of the same class"` prints, showing that the dynamically created array classes are reusable.

The third type is the element type. In terms of an array, an **element** must be understood to be any object stored in an array *that is not a dimensional node*. Dimensional nodes are discussed in 6.17 Multimaps and Multidimensional Arrays. Basically, they are arrays stored in other arrays. *They are not elements of the array. They are part of the array infrastructure.* You cannot, however, make the blanket statement that anything stored in an array *other than another array* is an element of that array, because if the component type is `Object`, the elements of an array can indeed be arrays. For example,

```
Object[] aa = {new int[5], new String[5]};
```

This is not a multidimensional array, which is obvious because the array type has only one pair of empty brackets. It is literally an array of arrays. Such declarations, however, are rare.

The **element type** is the class type of objects stored in an array. The element type must be assignment-compatible with the component type, otherwise an `ArrayStoreException` is thrown. The normal rules of assignment compatibility apply when assigning an element to one of the components of an array. For example,

```
Number[] numbers = {new Integer(2), new Long(2), new Double(3)};
```

In this example the component type is `Number`, the array type is `Number[]`, and the element types are `Integer`, `Long`, and `Double`, all of which are assignable to the component type. As this example shows, the element types in an array (or any container) are not necessarily the same. They are, however, always instances of the component type.

Components are variables. Elements are primitive values or objects. That is why the term *run-time type* is unnecessary. The term *element type* means the same thing.

If you have any problem with this usage distinction, remember that *component* always refers to the unnamed variables in an array, not to what is stored in them. The *elements* are what is stored in them.

6.3 Arrays

Arrays are the simplest and most widely used of all the container classes. They are different from any other container in a number of ways. Some of these differences are beneficial. Some are not. What are the pros and cons? The cons are

- *Interoperability*: Arrays do have an interface, albeit a very primitive one (array access expressions, `clone()`, and `length`). This interface does not remotely resemble any of the core collection interfaces. See 6.4 A Bridge over Troubled Waters (the `toArray` Methods) for a closely related discussion

- *Fixed Length*: Arrays are fixed-length. Once an array is created the length never changes. Most other containers are variable-length (or resizable). They either grow naturally every time an element is added (linked lists and binary trees) or they have a fixed-capacity, which, when exceeded, causes the container class to allocate a new and larger container, then move all of the elements or entries from the old container to the new one (`Array-List` and hash tables). Note that `ArrayList` is sometimes called a **resizable array**

- *Array Components Are Modifiable*: Array components are always unnamed variables (*variables* being the operative word). There is no way to make array components `final`. Anyone who has a reference to an array can store different values in the array, whereas it is a relatively simple matter to make a container in the collections framework unmodifiable

The pros are

- *Speed*: Arrays are generally faster than any of the other containers in the `java.util` package. This is not the case, however, when comparing array access expressions to the `get(Object o)` method in `ArrayList`. The `get(Object o)` method performs a bounds check and then returns the value of an array access expression. For example,

```
public Object get(int index) {
    if (index < 0 || index >= size)
        throw new IndexOutOfBoundsException(
        "Index: "+index+", Size: "+size);
    return elementArray[index];
}
```

The extra cost of accessing an `ArrayList` is an extra bounds check. This is a small constant. That is why interoperability is listed as the first *con*. Start using arrays and (short of a major rewrite) you are pretty much stuck with them

- *Compile-Time Type Checking*: All assignments to arrays are type checked at compile-time. If the component type is a reference type, they are also automatically checked at runtime. While there is a remote possibility of an `ArrayStoreException` being thrown at run time, this is less likely to happen than a `Class-CastException` when using untyped references. Furthermore, an `ArrayStoreException` can be systematically avoided by declaring array variables `final`.

- *No Wrapping of Primitives*: Containers in the collection framework use *untyped references*. That is, references to the elements in a `Collection` or to the keys and values in a `Map` are always stored in `Object` type variables, whereas the component type of an array can be any type, including the primitive data types. One very important consequence of this difference is that primitive values must be wrapped in a primitive type wrapper before adding them to any container other than an array. Unnecessarily creating objects is always a serious performance issue.

There is one other difference that is neither pro nor con. The dynamically created array classes do not implement either the `Enumeration` or `Iterator` interfaces as do the more complex container classes. Instead, a `for` loop is used to iterate over the elements of an array. To summarize, the pros are that arrays are super fast, can store primitive values, and assignments to components are type checked at compile time. The cons are that arrays are fixed length, have an extremely limited interface, and the components are always modifiable.

If you need to add or remove elements to a container after the initial loading of elements, arrays are probably not a good solution to your container problems because arrays are fixed length. If, however, you do not know how many elements will be loaded at run time, you can use an `ArrayList` and then dump the contents of the list into an array. For example,

```java
import java.io.*;
import java.util.*;
public class Test {
    public static void main(String[] args) throws IOException {
        File file = new File("doubles.dat");
        DataInputStream input = new DataInputStream
                            (new FileInputStream(file));
        int length = (int) file.length();
```

```
        if (length % 8 != 0)
            throw new IOException("file contaminated");
        int noRecords = length/8;
        List list = new ArrayList();
        for (int i=0; i < noRecords; i++)
            list.add(new Double(input.readDouble()));
        double[] values = new double[list.size()];
        Iterator iterator = list.iterator();
        int index = 0;
        while(iterator.hasNext())
            values[index++] = ((Double)iterator.next()).doubleValue();
    }
}
```

This program reads a file named `doubles.dat`, which contains a bunch of random numbers written using the `writeDouble(double v)` method in `DataOutputStream`. Hence, the record length is calculated at eight bytes. The random numbers are wrapped in a `Double` and then loaded into `ArrayList`. After loading all of the numbers the list is dumped into an array.

The `list(FilenameFilter filter)` method in the `File` class, which lists all of the file and subdirectory names in the target directory, uses this programming technique. A resizable array is needed because the number of files or subdirectories is unknown. Here is one possible implementation:

```
public String[] list(FilenameFilter filter) {
    String allNames[] = list();
    if ((allNames == null) || (filter == null)) {
        return allNames;
    }
    ArrayList filteredNames = new ArrayList();
    for (int i = 0 ; i < allNames.length ; i++) {
        if (filter.accept(this, names[i])) {
            filteredNames.add(names[i]);
        }
    }
    return (String[])(filteredNames.toArray(new String[0]));
}
```

What makes this example from the core API interesting is that the list of file names begins as a `String[]` (which is returned by the no-argument `list()` method). It is then filtered into an `ArrayList`, which is finally converted back into a `String[]` because that is the result type. Therefore, instead of an `ArrayList` to `String[]` container conversion, you have `String[]` to `ArrayList` to `String[]` container conversion, emphasizing the value of this programming technique.

6.3.1 The Canonical Form of the `for` Loop

Arrays are enumerated using the following **canonical** form of a `for` loop:

```
for (int i=0; i < arrayName.length; i++)
{ ... }
```

For example,

```
class Test {

    public static void main(String[] args) {
        int[] placeValues = new int[8];
        placeValues[0] = 1;
        for (int i = 1; i < placeValues.length; i++)
            placeValues[i] = placeValues[i-1] << 1;
        int total = 0;
        for (int i = 0; i < placeValues.length; i++) {
          total += placeValues[i];
          System.out.println(placeValues[i]);
        }
        System.out.println();
        System.out.println(total == Byte.MAX_VALUE + Math.abs(Byte.MIN_VALUE));
    }
}
```

Executing this program prints

```
1
2
4
8
16
32
64
128

true
```

In every iteration of the loop the Boolean expression in the `for` loop header, which includes a field access expression for the length of the array, must be evaluated.

The question is sometimes asked: should the field access expression in a loop control mechanism such as `i < placeValues.length` be taken out of the loop. For example,

```
int length = placeValues.length;
for (int i = 1; i < length; i++)
    placeValues[i] = placeValues[i-1] << 1;
```

This is a special case of the more general idea that *stack variables* (read *local variables*) are more efficient than field access expressions when coded in a loop.

This terminology is not sanctioned in either the *JLS* or *JVMS*. The `this` keyword, local variables, and parameters are all stack variables in the sense that they are allocated on the stack, in what is properly referred to as the *local variable array*. Using a **stack variable** means nothing more or less than assigning the value of a field (typically long-term state stored in an instance variable) to a local variable before using it in a loop. Thus at the point that `placeValues.length` is assigned to `length` in the above example, the local variable `length` becomes a so-called stack variable. This is a controversial performance optimization, made even more so by the fact that there are a few examples of using stack variables in the core API.[2] If it's good for the goose, it's good for the gander.

> Application programmers should strive to write readable code that is as efficient as possible without thinking in terms of how the JVM is implemented.

There is a growing consensus that not only is using stack variables an unnecessary performance optimization, but doing so could actually hinder a JVM implementor, whose job it is to make such performance optimizations for all Java programs. As controversial as it may sound to some very talented programmers, performance optimizations such as these are not in the problem domain of an application programmer, especially not a mainstream business application programmer for whom maintenance costs are as real as CPU cycles. Performance optimizations such as these are clearly in the problem domain of a system programmer.

Dealing with a major design flaw affecting all of Sun's early JVMs or working around a bug in the core API is one thing. Performance tuning an application based on an imperfect knowledge of a limited number of JVM implementations is counterproductive in the long haul. You must remember that there has not even been time enough in the life cycle of the Java platform for a major release (2.0, 3.0, 4.0, etc.), which most likely is going to include significant changes in the JVM, making ever more efficient implementations possible over the next decade. That is what I mean by *the long haul*. What I am talking about here is performance optimizations based on

---

2. I first encountered this in the source code for the `trim()` method in the `String` class, which, as of the 1.3 release, uses stack variables. The comment at the end of the line in which the field is assigned to a local variable before being used in a loop reads "avoid getfield opcode."

JVM implementation details that are intensely scrutinized on an ongoing basis. Such implementation details are likely going to be subject to continued, rapid development, particularly at this point in the life cycle of the Java platform.

This is not like it was with C. The C and C++ programming languages are developing at a Darwinian pace compared to the new Java technology juggernaut. It takes a very smart programmer to compensate for, or take advantage of, imperfections in an implementation of the C and C++ programming languages. Compensating for, or taking advantage of, comparable imperfections in a JVM requires just as much knowledge of the Java platform but is not as likely to be a problem tomorrow. Notice I said "a" JVM, because there are many JVM implementations. Their number and diversity will only increase as time passes. For example, the fully object-oriented HotSpot technology is a vast improvement over previous JVM implementations, and yet was introduced in a minor release. What of things to come? Simply put, the JVM is a moving target. The problem you solve today may not be a problem tomorrow.

What might be a problem tomorrow (or the day after), however, is the code you wrote to compensate for, or take advantage of, the imperfections in yesterday's JVM. No performance optimization could better frame this issue than the use of stack variables. Either it is a valid performance optimization or it is not. There is no in-between because to argue that a Java programmer should be performance tuning for a particular JVM implementation runs counter to the entire philosophy of the Java platform, and unnecessarily burdens mainstream business application programmers with the very same kind of system programming concerns as garbage collection all over again. Even understanding the issues involved requires an advanced understanding of JVM theory and design, but the issue is not about how much an application programmer knows about the JVM. The issue is performance optimizations in mainstream business applications given the rapid development of the Java platform and the average life cycle of a Java application. There are already indications that using stack variables can be a performance problem, not a performance optimization given what system programmers are doing in the most recent advances in JVM technology.

6.3.2 Array Classes Are Dynamically Created

Array classes are dynamically created when an array initializer or array creation expression is evaluated. The component type of an array can be any data type and the component type is part of the array type. By extension there is a potentially unlimited number of array types. One says that array types are **orthogonal** to the type system, which in mathematical terms means that for every type there is a corresponding array type. It is not possible to write the source code for a potentially unlimited number of array types. You must know the component type and the number of dimensions before creating an array class. This is precisely why array classes must be dynamically created. You can do this yourself using the `newInstance(Class componentType, int length)` method in the `java.lang.reflect.Array` class. Here is an example from a package-private class method in the `java.awt.AWTEventMulticaster` class in the core API:

```
static EventListener[] getListeners(EventListener l, Class listenerType) {
    int n = getListenerCount(l);
    EventListener[] result = (EventListener[])Array.newInstance(listenerType, n);
    populateListenerArray(result, l, 0);
    return result;
}
```

Dynamically created array classes such as these do not have class names. If you invoke the `getName()` method for one of the dynamically created array classes, the value returned is a *descriptor* for the two arguments passed to the `newInstance(Class componentType, int length)` method in the `java.lang.reflect.Array` class. For example,

```
public class Test {
    public static void main(String[] args) {
        int[][][] array = new int[3][2][5];
        System.out.println(array.getClass().getName());
    }
}
```

Executing this program prints `[[[I`. Descriptors are a special notation system used to encode type information in a class file. They are designed to save space. There are many different kinds of descriptors: field descriptors, method descriptors, parameter descriptors, and return descriptors, not just those used to encode array types. Because the dynamically created array classes do not have class names, the descriptors are used everywhere that a class name would normally be used, which explains why they are returned by the `getName()` method in the `Class` class.

The left brackets in an array type descriptor indicate the number of dimensions and the capital letter indicates the component type. For example, `[ [ [I` is a three-dimensional array of `int`. There is a capital letter for each of the primitive data types. If the component type is a reference type, the capital letter `L` is used followed by a fully qualified reference type name (using forward slashes rather than periods as separators) and then a semicolon. For example,

```
[Ljava/lang/Object;
```

This is an array type descriptor for a one-dimensional array of `Object`. That invoking the `getClass()` method for one of the dynamically created array classes returns a descriptor is something of a fluke. They were never intended to be seen by application programmers.

6.3.3 The Members of an Array Type

The members of any reference type are fields, methods, and member types. Those members are either declared or inherited. The problem with defining the members of an array in terms of *declared* members, however, is that there is no source code or API docs for the dynamically created array classes. Therefore, someone has to tell you what members are declared in those classes. As stated in the *JLS*, the members of an array type are specifically

- The `public final` field `length`, which contains the number of components of the array (`length` may be positive or zero)
- The `public` method `clone`, which overrides the method of the same name in class `Object` and throws no checked exceptions
- And all the members inherited from class `Object`; the only method of `Object` that is not inherited is its `clone` method

An array thus has the same `public` fields and methods as the following class:

```
class A implements Cloneable java.io.Serializable {
    public final int length = X;
    public Object clone() {
        try {
            return super.clone();
        } catch (CloneNotSupportedException e) {
            throw new InternalError(e.getMessage());
        }
    }
}
```

[end of quotation] [3]

Note that the only inaccessible member of one of the dynamically created array classes is the protected `finalize()` method inherited from the `Object` class, which is never invoked. Thus, one can generalize and say that all of the members of an interface or array type are `public`.

6.3.4 Array Type Variable Declarations

The syntax for array type variable declarations is shown in Table 6-1.

The following are some array type variable declarations from the core API:

```
/** The value is used for character storage. */
    private char value[];

/** A table of hex digits */
private static final char[] hexDigit = {
  '0','1','2','3','4','5','6','7','8','9','A','B','C','D','E','F'
};


/**
 * The array buffer into which the elements of the ArrayList are stored.
 * The capacity of the ArrayList is the length of this array buffer.
 */
private transient Object elementData[];
```

Table 6-1: The Four Parts of an Array Type Variable Declaration

Part			Notes
1	Field or local variable modifiers		Field modifiers are the access modifiers `public`, `protected`, and `private`, `static`, `final`, `transient`, and `volatile`. The only local variable modifier is `final`.
2	Type name		This is the component type.
3	Brackets		The empty pairs of brackets indicate the number of dimensions (or *the depth of array nesting* as stated in the *JLS*).
4	Variable declarator	Identifier	The name of the field or local variable.
		Brackets	Placement of some or all of the brackets after the identifier (that is, in a variable declarator) is optional.
		Variable initializer	Array initializer or array creation expression, but usually not an anonymous array.

---

3. James Gosling, Bill Joy, Guy Steele, and Gilad Bracha, *The Java Language Specification, Second Edition* (Boston: Addison-Wesley, 2000), §10.7, "Array Members."

Note that declaring an array type variable `final` means that the array variable will always reference the same array. It does not mean that the array components cannot be changed.

The placement of the brackets in an array type variable declaration is optional. In order to understand why the placement of brackets is optional, you must realize that placing them after the identifier puts them in a variable declarator. The whole idea of a variable declarator is to allow you to declare more than one variable with the same modifiers and type. In addition to having the same modifiers and component type, all of the variable declarators in an array type variable declaration have at least the number of dimensions as indicated by the empty brackets after the component type. In order to make variable declarators as independent from one another as possible, language designers have also allowed the brackets used in the array type to be placed in the variable declarator, thus allowing programmers to declare multiple array variables, all of which have the same modifiers and component type, but which may have different array types. This is now called **mixed notation**. Figure 6-1 is an example of mixed notation.

That was the intent of the language designers. The term *mixed notation*, however, is pejorative. No one wants to use variable declarators like that. The unintended consequence of this language design decision is that there are now two camps of programmers on the issue of bracket placement in array type variable declarations and mixed notation is sort of a *no man's land* between the two. The first camp emphasizes the array type. For these programmers, placing the brackets after the identifier obscures the array type. The second camp thinks more about the fact that the identifier is never used without brackets following (except in an array type variable declaration by the first camp). An array name without brackets looks

first camp   second camp   mixed notation

Figure 6-1: Mixed notation.

naked to these programmers and they can dismiss the array type argument by regarding the type name as the component type. Both camps are right. It is noteworthy that the authors of *The Java Programming Language* state that placing the brackets next to the type name "is generally preferable, because it places the type declaration entirely in one place."[4] I agree, but this is purely a matter of style.

What is not a matter of style, I would say, is the use of mixed notation.

6.3.5 Initializing Array Type Variables

The choices of initialization in Figure 6-1 are an array initializer or an array creation expression, both of which are discussed in the following subsections. Using an anonymous array in a variable initializer, however, betrays an ignorance of the difference between array initializers and anonymous arrays. For example,

```
String[] strings = {"variable", "initializers", "for", "arrays"};
String[] strings = new String[] {"variable", "initializers", "for", "arrays"};
```

These variable declarations are equivalent. The second declaration uses an anonymous array, which is not necessary in a variable initializer. Just use an array initializer as in the first declaration.

Initializing an array is a three-step process:

1. Declaring the array variable,
2. Creating an array and assigning it to the array variable (which is usually done in a variable initializer), and
3. Loading the array.

The first two steps are largely the same for any reference type variable. The only difference is that the object is an array. The third step is what makes arrays different. Arrays must be loaded before they can be used. For small arrays an array initializer can be used to both create an array and load the elements. Larger arrays are usually loaded using a `for` loop. If the array variable is a field the `for` loop can be placed in an initialization block to make sure the array is loaded during class or instance initialization. Another option is to invoke a method that loads the array either in the variable initializer or in an initialization block. In any case, the array is going

---

4. Ken Arnold and James Gosling, *The Java Programming Language, Second Edition* (Reading: Addison-Wesley, 1998), §5.8, "Array Variables."

to be loaded during class or instance initialization in one of the special initialization methods, so all of these options are purely a matter of style.

6.3.5.1 Array Initializers

An **array initializer** is a comma-separated list of expressions enclosed in braces. A trailing comma after the last expression in an array initializer is ignored, which makes it easier to manage long, vertical lists of comma-separated expressions. (You can cut and paste without worrying about removing the comma after the last expression in the list.) Here is a typical example of an array initializer:

```
static final int[] DAYS_IN_MONTH = {31,28,31,30,31,30,31,31,30,31,30,31};
```

This is a special syntax that can only be used in variable initializers for arrays. The array is implicitly created when the array initializer is evaluated. The size of the array is determined by the number of expressions. They are evaluated from left to right and the values are used to initialize the corresponding component of the array. A compiler error is generated if the type of an expression in an array initializer is not assignment compatible with the component type. That is part of the compile-time type checking for arrays.

Array initializers can be nested to initialize multidimensional arrays. See 6.17 Multimaps and Multidimensional Arrays for an example.

6.3.5.2 Array Creation Expressions

Arrays are explicitly created using an **array creation expression**. The general form of an array creation expression is

```
new componentType[dimensionExpression]…
```

The ellipses are for multidimensional arrays that have two or more dimension expressions enclosed in brackets. For example,

```
float[][] matrix = new float[3][3];
```

Note that a two dimensional array is often referred to as a **matrix**. Likewise, one-dimensional arrays are sometimes referred to as **vectors**, as in the Vector class (the implementation of which is a one dimensional array of Object).

Class instance creation expressions are similar to array creation expressions in that both begin with the new keyword. I can remember a distinct uneasiness the first time I saw the new operator in front of a primitive data type. It was confusing because I knew the new operator was used to create objects and that primitive data types were not objects. So what does something like *new int* mean? It means that you should keep looking to the right to see the bracketed dimension expression(s) because the only time you will ever see the new keyword in front of a primitive data type is in an array creation expression.

The dimension expression specifies the number of components (or unnamed variables) in an array. If the value of the dimension expression is a negative number, a NegativeArraySizeException is thrown. The value of the dimension expression is used to initialize the length field. In other words, the value of the dimension expression and the length of an array are one and the same. Arrays cannot be longer than Integer.MAX_VALUE, because the type of a dimension expression must be int or one of the smaller integral types. The byte, short, and char types are promoted to int when used in a dimension expression. The use of a long or floating-point type in a dimension expression generates a compiler error. This implicitly limits the size of an array in the Java programming language to Integer.MAX_VALUE, which, as you may recall from Chapter 4, is about two billion elements (2,147,483,647 to be exact). That is large enough for most mainstream business applications.

6.3.5.2.1 Automatic Initialization of Array Components

The components of the array are comparable to fields in nonarray classes in that they are automatically initialized to standard default values. For example,

```java
public class Test {
    public static void main(String[] args) {
        String[] strings = new String[10];
        System.out.println(strings[0]);
    }
}
```

Executing this program prints null, which is the standard default value for reference data types such as String. Notice that there is no definite assignment problem accessing the component. Array variables may be local, but never the components of an array. They are always initialized to standard default values during class initialization.

The standard default value of `null` used to initialize reference type array components can be useful in determining how many objects are in an array. For example,

```java
import java.math.BigInteger;
class Test {
    public static void main(String[] args) {
        Number[] numbers = new Number[5];
        numbers[0] = new Integer(25);
        numbers[1] = new Double(25.0);
        numbers[2] = new BigInteger("25");
        System.out.println("length = " + numbers.length);
        int index = 0;
        while(index < numbers.length) {
            if (numbers[index] == null)
                break;
            index++;
        }
        System.out.println("no. elelments = " + index);
    }
}
```

Executing this program prints

```
length = 5
no. elelments = 3
```

The `toArray(Object[] a)` method discussed in 6.4 A Bridge over Troubled Waters (the `toArray` Methods) does essentially the same thing by writing `null` to the first component after the copied collection (assuming the `length` of the array passed is greater than the `size()` of the collection copied).

6.3.6 Array Access Expressions

Access to the components (or unnamed variables) in an array is by definition an **array access expression**. The value and type of an array access expression are the same as the element accessed. This means that the type of an array access expression is not necessarily the same as the component type.

Array access expressions have two subexpressions: the **array reference expression** and the **index expression**. The general form of an array access expression is

```
primaryExpression[IndexExpression]
```

The primary expression to the left of the brackets is the array reference expression, which is usually just the name of an array variable. If the primary expression evaluates to `null`, a `NullPointerException` is thrown. It is possible, however, to invoke a method that returns a reference to an array. For example,

```
System.out.println("XYZ".toCharArray()[2]);
```

This line of code prints

```
z
```

The array reference expression is `"XYZ".toCharArray()`.

Array index expressions are discussed in the following subsection.

6.3.6.1 Array Index Expressions

Zero-origin integers called **indices** are used to access elements in linear data structures such as arrays in all programming languages. **Zero-origin** means the first element in the array or other linear struture has an index value of zero, the second element has an index value of one, the third element has an index value of two, and so on. The last element in an array has an index value equal to the length of the array minus one, which explains why the canonical form of the `for` loop uses `i < arrayName.length` as a loop control mechanism. The type of an index expression must be `int` or one of the smaller integral types. The `byte`, `short`, and `char` types are promoted to `int` when used in an index expression. Using a `long` or floating-point type in an index expression generates a compiler error. As a general rule, only integer literals and `int` type variables should be used to index an array.

The dynamically created array classes include a bounds check that is executed every time an array access expression is evaluated. A **bounds check** means that the index value passed must be between `0` and `arrayName.length - 1` inclusive. If the value of an index expression is *out of bounds*, an `ArrayIndexOutOfBoundsException` is thrown. The `get(int index)` method in the `ArrayList` class has what might at first look like a redundant bounds check. Here is the implementation:

```
public Object get(int index) {
    //THIS IS A BOUNDS CHECK
    if (index < 0 || index >= size)
        throw new IndexOutOfBoundsException("Index: " + index +
                                            ", Size: " + size);
    //ARRAY ACCESS EXPRESSION
    return elements[index];
}
```

Why do a bounds check in `ArrayList` if the dynamically created array classes do the same thing? The answer is that the array used to store the elements in an `ArrayList` has extra capacity. The same index value that throws an `IndexOutOfBoundsException` in the `get(Object o)` method of an `ArrayList` might return `null` when used in the `return elements[index]` statement. In other words, the cost of having extra capacity in the backing array is an extra bounds check in `ArrayList`.

6.4 A Bridge over Troubled Waters (the `toArray` Methods)

The collections framework was not completed until the 1.2 release. By that time there were other collections frameworks in use. In addition, arrays were more heavily used than they are now. Those array-based APIs will be around for a long time, if not for the lifetime of the Java platform. While Sun cannot be expected to do anything to legitimize the stopgap collection frameworks that came into use before the 1.2 release, the collections framework does include the following overloaded `toArray` methods for converting a `Collection` to an array. They are thought of as a *bridge* between the older array-based APIs and newer, collection-based APIs:

```
public Object[] toArray()
public Object[] toArray(Object[] a)
```

These methods are declared in the `Collection` interface, and are used when invoking an older method or constructor that expects an array instead of a `Collection`. The no-argument `toArray()` method is not very useful because the class of the array returned is always `Object[]`.

Although the result type of the `toArray(Object[] a)` method is also `Object[]`, the class of the array returned is always the same as the class of the array passed at run time. For example,

```
import java.util.*;
public class Test {
    public static void main(String[] args) {
        ArrayList list = new ArrayList();
        list.add("element");
        list.add("type");
        list.add("is");
        list.add("String");
        System.out.println(list.toArray(new String[0]).getClass().getName());
    }
}
```

Executing this program prints

```
[Ljava.lang.String;
```

This is the name (actually a descriptor) of the dynamically created `String[]` class. The same `String[]` array type can be used in a cast operator so that the component type of the array returned is the same as the element type. For example,

```
import java.util.*;
public class Test {
    public static void main(String[] args) {
        ArrayList list = new ArrayList();
        list.add("the");
        list.add("element");
        list.add("type");
        list.add("is");
        list.add("String");
        String[] array = (String[]) list.toArray(new String[0]);
        for (int i=0; i < array.length; i++)
            System.out.print(array[i].toUpperCase() + " ");
    }
}
```

Executing this program prints

```
THE ELEMENT TYPE IS STRING
```

This is how you convert a set or list to an array.

If the length of the array passed to the `toArray(Object[] a)` method is less than the number of elements in the target collection, a new array will be allocated in which to return the elements. Normally a dummy array with a length of zero is passed as in the following line of code from the example above:

```
String[] array = (String[]) list.toArray(new String[0]);
```

If, however, the length of the array passed is equal to or greater than the number of elements in the target collection, the same array is returned after loading all the elements. There are two possibilities. Either the array is the same size as the set or list, or larger. If larger, after copying the last element from the set or list, the next array component is set to `null` to indicate the last of the elements copied (which is not very useful if there are `null` elements in the set or list copied).

If any of the elements in the collection are not assignment-compatible with the component type of the array passed, an `ArrayStoreException` is thrown. For example,

```
import java.util.*;
public class Test {
```

```
    public static void main(String[] args) {
        ArrayList list = new ArrayList();
        list.add(new Integer(0));
        list.add(new Long(0L));
        list.add(new Double(0.0));
        list.add(new Character('a'));
        Number[] numbers = (Number[]) list.toArray(new Number[0]);
        for (int i=0; i < numbers.length; i++)
            System.out.println(numbers[i].intValue());
    }
}
```

This program compiles but throws an `ArrayStoreException` at run time because the `Character` class does not extend `Number`.

An iterator is used to load the array. Consequently, the order of elements in the array are in the same order as they would be returned by the iterator for a given collection.

6.5 Untyped References versus Parameterized Types

When used as a component type in an array or other container, `Object` is a generic reference type in which references to any class of objects can be stored. I refer to this use of the `Object` class as an **untyped reference**. This section discusses the problem of untyped references and how parameterized types will solve that problem. Before starting, Table 6-2 lists some important URLs for parameterized types.

Table 6-2: Important URLs for Parameterized Types

Name	URL
GJ Home Page	www.cs.bell-labs.com/who/wadler/pizza/gj/
JSP #000014	java.sun.com/aboutJava/communityprocess/jsr/jsr_014_gener.html
Bug ID 4064105[a]	developer.java.sun.com/developer/bugParade/bugs/4064105.html

a. Number two in the Top 25 RFEs (Requests For Enhancements) as of this writing.

The problem of untyped references is very straightforward. It is illustrated here using an array:

```
class Test {
    public static void main(String[] args) {
        Object[] array = {"no","compile-time", "type", "checking"};
        String s;
        for (int i=0; i < array.length; i++) {
```

```
            s = (String) array[i];
            System.out.print(s.toUpperCase() + " ");
        }
    }
}
```

Executing this program prints

NO COMPILE-TIME TYPE CHECKING

There is nothing wrong with this program as written. Were something other than a `String` inadvertently added to the `array`, however, no compiler error would be generated even though a `ClassCastException` would be thrown at run time. The essential problem is a lack of compile-time type checking of assignments to an `Object` type variable. The only type check performed for assignments to `Object` type variables is for primitive types. Any reference type can be assigned to an `Object` type variable because everything is an `Object`. The same is true for all of the container classes in the `java.util` package (that is, for all untyped references). The strong type checking in the Java programming language cannot solve the problem of untyped references.

A cast operator is required when removing elements from such a container. In doing so there is an assumption that all of the objects in the array are instances of the type name in the cast operator. If a different type object is added by mistake, a `ClassCastException` is thrown at run time. (Assumptions are never good in computer programming.) For example,

```
import java.util.*;
class Test {
    public static void main(String[] args) {
        ArrayList list = new ArrayList();
        list.add("no");
        list.add("compile-time");
        list.add("type");
        list.add("checking");
        list.add(new Integer(0));
        Iterator iterator = list.iterator();
        while (iterator.hasNext()) {
            String s = (String) iterator.next();
            System.out.print(s.toUpperCase() + " ");
        }
    }
}
```

Executing this program throws a `ClassCastException` and there is nothing you can do about it other than being very careful when adding elements to a container class that uses untyped references (which until parameterized types are added to the language is all of them). Although the essential problem is a lack of compile-time type checking when adding elements to the container, the `ClassCastException` is not thrown until an attempt is made to use that element as if it were the same type as the others. Inasmuch as the component type of all the containers in the collections framework is `Object`, there is nothing you can do to solve this problem short of creating a custom implementation as explained in 6.16 Custom Implementations of the Core Collection Interfaces. The problem of untyped references applies equally to all of the container classes in the collections framework as well as to legacy containers.

Having just read the sections on arrays, I expect you are wondering why anyone would use `Object` as a component type for strings. The problem is easily solved by changing the component type to `String`. For example,

```
class Test {
    public static void main(String[] args) {
        String[] arrayOfString = {"no","compile-time",
                                  "type", "checking"};
        for (int i=0; i < arrayOfString.length; i++) {
            System.out.print(arrayOfString[i].toUpperCase() + " ");
        }
    }
}
```

This program does the same thing as the original example, is slightly more efficient, and does not throw a `ClassCastException`. However, this only works for arrays. Programmers who come from languages that have parameterized types are used to solving this problem for the more complex container classes just as easily.

Parameterized types solve the problem by passing type information to the container class. As parameterized types are likely to be implemented in the Java programming language, the **type parameter** is placed inside less-than and greater-than signs so as to differentiate them from method and constructor parameters, which are placed in parentheses (and in the context of a discussion of parameterized types are referred to as **value parameters**). The following example is a futuristic look at the Java programming language:

```
import java.util.*;
class Test {
    public static void main(String[] args) {
        ArrayList<String> list = new ArrayList<String>();
        list.add("no");
        list.add("compile-time");
        list.add("type");
        list.add("checking");
        Iterator iterator = list.iterator();
        while (iterator.hasNext()) {
```

```
        System.out.print(iterator.next().toUpperCase() + " ");
    }
}
```

This program does the same thing as the last example and does not throw a `ClassCastException`. `ArrayList<String>` is the parameterized type name. Attempting to add anything other than a `String` to `ArrayList<String>` will generate an incompatible types compiler error rather than throwing a `ClassCastException` at run time.

If you want to truly understand parameterized types, understand this: parameterized types are not being added to simplify the language. They introduce as much complexity—I would say considerably more—than what they replace, which is nothing more than a few cast expressions. All of those type checks are neatly tucked away where you cannot see them, but they are still there. I feel confident in saying that the only reason why the software engineers at Sun, including Dr. Gosling, would consent to parameterized types becoming part of the language is so that applications do not throw a `ClassCastException` at run time. You just cannot have a programming language that has run-time exceptions more or less built in to something as basic as a container, which is what we have now. Critical systems need the reliability of knowing for sure that something as basic as a container is not going to crash the system, especially when human lives are at stake. This is why parameterized types must be added to the language. They are ugly but essential.

Parameterized types are moving slowly through the Java Community Process, but they are sure to be part of the core API sometime in the next couple of years. I would venture to guess that Generic Java (GL) will be the implementation choice given that Gilad Bracha, who wrote the changes for the second edition of the *JLS*, is one of the GL developers, and both Guy Steele and Dr. Gosling have publicly indicated their approval of the GL design. I like the GL design too.

6.5.1 What Is Run-Time Type?

The term **run-time type** is not sanctioned in the *JLS*. The original *JLS* flatly contradicts this usage.

> Sometimes a variable or expression is said to have a 'runtime type' but that is an abuse of terminology; it refers to the class of the object referred to by the value of the variable or expression at run time, assuming that the value is not `null`. Properly

speaking, type is a compile-time notion. A variable or expression has a type; *an object or array has no type,* but belongs to a class [emphasis added]. [5]

It is never easy to fly in the face of conventional wisdom. The terms *run-time type*, **run-time type identification**, and the acronym **RTTI** are well established. Hence, the second edition of the *JLS* softens this passage.

> Sometimes a variable or expression is said to have a "run-time type". This refers to the class of the object referred to by the value of the variable or expression at run time, assuming that the value is not null.[6]

Furthermore, the name of the section quoted was changed from "Variables Have Types, Objects Have Classes" to "Types, Classes, and Interfaces." These terms are a carry over from the type system in the

C programming language. I am strongly opposed to their continued use in the Java programming language, particularly the term *run-time type identification*. The term suggests something much more complicated than the reality of differentiating between untyped references and the class of the object stored in a container.

The same terminological distinction is made in reference to arrays when we speak of the component type versus the element type. The element type is the class of the object stored in the array, which is precisely how *run-time type* is being used. Why do we need both element type and run-time type? The preferred term for the objects stored in a container is *element*, which makes element type a much more natural term in comparison to run-time type. For example,

```
List list = new ArrayList();
list.add("Alfa"):
list.add("Baker"):
list.add("Alfa"):
```

In this example the element type is `String`. Why complicate things by saying that the run-time type is `String`? Doing so turns a simple terminological distinction into something that sounds like a complicated run-time mechanism. The only *mechanism* for RTTI is the `instanceof` operator.

---

5.   James Gosling, Bill Joy, and Guy Steele, *The Java Language Specification* (Reading: Addison-Wesley, 1996), §4.5.5, "Variables Have Types, Objects Have Classes."
6.   Gosling et al., §4.5.6, "Types, Classes, and Interfaces."

Type systems are much simpler than they used to be. We really do not need all of the C baggage that comes along with the term *run-time type*.

6.6 Time Complexities (or Big-O Notation)

If looping through a container, the time needed to complete an operation depends on the number of elements in the container. The more elements, the longer it takes. Container design puts a premium on performance that is not tied to the number of elements in the container at any given time because that means the larger the container, the slower the operation. This has developed into a science in which container performance is measured in terms of a **time complexity**, which is the subject of this section.

The basic unit of measurement in time complexities is **constant time**, which is expressed as $O(1)$ using **Big-O notation**. I use a fixed font when discussing Big-O notation, but that is only my personal preference. All time complexities have a name and most can also be expressed using Big-O notation. Another example is linear time, which is expressed as $O(n)$. The O stands for operation, which always means a container operation. All of the methods declared in a container class are *operations* in this context.

The API docs express $O(\log n)$ time as $\log(n)$ and $O(n \log n)$ as $n \log(n)$. The O is implicit. I prefer the explicit O. The n is the number of elements in the container. Logarithms are always base two in this context. For example, $O(\log n)$ is the same as $O(\log_2 n)$. In this case, almost all technical writers and software engineers assume base two logarithms rather than use the explicit subscript. The logarithmic and linear logarithmic time complexities are always used in reference to *binary* searches and balanced *binary* trees, which is why they are always log base two.

Generally speaking, each container operation has one main loop. There may be loops within the main loop (as is always the case in quadratic time), but there is one main loop. The code before and after the loop in a container operation is amortized constant time, as discussed in the next section. The code inside the loop is the **constant factor** used in time complexities.

All other time complexities are expressed as multiples of the constant factor. In other words, all time complexities are a measurement of how many times the main loop in a container operation must be executed.

Linear time, for example, means the main loop must be executed once for every element in the container. Linear time is very good if you are processing all of the elements in a container. In fact, if you are processing all of the elements in a container, linear time is the best possible time complexity. Linear time is very bad if you are only trying to access one of the elements in a container because access times are ideally constant, not dependent on the number of elements in a container.

The following is a complete list of time complexities mentioned in the API docs for the `java.util` package:

- Constant time or O(1)

- Amortized constant time

- Logarithmic time or O(log n)

- Linear time or O(n)

- Linear logarithmic time or O(n log n)

- Quadratic time or O(n2)

The time complexities in this list are ordered in terms of their *cost* from the least expensive to the most expensive operations. Constant time is the fastest time for any given container operation. Quadratic time is generally the slowest. The more costly linear logarithmic and quadratic time container operations sometimes cannot be avoided. Familiarize yourself with this list because they are likely to be mentioned in any discussion of the general-purpose containers in the `java.util` package.

The following program includes an example for each of the time complexities mentioned in the collections framework except for amortized constant time:

```
import java.text.DecimalFormat;
class Test {

    static final int CONSTANT_TIME = 1;
    static int logn, linear, nlogn, quadratic;
    static DecimalFormat formatter = new DecimalFormat("000000000");

    public static void main(String[] args) {

        System.out.println();
        System.out.println("        The Relative Cost of a " +
                    "Container Operation");
        System.out.println();
        System.out.println("   n      constant    log(n)" +
                    "   linear   n log(n)  quadratic");
```

```
          System.out.println("--------- --------- --------- " +
                             "--------- --------- ---------");
          timeComplexity(10);
          timeComplexity(25);
          timeComplexity(50);
          timeComplexity(100);
          timeComplexity(500);
          timeComplexity(1000);
          timeComplexity(5000);
        }
      static void timeComplexity(int n) {

          logn = linear = nlogn = quadratic = 0;

          for (int i=0; i < n; i++)
            linear += CONSTANT_TIME;

          for (int j=0; j < n; j++)
            for (int i=0; i < n; i++)
              quadratic += CONSTANT_TIME;

          int nodes = 1;  //root node
          while (nodes <= n) {
            logn += CONSTANT_TIME;
            nodes *= 2;  //balanced tree
          }

          nodes = 1;
          while (nodes <= n) {
            for (int i=0; i < n; i++)
              nlogn += CONSTANT_TIME;
            nodes *= 2;
          }

      System.out.print(suppressLeadingZeros(formatter.format(n) + " "));
      System.out.print(suppressLeadingZeros(formatter.format(CONSTANT_TIME) + " "));
      System.out.print(suppressLeadingZeros(formatter.format(logn) + " "));
      System.out.print(suppressLeadingZeros(formatter.format(linear) + " "));
      System.out.print(suppressLeadingZeros(formatter.format(nlogn) + " "));
      System.out.println(suppressLeadingZeros(formatter.format(quadratic)));
      }
      public static String suppressLeadingZeros(String s) {
        int i=0;
        while (s.charAt(i)=='0')
          i++;
        return s.substring(0,i+1).replace('0', ' ') + s.substring(i+1);
      }
    }
}
```

Executing this program prints

```
The Relative Cost of a Container Operation
```

n	constant	log(n)	linear	n log(n)	quadratic
10	1	4	10	40	100
25	1	5	25	125	625
50	1	6	50	300	2500

100	1	7	100	700	10000
500	1	9	500	4500	250000
1000	1	10	1000	10000	1000000
5000	1	13	5000	65000	25000000

Note that the O(log n) and O(n log n) examples are intended to simulate the cost of accessing a balanced binary tree, which is why nodes starts at one and is multiplied by two each iteration instead of using n and dividing by two, as would an example of the same time complexity intended to simulate the cost of a binary search (*divide and conquer*) algorithm.

6.6.1 Constant Time Operations

Another use of the term *constant time* is in reference to a **constant time operation**. For example,

```
public Object get(int index) {
    //THIS IS A BOUNDS CHECK
    if (index < 0 || index >= size)
        throw new IndexOutOfBoundsException("Index: " + index +
                                    ", Size: " + size);
    //ARRAY ACCESS EXPRESSION
    return elements[index];
}
```

This is one possible implementation of the get(int index) method in the ArrayList class. *This method runs in constant time because there are no loops involved.* The constant time for this operation is very low. There is a bounds check followed by an array access expression. Few container operations are as fast.

The most important constant time operations in the collections framework are summarized in Table 6-3. Notably absent from this table are the random access methods in LinkedList. While linked lists are touted for their constant time performance when adding elements to, or removing them from, either the beginning or middle of a list, a ListIterator must be used to achieve that level of performance. This is explained in detail in 6.10.1.1 ArrayList versus LinkedList.

6.6.2 Amortized Constant Time

Any code that is executed once for all of the elements accessed runs in what is called **amortized constant time**. For example, the code to balance a binary tree runs in amortized constant time. This time complexity is described as *amortized* because the cost of executing the code is spread

Table 6-3: Important Constant Time Operations

General Purpose Implementation	Method
ArrayList[a]	remove(Object o)
	get(int index)
	add(Object o)
	add(int index, Object element)
	set(int index, Object element)
ListIterator for a LinkedList	add(Object o)
	remove()
	set(Object o)
HashMap[b]	get(Object key)
	put(Object key, Object value)
	containsKey(Object key)
	remove(Object key)
HashSet[b]	add(Object o)
	contains(Object o)
	remove(Object o)

a. remove(int index) is not constant time because of element shifting.
b. This assumes a minimum of hash collisions (discussed below).

out over all of the elements accessed. This means code that runs in amortized constant time is never in the main loop, except if conditionally executed. Balancing a binary tree is such an example. The balanceTree(Node node) method is conditionally executed in the main loop of the put(Object key, Object value) method in TreeMap. Nevertheless, it runs in amortized constant time because it is not invoked in every loop (only when the binary tree needs to be balanced).

There is a single reference to amortized constant time in the collections framework in reference to the *add operation* in ArrayList.

> The add operation runs in *amortized constant time*, that is, adding n elements requires $O(n)$ time.[7]

This quotation is somewhat misleading in that "adding n elements requires $O(n)$ time" suggests constant time, not amortized constant time. I will explain this use of *amortized constant time* so as not to confuse the reader.

---

7. API docs for the java.util.ArrayList class.

There are actually four `add` methods for an `ArrayList`:

```
public boolean add(Object o)
public void add(int index, Object element)
public boolean addAll(Collection c)
public boolean addAll(int index, Collection c)
```

Adding elements to an `ArrayList` is described as amortized constant time because of how the `addAll(int index, Collection c)` bulk operation is implemented. A very poorly implemented `add-All(int index, Collection c)` method might shift the elements in the array after each object in the `Collection` is added to the beginning or middle of the list. By referring to the `add` operation in an `Array-List` as amortized constant time, Bloch is pointing out that, instead of expanding the backing array to make room for one element at a time, the array is expanded to make room for however many elements are in the `Collection` passed. Thus, the cost of element shifting (or expanding the array) is amortized over the number of elements added. This makes it possible to generalize and say that "adding n elements requires $O(n)$ time." But this is only a specific instance of the more general rule that conditionally executed code in the main loop of a container operation is executed in amortized constant time. Both of the `addAll` bulk operations actually run in linear time, as do most, if not all, of the other bulk operations. As for the `add(Object o)` and `add(int index, Object element)` methods in an `ArrayList`, they run in constant time.

6.6.3 Logarithmic Time

The *log* in `O(log n)` and `O(n log n)` is short for logarithm. Using logarithms is like starting with the answer to an exponential problem and working backwards. For example,

$$2^5 = 32$$
$$\log_2 32 = 5$$

32 is n, or the number of elements in the container. If you know the log of n, then you know how many times the main loop in the container opertion will execute. The answer in this case is five times. It's that simple. The $_2$ subscript in $\log_2$ is usually dropped in this context. It is understood that the log base is two. Here is another example without the subscript:

$$2^{12} = 4096$$
$$\log 4096 = 12$$

In this example the main loop of a container operation will execute 12 times for a container of 4,096 elements.

There are logarithm tables just like there are multiplication tables. Table 6-4 is a logarithm table for time complexities. Notice that quadratic time or n log(n) is the product of multiplying the first two columns.

6.6.4 Linear Time

After constant time, **linear time** is the next easiest to understand. Linear means "Of, relating to, or resembling ... a line."[8] Here we think of all of the elements in a container as being in a line. Linear time is usually a for loop or iterator that executes the container operation for every element in the container. Here is an example from the core API,

```
public static void fill(List list, Object o) {
    for (ListIterator i = list.listIterator(); i.hasNext(); ) {
        i.next();
        i.set(o);
    }
}
```

Table 6-4: Logarithm Table for Time Complexities[a]

n	1+log(n)	n log(n)
1	1	1
2	2	4
4	3	12
8	4	32
16	5	80
32	6	192
64	7	448
128	8	1024
256	9	2304
512	10	5120
1,024	11	11264
2,048	12	24576
4,096	13	53248

a. One is added to the actual value of log(n) to loosely represent the root node.

---

8.   Webster's online edition (www.m-w.com/cgi-bin/dictionary).

Linear time is expressed as `O(n)`, the constant factor multiplied by the number of elements in the container. It is also expressed as "time proportional to the size of the collection" or "linear time in the map size" in the API docs for the collections framework. For example, the `contains-Value(Object key)` method is described as "linear time in the map size." It iterates over `entrySet()` until the value is found. However, in time complexities, the worst case scenario is always used. So we assume that the value is either not found or is in the very last entry searched. Thus, "time proportional to the size of the collection" or "linear time in the map size" is just a different way of saying linear time (and then hoping for the best possible results). Linear time is when container operations start to get costly. It is always better to do something in constant time or logarithmic time if possible.

6.6.5 Quadratic Time

Quadratic time is the square root of `n`. That is what *quadratic* means. Square roots answer the question: what number times itself is equal to `n`? The following `n` and the corresponding quadratic times are from the example in 6.6 Time Complexities (or Big-O Notation).

10	100
25	625
50	2500
100	10000
500	250000
1000	1000000
5000	25000000

This is the worst time complexity mentioned in the API docs for the collections framework. It is mentioned only twice. Once is a warning to programmers extending `AbstractList`. See 6.16.1.2 `AbstractList` for a discussion. The other is the following quotation from the API docs for the overloaded `shuffle` methods in the `Collections` utility class.

> This method runs in linear time for a "random access" list (which provides near-constant-time positional access). It may require quadratic time for a "sequential access" list.[9]

You want to think twice before shuffling a `LinkedList` (which is the general-purpose implementation of a sequential access list).

---

9. API docs for the overloaded `shuffle` method in the `java.util.Collections` class.

Let us examine this method up close so that you have a better idea of what quadratic time means. Here is the loop in the `shuffle(List list)` method:

```
for (int i=list.size(); i>1; i--)
    swap(list, i-1, rnd.nextInt(i));
```

The `swap` method looks like this:

```
private static void swap(List a, int i, int j) {
    Object tmp = a.get(i);
    a.set(i, a.get(j));
    a.set(j, tmp);
}
```

This loop is going to execute 52 times if I shuffle a deck of cards regardless of the `List` implementation used. In this case the difference between the linear time of an `ArrayList` and the quadratic time of a `LinkedList` are the two `get(int index)` method operations in each iteration of the loop. That is a constant time operation in a `ArrayList`, hence the `shuffle(List list)` method is what it appears to be, namely, a linear time container operation. As discussed in 6.10.1.1 `ArrayList` versus `LinkedList`, the same `get(int index)` method in a `LinkedList` runs in $O(n/2)$, or half-linear time. Thus, two invocations of the `get(int index)` method equals n. If the main loop in the shuffle operation is a linear operation invoking another linear operation, that is n times n, or quadratic time. In this case, instead of the main loop in the shuffle operation executing 2,704 times, it is the following loop in the `get(int index)` method of a `LinkedList` that must execute that many times:

```
if (index < size/2) {
    for (int i = 0; i <= index; i++)
        e = e.next;
} else {
    for (int i = size; i > index; i--)
        e = e.previous;
}
```

In this case the constant factor is a single assignment statement. Nevertheless, the equivalent code in the `get(int index)` method of a `ArrayList` is an even faster array access expression that only has to execute 52 times. That is a huge performance difference in the invocation of a single `suffle(List list)` method. That is also why a knowledge of time complexities is so important. You must understand these terms in order to intelligently discuss the relative performance of container operations.

6.7 The Equivalence Relationship and Elements

As discussed in 4.11.1 Reference Equality versus the Equivalence Relationship, an equivalence relationship in the Java programming language is expressed as `x.equals(y)`. What is the significance of equivalence relationships to the collections framework? In a word, sameness.

Two elements x and y are the same if `x.equals(y)`. It does not matter if x and y are different objects. They are the same element.

More formally, two elements, x and y, are the same if the following expression evaluates to `true`:

```
x==null ? y==null : x.equals(y)
```

The more formal definition of sameness allows for the possibility of `null` references in a container. Note that if `x==null`, `x.equals(y)` would throw a `NullPointerException` were it not for the conditional operator. This is precisely the definition of a **duplicate element** in the collections framework.

In order to help you appreciate how important equivalence relationships are to the collections framework, the following is a complete list of methods that use `x==null ? y==null : x.equals(y)` as the basis for determining if an element is in a container.

- All of the `contains(Object o)` and `containsAll(Collection c)` methods in the `Collection` interface and the `containsValue(Object o)` method in the `Map` interface
- The `add(Object o)` method in the `Set` interface
- All of the `remove(Object o)` and `removeAll(Collection c)` methods in the `Collection` interface
- The `indexOf(Object o)` and `lastIndexOf(Object o)` methods in the `List` interface

- The `equals(Object o)` method for all of the core collection interfaces including the `Map.Entry` interface as well as the `equals(Object[] a, Object[] a2)` method in the `Arrays` utility class (used to determine if two containers have the same elements or if two maps have the same values)

- Equivalence relationships are indirectly used in an implementation of the `Comparator` interface

Reference equality is seldom used in the collections framework and never to compare objects.

6.8 Duplicate Elements

Much of the terminology of the collections framework is derived from set theory in mathematics. For example, in mathematics, a set is defined as a collection of objects. The objects are called elements or members of the set. In object-oriented programming the term **elements** is preferred so as not to confuse them with the members of a class or interface.

The term *set* has a specific meaning in mathematics that is different from everyday usage such as a *set of dishes*. *Duplicate elements are not permitted in a set*. That there are no duplicate elements in a set has important consequences for the `add(Object o)` method in the `Collection` interface, which is the superinterface of both `Set` and `List`. The specification for that method reads in part

> Ensures that this collection contains the specified element ...
> Returns `true` if this collection changed as a result of the call.
> (Returns `false` if this collection does not permit duplicates and already contains the specified element.)

There are three possible results when invoking the `add(Object o)` method for a set or list.

1. If a set already contains the object, `false` is returned and the set is unchanged.
2. If a set does not contain the object, the object is added to the set and `true` is returned.
3. The object is appended to the end of a list.

Note that an invocation of the `add(Object o)` method for a list always returns `true`.

Here is an example of a set that already contains the object being added:

```java
import java.util.*;
class Test {
  public static void main(String[] args) {
      final Integer TWO = new Integer(2);
      Set set = new HashSet();
      set.add(TWO);
      set.add(TWO);
      set.add(TWO);
      set.add(TWO);
      int total = 0;
      for (Iterator itr=set.iterator(); itr.hasNext();)
          total += ((Integer)itr.next()).intValue();
      System.out.println("total = " + total);
      System.out.println(set.add(TWO));
  }
}
```

Executing this program prints

```
total = 2
false
```

Notice that the `add(Object o)` method returns `false`. In this example each instance of `Integer` added to the set has the same value, which means they are the same element using the equivalence relationship. (In this example they are actually the same object, but that is irrelevant.) Only the first `add(Object o)` method invocation actually adds an element to the set.

The whole purpose of a set is to make sure there are no duplicate elements. Only lists can have duplicate elements. For example,

```java
import java.util.*;
class Test {
  public static void main(String[] args) {
      final Integer TWO = new Integer(2);
      List list = new ArrayList();
      list.add(TWO);
      list.add(TWO);
      list.add(TWO);
      list.add(TWO);
      int total = 0;
      for (Iterator itr=list.iterator(); itr.hasNext();)
          total += ((Integer)itr.next()).intValue();
      System.out.println("total = " + total);
      System.out.println(list.add(TWO));
  }
}
```

Executing this program prints

```
total = 8
```

```
true
```

This is essentially the same program as the original but uses a `List` instead of a `Set`.

One very common trick that takes advantage of the fact that sets do not allow duplicate elements is the following:

```
list = new List(new HashSet(list)); // no dups operation for lists
```

This line of code removes all of the duplicate elements from a list.

6.8.1 Using Mutable Objects as Elements in a `Set` or Keys in a `Map`

Both the API docs and Bloch warn against using mutable objects as the elements in a set.

> Great care must be exercised if mutable objects are used as set elements. The behavior of a set is not specified if the value of an object is changed in a manner that affects equals comparisons while the object is an element in the set. A special case of this prohibition is that it is not permissible for a set to contain itself as an element.[10]

> All other things being equal, immutable types are the way to go, especially for objects that will be used as elements in `Sets`, or keys in `Maps`. These collections will break if you modify their elements or keys while they're in the collection.[11]

If a mutator method were to change the value of an instance variable used in the implementation of the `equals(Object o)` method for that class, it is possible that a set could contain duplicate elements or that a map could contain duplicate keys as a result. Note that the invoker of the mutator method may be completely oblivious to the fact that the object is an element in a set or a key in a map. The effect on the behavior of a duplicate element or key is no less devastating. It "breaks" the interface contract for a `Set` or `Map` in the worst way. This is usually not a problem for maps because strings, which are often used as keys, are immutable.

---

10. API docs for the `java.util.Set` interface.
11. Bloch, "Writing Your Own Comparable Types," *interfaces/order.html*.

6.9 The Collections Framework

The collections framework was added to the core API in the 1.2 release. It has three main parts.

- The six core collection interfaces

- Two general-purpose implementations of the `List` interface and one each of the `Set`, `Map`, `SortedSet`, and `SortedMap` interfaces. The sixth core collection interface is `Collection`, which has no general-purpose implementation because the main purpose it serves is the interoperability of the `Set` and `List` subinterfaces

- The `Collections` utility class

Your focus in studying the collections framework should be on learning how to use the six core collection interfaces discussed in the following subsections. Bloch describes their importance as follows.

> The core collection interfaces are the heart and soul of the collections framework. When you understand how to use these interfaces, you know most of what there is to know about the framework.[12]

All you need to know about the general-purpose implementations is which one to use.

The six core collection interfaces do not have a common superinterface. `Collection` and three subinterfaces are in one interface hierarchy and `Map` and one subinterface are in a separate interface hierarchy. Nevertheless, the three methods in Table 6-5 are declared in both the `Collection` and `Map` interfaces and have the same semantics.

Because these methods are shown here, they are not repeated in the API tables for the `Collection` and `Map` interfaces below.

6.9.1 Bulk Operations

A **bulk operation** is passed a `Collection` of objects. With one exception, the name of a bulk operation is the same as the corresponding non-bulk method with `All` added to the end of the method name. For example, instead of adding a single `Object` to a container as does `add(Object`

---

12. Bloch, "Introduction to the lesson on interfaces," *interfaces/index.html*.

Table 6-5: Methods for All Sets, Lists, and Maps

Method Header	Short Description
int **size**	Returns the number of elements in the target set or list, or the number of entries in the target map. In the case of a set, the number of elements in the set is the set's *cardinality*.
boolean **isEmpty**	Returns `true` if the target set or list has no elements, or the target map has no entries.

void
clear
	BULK OPERATION:
	Removes all of the elements in the target set or list, or all of the entries in the target map. Here is one possible implementation for a set or list:
	
	```\nIterator iterator = iterator();\nwhile (iterator.hasNext()) {\n iterator.next();\n iterator.remove();\n}\n```
	
	Note that the no-argument `remove()` method invoked in the `while` loop is declared in the `Iterator` interface. It removes the last element returned by the iterator. The same bulk operation in a map can be implemented as follows,
	
	```\nmap.entrySet().clear();\n```
	
	The `Set` returned by the `entrySet` method in a map is used to remove all of the entries in the map.

o), the bulk operation `addAll(Collection c)` adds a `Collection` of objects. Most bulk operations are declared in the `Collection` interface. They are generally implemented by invoking the corresponding nonbulk method in a loop.

Here is a complete list of the bulk operations in the `Collection` interface:

```
containsAll(Collection c)
addAll(Collection c)
removeAll(Collection c)
retainAll(Collection c)
clear()
```

Using `Collection` as the parameter type in bulk operations is an important example of the principle of maximum generality as discussed in 6.9.2 The Principle of Maximum Generality. Any `Set` or `List` can be passed to a bulk operation.

The result type of bulk operations varies. The result type of `clear()` and `putAll(Map t)` is `void`. The result type of `containsAll(Collection c)` is `boolean`. A return value of `true` means that the target container is a subset or sublist. The other bulk operations also have a `boolean` result type, but for a different reason. The possibility exists that invoking `addAll(Collection c)`, `removeAll(Collection c)`, and `retainAll(Collection c)` may not result in a change to the target container. In that case `false` is returned. Normally `true` is returned.

Bulk operations are closely related to set theory in mathematics, as shown in Table 6-6. Most people learned some set theory in high school when introduced to "set intersection" and "set union" through the familiar Venn diagrams in Figure 6-2. For the sake of completeness, a **symmetric set difference** is coded as follows:

```
Set answer = new HashSet(s1)
answer.addAll(s2);
Set temp = new HashSet(s1);
temp.retainAll(s2);
answer.removeAll(temp);
```

What you have in the end is a union minus the intersection (that is, all of the elements except for those in both sets).

I am not sure how valuable this information is to Java programmers, but it is now customary to mention Venn diagrams in a chapter on the collections framework. Perhaps the Venn diagram for an intersection is useful because the method name `retainAll` is not intuitive. They also help to show that *bulk operations are destructive*. In fact, three of the bulk operations have a `boolean` result type that is used to indicate if the collection was modified as a result of executing the bulk operation. Those are the `addAll(Collection c)`, `retainAll(Collection c)`, and `removeAll(Collection c)` methods.

For every destructive bulk operation, however, there is usually an easy way to make it nondestructive. For example,

```
Set union = new HashSet(s1);
union.addAll(s2);                // non-destructive union

Set intersection = new HashSet(s1);
intersection.retainAll(s2);      // non-destructive intersection
```

Table 6-6: Bulk Operations and Set Theory

Bulk Operation	Math Symbol	Definition
`containsAll(Collection c)`	$a \subset b$	A **subset** means that every element in one set is also in the other.
`addAll(Collection c)`	$a \cup b$	A **union** is all of the elements is either or both sets.
`retainAll(Collection c)`	$a \cap b$	An **intersection** is all of the elements in both sets.
`removeAll(Collection c)`	$a \therefore b$	The **asymmetric difference** is all of the elements in one set that are not in the other.
`clear()`	$\varnothing$	The **empty set**.

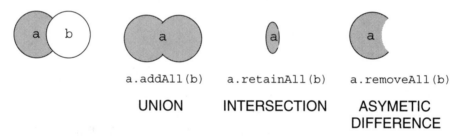

a.addAll(b)	a.retainAll(b)	a.removeAll(b)
UNION	**INTERSECTION**	**ASYMETIC DIFFERENCE**

Figure 6-2: Venn diagrams.

```
Set difference = new HashSet(s1);
difference.removeAll(s2);          // non-destructive asymmetric set difference

list1.addAll(list2);               // destructive list concatenation

List list3 = new ArrayList(list1);
list3.addAll(list2);               // non-destructive list concatenation
```

All of these nondestructive operations start by using a copy constructor.

The only bulk operation for maps is `putAll(Map t)`. The `key-Set()` and `entrySet()` methods, however, can be used to mimic bulk operations in a `Map`. For example,

```
a.entrySet().containsAll(b.entrySet()))    // submaps
a.putAll(b)                                // union
a.keySet().retainAll(b.keySet())           // intersection
a.keySet().removeAll(b.keySet())           // asymmetric difference
```

Note that the submap example uses `entrySet()`. It could just as easily use `keySet()` if you do not care about the values to which the keys map. The `keySet()`, `values()`, and `entrySet()` methods are powerful tools when used in combination with bulk operations, copy constructors, and other methods such as `equals(Object o)`.

6.9.2 The Principle of Maximum Generality

Regardless of the implementation, which may be one of the general-purpose implementations in the `java.util` package or a custom implementation, collection variables should always be declared to have one of the six core collection interface types. Here are some common examples:

```
Set set = new HashSet();
List list = new ArrayList();
Map map = new HashMap();
```

As stated by Bloch,

> This is a *strongly* recommended programming practice, as it gives you the flexibility to change implementations merely by changing the constructor. If the variables used to store a collection, or the parameters used to pass it around, are declared to be of the collection's implementation type rather than its interface type, then *all* such variables and parameters must be changed to change the collection's implementation type. Furthermore, there's no guarantee that the resulting program will work; if the program uses any nonstandard operations that are present in the original implementation type but not the new one, the program will fail.[13] Referring to collections only by their interface keeps you honest, in the sense that it prevents you from using any nonstandard operations.[14]

Inasmuch as Bloch designed and implemented the collections framework, I consider this to be a very important quotation. Elsewhere in *The Java Tutorial* he says,

> If your API contains a method that requires a collection on input, it is of paramount importance that you declare the relevant parameter type to be one of the collection *interface* types. **Never** use an implementation type, as this defeats the purpose of an interface-based collection framework, which is to allow col-

---

13. There are very few "nonstandard operations." This means methods declared in a general-purpose implementation but not in the corresponding core collection interface. These methods are summarized in Tables 6-15 and 6-20.
14. Bloch, "Basic Operations," *interfaces/set.html*.

lections to be manipulated without regard to implementation details.

Further, you should always use the least specific type that makes sense. For example, don't require a `List` or a `Set` if a `Collection` would do. It's not that you should never require a `List` or a `Set` on input; it is correct to do so if a method depends on some property of one of these interfaces. For example, many of the algorithms provided by the Java platform require a `List` on input because they depend on the fact that lists are ordered. As a general rule, however, the best types to use on input are the most general: `Collection` and `Map`.[15]

The last paragraph leads to what I call the **principle of maximum generality**, which simply means you should use `Collection` and `Map` as parameter types whenever possible. You need only look as far as the copy constructors and bulk operations in the general-purpose implementations to appreciate how important this is.

Result types are another matter altogether. *Generality* is achieved by whoever invokes the method. For example, if your method returns a `TreeMap`, whoever invokes that method is free to assign the return value to a `Map` type variable. Your job in determining the result type is to be as specific as possible (that is, to tell the user as much as you can about the class of object returned), *which is the opposite of the principle of maximum generality.*

If you follow the rule of not using general-purpose implementations as type names in variable declarations, then changing implementations is as simple as changing the class name in a single class instance creation expression. For example,

```
import java.util.*;
class Test {
  public static void main(String[] args) {
      Set quotes = new HashSet();
      quotes.add("I came, I saw, I conquered.");
      quotes.add("Come unto me, all ye that labour and are heavy laden, " +
              "and I will give you rest.");
      quotes.add("There is nothing either good or bad, " +
              "but thinking makes it so.");
      for (Iterator itr=quotes.iterator(); itr.hasNext();)
         System.out.println(itr.next());
  }
}
```

15. Bloch, "In-Parameters," *interoperability/api-design.html.*

Executing this program prints

```
I came, I saw, I conquered.
Come unto me, all ye that labour and are heavy laden, and I will give you rest.
There is nothing either good or bad, but thinking makes it so.
```

Simply by changing the implementation from `HashSet` to `TreeSet` in the class instance creation expression, the same program prints

```
Come unto me, all ye that labour and are heavy laden, and I will give you rest.
I came, I saw, I conquered
There is nothing either good or bad, but thinking makes it so.
```

The quotations will now print in alphabetical order. The ability to quickly and easily change implementations is important when working with containers. According to the original "Collections Framework Overview," this is one of the "primary advantages" of the collections framework.

> **Increases performance** by providing high-performance implementations of useful data structures and algorithms. Because the various implementations of each interface are interchangeable, programs can be easily tuned by switching implementations.[16]

For example, if you discover after the fact that you are frequently adding elements to or removing them from either the beginning or middle of an `ArrayList`, changing the implementation to a `LinkedList` is going to be critically important. See 6.10.1 Choosing a General-Purpose Implementation for a closely related discussion. See also 6.9.3.1 The Interoperability of Collection Implementations.

6.9.3 The `Collection` Interface

`Set` and `List` are the principle interfaces in the `Collection` hierarchy, as shown in Figure 6-3.

The `Collection` interface is summarized in Table 6-7. There are no general-purpose implementations of the `Collection` interface in the collections framework. *Its primary purpose is the interoperability of all set and list implementations.* Were the `Collection` interface directly implemented (most likely as an `AbstractCollection` subclass), it would be an unordered collection that allows duplicates. The name of such a col-

---

16. API docs for the 1.2 release, document entitled "Collections Framework Overview."

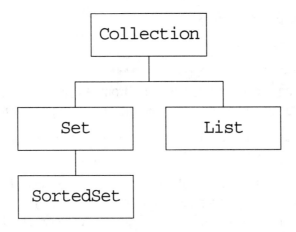

Figure 6-3: The Collection hierarchy.

Table 6-7: Methods for All Sets and Lists

Method	Short Description
`boolean` **contains** `Object o`	Returns `true` if the object is equal to one of the elements in the target collection.
`boolean` **containsAll** `Collection c`	BULK OPERATION: Returns `true` if all of the objects in `c` are equal to one of the elements in the target collection. Here is one possible implementation: ```\nIterator iterator = c.iterator();\nwhile (iterator.hasNext()) {\n if(!contains(iterator.next()))\n return false;\n}\nreturn true;\n``` The order of the elements does not matter, not even for a list. In mathematical terms, if both collections are sets, `c` is a *subset* of the `this` set.

Table 6-7: Methods for All Sets and Lists (Continued)

Method	Short Description
`boolean` **add** `Object o`	Returns `true` if the object is added to the target collection or `false` if the target set is unchanged. A target list will always return `true`. There are three possibilities. If the target collection is a set and the set does not contain an element equal to the object, it will be added and `true` returned. If the target set already contains an element equal to the object, the target set is unchanged and `false` is returned. The third possibility is that the target collection is a list, in which case the object is appended to the end of the list and `true` is always returned.

`boolean` **addAll** `Collection c`	BULK OPERATION: Adds any element in `c` that is not already an element in the target collection. Returns `true` if any elements are added or `false` if the target collection is unchanged. Here is one possible implementation for a set,
	
	```\nboolean changed = false;\nIterator iterator = c.iterator();\nwhile (iterator.hasNext()) {\n if(add(iterator.next()))\n changed = true;\n}\nreturn changed;\n```
	
	In mathematical terms, if both collections are sets, the result is a union of the two sets. If the target collection is a list the elements are appended to the end of the list *in the same order in which they are returned by the iterator*. For example,
	
	```\nboolean changed = false;\nint index = 0;\nIterator iterator = c.iterator();\nwhile (iterator.hasNext()) {\n add(index++, iterator.next());\n changed = true;\n}\nreturn changed;\n```
	
	The `add(int index, Object element)` method used in this example is unique to lists.

Table 6-7: Methods for All Sets and Lists (Continued)

Method	Short Description
boolean **remove** Object o	Removes *at most one element* from the target collection. If there is no element in the target collection equal to o, the collection is unchanged and `false` is returned. The possibility exists that a target list may contain more than one element equal to o, in which case the *first occurrence* of o is removed. *First occurrence* means the o with the smallest index value.
boolean **removeAll** Collection c	BULK OPERATION: Removes *at most one element* from the target collection for each element in c. Returns `true` if any elements are removed or `false` if the target collection is unchanged. Here is one possible implementation: ```java\nboolean changed = false;\nIterator iterator = iterator();\nwhile (iterator.hasNext()) {\n if(c.contains(iterator.next())) {\n iterator.remove();\n changed = true;\n }\n}\nreturn changed;\n``` As with the `remove(Object o)` method, there exists the possibility that a target list may contain more than one element equal to a given element in c, in which case the *first occurrence* of that element is removed. *First occurrence* means the element with the smallest index value. This method works the same for sets and lists. `AbstractList` has an somewhat more efficient implementation than what is shown here. In mathematical terms, if both collections are sets, the result is a *asymmetric set difference* of the two sets.

Table 6-7: Methods for All Sets and Lists (Continued)

Method	Short Description

boolean **retainAll** Collection c	BULK OPERATION:
	
	Removes any element in the target collections that is not equal to an element in c. Returns true if any elements are removed or false if the target collection is unchanged. Here is one possible implementation:
	
	``
	boolean changed = false;
	Iterator iterator = iterator();
	while (iterator.hasNext()) {
	    if(!c.contains(iterator.next())) {
	       iterator.remove();
	       changed = true;
	    }
	}
	return changed;
	``
	
	Except for the ! in the if statement (which is admittedly a big difference), the implementation of this method is the same as removeAll(Collection c) method. This method works the same for sets and lists. In mathematical terms, if both collections are sets the result is an *intersection* of the two sets.

Iterator **iterator**	Returns an implementation of the Iterator interface. The contract for this method in the Collection interface states that "there are no guarantees concerning the order in which the elements are returned (unless this collection is an instance of some class that provides a guarantee)."[a] The List subinterface provides such a guarantee: "Returns an iterator over the elements in this list in proper sequence."[b] Iterators are discussed in 6.13 Iterators. Note that if the target collection is a List, this method actually returns an instance of the ListIterator class.
Object[] **toArray** Object[] **toArray** Object[] a	Converts the collection to an array. The order of the elements in the array is determined by the iterator used to create the array. Hence, the elements of the array created from a target *list* are always in the same order as the list. These methods are discussed in 6.4 A Bridge over Troubled Waters (the toArray Methods).

a. API docs for the iterator() method in the java.util.Collection interface.
b. API docs for the iterator() method in the java.util.List interface.

lection is a **bag**. The idea is something like a grocery bag into which you can throw any kind of object. They are not very common.

6.9.3.1 The Interoperability of `Collection` Implementations

The term *interoperability* is an imposing one. It has a military origin, which according to *Webster's*, can be dated to 1977.[17] On the battlefield a premium is placed on weapon systems being interoperable, which means that parts from one kind of weapon system can be used to repair or replace the same part of a different weapon system. This is sometimes referred to as cannibalizing a plane or other major weapon system.

In computer science the term interoperability is best understood to mean the ability to pass data between unrelated APIs. Interoperability in the collections framework is achieved by always using one of the six core collection interface types to reference containers. Thus **interoperability** is defined as the use of common interface types to reference containers.

The standard constructors used in the collections framework are an important example of achieving interoperability through the use of common interface types. As stated in the `Collection` interface,

> All general-purpose `Collection` implementation classes (which typically implement `Collection` indirectly through one of its subinterfaces) should provide two "standard" constructors: a void (no arguments) constructor, which creates an empty collection, and a constructor with a single argument of type `Collection`, which creates a new collection with the same elements as its argument. In effect, the latter constructor allows the user to copy any collection, producing an equivalent collection of the desired implementation type. There is no way to enforce this convention (as interfaces cannot contain constructors) but all of the general-purpose `Collection` implementations in the SDK comply.[18]

The constructors that copy a collection are referred to as **copy constructors** throughout this chapter. Copy constructors are an important part of the overall design of the collections framework. They make it possible to instantiate any of the general-purpose implementations or a custom implementation of the core collection interfaces and to initialize that collection

---

17. *Webster's online edition (www.m-w.com/cgi-bin/dictionary)*.
18. API docs for the `java.util.Collection` interface.

with all the elements from another collection. In particular, a set or list can be initialized with the elements of any other set or list, regardless of the implementation details. For example,

```
import java.util.*;
class Test {
    public static void main(String[] args) {
        List names = new ArrayList();
        names.add("Peter");
        names.add("Paul");
        names.add("Mary");
        names.add("Peter");
        Set set = new HashSet(names);
        Iterator iterator = set.iterator();
        while (iterator.hasNext())
            System.out.println(iterator.next());
    }
}
```

Executing this program prints

```
Paul
Mary
Peter
```

A set does not allow duplicates, so the second Peter was not added. The copy constructors are discussed along with all the other standard constructors in 6.16.4 Standard Constructors. See also 6.9.2 The Principle of Maximum Generality.

6.9.3.2 The `Set` Interface

There are no methods for sets only. Were it not for subtle changes in the interface contract, the `Set` interface could be declared as follows:

```
package java.util;
public interface Set extends Collection { }
```

This is sometimes called *pure inheritance*. No behavior is added. There is only a specialization of the inherited behavior. For example, the API docs for the `add(Object o)` method in the `Collection` interface reads in part

> Ensures that this collection contains the specified element ....
> Returns `true` if this collection changed as a result of the call.
> (Returns `false` if this collection does not permit duplicates
> and already contains the specified element.)

The API docs for the same method in the `Set` interface states:

> Adds the specified element to this set if it is not already present
> .... More formally, adds the specified element, `o`, to this set if it

contains no element e such that `(o==null ? e==null
: o.equals(e))`. If this set already contains the specified element, the call leaves this set unchanged and returns `false`. In combination with the restriction on constructors, this ensures that sets never contain duplicate elements.

Other than the `add(Object o)` method not allowing duplicate elements, the only other methods in the `Set` interface regarded as having a substantially different interface contract are the `equals(Object o)` and `hashCode()` methods, which are discussed in 6.9.5 Housekeeping Methods for Containers. None of the other methods in the `Set` interface substantially change the interface contract as specified in the `Collection` superinterface.

6.9.3.2.1 The *SortedSet* Interface The elements in a `SortedSet` are maintained in ascending order. In order for a `SortedSet` implementation to be able to sort the elements as they are added, either the element type must implement the `Comparable` interface or a `Comparator` must be used when creating the `SortedSet`. For example,

```
import java.util.*;
class Test {
   public static void main(String[] args) {
      SortedSet set = new TreeSet();
      set.add(new Object());
      set.add(new Object());
   }
}
```

Attempting to execute this program throws a `ClassCastException` because the `Object` class does not implement the `Comparable` interface. (A method in the `TreeSet` class is trying to convert one of the elements to the `Comparable` type in order to invoke the `compareTo(Object o)` method.)

The ascending order maintained by a `SortedSet` is reflected in the following.

- Iterations are guaranteed to be in ascending order

- Arrays returned by either `toArray()` or `toArray(Object[] a)` are in ascending order

- Although not specified in the interface contract of the `toString()` method, string representations of sorted sets are also in ascending order

There are several methods unique to the `SortedSet` interface. They are summarized in Table 6-8.

6.9.3.3 The *List* Interface

Lists have two defining characteristics. The first is that there can be duplicate elements in a list. The second is that users have precise control over the order of elements in a list. *Precise control over the order of elements does not mean that lists are sorted.* To sort a list you must invoke one of

Table 6-8: Methods for Sorted Sets Only (`TreeSet`)

Method	Short Description

Comparator
comparator
	Returns `null` unless a `Comparator` was used to create the target set, in which case a reference to the `Comparator` is returned. This makes it possible to create another set with the same total ordering. For example,
	
	``
	TreeSet newSet;
	if (set.comparator() == null)
	    newSet = new TreeSet();
	else
	    newSet = new TreeSet(set.comparator());
	``

Object **first** Object **last**	Returns the first or last element in the target set. These are called the endpoints.
SortedSet **subSet** Object fromElement Object toElement	These methods return a range view of the target set (otherwise known as a subset). Range views are discussed in 6.12.3 Range Views (Sublists, Subsets, and Submaps).
SortedSet **headSet** Object toElement	
SortedSet **tailSet** Object fromElement	

the `sort` methods in the `Collections` utility class. Lists initially maintain the order in which elements are added. I refer to that as the **entry order**, which, of course, is different from the ascending or descending order of a sort. If you invoke the `add(Object o)` method, the element is appended to the end of the list. There are also the `add(int index, Object element)` and `add(int index, Collection c)` methods for adding one or more elements to the front of a list or inserting them into the middle. If you want a container to maintain the order in which elements are added, use one of the general-purpose `List` implementations else an array.

Although `ArrayList`, which is the most commonly used `List` implementation, is backed by an array, that is not necessarily true of all `List` implementations. Specifically, `LinkedList`, which is the other general-purpose implementation of the `List` interface, is not backed by an array. Nevertheless, lists use the same `int` type, zero-origin indexes, as do arrays. The only difference is the name of the exception thrown if the index is out of bounds. Table 6-9 shows all three of the run-time exceptions thrown by a bounds check in the core API. The general-purpose `List` implementations as well as all the other container classes in the collections framework throw the simpler `IndexOutOfBoundsException`. The random access methods in Table 6-10 are unique to the `List` interface. Note that the preferred terminology in the API docs is that an `index` parameter is the *specified position* in a list.

Table 6-9: Bounds Checking Exceptions

Use	Exception Name
Random access methods in the `List` interface	`IndexOutOfBoundsException`
Array access expressions	`ArrayIndexOutOfBoundsException`
Random access methods in the `String` class	`StringIndexOutOfBoundsException`

6.9.4 The `Map` Interface

A **map** is simply a table in which each row is referred to as an **entry**. There are two columns. One is the key and the other is the value to which it *maps*. For example,

Table 6-10: Random Access Methods for Lists Only[a]

Method	Short Description
Object **get** int index	Returns the element in the target list at the specified position.
Object **set** int index Object element	Replaces the element in the target list at the specified position with a reference to the element parameter. Returns a reference to the object that is replaced, as does the remove(int index) method.
void **add** int index Object element	The specification for this method is the same as the add(Object o) method in the Collection interface, only the element is inserted into the target list at the specified position instead of being appended to the end of the list. Note that the result types are also different because, unlike sets, the object will always be added to a list. Therefore, there in no need for a boolean result type.
| boolean<br>**addAll**<br>int index<br>Collection c | BULK OPERATION:<br>The specification for this method is the same as the addAll(Collection c) method in the Collection interface, only the elements are inserted into the target list starting at the specified position instead of being appended to the end of the list. Returns true if the target list is changed. The only reason why the target list would be unchanged is if c were empty. The elements are inserted into the list *in the same order in which they are returned by an iterator.* For example,<br><br>```java
boolean changed = false;
int index = 0;
Iterator iterator = c.iterator();
while (iterator.hasNext()) {
    add(index++, iterator.next());
    changed = true;
}
return changed;
```<br>In mathematical terms, if both collections are sets, the result is a union of the two sets. |
```

Table 6-10: Random Access Methods for Lists Only[a] (Continued)

Method	Short Description
Object **remove** int index	Removes the element in the target list at the specified position. As does the set(int index, Object element), returns a reference to the object that is replaced. The specification for this method is significantly different from the remove(Object o) method inherited from the Collection superinterface in that this removal operation is positional instead of based on an equivalence relationship. Unless an exception is thrown, the object is always removed. This explains the change in the result type from boolean to Object.
int **indexOf** Object o int **lastIndexOf** Object o	Returns the index of the first or last occurrence of any object in the target list equal to o or -1 if there is no such element in the list.
List **subList** int fromIndex int toIndex	This method returns a range view of the list (otherwise known as a sublist). Range views are discussed in 6.12.3 Range Views (Sublists, Subsets, and Submaps) below.
ListIterator **listIterator** ListIterator **listIterator** int index	Returns an implementation of the ListIterator interface. List iterators are discussed in 6.13.1 List Iterators.

a. All of these methods except indexOf(Object o), lastIndexOf(Object o), and the no-argument listIterator() throw IndexOutOfBoundsException.

```
import java.util.*;
class Test {
    public static void main(String[] args) {
        Map map = new HashMap((Map) System.getProperties());
        map.put("user.name", "Billy Bob Thornton");
        Iterator i = map.entrySet().iterator();
```

```
    while (i.hasNext()) {
        Map.Entry e = (Map.Entry) i.next();
        if (((String) e.getKey()).startsWith("user"))
            System.out.println(e.getKey() + "=" + e.getValue());
        else
            i.remove();
    }
  }
}
```

This program invokes the `entrySet()` method in order to view the `Map` as a set of `Map.Entry` instances. The entries in a map are a set because the `Map` interface does not allow duplicate keys. This is one of three collection views of a map, all of which are discussed in 6.12.4 Collection Views of a Map. Executing this program prints

```
user.language=en
user.name=Billy Bob Thornton
user.dir=C:\Java\classes
user.region=US
user.timezone=
user.home=C:\WINDOWS
```

This is a map of all the user system properties. I prefer to use system properties in map examples. The `Properties` class has been "retrofitted" to implement the `Map` interface, making it relatively easy to load system properties into a map. Dictionaries and telephone books are others commonly used as examples of maps, as the term is used in computer science. What all maps have in common is that you must know the key in order to find the value to which it maps. Every key maps to the value added to the map at the same time as the key when the `put(Object key, Object value)` method is invoked.

Table 6-11 is a graphical representation of the `HashMap` created in this example. This is more commonly referred to as a *table*, hence the `Hashtable` class name.

The keys in a map are a set. Therefore, the behavior of the `put(Object key, Object value)` method in a map is analogous to the `add(Object o)` method in a set. If the key already exists the value passed is used to replace the value in the map. Otherwise, a new entry is added to the map. There is a common example used to illustrate this property of maps. It is called a **frequency table**. A frequency table is one in which the value is the frequency of the key. In the following example that means how many times a word occurs in a nursery rhyme:

```
import java.util.*;
```

Table 6-11: An Example of a Map^a

Key	Value
user.language	en
user.name	Billy Bob Thornton
user.dir	C:\Java\classes
user.region	US
user.timezone	null
user.home	C:\WINDOWS

a. A map is said to be a set of key-value pairs (versus a set of elements).

```
class Test {
  public static void main(String[] args) {
    final Integer ONE = new Integer(1);
    Map map = new HashMap();
    String s = "How much wood would a woodchuck chuck, " +
               "if a woodchuck could chuck wood?";
    StringTokenizer tokenizer = new StringTokenizer(s, " \n\r,?");
    while(tokenizer.hasMoreTokens()) {
      String key = tokenizer.nextToken();
      Integer count = (Integer)map.get(key);
      if (count == null)
        count = ONE;
      else
        count = new Integer(count.intValue() + 1);
      map.put(key, count);
    }
    System.out.println(map);
  }
}
```

Executing this program prints

```
{if=1, much=1, woodchuck=2, wood=2, would=1, chuck=2, a=2, How=1, could=1}
```

The Map interface hierarchy is depicted in Figure 6-4. Table 6-12 includes all of the methods in the Map interface except the size(), isEmpty(), and clear() methods discussed in Table 6-5.

The get(Object key), put(Object key, Object value), and remove (Object key) methods in the Map interface all suffer from the same problem. They have an Object result type in which a null return value is supposed to mean that the key did not exist in the map prior to invoking the method. That only works, however, if null is not allowed as a value in the map. All of the general-purpose implementa-

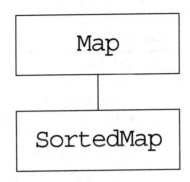

Figure 6-4: The Map interface hierarchy.

Table 6-12: Methods for Maps Only

Method	Short Description
boolean **containsKey** Object key	Returns true if the target map has a key or value equal to the object passed.
boolean **containsValue** Object value	
Object **get** Object key	If the target map has a key equal to the object passed, it returns the value to which that key maps. If there is no such key null is returned.
Object **put** Object key Object value	Did you ever wonder why they named this method *put?* It could not be named *add* because of the distinct possibility that a value may be *replaced.* In other words, *put* is a fudge. There are two possibilities: ❶ *putting* a new entry in the table in which case null is returned; and ❷ *putting* a new value in the table for a key that already exists (that is, mapping a key to a different value) in which case the replaced value is returned. In general, methods in the general collections framework always return a reference to an element that has been replaced.

Table 6-12: Methods for Maps Only

Method	Short Description
void **putAll** Map t	BULK OPERATION: Either adds all of the entries from t to the target map or replaces their values, depending on whether or not the key already exists. Here is one possible implementation: ```\nIterator iterator = t.entrySet().iterator();\nwhile (iterator.hasNext()) {\n Entry e = (Entry) iterator.next();\n put(e.getKey(), e.getValue());\n}\n```
Object **remove** Object key	Removes an entry from the target map or returns null if there is no such key.
Set **keySet** Collection **values** Set **entrySet**	These methods return a collection view of the map. Collection views are discussed in 6.12.4 Collection Views of a Map. Note that the result type of values() is Collection. That is the only example of a Collection implementation in the collections framework.

tion of the Map interface allows null as both a key and value, which means that a null return value could mean anything. Just because the general-purpose implementations allow null values, however, does not mean that there are null values in a map. If you know for sure that there are not, then a null return value means the key did not exist in the map prior to invoking the method. Otherwise, the containsKey(Object key) method must be invoked beforehand to determine if the key exists. Only then will you know how to interpret the return value from a get(Object key), put(Object key, Object value), or remove (Object key) method invocation. For example,

```
if (map.containsKey(key)) {
    map.remove(key);
    deleCount++;
} else {
    missingKeyCount++;
}
```

Once you add or remove the key it is obviously too late to invoke the `containsKey(Object key)` method, and you will not know how to interpret the return value of a `put(Object key, Object value)` or `remove (Object key)` method invocation.

6.9.4.1 The `SortedMap` Interface

The keys of a `SortedMap` are maintained in ascending order. In order for a `SortedMap` implementation to be able to sort the elements as they are added, either the element type must implement the `Comparable` interface or a `Comparator` must be used when creating the `SortedMap`. For example,

```
import java.util.*;
class Test {
    public static void main(String[] args) {
        SortedMap map = new TreeMap();
        map.put(new Object(), "value");
        map.put(new Object(), "value");
    }
}
```

Attempting to execute this program throws a `ClassCastException` because the `Object` class does not implement the `Comparable` interface. (A method in the `TreeMap` class is trying to convert one of the keys to `Comparable` in order to invoke the `compareTo(Object o)` method.)

The ascending order of a `SortedMap` is reflected in the following.

- The iterators returned by any of the collections views of a sorted map are guaranteed to be in ascending key order

- Arrays returned by either `toArray()` or `toArray(Object[] a)` are in ascending key order

- Although not specified in the interface contract of the `toString()` method, string representations of sorted maps are also in ascending key order

There are several methods unique to the `SortedSet` interface. They are summarized in Table 6-13.

Table 6-13: Methods for Sorted Maps Only (`TreeMap`)

Method	Short Description

Comparator
comparator
	Returns `null` unless a `Comparator` was used to create the target set, in which case a reference to the `Comparator` is returned. That makes it possible to create another set with the same total ordering. For example:
	
	``
	TreeMap newMap;
	if (map.comparator() == null)
	    newMap = new TreeMap();
	else
	    newMap = new TreeMap(map.comparator());
	``

Object **firstKey**	Returns the key for the first or last entry in the target map.
Object **lastKey**	
SortedSet **subSet** Object fromElement Object toElement	These methods return range views of the map (otherwise knows as submaps). Range views are discussed in 6.12.3 Range Views (Sublists, Subsets, and Submaps), below.
SortedSet **headSet** Object toElement	
SortedSet **tailSet** Object fromElement	

6.9.5 Housekeeping Methods for Containers

All of the containers in the collections framework override the following housekeeping methods:

```
public int hashCode();
public boolean equals(Object o);
public String toString();
```

The overriding implementations of these housekeeping methods in the container classes of the `java.util` package are discussed in order in the following subsections.

6.9.5.1 Hashing a Container

As might be expected, the hash code for a container is the sum of the hash codes for all of the elements. For example,

```
int hashCode = 0;
Iterator i = iterator();
while (i.hasNext()) {
    Object obj = i.next();
    hashCode = 31*hashCode + (obj==null ? 0 : obj.hashCode());
}
return hashCode;
```

Notice how this is consistent with the behavior of the `equals(Object p)` method discussed in the next section in that the `equals(Object o)` method compares all of the elements or entries in the container.

6.9.5.2 Equal Containers

There are a number of subtleties to consider when comparing containers for equality. Sets are easy. Sets are equal if they have the same elements. Lists, however, can have the same elements and not be equal because lists are the only container in which the order of elements is used in the definition of an equivalence relationship. For example,

```
import java.util.*;
class Test {
  public static void main(String[] args) {
      List ascending = new ArrayList();
      ascending.add("Alfa");
      ascending.add("Baker");
      ascending.add("Charlie");
      List descending = new ArrayList(ascending);
      Collections.reverse(descending);
      System.out.println(ascending.equals(descending));
  }
}
```

Executing this program prints `false` because these are not the same lists. Lists are not equal unless the elements are in the same order. Consequently, a set and list cannot be equal even if they contain exactly the same elements because sets are unordered.

The fact that a set and list cannot be equal also explains why some `Collection` implementations may have to use reference equality to implement the `equals(Object o)` method. The are two examples of this in the `Collections` utility class:

```
Collection unmodifiableCollection(Collection c)
Collection synchronizedCollection(Collection c)
```

The actual class of the object passed at run time is usually either `Set` or `List`. That type information is lost in the return value, which is a problem. As was just said, a set and list cannot be equal even if all of the elements are the same. To avoid the potential problem of unequal containers becoming equal as a result of the loss of some type information, the highly-specialized implementations of the `Collection` class returned by invoking one of these utility methods do not override the default implementation of the `equals(Object o)` and `hashCode()` methods in the `Object` class. This means that reference equality is used if two such views are compared.

Maps are not equal if any of the keys map to different values. It does not matter if the maps contain exactly the same keys. If all you want to know is if two maps have the same set of keys, use the `keySet()` method as follows:

```
a.keySet().equals(b.keySet())
```

If these maps have the same set of keys, `true` is returned regardless of the values to which those keys map. The same can be done with the values in a map using the `values()` method.

Finally, the `List` interface includes the following warning regarding the `equals(Object o)` and `hashCode()` methods.

> While it is permissible for lists to contain themselves as elements, extreme caution is advised: the `equals` and `hashCode` methods are no longer well defined on a such a list.[19]

6.9.5.3 The `toString()` Method in Container Classes

All sets and lists share a common `toString()` method that uses brackets to enclose a list of comma-separated elements, which are themselves converted to strings by invoking their `toString()` method. For example,

---

19. API docs for the `java.util.List` interface.

```
import java.util.*;
class Test {
  public static void main(String[] args) {
    List list = new ArrayList();
    list.add("Alfa");
    list.add("Baker");
    list.add("Charlie");
    System.out.println(list);
  }
}
```

Executing this program prints [Alfa, Baker, Charlie].

All maps share a common toString() method that is only slightly different from the toString() method for sets and lists. For example,

```
import java.util.*;
class Test {
  public static void main(String[] args) {
    Character a = new Character('a');
    Character b = new Character('b');
    Character c = new Character('c');
    Map map = new TreeMap();
    map.put(a, "Alfa");
    map.put(b, "Baker");
    map.put(c, "Charlie");
    System.out.println(map);
  }
}
```

Executing this program prints {a=Alfa, b=Baker, c=Charlie}. Notice the braces. Sets and lists have brackets instead.

6.10 General-Purpose Implementations

There are six general-purpose implementations as of this writing. There is always the possibility that the number of general-purpose implementations in the collections framework will increase in the future. For example, a multimap implementation could be added. However, the software engineers at Sun have to weigh the value of adding new general-purpose implementations against the *conceptual weight* they add to the collections framework. After all, it is a framework. Creating custom implementations based on one of the abstract implementations could not be easier. See also 6.17.1 Multimaps.

The general-purpose implementations are summarized in Table 6-14. Notice that the first word in a general-purpose implementation class name is an indication of the implementation (a Hash table, Array, or binary Tree) and the second word is the name of the interface implemented.

Table 6-14: General-Purpose Implementations

Interface	Class
Set	HashSet
List	ArrayList
	LinkedList
Map	HashMap
SortedSet	TreeSet
SortedMap	TreeMap

Except for `List` there is only one general-purpose implementation for each interface. This should tell you that there is a substantial difference between the two `List` implementations, `ArrayList` and `LinkedList`. That difference is discussed at length in 6.10.1.1 `ArrayList` versus `LinkedList`. As noted above, there are no general-purpose implementations of the `Collection` interface. The `values()` method in `HashMap` and `SortedMap` return a `Collection`, as do the `unmodifiableCollection(Collection c)` and `synchronizedCollection(Collection c)` methods in the `Collections` utility class. These are highly specialized implementations, however, and the only `Collection` implementations in the `java.util` package.

All of the general-purpose implementations have the following things in common.

- All optional operations are implemented
- `null` elements, keys, and values are allowed
- No synchronization
- Fail-fast iterators
- The `Serializable` and `Cloneable` interfaces are implemented

This regularity in the general-purpose implementations helps to compensate for the irregularity in views and brings a critically important sense of stability to the collections framework.

6.10.1 Choosing a General-Purpose Implementation

At the simplest level are what Bloch refers to as the **primary implementations** in the following quotation.

> ... one implementation is clearly the primary implementation: the one to use, all other things being equal.[20]

The primary implementations are shown in Table 6-15.

Table 6-15: Primary Implementations

Interface	Class
Set	HashSet
List	ArrayList
Map	HashMap

It is sometimes argued that it is faster to use a `HashSet` and then create a `TreeSet` when an ordered iteration is needed. For example,

```
Iterator iterator = new TreeSet(set).iterator();
```

Creating an ordered iteration of a `HashMap` using one of the collection views is not much more difficult. However, some very respectable software engineers and technical writers disagree. I will come back to the issue of `HashSet` versus `TreeSet` and `HashMap` versus `TreeMap` for ordered iterations shortly. The point here is that, if you start with a `HashSet` or `HashMap` and later want an ordered iteration, that is not a problem. Some programmers do so on purpose. The primary implementation you want to be most careful about is `ArrayList` (versus using a `LinkedList`). You can hardly go wrong with a decision to use the other two primary implementations, but not giving much thought as to which `List` implementation you should use can lead to serious performance problems.

Figures 6-5 and 6-6 comprise a two-part decision tree for choosing a container implementation. The first figure (arrays versus the collection framework) assumes that the performance of an array is more important than the guarantee of no duplicates in a set. If the element type is a reference type and performance is not critical, preference is given to the collections framework. By that I mean the decision tree suggests loading the elements

---

20. Bloch, "General Purpose Implementations," *implementations/ general.html*.

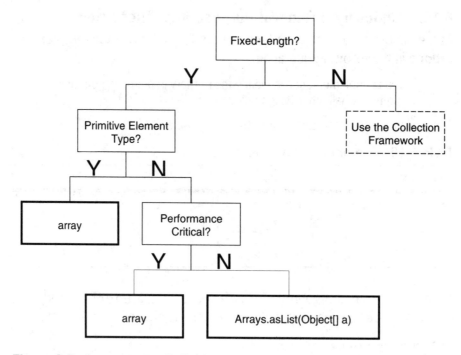

Figure 6-5: Array versus Collections Framework decision tree.

into an array but then invoking the `Arrays.asList(Object[] a)` method. The fixed-length `ArrayList` returned by that method maximizes performance while still using one of the core collection interfaces. The rationale for some of the decisions in the second figure is explained in the following subsections, particularly the questions of `ArrayList` versus `LinkedList`, `HashMap` versus `TreeMap`, and `HashSet` versus `TreeSet`.

6.10.1.1 *ArrayList versus LinkedList*

The `ArrayList` versus `LinkedList` decision is straightforward. You must always take into consideration the following:

- Random versus sequential access
- Adding elements to, or removing them from, either the beginning or middle of a list (which, however tedious, is the exact wording used throughout this chapter)

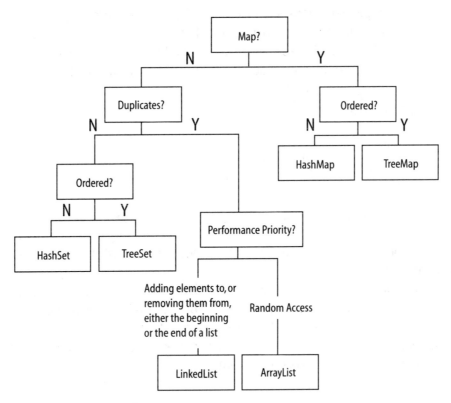

Figure 6-6: Collections Framework decision tree.

There is some overlap in these two in that some of the random access methods in the `List` interface add and remove elements. It is important to understand that the term **random access method** includes any method that uses an index to access the container. It doesn't matter if that method could be used to add elements to, or remove them from, either the beginning or middle of a list. The random access methods in the `List` interface are

```
get(int index)
set(int index, Object element)
add(int index, Object element)
addAll(int index, Collection c)
remove(int index)
```

The *Random Access* performance priority in Figure 6-6 refers to invoking these or any other random access methods that are passed an index value. (Usually, though, any discussion of "random access" refers to the random access methods in an `ArrayList`.)

`List` implementations such as `ArrayList` that store elements in an array are referred to as **random access lists**. The `get(int index)` or `set(int index, Object element)` methods are very fast because they are little more than array access expressions. For example,

```
public Object get(int index) {
    return elements[index];
}

public Object set(int index, Object element) {
    Object oldElement = elements[index];
    elements[index] = element;
    return oldElement;
}
```

These are implementations of the `get(int index)` or `set(int index, Object element)` methods in the `ArrayList` class with the bounds check removed. They are almost as fast as an array access expression.

Linked lists are either singly linked or doubly linked. The `LinkedList` class in the collections framework is a **doubly linked list**, which means that each element in the list includes a reference to the `previous` and `next` elements. The elements in a linked list are stored in data structures that are usually referred to as **nodes**. For example,

```
private static class Node {
    Object element;
    Node next
    Node previous;

    Node(Object element, Node next, Node previous) {
        this.element = element;
        this.next = next;
        this.previous = previous;
    }
}
```

Except for a change in the name of the class, this declaration is identical to the `private` nested top-level class used to implement the nodes in a `LinkedList`. The first node in a linked list is called the **head**. The last node is called the **tail**. All of the elements in the list have a `previous` and `next` node except the tail. The `next` field is `null` in the tail. The `previous` field in the head is a reference to the tail, which facilitates appending elements to the end of the list as well as backward iterations and also explains why the first and last nodes have special names. The head is the only node directly referenced by a `LinkedList`.

The nodes in a doubly linked list are shown in Figure 6-7. Notice that the `previous` field in the head points to the tail.

Linked lists are often referred to as **sequential access lists** because true random access is impossible given such an implementation. Random access implies the use of an index, say [99] for the 100th element in a list. In a linked list of several hundred elements, the only way to get to the 100th element is through the first 99. A reference to the 100th element is stored in the 100th node, and the only place a reference to the 100th node is stored is in the 99th and 101st nodes. You must always start at one end of the list and follow each of the links in order to find nth node in a linked list. This is the definition of **sequential access**. For example, a simplified implementation of the `get(int   index)` method (with the bounds check removed) looks like this:

```
public Object get(int index) {
    Node node = header;
    if (index < size/2) {
        for (int i = 0; i <= index; i++)
            node = node.next;
    } else {
        for (int i = size; i > index; i--)
            node = node.previous;
    }
    return node.element;
}
```

The worst case scenario is accessing elements in the middle of the list because the `get(int index)` method is smart enough to start from the

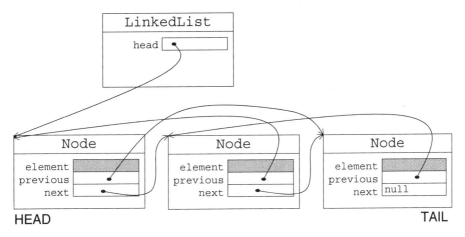

Figure 6-7: Doubly linked lists.

end of the list if the index is greater than `size/2` (as do all of the random access method implementations in `LinkedList`). That is half-linear time or `O(n/2)`, a time complexity not actually mentioned in the API docs.

Sequential access lists such as `LinkedList` are generally very slow. In *The Java Tutorial* Bloch says,

> If you frequently add elements to the beginning of the `List`, or iterate over the `List` deleting elements from its interior, you might want to consider `LinkedList`. These operations are constant time in a `LinkedList` but linear time in an `ArrayList`. But you pay a big price! Positional access is [`O(n/2)` time] in a `LinkedList` and constant time in an `ArrayList`. Furthermore, the constant factor for `LinkedList` is much worse. If you think that you want to use a `LinkedList`, measure the performance with both `LinkedList` and `ArrayList`. You may be surprised.[21]

As noted above, I use the phrase "adding elements to, or removing them from, either the beginning or middle of a list" throughout this chapter, always with the meaning that "this is what a `LinkedList` does well." It is a very carefully crafted phrase because it must exclude adding elements to, or removing them from, the end of a list (which `ArrayList` does faster than `LinkedList`). The phrase, however, is not a reference to any of the following methods for adding and removing objects in a list.[22]

```
add(Object o)
addAll(collection c)
add(int index, Object element)
addAll(int index, Collection c)
remove(Object o)
remove(int index)
removeAll(Collection c)
retainAll(Collection c)
clear()
```

These methods are very slow in a `LinkedList`. "How can that be?" you ask, "That is a complete list of all of the methods in the `List` interface that add or remove elements." True, and that is exactly the point.

---

21. Bloch, "List," *implementations/ general.html*. The API docs call this "time proportional to the index value," which can be interpreted to mean that larger index values require more time. As can be seen in the implementation of the `get(int index)` method, this is not the case. This is clearly `O(n/2)` time. Access is from either end of the list and time complexities are always worst-case scenarios.
22. An exception would be passing `add(int index, Object element)` and `remove(int index Object o)` an index of zero that would be adding an element to, or removing it from, the beginning of a list.

> A `ListIterator` must be used for constant time
> access when adding elements to, or removing them
> from, either the beginning or middle of a `LinkedList`.

This was first mentioned in reference to Table 6-2. It is somewhat counter-intuitive in that it is reasonable to assume that the following random access methods are used to "add elements to, or remove them from either the beginning or middle of a list."

```
add(int index, Object element)
addAll(int index, Collection c)
remove(int index)
```

This is not the case. As explained above, these are random access methods. With the exception of add(0, object) and remove(0), they should not be used to access a sequential access list. The correct way to add or remove elements from a sequential access list such as `LinkedList` is to use a `ListIterator`. That is the only constant-time performance you can get when adding elements to, or removing them from, either the beginning or middle of a list.

It is helpful to understand how a `LinkedList` uses an iterator to add and remove elements in constant time. Suppose that while iterating over a linked list I wanted to add an element. The following three lines of code from the add(Object o) method in `ListIterator` do the job:

```
Node newNode = new Node(element, nextNode, nextNode.previous);
newNode.previous.next = newNode;
newNode.next.previous = newNode;
```

That is a total of three assignment statements, which is a very low constant factor. Element removal using the remove() method in an iterator is also constant time with a very low constant factor. For example,

```
node.previous.next = node.next;
node.next.previous = node.previous;
```

The element being removed is stored in the node variable. Do not be confused by field access expressions such as node.previous.next. They are in the targetReference.fieldName general form, in which the targetReference is yet another field access expression. You do not normally see such constructs in an object-oriented programming language because of encapsulation (that is, private instance variables). If you have not previously studied the implementation of linked lists, take a minute to ponder what this code is doing. It is counterintuitive because `node` in effect removes itself from the list.

6.10.1.2 Element Shifting in an `ArrayList`

Removing an element from either the beginning or middle of an `Array-List` requires shifting all of the remaining elements with a higher index value. For example,

```
import java.util.*;
class Test {
  public static void main(String[] args) {
    ArrayList list = new ArrayList();
    list.add("Alfa");
    list.add("Alpha");
    list.add("Baker");
    list.add("Charlie");
    list.add("Delta");
    list.add("Echo");
    list.add("Foxtrot");
    list.remove("Alpha");
    System.out.println(list.get(1));
  }
}
```

Executing this program prints `Baker`. The elements `"Baker"` through `"Foxtrot"` were shifted to the left (collapsing the array) to close the gap between `"Alfa"` and `"Baker"`. This is referred to as **element shifting**. Element shifting is comparable to defragging your hard drive (which explains why it is a `native` method). The elements of a one-dimensional array must always be contiguous in memory, even in the Java programming language. Element shifting is depicted in Figure 6-8. Adding elements to either the beginning or middle of an `ArrayList` also requires shifting all the remaining elements with a higher index value

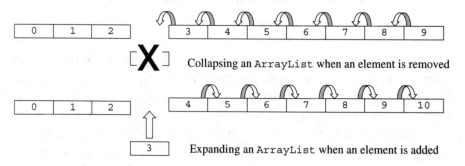

Collapsing an `ArrayList` when an element is removed

Expanding an `ArrayList` when an element is added

Figure 6-8: Element shifting in an `ArrayList`.

(expanding the array). The exact cost of adding elements to, or removing them from, either the beginning or middle of an `ArrayList` varies depending on where the element is added or removed and the size of the list. Time complexities are always worst case scenarios, however, which means that this would have to be characterized as linear time.

`System.arraycopy(Object src, int src position, Object dst, int dst position, int length)` is used to implement element shifting. This is a `native` method used throughout the core API, which implies that it is optimized in every conceivable way. Nevertheless, element shifting is very slow in comparison to adding elements to, or removing them from, either the beginning or middle of a `LinkedList`.

6.10.1.2.1 Stacks Stacks are linear data structures that are accessed from one end only. Which end does not matter. Because they are only accessed from one end, **stacks** are described as *LIFO* (*last-in, first-out*) data structures. At any given time the last object "pushed onto" the stack is going to be the first object "popped off." "Peeking" at an object on the top of a stack does not remove the object, as does "popping." Many analogies are used to help explain the design of stacks. I picture a roll of coins with one end open and the other closed.

The `Stack` class in `java.util` is a legacy implementation that subclasses the synchronized `Vector` class. `LinkedList` can also be used to implement a stack. For example,

```java
import java.util.*;
public class Stack extends LinkedList {

    public synchronized Object push(Object o) {
        add(o);
        return o;
    }
    public synchronized Object pop() {
        Object o = peek();
        remove(size() - 1);
        return o;
    }
    public synchronized Object peek() {
        int len = size();
        if (len == 0)
            throw new EmptyStackException();
        return get(len - 1);
    }
    public synchronized boolean empty() {
        return size() == 0;
    }
    public synchronized int search(Object o) {
```

```
        int i = lastIndexOf(o);
        if (i >= 0)
            return size() - i;
        return -1;
    }
}
```

Not only does this `Stack` class implement the same interface as `java.util.Stack`, the code is practically the same. The following program uses this `Stack` class:

```
public class Test {
    public static void main(String[] args) {
        Stack stack = new Stack();
        stack.push(new String("last-in"));
        stack.push(new String("first-out"));
        System.out.println("peeking = " + stack.peek());
        stack.pop();
        stack.pop();
        System.out.println(stack.isEmpty());
    }
}
```

Executing this program prints

```
peeking = first-out
true
```

6.10.1.2.2 Queues and Deques Queues are linear data structures that are accessed from both ends. The meaning of **queue** is this context is British in origin. Americans use *line* to mean the same thing. Objects are usually added to the tail of the list and removed from the head of the list, just like people *queue up* (British) or *get in line* (American).

Queues are used in computer programming for the same reason that people queue up or stand in line. The objects in a queue are waiting for some resource to become available. The usual example is a document waiting to be printed. A print queue, however, is more commonly referred to as a **printer spool**. This is an interesting term. Although not capitalized, *spool* is actually a highly contrived IBM acronym for *Simultaneous Peripheral Operation On-Line*. The mental picture is of a spool of thread on a sewing machine. The sewing machine determines when and how fast to feed the thread. The same is true of documents waiting to be printed. This is one of those terms that sounds more complicated than the actual code.

Deque (*double-ended queue*) is another IBM neologism. It is part acronym, part abbreviation, but in any case not capitalized. When using a deque, objects can be added to or removed from either end of the list.

This is simply a matter of how you choose to use a linked list. It could be a queue or deque, depending on which methods in Table 6-15 are invoked. For example,

```
LinkedList queue = new LinkedList();
```

This is the declaration of a collection variable that references a queue. It is assumed that only the `addLast(Object o)`, `getFirst()`, and `removeFirst()` methods would be invoked using the `queue` variable. If any of the other methods are invoked, especially the `addFirst(Object o)` or `removeLast()` methods, you should probably name the collection variable `deque`. In either case the implementation is a `LinkedList`.

There are no queue or deque implementations in the `java.util` package. There are a number of methods in the `LinkedList` class, however, that are specifically designed to allow a `LinkedList` to be used as either a queue or deque. These are shown in Table 6-16. These

Table 6-16: Queue and Deque Methods in `LinkedList`

Method	Short Description
void **addFirst** Object o	Adds an element to the beginning or end of the target list.
void **addLast** Object o	
Object **getFirst**	Returns the first or last element in the target list *without removing it*. This is equivalent to the `peek()` method in a stack.
Object **getLast**	
Object **removeFirst**	Removes and returns the first or last element in the target list.
Object **removeLast**	

are the only methods in the `LinkedList` class that are not also declared in the `List` interface. This means that the type of a collection variable used as a queue or deque must be `LinkedList`. This is an exception to the rule that core collection interface types should be used in the declaration of collection variables. This is not really a problem, however, because `LinkedList` is the only possible general-purpose implementation that can be used to implement a queue or deque.

6.10.1.3 *HashMap* and *Map.Entry*

As implemented in the collections framework, a hash table is an array of singly linked lists in which two or more entries with the same index value are linked together. The declaration of a hash table looks like this:

```
private Entry[] table;
```

The component type `Entry` is an implementation of the `Map.Entry` interface, which is declared in the body of the `Map` interface (and therefore does not need to be qualified). The following is a simplified implementation of the `Map.Entry` interface (without the housekeeping methods):

```
private static class Entry implements Map.Entry {
    int hashCode;
    Object key;
    Object value;
    Entry next;

    Entry(int hashCode, Object key, Object value, Entry next) {
        this.hashCode = hashCode;
        this.key = key;
        this.value = value;
        this.next = next;
    }
    public Object getKey() {
        return key;
    }
    public Object getValue() {
        return value;
    }
    public Object setValue(Object value) {
        Object oldValue = this.value;
        this.value = value;
        return oldValue;
    }
}
```

Notice that both the `hashCode` and `key` are stored in each entry.

The methods in `Map.Entry` are summarized in Table 6-17. There is only one way to get a reference to a `Map.Entry` object. That is to invoke

Table 6-17: The `Map.Entry` Interface[a]

Method	Short Description
Object **getKey**	Returns either the key or value of the target entry.
Object **getValue**	
Object **setValue** Object value	Replaces the value of the target entry with a reference to the specified object. As do all `set` methods that have a result type of `Object`, returns a reference to the object that is replaced.

a. The `equals(Object o)` and `hashCode()` methods were deliberately omitted. Their implementations are based on the key and value, as would be expected.

the `entrySet()` method in a `Map` implementation. The `Set` returned by that method is a set of `Map.Entry` objects. For example

```java
import java.util.*;
class Test {
    public static void main(String[] args) {
        HashMap map = new HashMap((Map) System.getProperties());
        Iterator i = map.entrySet().iterator();
        while (i.hasNext()) {
            Map.Entry e = (Map.Entry) i.next();
            if (((String) e.getKey()).equals("user.name")) {
                e.setValue("Billy Bob Thornton");
                System.out.println(e.getKey() + "=" + e.getValue());
            }
        }
    }
}
```

Executing this program prints

```
user.name=Billy Bob Thornton
```

For more details on how hash tables such as `HashMap` and `Hashtable` work, see 4.11.2 Understanding Hash Tables. A detailed description of hash tables had to be moved to that chapter in order to make the section on implementing the `hashCode()` method more meaningful.

6.10.1.3.1 The *Hash* in *HashSet* is a *HashMap*

While the interfaces for a `HashSet` and `HashMap` may be very different, the implementations are not. When you create a `HashSet`, what you are really creating is a `HashMap`. That much is obvious looking at the constructors and related instance variables in the `HashSet` class:

```
    private transient HashMap map;

    public HashSet() {
        map = new HashMap();
    }

    public HashSet(Collection c) {
        map = new HashMap(Math.max(c.size()*2, 11));
        addAll(c);
    }

    public HashSet(int initialCapacity, float loadFactor) {
        map = new HashMap(initialCapacity, loadFactor);
    }

    public HashSet(int initialCapacity) {
        map = new HashMap(initialCapacity);
    }
```

The value of each entry in the backing map is essentially ignored by using a dummy value, the declaration for which looks like this:

```
    private static final Object DUMMY_VALUE = new Object();
```

For example, the `add(Object o)` method for a `HashSet` is implemented as follows:

```
    public boolean add(Object o) {
        return map.put(o, DUMMY_VALUE) == null;
    }
```

Here you see an example of how `null` is used to distinguish between adding a new entry or replacing the value of a key. This works because all of the values in the backing map are DUMMY_VALUE, which is a reference to an object. In effect, `null` values are not allowed in the backing map.

As with the `add(Object o)` method, all of the other operations are delegated to the backing map. For example,

```
    public int size() {
        return map.size();
    }

    public boolean isEmpty() {
        return map.isEmpty();
    }

    public boolean contains(Object o) {
        return map.containsKey(o);
    }

    public boolean add(Object o) {
        return map.put(o, DUMMY_VALUE) == null;
    }

    public boolean remove(Object o) {
```

```
        return map.remove(o) == DUMMY_VALUE;
    }

    public void clear() {
        map.clear();
    }

    public Iterator iterator() {
        return map.keySet().iterator();
    }
}
```

This is nothing more than a *key set view of a map*, yet it would be too confusing to think of it as such. `HashSet` is a general-purpose implementation, not a view.

6.10.1.4 *TreeMap*

There are different motivations for studying the general-purpose implementations. List implementations must be studied to understand the difference between random and sequential access lists. Hash tables are studied in order to understand the constructor parameters used in performance tuning. The motivation for studying the implementation of balanced binary trees is to understand the importance of *guaranteed* logarithmic time. You must know enough about balanced binary trees to decide for yourself if guaranteed logarithmic time is fast enough to justify using a TreeMap or TreeSet when an ordered iteration is required. Some software engineers and technical writers think that logarithmic time is fast enough so that you should not hesitate to use a TreeMap or TreeSet when an ordered iteration is required. I am one of them. Others think that using a HashMap or HashSet and creating a TreeMap or TreeSet only when and if an ordered iteration is required is a performance optimization valid in at least some applications. The code for creating an ordered iterator from an unsorted HashSet is as follows:

```
Iterator iterator = new TreeSet(set).iterator();
```

That is an easy trick, but at what cost? The objective of this section is to discuss balanced binary trees so that you have a fuller understanding of logarithmic time and can make your own informed decision. Is this a valid performance optimization? That is an important question that you must answer for yourself in order to know which general-purpose implementation to use.

A **tree** is a data structure that has a root node, internal nodes, and leaf nodes. The appearance of such a data structure is that of an inverted tree with the **root node** at the top and the **leaf nodes** at the bottom. All of the other nodes are referred to as **internal nodes**.

The "Tree" in `TreeSet` and `TreeMap` is short for *binary* tree (or perhaps for *balanced* tree). A **binary tree** is a data structure in which each internal node has a **predecessor** or **parent node** and two **successor** or **child nodes**. The fields in which a reference to the successor nodes are stored are typically named `left` and `right`. That there are two such nodes explains the term *binary* tree. Here is an example of a `Node` class:

```
class Node implements Map.Entry {
    Object key;
    Object value;
    Node left = null;
    Node right = null;
    Node parent;

    Entry(Object key, Object value, Entry parent) {
        this.key = key;
        this.value = value;
        this.parent = parent;
    }

    public Object getKey() {
        return key;
    }

    public Object getValue() {
        return value;
    }

    public Object setValue(Object value) {
        Object oldValue = this.value;
        this.value = value;
        return oldValue;
    }
}
```

The housekeeping methods are omitted to simplify the `Node` class declaration. Each node represents an element in a `TreeSet` or an entry in a `TreeMap`. In a `TreeSet` nodes are strictly part of the implementation. In a `TreeMap`, however, references to nodes are returned to application programmers as instances of the `Map.Entry` interface when the `entrySet()` method is invoked. The `left` and `right` fields reference either a leaf node or an internal node. If they reference an internal node, that node is alternatively referred to as the left or right **subtree**. The definition of a **balanced binary tree** (or **balanced tree** for short) varies from one implementation to the next. The collections framework uses red-black trees for which the definition of *balanced* is that no leaf is more than twice as far from the root as any other leaf. Generally speaking, a *balanced tree* is one in which, for any given node, the left and right subtrees are close to the same size. The reason for balancing a binary search tree is to shorten the distance from the root node (which is the only node directly referenced in the `TreeMap` class) to any given leaf node. The shorter the distance to a leaf node, the less time required to access that node. The best possible access time for a perfectly balanced binary tree is logarithmic time, which explains the significance of guaranteed logarithmic time.

The distance from the root to any given leaf is important because the distance to the leaf node furthest away from the root is the worst case scenario used in time complexities. Figure 6-9 shows a red-black tree. This red-black tree has 25 nodes, which means that the time complexity is $\log(25)$, or five. Each time you stop on a node counts as one. Now start counting at one with the root node and count down to any leaf node. Is there guaranteed logarithmic time?

The important point to grasp about binary trees and logarithmic time is that as a binary tree grows *the number of nodes doubles with each increment in the time complexity.* You can see this in Table 6-3. This means that the larger the table, the more efficient logarithmic time is compared to linear time. Or you could say that as n grows, logarithmic time approaches linear time. The time-complexity graph in Figure 6-10 illustrates this point. Logarithmic time is shown as less efficient for very small n in this graph because of the additional overhead of a balanced binary tree.

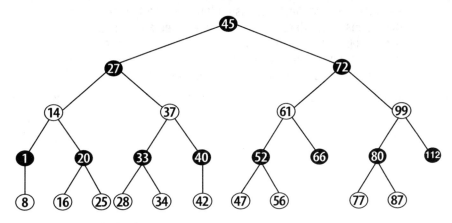

Figure 6-9: Red-black tree.

The white nodes would be red in a colored book. Colored nodes are unique to red-black trees, which is what the collections framework uses.

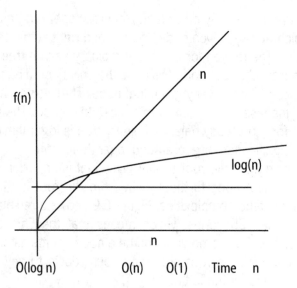

f(n)

n

log(n)

n

O(log n)　　　　O(n)　　O(1)　　Time　n

Figure 6-10: Time-complexity graph.

Now we are ready to answer the big question. Should `TreeSet` and `TreeMap` be freely used if an ordered iteration is required? More generally, is guaranteed logarithmic time fast enough that you should not have to second guess a decision to use `TreeSet` or `TreeMap`? Unfortunately, Bloch's comments on this question could be interpreted either way. In regard to `HashSet` versus `TreeSet` he says,

> It's very straightforward to decide which of these two to use. `HashSet` is much faster (constant time vs. log time for most operations), but offers no ordering guarantees. If you need to use the operations in the `SortedSet`, or in-order iteration is important to you, use `TreeSet`. Otherwise, use `HashSet`. It's a fair bet that you'll end up using `HashSet` most of the time.[23]

On the one hand he says that `HashSet` is "much faster," but on the other he says that `TreeSet` should be used if ordered iterations are required. These comments could easily be interpreted as justification for the performance optimization under consideration. In `HashMap` versus `TreeMap` he says:

---

23. Bloch, "Set," *implementations/general.html*.

> The situation for `Map` is *exactly* analogous to `Set`. If you need `SortedMap` operations or in-order `Collection`-view iteration, go for `TreeMap`; otherwise, go for `HashMap`.[24]

The "operations in the `SortedSet`" referred to in the first quotation are the methods in Table 6-8 and the "`SortedMap` operations" in the second quotation are the methods in Table 6-13. They are composed of `comparator()`, `first()` or `firstKey()`, `last()` or `lastKey()`, and the range views (subsets and submaps). If you need any of these methods, the choice must be `TreeSet` or `TreeMap`. Otherwise, the second quotation makes it clearer that Bloch considers the use of `TreeSet` or `TreeMap` when an ordered iteration requires a "straightforward" decision.

Adding an element to a `TreeSet` or putting an entry in a `TreeMap` is slower than adding an element to a `HashSet` or putting a entry in a `HashMap`. Assuming that `null` keys are not allowed, the constant factor for `HashMap` looks like this:

```
//compute index using hash code
hashCode = key.hashCode();
index = (hashCode & 0x7FFFFFFF) % hashTable.length;

//check to see if entry already in table
for (Entry e = hashTable[index] ; e != null ; e = e.next) {
    if ((e.hashCode == hashCode) && key.equals(e.key)) {
        Object old = e.value;
        e.value = value;
        return old;
    }
}

//add new entry
Entry e = new Entry(hashCode, key, value, hashTable[index]);
hashTable[index] = e;
return null;
```

The constant factor for the `put(Object key, Object value)` method in `TreeMap` looks like this:

```
Node node = root;
while (true) {
    int x = compare(key, node.key);
    if (x == 0) {
        return node.setValue(value);
    } else if (x < 0) {
        if (node.left != null) {
            node = node.left;
        } else {
            node.left = new Entry(key, value, node);
            return null;
```

---

24. Bloch, "Map," *implementations/general.html*.

```
      }
  } else {
    if (node.right != null) {
      node = node.right;
    } else {
      node.right = new Entry(key, value, node);
      balanceTree(node.right);
      return null;
    }
  }
}
```

The obvious difference is that `put(Object key, Object value)` is a constant time method in `HashMap`, whereas the same method in `TreeMap` executes a loop. The most time that loop would execute in a map with a million entries, however, is only 20 times. Keeping that in mind, I think it is fair to say the constant factor for `put(Object key, Object value)` in a `TreeMap` compares favorably with the constant time in a `HashMap`. Furthermore, I have seen a number of benchmark tests in which `TreeMap` or `TreeSet` performed reasonably well in comparison to a `HashMap` or `HashSet`. I think it would have been more prudent for Bloch to have said that a `HashSet` is *faster* than a `TreeSet` instead of *much faster*.

What about those software engineers and technical writers who suggest that using a `HashMap` or `HashSet` is faster, even when order iterations are required? Are they wrong? No. They contend that it is possible to recoup the cost of an iterator created by invoking `new TreeSet(set).iterator()` or `new TreeMap(map).iterator()`. The cost of such an iterator is linear logarithmic time because of the `addAll(Collection c)` method invocation in the `TreeSet(Collection c)` constructor or the `putAll(Map t)` method invocation in the `TreeMap(Map m)` constructor. Now consider Table 6-18 and Table 6-19. One thing we see from looking at these tables is that any activity against the faster `HashSet` or `HashMap` is like putting pennies in a penny bank towards the cost of one of those ordered iterations. Bulk operations are like putting in a handful of change. If the ordered iterations are few and the level of activity is high enough, a `HashSet` or `HashMap` is indeed the better choice. Note that you have to factor in the size of the hash table as well as the level of activity.

In the decision tree for the collections framework, I ask the question "Ordered?" If the answer is *Yes*, the decision tree branches to `TreeSet` or `TreeMap`. That is in keeping with Bloch's comments in *The Java Tuto-*

Table 6-18: `HashSet` **versus** `TreeSet` **Savings**

Method	Savings[a]

`add(Object o)`
`contains(Object o)`
`remove(Object o)`
	`O(log n)`

`addAll(Collection c)`
`containsAll(Collection c)`
`removeAll(Collection c)`[b]
	`c.size() * O(log n)`

`retainAll(Collection c)`	`O(n log n)`
`clear()`	none (`TreeMap.clear()` is actually faster)

a. Minus the constant for the comparable method in a `HashSet`.
b. Could also be `O(n log n)`.

Table 6-19: `HashMap` **versus** `TreeMap` **Savings**

Method	Savings[a]

`containsKey(Object key)`
`get(Object key)`
`put(Object key, Object value)`
`remove(Object key)`
	`O(log n)`

`putAll(Map t)`	`t.size() * O(log n)`
`containsValue(Object value)`	none
`clear()`	none (`TreeMap.clear()` is actually faster)

a. Minus the constant factor for the comparable method in a `HashMap`.

rial. Benchmark testing can help you decide if the performance optimization is worthwhile. Making the change is simple enough that you should at least consider the performance optimization in performance critical applications. Otherwise, I always opt for the simpler code to save on maintenance costs, which in this case means using a `TreeMap` or `TreeSet`.

6.10.1.4.1 The `Tree` in `TreeSet` is a `TreeMap` The relationship between `TreeSet` and `TreeMap` is comparable to that between `HashSet` and

HashMap in that there is only one implementation of a balanced binary tree in the collections framework. As with HashSet and HashMap, a TreeSet is implemented as a TreeMap that stores dummy values in all of the nodes. Again, you can see that in the TreeSet constructors and related instance variables:

```
private transient SortedMap m;  // The backing map
private transient Set keySet;   // A Set view of the SortedMap keys

public TreeSet() {
   this.m = new TreeMap();
   keySet = m.keySet();
}

public TreeSet(Comparator c) {
   this.m = new TreeMap(c);
   keySet = m.keySet();
}

public TreeSet(Collection c) {
   this.m = new TreeMap();
   keySet = m.keySet();
   addAll(c);
}

public TreeSet(SortedSet s) {
   this(s.comparator());
   addAll(s);
}
```

The value of each entry in the backing map is ignored by using a dummy value, the declaration for which looks like this:

```
private static final Object DUMMY_VALUE = new Object();
```

For example, the add(Object o) method for a TreeSet is implemented as follows:

```
public boolean add(Object o) {
   return map.put(o, DUMMY_VALUE) == null;
}
```

Here you see how null is used to distinguish between adding a new entry or replacing the value of a key. This works because all of the values in the backing map are DUMMY_VALUE, which is a reference to an object. In effect, null is not allowed as a value in the backing map.

As with the add(Object o) method, all the other operations are delegated to the backing map. For example,

```
public Iterator iterator() {
   return keySet.iterator();
}
```

```java
public int size() {
    return map.size();
}

public boolean isEmpty() {
    return map.isEmpty();
}

public boolean contains(Object o) {
    return map.containsKey(o);
}

public boolean remove(Object o) {
    return map.remove(o)==DUMMY_VALUE;
}

public void clear() {
    map.clear();
}

public boolean addAll(Collection c) {
    return super.addAll(c);
}

public SortedSet subSet(Object fromElement, Object toElement) {
    return new TreeSet(map.subMap(fromElement, toElement));
}

public SortedSet headSet(Object toElement) {
    return new TreeSet(map.headMap(toElement));
}

public SortedSet tailSet(Object fromElement) {
    return new TreeSet(map.tailMap(fromElement));
}

public Comparator comparator() {
    return map.comparator();
}

public Object first() {
    return map.firstKey();
}

public Object last() {
    return map.lastKey();
}
```

This is nothing more than a *key set view of a sorted map*, yet it would be too confusing to think of it as such. `TreeSet` is a general-purpose implementation, not a view.

6.10.2 Performance Tuning the General-Purpose Implementations

This section is about performance tuning. Mostly that means discussing nonstandard constructors. The `LinkedList`, `TreeSet`, and `TreeMap` class only have standard constructors, which are discussed in 6.16.4 Standard Constructors. They cannot be performance tuned. Table 6-20 lists the nonstandard, performance-tuning constructors. These performance tuning constructors are the subject of the following subsections.

There is one rule that applies not only to `ArrayList`, `HashMap`, and `HashSet`, but also to `StringBuffer` and other character-based containers.

Unless the container you are constructing is very small, you should always specify the initial capacity of a variable-length (or resizable) container.

Doing so is the easiest performance optimization you will ever code. If you do not specify an initial capacity, the container classes in the `java.util` package use a **default initial capacity** that is not part of the interface contract and therefore subject to change. The default initial capacity of an `ArrayList` is 10. For a `HashMap` or `HashSet`, the default initial capacity is 11. For very small lists or hash tables such as those used in the examples in this book, specifying an initial capacity is not necessary. Otherwise, you should always specify the initial capacity of an `ArrayList`, `HashMap`, or `HashSet`.

Table 6-20: Nonstandard, Performance-Tuning Constructors

General Purpose Implementation	Initial Capacity	Load Factor
`ArrayList`	`ArrayList` `int initialCapacity`	

`HashSet`	`HashSet`
	`int initialCapacity`
		`HashSet`
		`int initialCapacity`
		`float loadFactor`

`HashMap`	`HashMap`
	`int initialCapacity`
		`HashMap`
		`int initialCapacity`
		`float loadFactor`

6.10.2.1 Performance Tuning an *ArrayList*

There are two performance-tuning methods in the `ArrayList` class. These methods are summarized in Table 6-21. If you are playing by the rules and using core interface types everywhere, invoking these methods will require casting the target reference. For example,

```
static int trimToSize(List list) {
    if (list instanceof ArrayList) {
        ((ArrayList)list).trimToSize();
    }
    return list.size();
}

static void ensureCapacity(List list, int minimumCapacity) {
    if (list instanceof ArrayList) {
        ((ArrayList)list).ensureCapacity(minimumCapacity);
    }
}
```

These utility methods make it possible to performance tune any list. If the list is not an `ArrayList` no harm is done.

Table 6-21: Special Performance-Tuning Methods in `ArrayList`

Method	Short Description
void **ensureCapacity** int minCapacity	The size of the backing array will be at least `minCapacity` after invoking this method.
void **trimToSize**	Minimizes the storage requirements for an `ArrayList` by getting rid of any excess capacity. The size and the capacity of the array will be the same after invoking this method.

The `trimToSize()` method should only be used for lists that have considerably shrunk since the were originally allocated. Unlike the excess capacity in a hash table which adversely impacts iterators, the excess capacity in an `ArrayList` only wastes memory. If you want to improve the performance of an `ArrayList` by removing excess capacity, either use an array instead or do something like the following:

```
List list = Arrays.asList(list.toArray());
```

This is an expensive operation but creates a fixed-length `ArrayList` that out-performs the general-purpose `ArrayList` implementation. The `Arrays.asList(Object[] a)` method is discussed in 6.10.1 Choosing a General-Purpose Implementation.

The capacity of an `ArrayList` is increased by invoking the `ensureCapacity(int minimumCapacity)` method, which encapsulates the growth policy of an `ArrayList`. The growth policy is not part of the interface contract and is therefore subject to change. As of this writing, the size of the backing array is set to the `minimumCapacity` argument or increased by 150 percent + 1, whichever is greater.

The `ensureCapacity(int minimumCapacity)` method should be invoked before adding a lot of elements one at a time. In order to execute the following `Test` program, I saved `java.util.Array` to my `C:\Java\classes` development directory, replaced the `package` statement with `import java.util.*`, and added some diagnostic messages that make it very easy for you to see what is happening. These are the only changes I made, so what you are seeing here is exactly what `java.util.ArrayList` does. The `Test` program uses the default capacity `ArrayList()` constructor and then one that specifies an exact initial capacity.

```java
import java.util.*;
class Test {
    public static void main(String[] args) {
        List list;
        System.out.println();
        System.out.println("ArrayList list = new ArrayList()");
        System.out.println("--------------------------------");
        list = new ArrayList();
        load(list);

        System.out.println();
        System.out.println("ArrayList list = new ArrayList(100)");
        System.out.println("-----------------------------------");
        list = new ArrayList(100);
        load(list);
    }
    static void load(List list) {
        for(int i=0; i<100; i++)
            list.add(new Integer(i));
    }
}
```

Executing this program prints

```
ArrayList list = new ArrayList()
--------------------------------
```

```
ensureCapacity(11);
new Object[16];
copying elements from the old backing array...
ensureCapacity(17);
new Object[25];
copying elements from the old backing array...
ensureCapacity(26);
new Object[38];
copying elements from the old backing array...
ensureCapacity(39);
new Object[58];
copying elements from the old backing array...
ensureCapacity(59);
new Object[88];
copying elements from the old backing array...
ensureCapacity(89);
new Object[133];
copying elements from the old backing array...

ArrayList list = new ArrayList(100)
```

Now you can clearly see how utterly wasteful it is not to set the initial capacity for any but the smallest `ArrayList`.

You do not need to invoke the `ensureCapacity(int minimum-Capacity)` method before a bulk operation. The bulk methods invoke `ensureCapacity(int minimumCapacity)` using the size of the target list plus the size of the `Collection` passed as the `minimum-Capacity` argument. On the other hand, it would be more efficient to invoke `ensureCapacity(int minimumCapacity)` yourself before repeated invocations of a bulk operation, perhaps in a loop.

There is an alternative means of enlarging the size of an `ArrayList` using dummy elements as placeholders. For example,

```
list.addAll(Collections.nCopies(1000, null);
```

This is not the same as invoking `ensureCapacity(int minCapac-ity)`, but has the advantage of working for all lists without the use of a cast operator. See 6.15.7 Convenience Implementations for a discussion of the `Collections.nCopies(int n, Object o)` method.

6.10.2.2 Performance Tuning a `HashMap` or `HashSet`

Remember, `HashSet` is so called because the elements are stored in a `HashMap` that uses dummy values. The performance-tuning parameters discussed in this section are passed through as is to the backing `Hash-Map`. There are three goals when performance tuning a hash table:

1. *Access Times:* The number of hash collision that are a consequence of the table size (versus a poorly implemented hash algorithm) must be kept to a bare minimum. The `initialCapacity` argument must be at least greater than the number of entries.

2. *Efficient Iterations:* The capacity of the hash table must be minimized in order that iterations do not have to constantly iterate over empty buckets. The `initialCapacity` argument must be kept to a minimum.

3. *Predictable Behavior:* Rehashing should be the consequence of an unexpected increase in the number of entries.

Achieving all three of these goals in a given hash table is a delicate balancing act. Fortunately there is a standard formula that can be used. Before discussing that formula, there are a couple of performance related details about hash tables you must know.

The `put(Object key, Object value)` method is responsible for rehashing. It computes a threshold by multiplying the capacity of the map (either the initial capacity or the capacity after a previous rehashing) times the number of entries in the map. Once the threshold is passed the map is rehashed. Rehashing involves first allocating a new array, the capacity of which is twice the capacity of the previous hash table plus one. Next, the map entries must be moved from the old hash table to the new one. However, the entries cannot be copied to the same bucket in the new hash table because the capacity of the hash table is used in computing the index value of an entry (or the *bucket* in which the entry is stored). A larger hash table will result in a different index value for any given entry, which means that the index value for each of the entries must be recomputed before moving the entry to the new hash table. That's why it's called **rehashing**.

One of the most important details to understand when performance tuning a `HashMap` or `HashSet` is that *excess capacity in hash tables is bad for iterators.* The `HashSet` or `HashMap` iterators iterate over all the nodes in a map, not just over those for which there is an entry. Look back at Figure 4-13 and you will see that several of the buckets are empty (shown as `null` entries in the figire). An iterator doesn't know which buckets are empty and so must iterate over the entire collection view of a map in order to find all of the entries. As stated in the API docs for the `HashMap` class,

Iteration over collection views requires time proportional to the "capacity" of the HashMap instance (the number of buckets) plus its size (the number of key-value mappings). Thus, it's very important not to set the initial capacity too high (or the load factor too low) if iteration performance is important.[25]

The phrase "plus its size (the number of key-value mappings)" would read better if it said *plus any additional entries in collision lists (that is, buckets with more than one entry)*.

Access times are improved by increasing the capacity of a hash table because there are usually less hash collisions in larger hash tables. See 4.11.2.1 Hash Collisions for an example of this. Exactly how much excess capacity is required in this regard depends on the hash algorithm. For example, the Character class requires no excess capaicity in this regard because the hash code is the same as the character code, and therefore is distribution of the entires in a hash table is perfectly even. Such classes are the exception though.

What is the standard excess capacity used in the HashMap class (and therefore also in HashSet)? When the HashMap class rehashes a table, it doubles the current size of the map and adds one. Note also that the initial capacity of a set created using the HashSet(Collection c) copy constructor is c.size()*2 + 1 and the initial capacity of a map using the HashMap(Map t) copy constructor is t.size()*2 + 1. Why always add one? Two times anything is a even number and it is generally thought that you should set the capacity of a hash table to a prime number or, failing that, to an odd number. Bloch downplays the importance of this, however, in *The Java Tutorial*.

> If you accept the default load factor but you do want to specify an initial capacity, pick a number that's about twice the size that you expect the Set to grow to. If your guess is way off, it may have to grow or you may waste a bit of space, but either way it's no big problem. If you know a prime number of about the right size, use it. If not, use an odd number. Or use an even number. It doesn't really matter much; these things might make the Hash-Set perform a wee bit better, but nothing to write home about.[26]

---

25. API docs for the java.util.HashMap class.

26. Bloch, "Set," *implementations/general.html*

Note that the default size of a `HashSet` or `HashMap` is a prime number (eleven). The `HashCollisions` program in 4.11.2.1 Hash Collisions has a `prime(int n)` utility method that returns the closest prime for a given `int`. You can use that when allocating a `HashSet` or `HashMap`. Just pass the `prime(int n)` method a number twice the expected size of the map or set and let it do the rest for you.

The other performance-tuning parameter for `HashMap` and `HashSet` is the **load factor**. Load factors are usually less than `1.0f` (the `f` suffix is necessary because the parameter type for the load factor is `float`), which is interpreted as a percentage of the total capacity. For example, the default load factor is `0.75f`. This means the default behavior of hash tables in the core API is to rehash at 75 percent of the total capacity. A `HashMap` or `HashSet` with a capacity to hold up to 100 elements would be rehashed before or after the the 75th entry was added.

There is almost universal agreement that `0.75f` is a good default load factor for hash tables, but only when using two times the expected size of the hash table as the initial capacity. The standard formula used to performance tune hash tables is

---

Use the first prime number greater than or equal to two times the expected size of the hash table and the set the load factor to `0.75f`.

As an example of what can go wrong if you get do not understand these performance tuning parameters, suppose you want to load 100 entries into a hash table (either a `HashMap` or `HashSet`). You happen to know that the hash algorithm is one like the `Character` class so you set the initial capacity to 100, but forget to set the load factor also.

In order to execute the following `Test` program, I saved `java.util.HashMap` to my `C:\Java\classes` development directory, replaced the `package` statement with `import java.util.*`, and added some diagnostic messages that make it very easy for you to see what is happening. These are the only changes I made, so what you are seeing here is exactly what `java.util.HashMap` does. The `Test` program uses three possible class instance creation expressions for the `HashMap` class.

```
import java.util.*;
```

```
class Test {
    public static void main(String[] args) {
        Map map;
        System.out.println();
        System.out.println("HashMap map = new HashMap()");
        System.out.println("-------------------------");
        map = new HashMap();
        load(map);

        System.out.println();
        System.out.println("HashMap map = new HashMap(100, .99f)");
        System.out.println("-----------------------------------");
        map = new HashMap(100, .99f);
        load(map);

        System.out.println();
        System.out.println("HashMap map = new HashMap(100, 1.0f)");
        System.out.println("-----------------------------------");
        map = new HashMap(100, 1.0f);
        load(map);
    }
    static void load(Map map) {
        final String DUMMY_VALUE = "";
        for(int i=0; i<100; i++)
            map.put(new Integer(i), DUMMY_VALUE);
    }
}
```

Executing this program prints

```
HashMap map = new HashMap()
-------------------------
new HashMap(11, 0.75)
threshold = 8
rehashing ...
new HashMap(23, 0.75)
threshold = 17
rehashing ...
new HashMap(47, 0.75)
threshold = 35
rehashing ...
new HashMap(95, 0.75)
threshold = 71
rehashing ...
new HashMap(191, 0.75)
threshold = 143

HashMap map = new HashMap(100, .99f)
-----------------------------------
new HashMap(100, 0.99)
threshold = 99
rehashing ...
new HashMap(201, 0.99)
threshold = 198

HashMap map = new HashMap(100, 1.0f)
-----------------------------------
new HashMap(100, 1.0)
threshold = 100
```

Now you can clearly see how utterly wasteful it is not to set the load factor to `1.0f` when using an exact initial size.

Load factors greater than `1.0f` are unusual. They are used to make sure that hash tables are not rehashed. The price of using load factors greater than `1.0f` is a performance degradation that gets increasingly worse as the normal capacity of the table is exceeded.

6.11 Special-Purpose Implementations

As of this writing there is only one **special-purpose implementation** in the collection framework. That is the `WeakHashMap` added in the 1.3 release.

6.11.1 `WeakHashMap`

`WeakHashMap` is a special-purpose implementation of the `Map` interface added to the collections framework in the 1.3 release. It is essentially a `HashMap` in which the type of the keys is `WeakKey` instead of `Object`. `WeakKey` is a `private` nested top-level class that extends `WeakReference`. When the key is no longer referenced outside of the `Weak-HashMap`, the entry is automatically removed from the map by the garbage collector. The utility of `WeakHashMap` is explained as follows.

> Using `WeakHashMap` is beneficial for maintaining registry-like data structures, where the utility of an entry vanishes when its key is no longer reachable by any thread.[27]

Read the API docs to learn more about `WeakHashMap` class. They are very detailed.

6.12 Views

A **view** is a container that is returned by invoking a **view method** in the collections framework. If you count them based on their method names (that is, overloaded view methods count as 1), there are 23 views. The

---

27. JDK 1.1 release documentation,"Annotated Outline of Collections Framework."

result type of the method invoked determines the **view type**. *View types are always one of the six core collection interface types.* There is no exception to this rule.

There are five general categories of views:

- *Synchronized views* are thread safe. Synchronized views take the place of fail-safe iterators in a multithreaded application

- *Unmodifiable views* are read-only. This use of the terms *modifiable* and *unmodifiable* is at first bothersome to some programmers familiar with the concept of *mutable* and *immutable* objects. These are not just different terms for referring to mutable and immutable objects. There is indeed a difference, which is explained in 6.12.2 Unmodifiable Views

- *Range views of lists, sorted sets, and sorted maps* are more commonly referred to as sublists, subsets, and submaps

- *Collection views of maps,* the primary use of which is to iterate over the keys and values in a map. There is no `iterator` method in the `Map` interface. You must first invoke the `key-Set()`, `values()`, or `entrySet()` method to return a collection view of the map and then use that to invoke the `iterator()` method

- *List views of arrays* are fixed length. They allow you to maximize performance while still using one of the core collection interfaces

Each of these categories is discussed in order in the following subsections.

Views are highly-specialized implementations of one of the core collection interfaces. They are instances of `private` or package-private nested top-level classes, `private` member classes, anonymous classes, or helper classes (depending on complexity of the implementation), the declaration for which can be found in the same compilation unit as the corresponding view method. There are as many as 18 such classes. They are never mentioned in the API docs because they are not `public` classes. Nevertheless, these classes are instructive in that they are examples of custom implementations. For this reason tables in the following subsections include a column labeled *implementation details* that will tell you about the class that implements the view.

You will often hear the term *backed by* in discussions of the collections framework. Most of the time, when your read or hear about a container being backed by another container, the subject of that discussion is views. Views are themselves containers in that they always implement one of the six core collection interface types, but they are also said to be *backed by* another container. These highly specialized implementations of the core collection interfaces are sophisticated wrapper classes that *view* the container in which the elements, entries, keys, or values are actually stored as one of the following:

- Unmodifiable
- Synchronized
- A sublist, subset, or submap
- A collection (view of a map)
- A list (view of an array)

(This list corresponds to the five general categories of views above.) Bloch refers to only unmodifiable and synchronized views as *wrapper implementations*. There is what I consider to be a peculiar dichotomy in the collections framework in this regard. Only synchronized and unmodifiable views are described as wrapper implementations when, in fact, all views are wrappers.

The defining characteristic of a view is that the elements, entries, keys, or values are stored in a different container.

That is what you need to remember. The container in which the elements, entries, keys, or values are actually stored is called the **backing container**. A backing container may be more specifically referred to as a backing array, backing set, backing list, backing map, etc. The view wraps the backing container in which the elements, entries, keys, or values are actually stored. In that sense all views are wrapper implementations.

What makes the synchronized and unmodifiable views different is that they are also examples of the Decorator design pattern, and as such are comparable to stream decorators (or filters) in the `java.io` package. They are often referred to as *collection decorators*. A decorator is basically a wrapper that adds functionality. What decorators have in common with views is that they delegate to an instance of the class that is being decorated. *Likewise, all views delegate to the backing container.* I choose not to emphasize the fact that synchronized and unmodifiable views are examples of the Decorator design pattern, however, because doing so only detracts from the commonality of all views.

If the view method is one of a group of methods in either the `Collections` or `Arrays` utility class, the backing container is always the container passed to the utility method. Otherwise, the view method is an instance method and the backing container is the target object. This definition of *backing container* as the container in which the elements, entries, keys, or values are actually stored is extended to include the following.

- Iterators are sometimes said to be backed by the container over which they iterate

- Three of the general-purpose implementations are backed by other containers. An `ArrayList` is backed by an array, a `HashSet` is backed by a `HashMap`, and a `TreeSet` is backed by as `TreeMap`

These are nonview containers backed by other containers. They are not thought of as views or wrapper classes. They are just implemented in such a way that the elements or entries are stored in another type of container.

There is one universal truth for all views.

Any change in the view is reflected in the backing container and vice versa.

For example,

```
import java.util.*;
class Test {
    public static void main(String[] args) {
        String[] backingArray = {"", "and", ""};
        List list = Arrays.asList(backingArray);

        backingArray[0] = "before";
        list.set(2, "after");

        for(int i=0; i<backingArray.length; i++)
            System.out.print(backingArray[i] + " ");
        System.out.println();
        Iterator i = list.iterator();
```

```
            while (i.hasNext())
                System.out.print(i.next() + " ");
        }
    }
```

Executing this program prints

```
before and after
before and after
```

This program shows that changes to the list view are reflected in the backing array and vice versa.

That changes in the view are reflected in the backing container and vice versa is often expressed in the API docs as *writing through, reading through,* or *passing operations through* (*through* being the operative word). In at least one case the API docs say that an iterator *writes through* to the backing container. Here is a partial implementation of the class that implements a list view of an array *reading through* to the backing array:

```
private Object[] array;

public Object get(int index) {
    return array[index];
}
```

The `get(int index)` method uses the index to access the array. This is an example of "viewing" the container in which the elements are actually stored. In this example an array is viewed as an `ArrayList`. All views are more or less implemented like this.

Studying the implementation of a view, especially the synchronized and unmodifiable views, goes a long way towards demystifying the term *view*. To that end I include as examples possible implementations of three views. The purpose here is twofold. The first is to show how simple views are. The second is to show that all views have one thing in common. *They delegate to the backing container in which the elements are actually stored.*

I start with the unmodifiable views. The example is of the package-private `UnmodifiableCollection` class in the `Collections` utility class, an instance of which is returned when the `unmodifiableCollection(Collection c)` method is invoked:

```
static class UnmodifiableCollection
            implements Collection, java.io.Serializable {

    Collection modifiable;
    UnmodifiableCollection(Collection modifiable) {
        this.modifiable = modifiable;
    }
```

```
//DELEGATED RESPONSIBILITIES
public int size() { return modifiable.size(); }
public boolean isEmpty() { return modifiable.isEmpty(); }
public boolean contains(Object o) { return modifiable.contains(o); }
public Object[] toArray()  { return modifiable.toArray(); }
public Object[] toArray(Object[] a) { return modifiable.toArray(a); }
public boolean containsAll(Collection c) {
    return modifiable.containsAll(c);
}

public Iterator iterator() {
    return new Iterator() {
            Iterator i = modifiable.iterator();
            public boolean hasNext() { return i.hasNext();}
            public Object next()  { return i.next(); }
            public void remove() { throw unsupported; }
    };
}

private static UnsupportedOperationException unsupported =
            new UnsupportedOperationException();

//UNSUPPORTED OPERATIONS
public boolean add(Object o){ throw unsupported; }
public boolean remove(Object o) { throw unsupported; }
public boolean addAll(Collection c) { throw unsupported; }
public boolean removeAll(Collection c) { throw unsupported; }
public boolean retainAll(Collection c) { throw unsupported; }
public void clear() { throw unsupported; }
}
```

(Notice that even the iterator is delegated. The unmodifiable container iterator is iterating over an iterator.) What makes this implementation unmodifiable is that all of the modification methods including the `remove()` method in an `Iterator` (or the `add(Object o)`, `remove` or `set(Object o)` methods in a `ListIterator`) unconditionally throw an `UnsupportedOperationException`.

The synchronization decorators are very similar. Instead of throwing an `UnsupportedOperationException`, they change all of the method invocation expressions that delegate responsibilities into `synchronized` statements. For example,

```
import java.util.*;
class SynchronizedCollection implements Collection, java.io.Serializable {

    Collection unsynchronized;
    SynchronizedCollection(Collection unsynchronized) {
        this.unsynchronized = unsynchronized;
    }

    public synchronized int size() {
        return unsynchronized.size();
    }
```

```
        public synchronized boolean isEmpty() {
            return unsynchronized.isEmpty();
        }
        public synchronized boolean add(Object o) {
            return unsynchronized.add(o);
        }
        public synchronized boolean remove(Object o) {
            return unsynchronized.remove(o);
        }
        public synchronized boolean contains(Object o) {
            return unsynchronized.contains(o);
        }
        public synchronized Object[] toArray() {
            return unsynchronized.toArray();
        }
        public synchronized Object[] toArray(Object[] a) {
            return unsynchronized.toArray(a);
        }

        //THE ITERATOR IS N-O-T SYNCHRONIZED
        public Iterator iterator() {
            return unsynchronized.iterator();
        }

        public synchronized boolean containsAll(Collection c) {
            return unsynchronized.containsAll(c);
        }
        public synchronized boolean addAll(Collection c) {
            return unsynchronized.addAll(c);
        }
        public synchronized boolean removeAll(Collection c) {
            return unsynchronized.removeAll(c);
        }
        public synchronized boolean retainAll(Collection c) {
            return unsynchronized.retainAll(c);
        }
        public synchronized void clear() {
            unsynchronized.clear();
        }
    }
```

As with unmodifiable views, this is a straightforward solution to the problem.[28]

The next thing I want to discuss about synchronized and unmodifiable views is best remembered as *every view after their kind* (which alludes to similar quotations from *Genesis* in the Bible). An iterator created using an unmodifiable view cannot be used to modify the backing collection because all of the modification methods in the iterator throw an Unsup-

---

28. This implementation uses `synchronized` methods. The actual implementations in the collections framework use `synchronized` statements because the mutex for an empty collection or `Vector` is not the synchronized view. Both of these, however, are exceptional cases, and this implementation is much easier to read.

`portedOperationException`. For example, a list iterator created by an unmodifiable view would look like this:

```
public ListIterator listIterator() {
    return new ListIterator() {
        ListIterator i = list.listIterator();
        public boolean hasNext()     {return i.hasNext();}
        public Object next()         {return i.next();}
        public boolean hasPrevious() {return i.hasPrevious();}
        public Object previous()     {return i.previous();}
        public int nextIndex()       {return i.nextIndex();}
        public int previousIndex()   {return i.previousIndex();}
        //UNSUPPORTTED OPERATIONS
        public void remove() {
            throw new UnsupportedOperationException();
        }
        public void set(Object o) {
            throw new UnsupportedOperationException();
        }
        public void add(Object o) {
            throw new UnsupportedOperationException();
        }
    };
}
```

Likewise, all of the methods in an iterator created using a synchronized view are synchronized.

If an unmodifiable view is used to create yet another view of the same collection, the other view is wrapped in an unmodifiable view. For example, here is an implementation of the `subList(int fromIndex, int toIndex)` method in the same `UnmodifiableList` class:

```
public List subList(int fromIndex, int toIndex) {
    return new UnmodifiableList(list.subList(fromIndex, toIndex));
}
```

The same method in a `SynchronizedList` implementation would look like this:

```
public synchronized List subList(int fromIndex, int toIndex) {
    return new SynchronizedList(list.subList(fromIndex, toIndex));
}
```

Every view after their kind is, of course, a critically important part of the overall design of the views in the collections framework.

The `get(Object o)` method from a list view of an array was used above as an example of delegating to a backing container. That view is the last of the three view implementations discussed in this chapter. The main purpose here is to show that other views are not substantially different from the synchronized and unmodifiable views. This is a `private` nested top-level class declared in the `Arrays` utility class, an instance of which is returned when the `Arrays.asList(Object[] a)` method is invoked. The name of this class happens to be `ArrayList`, but is not to be confused with `java.util.ArrayList`. (The names of classes that implement views are of no real consequence. They are what I refer to as implementation only classes, which means that you never see them except as an instance of a superclass or an interface. In this case you never see the classes that implement views except as instances of one of the six core collection interface types.)

```java
private static class ArrayList extends AbstractList
                         implements java.io.Serializable {
    private Object[] array;
    ArrayList(Object[] array) {
        if (array==null)
            throw new NullPointerException();
        this.array = array;
    }
    public int size() { return array.length; }
    public Object[] toArray() { return (Object[]) array.clone(); }
    public Object get(int index) { return array[index]; }
    public Object set(int index, Object element) {
        Object oldElement = array[index];
        array[index] = element;
        return oldElement;
    }
    public int indexOf(Object o) {
        if (o==null) {
            for (int i=0; i<array.length; i++)
                if (array[i]==null)
            return i;
        } else {
            for (int i=0; i<array.length; i++)
            if (o.equals(array[i]))
            return i;
        }
        return -1;
    }
    public boolean contains(Object o) {
        return indexOf(o) != -1;
    }
}
```

That is the last of the three implementations. Now you should have a good idea of what the term *view* means.

The remainder of this section discusses what I refer to as the relative *stability* of a view. Some views should be used as soon as they are created, much like iterators. Others can be saved and used over and over again. Still others more or less replace the backing container, which means that you have no choice but to continue to use them. Table 6-22 shows the relative stability of views. Sublists are like butterflies, a thing of beauty that lasts for but a day. As stated by Bloch in *The Java Tutorial*:

> While the `subList` operation is extremely powerful, some care must be exercised when using it. The semantics of the `List` returned by `subList` become undefined if elements are added to or removed from the backing `List` in any way other than via the returned `List`. Thus, it's highly recommended that you use the `List` returned by `subList` only as a transient object, to perform one or a sequence of range operations on the backing `List`. The longer you use the `subList` object, the greater the probability that you'll compromise it by modifying the backing `List` directly (or through another `subList` object).[29]

This quotation is somewhat dated. A number of changes have been made since it was written. Now sublists are no different from fail-fast iterators in that they will throw a `ConcurrentModificationException` if the backing list is structurally modified. More on this subject later. As an example of using a sublist as a *transient object*, consider the following line of code:

```
list.subList(from, to).clear();
```

When used like this there is no chance of the backing list being structurally modified while the sublist is in use except in a multithreaded application.

Collection views of a map are especially interesting in this regard. They are anonymous classes loaded, linked, and initialized the first time they are used. A reference to the collection view is stored in a `transient` field in the backing map. Repeated invocations of the `keySet()`, `values()`, or `entrySet()` method for a given map returns the same view. For example,

Table 6-22: The Relative Stability of Views

As Fleeting as an Iterator	Designed for Continual Use	More or Less Replaces the Backing Container
Sublists	Subsets and submaps (including headsets, tailsets, headmaps, and tailmaps) Collection views of a map	Synchronized views Unmodifiable views List view of an array

---

29. Bloch, "The List Interface," *implementations/wrapper.html*.

```
    private transient Set entrySet = null;

    public Set entrySet() {
        if (entrySet == null) {
            entrySet = new AbstractSet() { ... };
        }
        return entrySet;
    }
```

This is the `entrySet()` method (with the anonymous class body omitted).
The `keySet()` and `values()` methods have similar implementations. As
an application programmer you have no choice but to continue using the
same collection view of a map because, even if you invoke `entrySet()`,
`keySey()`, or `values()` again, you get back the same collection view.

6.12.1 Synchronized Views

The rationale for not synchronizing the general-purpose containers in the
collections framework is explained as follows in *The Java Tutorial*.

> The fact that the new implementations are unsynchronized repre-
> sents a break with the past: `Vector` and `Hashtable`, which
> were introduced in JDK 1.0, are synchronized. The new
> approach was taken because it was recognized that collections
> are frequently used in a manner where the synchronization is of
> no benefit. Such uses include single-threaded use, read-only use,
> and use as part of a larger data object that does its own syn-
> chronization. In general, it is good API design practice not to
> make users pay for a feature that they generally don't use. Fur-
> ther, unnecessary synchronization can result in deadlock under
> certain circumstances.[30]

There is a synchronized view for each of the six core collection interfaces.
They are returned by the methods in the `Collections` utility class listed
in Table 6-23. As you can see, the parameter types and result types are
the same.

You must always remember the following when working with synchronized views.

- The mutex is the synchronized view, not the backing container,
  which means that all access to the backing container must be
  through the view

---

30. Bloch, "General Purpose Implementations," *implementations/general.html*.

- The iterators of a synchronized view are not synchronized, nor can they be. Synchronized iterations are discussed in 6.13.5.1 The Definition of a Structural Modification

The only way to guarantee that there is no unsynchronized access to the backing container is to instantiate a synchronized view as follows:

```
List list = Collections.synchronizedList(new ArrayList());
```

Table 6-23: Synchronized Views

No.	Method	Implementation Details[a]
1	Collection **synchronizedCollection** Collection c	SynchronizedCollection implements Collection
2	Set **synchronizedSet** Set s	SynchronizedSet extends SynchronizedCollection implements Set
3	List **synchronizedList** List list	SynchronizedList extends SynchronizedCollection implements List
4	Map **synchronizedMap** Map m	SynchronizedMap implements Map
5	SortedSet **synchronizedSortedSet** SortedSet s	SynchronizedSortedSet extends SynchronizedSet implements SortedSet
6	SortedMap **synchronizedSortedMap** SortedMap m	SynchronizedSortedMap extends SynchronizedMap implements SortedMap

a. All implementations are package-private, nested top-level classes.

Bloch says "a collection created in this fashion is every bit as thread-safe as a 'normally' synchronized collection like a Vector."[31] This is not to say that you cannot synchronize an existing collection. Just be very careful about passing a reference to the backing container out of the method in which it is created.

The following excerpt from *The Java Tutorial* under the heading "Reasons to Write Your Own Implementations" is relevant to any discussion of synchronized views.

> **Highly Concurrent**: The built-in collections are not designed to support high concurrency. The synchronization wrappers (and the legacy implementations) lock the *entire* collection every time it's accessed. Suppose you're building a server and you need a `Map` implementation that can be accessed by many threads concurrently. It is reasonably straightforward to build a hash table that locks each bucket separately, allowing multiple threads to access the table concurrently (assuming they're accessing keys that hash to different buckets).[32]

This excerpt applies equally to `HashSet` and `HashMap` but to none of the other general-purpose implementations.

6.12.2 Unmodifiable Views

Another way to describe unmodifiable views is as read-only access for containers. An unmodifiable view is not the same as an immutable container. The terms *modifiable* and *unmodifiable* apply to views only. The containers in which the elements are actually stored are *mutable* or *immutable*.

> An **immutable container** is either a custom container or one of the general-purpose containers to which there are no references other than unmodifiable views.

For example,

```
List list = new ArrayList();
list.add("Alfa");
list.add("Baker");
list.add("Chalie");
...
list.add("Zebra");
list = Collections.unmodifiableList(list);
```

31. Ibid., "Synchronization Wrappers," *implementations/wrapper.html*.
32. Ibid., "Reasons to Write Your Own Implementation," *custom-implementations/index.html*.

Invoking the `Collections.unmodifiableList(list)` method creates an unmodifiable view of the list. The container becomes immutable the moment the view is assigned to the `list` variable, which is the only reference to the container.

There is one unmodifiable views for each of the six core collection interfaces. They are returned by methods in the `Collections` utility class in Table 6-24. Bloch says this about unmodifiable views in the *The Java Tutorial*.

Table 6-24: Unmodifiable Views

No.	Method	Implementation Details[a]
7	Collection `unmodifiableCollection` Collection c	`UnmodifiableCollection implements Collection`
8	Set `unmodifiableSet` Set s	`UnmodifiableSet extends UnmodifiableCollection implements Set`
9	List `unmodifiableList` List list	`UnmodifiableList extends UnmodifiableCollection implements List`
10	Map `unmodifiableMap` Map m	`UnmodifiableMap implements Map`
11	SortedSet `unmodifiableSortedSet` SortedSet s	`UnmodifiableSortedSet extends UnmodifiableSet implements SortedSet`
12	SortedMap `unmodifiableSortedMap` SortedMap m	`UnmodifiableSortedMap extends UnmodifiableMap implements SortedMap`

a. All implementations are package-private, nested top-level classes.

The unmodifiable wrappers have two main uses:

- To make a collection immutable once it has been built. In this case, it's good practice not to maintain a reference to the backing collection. This absolutely guarantees immutability.
- To allow "second-class citizens" read-only access to your data structures. You keep a reference to the backing collection, but hand out a reference to the wrapper. In this way, the second-class citizens can look but not touch, while you maintain full access.[33]

If an unmodifiable view is instantiated using the same idiom as a synchronized view, no elements could be added to the collection. For example,

```
import java.util.*;
class Test {
    public static void main(String[] args) {
        List list = Collections.unmodifiableList(new ArrayList());
        list.add("whatever");
    }
}
```

Attempting to execute this program throws an `UnsupportedOperationException`. The equivalent way to instantiate an unmodifiable view is to overwrite the reference as soon as all of the elements are added. For example,

```
import java.util.*;
class Test {
    public static void main(String[] args) {
        List list = new ArrayList();
        list.add("whatever");
        list = Collections.unmodifiableList(list);
    }
}
```

If you follow this suggestion there is no possibility whatsoever that the backing container can be modified. This includes any iterators or other views created using the unmodifiable view.

The reason I quoted Bloch is to add a note of caution about "keeping a reference to the backing container." There are no modification checks of the backing container. If you do keep a reference, *it cannot be used to make structural modifications while there are unmodifiable views in use.* For example,

```
import java.util.*;
class Test {
    public static void main(String[] args) {
        List list = new ArrayList();
```

---

33. Joshua Bloch, "Unmodifiable Wrappers", *implementations/wrapper.html*

```
            list.add("Alfa");
            list.add("Baker");
            list.add("Charlie");
            List readOnly = Collections.unmodifiableList(list);
            System.out.println(readOnly.get(0));
            System.out.println(readOnly.get(1));
            list.remove("Charlie");
            System.out.println(readOnly.get(2));
        }
    }
```

Attempting to execute this program prints the following before throwing an exception:

```
Alfa
Baker
Exception in thread "main" java.lang.IndexOutOfBoundsException: Index: 2, Size: 2
        at java.util.ArrayList.RangeCheck(Unknown Source)
        at java.util.ArrayList.get(Unknown Source)
        at java.util.Collections$UnmodifiableList.get(Unknown Source)
        at Test.main(Test.java:12)
```

(RangeCheck() is a private method in the ArrayList class, which for some unknown reason is flaunting method naming conventions.) There is an assumption that the backing container will not be structurally modified while an unmodifiable view is in use. The idea of *keeping a reference to the backing container* while "second-class citizens" have read-only access through one of the unmodifiable views must be tempered by the realization that structural modifications invalidate those views as much as they do any sublists or fail-fast iterators that are in use.

6.12.3 Range Views (Sublists, Subsets, and Submaps)

Sublists, subsets, and submaps support all of the optional operations that the backing container supports. In the case of the general-purpose implementations in the collections framework, this means all operations are supported. There are seven range views, one for lists and three each for sorted sets and sorted maps. They are shown in Table 6-25.

The range of indices or objects passed to the subList(int fromIndex, int toIndex), subSet(Object fromElement, Object toElement), and subMap(Object fromKey, Object toKey) methods is described as a **right-open interval**,[34] which is a mathematical term that means the fromIndex, fromElement, or

---

34. Bloch uses *half-open* interval in *The Java Tutorial. Right open* is more descriptive.

Table 6-25: Range Views

No.	Interface	Method	Implementation Details
13	List	List **subList** int fromIndex int toIndex	helper class `SubList` extends `AbstractList` (helper classes are by definition non-`public`)
14	SortedSet[a]	SortedSet **subSet** Object fromElement Object toElement	uses a `private TreeSet` constructor to create a `TreeSet` from a submap
15		SortedSet **headSet** Object toElement	uses a `private TreeSet` constructor to create a `TreeSet` from a headmap
16		SortedSet **tailSet** Object fromElement	uses a `private TreeSet` constructor to create a `TreeSet` from a tailmap
17	SortedMap	SortedMap **subMap** Object fromKey Object toKey	`private` member class `SubMap` extends `AbstractMap` implements `SortedMap`
18		SortedMap **headMap** Object toKey	`private` member class `SubMap` extends `AbstractMap` implements `SortedMap`
19		SortedMap **tailMap** Object fromKey	`private` member class `SubMap` extends `AbstractMap` implements `SortedMap`

a. These range views are an exception to the general rule that all views are highly specialized implementations of one of the core collection interfaces.

`fromKey` are inclusive, and the `toIndex`, `toElement`, or `toKey` are exclusive. For example,

```
class Test {
    public static void main(String[] args) {
        char[] alphabet = {'a','b','c','d','e','f','g','h','i',
```

```
                    'j','k','l','m','n','o','p','q','r',
                    's','t','u','v','w','x','y','z'};
      for (int i=0; i < alphabet.length; i++) {
          System.out.print(alphabet[i]);
      }
   }
}
```

The value `alphabet.length` is `26`, which is one more than the last
index value. If `alphabet.length` were equal to zero in the last example, nothing would have printed. Likewise, if the `from` and `to` arguments
in a range view are equal, the sublist, subset, or submap returned is
always empty. Do you see how this is consistent with the canonical form of
the `for` loop used to iterate over the elements in an array? Ranges in the
Java programming language are always expressed as right-open intervals
for the sake of consistency. Right-open intervals are discussed further in
6.12.3.1 Endpoints as Absolute Points in an Element-Space.

Head sets and tail sets are sets that include the first or last element in
an ordered map or set. The `headSet(toElement)` and `head-`
`Map(toKey)` methods are right-open intervals in which the `from` element or key is the head. The **head** is also returned by the `first()`
method in a sorted set or by the `firstKey()` method in a sorted map.
As is expected in a right-open interval, `toElement` and `toKey` are exclusive. The `tailSet(fromElement)` and `tailMap(fromKey)`
methods, however, are closed intervals in which the implied `toElement`
or `toKey` is the tail. The **tail** is also returned by the `last()` method in a
sorted set or by the `lastKey()` method in a sorted map.

The remainder of this section discusses how to use range views. The
most literal use of a range view is to wedge it between a target object (the
backing collection) and an instance method. For example,

```
list.subList(from, to).clear();
set.subSet(from, to).clear();
map.subMap(from, to).clear();
```

These statements clear all of the elements between `from` and `to`. Here is
another example:

```
int size = list.subList(from, to).size();
int size = set.subSet(from, to).size();
int size = map.subMap(from, to).size();
```

These statements tell you how many elements are in a range view.

The other principle use of range views is to obviate the necessity of
declaring range methods in the `Collections` utility class (such as

those found in the `Arrays` utility class). For example, consider the following methods in the `Arrays` utility class:

```
public static void sort(Object[] a)
public static void sort(Object[] a, int fromIndex, int toIndex)
public static void sort(Object[] a, Comparator c)
public static void sort(Object[] a, int fromIndex, int toIndex, Comparator c)
```

If there were something comparable to range views for arrays, this list of methods could be reduced to the following:

```
public static void sort(Object[] a)
public static void sort(Object[] a, Comparator c)
```

Here is an example of using a sublist to sort part of an `ArrayList`:

```java
import java.util.*;
class Test {
    public static void main(String[] args) {
        String[] array = {"Alfa","Baker","Charlie",
                          "Foxtrot","Echo","Delta"};
        List list = Arrays.asList(array);
        List sublist = list.subList(3, list.size());
        Collections.sort(sublist);   // range operation
        for(int i=0; i < array.length; i++)
            System.out.println(array[i]);
    }
}
```

Executing this method prints

```
Alfa
Baker
Charlie
Delta
Echo
Foxtrot
```

Any of the methods in the `Collections` utility class that have a core collection interface type parameter can be passed a range view (as in the above example sorting part of an `ArrayList`).

Subdividing a sorted set or sorted map into subsets and submaps using right-open intervals is easy. The following example of a two-volume dictionary is from *The Java Tutorial*:

```
SortedSet volume1 = dictionary.headSet("n");
SortedSet volume2 = dictionary.tailSet("n");
```

In set theory `volume1` and `volume2` are said to be *disjoint* sets. The intersection of disjoint sets is always the empty set. To split a range of objects into three or more subsets or submaps, use code such as the following:

```
SortedMap one   = mainMap.headMap(a);
SortedMap two   = mainMap.subMap(a,b);
SortedMap three = mainMap.tailMap(b);
```

You can see how easy it would be easy to further subdivide the map, adding more submaps between the head and tail map.

6.12.3.1 Endpoints as Absolute Points in an Element-Space

The `fromIndex` and `toIndex`, `fromElement` and `toElement`, and the `fromKey` and `toKey` in a range view are refered to as **endpoints**. The name of this section was inspired by the following Bloch quotation on the subject:

> [T]he endpoints of a range view of [a sorted set map] are absolute points in the element-space, rather than specific elements in the backing collection (as is the case for lists). A range-view of a sorted set is really just a window onto whatever portion of the set lies in the designated part of the element-space.[35]

Objects are ordered like the numbers on a number line, but instead of a number line there is the **element-space** (also known as a **domain**). In a sorted set or map all the objects in the element-space are guaranteed to be **mutually comparable**. This is a special term used only in reference to the `sort` methods in the `Arrays` and `Collections` utility classes and to sorted sets and maps. Our focus here is on the latter.

As each element is added to a sorted set or each entry to a sorted map, either the `compareTo(Object o)` method in the `Comparable` interface (natural ordering) or the `compare(Object o1, Object o1)` method in a `Comparator` is invoked to *automatically* sort the element. In doing so the element being added is compared to some or all of the elements already in the container. If any of them are not assignment compatible, a `ClassCastException` is thrown.

The class type that determines if all subsequent objects added to a container are *mutually comparable* is the class of the first `Object` added to the container.

---

35. Bloch, "Rangeview Operations," *interfaces/sorted-set.html*.

That is never the `Object` class because the `Object` class does not implement the `Comparable` interface and has no instance variables that could be sorted by a `Comparator`. If an `Object` class object were passed to a natural comparison method, a `ClassCastException` would be thrown. The significance of this is that mutually comparable objects are usually instances of a base class, the definition of which is a direct subclass of `Object`. What makes the term *mutually comparable* so special is that it is based on the element type, which means *the class type of the objects* stored in the container. Most terms related to assignment compatibility are concerned with *the type of a variable or expression*.

Because of how natural comparison methods are coded, this almost always means that all of the elements in a sorted set or map have the same element type. In other words, they are all the same class of objects. The element-space is ordered either according to the natural ordering for that class of objects or using the same `Comparator` passed to the constructor.

There is a fundamental difference between sublists and the other range views. The endpoints in a sublist must correspond to actual elements in the backing list. For example,

```
import java.util.*;
class Test {
    public static void main(String[] args) {
        List list = new ArrayList();
        List sublist = list.subList(0, 1);
    }
}
```

Attempting to execute this program throws an `IndexOutOfBounds` exception with a detailed error message of `"toIndex = 1"` because the `subList(int fromIndex, int toIndex)` method uses the indices passed to access the backing array.

Furthermore, the `fromIndex` and `toIndex` passed to the `subList(int fromIndex, int toIndex)` method can be invalidated in one of two ways by modifications to the backing list. The first is either invoking one of the `set` methods or reordering the elements in the backing list. For example,

```
import java.util.*;
class Test {
    public static void main(String[] args) {
        List list = new ArrayList();
        list.add("Alpha");
        list.add("Baker");
        list.add("Charlie");
```

```
        ListIterator iterator = list.listIterator();
        Collections.reverse(list);
        while (iterator.hasNext())
            System.out.println(iterator.next());
    }
}
```

Executing this program prints

```
Charlie
Baker
Alpha
```

No exception is thrown because these are not *structural* modifications. See 6.13.5.1 The Definition of a Structural Modification for a discussion.

The other modification is removing elements from the backing list, which is a structural modification. For example,

```
import java.util.*;
class Test {
    public static void main(String[] args) {
        List list = new ArrayList();
        list.add("Alpha");
        list.add("Baker");
        list.add("Charlie");
        ListIterator iterator = list.listIterator();
        list.remove("Baker");
        while (iterator.hasNext())
            System.out.println(iterator.next());
    }
}
```

Structural modifications immediately invalidate all sublists in use. Attempting to execute this program throws a `ConcurrentModification-Exception`.

This is not so with subsets and submaps. The endpoints passed to the `subSet(Object fromElement, Object toElement)` and `subMap(Object fromKey, Object toKey)` methods are stored in `Object` type fields and used as what Bloch describes as **absolute endpoints** in the element-space. The objects passed to `sub-Set(Object fromElement, Object toElement)` and `sub-Map(Object fromKey, Object toKey)` are stored in the view. For example,

```
private Object fromKey, toKey;
SubMap(Object fromKey, Object toKey) {
    this.fromKey = fromKey;
    this.toKey = toKey;
}
```

They represent endpoints in a range of values for that element type. These endpoints have meaning even if the subset or submap is empty. For example,

```
import java.util.*;
class Test {
    public static void main(String[] args) {
        SortedSet set = new TreeSet();
        Set subset = set.subSet("Alpha", "Omega\0");
        subset.add("Zeus");
    }
}
```

Attempting to execute this program throws the following exception.

```
Exception in thread "main" java.lang.IllegalArgumentException: key out of range
        at java.util.TreeMap$SubMap.put(Unknown Source)
        at java.util.TreeSet.add(Unknown Source)
        at Test.main(Test.java:6)
```

There was no problem creating the range view on top of an empty set. The `"Alpha"` and `"Omega\0"` strings were stored in the range view and subsequently used to determine that `"Zeus"` is out of range. This example involves `String` type parameters, which are a special case because of the lexicographical sort order. For an explanation of the `"Omega\0"` endpoint, see 5.5.1 Right-Open Intervals in `String` and `String-Buffer`.

6.12.4 Collection Views of a Map

The `Map` interface has only one method for accessing the values in a map. That is the `get(Object key)` method, which requires that you know the key. There is no method for accessing the keys. That would require an iterator, and the `Map` interface has no `iterator()` method. Instead, the `Map` interface has the three view methods in Table 6-26, which are commonly referred to as **collection views of a map**. The view type is either `Set` or `Collection`, which can then be used to invoke the `itera-tor()` method. For example,

```
Iterator iterator = map.entryView().iterator();
```

Collection views of a map exist primarily to create iterators. The rationale for this design is that, in addition to the iterator, you get the full power of the `Set` or `Collection` interface when working directly with the keys or values in a map. It is a very smart design.

Table 6-26: Collection Views of a Map

No.	Interface	Method Header	Implementation Details
20	Map	Set **keySet**	anonymous class extends AbstractSet
21		Collection **values**	anonymous class extends AbstractCollection
22		Set **entrySet**	anonymous class extends AbstractSet

The `entrySet()` method is particularly interesting in that it is the only way to get a reference to one of the nodes (a `Map.Entry` object) in the backing map. As stated in the API docs for the `Map.Entry` interface:

> A map entry (key-value pair). The `Map.entrySet` method returns a collection-view of the map, whose elements are of this class. The *only* way to obtain a reference to a map entry is from the iterator of this collection-view. These `Map.Entry` objects are valid *only* for the duration of the iteration; more formally, the behavior of a map entry is undefined if the backing map has been modified after the entry was returned by the iterator, except through the iterator's own `remove` operation, or through the `setValue` operation on a map entry returned by the iterator.[36]

This quotation raises an interesting point. When iterating over the entries in a map, you have two interfaces to work with: the `Iterator` interface, which allows you to remove entries; and the `Map.Entry` interface, which allows you to get and set the value of an entry. Thus, even though you are only interested in the keys or values, you may want to use the `entrySet()` method instead of `keySet()` or `values()` if at all possible to make your implementation more flexible. This subject is discussed further in 6.13.2 Using Collection Views to Iterate over a Map.

6.12.4.1 Using Collection Views to Add or Remove Entries

None of the collection views support `add` or `addAll` operations because of the backing map. The `put(Object key, Object value)` and

---

36. API docs for the `java.util.Map.Entry` interface.

`putAll(Map t)` methods are used to add entries to a map, not `add` or `addAll` methods. As stated in *The Java Tutorial*,

> The `Collection`-views *do not* support element addition under any circumstances. It would make no sense for the `keySet` and `values` views, and it's unnecessary for the `entrySet` view, as the backing Map's `put` and `putAll` provide the same functionality.[37]

Some software engineers and technical writers have observed that the `add(Object o)` method makes sense for the entry view as an alternative to the `put(Object key, Object value)` method. I think Bloch's last sentence in the quotation is something of a dodge in this regard. The real problem is that it would be too awkward to change from *put* to *add* for maps. Furthermore, the `addAll(Collection c)` method signature is wrong for maps. It would have to be `addAll(Map t)`, and there is no such animal in the `Set` interface. Throwing the `UnsupportedOperationException` is the only way to go.

There are five methods that remove elements from a `Set` or `Collection`. Four of them are defined in the `Collection` interface. Those are the `remove(Object o)`, `removeAll(Collection c)`, `retainAll(Collection c)`, and `clear()` methods. The fifth is the `remove()` method in an `Iterator`. If any of these methods are invoked using a collection view of a map, the corresponding entry in the backing map is removed, not just the key or value. You cannot remove just a key or value from a map.

If the view is a `Collection` view of the values in a map, the possibility exists that there is more than one such value in the map. If that is the case, only one map entry is removed. The question is, which one? For example,

```
import java.util.*;
class Test {
    public static void main(String[] args) {
        HashMap map1 = new HashMap();
        map1.put("1", "number");
        map1.put("2", "number");
        map1.put("3", "number");
        map1.put("a", "letter");
        map1.put("b", "letter");
        map1.put("c", "letter");
        TreeMap map2 = new TreeMap(map1);
```

---

37. Joshua Bloch, *The Java Tutorial*, "Collection Views," *interfaces/map.html*.

```
        Collection values1 = map1.values();
        Collection values2 = map2.values();
        values1.remove("number");
        values2.remove("number");
        System.out.println("HashMap...");
        Iterator i = map1.keySet().iterator();
        while (i.hasNext())
            System.out.println(i.next());
        System.out.println();
        System.out.println("TreeMap...");
        i = map2.keySet().iterator();
        while (i.hasNext())
            System.out.println(i.next());
    }
}
```

Executing this program prints

```
HashMap...
b
a
2
1
c

TreeMap...
2
3
a
b
c
```

You have no control of which entry is removed from a `HashMap`, which is a good reason not to attempt the removal of specific values using the collection view returned by the `values()` method of a `HashMap`. A `TreeMap` is more predictable because the first value in ascending order is the one removed.

6.12.5 List View of an Array

The view method in Table 6-27 is declared in the `Arrays` utility class.

The `Arrays.asList(Object[] a)` method is the only way to convert an array into one of the six core collection interfaces types. The type is `List` because arrays can have duplicate elements. This implementation of the `List` interface does not support any methods that could possibly add or remove elements or otherwise resize the list, hence the list returned is fixed length, just like the backing array.

Table 6-27: List View of an Array

No.	Class	Method	Implementation Details
23	`Arrays`	`List` **asList** `Object[] a`	`private` nested top-level class `ArrayList` extends `AbstractList` (This is not the same class as `java.util.ArrayList`.)

6.13 Iterators

An iterator is used to *iterate over the elements of a collection* (the phrase *the elements of* being optional) or to *traverse* a collection. You can also iterate *through* a collection instead of *over* it. Take your pick. I prefer the wording *to iterate over the elements of an array*.

`ListIterator` is a subinterface of `Iterator`. This section primarily discusses the `Iterator` base class in Figure 6-11.

Table 6-28 discusses the three methods in the `Iterator` interface. These methods are usually invoked in a `for` loop. For example,

```
static void printElements(Collection c) {
    for (Iterator i = c.iterator(); i.hasNext(); )
        System.out.println(i.next());
}
```

This style of coding encourages immediate use of the iterator. Notice the similarity to `int i=0` in the canonical form of the `for` loop. Bloch did that on purpose. The effect is to homogenize iteration over the elements, entries, keys, or values of any container. I think `while` loops are an elegant alternative. For example,

```
static void printElements(Collection c) {
    Iterator i = c.iterator();
    while (i.hasNext()) {
        System.out.println(i.next());
    }
}
```

However, this is purely a matter of style. I use both `for` and `while` loops for iteration. Sometimes one just looks better than the other.

Not all iterators are what they appear to be. The `iterator()` method in `LinkedList` always returns a `ListIterator`. The implementation of this method is as follows:

```
public Iterator iterator() {
    return listIterator();
```

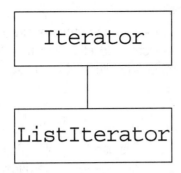

Figure 6-11: The `iterator` hierarchy.

Table 6-28: `Iterator` **Interface**

Method	Short Description
boolean **hasNext**	Returns `true` if there are more elements in the collection. This is what I call the *loop control mechanism*. It can be used to control the execution of a `for`, `while`, or `do` loop.
Object **next**	Returns a reference to the next element in the collection.
void **remove**	Removes the *current element*, the definition of which can be found in the section on list iterators. The `remove` method can only be invoked after the first `next` method invocation. Because it removes the element returned by the `next` method, it can only be invoked once in each iteration. IMPORTANT NOTE: If the target container is a map, this method always removes the map entry (regardless of which collection view is in use). You cannot remove just a key or value from a map. Only entries can be removed.

```
}
```

You should always invoke `listIterator()` for a `LinkedList`. Doing so offers greater flexibility in the implementation. The `ListIterator` interface is discussed in the following subsection.

6.13.1 List Iterators

A bidirectional `ListIterator` can move backwards and forwards over the elements in a list and can add elements to a list as well as remove them. There are two methods declared in the `List` interface that return a `ListIterator`:

```
public ListIterator listIterator()
public ListIterator listIterator(int index)
```

The second `ListIterator` is used in conjunction with the `hasPrevious()` and `previous()` methods to iterate backwards. For example,

```
import java.util.*;
class Test {
    public static void main(String[] args) {
        List list = new ArrayList();
        list.add("Alpha");
        list.add("Baker");
        list.add("Charlie");
        ListIterator iterator = list.listIterator(list.size());
        while (iterator.hasPrevious())
            System.out.println(iterator.previous());
    }
}
```

Executing this program prints

```
Charlie
Baker
Alpha
```

Note that a change in direction when iterating over the elements in a list causes the same element to be returned twice. For example,

```
import java.util.*;
class Test {
    public static void main(String[] args) {
        List list = new ArrayList();
        list.add("Alpha");
        list.add("Baker");
        list.add("Charlie");
        ListIterator iterator = list.listIterator();
        while (iterator.hasNext())
            System.out.println(iterator.next());
        while (iterator.hasPrevious())
            System.out.println(iterator.previous());
    }
}
```

Executing this program prints

```
Alpha
Baker
Charlie
```

```
Charlie
Baker
Alpha
```

The `hasNext()` and `next()` methods in `ListIterator` behave exactly as they do in an `Iterator`. They are therefore omitted from Table 6-29, which is the API table for the `ListIterator` interface. The `remove()` method also behaves exactly as it does in an `Iterator`, but is included in this table for reasons explained in the following subsection.

6.13.1.1 The Current Element in a `ListIterator`

The behavior of the `remove()` and `set(Object o)` methods in a `ListIterator` is defined in terms of the **current element**. The current element is the last element returned by either a `next()` or `previous()` method invocation. This is a precise definition. When an iterator is first created, there is no current element because neither the `previous()` nor `next()` methods have been invoked. Therefore, invoking either the `remove()` or `set(Object o)` method throws an `IllegalStateException`. For example,

Table 6-29: Methods for List Iterators Only[a]

Method	Short Description
`boolean` **`hasPrevious`**	Returns `true` if there are more elements in the target list moving in a backwards direction. This method is equivalent to the `hasNext()` method in a forward iteration.
`int` **`nextIndex`**	Returns the index of the next or previous element in the target list. As explained by Bloch,
`int` **`previousIndex`**	These [methods] are typically used for one of two purposes: To report the position where something was found, or to record the position of the `ListIterator` so that another `ListIterator` with identical position can be created.[b]
	In a forward iteration the `previousIndex()` method "report[s] the position where something was found" and `nextIndex()` "record[s] the position of the `ListIterator`."

Table 6-29: Methods for List Iterators Only[a] (Continued)

Method	Short Description
Object **next**	Returns the next or previous element in the target list, which then becomes the current element. Both `nextIndex` and `previousIndex` are incremented by the `next()` method and decremented by the `previous()` method.
Object **previous**	
void **add** Object o	Adds o to the target list using `nextIndex()` as the index value and then increments both `nextIndex` and `previousIndex`. The reason for doing so is twofold. Incrementing the indexes allows more objects to be added. It also means that any elements added to the target list will not be returned by the `next()` method in a forward iteration. They will, however, be returned by the `previous()` method in a backward iteration.
void **remove**	Removes the current element. Also decrements `nextIndex`, but only if the current element was returned by a `next()` method invocation (that is, only for a forward iteration).
void **set** Object o	Sets the value of the current element.

a. The `next()` and `remove()` methods are included in this table because of the definition of the current element in a list iterator.
b. Joshua Bloch, *The Java Tutorial*, "Iterators," *interfaces/list.html*.

```
import java.util.*;
class Test {
   public static void main(String[] args) {
      List list = new ArrayList();
      list.add("Alfa");
      list.add("Baker");
      list.add("Charlie");
      ListIterator iterator = list.listIterator();
      iterator.set("throws IllegalStateException");
   }
}
```

If either the `add(Object o)` or `remove()` methods are invoked, there is no current element until either `previous()` or `next()` are invoked again. *By extension, an added element is never the current element.* For example,

```java
import java.util.*;
class Test {
    public static void main(String[] args) {
        List list = new ArrayList();
        list.add("Alfa");
        list.add("Baker");
        list.add("Charlie");
        ListIterator iterator = list.listIterator();
        while(iterator.hasNext())
            iterator.next();
        iterator.add("Delta");
        iterator.set("throws IllegalStateException");
    }
}
```

The added elements become the new tail of the list, but not the current element. Here is an example involving the `remove()` method:

```java
import java.util.*;
class Test {
    public static void main(String[] args) {
        List list = new ArrayList();
        list.add("Alfa");
        list.add("Baker");
        list.add("Charlie");
        ListIterator iterator = list.listIterator();
        System.out.println(iterator.next());
        System.out.println(iterator.next());
        iterator.remove();
        iterator.set("throws IllegalStateException");
    }
}
```

Executing this program also throws an `IllegalStateException` because the current element is removed before the `set(Object o)` method is invoked.

The term *current element* is of my own making but is most useful in specifying the behavior of methods in the `ListIterator` class. As stated in the API table, the `remove()` method removes the current element from a list. Likewise, the `set(Object o)` method sets the value of the current element.

The index of the current element is returned by the `previousIndex()` method in a forward iteration, which is to be expected because the element has already been returned. For example,

```java
import java.util.*;
class Test {
    public static void main(String[] args) {
```

```
List list = new ArrayList();
list.add("Alfa");
list.add("Baker");
list.add("Charlie");
ListIterator iterator = list.listIterator();
System.out.println(iterator.next());
Object currentElement = iterator.next();
System.out.println("current element = " + currentElement);
System.out.println(iterator.previousIndex());
System.out.println(list.indexOf(currentElement));
    }
}
```

Executing this program prints

```
Alfa
current element = Baker
1
1
```

In a backward iteration the index of the current element is returned by the `nextIndex()` method. The `previousIndex()` and `nextIndex()` methods are discussed at length in the next section.

6.13.1.2 There are Two Indices in a `ListIterator`

A `ListIterator` uses two `private` indices, `nextIndex` and `previousIndex`, which are the same names as the corresponding accessor methods. The `previousIndex` is largely conceptual. It is always equal to `nextIndex` minus one. For a list iterator returned by the no-argument `listIterator()` method, the initial value of `previousIndex` is -1 and `nextIndex` is 0. For a list iterator returned by the `listIterator(int index)` method, the initial value of `previousIndex` is `index -1` and of `nextIndex` is `index`. This works for a backward iteration if you always invoke `listIterator(int index)` as follows:

```
ListIterator iterator = list.listIterator(list.size());
```

The size of the list is passed to the `ListIterator` constructor.

The `next()` method always uses `nextIndex` to access the target list. For example,

```
import java.util.*;
class Test {
    public static void main(String[] args) {
        Object currentElement = "none";
        List list = new ArrayList();
        list.add("Alfa");
        list.add("Baker");
```

```
        list.add("Charlie");
        ListIterator iterator = list.listIterator();
        while (iterator.hasNext())
            System.out.println(iterator.nextIndex() +
                "=" + iterator.next());
    }
}
```

Executing this program prints

```
0=Alfa
1=Baker
2=Charlie
```

The last thing the `next()` method does before returning is to increment both `nextIndex` and `previousIndex`. Likewise, the `previous()` method uses `previousIndex` to access the target list. The last thing `previous()` does before returning is decrement `nextIndex` or `previousIndex`.

The only other methods that change the values of `nextIndex` and `previousIndex` are `add(Object o)` and `remove()`. The index of an element added to the target list using the `add(Object o)` method of a list iterator is always `nextIndex`, even when adding elements in a backward iteration. For example,

```
import java.util.*;
class Test {
    public static void main(String[] args) {
        List list = new ArrayList();
        list.add("Alfa");
        list.add("Baker");
        list.add("Charlie");
        ListIterator iterator = list.listIterator();
        iterator.next();
        iterator.next();
        iterator.add("Delta");
        iterator = list.listIterator();
        while(iterator.hasNext())
            System.out.println(iterator.next());
    }
}
```

Executing this program prints

```
Alfa
Baker
Delta
Charlie
```

This is very intuitive, even when adding elements in a backward iteration. For example,

```
import java.util.*;
class Test {
    public static void main(String[] args) {
        List list = new ArrayList();
        list.add("Alfa");
        list.add("Baker");
        list.add("Charlie");
        ListIterator iterator = list.listIterator(list.size());
        iterator.previous();
        iterator.previous();
        iterator.add("Delta");
        iterator = list.listIterator();
        while(iterator.hasNext())
            System.out.println(iterator.next());
    }
}
```

Executing this program prints

```
Alfa
Delta
Baker
Charlie
```

Looking at these examples of a forward and backward iteration, ask yourself: "Where else would you expect the elements to be added?" There is no need for the *imaginary cursor* tradition started in either the API docs or *The Java Tutorial*. I think it only complicates a straightforward design.

The *imaginary cursor* aside, the only thing about the `nextIndex` and `previousIndex` design that requires explanation is that the `add(Object o)` increments the indices before returning. Consequently, you will never see elements added during a forward iteration. For example,

```
import java.util.*;
class Test {
    public static void main(String[] args) {
        List list = new ArrayList();
        list.add("Alfa");
        list.add("Baker");
        list.add("Charlie");
        ListIterator iterator = list.listIterator();
        System.out.println(iterator.next());
        System.out.println(iterator.next());
        iterator.add("Delta");
        System.out.println(iterator.next());
        System.out.println(iterator.hasNext());
    }
}
```

Executing this program prints

```
Alfa
Baker
Charlie
false
```

There is no reason for the iterator to return elements you just added, which explains this design. This was actually a last minute change made shortly before the First Customer Release (FCS). The explanation at the time was

> `ListIterator` Interface
>
> **Modified add semantics**. Previously, the newly added element was inserted after the cursor; now it's inserted before the cursor. In general, people do not want to see the element they added as the iteration continues, so they were forced to follow every call to `ListIterator.add` with an (extra) call to `ListIterator.next`. Worse, repeated calls to `ListIterator.add` caused the new elements to stack up backwards unless the caller threw in a call to next after each call to add. These calls to next after each insert are no longer necessary. In effect they're now done automatically.[38]

However, the same design causes added elements to be returned in a backward iteration. For example,

```
import java.util.*;
class Test {
    public static void main(String[] args) {
        List list = new ArrayList();
        list.add("Alfa");
        list.add("Baker");
        list.add("Charlie");
        ListIterator iterator = list.listIterator(list.size());
        System.out.println(iterator.previous());
        System.out.println(iterator.previous());
        iterator.add("Delta");
        System.out.println(iterator.previous());
        System.out.println(iterator.hasPrevious());
    }
}
```

Executing this program prints

```
Charlie
Baker
Delta
true
```

This behavior amounts to an assumption built-in to the `add(Object o)` method. This assumption is that elements are being added in a forward iteration.

---

38. API docs for the 1.2 release, document entitled "Collections Framework Overview."

If you reach the end of the list in a forward iteration, added elements become the new tail of the list. Do not, however, attempt to access those elements with the same iterator. For example,

```java
import java.util.*;
class Test {
    public static void main(String[] args) {
        List list = new ArrayList();
        list.add("Alfa");
        list.add("Baker");
        list.add("Charlie");
        ListIterator iterator = list.listIterator();
        while (iterator.hasNext()) {
            System.out.println(iterator.next());
        }
        iterator.add("Delta");
        iterator.add("Echo");
        iterator.add("Foxtrot");
        System.out.println(iterator.hasNext());
        System.out.println(iterator.next());
    }
}
```

Attempting to execute this program prints the following before throwing an NoSuchElementException:

```
Alfa
Baker
Charlie
false
Exception in thread "main" java.util.NoSuchElementException
        at java.util.AbstractList$Itr.next(Unknown Source)
        at Test.main(Test.java:16)
```

This behavior must be understood as an extension of the idea that iterators do not return elements added during the iteration. Consistency also dictates the design decision of what to do under the same circumstances in a backward iteration. The added elements are returned. For example,

```java
import java.util.*;
class Test {
    public static void main(String[] args) {
        List list = new ArrayList();
        list.add("Alfa");
        list.add("Baker");
        list.add("Charlie");
        ListIterator iterator = list.listIterator(list.size());
        while (iterator.hasPrevious()) {
            System.out.println(iterator.previous());
        }
        iterator.add("Delta");
        iterator.add("Echo");
        iterator.add("Foxtrot");
        System.out.println(iterator.hasPrevious());
        System.out.println(iterator.previous());
    }
}
```

This behavior makes the following generalization possible.

A forward iteration *never* returns added elements,
whereas a backward iteration *always* does.

This is a much-needed consistency.

6.13.2 Using Collection Views to Iterate over a Map

There is no `iterator()` method in the `Map` interface. First, a collection view of the map must be created by invoking the `keySet()`, `values()`, or `entrySet()` methods. This returns either a `Set` or `Collection`, which can then be used to iterate over the keys, values, or entries. Note that if you start with an unsorted map, the iterator is going to be unordered.

Does it cost any more to use an entry view than it does to use a key or value view? That is an important question because, for the purpose of iterating over a map, the entry view is much more powerful. The answer is an unqualified *No*. In fact, all three collection views return the same iterator. Here are the `iterator()` methods from each of the views:

```
public Iterator iterator() {
    return getHashIterator(KEYS);
}

public Iterator iterator() {
    return getHashIterator(VALUES);
}

public Iterator iterator() {
    return getHashIterator(ENTRIES);
}
```

You can guess which `iterator()` method goes with which collection view. There are three *types* of iterators, as determined by the following convenience constants:

```
private static final int KEYS = 0;
private static final int VALUES = 1;
private static final int ENTRIES = 2;
```

The `getHashIterator(int type)` method passes the type value to the `private HashIterator` class, which implements the `Iterator` interface. Regardless of the `type` passed, that implementation always iterates over the entries of a map. (It has to because if you use the iterator to remove a key or value from the map, the entry is removed, not just the key or value. As explained above, you cannot remove just a key or value from a map.) How is the `type` argument used? The `next()` method uses it as follows:

```
return type == KEYS ? node.key : (type == VALUES ? node.value : node);
```

The `node` variable is an instance of the `Node` class, which implements the `Map.Entry` interface. You see, the iterator for `keySet()` and `values()` is just a restricted `entrySet()` iterator. The question is, why use a restricted iterator?

There are times when you need to perform set operations on the keys of a map. If, however, a collection view is to be used only for iterations, consider using an entry view. For example,

```
Iterator i = m.entrySet().iterator();
while(i.hasNext()) {
    Map.Entry e = (Map.Entry) i.next();
    System.out.println(e.getKey() + ": " + e.getValue());
}
```

This gives you both the `Iterator` interface, which allows you to remove entries, and the `Map.Entry` interface. The latter includes access methods for the keys and values as well as the `setValue(Object value)` method. The `equals(Object o)` method can also be invoked should you need to compare two mappings to see if they are the same.

Note that the behavior of the `getValue()` and `setValue(Object value)` methods is undefined if the map entry is removed. That much should be obvious. That these methods cannot be invoked after the *current map entry* is removed is much like the concept of a *current element* discussed in reference to a list iterator.

6.13.3 A Poor Man's Collection

In the past `Enumeration` has been used to pass data to other methods and constructors. This use of an `Enumeration` is referred to as a **poor man's collection** (*poor* because an `Enumeration` can only be used once). It was not until the collections framework and the introduction of fail-fast iterators that the API docs began to openly discourage this coding practice.

A fail-fast `Iterator` should be used immediately. When `iterator()` or `listIterator()` is invoked, the `expectedModCount` in the iterator is set equal to the `modCount` in the backing container. For example,

```
int expectedModCount = modCount;
```

This variable initializer is executed when the `iterator()` or `listIterator()` method is invoked, in effect locking the backing container. A `ConcurrentModificationException` is thrown if the backing container is structurally modified while the iterator is in use. This pseudo lock is not released until you are done using the iterator. As with all locks, the shorter the duration of this lock-like mechanism referred to as *fail-fast iterators*, the less likelihood of contention.

That is why fail-fast iterators should be used immediately after invoking the the `iterator()` or `listIterator()` method that initializes the `expectedModCount` field. It also explains why using an iterator as a poor man's collection the way enumerations have been used in the past (that is, passing them around) is openly discouraged in the API docs. It follows that `Iterator` or `ListIterator` should not be used as parameter types. It is much better to use one of the six core collection interfaces as the parameter type in a method or constructor declaration, let users pass you a reference to the container or view, and invoke `iterator()` or `listIterator()` yourself immediately before using an iterator. This way you have the full functionality of the container or view at your disposal and the window of time in which the iterator effectively locks that backing container is minimized.

Here is where the `UnsupportedOperationException` can get tricky. If passed a reference to an unmodifiable view, attempting to invoke the `add(Object o)`, `remove()`, or `set(Object o)` methods in an `Iterator` or `ListIterator` (or any modification method for that matter) will throw an `UnsupportedOperationException`. This is roughly analogous to being passed a `null` reference. There is nothing you can do about it being a run-time exception. Just document that passing an unmodifiable collection will thrown an `UnsupportedOperationException`.

There is a method in the `Collections` utility class for converting one of the core collection interface types to an `Enumeration`:

```
public static Enumeration enumeration(Collection c)
```

As with other conversions from the collections framework to legacy containers, this method can be invoked right in the argument list when invoking one of the methods or constructors in an older API.

6.13.4 Synchronized Iterators

The synchronized views make no attempt to synchronize their iterators. This must be done by the application programmer. For example,

```
import java.util.*;
class Test {
    public static void main(String[] args) {
        List list = Collections.synchronizedList(new ArrayList());
        list.add("Alfa");
        list.add("Baker");
        list.add("Charlie");
        synchronized(list) {
            Iterator iterator = list.iterator();
            while (iterator.hasNext())
                System.out.println(iterator.next());
        }
    }
}
```

There are three things you should keep in mind about synchronized iterators. The most important thing to remember when synchronizing an iterator is that the mutex must always be the synchronized view. The second most important thing to remember is that the creation of the iterator must be in the synchronized block. For example,

```
import java.util.*;
class Test {
    public static void main(String[] args) {
        Map map = Collections.synchronizedMap(
                new HashMap((Map) System.getProperties()));
        Set entries = map.entrySet(); // no synchronization required
        synchronized (map) {
            Iterator i = entries.iterator();
            while (i.hasNext()) {
                Map.Entry e = (Map.Entry) i.next();
                if (((String) e.getKey()).startsWith("user"))
                    System.out.println(e.getKey() + "=" + e.getValue());
            }
        }
    }
}
```

Notice that the mutex is map, not entries, and that entries.iterator() is invoked in the synchronized block.

Those are the most important things to remember. Get them wrong and the iterator is not properly synchronized. The API docs for all of the synchronized views include the warning that "failure to follow this advice may result in nondeterministic behavior."[39]

The third thing is less important. Do you see how `map.entrySet()` is not in the `synchronized` block? This is because the view methods for a synchronized view are already synchronized (remember *every view after their kind*). Therefore, the view method does not need to be invoked in the synchronized block. This is true of all collections views of a map, subsets, sublists, submaps, headsets, headmaps, tailsets, tailmaps, etc. Only the `iterator()` and `listIterator()` methods must be invoked in the `synchronized` block.

6.13.5 Fail-Fast Iterators

Much is said about **fail-fast iterators** in the collections framework. All of the general-purpose implementations include a paragraph such as the following from the `LinkedList` class.

> The iterators returned by this class's `iterator` and `ListIt-erator` methods are *fail-fast*: if the list is structurally modified at any time after the iterator is created, in any way except through the Iterator's own `remove` or `add` methods, the iterator will throw a `ConcurrentModificationException`. Thus, in the face of concurrent modification, the iterator fails quickly and cleanly, rather than risking arbitrary, non-deterministic behavior at an undetermined time in the future.[40]

These paragraphs from the API docs for the general-purpose implementations, doubtless familiar to many readers, are the subject of several documentation bugs and are sure to be changed in a future release. One problem is the phrase in "the face of concurrent modification," which should read "in the face of structural modifications." This phrase alone is the source of much confusion, because structural modifications are not the same thing as concurrent modifications. For that matter, the `ConcurrentModificationException` exception name is misleading. Looking at bug reports on this subject, it is clear that the implementation was still maturing well after the 1.2 release, particularly in the area of sublists. I am sure that the idea of *limited concurrent modifications*, however, was formulated well in advance of the 1.2 release, suggesting that the

---

39. API docs for `synchronizedCollection(Collection c)`.
40. API docs for the `java.util.LinkedList` class.

choice to stick with the `ConcurrentModificationException` exception name was deliberate. The alternative would be to throw a `StructuralModificationException`.

Collection views of a map are a special case. The backing container is by definition a view. However, that in and of itself is not so unusual. The `iterator()` and `listIterator()` methods can be invoked for any view. What makes collection views of a map special is that structural modifications to the backing map affect not only the iterator, but also the `Map.Entry` objects used by the iterator. Remember, all collection views of a map return essentially the same iterator. The strongest structural modification warning for collections views is hidden away in the `Map.Entry` interface.

> These `Map.Entry` objects are valid *only* for the duration of the iteration; more formally, the behavior of a map entry is undefined if the backing map has been modified after the entry was returned by the iterator, except through the iterator's own `remove` operation, or through the `setValue` operation on a map entry returned by the iterator.[41]

In short, it's a bad idea to save references to `Map.Entry` objects when iterating over the entries in a map.

For the details on how fail-fast iterators are implemented see 6.16.2.1 `modCount`.

6.13.5.1 *The Definition of a Structural Modification*

The definition of a **structural modification** is the source of much confusion in understanding fail-fast iterators because setting the value of an element is not considered a structural modification. Specifically, the `set(int index, Object element)` method in the `List` interface, the `set(Object o)` method in the `ListIterator` interface, and the `setValue(Object value)` method in the `Map.Entry` interface do not increment the `modCount` variable used to implement fail-fast iterators. As stated in the API docs for the `ArrayList` class,

> A structural modification is any operation that adds or deletes one or more elements, or explicitly resizes the backing array;

---

41. API docs for the `java.util.Map.Entry` interface.

merely setting the value of an element is not a structural modification.[42]

The "explicitly resizes" comment is a reference to the `ensureCapacity(int minimumCapacity)` and `trimToSize()` methods in the `ArrayList` class. Why are `set` methods not structural modifications? That is a question that bothers many programmers.

Here you must differentiate between fail-fast iterators and synchronization. All of the synchronized views include a warning that iterators must be explicitly synchronized. For example,

```
synchronized(list) {
    Iterator iterator = list.iterator();
    while (iterator.hasNext())
      System.out.println(iterator.next());
}
```

If this is done there is no possibility whatsoever that one of the `set` methods can be invoked at the same time as an iteration is in progress. Therefore, the real question is, why are `set` methods not considered structural modifications *for the purpose of implementing fail-fast iterators?*

The problem is the `setValue(Object)` method in `Map.Entry` interface. This method is typically invoked in an iterator loop. For example,

```
Iterator i = m.entrySet().iterator();
while(i.hasNext()) {
    Map.Entry e = (Map.Entry) i.next();
    e.setValue(null);
}
```

Such an invocation of the `setValue(Object value)` method in the `Map.Entry` interface must be allowed. Otherwise, the method is useless because the only way to get a reference to a `Map.Entry` object is by invoking the `entrySet()` method, the primary use of which is to iterate over the entries in a map. To then define an invocation of the `setValue(Object value)` method as a concurrent modification would be a self-defeating design. This problem is a reference to one of these `Map.Entry` objects could be saved or passed to another method or otherwise used after the iteration is completed. That makes it difficult to impossible to say for sure if an invocation of that method is part of an iteration or a concurrent modification.

---

42. API docs for the `java.util.ArrayList` class.

The solution is the definition of *structural modifications* as opposed to concurrent modifications. For the sake of consistency, none of the `set` methods are structural modifications. It is possible to invoke a `set` method while an unsynchronized iterator is in use. The only damage done, however, is that a different element is returned than would have been before the `set` method was invoked. In short, concurrent modification is not only possible using fail-fast iterators, it is anticipated in their design. I refer to these as **limited concurrent modifications** to help me remember this aspect of the fail-fast iterator design.

Nothing like an `IndexOutOfBoundsException` is ever thrown as a result of these limited concurrent modifications. Therefore, to allow them at the API design level is actually a more flexible design. Programmers are always free to synchronize the iterator or otherwise assure that the only `set` method invoked while an iterator is in use is the one declared in the `ListIterator` interface. If multithreaded applications follow the advice on how to synchronize iterators in the next section, not only are limited concurrent modifications impossible, but synchronization effectively replaces the entire fail-fast iterator mechanism. In fact, in a properly synchronized multithreaded application, fail-fast iterators should be considered a *secondary system*.

6.13.5.1.1 *Structural Modifications and Views*

Fail-fast iterators are only part (albeit the most important part) of a much larger picture. A discussion of the entire `ConcurrentModificationException` mechanism necessarily includes views. For example, a sublist iterator is not actually fail fast. The sublist throws a `ConcurrentModification-Exception`, not the iterator, but you have probably never heard of a fail-fast sublist.

This section takes a careful look at the consequences of structural modifications of the backing container while a view (as opposed to an iterator) is in use. This is a much broader subject than just fail-fast iterators. An understanding of this subject necessarily requires a thorough understanding of how views are implemented. Therefore, if you have not read the section on views, please do so.

What I have found is that all of the views fall into one of the following four categories in terms of how the `ConcurrentModificationException` mechanism is implemented. They are listed here in the order in which structural modifications of the backing container are likely to throw an exception or otherwise result in program failure.

1.   The design of synchronized and unmodifiable views is such that there is what could be characterized as *an assumption* that structural modifications of the backing container are not possible.

2.   Range views of a list (sublists) are susceptible to structural modifications of the backing list because of their positional access methods. Consequently, they are as fail-fast as iterators.

3.   Collection views of a map and range views of a sorted set or map (subsets and submaps) are designed for continual use. Changes in the view are reflected in the backing container and vice versa. There are no positional access methods that could invalidate the view over time. Consequently, structural modifications are only an issue with the iterators. Why sublists are different from subsets or submaps in this regard is an interesting question. The answer is discussed at length in 6.12.3 Range Views (Sublists, Subsets, and Submaps).

4.   In the case of list views of an array, structural modifications of the backing array are not possible.

This list covers all of the views. Only the first two categories are discussed in the remainder of this section.

There is an assumption built into the design of synchronized and unmodifiable views that access to backing collections is strictly through the view. This assumption is very explicit in the case of a synchronized view. For example, all of the synchronization wrappers in the `Collections` utility class include the following warning.

> In order to guarantee serial access, it is critical that **all** access
> to the backing [container] is accomplished through the returned
> [synchronized view]. [43]

The reason why I characterize this as an assumption is that, as of this writing, none of API docs for the unmodifiable views include a structural modification warning. They are the only views in the collections framework

---

43. API docs for the `synchronizedCollection(Collection c)` method in the `java.util.Collections` class.

whose behavior is undefined in the face of structural modifications of the backing container that do not include such a warning. For example,

```
import java.util.*;
class Test {
    public static void main(String[] args) {
        List list = new ArrayList();
        list.add("Alfa");
        list.add("Baker");
        list.add("Charlie");
        List readOnly = Collections.unmodifiableList(list);
        int i = readOnly.indexOf("Charlie");
        list.remove("Baker");
        System.out.println(readOnly.get(i));
    }
}
```

Executing this program throws an `IndexOutOfBoundsException`. The view may be unmodifiable, but it can still throw an exception if the backing container is structurally modified. Suppose the `clear()` method is invoked immediately after an unmodifiable view is returned. That is why I characterize the lack of a structural modification warning in the API docs for the unmodifiable collections decorators as an *assumption*.

The views that are most susceptible to concurrent modification are range views of a list (sublists). The API docs include the following warning.

> The semantics of the list returned by this method become undefined if the backing list ... is structurally modified in any way other than via the returned list.[44]

For example,

```
import java.util.*;
class Test {
    public static void main(String[] args) {
        List list = new ArrayList();
        list.add("Alfa");
        list.add("Baker");
        list.add("Charlie");
        list.add("Delta");
        list.add("Echo");
        list.add("Foxtrot");
        List sublist = list.subList(3, list.size());
        list.remove("Delta");
        System.out.println(sublist.get(0));
    }
}
```

---

44. API docs for the `subList(int fromIndex, int toIndex)` method in the `java.util.List` interface.

Executing this program throws a `ConcurrentModificationExcep-`
`tion` just like an iterator would under the same circumstances. As stated
above, the iterators in a sublist do not throw a `ConcurrentModifica-`
`tionException`. The sublist does instead. They are in fact fail-fast.

6.13.6 Iterating Backwards Through a `TreeSet` or `TreeMap`

Only `ListIterator`(s) are bidirectional. Of course, the notion of iterating backwards through a `Set` or `Map` is meaningless because those containers are unordered. However, iterating backwards through a
`SortedSet` or `SortedMap` is useful. It is interesting to note that Bloch
refers to the fact that a `SortedSet` does not have a bidirectional iterator
as a "deficiency" in that interface.

There are two options. The first uses a copy constructor to create a
list, invokes the `listIterator()` method, and then uses the `List-`
`Iterator` to iterate backwards through a copy of the `SortedSet` or
the keys of a `SortedMap`. For example,

```
import java.util.*;
class Test {
    public static void main(String[] args) {
        SortedSet sortedSet = new TreeSet();
        sortedSet.add("Baker");
        sortedSet.add("Alfa");
        sortedSet.add("Charlie");
        synchronized(sortedSet) {
            ListIterator i = Collections.unmodifiableList(
                    new ArrayList(sortedSet)).listIterator(sortedSet.size());
            while(i.hasPrevious())
                System.out.println(i.previous());
        }
    }
}
```

Executing this program prints

```
Charlie
Baker
Alfa
```

The copy is unmodifiable precisely because it is a copy. You do not want
someone to think they can use it to modify the original container. Thus, this is
a limited solution in that it is necessarily read only. The iteration must be synchronized because it is not fail fast. It cannot detect structural modifications
of the `TreeSet` used to create the `List`. By changing `new ArrayL-`
`ist(sortedSet)` to `new ArrayList(sortedMap.entrySet())`,
the same code can be used for a `SortedMap`.

The second option is suggested by a line of code in *The Java Tutorial*:

```
import java.util.*;
class Test {
   public static void main(String[] args) {
      SortedSet sortedSet = new TreeSet();
      sortedSet.add("Baker");
      sortedSet.add("Charlie");
      sortedSet.add("Alfa");
      String predecessor = (String)sortedSet.last();
      backwardsIteration:
      while (true) {
         try {
            System.out.println(predecessor);
            predecessor = (String)sortedSet.headSet(predecessor).last();
         } catch (NoSuchElementException e) { break backwardsIteration; }
      }
   }
}
```

Executing this program prints

```
Charlie
Baker
Alfa
```

Needless to say, this is a very expensive operation. The initial value of `predecessor` can be any element in the `SortedSet`. By changing `sortedSet.headSet(predecessor).last()` to `sortedSet.headMap(predecessor).lastKey()`, the same code can be used for iterating backwards through the keys of a `SortedMap`.

6.14 Al-Khwarizmi Concerning the Hindu Art of Reckoning

The next section discusses the **algorithms** in the `Arrays` and `Collections` utility classes. Allow me a lengthy digression to discuss the term *algorithm* (or do not and bypass this section), which is most often used in reference to the utility methods about to be discussed. This term means many things to many people. It was originally a mathematical term, the etymology of which can be traced back to an Iranian mathematician and astronomer named Mohammed ibn-Musa Al-Khwarizmi who lived in Baghdad circa 850-780 BC in what is now known as the first golden age of Islamic science. He wrote, among other important works, an arithmetic treatise entitled *Al-Khwarizmi Concerning the Hindu Art of Reckoning*, the only surviving copy of which is a Latin translation entitled *Algoritmi de* *numero Indorum. Algorithm* is a Latin translation of the name *Al-Khwarizmi* from the title of that surviving copy.

I believe the popularity of the term in computer programming dates back to the publication of the now-famous book written by Niklaus Wirth in 1975 entitled *Algorithms + Data Structures = Programs*. As used by computer programmers, however, the term is usually reserved for functions, procedures, or methods that solve problems related to containers. These containers may be anything from a simple array in the case of a *sort algorithm* to the heap in the case of a *garbage collection algorithm*. These are exactly the kinds of iterative problem-solving methods found in the `Arrays` and `Collections` utility classes. I include this definition of algorithms so that you will understand the tendency on the part of a large number of software engineers and technical writers to refer to the methods in the `Arrays` and `Collections` utility classes as algorithms instead of just utility methods.

6.15 Utility Methods for `Arrays` and Other `Collections`

All of the methods (or algorithms) in the `Arrays` and `Collections` classes are discussed in the following subsections except for the synchronized and unmodifiable views and the `enumeration(Collection c)` method discussed in 6.13.3 A Poor Man's Collection. The only utility method in the `Arrays` class not discussed in the following subsections is the `asList(Object[] a)` method discussed in 6.12.5 List View of an Array. The section on copying has been extended to include cloning of the general-purpose implementations because the subjects are so closely related.

6.15.1 Sorting Containers

There are three subsections in which the sorting of arrays, lists, sets, and maps is discussed. Arrays are sorted using the overloaded `sort` methods in the `Arrays` utility class. Lists are sorted using the overloaded `sort` methods in the `Collections` utility class. There are no utility methods for sorting sets and maps. However, they can still be sorted easily. The idiom for doing so is discussed in 6.15.1.3 Sorting Sets and Maps.

All of the `sort` methods for objects throw a `ClassCastException` if the elements in a container are not mutually comparable. The term *mutually comparable* is discussed at length in 6.12.3.1 Endpoints as Absolute Points in an Element-Space. A `ClassCastException` usually means that there is more than one element type in the collection (or perhaps that the wrong `Comparator` was used). Another reason why a sort would throw a `ClassCastException` is if no `Comparator` were used and the element type has no natural ordering.

6.15.1.1 *Sorting an Array*

Sorting an array is easy. Just invoke `Arrays.sort(arrayName)`. Here is a complete list of fully overloaded `sort` methods in the `Arrays` class:

```
public static void sort(long[] a)
public static void sort(long[] a, int fromIndex, int toIndex)
public static void sort(int[] a)
public static void sort(int[] a, int fromIndex, int toIndex)
public static void sort(short[] a)
public static void sort(short[] a, int fromIndex, int toIndex)
public static void sort(char[] a)
public static void sort(char[] a, int fromIndex, int toIndex)
public static void sort(byte[] a)
public static void sort(byte[] a, int fromIndex, int toIndex)
public static void sort(double[] a)
public static void sort(double[] a, int fromIndex, int toIndex)
public static void sort(float[] a)
public static void sort(float[] a, int fromIndex, int toIndex)
public static void sort(Object[] a)
public static void sort(Object[] a, int fromIndex, int toIndex)
public static void sort(Object[] a, Comparator c)
public static void sort(Object[] a, int fromIndex, int toIndex, Comparator c)
```

The range methods (that have `fromIndex` and `toIndex` parameters) were added at the last minute before the FCS release with the following explanation.

> These calls are useful in conjunction with array-based data structures where only a part of the array is "active" at any given time.[45]

The same sort for a container in the collections framework would be accomplished by means of a range view.

---

45. API docs for the 1.2 release, document entitled "Collections Framework Overview."

6.15.1.2 Sorting a List

In order for a list to be sorted, it must be modifiable. There are three methods for sorting a list. The first uses the natural ordering of the element type, the second accepts a `Comparator` to override the natural ordering (that is, for ad hoc sorts), and the third reverses the existing order:

```
public static void sort(List list)
public static void sort(List list, Comparator c)
public static void reverse(List l)
```

As explained above, in the case of a `sort(List list)` method (which uses default ordering), if any of the elements in the list do not implement the `Comparable` interface, a `ClassCastException` is thrown. For both sorts, the elements in the list must be mutually comparable. All sorts in the `java.util` package are stable.

The `reverse(List l)` method should not be confused with a descending sort using the `Comparator` returned by the `Collections.reverseOrder()` method. The `reverse(List l)` method reverses the existing order, which could be entry order, ascending order, descending order, or even no order (the list having been shuffled). The `Collections.reverseOrder()` method always reverses the natural ordering. In fact, using the `Comparator` returned by that utility method to sort element types that do not implement the `Comparable` interface will throw a `ClassCastException`.

6.15.1.3 Sorting Sets and Maps

The only sort methods in the `Collections` utility class are for lists. Why? The general-purpose implementations of a `Set` and `Map` in the collections framework use a hash table in which to store elements. *Hash tables cannot be sorted.* If you want a sorted set or map, use a `TreeSet` or `TreeMap`.

The `TreeSet` and `TreeMap` general-purpose implementations are said to be automatically sorted. What this means is that the `compareTo(Object o)` method in the `Comparable` interface or the `compare(Object o1, Object o2)` in a `Comparator` is used every time an object is added to the container to determine exactly where to store that object in relation to the others already in the container. Then, when an iterator is used, the object graph is traversed in such a way that the elements or entries are returned in order. If you need to maintain a sorted set or map in an order other than the natural ordering, the following constructors must be used:

```
public TreeSet(Comparator c)
public TreeMap(Comparator c)
```

For example,

```
SortedSet set = new TreeSet(Colections.reverseOrder());
```

The following copy constructors use either the same `Comparator` or the natural ordering of the `SortedSet` or `SortedMap` copied:

```
public TreeSet(SortedSet s)
public TreeMap(SortedMap m)
```

All four of these are standard constructors as discussed in 6.16.4 Standard Constructors.

6.15.2 Searching

Searches of the containers in the `java.util` package are either linear or binary. Binary searches run in logarithmic time. Linear searches run in linear time. Which search algorithm you use depends on the container searched. Only random access lists and arrays that are sorted can be searched using the faster binary search algorithm. Unsorted random access lists, as well as all sequential access lists, sets, and maps must be searched using the slower linear search algorithms.

The names of the overloaded binary search methods in the Arrays and `Collections` utility classes are `binarySearch`. No surprise there. The names of the linear search methods, however, are `indexOf` and `lastIndexOf` in the `List` interface, `contains` in the `Set` interface, and `containsKey` or `containsValue` in the `Map` interface. That these methods search their respective containers is not as immediately obvious based on their method name. Furthermore, instead of returning an index for the element or entry, the `contains` methods return a `boolean` value.

The `contains(Object o)` method is the only method for searching a set. When searching a sequential access list, you have the choice of an `int` type index result type when using either the `indexOf(Object o)` or `lastIndexOf(Object o)` method or a `boolean` result type when using `contains(Object o)`. Normally a binary search is used to search random access lists because the binary search algorithm is so much faster. The API docs for the `List` interface includes the following warning:

> The `List` interface provides two methods to search for a specified object. From a performance standpoint, these methods should be used with caution. In many implementations they will perform costly linear searches.[46]

Though not immediately obvious, this warning applies to `indexOf(Object o)`, `lastIndexOf(Object o)`, and `contains(Object o)`. The `contains(Object o)` method in both of the general-purpose `List` implementations is implemented by invoking `indexOf(Object o)`. There are two methods for searching a map. One is the `containsKey(Object key)` method and the other is `containsValue(Object value)`. All of the methods used to search arrays and other containers in the `java.util` package are discussed in the following subsections.

6.15.2.4 *Binary Searches of Random Access Lists and Arrays*

There are two groups of `binarySearch` methods to consider. The first group of two `binarySearch` methods are for lists and are declared in the `Collections` utility class. The second group of methods for arrays are declared in the `Arrays` utility class. Notice that there are two methods for searching objects in both the `Arrays` and `Collections` utility classes: one that assumes natural ordering and the other can be passed a `Comparator`.

```
public static int binarySearch(List list, Object key)
public static int binarySearch(List list, Object key, Comparator c)

public static int binarySearch(long[] a, long key)
public static int binarySearch(int[] a, int key)
public static int binarySearch(short[] a, short key)
public static int binarySearch(char[] a, char key)
public static int binarySearch(byte[] a, byte key)
public static int binarySearch(double[] a, double key)
public static int binarySearch(float[] a, float key)
public static int binarySearch(Object[] a, Object key)
public static int binarySearch(Object[] a, Object key, Comparator c)
```

Never invoke one of these `binarySearch` methods unless the list or array is sorted in ascending order. That usually means invoking one of

---

46. API docs for the `java.util.List` interface.

the overloaded `sort` methods in the same `Arrays` or `Collections` utility class, but the array or other container may have been loaded in ascending order in the first place (obviating the need for a sort). For example,

```java
import java.util.*;
class Test {
    public static void main(String[] args) {
        char[] array = new char[] {'a', 'b', 'c', 'e', 'd', 'f'};
        System.out.println(Arrays.binarySearch(array, 'e'));
        Arrays.sort(array);
        System.out.println(Arrays.binarySearch(array, 'e'));
    }
}
```

Executing this program prints

```
-6
4
```

The return value before sorting the primitive type array incorrectly indicates that the character `'e'` is not in the array. Note that the value -6 is referred to as an *insertion point*. Insertion points are discussed below. The correct index for the character `'e'` in the sorted array is four. The return value for a binary search in meaningless unless the array or other container is sorted. When searching objects, a `Comparator` can be used so long as it is used to both sort and then search the array or other container. For example,

```java
import java.util.*;
class Test {
    public static void main(String[] args) {
        List list = new ArrayList();
        list.add("Alfa");
        list.add("Baker");
        list.add("Charlie");
        list.add("Delta");
        list.add("Echo");
        list.add("Foxtrot");
        Comparator reverse = Collections.reverseOrder();
        System.out.println(Collections.binarySearch(list, "Echo", reverse));
        Collections.sort(list, reverse);
        System.out.println(Collections.binarySearch(list, "Echo", reverse));
    }
}
```

Executing this program prints

```
-1
1
```

You simply cannot use a binary search algorithm unless the elements are sorted in the same order they are being searched.

All of the `binarySearch` methods in both the `Collections` and `Arrays` utility classes return an `int`. The API docs for all `binary-Search` methods use the exact same wording to explain the index value returned.

> **Return**s: index of the search key, if it is contained in the list; otherwise, `(-(insertion point) - 1)`. The insertion point is defined as the point at which the key would be inserted into the list: the index of the first element greater than the key, or `list.size()`, if all elements in the list are less than the specified key. Note that this guarantees that the return value will be >= 0 if and only if the key is found.[47]

Bloch has this to say in *The Java Tutorial*:

> This admittedly ugly formula was chosen to guarantee that the return value will be >= 0 if and only if the search key is found. It's basically a hack to combine a boolean ("found") and an integer ("index") into a single `int` return value.[48]

The return value for a `binarySearch` method is sometimes referred to as an **insertion point**, depending on how it is being used. There are three possibilities:

1. The first possibility is that you only want to know if an element is in the list. A return value >= 0 is the same as `true` when invoking `contains(Object o)` on a sequential access list.

2. The second possibility is that you want to retrieve the element after determining that it is in the list. In this case, the return value is the same as invoking the `indexOf(Object o)` method for a sequential access list.

3. The third possibility is that you want to add an element if and only if it is not already in the list (much like adding an element to a set). Remember, lists allow duplicates, so the list must be searched to determine if the element is already in the list. Furthermore, because the list is already sorted, you do not want to

---

47. API docs for all of the overloaded `binarySearch` methods in the `java.util.Array` and `java.util.Collections` classes.
48. Bloch, "Searching," *algorithms/index.html*.

disturb that order when adding an element. This is when the `binarySearch` return value is referred to as an *insertion point*. Before using it as such, however, remember to negate the return value and then subtract one. For example,

```
int index = Collections.binarySearch(list, key);
if (index < 0)
   list.add(-index-1, key);
```

This is indeed ugly, but it works.

Note that using the return value from a `binarySearch` method as an insertion point in an array would be even uglier (because you would have to do your own element shifting). You should consider using an `ArrayList` instead.

6.15.2.5 *Linear Searches of Sequential Access Lists, Sets, and Maps*

Only random access lists such as `ArrayList` should be searched using a binary search algorithm. Sequential access lists such as `LinkedList` should be searched using either the `contains(Object o)` or `indexOf(Object o)` method, depending on which result type you want. Both methods are linear searches, but that cannot be helped when searching a sequential access list.

If a sequential access list is passed to one of the `binarySearch` methods in the `Collections` class, the method reverts to a linear search. The core API makes this determination using the class of the `List` passed. If the `list` parameter is an instance of `Abstract-SequentialList`, it is assumed to be a sequential access list. Otherwise, it is assumed to be a random access list and a binary search is performed. In both cases the search algorithm used is the fastest for the given implementation. Make sure you extend `AbstractSequential-List` if you ever design a custom sequential access list. Otherwise, searching the list may be very slow.

That brings up an interesting point. It is sometimes said that if you are passed a `List` and do not know if it is a random access list or a sequential access list (that is, if you do not know anything about the implementation of the list) you should err on the side of caution and do the following.

- If at all possible, remove elements from the end of the list rather than from the beginning.

- Always use an iterator rather than indexing in a `for` loop

Using a `for` loop to randomly access the elements of a `LinkedList` is so disastrous that you should probably make it a rule never to use something like `for (int=0; i < list.size(); i++)` to iterate over a nonarray container unless there is a compelling reason to do so, in which case you should make sure the list is not a sequential access list such as `LinkedList`. How do you do that? If it's good for the goose, it's good for the gander. Use the same `AbstractSequentialList` type check as Bloch does in the `binarySearch` methods.

There are no search methods for sets and maps, just as there are no sort methods for set or maps. Every time you invoke the `contains(Object o)` method of a set, you are in effect searching the set to determine if an object is already an element of the set. The same is true of a map. Every time you invoke `containsKey(Object key)`, `containsValue(Object value)`, `get(Object key)`, or even `put(Object key, Object value)`, you are searching the map.

6.15.3 Cloning versus Copying a Container

With the exception of `WeakHashMap`, all of the containers in the `java.util` package (including arrays) implement the `Clonable` interface. In the case of the general-purpose implementations, this begs the question: what is the difference between cloning a container and using one of the following copy constructors?

```
public ArrayList(Collection c)
public LinkedList(Collection c)
public HashSet(Collection c)
public HashMap(Map t)
public TreeSet(SortedSet s)
public TreeMap(SortedMap m)
```

The short answer is that there is little or no difference because the copy constructors are shallow copies. In the case of an `ArrayList`, `HashSet`, or `HashMap`, however, the copy constructors increase the capacity of the container. Therefore, if you want a true clone of one of those three containers, use the `clone()` method.

The objects referenced by the elements, keys, or values in a container are not part of the container. The container is an array, hash table, linked list, or balanced binary tree used to group these objects. Copying the con-

> Whether you clone or copy a container, the result is
> always a shallow copy. Shallow copies are the norm
> when cloning or copying a container.

tainer does not mean copying all of the objects referenced by the elements, keys, or values.

That would be like cloning yourself every time you joined a new club, team, church, or other group. Think in terms of the physical container in memoɪy. The objects referenced are not part of the physical container. A container in memory is a container of references. That makes it more obvious that any container whatsoever, be it an original, a copy, or a copy of a copy a hundred times removed, is going to "see" changes to a mutable object. Furthermore, which reference in which container makes the change is completely irrelevant because mutable objects can be changed using references that are not in a container.

In a shallow copy of a container, references are merely copied. That means both the original and cloned container reference the same object. Were the references used to clone the objects instead of merely copying the reference, the copy would be what most programmers refer to as a deep copy of the container. I would argue that all copies or clones of a container are in fact deep copies because the objects referenced are not really part of the container; they are merely stored in the container. If you want to clone all of the objects referenced by a container, that is something entirely separate from the issue of cloning or copying the container. While this may not be the way most programmers think in terms of cloning or copying an container, it is notably that shallow copies of a container are the generally accepted norm, unlike any other kind of object in which a deep copy is generally expected. Maps are interesting in this regard. When cloning a map, the entries are cloned because a `Map.Entry` object (or node) is considered part of the map. The `clone()` method for `Map.Entry`, however, is also *shallow* in that references to the key and value are copied instead of being used to clone the object referenced. That means that a cloned map references all of the same keys and values as the original map, just like any other container.

Code such as the following must be used to create a *deep copy* of an array:

```
for(int i=0; i < array.length; i++) {
```

```
        array[i] = (Widget) array[i].clone();
}
```

Likewise, iterators are used to make a deep copy of a container in the collections framework. The `clone()` method is invoked for all of the elements, replacing the original with a reference to the clone.

Besides the `clone()` method and the copy constructors, there is a `copy(List dest, List src)` method in the `Collections` utility class. This method is the `List` analogue of the `System.arraycopy` method discussed in the following subsection. The main difference is the `src_position`, `dst_position`, and `length` parameters, which are not required in the `copy(List dest, List src)` method because of sublists. This method copies all of the elements from the `src` list to the same position in the `dest` list. An `IndexOutOfBounds-Exception` is thrown if the destination list is not at least as long as the source list. If it is longer the other elements in the destination list are unchanged as a result of invoking this method.

6.15.3.1 *System.arraycopy*

This method is used to copy arrays or subsequences of array components from a source array to a destination array. The entire method signature is fairly long:

```
arraycopy(Object src,
          int src_position,
          Object dst,
          int dst_position,
          int length)
```

This is one of a handful of methods in the core API that have parameter lists so long as to defy the use of the entire method signature. Hence, the name of this section. In this case, using just the method name is not a problem because `System.arraycopy` is so important that most programmer know immediately what is meant. The `src` parameter is the source array. The `dst` parameter is the destination array. The first element copied is `src[src_position]`. It is copied to `dst[dst_position]`, then both of the `src_position` and `dst_position` indices are incremented. The operation continues until `length` elements are copied. The `length` parameter is always the number of elements copied.

An invocation such as the following copies all of the elements in the source array:

```
arraycopy(src, 0, dst, 0, src.length);
```

This invocation appends all of the elements from the source array to the end of the destination array:

```
arraycopy(src, 0, dst, dst.length, src.length);
```

The length of the source and destination arrays do not need to be the same. If the destination array is not long enough, however, an `IndexOutOfBoundsException` is thrown. An `ArrayStoreException` may also be thrown if the elements in the source array are not assignable to the component type of the destination array.

It is possible that the source and destination arrays are the same. For example, this method is used to implement element shifting in the `ArrayList` class.

6.15.4 Shuffling

The following overloaded methods were not named `shuffle` *by chance*:

```
public static void shuffle(List list)
public static void shuffle(List list, Random rnd)
```

Bloch describes their usefulness as follows.

> This algorithm is useful in implementing games of chance. For example, it could be used to shuffle a `List` of `Card` objects representing a deck. Also it's useful for generating test cases.[49]

The first of the two methods uses `java.util.Random` as a default source of randomness. That class is described as a *pseudorandom* number generator, which explains the second method. It allows you to subclass `Random` and use a different algorithm for random number generation. Not many programmers will be doing that.

Who can resist this temptation to write the rudimentary software for a slot machine?

```
import java.util.*;

class Deck {
```

---

49. Bloch, "Shuffling," *algorithms/index.html*.

```
        private static final String[] cards = {
            "2 of Clubs","3 of Clubs","4 of Clubs","5 of Clubs",
            "6 of Clubs","7 of Clubs","8 of Clubs","9 of Clubs",
            "10 of Clubs","Jack of Clubs","Queen of Clubs",
            "King of Clubs","Ace of Clubs","2 of Hearts",
            "3 of Hearts","4 of Hearts","5 of Hearts","6 of Hearts",
            "7 of Hearts","8 of Hearts","9 of Hearts","10 of Hearts",
            "Jack of Hearts","Queen of Hearts","King of Hearts",
            "Ace of Hearts","2 of Diamonds","3 of Diamonds",
            "4 of Diamonds","5 of Diamonds","6 of Diamonds",
            "7 of Diamonds","8 of Diamonds","9 of Diamonds",
            "10 of Diamonds","Jack of Diamonds","Queen of Diamonds",
            "King of Diamonds","Ace of Diamonds","2 of Spades",
            "3 of Spades","4 of Spades","5 of Spades","6 of Spades",
            "7 of Spades","8 of Spades","9 of Spades","10 of Spades",
            "Jack of Spades","Queen of Spades","King of Spades",
            "Ace of Spades"};
        private List deck;
        private int cardIndex;

        public Deck() {
            deck = Arrays.asList(cards);
            Collections.shuffle(deck);
            Collections.shuffle(deck);   // why not?
            cardIndex = deck.size() - 1; //deal from end of list for speed
        }

        public void deal(int n, String[] names) {
            if (cardIndex+1 < n*names.length)
                throw new IllegalArgumentException("not enough cards");
            for(int i=0; i < names.length; i++) {
                System.out.println(names[i].toUpperCase());
                for(int j=0; j < n; j++) {
                    int nextCard = deck.size() - 1; //deal from end of list for speed
                    System.out.println(deck.get(cardIndex--));
                }
                System.out.println();
            }
        }
    }
```

Now for a hand of five card stud,

```
import java.util.*;
class Test {
    public static void main(String[] args) {
        Deck deck = new Deck();
        deck.deal(5, new String[] {"dealer", "me"});
    }
}
```

Here is a sample hand:

```
DEALER
6 of Clubs
10 of Hearts
7 of Hearts
Jack of Clubs
```

```
Jack of Spades

ME
7 of Spades
Ace of Diamonds
Queen of Hearts
5 of Clubs
4 of Hearts
```

You could easily modify this program to read the keyboard using standard I/O and deal five card draw.

6.15.5 Filling

The `fill` methods are used to reinitialize a list or to both initialize or reinitialize an array, perhaps with standard default values such as 0, the NULL character, `false`, or `null` values. After invoking any of the `fill` methods, all of the elements in the array or list are equal to the object or other value passed. These methods cannot be used to initialize an empty list because they do not add elements to the list. To initialize an empty list use the `Collections.nCopies(int n, Object o)` method discussed in 6.15.7 Convenience Implementations.

The following `fill` method for lists is declared in the `Collections` utility class:

```
public static void fill(List list, Object o)
```

Sublists are used for range operations. Here is a complete list of the fully overloaded `fill` methods declared in the `Arrays` utility class:

```
public static void fill(long[] a, long val)
public static void fill(long[] a, int fromIndex, int toIndex, long val)
public static void fill(int[] a, int val)
public static void fill(int[] a, int fromIndex, int toIndex, int val)
public static void fill(short[] a, short val)
public static void fill(short[] a, int fromIndex, int toIndex, short val)
public static void fill(char[] a, char val)
public static void fill(char[] a, int fromIndex, int toIndex, char val)
public static void fill(byte[] a, byte val)
public static void fill(byte[] a, int fromIndex, int toIndex, byte val)
public static void fill(boolean[] a, boolean val)
public static void fill(boolean[] a, int fromIndex, int toIndex, boolean val)
public static void fill(double[] a, double val)
public static void fill(double[] a, int fromIndex, int toIndex,double val)
public static void fill(float[] a, float val)
public static void fill(float[] a, int fromIndex, int toIndex, float val)
public static void fill(Object[] a, Object val)
public static void fill(Object[] a, int fromIndex, int toIndex,Object val)
```

As you can see, there is an overloaded `fill` method for every array type.

6.15.6 The Minimum and Maximum Elements

These methods work for any `Collection`, not just lists. Using a collection view of a map, they can also be applied to the keys and values in a map:

```
public static Object min(Collection coll)
public static Object max(Collection coll)

public static Object min(Collection coll, Comparator comp)
public static Object max(Collection coll,Comparator comp)
```

Unlike a `binarySearch`, the collection does not have to be sorted. However, all of the elements must be mutually comparable and have a natural ordering if a `Comparator` is not used. If the collection is a `TreeSet` or `TreeMap` sorted according to a `Comparator`, the second methods are usually invoked as follows:

```
min(coll, coll.comparator())
max(coll, coll.comparator())
```

The `min(Collection coll)` and `max(Collection coll)` can be invoked for a collection sorted according to a `Comparator`. However, they always return the minimum and maximum elements according to the natural ordering. If the `min(Collection coll)` and `max(Collection coll)` methods are invoked and there is no natural ordering, a `ClassCastException` is thrown. If the collection is empty, a `NoSuchElementException` is thrown.

When used with strings you may want to use the `Comparator` referenced by `String.CASE_INSENSITIVE_ORDER`. For example,

```
String min = (String) Collections.min(list, String.CASE_INSENSITIVE_ORDER)
String max = (String) Collections.max(list, String.CASE_INSENSITIVE_ORDER)
```

There are no methods for finding the minimum or maximum element in an array. However, the following code can be easily modified to work with any array type:

```
public static Object min(Object[] a) {
    Comparable candidate = (Comparable)a[0];
    for(int i=1; i < a.length; i++) {
        Comparable next = (Comparable)a[i];
            if (next.compareTo(candidate) < 0)
                candidate = next;
    }
    return candidate;
}

public static Object min(Object[] a, Comparator comp) {
    if (comp==null)
        return min(a);
```

```
        Object candidate = a[0];
        for(int i=1; i < a.length; i++) {
            Object next = a[i];
            if (comp.compare(next, candidate) < 0)
                candidate = next;
        }
        return candidate;
    }

    public static Object max(Object[] a) {
        Comparable candidate = (Comparable)a[0];
        for(int i=1; i < a.length; i++) {
            Comparable next = (Comparable)a[i];
            if (next.compareTo(candidate) < 0)
                candidate = next;
        }
        return candidate;
    }

    public static Object max(Object[] a, Comparator comp) {
        if (comp==null)
            return max(a);

        Object candidate = a[0];
        for(int i=1; i < a.length; i++) {
            Object next = a[i];
            if (comp.compare(next, candidate) > 0)
                candidate = next;
        }
        return candidate;
    }
```

They are modelled on the same methods in the `Collections` utility class. Apparently they were considered too basic to implement in the `Arrays` utility class. Nevertheless, I think it is useful to have a pattern for finding the minimum or maximum element in arrays of objects.

6.15.7 Convenience Implementations

There are three kinds of **convenience implementations**:[50]

- Empty containers
- Singletons
- Containers used to initialize other containers

The first of the two convenience implementations are for fields and methods in the `Collections` utility class. The containers they represent are

---

50. Bloch includes list views of an array (the `Arrays.asList(Object[] a)` method) in this section, whereas I include it in the section on views.

immutable and serializable. The first of the two convenience implementations are for passing 0 or one element where a `Collection`, `Set`,
`List`, or `Map` is expected. The container sets are referenced by the following fields:

```
public static final Set EMPTY_SET
public static final List EMPTY_LIST
public static final Map EMPTY_MAP
```

There are three singleton methods, one each for a `Set`, `List`, or `Map`:

```
public static Set singleton(Object o)
public static List singletonList(Object o)
public static Map singletonMap(Object key, Object value)
```

The reason why `singleton(Object o)` is not named `singleton-Set(Object o)` is that it was originally the only singleton method. The
others were added in the 1.3 release. The original `singleton(Object
o)` method is used to remove multiple occurrences of the same element
from a list. For example,

```
list.removeAll(Collections.singleton(element));
```

The same thing can be done to remove multiple entries from a map that
have the same value. For example,

```
map.values().removeAll(Collections.singleton(value));
```

Empty sets and singletons can be used anywhere a container is expected.

The other convenience implementation is returned by the following
method:

```
public static List nCopies(int n, Object o)
```

This is an interesting implementation that basically lies about its size. An
invocation of the `size()` method for the returned list will return `n`, but
there is no collection. In fact, an `nCopies` implementation has only two
fields in which the method parameters are stored:

```
int n;
Object element;
```

What makes this implementation useful is that the copy constructors and
bulk operations always use iterators. An iterator for an `nCopies` implementation keeps returning a reference to the same `element` `n` number
of times.

An `nCopies` implementation has two uses. The first is to initialize a
new list using a copy constructor. For example,

```
List list = new ArrayList(Collections.nCopies(1000, null));
```

`null` does not have to be the initial value of elements in a list. A reference to any object can be passed. Note that any container in which default values are stored can be used in conjunction with a copy constructor to initialize a set, list, or map. The second use is to expand the size of a list. For example,

```
list.addAll(Collections.nCopies(1000, null));
```

The `addAll(int index, Collection c)` method can be used to expand the middle of a list. The `ArrayList` class has an `ensureCapacity(int minimum-Capacity)` method. However, ensuring the *capacity* of a list and expanding the actual size of the list are two different things.

6.15.8 An `equals` Method for Arrays

These methods are comparable to the `equals(Object o)` method in any of the other container classes. They return true if the array contains the same elements in the same order. The length of the two arrays must be equal:

```
public static boolean equals(long[] a, long[] a2)
public static boolean equals(int[] a, int[] a2)
public static boolean equals(short[] a, short a2[])
public static boolean equals(char[] a, char[] a2)
public static boolean equals(byte[] a, byte[] a2)
public static boolean equals(boolean[] a, boolean[] a2)
public static boolean equals(double[] a, double[] a2)
public static boolean equals(float[] a, float[] a2)
public static boolean equals(Object[] a, Object[] a2)
```

Thus, the concept of equals is consistent for all of the containers in the `java.util` package.

6.16 Custom Implementations of the Core Collection Interfaces

There are four possible starting points for a custom implementation:

- Implementing a core collection interface from scratch (rare)
- Extending a general-purpose implementation
- Wrapping a general-purpose implementation (as do views)
- Extending one of the abstract implementations in the collections framework

I do not even discuss the first possibility. There are examples of extending and wrapping a general-purpose implementation in the following subsections. One is an extension of `HashMap` that does not allow `null` keys and the other is an `ArrayList` wrapper in which the component type of the backing array is `String` instead of the untyped reference `Object`. Therefore, assignments are type checked at compile time. This is sometimes called a **type-safe container**. I do not recommend this approach because parameterized types are sure to be added to the language in the near future. The abstract implementations are discussed in the following subsection.

6.16.1 Abstract Implementations

The abstract implementations more than anything else are what make the collections framework a *framework*. They are often referred to as **skeletal implementations** and are thoughtfully designed to minimize the work required to implement a core collection interface without making any gross assumptions about the implementation. What are *gross assumptions*? This is an important question. The abstract implementations throw an `UnsupportedOperationException` for any method that would make the collection modifiable or variable length. Exactly which methods those are is discussed in 6.16.2 Optional Operations.

All of the general-purpose implementations extend one of the abstract implementations, which makes them good examples of how to write a custom implementation. The abstract implementations class hierarchy is depicted in Figure 6-12. Note that sequential access lists extend `AbstractSequentialList` and not `AbstractList`. This harks back to when it was said earlier in this chapter that these implementations of the `List` interface are very different. If a custom implementation of a sequential access list does not extend `AbstractSequentialList`, the overloaded `binarySearch` methods will perform a binary search on the container, which would run in quadratic time.

All implementations are expected to include the standard constructors discussed in 6.16.4 Standard Constructors. The requirement for standard constructors cannot be enforced because constructors are not members of a class. Nonetheless, this is a requirement for a "well-behaved" container.

The following housekeeping methods are always free when extending an abstract implementation:

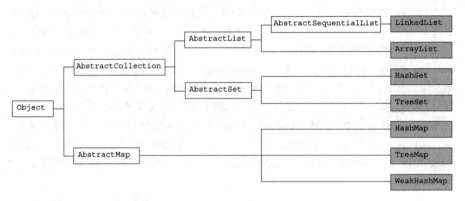

Figure 6-12: Abstract implementations class hierarchy.

```
hashCode()
equals(Object o)
toString()
```

Another always-free method is `isEmpty()`, which is built on top of `size()`. With the exception of `AbstractMap`, `size()` is one method that must always be implemented. In `AbstractMap`, `size()` is implemented on top of the foundation method.

The term **foundation method** is of my own making, but in keeping with Bloch's *built on top of* language. Once you understand what foundation methods are, you pretty much understand the design of the abstract implementations. Not counting the `size()` method, each of the abstract implementations has exactly one foundation method. The `size()` method is actually a second foundation method in all but the `Abstract-Map` class. I like to be able to say that there is only one foundation method in each of the abstract implementations, so I discount the importance of this method. Besides that, `size()` is a simple method to implement for any container.

For the purpose of discussing the abstract implementations, all of the other methods declared in the core collection interfaces are one of the following:

- Basic operations
- Optional operations
- View methods
- Iterators

A **basic operation** is always fully implemented. For example,

```
public boolean isEmpty() {
    return size() == 0;
}
```

This is an example of an `isEmpty()` method for a `Collection`. It is *built on top of* the `size()` method. Though not always as simple as the `isEmpty()` method, all of the basic operations are built on top of the foundation method for their respective abstract implementation.

The basic operations of a container never need to be coded.

Most of the optional operations are also fully implemented. The difference is that they are built on top of other optional operations instead of the foundation method. Those other optional operations they are built on top of are the truly optional operations that must be coded by hand. Their default implementations unconditionally throw an `UnsupportedOperationException`. A concise list of the truely optional operations that must be coded by hand can be found in 6.16.2 Optional Operations. That section differentiates between optional operations that are fully implemented and those that unconditionally throw an `UnsupportedOperationException`.

The idea of an *optional* operation being *fully implemented* may sound confusing at first. The design is actually very simple. As I have already said, fully implemented optional operations are built on top of other optional operations that unconditionally throw an `UnsupportedOperationException`. What makes fully implemented optional operations *optional* is that they do not catch that exception, in effect saying that *until you implement the other optional operation that I am built on top of, I am not supported*. Therefore, until you implement the optional operation that unconditionally throws an `UnsupportedOperationException`, all the optional operations that are built on top of it behave as if they unconditionally throw an `UnsupportedOperationException`. The relationship between optional operations that unconditionally throw an `UnsupportedOperationException` and fully implemented optional operations is analogous to the relationship between the foundation method and the basic operations.

Note that if I say an optional operation is *built on top* of another optional operations, I am always referring to a fully implemented optional operation. There are no exceptions to this rule. Optional operations that unconditionally throw an `UnsupportedOperationException` are not built on top of anything.

View methods are not discussed in the following subsections because they represent classes that are always fully implemented. If the backing container throws an `UnsupportedOperationException`, then so does the view.

The `iterator()` and overloaded `listIterator` methods are an important part of this discussion. The minimum implementation of the `Iterator` interface is the `hasNext()` and `next()` methods. I call this a **basic iterator**, whereas a **fully functional iterator** is one that implements the `remove()` method. The default implementation of that method in a basic iterator throws `UnsupportedOperationException`.

The definition of a basic iterator changes somewhat with list iterators. In addition to the `next()` and `hasNext()` methods, the `previous()`, `hasPrevious()`, `next-Index()`, and `previousIndex()` methods are implemented. The `add(Object o)`, `remove()`, and `set(Object o)` methods are only implemented in a fully functional list iterator. These distinctions between a basic iterator and a fully functional iterator are important in the context of a discussion of the abstract implementations

A container that supports only the basic operations is a **basic container**, or what might be described as a minimum implementation of one of the core collection interfaces. Generally speaking, the `iterator()` or `listIterator()` method for a basic container returns only a basic iterator. Such a container does not support any of the optional operations, including those in the `Iterator` and `ListIterator` interfaces. That would necessarily be a custom implementation because, as stated above, the general-purpose implementations support all of the optional operations and the `iterator()` and `listIterator()` methods for those containers always return fully functional iterators.

6.16.1.1 `AbstractCollection` and `AbstractSet`

I start with `AbstractCollection` and `AbstractSet`, which are one and the same in this regard. The foundation method is

```
public abstract Iterator iterator()
```

The container is either a basic container or fully functional, depending on how you implement the foundation method. All of the following basic operations are built on top of a basic iterator:

```
public boolean contains(Object o)
public boolean containsAll(Collection c)
public Object[] toArray()
public Object[] toArray(Object[] a)
```

The following optional operations are built on top of a fully functional iterator:

```
public boolean remove(Object o)
public boolean removeAll(Collection c)
public boolean retainAll(Collection c)
public void clear()
```

In other words, by implementing the `remove()` method in the iterator you in effect "turn on" all of these methods without having to write a single additional line of code.

That covers the entire `Collection` and `Set` interfaces except for the following two methods:

```
public boolean add(Object o)
public boolean addAll(Collection c)
```

As with most bulk methods, `addAll(Collection c)` is built on top of `add(Object o)`, which is an optional operation discussed in 6.16.2 Optional Operations. Now I will do the same thing for the other abstract implementations.

6.16.1.2 *AbstractList*

The foundation method for a random access list is

```
public abstract Object get(int index)
```

The only methods that are built directly on top of the foundation method are the iterators

```
public Iterator iterator()
public ListIterator listIterator()
public ListIterator listIterator(int index)
```

The following basic operations are built on top of only those iterators:

```
public boolean contains(Object o)
public boolean containsAll(Collection c)
public Object[] toArray()
public Object[] toArray(Object[] a)
public int indexOf(Object o)
public int lastIndexOf(Object o)
```

The iterators that are built on top of the foundation method are fully functional. However, they invoke optional operations that unconditionally throw an `UnsupportedOperationException`. In effect, they are basic iterators until the following optional operations are implemented:

```
public void add(int index, Object element)
public Object remove(int index)
public Object set(int index, Object element)
```

You can see how the `add(Object o)`, `remove()`, and `set(Object o)` methods in a `ListIterator` correspond to the optional operations in this list. Implement these three optional operations and the iterators in effect become fully functional. All of the following optional operations are in turn built on top of fully functional iterators:

```
public boolean add(Object o)
public boolean addAll(Collection c)
public boolean addAll(int index, Collection c)
public boolean remove(Object o)
public boolean removeAll(Collection c)
public boolean retainAll(Collection c)
public void clear()
```

That covers all of the `List` methods. Basically, with a random access list you have to implement `size()`, `get(int index)`, and the three optional operations listed above, and everything else comes free.

There are two other methods, however, that you should override. The `clear()` and the `protected removeRange(int fromIndex, int toIndex)` methods in `AbstractList` are written for a sequential access list. You should override either the `clear()` or `removeRange(int fromIndex, int toIndex)` method. `ArrayList` does both. It overrides `removeRange(int fromIndex, int toIndex)` with a random access implementation for the sake of subclasses and implements a very smart `clear()` method that sets all of the elements to `null` in a `for` loop, and then sets `size` to `0`. If you subclass `AbstractList` and fail to override either of these methods, you are subject to the following warning.

> This implementation gets a list iterator positioned before `from-Index`, and repeatedly calls `ListIterator.next` followed by `ListIterator.remove` until the entire range has been removed. *Note: if `ListIterator.remove` requires linear time, this implementation requires quadratic time.*[51]

---

51. API docs for the `protected removeRange(int fromIndex, int toIndex)` method in the `java.util.AbstractList` class.

This doc comment is a warning to programmers writing a custom implementation of a random access list that extends `AbstractList`. The `remove(Object o)` method in an iterator for a random access list requires linear time.

6.16.1.3 *AbstractSequentialList*

The foundation method for a sequential access list is a specific `listIterator()` method:

```
public abstract ListIterator listIterator(int index)
```

The other iterators are built directly on top of `listIterator(int index)`. For example,

```
public Iterator iterator() {
    return listIterator();
}

public ListIterator listIterator() {
    return listIterator(0);
}
```

The API docs make the following observation about the foundation methods in `AbstractList` and `AbstractSequentialList`.

> This class is the opposite of the `AbstractList` class in the sense that it implements the "random access" methods (`get(int index)`, `set(int index, Object element)`, `set(int index, Object element)`, `add(int index, Object element)` and `remove(int index)`) on top of the list's list iterator, instead of the other way around.[52]

The container is either a basic container or fully functional, depending on how you implement the foundation method. The following basic operations are built on top of a basic iterator:

```
public boolean contains(Object o)
public boolean containsAll(Collection c)
public Object[] toArray()
public Object[] toArray(Object[] a)
public int indexOf(Object o)
public int lastIndexOf(Object o)
public Object get(int index)
```

The following optional operations are built on top of a fully functional iterator:

---

52. API docs for the `java.util.AbstractSequentialList` class.

```
public boolean add(Object o)
public void add(int index, Object element)
public boolean addAll(Collection c)
public boolean addAll(int index, Collection c)
public boolean remove(Object o)
public boolean removeAll(Collection c)
public Object remove(int index)
public boolean retainAll(Collection c)
public Object set(int index, Object element)
public void clear()
```

That covers all of the `List` methods. Basically, with a sequential access list all you have to implement is `size()` and `listIterator(int index)` and everything else comes free.

6.16.1.4 *The `AbstractMap` Class*

The foundation method for a map is

```
public abstract Set entrySet()
```

All of the following basic operations are built directly on top of the foundation method. Notice that the list starts with `size()`:

```
public int size()
public boolean containsValue(Object value)
public void clear()
public Set keySet()
public Collection values()

public boolean containsKey(Object key)
public Object get(Object key)
public Object remove(Object key)
```

However, the default implementations of `containsKey(Object key)`, `get(Object key)`, and `remove(Object key)` surprisingly iterate over the `entrySet()`. This means that they run in linear time instead of constant time. We expect that for `containsValue(Object value)`, but not for `containsKey(Object key)`, `get(Object key)`, and `remove(Object key)`. The API docs for all three of these methods say "many implementations will override these methods." That is an understatement.

Maps have only one optional operation:

```
public Object put(Object key, Object value)
```

That `put(Object key, Object value)` is an optional operation seems strange at first. It has to be different in order to be consistent with the rule that abstract implementations are unmodifiable. The following bulk operation is built on top of the optional operation:

```
public void putAll(Map t)
```

That is all of the methods for the `Map` interface. Figure out how to implement `entrySet()` and `put(Object key, Object value)` and everything else is done for you. Well, not really. Most implementation will in fact override `containsKey(Object key)`, `get(Object key)`, and `remove(Object key)`, which means that custom implementations of the `Map` interface requires a little more work.

6.16.2 Optional Operations

An **optional operation** is a mutator method that makes a container either modifiable or variable length. Modifiable means you can set the value of an element in a set or list or replace a value in a map. Variable length means that elements can be added to or removed from a set or list or new entries can be added to a map. To differentiate between these mutator methods, those that set the value of an element in a set or list or replace a value in a map are called *set methods*. Those that change the add or remove elements are called *size methods*. The `put(Object key, Object value)` method is an exception. It is both a set and size method. This is not a very precise term, and I do not recommend the use of it outside of this discussion of optional operations.

As already explained in 6.16.1 Abstract Implementations, most of the methods that are described as *optional operations* are *fully implemented*, highly efficient implementations that do not require coding. If they throw an `UnsupportedOperationException`, it is because some other method they invoke is not implemented. The `UnsupportedOperation-Exception` is passed through. I do not include fully implemented methods in my definition of unsupported operations, regardless of the fact that they make the container modifiable or variable length. You do not have an *option* to implement these methods. They are already fully implemented. Moreover, in most cases their implementations are used in the general-purpose implementations. That is, they are not just default implementations. They are high-performance, production-ready implementations. An optional operation is therefore further defined as one that is implemented as follows in the abstract implementations:

```
throw new UnsupportedOperationException();
```

Table 6-30: `Collection` and `Set` **Optional Operations**

Method	Foundation Method	Size Method	Size Method
int **size**	✔		
Iterator **iterator**	✔		
boolean **add** Object o			✔
Iterator Methods			
void **remove**			✔

Table 6-31: `List` **Optional Operations**

Method	Foundation Method	Size Method	Size Method
int **size**	✔		
Object **get** int index	✔		
Object **set** int index Object element		✔	
void **add** int index Object element			✔

Table 6-31: `List` **Optional Operations (Continued)**

Method	Foundation Method	Size Method	Size Method
Object **remove** int index			✔
ListIterator Methods			
void **set** Object o		✔	
void **add** Object o			✔
void **remove**			✔

Table 6-32: `Map` **Optional Operations**

Method	Foundation Method	Modification Method	Size Method
Set **entrySet**	✔		
Object **put** Object key Object value		✔	✔

There are few such optional operations. They are summarized in Tables 6-30, 6-31, and 6-32. I have included the foundation methods and `size()` so that these tables represent a complete list of the methods that must be implemented in order to create fully working containers. Now *that* is a framework! Implementations are responsible for documenting which of the optional operations they support.

6.16.2.1 `modCount`

Implementing any of the optional operations discussed in the previous section with methods named `add`, `remove`, or `put` includes the responsibility of incrementing the `protected modCount` variable, that is if fail-fast iterators are desired. It is really as simple as `modCount++`. In the case of the `add(int index, Object element)` method in an `Array-List` or the `add(Object o)` method in a `ListIterator` for an `ArrayList`, invoking `ensureCapacity(size + 1)` increments `modCount` for you. *Do not increment it yourself!*

If you are incrementing any of the optional operations for an iterator, or implementing an iterator from scratch, all of the methods must check to make sure that the backing container has not been structurally modified. That is a little more involved. The `expectedModCount` field is declared the same as it is in the general-purpose implementations:

```
int expectedModCount = modCount;
```

It should be incremented by any of the `add` or `remove` methods in an iterator.

The fail-fast iterator mechanism is very simple. All of the methods that structurally modify a container increment `modCount`. When an iterator is first created, it assigns the value of `modCount` to `expectedMod-Count`, which only the iterator increments. Every time an `add` or `remove` method in the iterator is invoked, `expectedModCount` is incremented. If the iterator is making the only structural modifications to the backing container, then `modCount` and `expectedModCount` should remain equal. All you have to do is check. The collections framework uses a method such as the following:

```
final void checkForComodification() {
    if (modCount != expectedModCount)
        throw new ConcurrentModificationException();
}
```

The trick is in knowing when to invoke `checkForComodification()`. I suggest carefully studying one of the iterators in an abstract implementation before doing this yourself.

6.16.3 Restricted Containers

The idea of **restricted containers** was introduced as follows in "Collections Framework Overview" document of the 1.2 release.

Some implementations may restrict what elements (or in the case of `Maps`, keys and values) may be stored. Possible restrictions include requiring elements to:

- Be of a particular type
- Be non-`null`
- Obey some arbitrary predicate

Attempting to add an element that violates an implementation's restrictions results in a run-time exception, typically a `Class-CastException`, an `IllegalArgumentException`, or a `NullPointerException`. Attempting to remove or test for the presence of an element that violates an implementation's restrictions may result in an exception, though some "restricted collections" may permit this usage.[53]

Extending one of the general-purpose implementations and making modifications so that `null` values cannot be stored should be fairly straightforward. For example,

```
import java.util.*;
class RestrictedMap extends HashMap {
    public RestrictedMap(int initialCapacity, float loadFactor) {
        super(initialCapacity, loadFactor);
    }
    public RestrictedMap(int initialCapacity) {
            super(initialCapacity, 0.75f);
    }
    public RestrictedMap() {
            super(11, 0.75f);
    }
    public RestrictedMap(Map t) {
        super(t);
    }

    public Object put(Object key, Object value) {
        if (key == null)
            throw new NullPointerException();
        else
            return super.put(key, value);
    }
}
```

Implementing a wrapper class that has the same interface as a `Set`, `List`, or `Map` but does not use untyped references is more involved. It should be understood that doing so is a stopgap measure until parameterized types are added to the language. Nevertheless, I want to provide at least one example of such a wrapper:

---

53. API docs for the 1.2 release, document entitled "Collections Framework Overview."

```java
import java.util.*;
import java.io.File;

public class FileList implements Cloneable, java.io.Serializable {

    private ArrayList l;
    public FileList() {
        l = new ArrayList();
    }
    public FileList(int initialCapacity) {
        if (initialCapacity < 0)
            throw new IllegalArgumentException("Illegal Capacity: "+
                                               initialCapacity);
        l = new ArrayList(initialCapacity);
    }
    public FileList(Collection c) {
        checkCollection(c);
        l = new ArrayList(c);
    }
    public FileList(FileList fl) {
        l = new ArrayList(fl.l);
    }

    public void trimToSize() {
        l.trimToSize();
    }
    public void ensureCapacity(int minCapacity) {
        l.ensureCapacity(minCapacity);
    }

    public int size()                { return l.size(); }
    public boolean isEmpty()         { return l.isEmpty(); }
    public boolean contains(File f)  { return l.contains(f);}
    public int indexOf(File f)       { return l.indexOf(f); }
    public int lastIndexOf(File f)   { return l.lastIndexOf(f); }
    public boolean add(File f)       { return l.add(f); }
    public boolean remove(File f)    { return l.remove(f); }

    public File get(int index)          { return (File)l.get(index); }
    public File set(int index, File f)  { return (File)l.set(index, f); }
    public File remove(int index)       { return (File)l.remove(index); }

    public void add(int index, File f) { l.add(index, f); }

    public Iterator iterator()                { return l.iterator();  }
    public ListIterator listIterator()        { return l.listIterator(0); }
    public ListIterator listIterator(int index) { return l.listIterator(index); }

// BULK OPERATIONS

    public boolean addAll(Collection c) {
        checkCollection(c);
        return l.addAll(c);
    }
    public boolean addAll(int index, Collection c) {
        checkCollection(c);
        return l.addAll(index, c);
    }
    public boolean containsAll(Collection c) {
```

```
          checkCollection(c);
          return l.containsAll(c);
      }
      public boolean removeAll(Collection c) {
          checkCollection(c);
          return l.removeAll(c);
      }
      public boolean retainAll(Collection c) {
          checkCollection(c);
          return l.retainAll(c);
      }
      public void clear() { l.clear(); }


      public boolean addAll(FileList fl) {
          return l.addAll(fl.l);
      }
      public boolean addAll(int index, FileList fl) {
          return l.addAll(index, fl.l);
      }
      public boolean containsAll(FileList fl) {
          return l.containsAll(fl.l);
      }
      public boolean removeAll(FileList fl) {
          return l.removeAll(fl.l);
      }
      public boolean retainAll(FileList fl) {
          return l.retainAll(fl.l);
      }

// MISC
      public File[] toArray() {
          File[] newArray = new File[l.size()];
          int index=0;
          ListIterator i = l.listIterator();
          while(i.hasNext())
             newArray[index++] = (File)i.next();
          return newArray;
      }
      private void checkCollection(Collection c) {
          Iterator iterator = c.iterator();
          while(iterator.hasNext())
             if (!(iterator.next() instanceof File))
                throw new ClassCastException();
      }

// Housekeeping Methods
      public String toString() { return l.toString(); }
      public boolean equals(Object o) {
          if (o == this) return true;
          if (o == null) return false;
          if (o.getClass() != this.getClass())
              return false;
          FileList other = (FileList)o;
          return l.equals(other.l);
      }
      public int hashCode() { return l.hashCode(); }
      public Object clone() {
```

```
try {
    FileList clone = (FileList)super.clone();
    clone.l = (ArrayList) l.clone();
    return clone;
} catch (CloneNotSupportedException e) {
    throw new InternalError();
}
    }
  }
}
```

There are a few things to notice. The constructors and bulk operations that have a `Collection` parameter type have been kept. I simply iterate over the collection type checking each of the elements before delegating to the backing list. That opens the door to run-time exceptions, which is why you might just want to wait for parameterized types.

At first I wanted this to be a complete example and it is, except for the `toArray(Object a[])` method (which makes no sense in a container that does not use untyped references) and the overloaded `subList` methods. Implementing the overloaded `subList` methods would double the size of this already lengthy example. Otherwise, I believe this example is production ready. All you should need to do is change all occurrences of `File` to whatever type you want to use.

6.16.4 Standard Constructors

The **standard constructors** are a special programming convention used in the collections framework to support interoperability. All of the general-purpose implementations have no-argument and copy constructors. As stated in the `Collection` interface,

> All general-purpose `Collection` implementation classes
> (which typically implement `Collection` indirectly through one
> of its subinterfaces) should provide two "standard" constructors:
> a void (no arguments) constructor, which creates an empty col-
> lection, and a constructor with a single argument of type `Col-`
> `lection`, which creates a new collection with the same
> elements as its argument. In effect, the latter constructor allows
> the user to copy any collection, producing an equivalent collec-
> tion of the desired implementation type. There is no way to
> enforce this convention (as interfaces cannot contain construc-
> tors) but all of the general-purpose `Collection` implementa-
> tions in the SDK comply.[54]

---

54. API docs for the `java.util.Collection` interface.

The `Map` interface says essentially the same thing.

> All general-purpose map implementation classes should provide
> two "standard" constructors: a void (no arguments) constructor
> which creates an empty map, and a constructor with a single
> argument of type `Map`, which creates a new map with the same
> key-value mappings as its argument. In effect, the latter construc-
> tor allows the user to copy any map, producing an equivalent
> map of the desired class. There is no way to enforce this recom-
> mendation (as interfaces cannot contain constructors) but all of
> the general-purpose map implementations in the SDK comply.[55]

Here are both of the standard constructors for the `HashSet`, `Array-List`, `LinkedList`, and `HashMap` classes:

```
HashSet()
HashSet(Collection c)

ArrayList()
ArrayList(Collection c)

LinkedList()
LinkedList(Collection c)

HashMap()
HashMap(Map t)
```

In the case of the `HashSet(Collection c)`, `ArrayList(Collection c)`, and `LinkedList(Collection c)` constructors, using `Collection` as the parameter type in the copy constructor is an important example of the principle of maximum generality. In all three cases, any `Set` or `List` can be copied.

The `SortedSet` and `SortedMap` interfaces doubles that require-ment to allow for a `Comparator` to be passed to the constructor. In the case of an empty set or map the `Comparator` is explicitly passed to the constructor. In the case of a `SortedSet` or `SortedMap` the `Comparator` is implicitly passed as a member of the set or map. It is accessed using the `comparator()` method. Here are all four standard construc-tors for the `TreeSet` and `TreeMap` classes:

```
public TreeSet()
public TreeSet(Collection c)
public TreeSet(Comparator c)
public TreeSet(SortedSet s)

public TreeMap()
```

---

55. API docs for the `java.util.Map` interface.

```
public TreeMap(Map m)
public TreeMap(Comparator c)
public TreeMap(SortedMap m)
```

Note that it is the compile-time type of the constructor argument that
determines which constructor is invoked. This is important because it is
possible for a `Map` type variable to reference a `SortedMap`. The same is
true of `Set` and `SortedSet`. As always with `Comparator` arguments,
if the value passed is `null`, the natural ordering of the element type is
used by default.

6.17 Multimaps and Multidimensional Arrays

Multimaps are to maps what multidimensional arrays are to arrays. Both
are discussed in the following subsections. Note that there is no Multimaps
of Varying Length section like there is Multidimensional Arrays of Varying
Length section because most multimaps do vary in size, including the
example in this chapter. Only multidimensional arrays of varying length are
unusual.

6.17.1 Multimaps

A **multimap** is a map in which the value is another container. There is still
a one-to-one correspondence between keys and their values, but the fact
that the value is a container (array, `Set`, `List`, or another `Map`) in effect
makes for a one-to-many correspondence between the keys in a map and
the elements in the other containers.

 Just glance over the following program. Most of it displays instructions
to the console. It is shown here for the sake of completeness. The class
we are interested in is `SystemProperty`:

```
import java.util.*;
import java.io.*;
import SystemProperty.Property;

class SysProps {

    public static void main(String[] args) throws IOException {

        System.out.println();
        System.out.println();
        System.out.println("PROGRAM INSTRUCTIONS");
        System.out.println("--------------------");
        System.out.println("You can enter either the name of a ");
        System.out.println("system property (e.g., user.name)");
```

```
            System.out.println("to display an individual system property,");
            System.out.println("or one of the following codes to display");
            System.out.println("a group of system properties. Then press");
            System.out.println("the Enter key.");
            System.out.println();
            displayCodes();
            BufferedReader in = new BufferedReader
                                (new InputStreamReader(System.in));
            loop: while (true) {
                String s = in.readLine();
                if (s.equals(""))
                    break loop;
                List list = SystemProperty.getPropertyList(s); //may return null
                if (list == null) {
                    String value = System.getProperty(s);
                    if (value == null)
                        System.out.println("No such system property: " + s);
                    else
                        System.out.println(s + ": " + value);
                } else {
                    for(Iterator i = list.iterator(); i.hasNext();) {
                        Property property = (Property) i.next();
                        System.out.println(property.getDescription() +
                                    ": " + property.getValue());
                    }
                }
                displayCodes();
            }
        }

        static void displayCodes() {

            System.out.println();
            System.out.println("Code    Description");
            System.out.println("----    -----------");
            System.out.println("user    user");
            System.out.println("jre     Java Runtime Environment");
            System.out.println("cp      bootstrap, extension, and user classpaths");
            System.out.println("jvm     Java Virtual Machine");
            System.out.println("os      operating system");
            System.out.println("fs      file system");
            System.out.println("dir     directories");
            System.out.println("awt     AWT");
            System.out.println();
            System.out.println("PRESS ENTER ON EMPTY LINE" +
                        " TO END THE PROGRAM");
            System.out.println();
        }
    }
```

The SystemProperty class used in this program includes an example of a multimap in which the value of each entry in a HashMap is a List, an ArrayList to be exact. Although there should be no duplicate values, a list is used for the sake of maintaining entry order. I load the system properties into each of the lists in the same order that I want them to display. Notice at the top of the loadProperties() method how easy it is to create and load a multimap. Another interesting detail is that all of the lists in the multimap are local variables. They never leave the `loadProperties()` method except as values in the `sysProps` multimap:

```java
import java.util.*;
final class SystemProperty {
    private SystemProperty(){};
    private static final HashMap sysProps = new HashMap(23);
    static { loadProperties(); }
    public static List getPropertyList(String key) {
        return (List)sysProps.get(key);
    }
    private static void loadProperties() {

    //AWT
    List awt = new ArrayList();
    awt.add(new Property("awt.toolkit", "AWT Toolkit"));
    awt.add(new Property("java.awt.fonts", "AWT font library"));
    awt.add(new Property("java.awt.graphicsenv", "AWT graphics environment"));
    awt.add(new Property("java.awt.printerjob", "AWT printer job"));
    sysProps.put("awt", awt);

    //JRE
    List jre = new ArrayList();
    jre.add(new Property("java.runtime.name", "Java runtime name"));
    jre.add(new Property("java.runtime.version", "Java runtime version"));
    jre.add(new Property("java.vendor", "JRE vendor"));
    jre.add(new Property("java.vendor.url", "JRE vendor URL for home page"));
    jre.add(new Property("java.vendor.url.bug",
                        "JRE vendor URL for reporting bugs"));
    jre.add(new Property("java.version",
                        "JRE version number (same as the JDK version number)"));
    jre.add(new Property("java.specification.name", "JRE spec name"));
    jre.add(new Property("java.specification.vendor", "JRE spec vendor"));
    jre.add(new Property("java.specification.version", "JRE spec version"));
    sysProps.put("jre", jre);

    //JVM
    List jvm = new ArrayList();
    jvm.add(new Property("java.vm.name", "JVM implementation name"));
    jvm.add(new Property("java.vm.specification.name", "JVM spec name"));
    jvm.add(new Property("java.vm.specification.vendor", "JVM spec vendor"));
    jvm.add(new Property("java.vm.specification.version", "JVM spec version"));
    jvm.add(new Property("java.vm.vendor", "JVM vendor"));
    jvm.add(new Property("java.vm.version", "JVM implementation version"));
    jvm.add(new Property("java.vm.info", "JVM mode"));
    jvm.add(new Property("java.class.version", "major and minor version numbers"));
    sysProps.put("jvm", jvm);

    //DIRECTORIES (dir)
    List dir = new ArrayList();
    dir.add(new Property("java.home", "installation directory"));
    dir.add(new Property("user.dir", "current working directory"));
    dir.add(new Property("user.home", "user's \"home\" directory"));
    dir.add(new Property("java.io.tmpdir", "I/O temp directory"));
    dir.add(new Property("java.library.path", "binary directory"));
    sysProps.put("dir", dir);

    //CLASS PATH (cp)
    List cp = new ArrayList();
```

```java
cp.add(new Property("sun.boot.library.path", "bootstrap classpath (JRE)"));
cp.add(new Property("sun.boot.class.path", "bootstrap classpath (JDK only)"));
cp.add(new Property("java.ext.dirs", "extension classpath"));
cp.add(new Property("java.class.path", "user classpath"));
sysProps.put("cp", cp);

//FILESYSTEM (fs)
List fs = new ArrayList();
fs.add(new Property("file.encoding", "file encoding"));
fs.add(new Property("sun.io.unicode.encoding", "Unicode encoding"));
fs.add(new Property("file.encoding.pkg", "file encoding package"));
fs.add(new Property("file.separator", "platform-dependent file separator"));
fs.add(new Property("path.separator", "platform-dependent path separator"));
fs.add(new Property("line.separator", "platform-dependent line separator"));
sysProps.put("fs", fs);

//OPERATING SYSTEM (os)
List os = new ArrayList();
os.add(new Property("os.name", "operating system name"));
os.add(new Property("os.version", "operating system version"));
os.add(new Property("os.arch", "operating system architecture"));
os.add(new Property("sun.cpu.endian", "endianess"));
os.add(new Property("sun.cpu.isalist", "CPU \"is a\" list"));
sysProps.put("os", os);

//USER
List user = new ArrayList();
user.add(new Property("user.name", "User's account name"));
user.add(new Property("user.language", "User's Language"));
user.add(new Property("user.region", "User's Region"));
user.add(new Property("user.timezone", "User's Timezone"));
sysProps.put("user", user);

//check for invalid or new system properties while loading current values
Enumeration keys = System.getProperties().propertyNames();
boolean newSysProps = false;
String name, value;
keySearch: while (keys.hasMoreElements()) {
    String key = (String)keys.nextElement();
    Iterator iterator = sysProps.values().iterator();  // NOTICE THIS
    while (iterator.hasNext()) {
        List list = (List)iterator.next();              // AND THIS
        for(Iterator i=list.iterator(); i.hasNext();) {
            Property property = (Property) i.next();
            name = property.name;
            value = System.getProperty(name);
            if (value == null)
                throw new IllegalArgumentException(name +
                            " is not a system property");
            if (name.equals(key)) {
                property.value = value;
                continue keySearch;
            }
        }
    }
    if (!newSysProps) {
        System.out.println();
        System.out.println("UPDATE SystemProperty.java " +
                    "FOR NEW SYSTEM PROPERTIES...");
        newSysProps = true;
    }
    System.out.println(key + ": " + System.getProperty(key));
```

```
        }
    if (newSysProps)
        System.exit(0);
    }

    static class Property {

        String name;
        String value = null;
        String desc;

        Property (String name, String desc) {
            this.name = name;
            this.desc = desc;
        }
        public String getDescription() { return desc; }
        public String getValue() { return value; }
    }
}
```

This class includes code that iterates over the values of a multimap, converting each value to a `List` and then iterating over the list. Each list is a different grouping of system properties. In effect, the class adds a layer of organization absent in the `java.util.Properties` class. Multimaps are fairly easy to implement.

6.17.2 Multidimensional Arrays

Multidimensional arrays in older programming languages are allocated as blocks of physically contiguous memory. For example, `int[3][2][5]` would be allocated as shown in Figure 6-13. Java does not allocate multidimensional arrays as blocks of contiguous memory. This leads some software engineers and technical writers to conclude that "Java does not support multidimensional arrays."[56] Even Patrick Naughton says "There aren't really multidimensional arrays in Java."[57] These conclusions are not

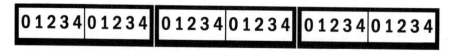

Figure 6-13: Contiguous memory multidimensional array.

56. Laura Lemay and Charles L. Perkins, *Teach Yourself Java in 21 Days, First Edition* (Indianapolis: Sams.net, 1996), 83.
57. Patrick Naughton, *The Java Handbook* (Berkeley: McGraw-Hill, 1996), 64.

supported in the original *JLS*, which does use the term *multidimensional array*, albeit sparingly.

> A clone of a multidimensional array is shallow …[58]

It would be more accurate to say that there are no multidimensional array *objects* in Java. Array objects are always single-dimensional. This may change soon. Java Specification Request 83 (JSR-000083), "Java Multiarray Package," is in the works. The summary for the JSR reads as follows.

> This JSR proposes a package implementing true rectangular multidimensional arrays for Java.[59]

You can read more about this JSR at *java.sun.com/aboutJava/communityprocess/jsr/jsr_083_multiarray.html*.

How are multidimensional arrays implemented at present then? The old mental model of dimensions as logical subdivisions of physically contiguous memory is replaced in the Java programming language by what is best thought of as a *root node* and *dimensional nodes* in the new mental model of a search tree. Array variables never directly reference more than one array object. That is the **root node**. The definition of **dimensional nodes** is any array other than a root node in which the component type is an array type. This is a precise definition. The **leaf nodes** are the actual arrays in which the elements are stored. Just as one speaks of the subtrees in a binary tree, the arrays referenced by a root node or dimensional node are referred to as **subarrays**, which may be other dimensional nodes or leaf nodes. For example, the rest of that quotation from the original *JLS* reads

> A clone of a multidimensional array is shallow, which it to say that it creates a single new array. Subarrays are shared.[60]

Instead of there being just two subarrays (as there are two subtrees in a binary tree), the number of subarrays is determined by the length of the root node or dimensional node. *The root node, dimensional nodes, and leaf nodes may be allocated anywhere on the heap and are not necessarily contiguous.* The same `int[3][2][5]` multidimensional array would be allocated as shown in Figure 6-14.

Now consider the following array declaration:

---

58. Gosling, Joy, and Steele, §10.7, "Array Members."
59. Jose E. Moreira et al., JSR-000083, "Java Multiarray Package," *java.sun.com/aboutJava/communityprocess/jsr/jsr_083_multiarray.html*
60. Gosling, Joy, and Steele, §10.7, "Array Members."

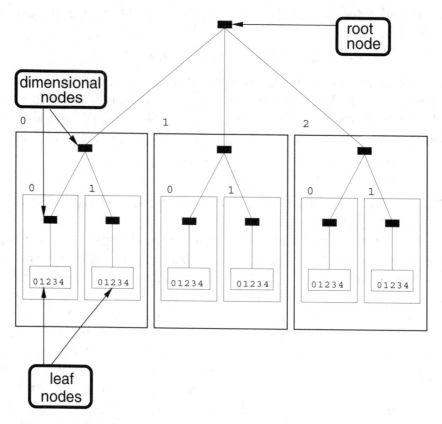

Figure 6-14: Java multidimensional array.

```
int [] [] [] array = new int [3] [2] [5] ;
```

The way to read an array creation expression for a multidimensional array is to look at the rightmost pair of brackets. This is the number of elements in each of the leaf arrays. Multiply the value of the dimension expressions inside of the remaining pairs of brackets together. The product is the total number of leaf nodes. Multiplying the total number of leaf nodes by the number of elements in each leaf node gives the storage capacity of a multidimensional array. For the above array declaration,

- Each leaf node has five elements
- There are 3 x 2 = 6 leaf nodes
- There are 6 x 5 = 30 components in this multidimensional array

This only works if there are the same number of subarrays in each of the dimensional nodes and the same number of elements in the leaf nodes, which is not necessarily the case.

6.17.2.1 *Multidimensional Arrays of Varying Length*

The array creation expression `new int[3][2][5]` is evaluated at run time as follows:

```
int[][][] a = new int[3][][];

for (int d1=0; d1 < a.length; d1++){
      a[d1] = new int[2][];
      for (int d2=0; d2 < a[d1].length; d2++){
              a[d1][d2] = new int[5];
      }
}
```

Note that an array creation expression for a multidimensional array must always include, at a minimum, the dimensional expression for the root node (that is, the left-most pair of brackets cannot be empty). Such a declaration represents a multidimensional array, the creation of which is not yet complete. To be precise, the creation of subarrays is deferred for one reason or another. As you can see in the innermost `for` loop, `d1` represents the root node and `d2` represents the dimensional nodes. If the above loop were written out as a series of individual array creation expressions (sometimes referred to as *unrolling* a loop), it would look like this:

```
int[][][] a = new int[3][][];     //root node

a[0] = new int[2][];       //dimensional node
a[0][0] = new int[5];
a[0][1] = new int[5];
a[1] = new int[2][];       //dimensional node
a[1][0] = new int[5];
a[1][1] = new int[5];
a[2] = new int[2][];       //dimensional node
a[2][0] = new int[5];
a[2][1] = new int[5];
```

As stated above, the number of subarrays for a root node or dimensional node is the `length` attribute of the array. For example, `a.length` is equal to three, `a[0].length` is equal to two, and `a[0][0].length` is equal to five.

When a multidimensional array is allocated using a single array creation expression, the length of each dimensional node at a given level in the search tree as well as the length of the leaf nodes are the same. However, subarrays can have any length if they are allocated separately. For example,

```
int[][][] a = new int[3][][];     //root node

a[0] = new int[1][];      //dimensional node
a[0][0] = new int[10];
a[0][1] = new int[20];
a[1] = new int[2][];      //dimensional node
a[1][0] = new int[100];
a[1][1] = new int[200];
a[2] = new int[3][];      //dimensional node
a[2][0] = new int[1000];
a[2][1] = new int[2000];
```

Array initializers can also be used to create multidimensional arrays of varying lengths. For example,

```
char[][][] alphabet =
{
{{'A','B','C','D','E','F'},{'G','H','I'}},
{{'J','K','L'},{'M','N','O'},{'P','Q','R'}},
{{'S','T','U'},{'V','W','X','Y','Z'}}
};
```

In this multidimensional array `alphabet[0][0][5] = 'F'`, but this is the only leaf node in which an index value of five can be used. Likewise, `alphabet[1][2][2] = 'R'`, but `alphabet[0][2][0]` throws an `ArrayIndexOutOfBoundsException`. Processing a multidimensional array of varying lengths requires the use of the `length` fields to determine the number of subarrays or components. For example, the `alphabet` array can be printed with the following nested `for` statement:

```
for (int i=0; i < alphabet.length; i++)
    for (int j=0; j < alphabet[i].length; j++)
        for (int k=0; k < alphabet[i][j].length; k++)
            System.out.print(alphabet[i][j][k]);
```

The diagnostic message prints

```
ABCDEFGHIJKLMNOPQRSTUVWXYZ
```

The same nested `for` statement will process any three dimensional array. If a multidimensional array has more or less dimensions, you need only add or remove additional nested `for` statements.

6.18 Legacy Containers

Prior to the Java 1.2 release there were only two general purpose-containers available in the `java.util` package. Those were `Vector` and

`Hashtable`. A `Vector` is essentially a synchronized `ArrayList`, and a `Hashtable` is a synchronized `HashMap`. These **legacy containers** should not be used in new code. They will always be a part of the language, however, because they are used as result and parameter types in a significant number of methods in the core API written prior to the 1.2 release.

Sun has consistently placed a premium on backwards compatibility throughout the evolution of the Java programming language, which means that the legacy containers are here to stay and you need to be familiar with them. I do not include API tables for these containers but focus on the few things you need to know to convert from and to legacy containers. The details of their interfaces can be learned using the API docs.

One of the benefits of having "retrofitted" the legacy containers is that they can be used as constructor arguments to create one of the general-purpose implementations in the collections framework. There have been many examples of creating a `HashMap` from the system's property object, which is a `Hashtable`. Likewise, an `ArrayList` can be created as follows:

```
List list = new ArrayList(vector);
```

Thus, if you invoke a method that returns a `Vector` or `Hashtable`, you can easily convert it to one of the core collection interface types. Going in the other direction is just as easy. This is usually required when invoking an older method or constructor. You can create the older container in the argument list. For example,

```
oldMethod(new Vector(c));
```

The `c` argument can be any `Set` or `List`, including a `TreeSet`.

```
oldMethod(new Hashtable(m));
```

The `c` argument can be any `Set` or `List`, including a `TreeSet`.

The `m` argument can be any `Map`, including a `TreeMap`. See 6.13.3 A Poor Man's Collection, for converting from and to an `Enumeration`.

Index

Symbols

" (quotation mark) 27
$ (dollar sign) 11
% (percent sign) 446
+ (plus sign) 30
+ operator 369
+= operator 362
, (comma) 42
. (period) 42
; (semicolon) 42
== (reference equality operator) 260–262
? (question mark) 446
\ (backslash) 27
_ (underscore) 11
' (apostrophe) 27

Numerics

32-bit pointers 181
64-bit pointers 181
64-bit systems 181

A

abnormal program termination 389–390
absolute endpoints 583
absolute pathname 81
abstract implementations 629–632
abstract keyword 15
abstract method modifiers 99
abstract modifiers 95
AbstractCollection class 632–633
AbstractList class 633–635
    clear() method in 634
    remove-Range(int fromIndex, int to-Index) method in 634
    See also classes
AbstractMap class 636–637
AbstractMethodError 69
AbstractSequentialList class 635–636
AbstractSet class 632–633
accessor methods 300
    in ResourceBundle class 430

public 237
acute accent 353
add rule 424
add(BigDecimal val) method 225
add(BigInteger val) method 222
add(First Object o) method 541
add(int field, int value) method 415, 416
add(int index Object element) method 519
add(Object o) method 494, 500
    description of 511, 592
    in LinkedList Iterator 494
    in Set interface 499
addAll(Collection c) method 505, 511
addAll(int index, Collection c) method 495, 519
addAll(Map t) method 586
addition operations 370
addLast(Object o) method 541
Albania 403
Albanian language 399, 403
Algeria 400
algorithms 465, 610
Al-Khwarizmi, Mohammed ibn-Musa 610
alphabet 36
AM_PM field 409, 417
    default symbol 454
amortized constant time 491, 493–495
anonymous classes 112
    as optional class bodies 121
    orphaned 137
    using 126–128
    vs. local classes 121–123
    See also classes
API (application programming interface) 483
apostrophe (') 27
append methods 340
<applet> tag 42
application programming interface (API) 483

Byte class 68, 374
byte keyword 15
bytecodes 150
byteValue() accessor method 237
byvalue keyword 16

C

C programming language 20
    type system in 489
C++ programming language 20
C0 control characters 22–24
cached hash code optimization 275
Calendar class 406
    date fields in 416–419
    inconsistent information policy in
        413–414
    methods in 407
    setTimeZone(TimeZone zone)
        method in 458
    time fields in 416–419
    See also classes
Canada 401, 402
canonical mappings 354
canonical names 70
capacity 323
capacity() method 323
cardinality 504
carriage return 4, 6, 24
case 244–248
case keyword 15
case mappings 328–330
cast keyword 16
cast operator 43, 362, 486
Catalan language 398, 400
catch keyword 15
ceiling 188
Center for Java Technology 429
Central Standard Time (CST) 457
char [] array
    conversion to String 334–336
    sharing 380–381
char data type 17, 18, 219
char keyword 15
character buffer 367

Character class 4
    declarations in 36
    hashCode( ) method in 253
    importing 68
    isSpace(char ch) method in 337
    Unicode utility methods in 245
    See also classes
character encoding string 336
character literals 17
character string 324
character types 248–249
Character.getType (char ch) method
    248
Character.isJavaIdentifierStart(char ch)
    method 11
Character.isLetter(char ch) method
    348
Character.Subset class 284
CharacterArrayWriter 347
CharacterIterator interface 342–345
    description of 343
    getting the index in 344
    setting the index in 344
characters 18
    accessing 332–334
    control 22–24
    converting to numbers 251
    line separators 23–26
    NULL 21–22
    ordinary 360
    paragraph separators 26
    special 26–27
charAt(int index) method 146, 332
charValue() method 237
checked exceptions 327
checkForComodification() method 640
child nodes 546
Chile 401
China 403
Chinese language 399, 403
circled digits 51
circumflex accent 353
class bodies 51
class body declarations 48–49

classpath formulas 82–83
   complex 84–86
   simple 83
clear() method 421, 608
<clinit> method 53–54, 56
clone() method 259, 294–298, 620
   method contract for 294–295
Cloneable interface 68, 298–299
CloneNotSupportedException 69, 295, 298–299
cloning 294–298
   bitwise copy 295
   containers 619–621
   deep copy 297
   shallow copy 296
   See also copying
collection decorators 564
Collection interface 98, 509–513
   addAll(Collection c) method in 511
   bulk operations in 504
   contains(Object o) method in 499, 510
   containsAll(Collection c) method in 499, 510, 511
   iterator 513
   methods in 483, 503
   remove(Object o) method in 499, 512, 513
   removeAll(Collection c) method in 499
   toArray method in 513
   See also interfaces
collection interface type variables 464
collection variables 464
collection views 563
   in adding entries 585–587
   iterating over maps using 599–600
   of maps 571, 584–585
   in removing entries 585–587
collections 463
collections framework 463–465
   duplicate elements in 499
   equivalence relationship in 499–500

   main parts of 503
Collections utility class
   binary search methods in 614–616
   in collections framework 503
   compareTo(Object o) method 301
   copy(List dest, List src) method in 620
   fill method in 624
   sort algorithms in 314
Collections.reverseOrder() utility method 314
collision list 269
Colombia 401
.com 62
COMBINING_SPACING_MARK character type 250
comma (,) 42
comments 3
   multi-line 8
   single-line 8
common ancestor class. See Object class
Comparable interface 68, 229, 300, 304–309
   compareTo(Object o) method in 581
   See also interfaces
Comparator interface 300, 310–312
   compare(Object o1, Object o1) method in 581
   equivalence relationships in 500
   specifications of 331
   uses of 310
   See also interfaces
comparators
   reverse-order 314
   uses of 310
compare(Object o1, Object o1) method 581
compare(Object o1, Object o2) method 300, 310
compareTo() method 259
compareTo(BigDecimal val) method in BigInteger class 222

java.util.Locale class 144
javac compiler 50
javax.swing packages 465
javax.swing.JSlider class 128
JDK (Java Development Kit) 62
Jordan 400
JVM (Java Virtual Machine)
   intern mechanism in 377
   memory allocation in 257
   method area of 140
   pool of strings in 377
   setting the default locale by 395

K

keyboards
   limited interfaces of 12
   reading 388–389
keys 262–263, 521
keySet() method 572
   description of 524
   in bulk operations for maps 506
   in Map interface 585
keystrokes 388
keyword class 28
keywords 2, 15–16
   names 171–172
   static 117–119
   super 149–152, 174–175
   this 149–152
keywordthrows 15
Korean language 398, 402
Kuwait 400

L

labels 13
language code 391
languages 391–403
last method 517
lastIndexOf(Object o) method 500, 520
lastKey method 526
Latin script 246
Latin-1 diacritics 353
Latvia 402
Latvian (Lettish) language 398, 402
leaf nodes 546, 651

Lebanon 400
legacy containers 655
length() method 146, 323
lexical analysis 347–361
lexical structure 2
Libya 400
limited concurrent modifications 605
line feed 4, 6, 24
line separators 23–26
line terminators. See line separators
line wrapping 356
line.separator system property 23
LINE_SEPARATOR character type 250
linear data structures 539
linear logarithmic time 491
linear searches 614
   of maps 618–619
   of sequential access lists 618–619
   of sets 618–619
linear time 491, 496–497
LinkageError 69
linked lists
   elements in 534
   nodes 534
LinkedList class
   add(First Object o) method in 541
   addLast(Object o) method in 541
   vs. ArrayList class 532–537
   getFirst method in 541
   getLast method in 541
   implementing stacks in 539
   iterator() method in 589
   removeFirst method in 541
   removeLast method in 541
lira 395
List interface 98, 517–518
   add(int index Object element)
     method in 519
   addAll(int index Collection c) meth-
     od in 519
   get(int index) method in 519
   indexOf(Object o) method in 500, 520
   lastIndexOf(Object o) method in
     500, 520

military time 421, 441, 454
MILLISECOND field
    default symbol 454
milliseconds 405–406
min(Collection coll) method 311, 625
MIN_VALUE constant 188
MIN_VALUE field 32
minimum elements 625–626
minus sign (-) 446
MINUTE field 454
minutes 406
MissingResourceException 404
mixed notation 477
modCount 640
modern scripts 246
MODIFIER_LETTER character type 249
MODIFIER_SYMBOL character type 250
modifiers 15
    class 90
    static 140–143
monetary values 233–235
MONTH field 416, 417
    default symbol 450
    setting 414–415
Morocco 400
movePointLeft(int n) method 226
movePointRight(int n) method 226
multidimensional arrays 650–652
    of varying lengths 653–654
multi-line comments 8
multimaps 646–650
multiple current instances 163–167
multiply(BigDecimal val) method 225
multiply(BigInteger val) method 222
mutable objects 502
mutator methods 321–322
mutex 572, 602

N

named constants 16
names 9, 12–14
    syntactic classification of 13
naming 12–14
NaN (Not-a-Number) constant 204, 243

native keyword 15
natural numbers 183
natural ordering 302
    chronological 305
    in compareTo(Object o) method 308
    lexicographic 305
    locale-specific lexicographic 305
    signed numerical 305
    system-dependent lexicographic
        on pathname 305
    unsigned numerical 305
negate() method 222
negative circled digits 51
negative numbers 445
negative zero 204
NegativeArraySizeException 69, 324,
    480
nested interfaces 49, 124
    in class body declarations 141,
        48, 51
    importing 70, 74–75
nested top-level classes 49
    in class body declarations 51, 141
    description of 112
    importing 70, 74–75
    See also classes
nested types 167–168
    names 170
    uses of 168
.net 62
Netherlands 402
network codes 26
network protocols 26
new keyword 15, 43, 171–172
New Zealand 401
newInstance(Class componentType, int
    length) method 474
newLength argument 322
newLine() method 26
newMonths) method 450
next() method 351
    description of 591
    in Iterator interface 589
    in ListIterator interface 590

in rehashing 558
in Map interface 521, 522
in TreeMap 494, 549
putAll(Map t) method 506, 585
description of 524

Q

Qatar 400
quadratic time 490–491, 497–499
qualified names 71
qualifying instances 171
default 172–174
qualitative sampling 287
quantitative sampling 287
question mark (?) 446
queues 540–542
quotation mark (") 27
quoteChar method 360
quoted strings 360

R

radix 35–38
conversion methods 35
specifiers 36
radix point 34
random access lists 534
binary searches of 615–618
random access method 533
range views 563, 577–580
using 579–580
RangeCheck() method 577
readJavaFormatString(s) method 240
readline() method 389
real numbers 183
record separator 6
redirect(String fileName) method 383
redundant imports 67
reference data types 178
reference equality
vs. equivalence relationship 260–262
operator (==) 260–262
references 181
null 221
regionMatches method 331

rehashing 558
relational operators 229
and inexact results 231
remainder(BigInteger val) method 222
remove (Object key) method 522
remove() method 592
description of 589
element removal using 537
in LinkedList Iterator 494
remove(int index) method 520
remove(Object key) method 494, 524
remove(Object o) method 494, 499, 512
removeAll(Collection c) method 499, 505, 512
removeFirst method 541
removeLast method 541
replace(char oldChar, char newChar) method 338, 341
replace(int start, int end, String str) method 338, 341
reserved words 16
resizable arrays 468
ResourceBundle class 404
accessor methods in 430
rest keyword 16
restricted containers 640–644
retainAll(Collection c) method 505, 513
return keyword 15
reusable objects 50
class body declarations in 93–94
reverse order comparator 314
reverse order sorts 302–303
reverse() method 341
reversed domain names 60
right-open intervals 577
in String class 326–327
in StringBuffer class 326–327
ring above 353
Ritchie, Dennis 382
roll rule 425
roll(Calendar.DATE, true) method 426
roll(int field, boolean up) method 415
roll(int field, int value) method 415, 423, 426

setDigit(char digit) method 446
setEras(String[] newEras) method 449
setErr method 385
setGroupingSeparator(char grouping-Separator) method 446
setIn method 385
setInfinity() method 446
setInternationalCurrencySymbol() method 447
setLength(int newLength) method 322
setMaximumIntegerDigits(int newValue) method 437
setMinimumFractionDigits(int newValue) method 437
setMinusSign() method 446
setMonetaryDecimalSeparator() method 446
setNaN() method 446
setOut method 385
setPatternSeparator() method 447
setPercent() method 446
setScale() method 228
setShortMonths(String[] newShortMonths) method 450
setText methods 351
setTime(Date date) method 408
setTime(long time) method 406
setTimeInMillis(long millis) method 408
setTimeZone(TimeZone zone) method 458
setValue(Object value) method 600
setZeroDigit() method 446
shadowed fields 159–161
shadows 78
shallow copy 296, 619
shiftLeft(int n) method 222
shiftRight(int n) method 222
Short class 68, 374
short keyword 15
shortValue() accessor method 237
shuffle(List list) method 498
shuffling 622–623
significands 38
    floating-point types and 208–211
    storing values in 205

significant digits 193–195
simple classpath formulas 83
SimpleDateFormat class 431
    applyPattern(String pattern) method in 442–445
sin method 14
single-line comments 8
singleton(Object o) method 627
singletons 626–627
single-type-import declarations 10, 64
size() method 627, 630
skeletal implementations 629
Slovak language 399, 402
Slovakia 402
Slovenia 403
Slovenian language 399, 403
Software Development Kit (SDK) 62–64
software engineers 14
SortedMap interface 98, 308
    ascending order of 525
    comparator() method in 311, 526
    firstKey method 526
    headSet(Object toElement) method 526
    iterating backwards through 608–609
    methods in 21
    subSet(Object fromElement, Object toElement) method 526
    tailSet(Object fromElement) 526
    See also interfaces
SortedSet interface 98, 308, 516–517
    comparator() method in 311, 517
    first method() in 517
    headSet(Object toElement) method in 517
    iterating backwards through 608–609
    last method() in 517
    methods in 21
    subSet(ObjectfromElement Object toElement) method in 517
    tailSet(Object fromElement) method in 517

void keyword 15
volatile keyword 15

W

WeakHashMap class 562
WeakKey class 562
WEEK_OF_MONTH field 417
    default symbol 452
WEEK_OF_THE_MONTH field 409
WEEK_OF_YEAR field 417
    default symbol 452
Western Europe 395
while keyword 15
white space 3–7, 429
    internationalized definition of 6
whole numbers 183
widening conversions 212
wild cards 65
Windows operating system 337
    EOF(End-of-File) marker in 388
word boundaries 348, 354–356
    iterating over 354–356

WordCount program 355
would-be mutator methods 322
wrapper classes 236–238
    unmodifiable 575
wrapper implementations 564
writeDouble(double v) method 470

Y

YEAR field 417
    default symbol 449
years 406
Yemen 400
Yugoslavia 393, 402, 403

Z

zero 188
    rounding away from 227
    rounding towards 227
zero-origin integers 482–483
zone ID 456
ZONE_OFFSET field 417, 428

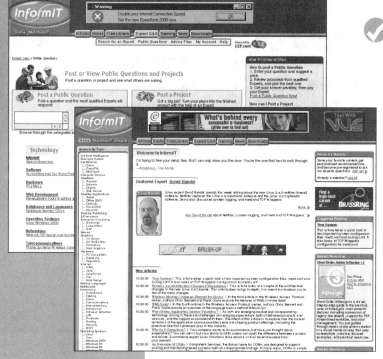
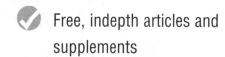